Perspectives and Considerations on the Evolution of Smart Systems

Maki K. Habib
American University in Cairo, Egypt

A volume in the Advances in Systems Analysis,
Software Engineering, and High Performance
Computing (ASASEHPC) Book Series

Published in the United States of America by
IGI Global
Engineering Science Reference (an imprint of IGI Global)
701 E. Chocolate Avenue
Hershey PA, USA 17033
Tel: 717-533-8845
Fax: 717-533-8661
E-mail: cust@igi-global.com
Web site: http://www.igi-global.com

Library of Congress Cataloging-in-Publication Data

Names: Habib, Maki K., 1955- editor.
Title: Perspectives and considerations on the evolution of smart systems / edited by Maki K. Habib.
Description: Hershey, PA : Engineering Science Reference, [2023] | Includes bibliographical references and index. | Summary: "Perspectives and Considerations on the Evolution of Smart Systems discusses the latest edge development that informs and facilitates the next level of development. It highlights how the evolving technologies and techniques are going to impact the developments in the field considering climate, environment, circular economy, and ecosystems. Covering topics such as dynamic difficulty adjustment, intelligent control, and serious games, this premier reference source is an excellent resource for engineers, computer scientists, IT professionals, developers, data analysts, students and educators of higher education, librarians, researchers, and academicians"-- Provided by publisher.
Identifiers: LCCN 2022057765 (print) | LCCN 2022057766 (ebook) | ISBN 9781668476840 (h/c) | ISBN 9781668476857 (s/c) | ISBN 9781668476864 (eISBN)
Subjects: LCSH: Expert systems (Computer science)
Classification: LCC QA76.76.E95 P46 2023 (print) | LCC QA76.76.E95 (ebook) | DDC 006.3/3--dc23/eng/20230123
LC record available at https://lccn.loc.gov/2022057765
LC ebook record available at https://lccn.loc.gov/2022057766

This book is published in the IGI Global book series Advances in Systems Analysis, Software Engineering, and High Performance Computing (ASASEHPC) (ISSN: 2327-3453; eISSN: 2327-3461)

British Cataloguing in Publication Data
A Cataloguing in Publication record for this book is available from the British Library.

All work contributed to this book is new, previously-unpublished material. The views expressed in this book are those of the authors, but not necessarily of the publisher.

For electronic access to this publication, please contact: eresources@igi-global.com.

Advances in Systems Analysis, Software Engineering, and High Performance Computing (ASASEHPC) Book Series

Vijayan Sugumaran
Oakland University, USA

ISSN:2327-3453
EISSN:2327-3461

MISSION

The theory and practice of computing applications and distributed systems has emerged as one of the key areas of research driving innovations in business, engineering, and science. The fields of software engineering, systems analysis, and high performance computing offer a wide range of applications and solutions in solving computational problems for any modern organization.

The **Advances in Systems Analysis, Software Engineering, and High Performance Computing (ASASEHPC) Book Series** brings together research in the areas of distributed computing, systems and software engineering, high performance computing, and service science. This collection of publications is useful for academics, researchers, and practitioners seeking the latest practices and knowledge in this field.

COVERAGE

- Parallel Architectures
- Virtual Data Systems
- Distributed Cloud Computing
- Computer Graphics
- Engineering Environments
- Computer Networking
- Performance Modelling
- Enterprise Information Systems
- Software Engineering
- Metadata and Semantic Web

IGI Global is currently accepting manuscripts for publication within this series. To submit a proposal for a volume in this series, please contact our Acquisition Editors at Acquisitions@igi-global.com or visit: http://www.igi-global.com/publish/.

Titles in this Series

For a list of additional titles in this series, please visit: www.igi-global.com/book-series

Neuromorphic Computing Systems for Industry 4.0
S. Dhanasekar (Department of ECE, Sri Eshwar College of Engineering, India) K. Martin Sagayam (Karunya Institute of Technology and Sciences, India) Surbhi Vijh (ASET, Amity University, Noida, India) Vipin Tyagi (Jaypee University of Engineering and Technology, India) and Alex Norta (Tallinn University, Esonia)
Engineering Science Reference • © 2023 • 377pp • H/C (ISBN: 9781668465967) • US $270.00

Business Models and Strategies for Open Source Projects
Francisco José Monaco (Universidade de São Paulo, Bazil)
Business Science Reference • © 2023 • 339pp • H/C (ISBN: 9781668447857) • US $270.00

Advanced Applications of Python Data Structures and Algorithms
Mohammad Gouse Galety (Department of Computer Science, Samarkand International University of Technology, Uzbekistan) Arul Kumar Natarajan (CHRIST University (Deemed), India) and A. V. Sriharsha (MB University, India)
Engineering Science Reference • © 2023 • 298pp • H/C (ISBN: 9781668471005) • US $270.00

Handbook of Research on Machine Learning-Enabled IoT for Smart Applications Across Industries
Neha Goel (Raj Kumar Goel Institute of Technology, India) and Ravindra Kumar Yadav (Raj Kumar Goel Institute of Technology, India)
Engineering Science Reference • © 2023 • 542pp • H/C (ISBN: 9781668487853) • US $345.00

Quantum Computing and Cryptography in Future Computers
Shyam R. Sihare (Dr. APJ Abdul Kalam Govt. College, India)
Engineering Science Reference • © 2023 • 300pp • H/C (ISBN: 9781799895220) • US $270.00

Handbook of Research on Integrating Machine Learning Into HPC-Based Simulations and Analytics
Belgacem Ben Youssef (King Saud University, Saudi Arabia) and Mohamed Maher Ben Ismail (King Saud University, Saudi Arabia)
Engineering Science Reference • © 2023 • 400pp • H/C (ISBN: 9781668437957) • US $325.00

Machine Learning Algorithms Using Scikit and TensorFlow Environments
Puvvadi Baby Maruthi (Dayananda Sagar University, India) and Smrity Prasad (Dayananda Sagar University, India)
Engineering Science Reference • © 2023 • 320pp • H/C (ISBN: 9781668485316) • US $270.00

IGI Global
PUBLISHER of TIMELY KNOWLEDGE

701 East Chocolate Avenue, Hershey, PA 17033, USA
Tel: 717-533-8845 x100 • Fax: 717-533-8661
E-Mail: cust@igi-global.com • www.igi-global.com

Table of Contents

Detailed Table of Contents

Chapter 1
Alessandro Massaro, LUM Enterprise Srl, Bari, Italy & Dipartimento di Management,
Finanza e Tecnologia, Università LUM "Giuseppe Degennaro", Bari, Italy

The book chapter is focused on the definition of efficient models to apply to production processes. Specifically, starting to business process modelling and notation (BPMN) approach, are defined rules and methods to integrate artificial intelligence (AI) and innovative key performance indicators (KPIs) for task checkpoints implementing a dynamic and intelligent decision-making approach. The whole theoretical mechanism constitutes a decision support system (DSS) model supporting risk analyses including aspects related to organization, predictive maintenance, and the use of technologies in the era of Industry 5.0. Particular attention is addressed on methods about the efficient monitoring of production processes by means process mining (PM) workflows. Different examples are provided in the book chapter, by enhancing the aspect related to the DSS logics and implementation of logic conditions. The discussed model opens a new topic about intelligent BPMN and process engineering including AI facilities strengthening decisions in operating processes.

Chapter 2
Tomohiro Yamaguchi, Nara College, National Institute of Technology, Japan

The mission of this chapter is to add an explainable model to multi-goal reinforcement learning toward an autonomous smart system to design both complex behaviors and complex decision making friendly for a human user. At the front of the introduction section, and a relation between reinforcement learning including an explainable model and a smart system is described. To realize the explainable model, this chapter formalizes the exploration of various behaviors toward sub-goal states efficiently and in a systematic way in order to collect complex behaviors from a start state towards the main goal state. However, it incurs significant learning costs in previous learning methods, such as behavior cloning. Therefore, this chapter proposes a novel multi-goal reinforcement learning method based on the iterative loop-action selection strategy. As a result, the complex behavior sequence is learned with a given sub-goal sequence as a sequence of macro actions. This chapter reports the preliminary work carried out under the OpenAIGym learning environment with the CartPoleSwingUp task.

    Juan Ignacio Vargas-Bustos, Universidad Veracruzana, Mexico
    Ericka Janet Rechy-Ramirez, Universidad Veracruzana, Mexico

Serious games have been used for assisting people in physical rehabilitation for hands. People might have different degrees of mobility in their hands; consequently, it would be convenient that the game could be adapted according to the range-of-motion in performing hand movements. This study implemented a serious game for hand rehabilitation with two play modes. Mode one does not adjust the game difficulty; whereas mode two adjusts the game difficulty according to the player's range-of-motion in performing flexion, extension, ulnar, and radial deviations. The game difficulty was adjusted using fuzzy logic to compute positions at which the rewards will be displayed at the game scene (easy, medium, and difficult positions to collect the rewards). Four participants played both modes. Two-tailed t-tests revealed that there were no significant differences between both modes in terms of rewards collected ($p = 0.6621$), play time ($p = 0.8178$), and "game engagement questionnaire" score ($p = 0.1383$).

    Oluwaleke Umar Yusuf, The American University in Cairo, Egypt
    Maki K. Habib, The American University in Cairo, Egypt

This chapter presents a detailed introduction to the decentralized data processing and storage paradigm called blockchain technology, delving into its fundamental concepts, foundational principles, and advantages. A literature review is conducted, detailing existing research areas, and enabling technologies driving further research and development into the technology. The two-way fusion of machine learning – another data-driven technology – is considered, wherein one technology addresses limitations and drawbacks within the other. The existing applications of blockchain technology within various domains are discussed, along with some identified research challenges and future trends. A case study is also provided to demonstrate the integration of blockchain technology into the internet of vehicles domain.

    Chabi Gupta, School of Commerce, Finance and Accountancy, Christ University, India

It is smart for investors to plan for a drop that may be accompanied by a recession in the late stages of a bull market. The authors examine a variety of passive and active strategies, as well as their success in different crises. However, while choosing the best of strategies in the worst of circumstances, investors must be cautious in defining 'best.' It's critical to comprehend not only the long-term performance but also the whole cost of putting various preventive measures in place. The authors analyse popular strategies like technical analysis, fundamental analysis, relying on financial news, seeking professional advice, tips from trade experts, and self-intuition while making portfolios. Our findings indicate that every investment is unique. Some defensive methods will be more effective than others in each case. As a result, diversification across several viable strategies may be the wisest course of action.

Chapter 6

Morteza Mohammadzaheri, Birmingham City University, UK
Mojtaba Ghodsi, University of Portsmouth, UK
Hamidreza Ziaiefar, University of South-Eastern Norway, Norway
Issam Bahadur, Sultan Qaboos University, Oman
Musaab Zarog, Sultan Qaboos University, Oman
Mohammadreza Emadi, Sultan Qaboos University, Oman
Payam Soltani, Birmingham City University, UK
Amirhosein Amouzadeh, Sultan Qaboos University, Oman

This chapter equitably compares five different artificial intelligence (AI) models and a linear model to tackle two real-world engineering data-driven modelling problems with small number of experimental data samples, one with sparse and one with dense data. The models of both cases are shown to be highly nonlinear. In the case with available dense data, multi-layer perceptron (MLP) evidently outperforms other AI models and challenges the claims in the literature about superiority of fully connected cascade (FCC). However, the results of the problem with sparse data shows superiority of FCC, closely followed by MLP and neuro-fuzzy network.

Chapter 7

P. Senthil Kumar, Mohan Babu University, India

It proposes the PSK (P. Senthil Kumar) method for solving intuitionistic fuzzy solid transportation problems (IFSTPs). In our daily life, uncertainty comes in many ways, e.g., the transportation cost (TC) is not a fixed one, it varies from time to time due to market conditions (i.e., the price of diesel is depending on the cost of crude oil), mode of the transportation, etc. So, to deal with the TP having uncertainty and hesitation in TC, in this chapter, the author divided IFSTP into 4 categories and solved type II- IFSTP by using TIFNs. The model of type II- IFSTP and its relevant CSTP both are presented. The PSK method is presented clearly with the proof of some theorems and corollary. To illustrate the PSK method with proposed models, the numerical experiment and its related graphs are presented. Real-life problems are identified and solved by the PSK method with MATLAB and LINGO software. Analysis, discussion, merits, and demerits of the PSK method are all presented. A valid conclusion and recommendations are given. Finally, some of the future research areas are also suggested.

Chapter 8

Patricia R. Cristaldo, GIBD, Argentina
Daniela Lopez De Luise, CI2S Labs, Argentina
Lucas La Pietra, GIBD, Argentina

This chapter presents an overview of the project management field, and a set of metrics useful to evaluate the goodness of different project management methodologies considering specific features of the enterprise, project, and goals. It is a multidisciplinary problem that covers the technical analysis of main methodologies, requirements, and management perspectives. It aims to translate semantical and subjective appreciations into a combination of well-determined equations giving an approximation through automatic processing, and a systematic appreciation. The confidence levels are introduced in the indicators associated with the metrics. The entire approach considers information taken from documents and tacit biases made explicit through a questionary specifically defined. As will be shown below, one of the benefits of using these metrics is the possibility of assessing the strong association between project success and documents' scope quality. Also, a number of parameters are relevant to select a management methodology and to improve risk determination.

Chapter 9

Noman Islam, Karachi Institute of Economics and Technology, Karachi, Pakistan
Muhammad Furqan Zia, Koc University, Istanbul, Turkey
Darakhshan Syed, Bahria University, Pakistan

Cognitive radio ad hoc network (CRAHN) is an emerging discipline of network computing. It combines the advantages of cognitive radio networks and mobile ad hoc networks. This chapter starts with an overview of various research issues of CRAHN along with representative solutions for these research issues. Among the various research issues presented, security is discussed in detail due to its prime importance. A review of existing literature reveals that not much work on security has been reported for cognitive radio networks. Specifically, an overview of security issues in CRAHN, presented in this article, is a novel work of this kind. A major part of this article highlights the importance of security in CRAHN and presents an overview of major security issues and the solutions proposed to address these issues in CRAHN.

Chapter 10

Afnan Khaled Elhamshari, The American University in Cairo, Egypt
Maki Habib, The American University in Cairo, Egypt

For the past few decades, the scientific community has been paying attention to energy harvesters to reduce the use of batteries as the main power source for IoT devices and MEMS. Energy harvesters allow for the use of ambient energy, mostly a by-product of an application, to generate electricity while relying on batteries as a backup option to store the excess energy. This chapter includes a review of each energy harvester type, subtype, configuration, usage, and power output to understand the different kinds of energy harvesters and motivate a discussion between their advantages and limitations. The chapter also discusses the advantages and the limitations of current storage options for energy harvesting and how applications can benefit from future research in this area. The chapter concludes with a discussion of the challenges and future opportunities still open in the field of energy harvesters to obtain more reliable, cleaner, and cheaper energy sources.

Chapter 11

Ali Selamat, Universiti Teknologi Malaysia, Malaysia & Hradec Kralove University, Czech Republic

Nguyet Quang Do, Universiti Teknologi Malaysia, Malaysia

Ondrej Krejcar, Hradec Kralove University, Czech Republic

The past decade has witnessed the rapid development of natural language processing and machine learning in the phishing detection domain. However, there needs to be more research on word embedding and deep learning for malicious URL classification. Inspired to solve this problem, this chapter aims to examine the application of word embedding and deep learning in extracting features from website URLs. To achieve this, several word embedding techniques, such as Keras, Word2Vec, GloVe, and FastText, were used to learn feature representations of webpage URLs. The obtained feature vectors were fed into a deep-learning model based on CNN-BiGRU for extraction and classification. Two different datasets were used to conduct numerous experiments, while various metrics were utilized to evaluate the phishing detection model's performance. The obtained findings indicated that when combined with deep learning, Keras outperformed other text embedding methods and achieved the best results across all evaluation metrics on both datasets.

Chapter 12

Ali Shaheen, Dakota State University, USA

Omar El-Gayar, Dakota State University, USA

Agriculture is one of the high labor occupations around the globe. To meet the population growth and its demand, with the increase in labor cost, there is a need to explore efficient autonomous systems which may replace the traditional methods. Computer vision, edge, and deep learning (DL) models have become a promising area of research. This new paradigm of deep edge intelligence is most appropriate for agriculture activities where real-time decision-making is very important. In this chapter, the authors conduct a systematic literature review on deep learning-aided edge intelligence (EI) applications in agriculture to gather the evidence for prospects of DL at edge in agriculture. They discuss how DL models have shown outstanding performance within limited time and computation resources, and also provide future research directions to enhance the viability and applicability of complex deep learning (DL) models deployed at edge devices in agricultural applications.

Chapter 13

S. A. Karthik, BMS Institute of Technology and Management, India

R. Hemalatha, St. Joseph's College of Engineering, India

R. Aruna, AMC Engineering College, India

M. Deivakani, PSNA College of Engineering and Technology, India

R. Vijaya Kumar Reddy, Koneru Lakshmaiah Education Foundation, India

Sampath Boopathi, Muthayammal Engineering College, India

The internet of things (IoT) has the potential to transform healthcare by fusing the most significant technological and scientific advances in the fields of automation, mobility, and data analytics to improve patient care. IoT links sensors, actuators, and other devices to a network in order to collect and disseminate communication messages that an organization may then evaluate. To track health parameters, the suggested paradigm focuses on sensors, communications protocols, and cloud technologies. The study looks at the crucial elements of a healthcare IoT system. For the control, security, and protection of IoT networks, data confidentiality and authentication are crucial. For the purpose of resolving security challenges, flexible infrastructure is necessary. The goal of the chapter is to discuss IoT security concerns in healthcare devices and offer recommendations for future research to enhance the use of IoT devices.

Preface

In today's rapidly advancing technological landscape, smart and embedded systems have emerged as a critical field, synergizing sensing, actuation, control functions, and smartness to automate processes, monitor real-time systems, and make well-informed decisions. These systems can collect data and represent knowledge, analyze situations under different conditions, reason, and act upon them promptly. Connectivity, networking capabilities, and the incorporation of intelligent learning techniques, including machine learning, deep learning, and data analytics, have significantly driven the evolution of smart systems. This book *Perspectives and Considerations on the Evolution of Smart Systems* explores the contributions of IoTs, CPSs, WSNs, AI and machine learning, and real-time embedded systems to developing smart systems with advanced capabilities. It also highlights the impact of evolving technologies and techniques on various aspects such as climate, environment, circular economy, and ecosystems.

As the editor of this book, I recognize the significance of smart systems in shaping different aspects of human life, industries, and the environment. This publication contributes to the development of the field, introducing the latest advancements and cutting-edge developments that inform and facilitate the next level of progress. Our objective is to provide a comprehensive resource that assists researchers and professionals in understanding and exploring the multifaceted domain of smart systems.

This book is designed to cater to many readers, including engineers, computer scientists, investigators, researchers, IT professionals, developers, data analysts, professors, and students. It covers a diverse range of topics and challenges associated with the field of intelligence and smart systems, including design, architectures, technology, sensing, control, autonomy, energy efficiency, connectivity, networking capabilities, machine learning, deep learning, distributed systems, human-machine interface, system integration, knowledge representation, data analytics, IoT, CPS, WSN, industry 4.0/5.0, intelligence, robotics, mechatronics, embedded systems, innovation, bioinspiration, sustainability, edge computation, digital and virtual connectivity, environment, and applications across various domains.

Each chapter explores different dimensions of smart systems, presenting the latest research, methodologies, and advancements in the respective areas. The aim is to foster innovation, collaboration, and knowledge exchange among the readers by addressing the challenges and opportunities within this dynamic field.

Chapter 1 provides a comprehensive exploration of efficient models for production processes, focusing on the integration of Artificial Intelligence (AI) and innovative Key Performance Indicators (KPIs) within a Business Process Modelling and Notation (BPMN) approach. The chapter emphasizes the development of a Decision Support System (DSS) model that supports risk analysis and predictive maintenance while incorporating Process Mining (PM) workflows for efficient monitoring of production processes.

Chapter 2 focuses on multi-goal reinforcement learning and designing autonomous smart systems with complex behaviors and decision-making capabilities. The chapter introduces an explainable model that utilizes an iterative loop-action selection strategy to explore various behaviors efficiently. The preliminary work carried out under the OpenAIGym learning environment with the CartPoleSwingUp task is presented to demonstrate the potential of the proposed approach.

Chapter 3 delves into the implementation of serious games for hand rehabilitation, particularly addressing the adaptation of game difficulty based on the player's range of motion in hand movements. The chapter discusses the use of fuzzy logic to adjust game difficulty and presents findings from participants who played both modes of the serious game.

Chapter 4 offers an in-depth introduction to Blockchain Technology, exploring its fundamental concepts, advantages, and existing applications. The chapter also investigates the fusion of Machine Learning with blockchain technology and discusses research challenges and future trends in this domain. A case study demonstrates the integration of blockchain technology into the Internet of Vehicles.

Investment strategies and their effectiveness in different crises are examined in Chapter 5. The chapter highlights the importance of understanding the uniqueness of each investment and the need for diversification across multiple strategies. Various popular investment strategies are analyzed to provide insights for investors, such as technical analysis, fundamental analysis, and seeking professional advice.

Chapter 6 presents a comparative analysis of different Artificial Intelligence (AI) models, including a linear model, to address real-world engineering data-driven modeling problems with sparse and dense data. The chapter evaluates each model's performance and identifies specific models' superiority in different scenarios.

Chapter 7 introduces the PSK method for solving intuitionistic fuzzy solid transportation problems (IFSTPs) using TIFNs (Type-2 Intuitionistic Fuzzy Numbers). The chapter provides a clear explanation of the PSK method, along with theorem proofs and numerical experiments. Real-life problems are solved using the PSK method, and its merits, demerits, and future research areas are discussed.

An overview of Project Management and the evaluation of project management methodologies are presented in Chapter 8. The chapter introduces metrics and indicators to assess different methodologies, considering specific enterprise, project, and goal features. The approach incorporates information from documents and tacit biases through a defined questionnaire, enabling a systematic evaluation of project success.

Chapter 9 explores the research issues and security aspects of Cognitive Radio Ad Hoc Networks (CRAHN). The chapter provides an overview of CRAHN, explicitly focusing on security issues. Existing literature on security in CRAHN is reviewed, highlighting the importance of security in this emerging discipline.

Energy harvesters and their applications in reducing the use of batteries for IoT devices and MEMS are investigated in Chapter 10. The chapter reviews different energy harvester types, configurations, power outputs, and storage options. Challenges and future opportunities in the field of energy harvesters are discussed.

Chapter 11 focuses on applying word embedding and deep learning in extracting features from website URLs for malicious URL classification. The chapter examines various word embedding techniques and evaluates their performance in combination with deep learning models. Experimental results demonstrate the effectiveness of the proposed approach in phishing detection.

In Chapter 12, the authors conduct a systematic literature review on deep learning-aided edge Intelligence (EI) applications in agriculture. The chapter discusses how deep learning models deployed at edge devices can enhance real-time decision-making in agricultural applications. Future research directions are identified to enhance further the viability and applicability of complex deep-learning models in agriculture.

Chapter 13 delves into the crucial elements of a healthcare IoT system, focusing on sensors, communication protocols, and cloud technologies. The chapter addresses the security concerns associated with healthcare IoT devices and provides recommendations for enhancing IoT device usage in healthcare.

Each chapter in this edited reference book contributes unique insights and expertise to the field of smart systems. This collection of chapters will provide readers with a comprehensive understanding of the evolving landscape of smart systems and inspire further research and innovation in this rapidly advancing domain.

I sincerely thank all the contributors who have shared their expertise and insights in this book. Their valuable contributions have shaped this publication into a comprehensive reference, offering a multidimensional perspective on the evolution of smart systems.

I hope that *Perspectives and Considerations on the Evolution of Smart Systems* will be an enlightening resource, providing readers with the necessary knowledge and inspiration to contribute to developing and applying smart systems. May this book ignite curiosity, spark new ideas, and contribute to advancing this transformative field.

Maki K. Habib
American University in Cairo, Egypt

Chapter 1
Process Mining in Production Management, Intelligent Control, and Advanced KPI for Dynamic Process Optimization:
Industry 5.0 Production Processes

Alessandro Massaro
https://orcid.org/0000-0003-1744-783X

LUM Enterprise Srl, Bari, Italy & Dipartimento di Management, Finanza e Tecnologia, Università LUM "Giuseppe Degennaro", Bari, Italy

ABSTRACT

The book chapter is focused on the definition of efficient models to apply to production processes. Specifically, starting to business process modelling and notation (BPMN) approach, are defined rules and methods to integrate artificial intelligence (AI) and innovative key performance indicators (KPIs) for task checkpoints implementing a dynamic and intelligent decision-making approach. The whole theoretical mechanism constitutes a decision support system (DSS) model supporting risk analyses including aspects related to organization, predictive maintenance, and the use of technologies in the era of Industry 5.0. Particular attention is addressed on methods about the efficient monitoring of production processes by means process mining (PM) workflows. Different examples are provided in the book chapter, by enhancing the aspect related to the DSS logics and implementation of logic conditions. The discussed model opens a new topic about intelligent BPMN and process engineering including AI facilities strengthening decisions in operating processes.

DOI: 10.4018/978-1-6684-7684-0.ch001

1. INTRODUCTION: BACKGROUND AND BPMN FRAMEWORK

Process Mining (PM) is an important research topic of management engineering concerning the implementation of Industry 5.0 production processes using self-adaptive mechatronic facilities. Possible applications are in quality control and production efficiency processes enabling automatic setting and calibration of machine parameters.

Specifically, the PM is a 'proof of concept' that is born as Industry 5.0 perspective (Massaro, 2021 a): modern industrial process workflows are characterized by Artificial Intelligence (AI) decision making phases enabling specific sub-processes. The initial concept was later expanded to Business Process Modelling and Notation (BPMN) modelling of operations of production machines (Massaro, 2022 a) and to risk assessment in industrial scenario (Massaro, 2022 c). A recent study highlights the importance and the utility of PM in industrial manufacturing processes requiring advanced mechatronic systems (Massaro, 2023). The goal of this chapter is just to provide elements about the matching between AI-based mechatronic systems and PM model execution.

PM is a particular BPMN workflow representation based on AI algorithms behaving as process decision making. The PM can be implemented to enable the entire process of automation and control. The control and the actuation processes can be performed by Decision Support Systems (DSSs) which play an important role in the automatic decision-making processes, especially when a robotic action must be performed (Massaro, 2021a). DSS workflows can be designed and integrated into process workflows embedding AI engines (Massaro, 2021b). The workflows sketch actions and working activities in operative processes. BPMN is tool adopted to design workflow modelling processes (Massaro, 2021c), and it is suitable to highlight DSSs functions in operative workflows (Massaro, 2022 a). The DSSs are modelled as a part of the whole BPMN process referred to the AI-based decision making sub-process.

1.1 BPMN Main Symbols

The main BPMN symbols useful to design a process are listed in Table 1. The symbols are classified as events, tasks and gateways. All the symbols are linked constituting workflows modelling a process or a sub-process. The workflows are contained into pools (containers of workflows dedicated to a specific actor of the system). A full process could be composed by different pools, since a simpler system could require only one pool. Different pools are graphically arranged into a sequential vertical scheme. A pool refers to a system of actors or to a software platform such as a portal addressing the actions to do by means a dropdown menu representing the phases of a process.

The digital BPMN model is the first step to digitize processes in companies oriented on digital transformation.

Table 1. BPMN legend: summary of main BPMN symbols and their description

Main BPMN Symbols	Description
Events	Events of a process or of a sub-process
	Start: the process begin by this symbol indicating the starting point of a process or of a sub-process workflow contained into a pool. This symbol can be omitted in simplified workflows referring to the *Start* of a sub-process.
	Intermediate start: the starting point of a sub-process starts with an intermediate process enabled typically by a request (the intermediate process is enabled only if it is required and generally does not represent the starting point of the main process).
	Timer start: the time symbol indicates a periodic action or a specific time to perform a task (typically, a feedback interconnecting this symbol indicates a periodic action controlling a specific task).
	Message start: a process or a sub-process can be initiated by means of a notification (e-mail, message or call) containing information about the tasks to develop. This symbol is adopted also to indicate the information traceability.
	Intermediate message: during a process or a sub-process is enabled a notification (message, e-mail or call); this symbol can be contained into the task symbol (task triggered by a notification).
	End: end of a process or of a sub-process.
	End with a notification: the process or the sub-process terminates with a notification (e-mail, call, chat, message, etc.).
Tasks	Actions of a process or of a sub-process (the tasks can be performed by a human or by a machine).
	Generic task: each action of a worker or of a software or hardware platform are modelled by rectangular boxes to be linked to form a workflow.
	Sub-process: symbol collapsing a sub-process (simplification of a sub-process which is not important to represent in details); this symbol typically indicates a sub-process which it is not important to highlight (the attention is focused on the other tasks).
	Receive a task: the task is enabled by a notification.
Gateways	Logic conditions and workflow splitting actions
	Exclusive: logic condition indicating a simple check having as output simple conditions ('Yes' or 'Not', '<' or '>', etc.); this gateway represents a basic decision making symbol.
	Exclusive: logic condition indicating a simple check having as output simple conditions ('Yes' or 'Not', '<' or '>', etc.); this gateway represents a basic decision making symbol.
	Parallel: this condition indicates a splitting of processes or of sub-processes independently to a logic condition.
	Exclusive Event based: this symbols is a checkpoint typically used when a strong check based on a detailed decision is required (for example when a sign of a responsible is required); this symbol indicates a deeper decision-making.
	Complex: this symbol allows to implement complex logics as for logics characterizing logic ports (for example for the implementation of truth tables).

1.2 Digital Transformation in Industries

A simple way to trace the digital transformation process of a company is to map by trough BPMN all the processes involved in both horizontal and vertical integration of industrial facilities. Basic topics are facilities and applications regarding document dematerialization and in general digital maturity. Digital maturity can be quantitatively estimated by assigning a score about the usability of software typically adopted in company such as Enterprise Resource Planning (ERP), Customer Relationship Management (CRM), and Project Management (PM). Other important topics of digital transformation are data security, supply chain traceability and Big Data analytics. Security procedures can be applied for digital data control and for identification of workers into a hierarchal system. Some digital systems such as Radio Frequency Identification (RFID), Beacon, Barcode, QR code, Global Positioning System (GPS), and blockchain can be used for worker and for product traceability thus optimizing warehouse intralogistics and security. Big Data and AI technologies are fundamental for the implementation of Industry 5.0 facilities and are considered as important research topics for the production upgrade.

Table 2. Topics of the digital transformation

Industry Digital Transformation	Description
Data security	• Cybersecurity applied on digital data of the industry; • access control of the backend system; • authentication systems. A possible implementation is related to the development of AI tools classifying and detecting risks (Massaro, Gargaro et al. 2020).
Worker recognition and security	• Worker identification: face recognition, biometric recognition, RFID detection, badge recognition, etc. (Massaro, Gargaro et al. 2020); • process planning: hierarchy designation procedure, activities planning safety standards, security systems adoption, security procedures (Massaro 2022 c).
Traceability	• Supply chain traceability technologies: barcode, QRcode, RFID, beacon, GPS, blockchain, etc. (Massaro 2021 a); • traceability of products; • supply chain monitoring; • semi-product monitoring (check of the working phases); • human resources tracking.
Big Data Analytics	• Data collection in Big Data systems; • data fusion approaches integrating open data sources; • AI data processing (Massaro 2023); • MapReduce technology (system scalability); • Not Only SQL (NOSQL) technology; • Quantum computing.
Artificial Intelligence (AI)	• AI supervised algorithms (data classification and forecasting); • AI unsupervised algorithms (data clustering); AI represents the evolution of data processing from Industry 4.0 to Industry 5.0 (Massaro 2021 a).
Digital maturity	• Hardware tools; • software tools. Identification of the most important digital tools or facilities improving the digital transformation of the company (Magaletti et al. 2023).
Document dematerialization	• Document digitalization; • document retrieval (documents with metadata or indexed to facilitate the retrieval process); • informatics expert agents (Barbuzzi et al. 2020) able to recognize document features (sign, layout, rub stamp, etc.).

Some main topics of the digital transformation are more detailed in Table 2.

The new frontier of digital transformation is the implementation of intelligent and automated digital decision making engine. In this scenario, PM models are mainly characterized by a computational DSS core capable to automatically decide the process or the sub-process to execute. We observe that PM and DSS are connected and not necessarily integrated because typically DSS behaves as a 'standalone' engine. PM can deploy also complex logic rules (Boolean logics involving a large number of variables) or forecasting algorithms. The PM engine is the "intelligent core" of the digitised processes achieving decision-making by means of advanced data processing algorithms based on Boolean logics or on data clustering (unsupervised AI algorithms), or on data classification/prediction (supervised AI algorithms), or on other techniques and intelligent Key Performance Indicators (KPIs) suitable for the specific case study.

1.3 Processes and Actors Involved in PM

Industry 5.0 processes can be modelled by PM having the goal to upgrade and to optimize all the activities of the whole manufacturing supply chain. In Table 3 are listed some typical processes and sub-processes involved in PM by considering possible professional skills (system's actors) into the whole industrial scenario.

1.4 Preliminary Approaches to Design BPMN Digital Processes

All processes and sub-processes can be modelled by BPMN workflows as the simplified one illustrated in Figure 1 showing a main process (process to focus the attention) and integrating a sub-process (sub-process which can be collapsed into a unique task symbol, and which is not important to describe). The BPMN is a versatile approach to simulate different operating scenarios fixing responsibilities for different actions to perform related to a process or to a sub process. This implies an increase of responsibility of human resources. Furthermore, the BPMN workflows establish for each role the task to execute, thus increasing the possibility to control more easily the activities. Different tools can be adopted to facilitate the preliminary definition of requirements of a BPMN process. One of these tool is the Unified Modelling Language (UML): specifically, the Use Case Diagram (UCD) helps to define the actors of the systems and the main functions to assign to the task of the process; UCD is also useful to the beginning of the process design; the Sequence Diagram (SD) facilitates the comprehension of the timing of the executions of the process tasks and it is indicated to further explain the timing of actions for each phase. Other typologies of more simple flowcharts can be firstly adopted to facilitate the design of the BPMN workflow: basic informatics flowchart are indicated especially for the definition of the links linking the different pools of a macro-process.

A BPMN workflow is characterized by the following features:

- **Workflow Complexity:** the complexity level of a workflow is the number of tasks managed by a single actor of the system (a low number of tasks indicates a low complexity).
- **Interdependence:** the interdependence between different pools is the number of the links between the task of different actors of the system (a low number of links indicates a low interdependence);
- **Graphical Simplification:** the simplification is quantified as the number of the simplified sub-processes contained in a main process (see sub-process simplification in Figure 1).

Table 3. PM application fields and involved processes

PM application field	Processes and sub-processes involved	Actors involved in the process
Production	• Project management; • Reverse engineering; • Rapid prototyping; • Additive manufacturing; • Industry 4.0/Industry 5.0; • Warehouse stock management; • Worker security; • Internet of Things (IoT); • Human Machine Interface (HMI); • Sensing and actuation (self-adaptive); • Production efficiency; • Predictive maintenance; • Supply chain district management; • Cloud machine control; • Energy management; • Quality assessment/management.	• Technician; • Project Manager; • Simple worker; • Computer scientist; • Data Analyst; • Production Engineer; • Mechanical Engineer; • Electronic Engineer; • Energy Manager; • Measurer; • Management Engineer; • Quality Manager; • Security responsible; • Production manager; • Product manager; • Information; • R&D Chief.
Human resources (HR)	• HR selection; • HR training; • Organizational models; • Project management; • Worker security; • Change management.	• Project Manager; • Worker recruiter; • Management Engineer; • Chief Executive Officer (CEO).
Services	• Business management; • HR management; • Business models; • Logistics; • Risk analysis; • Customer care.	• Agent; • Worker recruiter; • Management Engineer; • Economist; • Data scientist; • Data analyst; • Project Manager.
Marketing	• Strategic marketing; • Dynamic pricing; • Customer care; • Customer clustering; • Recommender systems; • Business Intelligence.	• Economist; • Computer Scientist; • Data analyst; • Data scientist.

Figure 1. Schematic BPMN simplification of a sub-process with a task (all the sub-process is collapsed into a unique task)

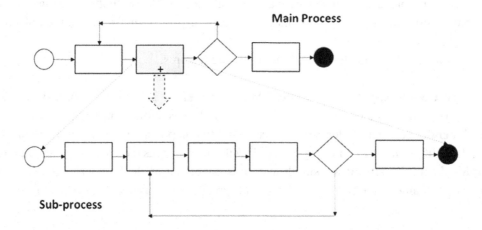

A hypothetical metric to adopt for the three features is a scale with the following qualitative five values: very low, low, average, high, very high (other scale of values can be adopted depending on the desired accuracy). This metric is useful for project managers to pass from a "AS IS" workflow to a "TO BE" one with the goal to decrease the workflow complexity and to increase the interdependences by simplifying as much as possible the workflow (a high value of 'Graphical Simplification' means greater ease in understanding the workflow). A consulting report typically will contain the above described features and the adopted BPMN legend (similar to the legend illustrated in Table 1).

The process mapping is performed following the steps of Figure 2 summarized as:

- **Phase 1:** analysis of the company organization chart indicating the main sectors of the industry and the related responsible for each sector;
- **Phase 2:** the Phase 1 allows to select the managers of areas to interview for the "AS IS" and "TO BE" process maps which will be sketched by BPMN workflows; the confidence level of the interviews are related to the capability of the interviewer (project manager) to understand the various meanings and implications of the answers (matching between polysemy, natural language, and technical knowledge of the interviewer about the specific topic);
- **Phase 3:** often the planning of the interviews to perform allows to update the organization chart of the company; this aspect is usual for industries in continuous evolution concerning outcomes of product or of services;
- **Phase 4:** the performed interviews allow the mapping of the "AS IS" processes of the company, by defining at the same time possible bottlenecks or critical points to be solved; during the interviews are yet hypothesized some solutions to problems; the preliminary feedbacks of the proposed solutions of the managers are important to anticipate and to share possible "TO BE" scenarios;
- **Phase 5:** the final phase is the "TO BE" workflow representing the perspectives of the analysed process adding new digital technologies or applying new models (as for the change management).

All the phases of the process mapping are addressed by through a preliminary requirements analysis (requirements deduced by needs). The proposed scheme is a main reference approach and is not a universal criterion: each case study could require a specific approach matching with the framework to analyse. The questionnaires for the interviews are designed for the specific sector and process to map. The experience to find new useful solutions facilitates the increase of the knowledge of technologies for the company workers: a deep analysis of solutions and models will increase the efficacy of the proposed technological solutions suggested in the modelled "TO BE" process.

1.5 PM Goals and Implementation Tools

The goal of the chapter is to provide new elements about the process modelling and process mapping merging AI and electronics (PM models) to design intelligent automated processes for control and actuation of production machines in manufacturing. The framework to consider is the design of innovative BPMN workflows for KPI evaluation and for logic control of machine and production robots. The challenge addressed in the research is the application of methods and tools usable to design PM models starting to the process mapping concept.

Figure 2. Phases of a consulting mapping "AS IS" and "TO BE" processes of a company

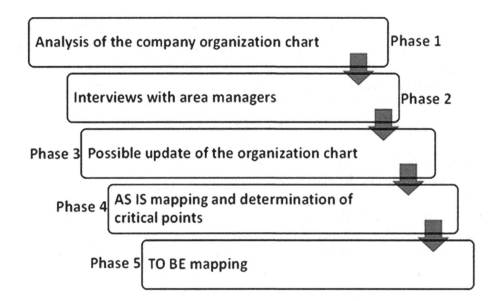

Actually, production processes are 'static' (production executed by fixed machine parameters). PM models are useful to solve problems in advanced production systems (Massaro, 2023) due to the static approach, such as: difficult control of synchronization of all machines/robots of production lines, absence of automation in machine parameter setting, and absence of product quality prediction and control. The PM is a dynamic technique suitable to control defects by setting automatically machines, enabling predictive maintenance, and tailoring different advanced technologies of Industry 5.0 such as Quantum Computer, Edge Computing, and Big Data analytics. The limitation of PM is mainly in the matching with real production of supply chains which include obsolete machines.

The goal of the proposed research is to provide elements and tools proving the possibility to design PM models in manufacturing processes. Specifically, in the next section of the chapter are provided more details about symbols and workflows modeling a PM electronic framework including description of DSS engine logics. Furthermore, it is discussed an example of implementation of a PM model by means of Konstanz Information Miner (KNIME) tool executing decision making rules by means the application of an "OR"/"AND" logic circuits.

2. PROCESS MINING ELEMENTS AND WORKFLOW DESIGN ASPECTS

Industry 5.0 facilities are mainly addressed on the automation of production and on self-adaption of processes by AI. The electronic components of the mechatronic systems implement specific functions such as robotic motion (sensing and actuation systems) and machine parameter monitoring. These functions can be represented by workflows such as BPMN ones modelling input and output signals of electronic components. An automated and intelligent decision making of a machine is then implemented by designing specific logic rules of the whole electronic/mechatronic system. Logic ports are suitable to execute logic rules and AI circuits (Massaro, 2022 a) and can be modelled by BPMN workflows. The integration of the logic conditions in the BPMN defines the PM model.

2.1 BPMN Workflows Modelling Logic Ports in Electronics

An innovative approach tailoring PM models is the implementation of logic rules capable to select a process or a sub-process or to perform a decision-making splitting a workflow (decision of tasks to perform indicating a specific signal to control). By considering the basic circuital elements of "AND" and of "OR" logic ports of Figure 3, it is possible to define all the logics rules characterizing a process workflow. The Boolean logic is applied also to model complex rules based for example on a combined evaluation of production parameters overcoming specific thresholds. In this way, a machine process can be also modelled by a logic 'electronic' circuit characterized by input and output ports, where the input ports are the task's parameters (inputs or conditions influencing a machine process), and the output ports are solutions enabling a decision or a task (enabled port means enabling a machine decision or a parameter setting).

Figure 3. Examples of the "AND" (left) and "OR" (right) logic ports

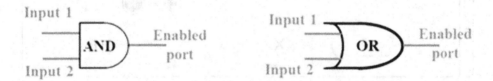

In order to design machine logic circuits by BPMN approach, it is necessary to "explode" the "AND" and of "OR" logic ports by means the symbols of Table 1. In Figure 4 are illustrated the BPMN "translations" of both the ports of Figure 3. The "AND" logic port is modelled by two conditions as input parameters of the ports ('Condition A' and 'Condition B' or equivalently 'Input 1' and 'Input 2' of Figure 3), besides the "Exclusive" gateway is able to provide the results about a checking phase (answering to the question: "is the condition satisfied?"). Finally, a "Complex Multiplier" gateway allows to execute the final decision related the table of truth of the "AND" logic as:

- (Yes, Yes) or equivalently (1,1): enabling the output port;
- (No, No) or equivalently (0,0): disabling the output port;
- (No, Yes) or equivalently (0,1): disabling the output port;
- (Yes, No) or equivalently (1,0): disabling the output port;

As for the "AND" port, also the "OR" port is characterized by two conditions as input parameters of the ports ('Condition A' and 'Condition B' or equivalently 'Input 1' and 'Input 2' of Figure 3) and by the "Exclusive" gateways able to provide the results about the condition checking. In this case, the "Parallel" gateway combines the unique condition related the port disabling action, besides the "Logic Multiplier" combines the other combinations enabling the output port. The table of truth of the "OR" logic is:

- (Yes, Yes) or equivalently (1,1): enabling the output port;
- (No, No) or equivalently (0,0): disabling the output port;
- (No, Yes) or equivalently (0,1): enabling the output port;
- (Yes, No) or equivalently (1,0): enabling the output port.

Figure 4. Examples of the "AND" (above) and "OR" (below) logic ports modelled by BPMN

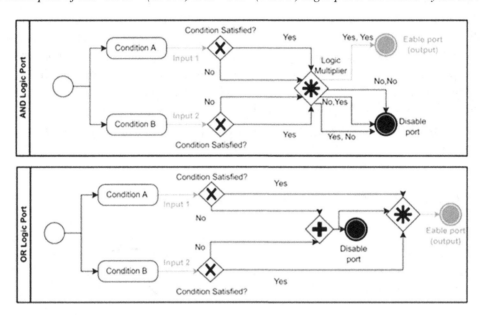

The "Exclusive Event Based" symbol of Figure 5 can be adopted to enclose all symbols of the Figure 4 thus simplifying the whole logic port workflow: the scheme of Figure 5 with two input ports and two output ports is able to simplify the workflows of Figure 4 behaving as a 2x2 black box. The use of the "Exclusive Event Based" symbol is also mainly indicated to represent a deeper checkpoint.

2.2 Examples of AI-PM Models Oriented on KPIs Evaluation

The logic ports and the BPMN symbols are suitable for the modelling of KPIs: the decision making about production quality and production efficiency can be modelled by a BPMN process introducing checkpoints according to the standard ISO: 9001-2015. The task of KPI evaluation enabling decision making is a part of the whole process workflow. The KPI metric is classified as "qualitative" or "quantitative". In Figure 6 is illustrated an example of a BPMN model of a production quality process control integrating a KPI evaluation. The workflow is structured as follows:

- the KPI monitoring process starts with the KPI evaluation (for example by checking a defect by means of a measurement instrument or by image vision technique);
- if the checkpoint provides a positive result, the process continues and periodically is estimated the same KPI controlling quality, besides digital data of measurements are stored into a database system;

Figure 5. "Exclusive event based" having five input ports and three output ports. All the disconnected inputs are processed by the "Exclusive Event Based" gateway behaving as a decision making selecting three main outputs. The automatism of the decision making switches the output according to the specific AI input data processing (Industry 5.0 scenario about the self-adapting of the output process).

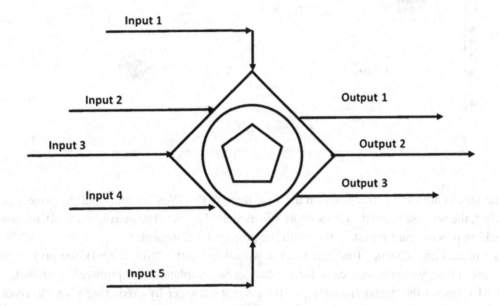

- if the checkpoint provides a negative result, the production process is reengineered to avoid again defects, and data are stored into the system database to trace historical data of product quality;
- an AI engine (core of the PM workflow) is useful to classify or to predict defects thus supporting risk assessment about product quality (the PM is characterised by AI algorithms suitable to extract defect features from a product or semi-product image);
- a procedure reporting quality trend and quality prediction is continually triggered to control the production risk concerning defects.

The same PM model of Figure 6 can be also applied to control production machine malfunctions by enabling predictive maintenance procedures (AI prediction of machine failures). The KPIs are suitable also to control working environment conditions (controlling alerting variables such as gas, smoke, temperature, etc.) by defining hazard levels in the risk assessment.

In the second theoretical example, the PM model is applied in the Figure 7 representing a project management process. The BPMN workflow is actuated by a project manager controlling periodically project results. The workflow is structured as follows:

- a project manager periodically controls results and the risk prediction supporting the risk analysis (AI forecasting predicting risks);
- in the case of a positive check the development of the process continues and the results are again periodically checked;

Figure 6. PM model implementing a KPI monitoring process: BPMN workflow modelling a quality checkpoint integrating a KPI decision making function

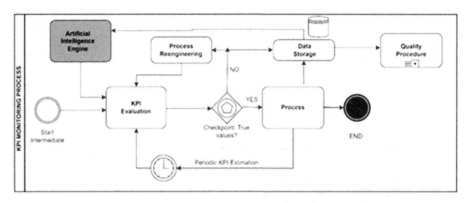

- if the results are "True" (indicated in the workflow by the "Yes" output) and the project period is the last, the process ends (the check control is modelled by the "Exclusive" symbol), otherwise the checking process continues together with the project development;
- if the results are "Untrue" (indicated in the workflow by the "No" output), the project manager allocates other human resources or further budget to complete or to optimize the project;
- the AI supports the decision making of the project manager by predicting possible risks correlated with the project development (risk of malfunctions of tools and machines, unavailability of materials, etc.).

As dashboards indicating KPIs different plots such as the radar chart and target chart (see examples in Figure 8). The dashboards are also important to highlight industry target (target chart), or to observe the actual and the future digital impacts (Massaro, 2022 b) in digital transformation processes (radar chart).

AI supervised algorithms typically used for variable classification and prediction are Artificial Neural Networks (ANN), Convolutional Neural Networks (CNN), Long Short Term Memory (LSTM) networks, and Recurrent Neural Network (RNN). The AI unsupervised models are more indicated for clustering analysis when a large number of variables are considered. Data clustering techniques are k-Means and Fuzzy c-Means (clustering scoring the data membership to each cluster).

Figure 7. PM BPMN model: example of a process management process executed by a project manager

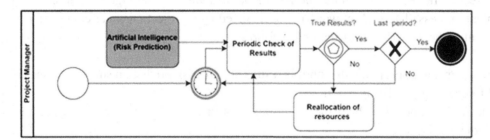

Figure 8. (Left) target chart; (right) radar chart indicating KPIs values

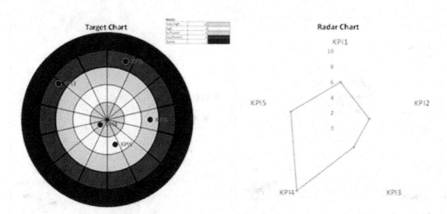

3. EXAMPLE OF IMPLEMENTATION AND EXECUTION OF PM MODEL

A possible way to implement PM models is to "translate" the BPMN model by trough a KNIME workflow. KNIME is an open source tool suitable to model the data processing tasks and fluxes as workflows constituted by blocks (or nodes) and links interconnecting nodes. The KNIME workflow of Figure 9 is an example of implementation of a complex logic condition composed by "AND" and "OR" logic ports structuring the decisional circuit of Figure 9. The whole analysed logic circuit can be simplified by a black box having three input ports and one output port (final enabled port). An alternative way to represent the logic ports are the BPMN schemes of Figure 4, where the final output signal Y is the process to enable (signal '1') or disable (signal '0') by means an output controlled port. The proposed theoretical example is characterized by three input ports ('Input 1', 'Input 2', and 'Input 3') and by a single 'Y' output port. The KNIME workflows is structured as follows:

- Three 'Excel reader' nodes are the input signals ('Input 1', 'Input 2', and 'Input 3');
- Two 'Column Appender' nodes are able to merge the input values into an unique matrix;
- The 'Math Formula' block implements the logic AND multiplication (A=Input 3= Input 1 * Input 2 as it is a multiplication operation between '1' and '0' values);
- The 'Rule Engine' block estimating the final output value Y= A OR B.
- The 'Missing Value' block is applied to set the missing values of the table as the corresponding '0' (artifice to have the final truth table in correct form with '0' and '1' values).

In Figure 11 is illustrated a screenshot representing the KNIME workflow "Truth" table output of the circuit of Figure 10: the first three columns are the input signals loaded in the local repository to be processed, besides the fourth and the fifth columns are the results of the "AND" and of the "OR" logic port outputs of Figure 10, respectively.

We observe that the Boolean algorithms are the KNIME pre-set Boolean functions implemented into the KNIME 'Math Formula' and 'OR' blocks of Figure 9. The KNIME tool is able to further combine more "AND" and "OR" logic ports to construct more complex logic networks (advantage for the deployment of complex logics).

Figure 9. PM model implemented by a KNIME workflow

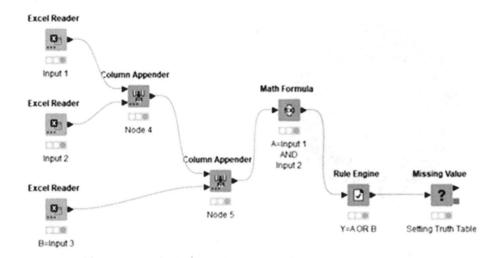

Figure 10. Circuit with logic ports implemented by the workflow of Figure 9 and related black box simplified model

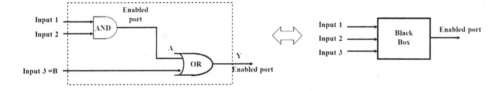

Figure 11. Table of the final truth table (table output of the 'missing value' block of the workflow of Figure 9)

Output table - 3:8 - Missing Value (Setting Truth Table)

File   Edit   Hilite   Navigation   View

Table "default" - Rows: 14   Spec - Columns: 5   Properties   Flow Variables

Row ID	Input 1	Input 2	Input 3	D Input 1 AND Input 2	Final OR (Y)
Row0	1	0	1	0	1
Row1	1	0	1	0	1
Row2	1	1	1	1	1
Row3	1	0	1	0	1
Row4	0	0	0	0	0
Row5	1	1	0	1	1
Row6	1	1	0	1	1
Row7	0	1	1	0	1
Row8	0	1	1	0	1
Row9	0	1	1	0	1
Row 10	1	1	0	1	1
Row 11	1	1	1	1	1
Row 12	0	0	1	0	1
Row 13	1	0	0	0	0

4. CONCLUSION

The book chapter is focused on an innovative approach to model PM process by means BPMN and an open source tool executing processes. The first part of the chapter describes the meaning of main BPMN symbols usable to design a PM-BPMN workflow. The attention is then moved to the modelling of "AND" and "OR" logic ports as examples of logic rules constituting PM decision-making processes. The described examples highlight that the PM models are typically characterized by a decision-making performed by an AI algorithm, being the forecasting of risks an important aspects to reinforce decisions for production and for safety management.

The advantages of AI implementation in PM models are mainly in the possibility to improve the decision making by optimizing the accuracy of the response. Specifically, the efficiency of AI supervised algorithms are in the optimization of the training models. A disadvantage is to have a large volume of digital data to process which typically are not available (large input dataset are required to optimize the training models). The proposed methodology is structured into two phases: the first one is significant to design digitally processes by means of BPMN models integrating AI and logic rules, and the second one is an example of the execution of the decision making model by means the KNIME tool. The discussed tools are elements important for the digital transformation of industries addressing the standard processes on a data mining/data driven process intelligently managing production, quality and safety. Perspectives about PM applications are in the Industry 5.0 scenario triggering AI algorithms to activate tasks and allowing a self-adaption processes controlled automatically by an AI engine. The new challenge is to design innovative manufacturing production processes based on intelligent control of production. The process design of digital fluxes is a good solution for the tailoring of innovative manufacturing supply chains in Indutry 5.0. A possible gap between PM design and PM implementation is in the flexibility of hardware and software components about computational time, availability of open systems for the interconnection of different advanced technologies, and the knowledge in AI-based programming. Actually, the PM has been successfully applied to human resource organizational models in healthcare processes (Rosa et al. 2023). The next step is to apply this technique in industrial electronic systems matching with Programmable Logic Controller (PLC) protocols.

ACKNOWLEDGMENT

The author gratefully thanks the staff of "Ingegneria Gestionale" of LUM University "Giuseppe Degennaro".

REFERENCES

Barbuzzi, D., Massaro, A., Galiano, A., Pellicani, L., Pirlo, G., & Sageese, M. (2020). Multi-Domain Intelligent System for Document Image Retrieval. *International Journal of Adaptive and Innovative Systems*, 2(4), 282–297. doi:10.1504/IJAIS.2019.108381

Magaletti, N., Massaro, A., Cosoli, G., & Leogrande, A. (2023). Smart District 4.0 Project: Validation of Results and Exploitation Perspectives. G. Agapito et al. (Eds.): ICWE 2022 Workshops, (pp. 149-159). IEEE.

Massaro, A. (2020). Image Processing and Post-Data Mining Processing for Security in Industrial Applications: Security in Industry. Handbook of Research on Intelligent Data Processing and Information Security Systems. IGI Global. doi:10.4018/978-1-7998-1290-6.ch006

Massaro, A. (2021 a). *Electronic in Advanced Research Industry: From Industry 4.0 to Industry 5.0 Advances*. Wiley. doi:10.1002/9781119716907

Massaro, A. (2021 b). *Electronic and Reverse Engineering*. Wiley. doi:10.1002/9781119716907.ch8

Massaro, A. (2021 c). *Information Technology Infrastructures Supporting Industry 5.0 Facilities*. Wiley. doi:10.1002/9781119716907.ch2

Massaro, A. (2022a). Advanced Control Systems in Industry 5.0 Enabling Process Mining. *Sensors (Basel)*, *22*(22), 1–18. doi:10.339022228677 PMID:36433272

Massaro, A. (2022c). Multi-Level Decision Support System in Production and Safety Management. *Knowledge (Beverly Hills, Calif.)*, *2*(4), 682–701.

Massaro, A. (2023). Advanced Electronic and Optoelectronic Sensors, Applications, Modelling and Industry 5.0 Perspectives. *Applied Sciences (Basel, Switzerland)*, *13*(7), 1–26. doi:10.3390/app13074582

Massaro, A., Cosoli, G., Magaletti, N., & Costantiello, A. (2022b). A Search Methodology Based on Industrial Ontology and Machine Learning to Analyze Georeferenced Italian Districts. *Knowledge (Beverly Hills, Calif.)*, *2*(2), 243–265.

Massaro, A., & Galiano, A. (2020). Image Processing and Post-Data Mining Processing for Security in Industrial Applications: Security in Industry. Handbook of Research on Intelligent Data Processing and Information Security Systems. IGI Global. doi:10.4018/978-1-7998-1290-6.ch006

Massaro, A., Gargaro, M., Dipierro, G., Galiano, A. M., & Buonopane, S. (2020). Prototype Cross Platform Oriented on Cybersecurity, Virtual Connectivity, Big Data and Artificial Intelligence Control. *IEEE Access: Practical Innovations, Open Solutions*, *8*, 197939–197954. doi:10.1109/ACCESS.2020.3034399

Rosa, A., Massaro, A., & McDermott, O. (2023). Process Mining Applied to Lean Management Model Improving Decision Making in Healthcare Organizations. In 18th International Forum on Knowledge Asset Dynamics, Matera, Italy.

KEY TERMS AND DEFINITIONS

Artificial Intelligence (AI) Engine: AI algorithms integrated in a PM model and predicting or classifying process's variables.

Data-Driven Process: Data driving a process or a sub-process.

Decision Making: A process enabled by a decision performed by a logical condition or by a key performance estimation.

Decision Support System (DSS): A system constituted by algorithms or by intelligent decision-making procedures supporting the decision about the process to execute.

KPI (Key Performance Indicator): Parameter estimated to check efficiency, risk, and quality.

Process Mining (PM): Processes integrating logic rules or AI outputs as decision-making.

Quality Assessment: The definition of hazard risk levels by means of the application of a PM model.

Chapter 2
The Explainable Model to Multi–Objective Reinforcement Learning Toward an Autonomous Smart System

Tomohiro Yamaguchi

Nara College, National Institute of Technology, Japan

ABSTRACT

The mission of this chapter is to add an explainable model to multi-goal reinforcement learning toward an autonomous smart system to design both complex behaviors and complex decision making friendly for a human user. At the front of the introduction section, and a relation between reinforcement learning including an explainable model and a smart system is described. To realize the explainable model, this chapter formalizes the exploration of various behaviors toward sub-goal states efficiently and in a systematic way in order to collect complex behaviors from a start state towards the main goal state. However, it incurs significant learning costs in previous learning methods, such as behavior cloning. Therefore, this chapter proposes a novel multi-goal reinforcement learning method based on the iterative loop-action selection strategy. As a result, the complex behavior sequence is learned with a given sub-goal sequence as a sequence of macro actions. This chapter reports the preliminary work carried out under the OpenAIGym learning environment with the CartPoleSwingUp task.

INTRODUCTION

The mission of this chapter is to add an explainable model to multi-goal reinforcement learning (Drugan 2017)(Yamaguchi 2022) toward an autonomous smart system to design both complex behaviors and complex decision making friendly for a human user. At the front of the introduction, a relation between reinforcement learning including an explainable model and a smart system is described.

DOI: 10.4018/978-1-6684-7684-0.ch002

Smart systems incorporate functions of sensing, actuation, and control in order to describe and analyze a situation, and make decisions based on the available data. In most cases the "smartness" of the system can be attributed to autonomous operation. To make systems smarter, third-generation smart systems combine "intelligence". To realize this, DARPA formulated the explainable artificial intelligence (XAI) program with the goal to enable end users to better understand, trust, and effectively manage artificially intelligent systems (Gunning, 2021). **Table 1** shows the issues on a smart system with explainable AI (XAI) mainly on learning capabilities. The research field of a smart system is expanded from data analytics to autonomous control task. This chapter focuses on the latter task. The characteristics of the autonomous control is that the model has multiple states and it handles state transitions with actions. Reinforcement learning is one of the machine learning methods to learn autonomous control associated with multiple decision making problems including state transitions.

Table 1. It is the issues on a smart system with explainable AI

machine learning task	machine learning method	problem
data analytics	supervised learning	classification
	unsupervised learning	clustering
autonomous control	reinforcement learning	multiple stage decision making

Therefore, this chapter describes the exploration of various behaviors toward sub-goal states in an efficient and systematic manner through the use of repeated loop-action. There are three main features. The first one is that the iterative loop-action simplifies the result of an action sequence. The second feature is that it explores the action space with a given sub-goal set as a guide for collecting behaviors toward one of the sub-goals. The third feature is that a macro action is learned from a collected behavior, which consists of a certain length of repeated loop-actions between two sub-goal states.

In recent years, deep reinforcement learning research has made significant progress by utilizing images as perceptual input (Mnih 2015). This has expanded the scope of application for reinforcement learning to include TV game play simulators, such as the Atari 2600 TV game machine from the 1970s. In several Atari 2600 TV games, deep reinforcement learners have successfully surpassed the highest score achieved by human experts using evaluation criteria such as maximizing the game score (Mnih 2015).

Reinforcement learning (RL) is a popular algorithm used for automatically solving sequential decision problems. It is commonly modeled as Markov decision processes (MDPs) (Puterman 1994). While there are numerous RL methods available, many of them focus on single-objective settings where the agent's goal is to determine a single solution based on an optimality criterion. However, it has become evident that learning becomes challenging in games that require context-based learning, such as anticipating future events (e.g., obtaining keys for later stages) or making choices at branching points that do not immediately generate rewards. In such cases, imitation learning methods that leverage action sequences from human experts, particularly those capable of handling context like the Decision Transformer (DT) method proposed by Chen (2021), are expected to be beneficial. Nevertheless, when dealing with unknown goals or environments, applying imitation learning can be difficult due to the lack of prior knowledge about the model's behavior sequences.

In the current deep reinforcement learning research (Plaat 2020), there are two major problems that pose significant challenges to practical application. The first problem is the reward sparse problem, where reinforcement learning struggles to make progress in vast learning state spaces due to the scarcity of reward states. When applying reinforcement learning methods to real-world tasks, continuous state spaces are often encountered. However, discovering the desired action sequence that leads to the goal through trial and error becomes difficult with traditional reinforcement learning methods, as the continuous state space is much larger than the discrete state space. To address this issue, one approach is to generate various sub-goals within the continuous state space and utilize the sequence of sub-goals as context to derive the desired action sequence. The second problem pertains to the challenge of consistently obtaining the desired result, namely the action sequence aligned with the given context. This difficulty arises from the inherent complexity of understanding the internal structure of the learning unit and accurately predicting the learning outcomes.

To address the aforementioned problems, this research establishes three main research goals. The first goal is to develop a method for automatically generating a sub-goal set consisting of initial states, the main goal state, and similar states associated with either the initial or main goal state. This approach aims to create a comprehensive set of sub-goals that can facilitate learning and exploration in the given task. The second goal is to implement an iterative loop action selection strategy that enables systematic exploration of a large learning space. By employing this strategy, the research aims to collect behavior sequences that transition to each sub-goal in the generated set. This exploration process facilitates the learning of macro-behaviors that transition between sub-goals, as well as the development of partial policies for each sub-goal. The third goal is to realize a multi-goal control mechanism that guides the execution of complex behavior sequences along arbitrary sub-goal sequences. This mechanism enables the agent to navigate through the task by following specific sub-goal sequences, allowing for more flexible and adaptable behavior generation. Overall, these research goals aim to overcome the challenges posed by sparse rewards, large state spaces, and the difficulty in deriving desired action sequences, by incorporating automatic sub-goal generation, systematic exploration, and multi-goal control into the learning process.

The learning task addressed in this research is multi-goal reinforcement learning, specifically focusing on the components of complex chain behaviors. The objective is to train an agent to learn and execute these complex behaviors by combining multiple sub-goals. The learning space in this task is defined by a continuous state vector space, which consists of multiple continuous values representing different aspects of the environment, and a discrete action space composed of a finite number of discrete actions that the agent can take. As a demonstration of multi-goal learning, the execution task in this research aims to achieve flexible execution of learned behaviors along a given arbitrary sub-goal sequence. The sub-goal sequence represents a chain of various techniques in gymnastics, and the agent's objective is to execute these techniques in the specified order. By addressing the learning and execution tasks in the context of multi-goal reinforcement learning, this research aims to develop methods and techniques that enable agents to learn and execute complex chain behaviors with a combination of sub-goals, thereby showcasing the flexibility and adaptability of the proposed approach.

This chapter presents a novel multi-goal reinforcement learning method that focuses on the automatic generation of sub-goals and systematic exploration of the action space using iterative loop action selection strategies. To assess the effectiveness of this proposed method, it is applied to the CartPoleSwingUp task, which is a standard benchmark environment in reinforcement learning research, available in OpenAIGym. Then, this chapter also presents the results of a preliminary experiment conducted on the CartPoleSwingUp task using the proposed method.

BACKGROUND OF THIS RESEARCH

This section describes the background and positioning of this research. In the field of deep reinforcement learning (DRL), there was initially a competition for high-speed learning methods. Recent research in DRL has expanded the base of the field by incorporating elemental technologies from existing reinforcement learning approaches, such as human-understandable model-based methods (Plaat 2020), multi-task DRL, and multi-objective DRL. **Table 2** presents the positioning of this research in addressing two key issues:

(a) The reward sparse problem in a vast learning state space.
(b) The challenges associated with deriving desired results.

Table 2. It is the positioning of this research

research issues	conventional methods	proposed method
(a) reward sparse problem	reward shaping, curriculum learning and sub-goal discovery	generate multiple sub-goals with similar initial and goal states
(b) learning desired results	offline learning from supervised data such as behavior cloning	online learning by systematic exploration

(a) Reward sparse problem in a vast learning state space:

In addressing the reward sparse problem in a vast learning state space, conventional methods include step-by-step goal setting and learning environment design, such as reward shaping (Ng 1999)(Devlin 2012) and curriculum learning (Forestier 2022), as well as sub-goal discovery methods (McGovern 2001) for hierarchical reinforcement learning (Plappert 2018)(Pateria 2021)(Hutsebaut-Buysse 2022), which are also considered in this research. It is important to note that curriculum learning (Soviany 2022) involves training machine learning models in a meaningful order, progressing from easy to hard samples. Many of these methods augment the continuous state space using large amounts of training data and employ approximate learning. However, due to this approximation-based augmentation, there is a risk of overlooking or ignoring unexpected states that are sporadically scattered (referred to as pitfalls) in the state space. This poses a fundamental weakness of deep learning methods, including deep reinforcement learning (DRL). It is worth mentioning that these unexpected states have recently gained attention as adversarial examples that can deceive AI systems in the field of deep learning. In contrast, the proposed method takes a different approach by generating multiple sub-goals and identifying behavior sequences that transition towards these sub-goals, rather than relying solely on data supplementation.

(b)   Problems that are difficult to derive desired results:

Regarding the problems that are difficult to derive desired results, conventional methods have proposed offline learning approaches (Kumar 2022) such as Behavior Cloning and imitation learning, which rely on supervised data from a large play history database of expert human players. However, when utilizing the play history database of human experts, there is a certain expectation of achieving task goals, but the extent of coverage in the learning process is crucial. On the other hand, when generating play history automatically through random action selection, it is possible to cover the learning range near the initial state. However, as the system explores further away from the initial state, it becomes increasingly challenging to achieve good task performance, resulting in a drawback. In essence, offline learning methods based on play history databases face challenges in both scenarios. In comparison, the proposed method takes a different approach. It does not rely on play history databases but instead discovers behavior sequences that transition towards sub-goals through online exploration. The sub-goal candidates are generated offline and used as learning data. This approach ensures both a consistent quality of training data and comprehensive coverage of the learning range, addressing the limitations of offline learning methods mentioned earlier.

IDENTIFICATION OF ACTION SPACE MODEL

This section describes the identification of the action space model based on the iterative loop action exploration strategy. Firstly, the method of generating sub-goal states in the abstract state space is introduced to address the issue of "reward sparsity in a vast learning state space." Secondly, a summary model is presented, which comprises a set of sub-goal states and action sequences that transition between these sub-goal states, aiming to solve the problem of "difficulties in deriving desired results." The proposed summary model is one of the explainable models in Explainable Reinforcement Learning researches (Puiutta 2020) (Dazeley 2023). Finally, the iterative loop action exploration strategy is proposed for systematic exploration of the discrete action space.

Generation of Sub-goal States in the Abstract State Space

This subsection explains the method used to generate sub-goal states in the abstract state space, aiming to approximate the entire continuous state space through discretization. To achieve this, the research emphasizes the initial state and the main goal state of the learning task. Firstly, for the initial state, logical operations are applied to transform and generate similar states in the neighborhood. Similarly, a similar operation is used to generate similar states of the goal state. Subsequently, a sub-goal set is created, consisting of the initial state, the goal state, and their respective similar states.

As an illustrated example, this section explains the Cart-pole Problem [1], which involves controlling an inverted pendulum by moving a cart left and right to keep the pole in an upward vertical direction. Specifically, the CartPoleSwingUp task is described, where the initial state of the pole is in a downward vertical direction, and the goal state is an upward vertical direction. **Figure 1** shows the CartPoleSwingUp environment and the tasks addressed in this research. In **Figure 1(a)**, a cart with a pole is shown. The cart-pole system consists of a pendulum with its center of gravity positioned above the pivot point. Although the system is inherently unstable, it can be controlled by manipulating the pivot point. The pole is connected to the cart through an un-actuated joint, allowing the cart to move along a frictionless track. The available actions in this environment are applying horizontal forces to the left or right to push the cart. There are four observable states: the position and velocity of the cart, and the angle θ and angular velocity ω of the pole. To focus on the behavior of the pole, this study simplifies the target state to only consider the pole angle θ and the angular velocity ω. The angle ω has specific values: $\omega=0$ for the downward vertical direction, $\omega=$Pi for the upward vertical direction, and $\omega=$|Pi|/2 for the horizontal direction.

Next, an overview of the CartPoleSwingUp task is provided. The objective of this task is to maintain balance of the cart-pole system by applying appropriate forces to the pivot point. **Figure 1(b)** illustrates the initial state of the task, where the pole is vertically downward ($\theta=0$) and its angular velocity is zero ($\omega=0$). In this state, the cart's velocity is also zero. **Figure 1(c)** depicts the goal state of the task, where the pole angle is approximately vertical upward ($\theta=180$ degrees) and the angular velocity is zero ($\omega=0$). The goal is to maintain the pole angle close to the vertical upward direction ($|\omega|<\varepsilon$) as the desired outcome of this task.

Figure 1. The CartPoleSwingUp environment and its tasks. 1(a) It is the Cart with the Pole, 1(b) It is the initial state of the task ($\theta=0$, $\omega=0$), 1(c) It is the target state of the task ($\theta=180$ degrees, $\omega=0$).

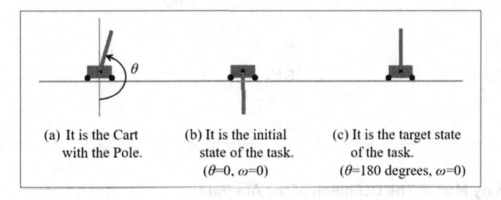

(a) It is the Cart with the Pole.

(b) It is the initial state of the task. ($\theta=0$, $\omega=0$)

(c) It is the target state of the task. ($\theta=180$ degrees, $\omega=0$)

Figure 2 shows the abstracted state space of the polar graph focusing both the pole angle θ and the pole angular velocity ω of the CartPoleSwingUp task. In **Figure 2**, let sg_0 be *the initial state* of the bar and sg_2 be *the main goal state* of it. First, the neighborhood state of sg_0 is generated as sg_1 by changing the range of angular velocity ω of sg_0 which is nearly equal 0 ($|\omega|<\varepsilon$) to $\varepsilon<|\omega|$. By the same operation, the neighborhood state of sg_2 ($|\omega|<\varepsilon$) is generated as sg_3 ($\varepsilon<|\omega|$). Then *the sub-goal set* $\{sg_0, sg_1, sg_2, sg_3\}$ is set.

In other words, the initial state sg_0 and the main goal state sg_2 are sub-goals contained within the abstract state represented by the small inner circle in **Figure 2**, expressed as $|\omega|<\varepsilon$. On the other hand, sg_1 and sg_3 are sub-goals generated as similar states within the abstract state outside of $|\omega|<\varepsilon$, depicted as the donut shape ($\varepsilon<|\omega|$) in **Figure 2**. Based on the above, sub-goals are generated to contribute to deriving various desired results. Additionally, after systematic exploration, if a state is found that partially resembles a sub-goal within an action sequence that does not reach any sub-goal, it is added to the sub-goal set. For example, this could be an unexpected state where $|\omega|<\varepsilon$ and θ is neither equal to 0 nor 180 degrees.

Figure 2. The abstracted state space of the polar graph focusing both the pole angle θ and the pole angular velocity ω of the CartPoleSwingUp task

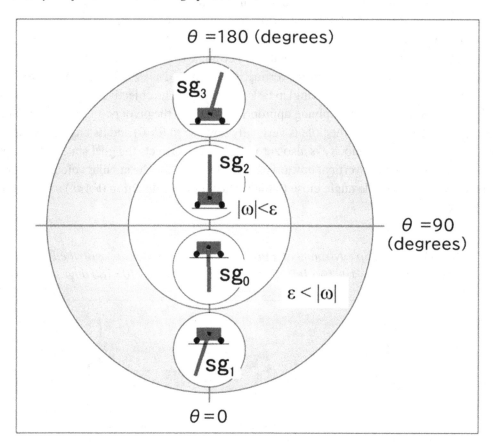

Summary Model: The Definition of the Abstract Model Based on Sub-Goal State Set

In order to generate a complex action sequence according to the context, it is desirable to use a clear and concise learning model that is easy for humans to handle. Therefore, this section describes *a summary model* consisting of multiple *sub-goals* and *macro-actions* (each of them is an action sequence) transitioning to each sub-goal.

Figure 3 shows an example of the summary model for the CartPoleSwingUp task. Let MA_{ij} be the macro action from sg_i to sg_j, this summary model consists of the set of sub-goals $\{sg_0, sg_1, sg_2, sg_3\}$ in the state space shown in Fig.1 plus the following five types of *macro-action* transitioning to sub-goals:

(1) MA_{01}, the transition from sg_0 to sg_1 is a swing from hanging.
(2) MA_{12}, the transition from sg_1 to sg_2 is a handstand from kicking up.
(3) MA_{21}, the transition from sg_2 to sg_1 is a swing from handstand.
(4) MA_{13}, the transition from sg_1 to sg_3 is a upward swing.
(5) MA_{31}, the transition from sg_3 to sg_1 is a downward swing.

Figure 3. An example of the summary model for the CartPoleSwingUp task

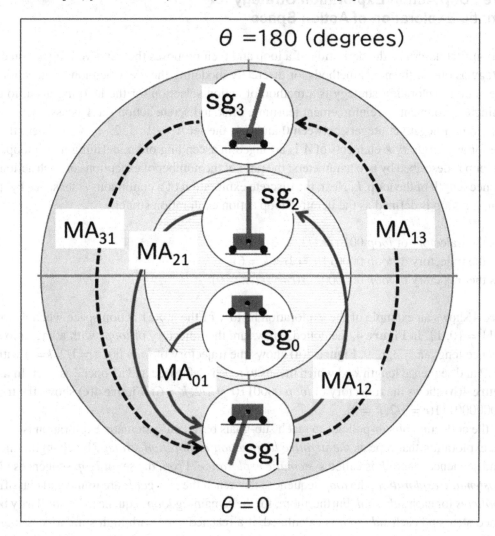

Using this summary model, the context of complex behavior can be represented by a chain of macro-actions that transition to each sub-goal based on the sub-goal sequence. For example, if the sub-goal sequence is (sg_0, sg_1, sg_2, sg_1, sg_3, sg_1, sg_2), the output from the model would be (MA_{01}, MA_{12}, MA_{21}, MA_{13}, MA_{31}, MA_{12}), representing the sequence of actions: swinging from hanging, performing a hand-stand from kicking up, swinging from handstand, performing an upward swing, performing a downward swing, and performing a handstand from kicking up.

At this time, it is evident that multiple partial policies can be selected for the part where the transition destination from sub-goal sg_1 differs for sg_2 and sg_3. Consequently, multipurpose policy control is described, wherein different learning outcomes are achieved. The solid line represents the partial policy (sg_1, sg_2), while the dotted line represents the partial policy (sg_1, sg_3)), with each sub-goal sg_2 and sg_3 being switched according to the goal. This generates a complex behavior sequence that cannot be controlled by a single policy.

Iterative Loop Action Exploration Strategy for Systematic Exploration of Action Space

This section first describes the definition of a loop and then proposes the iterative loop action exploration strategy as one of the novel methods for discretely modeling the identification of an action space. Here, the action exploration strategy is a method of action selection for the learning agent to explore the learning environment in reinforcement learning. First, a discrete action set A is assumed. When its elements are non-negative integers between 0 and n-1, the set $A = \{0, 1, 2, ..., n-1\}$. Then, the action sequence for any arbitrary k elements of A is arranged in ascending order, defining it as a loop. At this time, the loop is described by two parameters: the ratio of the number of executions of each action, r, and the sequence length of the loop, k. Next, the discrete exploration of a continuous state space by iterative execution of a loop is defined as the iterative loop action exploration strategy.

(a)   It is the trajectory of *loop* 001 ($r=1/2, k=3$).
(b)   It is the trajectory of *loop* 000011($r = 1/2, k = 6$).
(c)   It is the trajectory of *loop* 000000111($r = 1/2, k = 9$).

Figure 4 shows an example of the exploration history of the a0×a1 action space when action set A = {a0, a1} = {0, 1}. In **Figure 4**, the dotted arrows are the trajectory of *loops* with a0/a1 ratio $r = 1/2$ and sequence length k = 3, 6, 9. **Figure 4(a)** shows the trajectory of *loop* 001 ($r=1/2, k=3$) with a0/a1 ratio $r=1/2$ and sequence length $k=3$ which means to repeat "a0 twice and a1 once" as a set. In the same way, **Figure 4(b)** shows the trajectory of *loop* 000011($r = 1/2, k = 6$), **Figure 4(c)** shows the trajectory of *loop* 000000111($r = 1/2, k = 9$).

Next, the collection of sub-policies to reach sub-goals based on systematic exploration is described. First, the exploration that repeats *the iterative loop action exploration strategy* by changing the action ratio r and sequence length k is called s*ystematic exploration*. From the set of *loop* sequences obtained by this s*ystematic exploration*, the *loop* sequences that reach the *sub-goals* are found and classified into *partial policies* for each *sub-goal*. Furthermore, for the remaining *loop* sequence, the similarity between the reached state and each *sub-goal* is calculated, if a reached state with high similarity is found, it is added to the *sub-goal* set as an unexpected *sub-goal* candidate. This method is related to Hindsight Experience Replay (Andrychowicz 2017) (Manela, 2019), which successfully learns from failed episodes that do not reach their goals.

EXPERIMENTS

This section shows the authors' preliminary experimental results of the systematic exploration by the iterative loop action exploration strategy on the CartPoleSwingUp task.

Figure 4. The exploration history of the a0×a1 action space

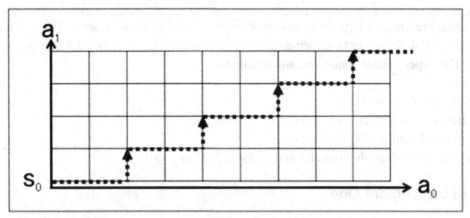

(a) the trajectory of *loop* 001 (*r*=1/2, *k*=3)

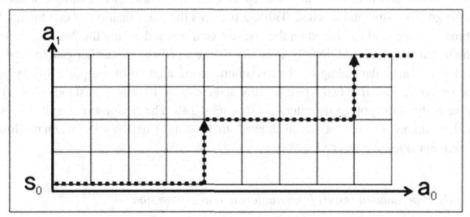

(b) the trajectory of *loop* 000011(*r* = 1/2, *k* = 6)

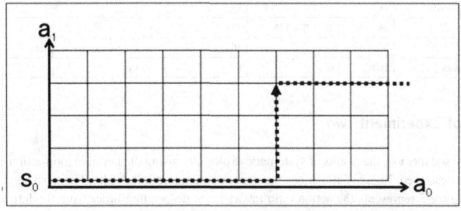

(c) the trajectory of *loop* 000000111(*r* = 1/2, *k* = 9)

Experimental Setup

This subsection presents the experimental conditions for learning environments. The continuous state space of the CartPoleSwingUp task focuses on two dimensions: the pole angle θ and the pole angular velocity ω. The experimental conditions are as follows:

- The number of actions is two.
- The start state of each episode is fixed to sg_0 ($\theta=0$, $\omega=0$).
- The episode length is 200 steps.
- The number of sub-goals to be checked is three, $\{sg_1, sg_2, sg_3\}$.

Results of Experiment One

As the baseline method, the results of random exploration through random action selection are described. Because most existing RL methods including deep RL methods explore by random action selection until some learning goal is found and reached. **Table 3** presents the classification of one hundred episodes into three types: sg_1, sg_2 and sg_3, based on the last sub-goal reached during the 200-step episode, starting from the initial state sg_0. Additionally, episodes that reached sg_1 are further categorized into small swings and large swings, depending on the maximum swing angle θ of the pole. Similarly, episodes that reached sg_2 are divided into two types: kicking up ($1 < |\omega| < 10$) and handstand ($|\omega| < 1$), based on the angular velocity of the pole in the interval $175 < |\theta| < 180$. The exploration results of one hundred episodes with randomly selected actions all showed small swings (max $|\theta| < 90$) when reaching sg_1, and there were zero episodes that reached sg_2 or sg_3.

Table 3. It is the experimental results from random action exploration

type of behavior	small swing	large swing	rotation	kicking up	handstand	total
last visited sub-goal	sg_1		sg_3	sg_2		
max θ (degrees)	$|\theta| < 90$	$90 < |\theta| < 175$	$175 < |\theta| < 180$			
ω	don't care		$10 < |\omega|$	$1 < |\omega| < 10$	$|\omega| < 1$	
number of episodes	100	0	0	0	0	100

Results of Experiment Two

As the proposed method, the results of systematic exploration using the iterative loop action exploration strategy are described. **Figure 5** illustrates the systematic exploration results. The horizontal axis of the graph in **Figure 5** represents the action ratio (a0/a1 ratio, descending order from the left) of the loop utilized for exploration, while the vertical axis represents the ratio (and number of occurrences) of each behavior as presented in **Table 3** within episodes with the same a0/a1 ratio.

Under the conditions of loop length $k = n(a0 + a1)$, where $n = 1, 2, 3, ...$ (n|($k \leq 200$)), each episode (200 steps) was executed once for each k. For instance, when the a0/a1 ratio is 1/2, the values of k include 3, 6, 9, ... 198, resulting in a total of 66 episodes. The bar graph indicates the following occurrences from the bottom:

- The small swing is 14 times.
- The large swing is 11 times.
- The kicking up is 11 times.
- The rotation is 18 times.
- The handstand is 12 times.

As depicted in **Figure 5**, several behaviors, such as kicking up or handstand, approach the main goal when the a0/a1 ratio is greater than 1/5 (left side of the graph). By comparing the experimental results with random action exploration, it becomes evident that the proposed method is more efficient in discovering behaviors that achieve the main goal. In contrast, when the a0/a1 ratio is less than or equal to 1/5 (right side of the graph), the majority of episodes exhibit large swings. This suggests that systematic exploration based on different action ratios can lead to different sub-goals and macro-behaviors.

Figure 5. The distribution of systematic exploration results in the CartPoleSwingUp task

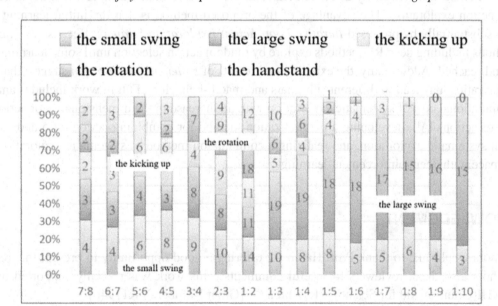

Discussions

This subsection discusses the theoretical significance of systematic exploration. The important point, theoretically, of the proposed systematic exploration is that the search results are independent for the combination of the action ratio (a0/a1 ratio) and loop length k. This means that it is possible to search in parallel. Therefore, if a mechanism is constructed to systematically explore the parameter space of "action ratio * loop length" in parallel, the computational cost associated with an increase in the number of dimensions of actions, specifically the number of actions |A|, will be reduced.

FUTURE RESEARCH DIRECTIONS

This section discusses the possibilities of this research, focusing on combining the proposed systematic exploration of the action space with deep reinforcement learning methods. Especially in the case of deep reinforcement learning, where image-based states are handled, the exploration cost due to random actions in the continuous state space becomes very large. On the other hand, the systematic search proposed in this study has the advantage of being able to discover interesting behaviors more efficiently than random action search.

CONCLUSION

This chapter proposed a novel multi-goal reinforcement learning method based on *systematic exploration* using the iterative loop action exploration strategy. The experimental results demonstrate that the proposed method can efficiently discover behaviors that achieve the main goal when compared with random action exploration. The advantage of the proposed method is that the initial learning cost is reduced substantially by proposed *Iterative Loop Action Exploration Strategy*. Because most existing RL methods including deep RL methods explore by random action selection until some learning goal is found and reached. Additionally, the experimental results of *systematic exploration* suggest that different action ratios may lead to different sub-goals and macro-behaviors. Future work includes analyzing the computational cost of systematic exploration with an increase in the dimensionality of actions (the number of actions |A|), developing a parallelization method for combining action ratio and sequence length in systematic exploration, and realizing a combination method of systematic exploration in the action space with deep reinforcement learning.

ACKNOWLEDGMENT

The authors would like to thank Prof. Habib for offering a good opportunity to present this research. The authors also thank reviewers for useful comments. This work was partially supported by JSPS KAKENHI(Grant-in-Aid for Scientific Research ©) [Grant Number 20K11946].

REFERENCES

Andrychowicz, M., Wolski, F., Ray, A., Schneider, J., Fong, R., Welinder, P., McGrew, B., Tobin, J., Abbeel, P., Zaremba W. (2017). *Hindsight Experience Replay, Advances in Neural Information Processing Systems 30*. NeurIPS. https://arxiv.org/pdf/1707.01495.pdf

Chen, L., Lu, K., Rajeswaran, A., Lee, K., Grover, A., Laskin, M., Abbeel, P., Srinivas, A. and Mordatch, I. (2021). Decision Transformer: Reinforcement Learning via Sequence Modeling. arXiv. https://arxiv. org/abs/2106.01345

Colas, C., Fournier, P., Sigaud, O., Chetouani, M., Oudeyer, P. (2019). CURIOUS: Intrinsically Motivated Modular Multi-Goal Reinforcement Learning. *Proc. of the 36th International Conference on Machine Learning, 2019.* arXiv. https://arxiv.org/pdf/1810.06284v4.pdf

Dazeley, R., Vamplew, P. and Cruz, F. (2023). *Explainable reinforcement learning for broad-XAI: a conceptual framework and survey.* Neural Computing and Applications. https://link.springer.com/article/10.1007/s00521-023-08423-1

Devlin, S. M., & Kudenko, D. (2012). Dynamic Potential-Based Reward Shaping. *Proceedings of the 11th International Conference on Autonomous Agents and Multiagent Systems (AAMAS 2012),* 433-440. https://eprints.whiterose.ac.uk/75121/1/aamas2012.pdf

Forestier, S., Portelas, R., Mollard, Y., Oudeyer, P. (2022). Intrinsically Motivated Goal Exploration Processes with Automatic Curriculum Learning. *Journal of Machine Learning Research, 23,* 1–41. https://arxiv.org/pdf/1708.02190v3.pdf

Gunning, D., Vorm, E., Wang, J.Y. and Turek, M. (2021). DARPA's explainable AI (XAI) program: A retrospective. *APPLIED AI LETTERS, 2*(4). Wiley Online Library. doi:10.1002/ail2.61

Hutsebaut-Buysse, M., Mets, K., & Steven Latré, S. (2022). Hierarchical Reinforcement Learning: A Survey and Open Research Challenges, *Machine Learning Knowledge, 4*(1), 172-221. https://www. mdpi.com/2504-4990/4/1/9

Kumar, A., Hong, J., Singh, A., Levine, S. (2022). When Should We Prefer Offline Reinforcement Learning Over Behavioral Cloning? The International Conference on Learning Representations (ICLR 2022). arXiv. https://arxiv.org/abs/2204.05618

Manela, B. (2019). Bias-Reduced Hindsight Experience Replay with Virtual Goal Prioritization. *Papers With Code.* https://paperswithcode.com/paper/bias-reduced-hindsight-experience-replay-with

McGovern, A., & Barto, A. G. (2002). *Automatic Discovery of Subgoals in Reinforcement Learning using Diverse Density.* Scholar Works. https://scholarworks.umass.edu/cgi/viewcontent. cgi?article=1017&context=cs_faculty_pubs

Mnih, Kavukcuoglu, K., Silver, D., Rusu, A. A., Veness, J., Bellemare, M. G., Graves, A., Riedmiller, M., Fidjeland, A. K., Ostrovski, G., Petersen, S., Beattie, C., Sadik, A., Antonoglou, I., King, H., Kumaran, D., Wierstra, D., Legg, S., & Hassabis, D. (2015). Mnih, V., Kavukcuoglu, K., Silver, D., Rusu, A. A., Veness, J., Bellemare, M. G., & Petersen, S. (2015). Human-level control through deep reinforcement learning. *Nature, 518*(7540), 529–533. doi:10.1038/nature14236 PMID:25719670

Ng, A. Y., Harada, D., & Russell, S.J. (1999). Policy invariance under reward transformations: Theory and application to reward shaping. *Proceedings of International Conference on Machine Learning (ICML-1999),* (pp. 278–287). EECS. https://people.eecs.berkeley.edu/~pabbeel/cs287-fa09/readings/NgHaradaRussell-shaping-ICML1999.pdf

Pateria, Subagdja, B., Tan, A., & Quek, C. (2021). Pateria, S., Subagdja, B., Tan, A., Quek, C., Hierarchical Reinforcement Learning: A Comprehensive Survey. *ACM Computing Surveys*, *54*(5), 1–35. doi:10.1145/3453160

Plaat, A., Kosters, W., & Preuss, M. (2020). *Deep Model-Based Reinforcement Learning for High-Dimensional Problems, a Survey*. arXiv. https://arxiv.org/pdf/2008.05598.pdf

Plappert, M., Andrychowicz, M., Ray, A., McGrew, B., Baker, B., Powell, G., Schneider, J., Tobin, J., Chociej, M., Welinder, P., Kumar, V., Zaremba. W. (2018). *Multi-Goal Reinforcement Learning: Challenging Robotics Environments and Request for Research, 2018*. arXiv. https://arxiv.org/pdf/1802.09464v2.pdf

Puiutta, E. & Veith, E. (2020). MSP, Explainable Reinforcement Learning. *Survey (London, England)* https://arxiv.org/pdf/2005.06247.pdf

Puterman, M. L. (1994). *Markov Decision Processes: Discrete Stochastic Dynamic Programming*. John Wiley & Sons, Inc. doi:10.1002/9780470316887

Soviany, P., Ionescu, R. T., Rota, P., Sebe, N. (2022). Curriculum Learning. *Survey (London, England)*, arXiv. https://arxiv.org/abs/2101.10382

ADDITIONAL READING

Drugan, M., Wiering, M., Vamplew, P., & Chetty, M. (2017). Special issue on multi-objective reinforcement learning. *Neurocomputing*, *263*(8), 1–2. doi:10.1016/j.neucom.2017.06.020

Drugan, M., Wiering, M., Vamplew, P., & Chetty, M. (2017). Multiobjective Reinforcement Learning: Theory and Applications. *Neurocomputing*, *263*(8), 1–86. doi:10.1016/j.neucom.2017.06.020

Herrmann, M. (2015). *RL 16: Model-based RL and Multi-Objective Reinforcement Learning*, University of Edinburgh, School of Informatics. https://www.inf.ed.ac.uk/teaching/courses/rl/slides15/rl16.pdf

Liu, C., Xu, X., & Hu, D. (2015). Multiobjective Reinforcement Learning: A Comprehensive Overview. *IEEE Transactions on Systems, Man, and Cybernetics. Systems*, *45*(3), 385–398. doi:10.1109/TSMC.2014.2358639

Mossalam, H., Assael, Y. M., Roijers, D. M., & Whiteson, S. (2016). *Multi-objective deep reinforcement learning*. arXiv preprint arXiv:1610.02707. https://arxiv.org/pdf/1610.02707.pdf

Natarajan, S., & Tadepalli, P. (2005). Dynamic preferences in multi-criteria reinforcement learning, In *Proceedings of the 22nd international conference on machine learning (ICML-2005)*, (pp. 601-608). ACM. 10.1145/1102351.1102427

Nguyen, T. T. (2018). A Multi-Objective Deep Reinforcement Learning Framework. arXiv. http:// arxiv.org/ftp/arxiv/papers/1803/1803.02965.pdf

Roijers, D. M., Vamplew, P., Whiteson, S., & Dazeley, R. (2013). A Survey of Multi-Objective Sequential Decision-Making [AI Access Foundation]. *Journal of Artificial Intelligence Research*, *48*, 67–113. doi:10.1613/jair.3987

Roijers, D. M., Whiteson, S., Vamplew, P., & Dazeley, R. (2015). Why Multi-objective Reinforcement Learning? *Proceedings of the 12th European Workshop on Reinforcement Learning (EWRL 2015)*, (pp. 1-2). IEEE.

Uchibe, E., & Doya, K. (2008). Finding intrinsic rewards by embodied evolution and constrained reinforcement learning. *Neural Networks*, *21*(10), 1447–1455. doi:10.1016/j.neunet.2008.09.013 PMID:19013054

Yamaguchi, T., Kawabuchi, Y., Takahashi, S., Ichikawa, Y. and Takadama, K. (2022). Formalizing Model-Based Multi-Objective Reinforcement Learning With a Reward Occurrence Probability Vector, in Habib, M.K. (ed.), Handbook of Research on New Investigations in Artificial Life, AI, and Machine Learning. IGI Global.

KEY TERMS AND DEFINITIONS

Abstract Space: It is a hypothetical space characterized by equal and consistent properties.

Action Exploration Strategy: It is a method of action selection for the learning agent to explore the learning environment in reinforcement learning.

Cart-Pole Problem: It is the control task of an inverted pendulum that moves a cart left and right to keep

CartPoleSwingUp Task: It is one of the OpenAIGym task of Cart-pole Problem in which the initial state of the pole is the downward vertical direction, and the goal state of it is the upward vertical direction.

Curriculum Learning: Training machine learning models in a meaningful order, from the easy samples to the hard ones.

Deterministic Policy: It is defined by a function that selects an action for every possible state.

eXplainable Reinforcement Learning (XRL): It is to cover research into explaining agent's decisions during temporally separated decision-making tasks.

Hindsight Experience Replay: It successfully learns from failed episodes that do not reach their goals by experience replay.

Loop Action: An action sequence for any k arbitrary elements of an action set is arranged in ascending order of action.

Markov Decision Process (MDP): It is a discrete time and a discrete state space stochastic control process. It provides a mathematical framework for modeling decision making in situations where outcomes are partly random and partly under the control of a decision maker.

Model-based Reinforcement Learning: The reinforcement learning algorithm which starts with directly estimating the MDP model statistically, then calculates the value of each state as $V(s)$ or the quality of each state action pair $Q(s, a)$ using the estimated MDP to search the optimal solution that maximizes $V(s)$ of each state.

Offline Learning: In machine learning field, it is the learning from an offline dataset pre-collected experience, without any online interaction.

Online Learning: In machine learning field, online means that a learner is connected to a learning environment. So, it is the learning that a learner directly learns in a learning environment. Note that in the education field, the meaning of offline learning is that a learner is required to travel to the training location, typically a lecture hall or classroom, which is different from the meaning of it in the machine learning field.

Partial Policy: It is defined by a function that selects an action for partial range of every possible state.

Potential-Based Reward Shaping: It is one of Reward Shaping which can signicantly improve the time needed to learn an optimal policy without change the optimal policy.

Reinforcement Learning: The popular learning algorithm for automatically solving sequential decision problems. It is commonly modeled as Markov decision processes (MDPs).

Reward Shaping: A framework that aims to improve the learning speed by adding an additional value to the normal reward value of reinforcement learning.

Reward Sparse Problem: The problem that reinforcement learning does not progress in a vast learning state space before acquiring a reward since the reward states are sparse.

Sub-goal: To decompose a learning problem into a set of simpler learning problems.

Summary Model: In this chapter, it is the model consisting of multiple sub-goals and macro-actions (each of them is an action sequence) transitioning to each sub-goal.

Systematic Exploration: It is the exploration which is done according to a fixed plan, in a thorough and efficient way.

the pole at the upward vertical direction.:

Chapter 3
Dynamic Difficulty Adjustment (DDA) on a Serious Game Used for Hand Rehabilitation

Juan Ignacio Vargas-Bustos
Universidad Veracruzana, Mexico

Ericka Janet Rechy-Ramirez
https://orcid.org/0000-0002-8401-1174
Universidad Veracruzana, Mexico

ABSTRACT

Serious games have been used for assisting people in physical rehabilitation for hands. People might have different degrees of mobility in their hands; consequently, it would be convenient that the game could be adapted according to the range-of-motion in performing hand movements. This study implemented a serious game for hand rehabilitation with two play modes. Mode one does not adjust the game difficulty; whereas mode two adjusts the game difficulty according to the player's range-of-motion in performing flexion, extension, ulnar, and radial deviations. The game difficulty was adjusted using fuzzy logic to compute positions at which the rewards will be displayed at the game scene (easy, medium, and difficult positions to collect the rewards). Four participants played both modes. Two-tailed t-tests revealed that there were no significant differences between both modes in terms of rewards collected ($p = 0.6621$), play time ($p = 0.8178$), and "game engagement questionnaire" score ($p = 0.1383$).

INTRODUCTION

Hands play a key role in daily activities. People use them to interact with the world. Nevertheless, due to accidents or medical conditions, people might lose mobility in their hands; consequently, they might require physical rehabilitation.

According to Walsh et al., (2002), "exercise forms a crucial part of a patient's motor rehabilitation in terms of upper and lower limb function as well as prevention of muscle atrophy" (p. 2).

DOI: 10.4018/978-1-6684-7684-0.ch003

The main problem in the traditional rehabilitation method is the lack of motivation in patients; therefore, the performances of the rehabilitation exercises might become frustrated and boring. To cope with this issue, robots have been used to assist people during their motor rehabilitation exercises. For instance, a review on robots employed as assistive technologies for rehabilitation on upper limb can be found in (Narayan et al., 2021). In the same vein, robots have been employed for lower limb motor rehabilitation (Alvarez-Perez et al., 2020; Hussain et al., 2017, Hussain et al., 2021).

On the other hand, researchers (Lohse et al., 2013) have studied that video games can be used as a therapeutic tool in physical rehabilitation due to their motivational and engagement properties (e.g., optimal challenge, rewards and feedback provided to the players). As can be seen, these games are focused on assisting people in their rehabilitation processes. These types of games are called serious games. According to Zyda (2005), a serious game can be defined as "a mental contest, played with a computer in accordance with specific rules, that uses entertainment to further government or corporate training, education, health, public policy, and strategic communication objectives" (p. 26).

It is important to remark that serious games have been used to assist therapists in the rehabilitation processes of patients on emotional health aspects (e.g., anxiety and depression (Abd-Alrazaq et al., 2022; Barnes & Prescott, 2018; Dias et al., 2018), autism spectrum disorder (Silva et al., 2021; Tsikinas & Xinogalos, 2019), phobias: acrophobia (Sharmili & Kanagaraj, 2020), spider phobia (Lindner et al., 2020)) and motor rehabilitation (e.g. ankle rehabilitation (Hendrickx et al., 2021, Feng et al., 2018), finger rehabilitation (Rahman, 2017; Aguilar-Lazcano & Rechy-Ramirez, 2020), shoulder rehabilitation (Viglialoro et al., 2020; Steiner et al., 2020)), so that the patients could be engaged to the rehabilitation and therapy. Additionally, virtual reality has been used in serious games for upper limb rehabilitation. For instance, Wang et al., (2022) conducted a review on game-based virtual reality systems for upper limb rehabilitation on people that have suffered a stroke to assess the effectiveness of these systems. As a result, authors found that games based on virtual reality for upper limb rehabilitation are more effective than traditional rehabilitation on people suffering cerebral apoplexy.

In terms of wrist motor rehabilitation, the majority of these games are controlled using rehabilitation exercises for the wrist (e.g., flexion, extension, ulnar and radial deviations, pronation and supination of the wrist). The wrist has two main joints, radiocarpal joint and midcarpal joint, that are involved in these rehabilitation exercises (see Figure 1). The intensities of the movements depend on the range-of-motion (ROM) that the patients might have in their hands. According to the American Physical Therapy Association (2001), the range-of-motion "is the arc of motion that occurs at a joint or a series of joints".

Several studies have been published on using serious games for hand rehabilitation. Some serious games are played using hand movements detected via cameras.

For instance, two games called SpongeBall and SpaceRace were played by using hand movements identified via a webcam and thermal camera (Evett et al., 2011). Computer vision was employed to recognize the hand movements. Specifically, in the SpongeBall game (i.e., a shooting target game), the player moves the hand and selects a ball by pinching on it, then places the ball at the desired position and opens the hand to throw the ball to the target. In the SpaceRace game, a ship is controlled using rotation (pronation and supination of the wrist) and translation hand movements; so that the ship navigates and avoids obstacles displayed at the game scene.

Other studies have used Leap motion controller (i.e., a sensor based on infrared cameras that provides X, Y, Z coordinates of the phalanges, wrist, palm and elbow) to detect hand movements that are employed to play the game.

Figure 1. Wrist joints

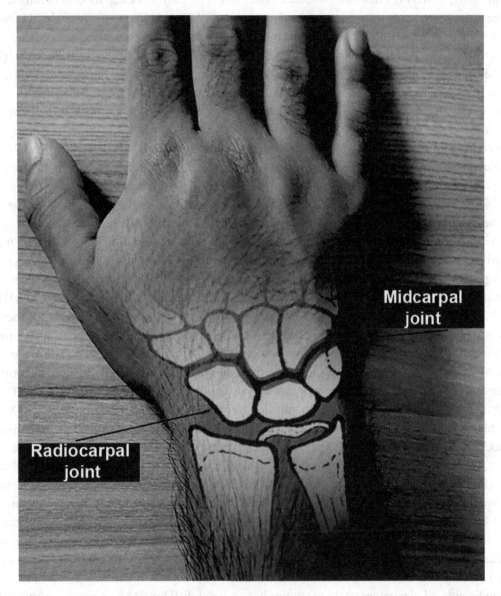

For example, Angry bird and spacecraft games were played using hand movements detected via a Leap motion controller (Elnaggar & Reichardt, 2016). In the Angry bird game, the player throws birds in order to destroy pigs; whereas in the spacecraft game, the player controls a spacecraft and destroys enemies. The same hand movements are used to play both games. Specifically, the player moves the hand to set the position of the bird (Angry bird game) or to control the spacecraft (Spacecraft game) and closes the hand to throw the bird to destroy the pigs (Angry bird game) or to shoot the enemies (Spacecraft game).

Other study (Rechy-Ramirez et al., 2019) has implemented a game, in which the player moves a ball into a maze using extension, flexion, pronation and supination of the wrist in order to collect cubes displayed at the game scene. The wrist movements were identified using data from a Leap motion controller and a Myo armband (i.e., a sensor based on electromyography signals).

Additionally, a study (Fernández-González et al., 2019) employed a Leap motion controller to play five games (the piano game –the user plays a virtual piano-; the reach game –the user should reach with the hand several cubes displayed at different positions at the game scene-; the grasp game –the user should grasp a cube and set it at other position using movements of flexion and extension fingers and fist closed-; the pinch game –the user should make a cube smaller by using a pinch movement-; and the flip game –the user moves the cube using pronation and supination movements-) in order to assess its effectiveness for upper limb rehabilitation in patients suffering mild-to-moderate stages of Parkinson's disease. Authors reported that a Leap motion controller might be used as a feasible rehabilitation tool to improve coordination and speed of movements for upper limbs in patients suffering Parkinson's disease.

Furthermore, studies have implemented serious games that are controlled via electromyography signals (i.e., muscular activity is collected and processed to detect hand movements). Specifically, in this regard, a study (Nasri et al., 2020) collected EMG (electromyography) signals via a Myo armband. These EMG signals were processed to identify seven hand movements (open hand, closed hand, victory sign, tap, wrist flexion, wrist extension and neutral). A convolutional neural network and gated recurrent unit were employed to classify the hand movements. Open hand and tap movements reported low classification accuracy percentages. Conversely, closed hand, victory sign, wrist flexion, wrist extension and neutral movements reported feasible classification accuracy percentages (i.e., a maximum error of ±0.05 was achieved). Consequently, the authors only used these five hand gestures to control the serious game. The key aim of the game was to control a ball via five commands (i.e., increase the ball speed, move the ball backwards, jump, make the ball bigger or smaller) in order to avoid obstacles and drop the ball into a basket so that a reward is reported at the game. Each command is associated with a hand movement.

Other study (Song et al., 2022) has implemented two serious games for hand rehabilitation ("find the sheep" game and "best salesman" game) controlled through 12 activities-of-daily-living (ADLs) hand movements taken from the Fugl Meyer Assessment (i.e., mass flexion, mass extension, hook-like grasp, thumb adduction, opposition, cylinder grip, spherical grip, wrist volar flexion, wrist dorsiflexion, forearm pronation, forearm supination, and neutral movement). Data from force myography (FMG), electromyography (EMG), and inertial measurement unit (IMU) sensors were combined in order to identify the hands movements. Authors reported an accuracy percentage of 81.0% using this data combination from the three sensors and a linear discriminant analysis as the classifier. At the "find the sheep" game, participants should find the sheep card and perform the hand movement associated with this card; whereas at the "best salesman" game, participants should execute hand movements to give food to customers as requested at the game.

As can be noticed, the games of these studies have a fixed difficulty to be played; consequently, patients might experience frustration or boredom. According to Czikszentmihalyi (1990), there should be a flow channel to experience a deep sense of enjoyment; that is, an equilibrium between boredom (too easy) and frustration (too hard). Based on this, the game difficulty can be adjusted in real time in order to keep the player's engagement, which is called DDA (Dynamic Difficulty Adjustment). One definition of DDA is provided by (Zohaib, 2018) as the "technique of automatic real-time adjustment of scenarios, parameters, and behaviors in video games, which follows the player's skill and keeps them from boredom (when the game is too easy) or frustration (when the game is too difficult)" (p. 2).

Some studies have adjusted the difficulty on the games in order to encourage the player's engagement. In this context, it can be seen that there are games played by moving a mouse with the hands or by performing hand movements detected through cameras and robotic systems.

Games With DDA That Are Played Using a Mouse

A game called Prehab is played via a mouse (Hocine et al., 2014; Hocine et al., 2015). Essentially, the player must eliminate enemies and collect gemstones and coins by moving a mouse with the hand. The game difficulty was adjusted using a Monte Carlo tree search to select an ability zone (i.e., an area in which the coins are displayed at easy, medium, difficult, very difficult and expert positions to be collected by the player) based on the player's abilities (fatigue and motivation).

Games With DDA That Are Played Using Cameras

These games use either a Kinect (i.e., sensor based on RGB and infrared cameras that provides the user's skeleton) or Leap motion controller (sensor based on infrared cameras that provides X, Y, Z coordinates of the phalanges, wrist, palm and elbow) to collect the data from the hand movements. Moreover, the game activities of these serious games were to collect objects from the game scene; to collect and place the objects at different positions at the game scene; and to move an avatar. Additionally, these games adjusted their difficulties using fuzzy systems, Q-learning, and computation of variables based on their behaviors in the previous level.

Other studies (Siegel & Smeddinck, 2012; Smeddinck et al., 2013) used a Kinect to identify arm and hand movements. These movements were employed to collect stars displayed sequentially at the game scene. The authors adjusted the game difficulty by adapting the time that the stars are available to be collected, and the amplitude of the movement that the player should perform to collect the stars. These adjustments were computed based on the player's performance of the previous level (i.e., based on rates of collected and non-collected stars as well as the completion time).

Similarly, Cardia da Cruz et al., (2020) proposed a game in which the player pops balloons that are moving at the game scene. The time at which the balloons were moving was adjusted using Q-learning. Moreover, the pinch hand movement was identified using data provided by a Leap motion controller.

Other study (Verhulst et al., 2015) implemented a game in which the player controls an avatar and touches objects with the hands. The hand movements were recognized using data provided by a Kinect. Furthermore, the game difficulty was adapted using thresholds for the player's anxiety and boredom. These emotions were identified by collecting electrocardiogram and electrodermal activity signals via a BItalino sensor. These signals were processed using support vector machines to recognize these emotions.

Games With DDA That Are Played Using Robotic Systems

Other studies have used robotic systems to control the game. For example, in a game called Nuts Catcher (Andrade et al., 2014; Andrade et al., 2018), the player moves a squirrel to right and left using extension and flexion of the wrist to collect nuts falling down from trees. A robotic system was implemented in order to detect these wrist movements. The robotic system has three degrees-of-freedom and is composed of three direct current (DC) motors, Maxon DC motor with encoders and a control drive-EPOS (Andrade et al., 2010). The game difficulty of this game was adjusted by applying Q-learning, so that game parameters such as the number of nuts falling down and the distance between the squirrel and the nut are modified (Andrade et al., 2014). Additionally, evolutionary algorithms were used to adjust the game difficulty (Andrade et al., 2018).

Contributions of this Research

As can be noticed, these games that adjust their game difficulties only employ hand movements such as pinch, grasp, moving the hand in four directions, flexion and extension of the wrist; however, hand movements such as pronation, supination, radial and ulnar deviations are needed in physical rehabilitation for the hand. Consequently, the key contributions of this study are:

- to propose a serious game with two play modes (play mode 1 and play mode 2) that could be controlled via wrist movements used for hand rehabilitation (i.e., flexion, extension, ulnar and radial deviations of the wrist). The play mode 1 does not adjust the game difficulty; whereas the play mode 2 adjusts the game difficulty (i.e., rewards are placed at the game scene at easy, medium and difficult positions to be collected by the player) according to the patients' ROM in performing the exercises. This adjustment is performed using fuzzy logic type I.
- To compare the performances of these two play modes in terms of the mean number-of-rewards collected, mean game score, mean play time, total play time and engagement score from the "Game Engagement Questionnaire".

METHODS

Sensor

A Leap Motion Controller (LMC) was used to detect the participant's hand movements (see Figure 2). LMC is a tracking sensor composed of two infrared cameras and three infrared LEDs. This sensor is able to collect X, Y, Z coordinates of the positions of the finger phalanges, palm, wrist and elbow. LMC has a 150 field of view with approximately eight cubic feet of interactive 3D space.

The Game

Gameplay

There are various taxonomies regarding game genres (Yuan et al., 2011; Arsenault, 2009). According to ESA (Entertainment Software Association, 2022), some game genres are: puzzle, action, arcade, shooter, sports, fighting, racing & vehicle simulation, strategy, and role-playing games. In this regard, the game is an "endless runner" game genre; that is, the player is moving continuously towards a specific direction while is avoiding killer enemies in order to be alive.

It can be seen from Figure 3 that the player (i.e., character on the red plane) must avoid obstacles (i.e., UFO) and collect rewards (i.e., bones) which are displayed at the game scene. Unity 2020.2.1f1 was used to implement the game.

Figure 2. Leap motion controller

Figure 3. Game scene

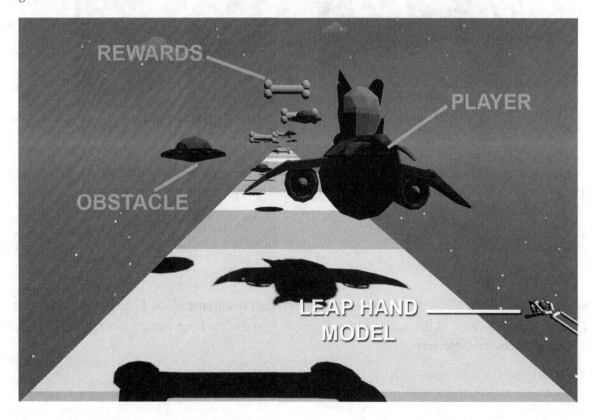

In order to control the red plane in the X and Y axes, the player should perform the following wrist movements (see Figure 4):

- ulnar deviation to move to the left (X axis),
- radial deviation to move to the right (X axis),
- flexion to move downward (Y axis), and
- extension to move upward (Y axis)

Figure 4. Wrist movements

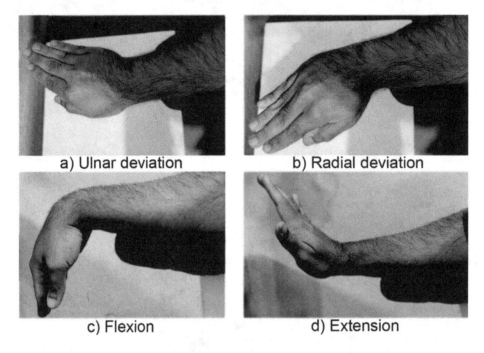

a) Ulnar deviation   b) Radial deviation

c) Flexion   d) Extension

Based on Herrera-Luna (2019), in order to identify the hand movements two angles were computed (FlExθ = for flexion and extension angles, and **D**eviationθ = deviation angle) using equations (1) and (2):

$$FlEx\theta = \cos^{-1} \frac{\left(\overrightarrow{WRIST} \cdot \overrightarrow{PALM} \right)}{\overrightarrow{WRIST} \cdot \overrightarrow{PALM}} \tag{1}$$

where $\overrightarrow{WRIST}$ is the 3D vector of the wrist position from one frame of the Leap motion controller; $\overrightarrow{PALM}$ is the 3D vector of the palm position from one frame of the Leap motion controller, and $FlEx\theta$ is the angle between these vectors.

$$Deviation\theta = \cos^{-1} \frac{\left(\overrightarrow{RING} \cdot \widehat{CW} \right)}{\overrightarrow{RING} \cdot \widehat{CW}} \tag{2}$$

where $\overrightarrow{RING}$ stands for a direction vector of the ring finger and $\widehat{CW}$ is a unit vector from a reference system placed on the centroid of the wrist.

Obstacles

Obstacles (non-player characters) of the UFO shape (see Figure 3) are displayed at the game scene in order to encourage the player to move from the start position. If the player collides with any of the obstacles, then the game is over and stops updating the player score.

Rewards

Rewards (non-player characters) with bone shapes (see Figure 3) are displayed at the game scene in order to motivate the player to move in four directions (up, down, right and left), so that the player can perform the four wrist movements. The player score is increased when the player collides with a bone.

Game Score

The game score is computed based on the play time (seconds) that the player was alive ($alive_{time}$) and the rewards that were collected (*bones*) during this time. Each reward gives five points. Specifically, the game score is computed via equation (3):

$$Game_{score} = alive_{time} + (bones*5) \tag{3}$$

The $alive_{time}$ and *bones* are reset to zero when the player collides with any obstacle (i.e., when the game is over).

Play Modes

The game has two play modes: one mode has a fixed degree of game difficulty (play mode 1) and the other adjusts the game difficulty (play mode 2).

Play Mode One: Without DDA

This play mode does not adjust the game difficulty according to the ROM; that is, the bones are displayed randomly at the game scene without considering the participant's ROM.

Algorithm. The game scene is set up as follows:

```
INPUTS:
NPC list: a list of 150 non-player characters (NPC) is created: 90 bones (re-
wards) and 75 UFOs (obstacles)
Every frame at Unity:
DO
IF NPC list is empty THEN
DO
- Create a list of 150 non-player characters (NPC): 90 bones (rewards) and 75
UFOs (obstacles)
END IF
IF NPC list is not empty THEN
DO
- Select randomly 25 non-player-characters from the NPC list
-Place randomly the 25 non-player-characters at an area delimited by the fol-
lowing coordinates (3.59, 9.08) and (-3.9, 1.38); i.e., an area that is easy
to collect the bones
-Discard the 25 non-player-characters from the NPC list
END IF
END
```

Play Mode Two: With DDA

At this mode, bones (rewards) are displayed at positions that are easy, medium or difficult to be collected by the player in order to adjust the game difficulty (i.e., DDA).

DDA Using Fuzzy Logic Type I. The DDA on the game was performed using fuzzy logic type I. This process mainly involves three steps: fuzzification, fuzzy inference, and defuzzification.

Fuzzification. At this step, the crisp value (crisp input) is translated into a fuzzy input using membership functions. The crisp value corresponds to the participant's ROM of the wrist movement (extension, flexion, ulnar deviation or radial deviation), which is computed using the data collected from the LMC.

Once that the participant's ROM of the wrist movement has been calculated (see Figure 5), membership functions are applied in order to obtain the fuzzy input.

Fuzzy logic uses degrees-of-membership (DOM) to represent the uncertainty. These DOM determine at what degree a variable belongs to a fuzzy set. These DOM range between zero and one. Furthermore, these DOM are computed using membership functions such as triangle, trapezoidal, Sigmoid and Gaussian functions (see Figure 6).

A trapezoidal membership function was used to compute the DOM of the participant's ROM of the wrist movement for each of the following fuzzy input sets (fuzzification step):

- Deficient
- Medium
- Good

Figure 5. Flexion ROM

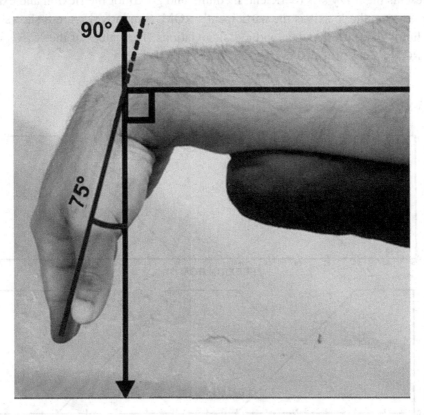

Figure 6. Membership functions

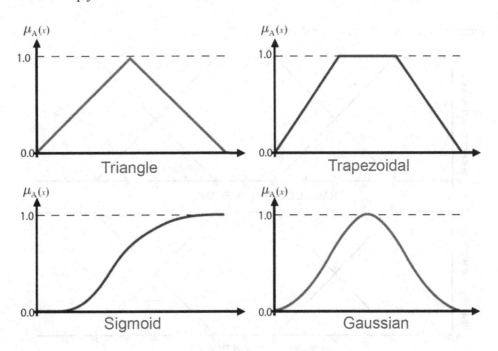

Figure 7 presents the fuzzy sets (deficient, medium, and good) for the flexion and extension movements. As can be seen, the X axis is the participant's ROM. Similarly, Figure 8 shows the fuzzy sets (deficient, medium, good) for the ulnar and radial deviations. The values of the X axis were fixed according to the ROM values provided in (Norkin, 2016).

Figure 7. Fuzzy sets for flexion and extension

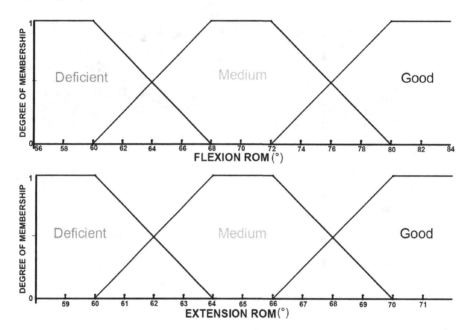

Figure 8. Fuzzy sets for radial and ulnar deviations

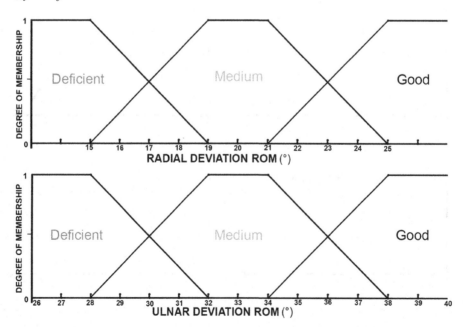

Specifically, the fuzzification is performed by computing the trapezoidal membership function on the participant's ROM using the following equation:

$$f(x;a,b,c,d) = \begin{cases} 0 & for \ x < a \\ \dfrac{x-a}{b-a} & for \ a \le x \le b \\ 1 & for \ b \le x < c \\ \dfrac{d-x}{d-c} & for \ c \le x < d \\ 0 & for \ d \le x \end{cases} \tag{4}$$

where:

- a is the x coordinate of the lower left corner of the trapezoidal.
- b is the x coordinate of the upper left corner of the trapezoidal.
- c is the x coordinate of the upper right corner of the trapezoidal.
- d is the x coordinate of the lower right corner of the trapezoidal.
- x is the value computed using the Leap Motion Controller.

At the end of this step, it is known at what degree-of-membership the participant's ROM belongs to the deficient, medium and good fuzzy sets (fuzzy input).

For example, a 75° of flexion ROM has the following DOM (see Figure 9 and equations (5)-(7)):

$$DOM_{Deficient} = 0 \tag{5}$$

$$DOM_{Medium} = \frac{d-x}{d-c} = \frac{80-75}{80-72} = 0.625 \tag{6}$$

$$DOM_{Good} = \frac{x-a}{b-a} = \frac{75-72}{80-72} = 0.375 \tag{7}$$

Fuzzy inference. At this step, rules are assessed to compute the fuzzy output (i.e., the game difficulty is easy, medium or hard). Specifically, the game difficulty is adjusted based on the position at which the bone is displayed at the game scene (see Figure 10), that is, the bones are displayed at positions that are easy, medium or difficult to be collected at the game scene.

The position of the bone is set using X, Y coordinates computed according to the DOM of the participant's ROM of the wrist movements (extension, flexion, ulnar deviation and radial deviation) in each fuzzy set (deficient, medium, good). The ROM of a flexion movement determines the negative y-coordinate of the position of the bone, whereas the ROM of an extension movement sets the positive y-coordinate. Conversely, the ROMs of the ulnar and radial deviations determine the negative and positive x-coordinates, respectively. Three fuzzy output sets (easy, medium, hard) are defined for the difficulty in X and Y coordinates (see Figure 11 and Figure 12).

Figure 9. a 75° of flexion ROM

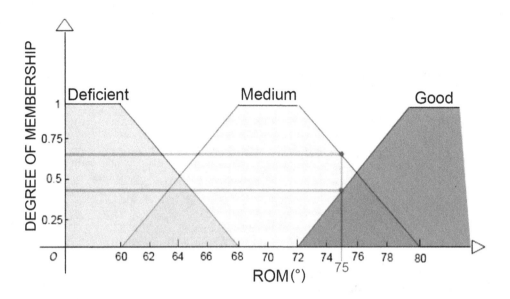

Figure 10. Position of the bone at the game scene

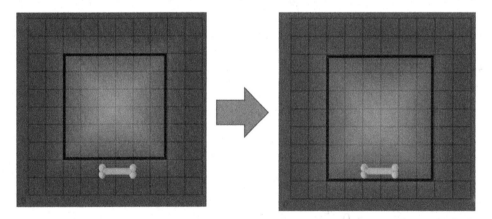

Additionally, the following twelve if-then rules were defined to compute the fuzzy output:

- If flexion_ROM is deficient then the negative_Y_difficulty is easy
- If flexion_ROM is medium then negative_Y_difficulty is medium
- If flexion_ROM is good then the negative_Y_difficulty is hard
- If extension_ROM is deficient then the positive_Y_difficulty is easy
- If extension_ROM is medium then positive_Y_difficulty is medium
- If extension_ROM is good then the positive_Y_difficulty is hard
- If ulnar_ROM is deficient then the negative_X_difficulty is easy
- If ulnar_ROM is medium then negative_X_difficulty is medium
- If ulnar_ROM is good then the negative_X_difficulty is hard

- If radial_ROM is deficient then the positive_X_difficulty is easy
- If radial_ROM is medium then positive_X_difficulty is medium
- If radial_ROM is good then the positive_X_difficulty is hard

Figure 11. Fuzzy sets for game difficulty in X coordinates

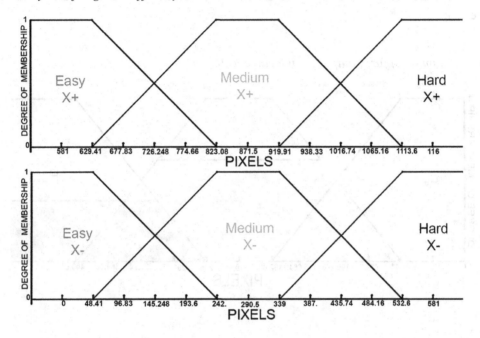

Figure 12. Fuzzy sets for the game difficulty in Y coordinates

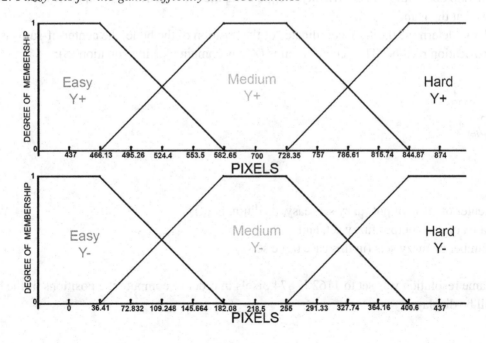

For the previous example (i.e., a 75° of flexion ROM), the following rules are activated:

- If flexion_ROM is medium then negative_Y_difficulty is medium
- If flexion_ROM is good then the negative_Y_difficulty is hard

Consequently, the fuzzy output has 0.625 DOM for "Medium Y-" and 0.375 DOM for "Hard Y-" (see Figure 13):

Figure 13. An example of fuzzy output for the game difficulty

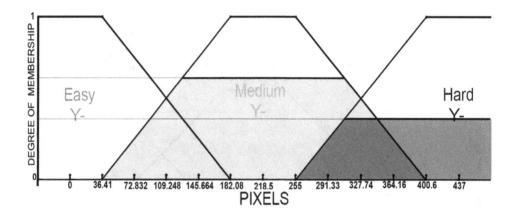

Defuzzification. Once that the fuzzy output is computed using the rules, a defuzzification process is performed to obtain the game difficulty (i.e., to compute the specific position at which the bone will be displayed at the game scene).

In order to determine the X, Y coordinates of the position of the bone, the center-of-sums is used as the defuzzification method. The center-of-sums (Z*) is computed using equation (8):

$$Z^* = \frac{\sum_{i=1}^{n} z_i A_i}{\sum_{i=1}^{n} A_i} \tag{8}$$

where:

z_i is the center of each output fuzzy set (easy, medium, hard);
A_i is the area of each output fuzzy set, and
n is the number of fuzzy sets (in this case three sets)

The game resolution was set to 1162 X 874 pixels in order to compute the positions of the bones at which will be displayed.

Once that the output value is computed (i.e., Z*), this is converted into Unity coordinates for the game scene using equations (9)-(12):

$$X+ = \frac{Z^*X20}{1162} - 10 \text{, if it is a radial deviation} \tag{9}$$

$$Y+ = \frac{Z^*X10}{874} \text{, if it is an extension} \tag{10}$$

$$X- = \frac{Z^*X10}{581} - 10 \text{, if it is an ulnar deviation} \tag{11}$$

$$Y- = \frac{Z^*X5}{437} \text{, if it is a flexion} \tag{12}$$

For the fuzzy output of the example (see Figure 13), A_i for "Medium Y-" and "Hard Y-" are obtained using the Thales' theorem (see equations (13)-(14)):

$$A_{\text{Medium-Y}} = 136.5975 \tag{13}$$

$$A_{\text{Hard-Y}} = 59.3775 \tag{14}$$

Furthermore, the centers of "Medium Y-" and "Hard Y-" are computed using equations (15) and (16):

$$Z_{\text{Medium}-Y} = \frac{36.41 + 400.6}{2} = 218.505 \tag{15}$$

$$Z_{\text{Hard}-Y} = \frac{255 + 437}{2} = 346 \tag{16}$$

Then the center-of sum is applied:

$$Z^* = \frac{(136.5975X218.505) + (59.3775X346)}{218.505 + 346} = 89.267 \tag{17}$$

Finally, this output value (Z*) is converted into Unity coordinates for the game scene as follows:

$$Y- = \frac{89.267X5}{437} = 1.021 \tag{18}$$

Algorithm. In order to compute the specific positions at which the bones will be displayed, the processes of fuzzification, fuzzy inference, and defuzzification are executed as follows:

```
INPUTS:
FlEx θ = flexion/extension angle
Deviationθ = deviation angle of the wrist
Pitch=Direction of movement in Y      //-1 or 1
Yaw= Direction of movement in X      //-1 or 1
FlEx θ = FlEx θ * Pitch
Deviationθ = Deviationθ * Yaw
IF FlEx θ > 0 THEN
DO
-Fuzzification: compute the degree-of-membership for the extension ROM given
FlEx θ
-Fuzzy inference: evaluate the rules
-Defuzzification: compute the center-of-sums on the fuzzy output
END IF
IF FlEx θ <0 THEN
DO
-Convert FlEx θ into a positive value (i.e., FlEx θ = FlEx θ * -1)
-Fuzzification: compute the degree-of-membership for the flexion ROM given
FlEx θ
-Fuzzy inference: evaluate the rules
-Defuzzification: compute the center-of-sums on the fuzzy output
END IF
IF Deviationθ >0 THEN
DO
-Fuzzification: compute the degree-of-membership for the radial deviation ROM
given Deviationθ
-Fuzzy inference: evaluate the rules
-Defuzzification: compute the center-of-sums on the fuzzy output
END IF
IF Deviationθ <0 THEN
DO
-Convert Deviationθ into a positive value (i.e., Deviationθ = Deviationθ * -1)
-Fuzzification: compute the degree-of-membership for the ulnar deviation ROM
given Deviationθ
-Fuzzy inference: evaluate the rules
-Defuzzification: compute the center-of-sums on the fuzzy output
END IF
DO
-Convert the output value (i.e., Z*(Pixeles)) into Unity coordinates at the
game scene (X+ for radial deviation, Y+ for an extension, X- for an ulnar
deviation, Y- for a flexion).
```

```
-Every 22 seconds, four bones are displayed at the game scene at the following
positions:
X-, Y-
X+, Y-
X+, Y+
X-, Y+
During this time period (i.e., 22 seconds), the game scene is set up using the
algorithm of the play mode 1. Furthermore, the player performs the four hand
movements (i.e., flexion, extension, ulnar and radial deviations); consequent-
ly, the four bones can be created.
END
```

GEQ Questionnaire

The "Game Engagement Questionnaire" proposed by Brockmyer et al., (2009) was used to measure the player's engagement (i.e., the involvement in the game) after finishing the game sessions. This questionnaire is composed of 19 items that aim to measure four emotional states:

- Immersion: the players are engaged to the game; however, they are aware of their environments. Only one item assesses this emotion in GEQ questionnaire (i.e., 5.26% of the questionnaire): "I really get into the game" (Brockmyer et al., 2009, p.629)
- Presence: this emotion is associated with spatial presence. According to Wirth et al., (2007) spatial presence can be defined as "the sensation of being physically situated within the spatial environment portrayed by the medium" (p. 497). Four out of the 19 GEQ items evaluate this emotion (i.e., 21.05% of the questionnaire). Some GEQ items are: "I lose track of time; Things seem to happen automatically" (Brockmyer et al., 2009, p.629).
- Flow: it is the sensation of enjoyment because there is an equilibrium between the skill and challenge to play the game. Nine GEQ items focused on this emotion (i.e., 47.37% of the questionnaire). Some of these items are: "I can't tell I'm getting tired; I play without thinking how to play" (Brockmyer et al., 2009, p.629).
- Absorption: it is the sensation of full engagement in the game. Five out of 19 GEQ items assess this emotion (i.e., 26.32% of the questionnaire). Some items for this emotion are: "I lose track of where I am; I feel spaced out" (Brockmyer et al., 2009, p.629).

The user can respond each item of the questionnaire using "No" (0 points), "Yes" (1 point) or "Maybe" (0.5 points). In order to obtain a percentage for each emotion (GEQ score for each emotion), the points corresponding to the questions of each emotion were added, and then the corresponding percentage was computed. Further details can be seen in (Brockmyer et al., 2009).

Participants

Four volunteers (two men and two women: mean age = 23.75 ± 0.43 years) participated in the experiments. The experiments were performed according to the 1964 Declaration of Helsinki and all volunteers signed a written consent to participate in the experiments. All participants were right handed. Two of the volunteers have experience in playing video games; whereas the remaining two have no experience.

Experiments

All participants executed the hand movements using the right hand. Each participant played each play mode for 15 minutes. During this play time, the participants played the play mode several times (sessions) because they could lose the game and this was restarted. Additionally, after each session, the participants could rest for one minute, if they wanted.

Table 1 shows the number of sessions that each participant played each play mode (i.e., the number of times that the player lost the game in each play mode during the 15 minutes) and the order in which the play modes were played. As can be seen, two subjects (A, D) tested first the play mode without DDA and the other two subjects played the game first using the play mode with DDA (B, C). In terms of the sessions, it can be noticed that only subject D lost the game fewer times using the play mode with DDA than the play mode without DDA. Conversely, the remaining subjects lost the game fewer times using the play mode without DDA than playing the play mode with DDA. Additionally, it can be seen that subject A almost lost the game the same times using both play modes.

Table 1. Number of sessions that each participant played each play mode and the order in which the play modes were played

Subject	First play mode used in the game	Number of sessions played in play mode 1 (without DDA)	Number of sessions played in play mode 2 (with DDA)
A	Mode 1	7	8
B	Mode 2	12	16
C	Mode 2	9	12
D	Mode 1	11	7

Three variables (game score, play time, number-of-bones collected) were obtained for each session for each subject. In order to analyze each variable, a mean of the values for each variable was computed per participant. Moreover, the total play time that each participant spent in each play mode was reported. Finally, the GEQ questionnaire was answered by all the participants at the end of playing each play mode.

Figure 14 presents the experimental setting. As can be seen, the participant placed the hand on a support that is 26 centimeters over the Leap Motion Controller. According to (Leap motion controller, n.d.), Leap motion controller has a tracking range depth between 10 and 60 centimeters. Before conducting the formal experiments, a participant tested the game without a hand support and trying to set the hand at least 10 centimeters above the Leap Motion Controller in order to visualize the hand properly. However, the participant reported discomfort and it was difficult to maintain the hand at this height without a support; consequently, the participant's hand was not visualized properly several times. Based on this, empirical experiments were performed using several supports of different heights (i.e., 18 centimeters, 20.5 centimeters and 26 centimeters) to analyze whether the participant's hands were visualized properly. As a result, the support with a height of 26 centimeters allowed a feasible visualization of the hand and it was the most comfortable to use.

Figure 14. Experimental setting

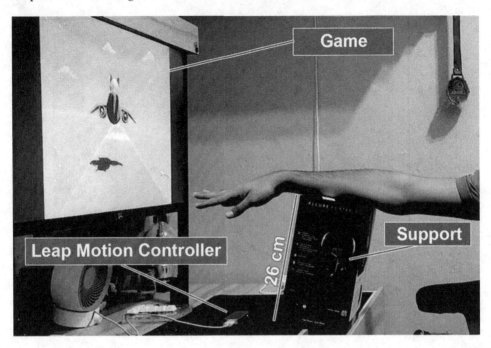

PRELIMINARY RESULTS

Figure 15 presents the mean number-of-bones (rewards) collected by the four subjects (A, B, C, D) using the two play modes during the 15 minutets. As can be seen, three subjects collected on average more bones using the "play mode 1: without DDA" (subject A = 18.4285 bones, subject B = 12.4166 bones, subject C = 13.7777 bones) than using the "play mode 2: with DDA" (subject A = 17.075 bones, subject B = 9.125 bones, subject C = 5.8666 bones). Conversely, only subject D collected on average more bones using the play mode with DDA (19 bones) than using the play mode without DDA (10.7272 bones).

In terms of the mean play time (seconds being alive) spending by the participants in each play mode, it can be seen from Figure 16 that two subjects (subject A, subject D) spending on average more time playing the play mode with DDA (subject A = 73.75 seconds, subject D = 124.5714 seconds) than the play mode without DDA (subject A = 68.2857 seconds, subject D = 60.9090 seconds). Furthermore, subject D played the mode with DDA on average more than twice the time that she played the mode without DDA. Conversely, subjects B and C played on average more time the play mode without DDA (subject B = 54.75 seconds, subject C = 66.4444 seconds) than the play mode with DDA (subject B = 37.625 seconds, subject C = 33.6 seconds). Additionally, subject C played the mode without DDA on average almost twice the time that he played the mode with DDA.

Figure 17 presents the total time played by each subject using both modes. It can be noticed that it has the same tendency that the mean play time; that is, subjects B and C spent more time playing the play mode without DDA (subject B = 657 seconds, subject C = 598 seconds) than the play mode with DDA (subject B = 527 seconds, subject C = 504 seconds). In contrast, subjects A and D played more time the play mode with DDA (subject A = 590 seconds, subject D = 872 seconds) than the play mode without DDA (subject A = 478 seconds, subject D = 670 seconds).

Figure 15. Mean number-of-bones collected by the four subjects in the two play modes

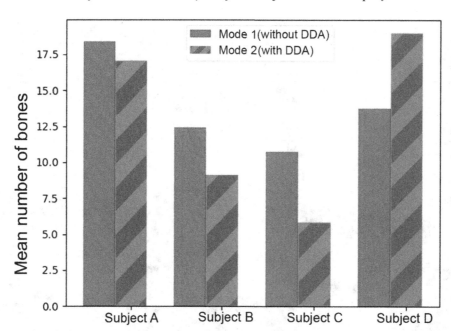

Figure 16. Mean play time (in seconds) of the four subjects in the two play modes

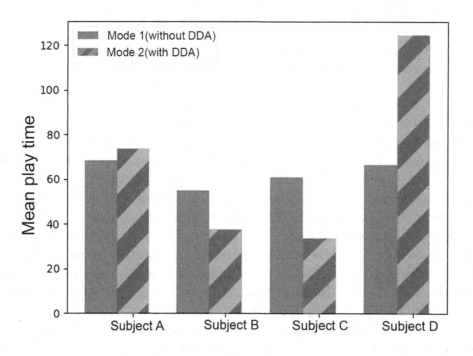

Figure 17. Total play time (in seconds) of the four subjects in the two play modes

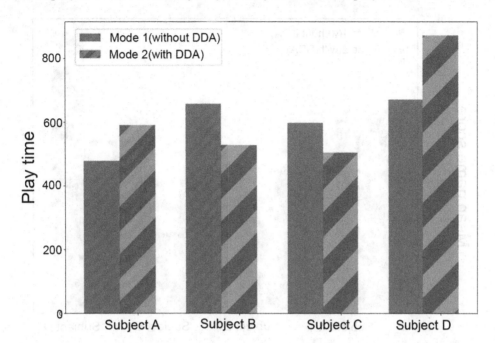

With regard to the mean game score reported in each play mode, it can be seen from Figure 18 that only subject D achieved on average a higher game score playing the game with DDA (219.5714 points) than the game without DDA (114.5454 points). Moreover, subject A reported on average almost the same game score playing both modes (game with DDA: 159.125 points, game without DDA: 160.4285 points). Subjects B and C achieved on average higher game scores playing the game without DDA (subject B = 116.8333 points, subject C = 135.3333 points) than playing the game with DDA (subject B = 83.25 points, subject C = 62.933 points).

Finally, the GEQ questionnaire was answered by the participants after finishing playing each play mode in order to analyze their emotions during their play time (i.e., each participant answered the questionnaire twice). The key aim of this questionnaire is to obtain a score on the engagement level between the player and the play mode.

Figure 19 shows the mean score for the GEQ questionnaire reported by the subjects in each play mode. As can be noticed, immersion reported the highest percentages in both play modes (play mode without DDA = 87.5%, play mode with DDA = 87.5%) followed by presence (play mode without DDA = 54.16%, play mode with DDA = 45.83%). Conversely, absorption obtained the lowest percentages (play mode without DDA = 17.5%, play mode with DDA = 10%). Additionally, it can be seen that three (absorption, flow and presence) out of the four emotions reported higher scores in the play mode without DDA than in the play mode with DDA.

Figure 18. Mean game score of the four subjects in the two play modes

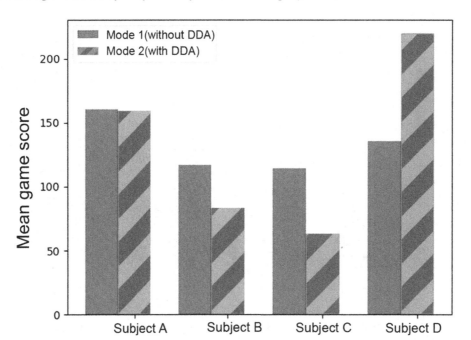

Figure 19. Percentages for each emotion (mood) of the GEQ questionnaire

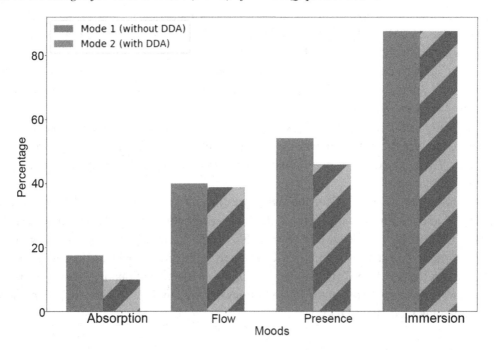

Statistical Analysis

Statistical tests were applied in order to analyze if there were significant differences between the play mode with DDA and the play mode without DDA in any of the five variables (mean play time, total play time, mean game score, mean number-of-bones collected, GEQ questionnaire score). All the statistical tests used a confidence interval alpha = 0.05. R *4.0.3* was employed to perform the statistical tests.

Firstly, Shapiro-Wilk tests were applied on the samples of each variable in each play mode to analyze whether they followed a normal distribution (p>= 0.05) or not (p< 0.05).

It can be noticed from Table 2, Table 3, Table 4, Table 5, and Table 6 that all the samples of the five variables (mean game score, mean number-of-bones collected, mean play time, total play time, and GEQ score) in the two play modes followed a normal distribution (p>= 0.05); consequently, two-tailed t-tests were applied to determine if there were significant differences (p<0.05) between the play modes or not (p >= 0.05) in any variable.

Table 2. Shapiro-Wilk statistics of the mean game score for the play modes with DDA and without DDA at α = 0.05 and critical value of W = 0.748

Play modes	Mean game score	
	Statistic	p-value
Play mode without DDA	0.88486	0.3598
Play mode with DDA	0.93032	0.5963

Table 3. Shapiro-Wilk statistics of the mean play time for the play modes with DDA and without DDA at α = 0.05 and critical value of W = 0.748

Play modes	Mean play time	
	Statistic	p-value
Play mode without DDA	0.93662	0.6339
Play mode with DDA	0.87982	0.3379

Table 4. Shapiro-Wilk statistics of the total play time for the play modes with DDA and without DDA at α = 0.05 and critical value of W = 0.748

Play modes	Total play time	
	Statistic	p-value
Play mode without DDA	0.87252	0.3077
Play mode with DDA	0.80234	0.1065

Table 5. Shapiro-Wilk statistics of the mean number-of-bones collected for the play modes with DDA and without DDA at α = 0.05 and critical value of W = 0.748

Play modes	Mean number-of-bones collected	
	Statistic	p-value
Play mode without DDA	0.92946	0.5912
Play mode with DDA	0.90534	0.458

Table 6. Shapiro-Wilk statistics of the GEQ score for the play modes with DDA and without DDA at α = 0.05. Critical value of W = 0.748

Play modes	GEQ score	
	Statistic	p-value
Play mode without DDA	0.98722	0.9428
Play mode with DDA	0.96545	0.8131

Table 7. Two-tailed t-tests at α = 0.05 of the five variables: mean game score, mean play time, total play time, mean number-of-bones collected, GEQ questionnaire score. Critical value t(3) = 3.182

Variable	T-test value	p-value
Mean game score	0.018764	0.9862
Mean play time	-0.25138	0.8178
Total play time	-0.28078	0.7971
Mean number-of-bones collected	0.48306	0.6621
GEQ score	2.0078	0.1383

As can be seen from Table 7, preliminary results revealed that there were no significant differences in any of the five variables (mean game score, mean number-of-bones collected, mean play time, total play time, GEQ score) between the play modes (p >= 0.05). A possible explanation for this might be that the main difference between both play modes is that only four bones (bonus) are created based on the player's ROM in the play mode with DDA. Based on these preliminary results, it would be convenient to create more bones according to the player's ROM in the play mode with DDA in order to be significant differences between the play modes.

DISCUSSION

Five variables (mean game score, mean number-of-bones collected, mean play time, total play time, and GEQ score) were considered to analyze the performances of both play modes (play mode 1: without DDA, and play mode 2: with DDA). Preliminary results revealed that the majority of the subjects (A, B, C) obtained higher mean game scores and mean number-of-bones collected (rewards) in the play mode without DDA than in the play mode with DDA. Similarly, half of the subjects (B, C) stayed alive more time (play time) on average using the play mode without DDA than the play mode with DDA. Conversely, only subject D reported higher mean game score, mean number-of-bones collected (rewards), mean play time and total play time (time being alive) using the play mode with DDA than using the play mode without DDA. Despite these preliminary findings, two-tailed t-tests revealed that there were no significant differences in any of the four variables (mean game score, mean number-of-bones collected, mean play time and total play time) between both play modes.

Regarding the GEQ questionnaire, immersion (i.e., the players are engaged to the game; nevertheless, they are aware of their environments) was the emotion that reported the highest percentages in both play modes (over 85%). Additionally, the other three emotions (absorption, presence and flow) reported higher percentages in the play mode without DDA than in the play mode with DDA. Similarly, a two-tailed t-test found no significant difference in the GEQ score on the play mode without DDA and the play mode with DDA.

Although this study implemented a play mode with DDA for hand rehabilitation; there are some limitations:

- only a GEQ questionnaire was used to assess the players' engagement on the play modes.
- the DDA in play mode 2 was adjusted only considering the player's ROM

- only one technique (fuzzy logic type I) was employed to perform the DDA in play mode 2.
- the player's performance is not recorded in the game.
- the evaluation of both play modes was performed with a small sample of participants as a preliminary study; consequently, we plan to increase the sample size in the upcoming assessment.

FUTURE RESEARCH DIRECTIONS

Further research, which take these limitations into account, will need to be undertaken. For instance, future research on:

- measuring the player's engagement using biosignals (such as breathing, electroencephalography or electrocardiogram signals); so that this information can be considered to perform the DDA as well.
- considering other game variables (e.g., player's speed) to compute the DDA.
- implementing games according to players' preferences based on their ages. For instance, it has been found in (Chesham et al., 2017) that elderly people prefer to play casual puzzle games.
- performing the DDA using other techniques such as Q-learning, fuzzy logic type II, or evolutionary algorithms.
- providing several hand movements employed in rehabilitation, so that the player could choose the movements used to control the game
- recording the player's performance.
- increasing the number of participants that tested both play modes.

CONCLUSION

This study implemented a game for hand rehabilitation controlled through four wrist movements: flexion, extension, ulnar and radial deviations. This game offers two play modes. The play mode 1 does not adjust the game difficulty; whereas the play mode 2 adjusts the game difficulty based on the player's ROM. Specifically, in the play mode 2, the rewards are displayed at positions that are easy, medium or difficult to collect by the player at the game scene taking into account the player's ROM in performing flexion, extension, ulnar and radial deviations of the wrist. This adjustment was performed using fuzzy logic type I. Basically, trapezoidal functions were applied to model the input and output fuzzy sets; twelve if-then rules were employed for the fuzzy inference and the center-of-sum was used for the defuzzification. Five variables (mean game score, mean number-of-rewards collected, mean play time, total play time, "Game Engagement Questionnaire" score) were compared in order to analyze the performances of both play modes. As a result, two-tailed t-tests found no significant differences between both modes in terms of mean number-of-rewards collected ($p = 0.6621$), mean play time ($p = 0.8178$), total play time ($p = 0.7971$), mean game score ($p = 0.9862$), and "Game Engagement Questionnaire" score ($p = 0.1383$).

REFERENCES

Abd-Alrazaq, A., Al-Jafar, E., Alajlani, M., Toro, C., Alhuwail, D., Ahmed, A., Reagu, S. M., Al-Shorbaji, N., & Househ, M. (2022). The effectiveness of serious games for alleviating depression: Systematic review and meta-analysis. *JMIR Serious Games*, *10*(1), e32331. doi:10.2196/32331 PMID:35029530

Aguilar-Lazcano, C. A., & Rechy-Ramirez, E. J. (2020). Performance analysis of Leap motion controller for finger rehabilitation using serious games in two lighting environments. *Measurement*, *157*, 107677. doi:10.1016/j.measurement.2020.107677

Alvarez-Perez, M. G., Garcia-Murillo, M. A., & Cervantes-Sánchez, J. J. (2020). Robot-assisted ankle rehabilitation: A review. *Disability and Rehabilitation. Assistive Technology*, *15*(4), 394–408. doi:10.1 080/17483107.2019.1578424 PMID:30856032

American Physical Therapy Association. (2001). Guide to physical therapist practice. Physical therapy, 81(1), 9–746.

Andrade, K. D. O., Fernandes, G., Caurin, G. A., Siqueira, A. A., Romero, R. A., & Pereira, R. D. L. (2014, October). Dynamic player modelling in serious games applied to rehabilitation robotics. *In 2014 Joint Conference on Robotics: SBR-LARS Robotics Symposium and Robocontrol* (pp. 211-216). IEEE. 10.1109/SBR.LARS.Robocontrol.2014.41

Andrade, K. O., Ito, G. G., Joaquim, R. C., Jardim, B., Siqueira, A. A., Caurin, G. A., & Becker, M. (2010, November). A robotic system for rehabilitation of distal radius fracture using games. *In 2010 Brazilian symposium on games and digital entertainment* (pp. 25-32). IEEE. 10.1109/SBGAMES.2010.26

Andrade, K. O., Joaquim, R. C., Caurin, G. A., & Crocomo, M. K. (2018). Evolutionary algorithms for a better gaming experience in rehabilitation robotics. [CIE]. *Computers in Entertainment*, *16*(2), 1–15. doi:10.1145/3180657

Arsenault, D. (2009). Video game genre, evolution and innovation. *Eludamos (Göttingen)*, *3*(2), 149–176. doi:10.7557/23.6003

Barnes, S., & Prescott, J. (2018). Empirical evidence for the outcomes of therapeutic video games for adolescents with anxiety disorders: Systematic review. *JMIR Serious Games*, *6*(1), e9530. doi:10.2196/games.9530 PMID:29490893

Brockmyer, J. H., Fox, C. M., Curtiss, K. A., McBroom, E., Burkhart, K. M., & Pidruzny, J. N. (2009). The development of the game engagement questionnaire: A measure of engagement in video game-playing. *Journal of Experimental Social Psychology*, *45*(4), 624–634. doi:10.1016/j.jesp.2009.02.016

Cardia da Cruz, L., Sierra-Franco, C. A., Silva-Calpa, G. F. M., & Barbosa Raposo, A. (2020, July). A Self-adaptive serious game for eye-hand coordination training. *In International Conference on Human-Computer Interaction* (pp. 385-397). Springer, Cham. 10.1007/978-3-030-50164-8_28

Chesham, A., Wyss, P., Müri, R. M., Mosimann, U. P., & Nef, T. (2017). What older people like to play: Genre preferences and acceptance of casual games. *JMIR Serious Games*, *5*(2), e7025. doi:10.2196/games.7025 PMID:28420601

Czikszentmihalyi, M. (1990). *Flow: the psychology of optimal experience*. Harper & Row.

Dias, L. P. S., Barbosa, J. L. V., & Vianna, H. D. (2018). Gamification and serious games in depression care: A systematic mapping study. *Telematics and Informatics, 35*(1), 213–224. doi:10.1016/j. tele.2017.11.002

Elnaggar, A., & Reichardt, D. (2016, December). Digitizing the hand rehabilitation using serious games methodology with user-centered design approach. *In 2016 International Conference on Computational Science and Computational Intelligence (CSCI)* (pp. 13-22). IEEE. 10.1109/CSCI.2016.0011

Entertainment Software Association. (2022). *2022 Essential Facts About the Video Game Industry. Player habits and preferences*. The ESA. https://www.theesa.com/resource/2022-essential-facts-about-the-video-game-industry/

Evett, L., Burton, A., Battersby, S., Brown, D., Sherkat, N., Ford, G., & Standen, P. (2011, November). Dual camera motion capture for serious games in stroke rehabilitation. *In 2011 IEEE 1st International Conference on Serious Games and Applications for Health (SeGAH)* (pp. 1-4). IEEE. 10.1109/ SeGAH.2011.6165460

Feng, J., Chen, K., Zhang, C., & Li, H. (2018, December). A virtual reality-based training system for ankle rehabilitation. *In 2018 IEEE International Conference on Progress in Informatics and Computing (PIC)* (pp. 255-259). IEEE. 10.1109/PIC.2018.8706143

Fernández-González, P., Carratalá-Tejada, M., Monge-Pereira, E., Collado-Vázquez, S., Sánchez-Herrera Baeza, P., Cuesta-Gómez, A., Oña-Simbaña, E., Jardón-Huete, A., Molina-Rueda, F., Balaguer-Bernaldo de Quirós, C., Miangolarra-Page, J., & Cano-de la Cuerda, R. (2019). Leap motion controlled video game-based therapy for upper limb rehabilitation in patients with Parkinson's disease: A feasibility study. *Journal of Neuroengineering and Rehabilitation, 16*(1), 1–10. doi:10.118612984-019-0593-x PMID:31694653

Hendrickx, R., van der Avoird, T., Pilot, P., Kerkhoffs, G., & Schotanus, M. (2021). Exergaming as a Functional Test Battery in Patients Who Received Arthroscopic Ankle Arthrodesis: Cross-sectional Pilot Study. *JMIR Rehabilitation and Assistive Technologies, 8*(2), e21924. doi:10.2196/21924 PMID:33949311

Herrera-Luna, I. (2019. *Fusión de características geométricas y señales electromiográficas para la identificación off-line de movimientos de muñeca utilizados en rehabilitación* [Unpublished dissertation, Universidad Veracruzana, Xalapa, Veracruz, México]. https://www.uv.mx/mia/files/2021/07/tesis-IHL-1.pdf

Hocine, N., Gouaich, A., & Cerri, S. A. (2014, April). Dynamic difficulty adaptation in serious games for motor rehabilitation. In *International Conference on Serious Games* (pp. 115-128). Springer, Cham. 10.1007/978-3-319-05972-3_13

Hocine, N., Gouaïch, A., Cerri, S. A., Mottet, D., Froger, J., & Laffont, I. (2015). Adaptation in serious games for upper-limb rehabilitation: An approach to improve training outcomes. *User Modeling and User-Adapted Interaction, 25*(1), 65–98. doi:10.100711257-015-9154-6

Hussain, S., Jamwal, P. K., & Ghayesh, M. H. (2017). State-of-the-art robotic devices for ankle re-rehabilitation: Mechanism and control review. *Proceedings of the Institution of Mechanical Engineers. Part H, Journal of Engineering in Medicine, 231*(12), 1224–1234. doi:10.1177/0954411917737584 PMID:29065774

Hussain, S., Jamwal, P. K., Vliet, P. V., & Brown, N. A. (2021). Robot assisted ankle neuro-rehabilitation: State of the art and future challenges. *Expert Review of Neurotherapeutics, 21*(1), 111–121. doi:10.108 0/14737175.2021.1847646 PMID:33198522

Leap Motion Controller. (n.d.) *Overview. Which hand tracking product is right for you? Leap Motion controller.* Ultra Leap. https://www.ultraleap.com/product/leap-motion-controller/

Lindner, P., Rozental, A., Jurell, A., Reuterskiöld, L., Andersson, G., Hamilton, W., Miloff, A., & Carlbring, P. (2020). Experiences of gamified and automated virtual reality exposure therapy for spider phobia: Qualitative study. *JMIR Serious Games, 8*(2), e17807. doi:10.2196/17807 PMID:32347803

Lohse, K., Shirzad, N., Verster, A., Hodges, N., & Van der Loos, H. M. (2013). Video games and rehabilitation: Using design principles to enhance engagement in physical therapy. *Journal of Neurologic Physical Therapy; JNPT, 37*(4), 166–175. doi:10.1097/NPT.0000000000000017 PMID:24232363

Narayan, J., Kalita, B., & Dwivedy, S. K. (2021). Development of robot-based upper limb devices for rehabilitation purposes: A systematic review. *Augmented Human Research, 6*(1), 1–33. doi:10.100741133-020-00043-x

Nasri, N., Orts-Escolano, S., & Cazorla, M. (2020). An semg-controlled 3d game for rehabilitation therapies: Real-time time hand gesture recognition using deep learning techniques. *Sensors (Basel), 20*(22), 6451. doi:10.339020226451 PMID:33198083

Norkin, C. C. (2016). *Measurement of joint motion: a guide to goniometry.* FA Davis.

Rahman, M. A. (2017). Web-based multimedia hand-therapy framework for measuring forward and inverse kinematic data. *Multimedia Tools and Applications, 76*(6), 8227–8255. doi:10.100711042-016-3447-6

Rechy-Ramirez, E. J., Marin-Hernandez, A., & Rios-Figueroa, H. V. (2019). A human–computer interface for wrist rehabilitation: A pilot study using commercial sensors to detect wrist movements. *The Visual Computer, 35*(1), 41–55. doi:10.100700371-017-1446-x

Siegel, S., & Smeddinck, J. (2012, September). Adaptive difficulty with dynamic range of motion adjustments in exergames for Parkinson's disease patients. *In International Conference on Entertainment Computing* (pp. 429-432). Springer, Berlin, Heidelberg 10.1007/978-3-642-33542-6_45

Silva, G. M., Souto, J. J. D. S., Fernandes, T. P., Bolis, I., & Santos, N. A. (2021). Interventions with serious games and entertainment games in autism spectrum disorder: A systematic review. *Developmental Neuropsychology, 46*(7), 463–485. doi:10.1080/87565641.2021.1981905 PMID:34595981

Smeddinck, J. D., Siegel, S., & Herrlich, M. (2013, May). Adaptive difficulty in exergames for Parkinson's disease patients. In Graphics Interface (pp. 141-148).

Song, X., van de Ven, S. S., Chen, S., Kang, P., Gao, Q., Jia, J., & Shull, P. B. (2022). Proposal of a wearable multimodal sensing-based serious games approach for hand movement training after stroke. *Frontiers in Physiology, 13*, 811950. doi:10.3389/fphys.2022.811950 PMID:35721546

Steiner, B., Elgert, L., Saalfeld, B., & Wolf, K. H. (2020). Gamification in rehabilitation of patients with musculoskeletal diseases of the shoulder: Scoping review. *JMIR Serious Games, 8*(3), e19914. doi:10.2196/19914 PMID:32840488

Tsikinas, S., & Xinogalos, S. (2019). Studying the effects of computer serious games on people with intellectual disabilities or autism spectrum disorder: A systematic literature review. *Journal of Computer Assisted Learning, 35*(1), 61–73. doi:10.1111/jcal.12311

Verhulst, A., Yamaguchi, T., & Richard, P. (2015, February). Physiological-based Dynamic difficulty adaptation in a theragame for children with cerebral palsy. *In Proceedings of the 2nd International Conference on Physiological Computing Systems (PhyCS-2015)* (pp. 164-171). Scitepress. 10.5220/0005271501640171

Viglialoro, R. M., Condino, S., Turini, G., Mamone, V., Carbone, M., Ferrari, V., Ghelarducci, G., Ferrari, M., & Gesi, M. (2020). Interactive serious game for shoulder rehabilitation based on real-time hand tracking. *Technology and Health Care, 28*(4), 403–414. doi:10.3233/THC-192081 PMID:32444586

Walsh, C. M., Gull, K., & Dooley, D. (2022). Motor rehabilitation as a therapeutic tool for spinal cord injury: New perspectives in immunomodulation. *Cytokine & Growth Factor Reviews*. doi:10.1016/j.cytogfr.2022.08.005 PMID:36114092

Wang, L., Chen, J. L., Wong, A. M., Liang, K. C., & Tseng, K. C. (2022). Game-Based Virtual Reality System for Upper Limb Rehabilitation After Stroke in a Clinical Environment: Systematic Review and Meta-Analysis. *Games for Health Journal, 11*(5), 277–297. doi:10.1089/g4h.2022.0086 PMID:36252097

Wirth, W., Hartmann, T., Böcking, S., Vorderer, P., Klimmt, C., Schramm, H., Saari, T., Laarni, J., Ravaja, N., Gouveia, F. R., Biocca, F., Sacau, A., Jäncke, L., Baumgartner, T., & Jäncke, P. (2007). A process model of the formation of spatial presence experiences. *Media Psychology, 9*(3), 493–525. doi:10.1080/15213260701283079

Yuan, B., Folmer, E., & Harris, F. C. Jr. (2011). Game accessibility: A survey. *Universal Access in the Information Society, 10*(1), 81–100. doi:10.100710209-010-0189-5

Zohaib, M. (2018). Dynamic difficulty adjustment (DDA) in computer games: A review. *Advances in Human-Computer Interaction, 2018*, 1–12. doi:10.1155/2018/5681652

Zyda, M. (2005). From visual simulation to virtual reality to games. *Computer, 38*(9), 25–32. doi:10.1109/MC.2005.297

ADDITIONAL READING

Boyle, E. A., Connolly, T. M., Hainey, T., & Boyle, J. M. (2012). Engagement in digital entertainment games: A systematic review. *Computers in Human Behavior, 28*(3), 771–780. doi:10.1016/j.chb.2011.11.020

Ponce-Cruz, P., Molina, A., & MacCleery, B. (2016). *Fuzzy Logic Type 1 and Type 2 Based on Lab-VIEW"! FPGA*. Springer. doi:10.1007/978-3-319-26656-5

Ross, T. J. (2009). *Fuzzy logic with engineering applications*. John Wiley & Sons.

Sharmili, S. S., & Kanagaraj, R. (2020). Live Beyond Fear: A Virtual Reality Serious Game Platform to Overcome Phobias. *In 2020 5th International Conference on Devices, Circuits and Systems (ICDCS)* (pp. 336-339). IEEE. 10.1109/ICDCS48716.2020.243592

Wiemeyer, J., Nacke, L., Moser, C., & Floyd'Mueller, F. (2016). Player experience. In *Serious games* (pp. 243–271). Springer. doi:10.1007/978-3-319-40612-1_9

KEY TERMS AND DEFINITIONS

Dynamic Difficulty Adjustment (DDA): The game difficulty is modified continuously in the game in order to avoid boredom or frustration on the player.

Engagement: it is the feeling of enjoying playing the game (i.e., the involvement in the game).

Fuzzy Logic: It was introduced by Lotfi Zadeh in 1965. Fuzzy logic could be employed to tackle data uncertainty through mainly three processes: fuzzification, fuzzy inference, and defuzzification.

Leap Motion Controller: It is a sensor based on infrared cameras and leds, which can identify X, Y, Z coordinates of the positions of the finger phalanges, palm, wrist and elbow.

Range-of-Motion: The number of degrees - arc - that a joint could achieve when it is moved from one position to another.

Rehabilitation: A process that is needed in order to recover mobility. This could be done using body movements or exercises.

Serious Game: It is a video game played against a computer, where its main purpose is beyond the entertainment (i.e., it is designed to tackle health problems or train people mainly).

Chapter 4
Evolution of Blockchain Technology:
Principles, Research Trends and Challenges, Applications, and Future Directions

Oluwaleke Umar Yusuf
The American University in Cairo, Egypt

Maki K. Habib
The American University in Cairo, Egypt

ABSTRACT

This chapter presents a detailed introduction to the decentralized data processing and storage paradigm called blockchain technology, delving into its fundamental concepts, foundational principles, and advantages. A literature review is conducted, detailing existing research areas, and enabling technologies driving further research and development into the technology. The two-way fusion of machine learning – another data-driven technology – is considered, wherein one technology addresses limitations and drawbacks within the other. The existing applications of blockchain technology within various domains are discussed, along with some identified research challenges and future trends. A case study is also provided to demonstrate the integration of blockchain technology into the internet of vehicles domain.

INTRODUCTION

The contemporary data processing and storage paradigm hinges upon centralized authorities for access, resolution, trust, and integrity. Blockchain Technology – also known as Decentralized Ledger Technology – aims to address the single-point-of-failure vulnerabilities introduced by such centralized authorities. A blockchain is a continuously growing data structure consisting of an immutable chain of blocks distributed among multiple authenticated nodes. Furthermore, no authoritative entity is required to validate

DOI: 10.4018/978-1-6684-7684-0.ch004

and ensure data authenticity, integrity, and security. Any form of digital (or digitalized) information can be stored on a blockchain to support various applications in different domains. Such digital information includes financial transactions, legal documentation, patient health records, supply chain, and logistical data, amongst others (Baiod et al., 2021; Casino et al., 2019; Hassan et al., 2020).

The origins of blockchain technology date back to 1991 when a paper (Haber & Stornetta, 1991) first appeared proposing the concept of attaching a time-stamp to a digital document. Building upon that paper and other related research work, a white paper (Nakamoto, 2009) was proposed in 2008, which established the utility of blockchain as a technology, popularizing the concept of secured peer-to-peer (P2P) transactions in the form of Bitcoin. Since then, blockchain technology has been implemented in capital markets, the Internet of Things, and supply chain management (Baiod et al., 2021; Casino et al., 2019; Zheng et al., 2019). In addition, blockchain technology has been proposed as a core component of smart cities (Salha et al., 2019), autonomous freight (Narbayeva et al., 2020), and the Internet of Vehicles (Mollah et al., 2021) in the near future.

Due to the relative immaturity and fast-paced innovation of blockchain technology, there is a lack of concise, up-to-date literature that provides an interested layperson with a detailed introduction to the technology and its potential to revolutionize diverse domains simultaneously. To this end, this chapter intends to provide a comprehensive overview of the evolution of blockchain technology underlying – from its fundamental concepts and foundational principles to its advantages for various applications. This is followed by a review of research areas and enabling technologies driving the continued development of blockchain technology. Next, we discuss some research challenges and detail the application of blockchain technology in various domains. We also examine a case study demonstrating the integration of blockchain technology into the Internet of Vehicles domain. Finally, we outline some future trends with blockchain technology.

FUNDAMENTAL CONCEPTS OF BLOCKCHAIN TECHNOLOGY

Blockchain Technology is built upon three fundamental concepts – blocks, nodes, and consensus protocols. The blockchain consists of *blocks* distributed across connected *nodes* governed by *consensus protocols* (Chandrayan, 2020; Malcom, 2021).

Blocks

The blockchain is a literal chain of blocks, each containing a block header and (transaction) data. The block header consists of metadata for identifying blocks in the chain and verifying the integrity of the blockchain using the hashes contained in each block. Depending on the application, the block data contains the actual system and user data. A block consists of three core elements, as demonstrated in Figure 1, as follows:

- **Data:** the data (or metadata) stored on the blockchain for a specific application.
- **Nonce:** a unique, randomly generated 32-bit number that contributes to the *hash* generation.
- **Hash:** a 256-bit number generated from the *nonce*, *data,* and the previous block's *hash* (denoted as *prev*). The blockchain is created and made immutable by including the *prev* value in the current hash.

Figure 1. Elements of a blockchain block
(Hassan et al., 2020)

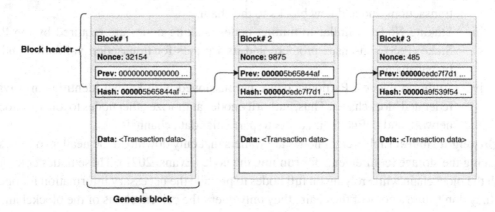

Nodes

Nodes are electronic devices – connected to the network and possessing an IP address – which serve as communication endpoints through which any user, application, or device interacts with the blockchain (Geroni, 2021). It is a common misconception that all nodes are thought to provide the same functionality or that each user interacting with the blockchain is considered a node (Geroni, 2021). Nodes are classified based on distinct roles played inside the blockchain ecosystem. The roles of nodes are protocol-specific – rather than software-specific – and are defined by the requirements of the blockchain application. As a result, nodes can participate in various activities, including transaction processing, block creation, and ledger management (Poston, 2022).

As shown in Figure 2, there are two main types of nodes, discussed as follows:

1. **Full Nodes:** Full nodes contain a complete copy of the blockchain's history, acting as servers in the decentralized blockchain network. Their main tasks include maintaining the consensus between other nodes, verifying transactions, storing the blockchain data, and providing access to the block-chain ledger.
    a. Pruned Full Node: This type of full node has a defined memory limit to hold the blockchain data. A pruned full node begins by downloading blocks from the beginning of the chain and continuously deletes older blocks to make room for newer blocks when the set limit is reached. The older blocks are not entirely erased; their headers and chain positions are retained to ensure continued chain integrity.
    b. Archival Full Node: This is the most common full node in blockchain implementations and discussions. It maintains the complete blockchain in its database. The only difference between pruned and archival full nodes is the hard drive space used. Archival nodes are further divided into the following categories:
        i. Masternodes: Masternodes are full nodes that do not possess the power to add new blocks to the blockchain but only maintain the blockchain ledger and validate the transactions.

ii. Mining Nodes: These nodes are specifically created to solve the complex mathematical functions required by consensus protocols such as Proof of Work (PoW) to validate transactions and add new blocks to the chain.

iii. Staking Nodes: Similar to mining nodes, staking nodes are required by the Proof of Stake (PoS) consensus protocol and its variants for transaction validation and ledger management.

iv. Authority Nodes: Participants are permissioned with known identities in private and federated blockchains. Thus, authority nodes authorize other nodes to join the blockchain network and define their access to particular data channels.

2. **Lightweight Nodes:** Lightweight nodes are wallets that only download the headers of blocks, thus reducing the storage requirements for running the node (Evans, 2022). These nodes communicate with the blockchain while relying on full nodes to provide the necessary information for operation. As they don't store a copy of the chain, they only query the current status of the blockchain for the newest block and broadcast transactions for processing.

Figure 2. Types of blockchain nodes

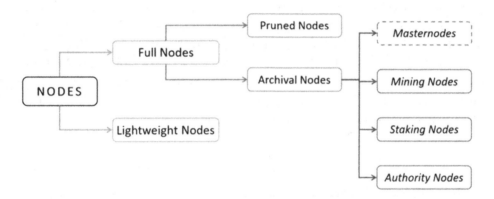

Consensus Protocols

Mining and staking nodes are archival full nodes responsible for validating transactions across the network and adding new blocks to the chain. These activities are coordinated and validated amongst the distributed nodes employing established *Consensus Protocols* (Bhardwaj, 2019). A consensus protocol is a fault-tolerant mechanism through which a distributed system's nodes collectively agree on the state of a collectively maintained record (Hassan et al., 2020). Depending on the specifics of the blockchain application, there are several consensus protocols, as shown in Figure 3, with the PoW and PoS variants most commonly used (Coinbase Team, 2022; Conway, 2022).

Figure 3. Types of consensus protocols
(Anwar, 2018)

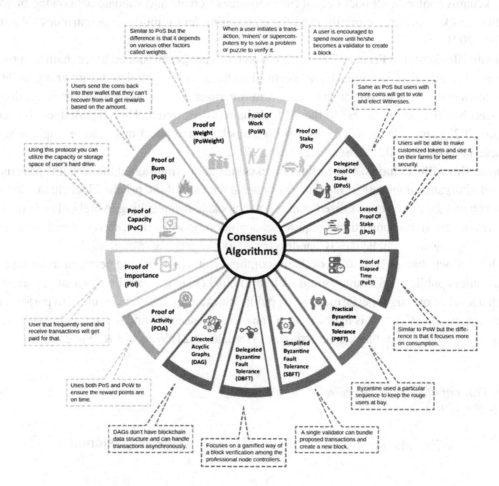

Types of Blockchain Structures

Figure 4 shows the types of blockchain structures available, characterized as permissionless or permissioned. Permissionless blockchains allow any user to join the blockchain network pseudo-anonymously and do not restrict the rights of the nodes on the blockchain network. On the other hand, permissioned blockchains restrict access to the network to specific users and may also restrict the rights of nodes on that network. The identities of the users of a permissioned blockchain are known to the other users of that permissioned blockchain (Wegrzyn & Wang, 2021).

Due to the large number of nodes, permissionless blockchains tend to be more secure against adversarial attacks, with longer transaction processing times than permissioned blockchains. Also, permissioned blockchains require a centralized authority to grant permission to nodes and create restrictions on the blockchain. This centralization introduces a single point of failure vulnerability to the system. A combination of permissionless and permissioned characteristics results in four types of blockchain structures – Public, Private, Consortium, and Hybrid – with various advantages, disadvantages, and use cases summarized in Figure 5 as follows:

1. **Public Blockchains:** Public blockchains are entirely open, decentralized, and permissionless. Public blockchains confer on all nodes equal rights to access, create and validate data on the blockchain. Public blockchains are primarily used for exchanging and mining cryptocurrency (Wegrzyn & Wang, 2021).

2. **Private Blockchains:** Private (managed) blockchains are permissioned blockchains controlled by a single organization and overseen by a central authority. The central authority grants node access to known users with varying rights to perform functions. Private blockchains are partially decentralized because public access to these blockchains is restricted. The Hyperledger (Hyperledger Team, 2022) umbrella project of open-source blockchain applications is an example of a private blockchain (Anwar, 2021; Wegrzyn & Wang, 2021).

3. **Consortium Blockchains:** Consortium blockchains are permissioned blockchains governed by a group of organizations rather than one entity, as in the case of the private blockchain. Consortium blockchains are more decentralized than private blockchains, resulting in higher levels of security. However, setting up consortiums requires cooperation between the different organizations, often presenting logistical challenges (Chandrayan, 2020; Wegrzyn & Wang, 2021).

4. **Hybrid Blockchains:** Hybrid blockchains combine features of private permission-based and permissionless public blockchain systems. A hybrid blockchain is controlled by a single organization with a level of oversight performed by the public blockchain, which is required to perform certain transaction validations. This hybridization enhances the security and transparency of the standard private and consortium blockchain structures (Iredale, 2021; Wegrzyn & Wang, 2021).

Figure 4. Types of blockchain structures
(Wegrzyn & Wang, 2021)

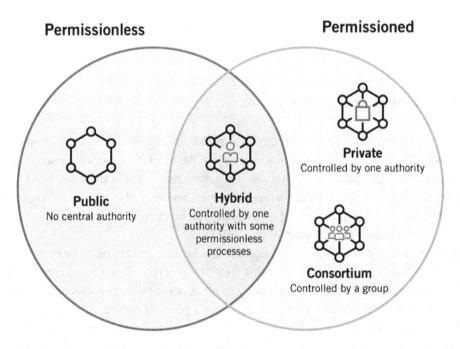

Figure 5. Advantages, disadvantages, and use cases of different blockchain structures
(Parizo, 2021)

	Public (permissionless)	Private (permissioned)	Consortium	Hybrid
ADVANTAGES	+ Independence + Transparency + Trust	+ Access control + Performance	+ Access control + Scalability + Security	+ Access control + Performance + Scalability
DISADVANTAGES	– Performance – Scalability – Security	– Trust – Auditability	– Transparency	– Transparency – Upgrading
USE CASES	▪ Cryptocurrency ▪ Document validation	▪ Supply chain ▪ Asset ownership	▪ Banking ▪ Research ▪ Supply chain	▪ Medical records ▪ Real estate

ADVANTAGES OF BLOCKCHAIN TECHNOLOGY

Figure 6 summarizes some of the advantages of blockchain technology. These advantages – decentralization, immutability, transparency, security, and traceability – are detailed as follows:

1. **Decentralization:** This is a core feature of blockchain technology. All operations performed on the blockchain network do not depend on centralized, third-party, authoritative entities for user access, user authentication, data integrity, and data security. Furthermore, the distributed network is robust as the failure or attack on an individual node does not cascade to the rest of the network. Thus, blockchain technology and applications built upon it are resilient to attacks, censorship, interference, and restrictions by outside parties (Edgar, 2021).
2. **Immutability:** A blockchain becomes immutable and tamper-proof by incorporating cryptographic hash algorithms, which create links between adjacent blocks. Changes to the blockchain are reflected in other nodes and must be validated with the consensus protocol before the altered version is accepted as the updated blockchain. Any questionable alteration to any block propagates across the entire blockchain, thus reducing the possibility of the altered blockchain being accepted by other nodes (Edgar, 2021; Lastbitcoder, 2022).
3. **Transparency:** Since it is an open-source, decentralized ledger, all historical transactions and operations on a blockchain are public to all nodes with access rights, thus lending credibility and integrity to the processes and data within the blockchain. In a public blockchain structure, all nodes have access rights. However, the centralized authority in a permissioned blockchain structure determines which nodes have access rights. This transparency suits the technology for applications involving information coordination amongst a large group of geographically distributed and (pseudo-)anonymous individuals (Hayes, 2022).
4. **Security:** A combination of decentralization, immutability, and transparency makes the blockchain secure. Copies of the entire blockchain are stored on and synchronized between multiple nodes without the oversight of some central entity, eliminating the potential single point of failure. Each node within the blockchain network is provided with a unique identity – in the form of public and private cryptographic keys – for user authentication and transaction verification. Most successful

blockchain attacks gained unauthorized access to the network using compromised private keys. Successful direct attacks against the blockchain are rare (Team DataFlair, 2018; Team Etoro, 2022).

5. **Traceability (Verifiability):** A consequence of the transparency and immutability of blockchain technology is the creation of an irreversible audit trail. Compared to contemporary data systems, this unbroken trail makes it relatively easy to track and resolve issues or disputes based on the blockchain's data. Also, the distributed nature of the network lends permanence to the information stored on a blockchain (Team DataFlair, 2018).

Figure 6. Advantages of blockchain technology

Decentralization	operations do not depend on centralized, third-party, authoritative entities
Immutability	any changes are reflected in all nodes and must be validated using the consensus protocol
Transparency	all historical transactions and operations are public to all nodes
Security	copies of the blockchain are stored on and synchronized between multiple nodes
Traceability	an irreversible and unbroken audit trail for tracking and resolving issues or disputes

FOUNDATIONAL PRINCIPLES OF BLOCKCHAIN TECHNOLOGY

The four commonly identified foundational technological principles which serve as the basis of blockchain technology are: distributed database, peer-to-peer network, computational logic, and immutable ledger (Baiod et al., 2021; Gupta, 2018; Malcom, 2021). These foundational principles are detailed as follows:

1. **Distributed Database:** Decentralized systems – incorporating distributed databases – store copies of the system information on all (or multiple) entities within the network, thus introducing redundancies into the system. In some cases, the system data can be stored off-chain while the associated metadata is stored on-chain and linked to the actual data using the block hash (Baiod et al., 2021; Gupta, 2018).

   However, as shown in Figure 7 (adapted from (BYJU'S Team, 2022; Lissounov, 2018)), contemporary systems offer client-server services which depend on a centralized entity for data storage and retrieval. This approach introduces a single point of failure with inherent drawbacks – which the decentralized approach aims to tackle – such as (Malcom, 2021):

   a. All the data is stored in one location, making it an easy target for potential attackers.

   b. All services are halted if the central entity is down (planned upgrade or unplanned outage).

   c. All the data is compromised if the central entity gets corrupted.

2. **Peer-To-Peer (P2P) Network:** A blockchain is maintained by a P2P network (Figure 7) of interconnected nodes with equal privileges who all have (shallow or full) copies of the blockchain data.

Thus, centralized authorities and other intermediaries are not required to maintain trust, ensure security and validate transactions within the blockchain. The nodes (peers) can pass the data of any transaction to the entire network. Once a data block is validated, it is added to the chain, and all nodes update their copies. If an attacker tries to modify the data on any local node, the rest of the network will not accept the altered block (Gupta, 2018; Malcom, 2021).

Figure 7. Client-server and peer-to-peer system architectures

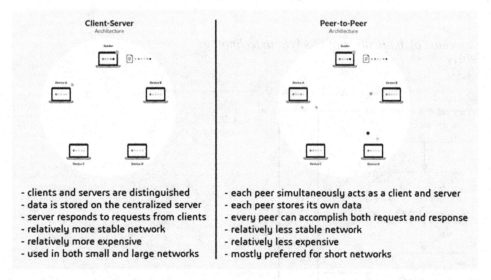

3. **Computational Logic:** Since a blockchain is a digital database, transactions between constituent nodes are guided by computational logic via pre-defined rules and protocols. This concept is especially beneficial in enterprise markets as the private blockchain offers nodes to help manage the permissions for accessing, submitting, and verifying transactions and data. Nodes within the blockchain need to agree on the validity of new blocks based on a pre-defined consensus protocol before the said blocks can be added to the chain. If all nodes are in agreement, the block is added to the blockchain. If different nodes find different chains valid, the longest chain is selected as the blockchain, the shorter chains are discarded, and all nodes update to the longest chain (Malcom, 2021).

4. **Immutable Ledger:** As illustrated in Figure 1, every block contains the previous block's hash, which means the entire blockchain must be modified to tamper with any block's record. This feature allows the chain to work as an immutable ledger – it is impossible to alter the data. The immutability of blockchain technology is derived from the *Cryptographic Hash Function,* which has a vital characteristic known as the *Avalanche Effect* – a slight change in the input reflects more significant changes in the hash. Any attempt to alter a block changes its hash drastically, with the changes cascading to subsequent blocks down the chain. The complete copy of the chain is modified, rendering it invalid (Baiod et al., 2021; Malcom, 2021).

LITERATURE REVIEW: RESEARCH AREAS

As a distributed database, blockchain technology can be integrated into any domain where data is shared between several collaborating entities. Figure 8 shows a flowchart of application-specific details that can be considered before implementing blockchain technology. The flowchart provides a rule of thumb for determining when – and what type of – blockchains are suitable for implementation. The available literature details the technological advancements, active research areas, enabling technologies, and real-world applications of blockchain technology.

Figure 8. Flowchart of application of blockchain technology
(Baiod et al., 2021)

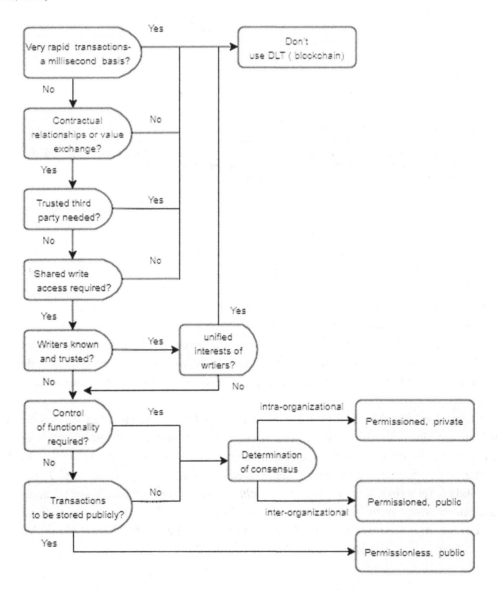

Healthcare

The healthcare sector is a problem-driven, data- and personnel-intensive domain where the ability to access, edit and trust the data emerging from its activities is critical for the entire sector's operations and achieving desired health outcomes. The most significant impact of blockchain within the healthcare sector relates to improving clinical trial management, regulatory compliance, and providing a decentralized framework for sharing Electronic Health Records (EHR) (Hasselgren et al., 2020). Compared to the traditional Distributed Database Management System (DDBMS), the key benefits of adopting blockchain technology in biomedical and healthcare applications include (Kuo et al., 2017):

1. **Decentralized Management:** Blockchain is suitable for applications where independently managed stakeholders (hospitals, providers, patients, and payers) wish to collaborate without ceding control to a central management intermediary.
2. **Immutable Audit Trail:** Blockchain only supports "create" and "read" functions, making it suitable as an unchangeable ledger to record critical information such as insurance claim records.
3. **Data Provenance:** Blockchain is suitable for managing critical digital assets (such as patient consent records) where changes in ownership are restricted to the owner, following cryptographic protocols.
4. **Robustness & Availability:** Blockchain achieves a high level of data redundancy at a relatively reduced cost, making it more suitable than a DDBMS for the preservation and continuous availability of important records such as EHRs.
5. **Security & Privacy:** Blockchain employs cryptographic algorithms (such as SHA-256 and ECDSA) for running consensus algorithms, generating user addresses for improved privacy, and generating high-security-level public and private keys as digital signatures for ownership verification.

The integration of blockchain technology in biomedical and healthcare applications aims to exploit the blockchain-stored data towards creating improved medical record management, enhanced insurance claim processes, and accelerated clinical/biomedical research. Such applications include health insurance, digitalization of medical services, clinical trial results, medical records and patient data storage, e-medicine, IoT, and medical supply chains, amongst others (Nair, 2020). However, some potential integration challenges involving transparency, confidentiality, speed, and scalability remain to be addressed (Kuo et al., 2017).

Big Data

Big Data is a new generation of technologies and architectures designed to analyze a large amount of data and capture its main characteristics through knowledge discovery and analytics. These datasets have huge sizes and dimensionalities and cannot be stored, managed, analyzed, and captured using conventional database tools (Deepa et al., 2021). Big data is typically characterized by 4-V features as follows:

1. **Volume**: Volume refers to the quantity of data, i.e., whether a dataset is considered big data. This feature leads to processing challenges regarding modularity, class imbalance, dimensionality, nonlinearity, and computing.

2. **Variety**: Variety represents the types of data (video, text, audio, etc.) and their compositions (structured, semi-structured data, and unstructured). The challenges caused by variety include data locality, heterogeneity, and noise.
3. **Velocity**: This feature refers to the speed of data generation, that is, how fast the data is generated to meet the demand.
4. **Veracity**: This feature refers to the quality aspect since the data can be collected from multiple sources, which may include low-quality and noisy samples.

Big data has found applications in many vertical domains, such as smart grid, mobile and e-health, transportation and logistics, and wireless and communication networking. However, big data also faces challenges such as data security and privacy, energy management, scalability of computing infrastructure, data management, data interpretation, real-time data processing, and big data intelligence. Blockchain has the potential to transform current big data systems by providing efficient security features and network management capabilities for enabling newly emerging big data services and applications (Deepa et al., 2021).

As shown in Figure 9, integrating blockchain technology with big data creates services in big data environments for the acquisition, storage, analytics, and privacy preservation of big data. Such services cover applications such as smart cities, smart healthcare, smart grids, intelligent transportation, and other big data projects. However, these services and applications are plagued by security, standardization, and complexity research challenges (Deepa et al., 2021).

Figure 9. Overview of blockchain services in big data environment
(Deepa et al., 2021)

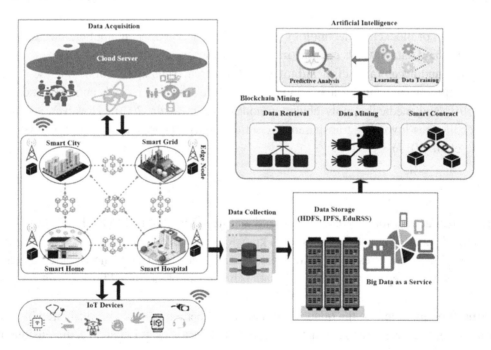

Digital Twins

For predictive maintenance, a promising solution is creating a virtual replica of the underlying product, process, or service. Such a replica can be used to analyze, predict, and optimize all operations before its real-world implementation. Following a closed loop, the simulation data is fed back to the physical object to calibrate the operations and enhance the system's performance. Such a bi-directional mapping between physical space (object) and virtual space (replica) is called Digital Twin (DT) (Suhail et al., 2021).

Formally, a DT is defined as an integrated multi-physics, multi-scale, probabilistic simulation mirroring a physical system based on models, sensors, historical data, etc. DTs can be leveraged to draw intelligent conclusions from data by identifying faults and recommending precautionary measures ahead of critical events. Integrating blockchain technology with DTs ensures secure data management and targets key challenges of disparate data repositories and untrustworthy data dissemination in industrial use cases (Suhail et al., 2021). The key benefits of blockchain-based DTs – such as that shown in Figure 10 – include the following:

- Trustworthy Sources
- Distributed Infrastructure
- Securing Digital Twins Data
- Data Traceability in Digital Twins
- Access Privileges of Digital Twins
- Safeguarding Product Lifecycle Data
- Automation Through Smart Contracts
- Combating the Problem of Counterfeits

However, the successful implementation of blockchain-based DTs is hindered by technical, logistical, and social challenges involving the representation of digital twins, expenditures on infrastructure, standardization efforts, ethical concerns, and legal issues, amongst others (Suhail et al., 2021).

LITERATURE REVIEW: ENABLING TECHNOLOGIES

An enabling technology is an innovation that can be applied to drive the radical and rapid development of subsequent derivative technologies, often in diverse fields ('Enabling Technology', 2022). Some technologies have driven ongoing research, development, and investment in blockchain technology, as follows:

Blockchain and Internet of Things (IoT)

The IoT ecosystem seamlessly interconnects myriad "things" (electronic or electrical devices) with different characteristics and functionalities in human-centric and machine-centric networks through the Internet. The principal aim is to maximize the benefits of data collected by various sensors and actuators embedded in these heterogeneous devices (Miraz, 2020). Currently, most IoT solutions rely on the centralized server-client paradigm, connecting to cloud servers through the Internet (Fernández-Caramés & Fraga-Lamas, 2018).

Figure 10. Framework for a blockchain-based digital twin
(Suhail et al., 2021)

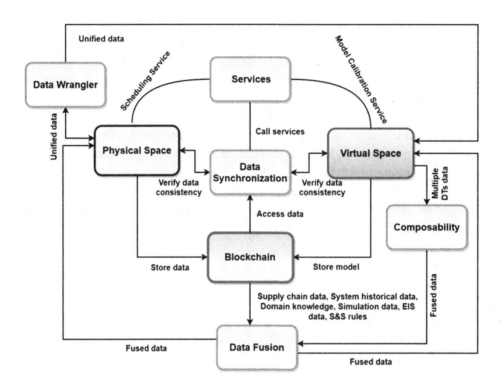

However, the significant number of connected devices and massive data traffic become bottlenecks in meeting the required Quality-of-Services (QoS) due to the computing, storage, and bandwidth constraints of IoT devices (Ferrag et al., 2019). The convergence of IoT and blockchain technology aims to transform major application areas of IoT by enabling a decentralized environment with anonymous and trustful transactions. With blockchain technology, IoT systems benefit from lower operational costs, decentralized resource management, and robustness against threats and attacks (Ferrag et al., 2019).

Note that a blockchain is not always the best solution for every IoT scenario. Traditional databases or Directed Acyclic Graph-based ledgers may better fit specific IoT applications. A generic flow diagram similar to that shown in Figure 8 can be used to determine the type of blockchain necessary depending on an IoT system's characteristics. Figure 11 shows IoT fields and use cases where blockchain technology can be applied. Some open questions and research challenges regarding blockchain-IoT integration include (Ferrag et al., 2019):

- Resiliency against Combined Attacks
- Dynamic and Adaptable Security Framework
- Compliance with GDPR
- Energy-efficient Mining
- Blockchain-specific Infrastructure
- Social Networks and Trust Management

Figure 11. Integration of blockchain technology and the internet of things
(Fernández-Caramés & Fraga-Lamas, 2018)

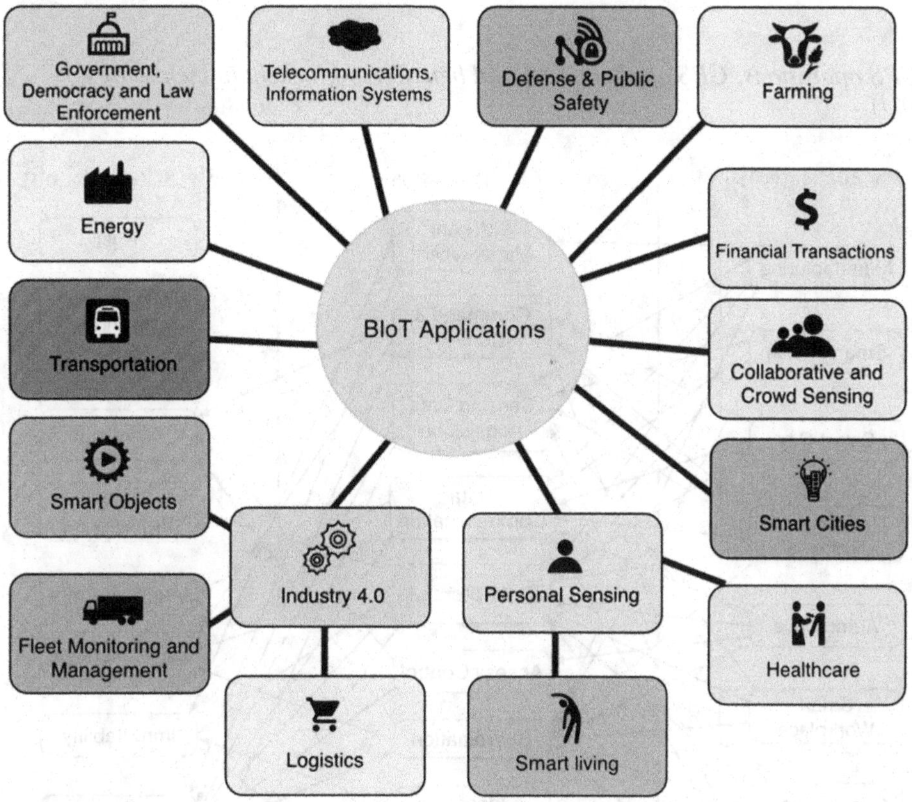

Blockchain and Cyber-Physical Systems (CPS)

CPS is based on systems incorporating cyber and physical systems to exchange real-time data. A CPS is a network of embedded systems comprising sensors, aggregators, and actuators capable of monitoring and controlling IoT-related processes and objects. CPS integrates sensing, networking, communication, control, and computation and has become essential for critical infrastructure, including water, energy, gas, healthcare, transportation, and smart grid systems (Khalil et al., 2021). Due to its mission-critical nature, CPS operations must be made fault-tolerant and secure while requiring timely delivery of messages and processing. CPS that spans multiple organizations would also require much stronger trust-level guarantees.

However, traditional CPS approaches suffer from several problems related to atomicity, fault tolerance, key management, and trust. By integrating with blockchain technology, CPS can enhance its security, dependability, and trust without involving any trusted third party or centralized control (Khalil et al., 2021; Zhao et al., 2021). Figure 12 shows nine basic CPS operations, their relationship with different CPS applications, and the benefits derivable from blockchain integrations. However, the integration of blockchain and CPS is not without challenges, with two apparent limitations (Zhao et al., 2021):

- The significant delay in reaching consensus in the blockchain.
- The inadequate throughput that current blockchain platforms can sustain.

Figure 12. CPS operations, CPS applications, and benefits to blockchain technology
(Zhao et al., 2021)

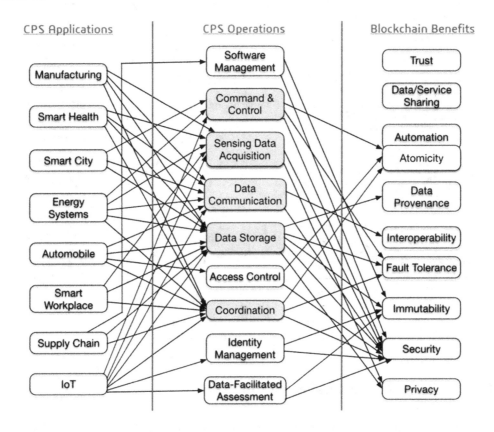

Blockchain and Internet of Vehicles (IoV)

IoV is a new paradigm within Intelligent Transportation Systems (ITS) driven by the confluence of smart vehicles, IoT, and AI. In the IoV ecosystem, vehicles are connected with other vehicles, people, and infrastructures through the Internet, so they can drive safely and intelligently by sensing and monitoring their environments. The development of IoV will generate massive amounts of data, which will require a proportional amount of computing and storage resources shared across vehicles in the network to support a wide range of applications and services (Mollah et al., 2021). However, some unique characteristics of the IoV ecosystem pose novel challenges when integrated with existing Internet technologies. Such unique characteristics include the following (Mollah et al., 2021):

- The high and diverse mobility of vehicles leads to difficulties in maintaining stable communication regardless of dedicated channels.

- The IoV ecosystem relies on a heterogeneous wireless communication network, where several wireless technologies coexist in complex and dynamic topologies.
- In emergency and safety-related vehicular applications, communication latency is critical to avoiding and responding to accidents.
- The extensive geographical range of vehicles, integration of various devices, protocols, and platforms across the ecosystem, and the capability of collaboration between IoV components pose considerable scalability, heterogeneity, and interoperability concerns, respectively.
- The dynamic and heterogeneous nature of IoV scenarios complicates the implementation of machine learning (ML) techniques for applications based on Artificial Intelligence (AI).

Figure 13. Integration of blockchain technology and the IoV

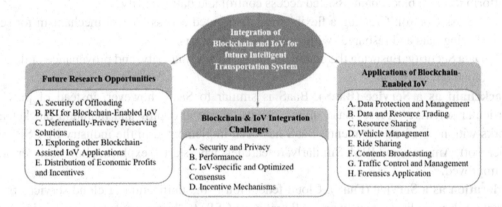

Blockchain technology can potentially provide innovative solutions for IoV application scenarios involving the real-time exchange of massive data generated by high-mobility vehicles where classic techniques are unlikely to be suitable and effective. Furthermore, the increasing connectivity and heterogeneity in such scenarios introduce unique attack vectors for malicious entities. As enumerated in Figure 13 (adapted from (Mollah et al., 2021)), integrating blockchain technology with the Internet of Vehicles is appealing for some applications. Such integration offers potential research opportunities and challenges to tackle (Mollah et al., 2021).

Blockchain and Cloud Technologies

Cloud is an on-demand, pay-as-you-go service paradigm facilitating the availability of shared resources for data storage and computation. Cloud computing solves the traditional resource management problem providing uninterrupted network access and resource pooling at significantly reduced costs. Cloud services are facilitated by cloud service providers (CSPs) – third parties that provide cloud storage, virtualization, networking components, data, and operating systems (Sarker et al., 2020). CSPs package these services in three fundamental service models:

1. Infrastructure-as-a-Service (IaaS)
2. Platform-as-a-Service (PaaS)
3. Software-as-a-Service (SaaS)

However, Cloud has some limitations, such as shared infrastructure problems, virtualization issues, API securities, privacy, and SLA (Service Level Agreement)-based legal issues. The integration of blockchain technology and the Cloud has received significant attention for tackling these limitations, ensuring efficiency, transparency, and security, and offering better cloud services in the form of novel service models. Blockchain integration with cloud platforms can be grouped into four service models as follows (Sarker et al., 2020):

- **Security as a Service (SECaaS)**: SECaaS aims to improve the security services within a cloud platform through blockchain-assisted access control and data security.
  - Access Control: Creating a flexible and distributed access control mechanism for securely sharing data and resources within cloud environments.
  - Data Security: Ensuring the confidentiality, privacy, integrity, and provenance of data within cloud environments.
- **Blockchain as a Service (BaaS)**: BaaS is similar to SaaS; however, instead of providing a particular software service, BaaS allows clients to create, deploy and maintain blockchain networks within cloud environments. BaaS has been implemented in the industry by CSPs such as Microsoft, Amazon, and IBM. Similarly, researchers have started exploring how such services can be improved.
- **Federation as a Service (FaaS)**: Cloud federation is the unification of cloud services from different CSPs with disparate networks, allowing the CSPs to share resources across their infrastructures and providing users with a more flexible service-delivery option with enhanced availability. FaaS explores the potential of blockchain technology for the secure, transparent, and accountable creation and management of cloud federations.
- **Management as a Service**: Cloud management can be referred to as the administrative controls encapsulating the process of evaluating and monitoring users, data, resources, applications, and services. The management as a service model focuses on managing tenants and other resources within a cloud environment using blockchain technology.

Cloud of Things (CoT)

Due to the limited resources of IoT devices, application tasks are often delegated to the cloud, giving birth to the Cloud of Things (CoT) paradigm. CoT provides a flexible, robust cloud computing environment for processing and managing IoT services, showing great potential to improve the system performance and efficiency of service delivery (Nguyen et al., 2020).

In this context, blockchain technology provides innovative solutions to address CoT challenges in decentralization, data privacy, and network security. At the same time, CoT offers elasticity and scalability functionalities to improve the efficiency of blockchain operations. The integration of blockchain and CoT – called BCoT – has been widely regarded as a promising enabler for various applications in different use-case domains, such as smart healthcare, smart city, smart transportation, and smart industry (Nguyen et al., 2020).

Blockchain and Edge Computing

Edge computing is an extension of cloud computing that pushes the frontier of computation power, data storage, and application services away from the centralized cloud to the edge servers of the network (Luo et al., 2020). Edge computing retains the core advantages of cloud computing and transfers real-time control and sensitive data storage to the edge servers, thus enabling applications with location awareness, low latency, heterogeneity, versatility, scalability, fault tolerance, privacy security, and improved Quality of Service (QoS), especially the compute-intensive and delay-sensitive ones (Luo et al., 2020; Yang et al., 2019). The edge computing architecture is generally divided into three levels, representing the computing capacity of edge computing elements and their characteristics, as follows (Luo et al., 2020; Yang et al., 2019):

1. **IoT Devices:** IoT devices at the *front-end* provide interactive and responsive connections of people and things in the network and are connected to one of the edge servers. However, resource requirements must be forwarded to the servers due to the limited capacity of these devices.
2. **Edge Servers:** Edge servers in the *near-end* can provide numerous resource requirements, such as real-time data processing, data caching, and computation offloading. Therefore, edge servers provide better performance for end users with a slight increase in latency.
3. **Cloud Servers:** Cloud servers in the *far-end* provide high-performance computing, big data analytics, and more data storage without strict real-time requirements.

Figure 14. The architecture of blockchain-enabled edge computing
(Luo et al., 2020)

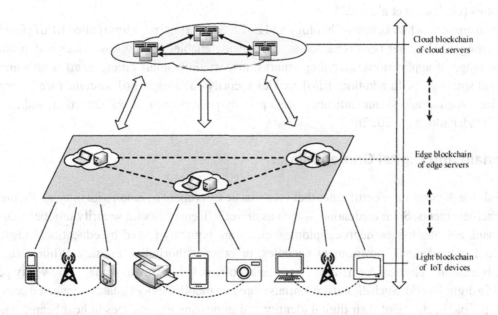

85

This architecture aims to execute the compute-intensive and delay-sensitive part of an application in the edge network, with some applications in the edge server communicating with the core cloud for data synchronization. Despite its benefits, the distributed structure of edge creates significant security and privacy challenges due to the interplay of heterogeneous edge servers and the migration of services across the edge servers (Yang et al., 2019). By integrating blockchain technology into the edge computing network – as shown in Figure 14 – the system can provide reliable access and control of the network, storage, and computation over many distributed edge and cloud servers. Consequently, the system's network security, data integrity, and computation validity can be considerably improved.

Likewise, the integration of edge computing provides the system with plenty of computing and storage resources distributed at the network edge, effectively offloading the blockchain storage and the mining computation from the devices with power, storage, and compute limitations (Yang et al., 2019). Blockchain technology has been integrated into edge computing-based IoT networks in applications such as smart cities, smart transportation, industrial IoTs, smart homes, and smart grids (Luo et al., 2020). However, some significant research challenges remain to be addressed involving Scalability, Consensus Optimization, Interoperability, Cost Standardization, self-organization, security, and resource management (Luo et al., 2020; Yang et al., 2019).

Edge of Things (EoT)

Edge computing has been recently proposed to support IoT by creating Edge of Things (EoT) networks by migrating computing and storage to the network's edge. In this regard, a better computing experience can be provided for users by eliminating the computational burden placed on resource-constrained IoT sensors and significantly reducing the communication overhead. Therefore, EoT can support location-aware distributed IoT applications to facilitate time-sensitive service delivery with reduced computation complexities (Gadekallu et al., 2022).

The convergence of blockchain technology and EoT leads to a new paradigm called BEoT (Blockchain Edge of Things). BEoT has been regarded as a promising enabler for future services and applications in a wide range of applications, including smart transportation, smart cities, smart healthcare, smart homes, and smart grids. In addition, BEoT tackles security challenges EoT systems face by providing key services, such as access authentication, data privacy preservation, attack detection, and trust management (Gadekallu et al., 2022).

Blockchain and Digital Credentials

Credentials are documents or certificates that verify basic facts about a person's identity, skills, qualifications, or achievements. Such credentials – such as driver's licenses, social security numbers, employee badges, bank account logins, degree diplomas, etc. – are typically issued by educational institutions, professional organizations, government agencies, or other authoritative entities. While today, most credentials exist in a physical form, digital credentials offer a better way to manage and verify personal identity in a digital world. Such digital credentials stored on mobile devices enable connected ecosystems – putting people in charge of their digital identity and improving experiences in healthcare, education, government services, and other areas (Kaplan et al., 2022).

Blockchain technology – with the underlying decentralized ledger and cryptographic protocols – forms the foundation for generating and securing digital credentials. The blockchain also acts as the trust anchor and registry for verifying digital credentials. When an individual shares a digital credential, the receiving organization can instantly verify it against the immutable records in the blockchain registry without needing to contact the original issuer. This paradigm facilitates data privacy, enables instant authentication, improves integrity, and helps build trust in the credentials. However, interoperability standards are needed for different blockchain networks to securely exchange verifiable credentials (Kaplan et al., 2022).

Within the education sector, the combination of blockchain technology and digital credentials has been proposed as a potential solution to the counterfeiting of diplomas and certificates. In addition, quality rankings of the degree-granting institutions can be appended to the digital diploma. This approach – with the growth in international mobility – could simplify the verification of qualifications for employers, universities, and students (Castro & Au-Yong-Oliveira, 2021). However, some key issues limit the wide-scale adoption of blockchain technology for education. Such barriers include a lack of governance, standards, and interoperability; trust and legitimacy; technological maturity; and policy and regulatory challenges (Grech et al., 2021).

RESEARCH CHALLENGES OF BLOCKCHAIN TECHNOLOGY

Knowledge Gaps

Some limitations of blockchain technology and its applications can be identified from the discussion on research areas and enabling technologies. These limitations expose gaps in current knowledge and viable areas for further research efforts, as follows:

1. **Latency:** Blockchain financial and cryptocurrency applications have significant latency issues and low rates of transactions compared to existing financial payment-processing networks. While permissioned blockchains perform better than permissionless ones, there is still a long way to go in reducing the time required to process blocks and confirm transactions (Casino et al., 2019; Yli-Huumo et al., 2016)

2. **Quantum Resilience:** Blockchain depends on the *Cryptographic Hash Function* for ledger immutability and public-key encryption for signing transactions. A quantum computer would require 2^{128} operations to crack the commonly used *SHA-256* hash algorithm, making *SHA-256* resistant to quantum attacks. However, *ECDSA* and other public-key encryption algorithms can be broken once a big enough quantum computer is built, rendering almost all blockchains insecure (Casino et al., 2019).

3. **Interoperability:** The fast growth of the blockchain ecosystem has led to a wide diversity of implementations and features. These heterogeneous solutions give rise to interoperability issues, thus hindering standardization and widespread adoption of the technology (Casino et al., 2019).

4. **Privacy & Confidentiality:** Privacy and confidentiality issues continue to plague blockchain applications because the information is stored as a public ledger. While anonymization and encryption-based mechanisms can be adopted to protect the confidentiality of the information, these mechanisms are often insufficient and limited by the specifics of the implementation (Casino et al., 2019).

5. **Smart Contracts (SCs):** Smart contracts running on blockchain networks are similar to programs and have the same problems. SCs often contain errors and vulnerabilities in the code that can be exploited to compromise the network's security. The programming paradigm of SCs makes their operation challenging to understand, thus easing the task of hiding illegal and nefarious activities (Casino et al., 2019).

Blockchain Adoption Challenges

As with every technology, there are pros and cons to balance when adopting the technology. The following are some barriers to the integration of blockchain technology:

1. **Legalities & Regulation:** Blockchain technology is relatively new, and the legal ramifications of its adoption are not fully worked out. Thus, the lack of concrete regulatory oversight makes it hard to map appropriate legal liabilities, slowing down overall technology adoption (Lastbitcoder, 2022; Team DataFlair, 2018).
2. **Data Portability:** Due to the inherent principles of blockchain technology, users are unable to transfer their records of transactions between different blockchains. Furthermore, there are no standards dictating how data is stored, public-private keys are generated, hash values are generated, and data is broadcast across peers within and across different blockchains (Jaikaran, 2018).
3. **Immaturity:** Blockchain technology has yet to inspire widespread confidence due to its immaturity. It is sometimes considered a fad for tech-savvy people. While several blockchain applications are doing great in different industries, there is still some ways before the technology garners enough confidence to attract massive investments and increased research interest (Lastbitcoder, 2022).
4. **Implementation Costs:** Blockchain technology represents relatively low costs for users; unfortunately, this implies high implementation costs for developers regarding hardware and software requirements during the application's initial development and final deployment. The time and cost of implementing a blockchain is a significant overhead that delays its mass adoption and implementation (Edgar, 2021; Team DataFlair, 2018).
5. **Energy Costs:** Some consensus protocols require time- and energy-intensive computations. Furthermore, keeping a real-time ledger also contributes to power consumption as every change on the blockchain is communicated with every node on the network simultaneously. This becomes a bigger problem the larger the size of the blockchain (Lastbitcoder, 2022; Team DataFlair, 2018).
6. **Storage Costs:** As the number of users (nodes) grows and the amount of data stored on the blockchain increases, the number of operations integrated into the blocks to be stored will also grow. Thus, the storage space required for the blockchain's full nodes will also increase to accommodate the complete ledger. This also increases the maintenance cost of the network (Edgar, 2021; Team DataFlair, 2018).
7. **Inefficient Validation & Mining Processes:** It is inefficient to have several network nodes validating the same transactions or mining for new blocks simultaneously since only one node will receive the reward derived from the mining or validation process. These inefficiencies – multiple nodes doing the same thing – imply a considerable waste of energy and are environmentally unsustainable (Edgar, 2021; Team DataFlair, 2018).

8. **Scalability:** One of the drawbacks of blockchain technology is the difficulty in scaling due to the fixed size of the blocks for storing information. Blockchain size limits are small by modern data storage standards, limiting the transaction-per-second (TPS) rate. A larger block size limit enables a higher TPS rate but may result in stales, and temporary chain splits (Bitstamp Team, 2021; Lastbitcoder, 2022).

BLOCKCHAIN TECHNOLOGY AND APPLICATION EVOLUTION

The following section explores some applications of blockchain technology encompassing custom blockchain implementations and blockchain integrations with existing systems. As a rule of thumb, blockchain integrations are advantageous to systems where (Marr, 2021a):

- There is a need to manage and secure digital relationships.
- A decentralized, shared system of record is required.
- A middleman or gatekeeper function is expensive or time-consuming.
- There is a need to record secure transactions, especially between multiple partners.
- Data is in constant flux, but records of past actions are required.

Figure 15 provides a comprehensive graphical representation of heterogenous blockchain-enabled applications in various domains, some of which are detailed as follows:

1. **Financial Applications:** Blockchain technology is currently applied to various financial fields, including business services, settlement of financial assets, prediction markets, and economic trans-actions. The global financial system has explored blockchain-enabled applications for financial assets, such as securities, fiat money, and derivative contracts (Casino et al., 2019; Zheng et al., 2019).
2. **Governance:** Governments over time have been entrusted with managing and holding official records of citizens and enterprises. Blockchain-enabled applications might change how local or state governments operate by disintermediating transactions and record keeping. The accountability, automation, and safety that blockchain offers for handling public records could eventually obstruct corruption and make government services more efficient (Casino et al., 2019; Swan, 2015).
3. **Healthcare:** Blockchain technology could play a pivotal role in the healthcare industry with ap-plications such as public healthcare management, longitudinal healthcare records, online patient access, sharing patients' medical data, user-oriented medical research, drug counterfeiting, and precision medicine. In particular, blockchain technology and smart contracts could solve problems of scientific credibility of findings in clinical trials and consent issues with patients (Baiod et al., 2021; Casino et al., 2019; Zheng et al., 2019).
4. **Supply Chain Management (SCM):** Blockchain has the potential to become a significant source of disruptive innovations in business and management by improving, optimizing, and automating business processes. Blockchain technology is expected to increase transparency and accountability in supply chain networks, thus enabling more flexible value chains (Casino et al., 2019).

Figure 15. Mind map of blockchain technology and its application evolution
(Casino et al., 2019)

5. **Logistics Management:** Logistics management is inherently associated with some complexity, with several entities simultaneously involved in synchronized activities involving various institutions such as plants, storage firms, shipping companies, and regulatory entities. Logistics management applications must be functional enough to facilitate planning, scheduling, coordinating, monitoring, and validating these activities (Baiod et al., 2021).

6. **Transportation Problems:** The transportation problem (TP) is an optimization problem where resources must be allocated from a supply point to a demand point in an optimal manner (Kumar, 2018). TPs have been formulated as intuitionistic fuzzy optimization problems due to imprecise information about costs, supplies, demands, and conveyances in the real world (Kumar, 2019). The application of blockchain technology in this domain can potentially reduce the uncertainties resulting from imprecise information, thus further pushing the optimality of computed solutions.

7. **Power and Energy Sectors:** The potential applications of blockchain technology in the power and energy sectors are far-reaching and may have an enormous impact on processes and platforms. For example, blockchain has the potential to reduce costs, enable new business models, and enhance the efficiency of utility billing processes. Blockchain technology may also be used to issue certificates

of origin, develop P2P energy transaction schemes, and establish energy management schemes for electric vehicles (Baiod et al., 2021; Casino et al., 2019).

8. **Internet of Things (IoT):** The primary aim of decentralized, blockchain-enabled IoT platforms is to provide secure and auditable data exchange in heterogeneous context-aware scenarios with many interconnected intelligent devices. Blockchain-enabled (automated and decentralized) IoT implementations have increased network scalability, improved management efficiency, reduced maintenance costs, and increased network security (Casino et al., 2019; Christidis & Devetsikiotis, 2016; Hassan et al., 2020). The Internet of Everything (IoE) extends the IoT paradigm by aggregating interconnected networks of data, things, people, and processes (Singh et al., 2020).

TWO-WAY FUSION: BLOCKCHAIN AND MACHINE LEARNING

Background

Machine Learning (ML) is a multi-disciplinary field focusing on understanding and building applications and algorithms that learn through experience (Tanwar et al., 2020). As a subset of Artificial Intelligence (AI), it is the ability to teach a computer using sample (training) data without programming it explicitly. ML algorithms are application-specific and dependent on the output required by the system. As shown in Figure 16, ML approaches are traditionally divided into three broad categories – depending on the nature of the "feedback" available to the learning system – as follows ('Machine Learning', 2022):

- **Supervised Learning:** The learning algorithm is presented with example inputs and their desired outputs, and the goal is to learn a general rule that correctly maps inputs to outputs.
- **Unsupervised Learning:** No labels are given to the learning algorithm, leaving it to discover hidden patterns and structure in the input data autonomously. The data samples are subsequently grouped into clusters depending on their similarity or dissimilarity.
- **Reinforcement Learning:** The learning algorithm interacts with a dynamic environment in which it must perform a specific goal. As it navigates its problem space, the algorithm is provided "feedback" that's analogous to rewards, which it tries to maximize.

However, other ML approaches have been developed which do not neatly fit into the categories mentioned above, instead sometimes combining features from the traditional approaches, as follows:

- **Semi-Supervised Learning:** This approach involves a mixture of supervised and unsupervised ML approaches. An unsupervised ML algorithm may be applied to discover the structure of input variables and make best-guess predictions for the unlabeled data. Said predictions serve as training data for the supervised ML algorithm, which is subsequently used to make predictions on unseen data (Tanwar et al., 2020).
- **Deep Learning (DL):** DL is a class of ML algorithms based on Artificial Neural Networks that use multiple layers to progressively extract higher-level features from the raw input. The learning process can be supervised, semi-supervised, or unsupervised as a model learns the latent space representation of the most basic form of data, i.e., images, text, and speech signals ('Deep Learning', 2022; Shafay et al., 2022).

Figure 16. Machine learning approaches and algorithms
(Karthikeyan & Priyakumar, 2022)

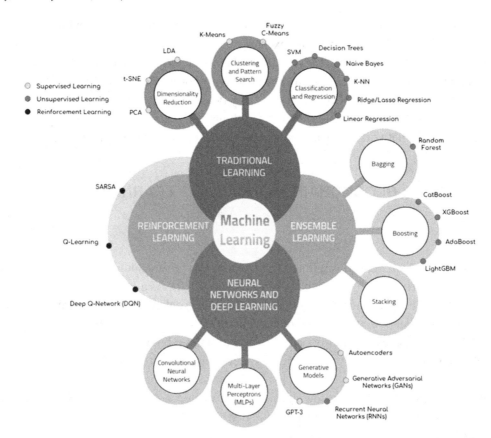

- **Federated Learning:** Federated Learning is an ML approach that trains an algorithm across multiple decentralized edge devices or servers holding local data samples without exchanging them. This approach contrasts traditional ML and DL techniques, where all the local datasets are uploaded to a centralized server, leading to data confidentiality and security challenges ('Deep Learning', 2022; Shafay et al., 2022).

By design, blockchain is a fault-tolerant technology that secures data, while ML focuses on utilizing data to train models and make accurate predictions. As ML and blockchain are both data-driven technologies, there is an increasing interest and research on integrating both technologies. From existing surveys on the integration of ML and blockchain technology (Chen et al., 2021; Liu et al., 2020; Shafay et al., 2022; Tanwar et al., 2020), existing research and applications integrate both technologies in one of two ways:

1. Using ML techniques to optimize blockchain systems and perform data analytics.
2. Implementing blockchain techniques for improved access and security of ML data and training.

Blockchain Techniques Within Machine Learning Systems

ML systems have gained significant traction in recent years due to their proven efficacy in making informed decisions. The efficacy and efficiency of ML systems are highly dependent on the availability and quality of the data used during the model training phase. However, existing ML systems are typically based on centralized servers for data storage and model training. They are thus vulnerable to the single point of failure problem and data alteration by adversarial agents. Furthermore, these systems fail to provide adequate operational transparency, traceability, security, and trusted data provenance (Shafay et al., 2022).

Figure 17. Key features of blockchain technology that can benefit machine learning
(Liu et al., 2020)

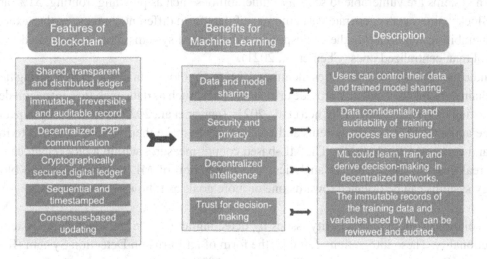

Due to its inherently distributed and immutable nature, blockchain technology is a natural tool for sharing and handling big data from various sources by incorporating smart contracts (Chen et al., 2021). Blockchain technology can efficiently ensure the integrity, security, and confidentiality of ML data and models against attacks, noise, and errors. Thus, the predictions made by such blockchain-based ML models are more trustworthy and accurate (Shafay et al., 2022). Furthermore, blockchain technology can be utilized to distribute computing powers, build IoT networks, and develop online predictive models with various data sources (Chen et al., 2021).

As illustrated in Figure 17, some benefits associated with the integration of blockchain technology with ML systems and applications include the following:

- Data security and privacy.
- Automated and trusted decision-making.
- Cumulative judgments and decentralized intelligence.
- Data and model sharing.
- Enhanced robustness.

In summary, blockchain technology can provide a stable, permanent, automated, and decentralized infrastructure for the critical data and models that ML systems and applications would acquire, process, and employ (Shafay et al., 2022). The combination of federated learning and edge computing to achieve a secure and decentralized ML approach is especially important when deploying deep learning systems – which require tremendous computing power – within the IoT domain. The type of blockchain structure – public, private, consortium, or hybrid – and consensus protocol adopted will depend on the specific ML system and application.

Machine Learning Techniques within Blockchain Technology Systems

The underlying foundational principles of blockchain technology – distributed database, P2P network, computational logic, and immutable ledger –ensure data security, privacy, and legitimacy. However, blockchain systems are vulnerable to security vulnerabilities such as phishing, routing, 51%, and Sybil attacks. Blockchain systems generate vast amounts of data from different sources, further exacerbating these vulnerabilities and making the corresponding distributed systems more complicated to monitor and control than centralized ones (Chen et al., 2021).

To handle the security vulnerabilities mentioned, ML technology can be integrated during the design of blockchain systems to efficiently provide critical services, such as data analytics, intrusion detection, and forecasting of system behaviors (Chen et al., 2021; Tanwar et al., 2020). The learning capabilities of ML can be applied to blockchain systems and applications to make them smarter, leading to improved security and consensus mechanisms. The ML-based countermeasures within a blockchain can be classified as real-time or historical data analytics. The integration of ML techniques within blockchain technology systems can be oriented towards one or more goals as follows:

- ML solutions handle data security issues by detecting attacks on the blockchain system and its functionality. These integrations can take the form of an Intrusion Detection System (IDS) or an Anomaly Detection System (ADS) (Tanwar et al., 2020).
- ML solutions monitor the blockchain system to find patterns in its data, nodes, and transactions. Transaction Entity Classification can be adopted in cryptocurrency applications to flag cyber-criminal activities or classify transaction entities (Chen et al., 2021).
- ML is used to create prediction models for decision-making and analysis. Such ML models have been applied to predicting the prices of several cryptocurrencies, such as Bitcoin, Ripple, and Ethereum (Chen et al., 2021; Tanwar et al., 2020).

Limitations and Challenges

As expected, some research challenges and practical limitations hinder the integration of machine learning and blockchain technologies. Some of these issues are native to blockchain technology and are further exacerbated by the integration of ML technology. The major ML-specific issues include:

1. **Integration Scalability:** A ML-integrated blockchain network will encounter scalability issues resulting from the large volume and velocity of transactions. These scalability issues involve increased internet bandwidth, computing power, and data storage requirements. Hence, the addition

of blocks and transactions to the blockchain needs to be decreased to meet inevitable user demands (Shafay et al., 2022; Tanwar et al., 2020).

2. **Security & Privacy:** One of the aims of ML integration is the improved security and privacy of blockchain systems through ML-based IDS. However, these security mechanisms depend on ML solutions that can deal with the large volume, high dimensionality, dynamic, and real-time nature of blockchain data and networks for different security or privacy issues (Liu et al., 2020).

3. **Storage Capacity:** Blockchain technology has always faced memory constraints due to the increasing size of the decentralized ledger as new blocks are added over time. Integrating ML solutions worsens the storage issue while reducing the efficacy and efficiency of the ML solutions and the entire blockchain system. However, ML (and DL) approaches can be employed for data compression as well as assisting in minimizing data redundancy on the blockchain (Shafay et al., 2022; Tanwar et al., 2020).

4. **Big Data Processing:** ML-based blockchain systems involve data collection and processing in which the raw data is usually large, noisy, and unlabeled. Such datasets pose significant storage, computing, and performance challenges and require further exploration to derive effective ML solutions. Furthermore, there are some issues with moving data and computing power onto the blockchain, including how to store these large-scale distributed data in a decentralized manner, discover and use data in huge data markets, and incentivize consumers to share their data on the blockchain (Liu et al., 2020).

5. **Economical ML:** ML approaches – especially DL – have been successful in various domains at the expense of high storage, computing, and financial costs during development and deployment. Thus, more research is needed to develop cost-efficient, resource-friendly, and high-performance ML frameworks for integration with blockchain systems (Shafay et al., 2022).

6. **ML-Specific Consensus Protocols:** When ML-based analytics are integrated into blockchain systems, the models must make quick predictions, as delays could lead to undesirable outcomes. In addition to energy and computing consumption issues, existing blockchain consensus protocols have latencies on the scale of seconds, which cascade to the ML model predictions. ML-specific consensus protocols can be designed to tackle the latency issue based on the proofs related to the data quality, optimization techniques, model hyperparameters, and model convergence time (Liu et al., 2020; Shafay et al., 2022).

CASE STUDY: BLOCKCHAIN FOR THE INTERNET OF VEHICLES

IoV represents the real-time data interaction between vehicles and between vehicles and infrastructures through smart devices, vehicle navigation systems, mobile communication technology, and information platforms. This concept has enabled easier collection, computing, and sharing of information about vehicles and infrastructures into Internet systems and other information platforms. Despite its advantages, the concept of IoV has certain limitations and challenges – such as centralization, heterogeneity, scalability, and interoperability – which cannot be tackled by conventional security and privacy methods (Jabbar et al., 2020; Mollah et al., 2021).

A particular challenge in the IoV, especially in Vehicle-to-Vehicle and Vehicle-to-Infrastructure communications, is to ensure fast, secure transmission and accurate recording of the data. To overcome the challenges of privacy and security in IoV networks, this case study – *Blockchain for the Internet of*

Vehicles: A Decentralized IoT Solution for Vehicles (DISV) Communication Using Ethereum (Jabbar et al., 2020) – adapted blockchain technology for Real-Time Application to solve Vehicle-to-Everything (V2X) communications problems.

System Overview

A prototype of DISV was developed and tested based on the following scenario: "if a driver is drowsy, the nearest cars should be alerted by a message via blockchain." As illustrated in Figure 18, the solution contains three layers – the perception, network, and application layers – and a workflow with three main steps, as follows:

1. The cars send data to the central server.
2. Based on the received data, the central server sends an invitation to connect to the blockchain layer.
3. The cars can securely share the data with other IoV participants in the same area.

Perception Layer

The perception layer is the physical layer. It consists of several IoT devices equipped with sensors designed to identify and collect information about the environment (i.e., physical parameters) and to detect nearby smart devices. The Android Application for Vehicles (AV) embedded into the perception layer collects and analyzes data about the trip, the vehicle, and the driver's behavior. The Android Application for Infrastructure (AP) simulates the role of IoT devices integrated into the roads, such as radars, traffic lights, and roadside electronic signs.

Figure 18. The architecture of the blockchain-based IoV DISV solution
(Jabbar et al., 2020)

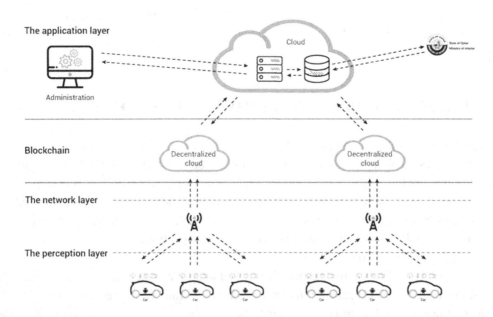

Network Layer

The network layer connects the sensors to other servers, network devices, and smart things and transmits and processes sensor data. A hybrid system gathers and stores sensor data locally before transmitting them to the server via Wi-Fi or mobile internet.

Application Layer

The application layer consists of two principal components: the central cloud server and the blockchain-based communication network.

1. **Central Cloud Server:** The central cloud delivers application-specific services to the end user. It sends the collected data – sensor data from IoT devices and other information from traffic authorities – to the web service for processing and analysis. The web service is responsible for interaction between different components of the IoT solution, such as web applications, database servers, IoT devices, and other embedded systems. The web application provides access to historical information about the driver, vehicle, and trips.
2. **Blockchain Network Layer:** The blockchain layer manages communication between cars. The car sends collected data to the central cloud server via a web service in each time slot. The data also includes the current location and the connection status to one of the existing blockchain layers. Subsequently, the central cloud server invites nearby IoT devices to establish communication through an available blockchain cloud. Each road section has a dedicated blockchain layer that sends messages to the connected IoT devices that accept the invitation.

Nominal Scenario

The nominal scenario of communication between IoT devices in the DISV is divided into two subprocesses: registration and messaging, as follows:

1. **Registration:**
    a. For every time slot (15 s), the IoT device sends the collected data to the central server via the Internet.
    b. The central cloud server saves the collected data in the database server. In addition, the server looks for IoT devices at nearby locations, such as road sections, roundabouts, and traffic signals.
    c. An invitation is sent to the devices in the same location to communicate through one of the available blockchain layers.
    d. After accepting the invitation, the second sub-process begins.
2. **Messaging:**
    a. The IoT devices are now connected and can share data through messages on the blockchain network.
    b. An IoT device can publish a message validated (mined) by the consensus protocol on the Ethereum network.

c.   The message is added to the smart contract so that every device connected to that blockchain layer can receive it.

The performance of the proposed solution was evaluated across the properties, including availability, execution time, cost, integrity, immutability, and security. All these properties must provide the highest performance to allow the solution's flawless operations. The solution's availability, integrity, immutability, and security depend on the core principles of blockchain technology and are further strengthened by deploying the solution on a private blockchain. The security vulnerabilities of the web framework and smart contract were minimized by incorporating recommended security requirements into the system. The evaluation results showed that DISV could be considered a real-time application and a solution for the main challenges of V2X communications and facilitate the data exchange and cooperation between vehicles, infrastructure, and other actors in the IoV ecosystem.

FUTURE TRENDS OF BLOCKCHAIN TECHNOLOGY

Global spending on blockchain technology amounted to $6.6 billion in 2021, and the market is forecasted to show an average annual growth rate of 56% from 2022 to 2029 (Horiachko, 2022). As shown in Figure 19, Companies from various industries actively participate in blockchain technology, with the banking, financial services, and insurance (BFSI) sectors leading the way. Some top trends with blockchain technology include:

1.   **Central Bank Digital Currencies (CBDCs)**: One of the latest trends in blockchain technology is the adoption of digital currencies by central banks of different countries (Horiachko, 2022). These digital currencies (tokens) operate alongside traditional currencies, allowing users to conduct transactions and manage their assets without relying on third-party service providers. The central banks can also control the circulating supply by keeping the token's value pegged to the country's traditional currency (Marr, 2021b).

Figure 19. Global blockchain market share by industry, 2021
(Horiachko, 2022)

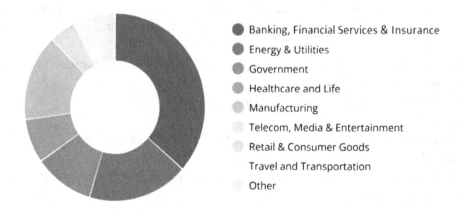

2. **Sustainable Blockchains**: Blockchains can potentially use a lot of energy and create high levels of carbon emissions, leading to increased emphasis on attempts to "greenify" blockchain. There are a few ways this can be done, including carbon offsetting, moving to less energy-intensive models of blockchain technology, and greater investments in generating renewable energy (Marr, 2021b; Sharma, 2020).

3. **Non-Fungible Tokens (NFTs)**: NFTs are cryptographic objects on the blockchain with special identification codes and metadata that differentiate them from one another. Unlike fungible currencies, NFTs cannot be sold or substituted for equivalency, thus bestowing ownership rights to asset holders (Sharma, 2020). The use of NFTs is expanding beyond online art into music, gaming, entertainment, fashion, and the metaverse (Marr, 2021b).

4. **Blockchain-as-a-Service (BaaS)**: BaaS is a robust solution that helps users to employ cloud services for building, using, and hosting blockchain projects at reduced costs and complexity. The concept involves services related to core infrastructural maintenance, such as installation, monitoring, and configuration. While companies like Amazon, Microsoft, and IBM are currently at the forefront of offering BaaS services to large-scale companies, more firms can be expected to cover the gap regarding medium and small-scale businesses (Horiachko, 2022; Sharma, 2020).

5. **Metaverse**: Metaverse is a 3D universe where several virtual ecosystems connect to form a more extensive cluster, allowing users to play, communicate and work together in a new paradigm. Metaverse combines augmented reality, virtual reality, and blockchain technology and promises to open a new era of technological innovation. With the growing attention and participation of tech companies in the metaverse, its integration with blockchain technology has become increasingly relevant (Horiachko, 2022; Sharma, 2020).

CONCLUSION

This paper presented an overview of the current state of blockchain technology, its development ecosystem, and application implementations. The basic premise of the technology – decentralized, immutable ledger – offers numerous advantages, which has seen the rapid and continued adoption of blockchain technology in numerous domains. Furthermore, blockchain technology is being developed alongside Big Data Analytics, Artificial Intelligence, Machine Learning, Virtual Reality, and Augmented Reality. The intersection of these cutting-edge technologies with blockchain technology seems inevitable and promising. However, as discussed in the research challenges and future trends, several integration barriers must be addressed, and knowledge gaps to be filled for blockchain technology to reach its full potential. Nevertheless, innovations from the developer and research communities continue to propel the technology to its next iteration.

REFERENCES

Anwar, H. (2018, August 25). Consensus Algorithms: The Root of Blockchain Technology. *101 Blockchains*. https://101blockchains.com/consensus-algorithms-blockchain/

Anwar, H. (2021, June 2). What is a Private Blockchain? Beginner's Guide. *101 Blockchains*. https://101blockchains.com/what-is-a-private-blockchain/

Baiod, W., Light, J., & Mahanti, A. (2021). Blockchain Technology and its Applications Across Multiple Domains: A Survey. *Journal of International Technology and Information Management*, *29*(4), 78–119. doi:10.58729/1941-6679.1482

Bhardwaj, C. (2019, October 21). Analysis of the Blockchain Consensus Algorithms. *Appinventiv*. https://appinventiv.com/blog/blockchain-consensus-algorithms-guide/

Bitstamp Team. (2021, August 18). *What is Block Size?* Bitstamp Blog. https://blog.bitstamp.net/post/what-is-block-size/

BYJU'S Team. (2022, November 8). *Difference between Client-Server and Peer-to-Peer Network*. BYJUS. https://byjus.com/gate/difference-between-client-server-and-peer-to-peer-network/

Casino, F., Dasaklis, T. K., & Patsakis, C. (2019). A Systematic Literature Review Of Blockchain-Based Applications: Current Status, Classification And Open Issues. *Telematics and Informatics*, *36*, 55–81. doi:10.1016/j.tele.2018.11.006

Castro, R. Q., & Au-Yong-Oliveira, M. (2021). Blockchain and Higher Education Diplomas. *European Journal of Investigation in Health, Psychology and Education*, *11*(1), 1. Advance online publication. doi:10.3390/ejihpe11010013 PMID:34542456

Chandrayan, P. (2020, September 21). BlockChain Principle, Type & Application & Why You Should Care About It? *SysopsMicro*. https://medium.com/the-programmer/blockchain-principle-type-application-why-you-should-care-about-it-249417b516cc

Chen, F., Wan, H., Cai, H., & Cheng, G. (2021). Machine Learning In/For Blockchain: Future and Challenges. *The Canadian Journal of Statistics*, *49*(4), 1364–1382. doi:10.1002/cjs.11623

Christidis, K., & Devetsikiotis, M. (2016). Blockchains and Smart Contracts for the Internet of Things. *IEEE Access : Practical Innovations, Open Solutions*, *4*, 2292–2303. doi:10.1109/ACCESS.2016.2566339

Coinbase Team. (2022, April 24). *What Is 'Proof Of Work' Or 'Proof Of Stake'?* https://www.coinbase.com/learn/crypto-basics/what-is-proof-of-work-or-proof-of-stake

Conway, L. (2022, February 18). *Proof-of-Work vs. Proof-of-Stake: Which Is Better?* Blockworks. https://blockworks.co/proof-of-work-vs-proof-of-stake-whats-the-difference/

Deepa, N., Pham, Q.-V., Nguyen, D. C., Bhattacharya, S., Prabadevi, B., Gadekallu, T. R., Maddikunta, P. K. R., Fang, F., & Pathirana, P. N. (2021). *A Survey on Blockchain for Big Data: Approaches, Opportunities, and Future Directions* (arXiv:2009.00858). arXiv. https://doi.org//arXiv.2009.00858 doi:10.48550

Edgar, T. (2021, June 29). Advantages and Disadvantages of Blockchain. *BBVA.CH*. https://www.bbva.ch/en/news/advantages-and-disadvantages-of-blockchain/

Evans, J. (2022, April 24). *Blockchain Nodes: How They Work (All Types Explained)*. Nodes.com. https://nodes.com/

Fernández-Caramés, T. M., & Fraga-Lamas, P. (2018). A Review on the Use of Blockchain for the Internet of Things. *IEEE Access : Practical Innovations, Open Solutions, 6*, 32979–33001. doi:10.1109/ACCESS.2018.2842685

Ferrag, M. A., Derdour, M., Mukherjee, M., Derhab, A., Maglaras, L., & Janicke, H. (2019). Blockchain Technologies for the Internet of Things: Research Issues and Challenges. *IEEE Internet of Things Journal, 6*(2), 2188–2204. doi:10.1109/JIOT.2018.2882794

Gadekallu, T. R., Pham, Q.-V., Nguyen, D. C., Maddikunta, P. K. R., Deepa, N., Prabadevi, B., Pathirana, P. N., Zhao, J., & Hwang, W.-J. (2022). Blockchain for Edge of Things: Applications, Opportunities, and Challenges. *IEEE Internet of Things Journal, 9*(2), 964–988. doi:10.1109/JIOT.2021.3119639

Geroni, D. (2021, April 5). Blockchain Nodes: An In-Depth Guide. *101 Blockchains*. https://101blockchains.com/blockchain-nodes/

Grech, A., Sood, I., & Ariño, L. (2021). Blockchain, Self-Sovereign Identity and Digital Credentials: Promise Versus Praxis in Education. *Frontiers in Blockchain, 4*. https://www.frontiersin.org/articles/10.3389/fbloc.2021.616779

Gupta, A. (2018, July 18). Introduction to Blockchain Technology. *GeeksforGeeks*. https://www.geeksforgeeks.org/blockchain-technology-introduction/

Haber, S., & Stornetta, W. S. (1991). How to time-stamp a digital document. *Journal of Cryptology, 3*(2), 99–111. doi:10.1007/BF00196791

Hassan, F. ul, Ali, A., Rahouti, M., Latif, S., Kanhere, S., Singh, J., AlaAl-Fuqaha, Janjua, U., Mian, A. N., Qadir, J., & Crowcroft, J. (2020). Blockchain And The Future of the Internet: A Comprehensive Review. *ArXiv:1904.00733 [Cs]*. https://arxiv.org/abs/1904.00733

Hasselgren, A., Kralevska, K., Gligoroski, D., Pedersen, S. A., & Faxvaag, A. (2020). Blockchain In Healthcare And Health Sciences—A Scoping Review. *International Journal of Medical Informatics, 134*, 104040. doi:10.1016/j.ijmedinf.2019.104040 PMID:31865055

Hayes, A. (2022, September 27). *Blockchain Facts: What Is It, How It Works, and How It Can Be Used*. Investopedia. https://www.investopedia.com/terms/b/blockchain.asp

Horiachko, A. (2022, June 10). *Top 9 Blockchain Technology Trends to Follow in 2022*. Softermii. https://www.softermii.com/blog/hot-trends-in-blockchain-app-development

Hyperledger Team. (2022, May 16). About – Hyperledger Foundation. *Hyperledger Foundation*. https://www.hyperledger.org/about

Iredale, G. (2021, January 6). What Are The Different Types of Blockchain Technology? *101 Blockchains*. https://101blockchains.com/types-of-blockchain/

Jabbar, R., Kharbeche, M., Al-Khalifa, K., Krichen, M., & Barkaoui, K. (2020). Blockchain for the Internet of Vehicles: A Decentralized IoT Solution for Vehicles Communication Using Ethereum. *Sensors (Basel), 20*(14), 3928. doi:10.339020143928 PMID:32679671

Jaikaran, C. (2018). *Blockchain: Background and Policy Issues*. Congressional Research Service.

Kaplan, A., Figge, H., & Hirsch-Allen, J. (2022). The Next Evolution Of Digital Identity: Scalable, Secure, And Trusted Digital Credentials. *IBM Institute for Business Value*. https://www.ibm.com/thought-leadership/institute-business-value/en-us/report/digital-identity

Karthikeyan, A., & Priyakumar, U. (2022). Artificial Intelligence: Machine Learning For Chemical Sciences. *Journal of Chemical Sciences*, *134*(1), 2. doi:10.100712039-021-01995-2 PMID:34955617

Khalil, A. A., Franco, J., Parvez, I., Uluagac, S., & Rahman, M. A. (2021). *A Literature Review on Blockchain-enabled Security and Operation of Cyber-Physical Systems* (arXiv:2107.07916). arXiv. https://doi.org//arXiv.2107.07916 doi:10.48550

Kumar, P. S. (2018). Search for an Optimal Solution to Vague Traffic Problems Using the PSK Method. In *Handbook of Research on Investigations in Artificial Life Research and Development* (pp. 219–257). IGI Global. doi:10.4018/978-1-5225-5396-0.ch011

Kumar, P. S. (2019). PSK Method for Solving Mixed and Type-4 Intuitionistic Fuzzy Solid Transportation Problems. [IJORIS]. *International Journal of Operations Research and Information Systems*, *10*(2), 20–53. doi:10.4018/IJORIS.2019040102

Kuo, T.-T., Kim, H.-E., & Ohno-Machado, L. (2017). Blockchain Distributed Ledger Technologies For Biomedical And Health Care Applications. *Journal of the American Medical Informatics Association : JAMIA*, *24*(6), 1211–1220. doi:10.1093/jamia/ocx068 PMID:29016974

Lastbitcoder. (2022, February 2). Advantages and Disadvantages of Blockchain. *GeeksforGeeks*. https://www.geeksforgeeks.org/advantages-and-disadvantages-of-blockchain/

Lissounov, K. (2018, June 28). *What's The Difference Between Peer-To-Peer (P2P) Networks And Client-Server?* Resilio Blog. https://www.resilio.com/blog/whats-the-difference-between-peer-to-peer-and-client-server

Liu, Y., Yu, F. R., Li, X., Ji, H., & Leung, V. C. M. (2020). Blockchain and Machine Learning for Communications and Networking Systems. *IEEE Communications Surveys and Tutorials*, *22*(2), 1392–1431. doi:10.1109/COMST.2020.2975911

Luo, C., Xu, L., Li, D., & Wu, W. (2020). Edge Computing Integrated with Blockchain Technologies. In D.-Z. Du & J. Wang (Eds.), *Complexity and Approximation: In Memory of Ker-I Ko* (pp. 268–288). Springer International Publishing., doi:10.1007/978-3-030-41672-0_17

Machine Learning. (2022). In *Wikipedia*. https://en.wikipedia.org/w/index.php?title=Machine_learning&oldid=1125574586#Approaches

Malcom, A. (2021, October 6). Blockchain Principles: Understanding Blockchain Technology. *Businesstechweekly.com*. https://www.businesstechweekly.com/finance-and-accounting/fintech/blockchain-principles/

Marr, B. (2021a, July 2). Why Use Blockchain Technology? *Bernard Marr*. https://bernardmarr.com/why-use-blockchain-technology/

Marr, B. (2021b, November 19). The 5 Biggest Blockchain Trends In 2022. *Forbes*. https://www.forbes.com/sites/bernardmarr/2021/11/19/the-5-biggest-blockchain-trends-in-2022/

Miraz, M. H. (2020). Blockchain of Things (BCoT): The Fusion of Blockchain and IoT Technologies. In S. Kim & G. C. Deka (Eds.), *Advanced Applications of Blockchain Technology* (pp. 141–159). Springer. doi:10.1007/978-981-13-8775-3_7

Mollah, M. B., Zhao, J., Niyato, D., Guan, Y. L., Yuen, C., Sun, S., Lam, K.-Y., & Koh, L. H. (2021). Blockchain for the Internet of Vehicles towards Intelligent Transportation Systems: A Survey. *IEEE Internet of Things Journal, 8*(6), 4157–4185. doi:10.1109/JIOT.2020.3028368

Nair, S. (2020, May 30). How AI & Blockchain Can Combine To Boost The Healthcare Industry. *Blockchain for Everyone*. https://medium.com/blockchain-for-everyone/how-ai-blockchain-can-combine-to-boost-the-healthcare-industry-bcfb6aef2b96

Nakamoto, S. (2009). *Bitcoin: A Peer-to-Peer Electronic Cash System*. Bitcoin. https://bitcoin.org/bitcoin.pdf

Narbayeva, S., Bakibayev, T., Abeshev, K., Makarova, I., Shubenkova, K., & Pashkevich, A. (2020). Blockchain Technology on the Way of Autonomous Vehicles Development. *Transportation Research Procedia, 44*, 168–175. doi:10.1016/j.trpro.2020.02.024

Nguyen, D. C., Pathirana, P. N., Ding, M., & Seneviratne, A. (2020). Integration of Blockchain and Cloud of Things: Architecture, Applications and Challenges. *IEEE Communications Surveys and Tutorials, 22*(4), 2521–2549. doi:10.1109/COMST.2020.3020092

Parizo, C. (2021, May 28). *What Are The 4 Different Types of Blockchain Technology?* SearchCIO. https://www.techtarget.com/searchcio/feature/What-are-the-4-different-types-of-blockchain-technology

Poston, H. (2022, April 24). *Blockchain Tutorial: Part 2—Nodes*. Ghost Vault. https://ghostvolt.com/articles/blockchain_nodes.html

Salha, R. A., El-Hallaq, M. A., & Alastal, A. I. (2019). Blockchain in Smart Cities: Exploring Possibilities in Terms of Opportunities and Challenges. *Journal of Data Analysis and Information Processing, 7*(3), 3. doi:10.4236/jdaip.2019.73008

Sarker, S., Saha, A. K., & Ferdous, M. S. (2020). *A Survey on Blockchain & Cloud Integration* (arXiv:2012.02644). arXiv. /arXiv.2012.02644 doi:10.1109/ICCIT51783.2020.9392748

Shafay, M., Ahmad, R. W., Salah, K., Yaqoob, I., Jayaraman, R., & Omar, M. (2022). Blockchain For Deep Learning: Review and Open Challenges. *Cluster Computing*. Advance online publication. doi:10.100710586-022-03582-7 PMID:35309043

Sharma, T. K. (2020, January 7). 5 Biggest Blockchain Trends In 2022. *Blockchain Council*. https://www.blockchain-council.org/blockchain/5-biggest-blockchain-trends/

Singh, P., Nayyar, A., Kaur, A., & Ghosh, U. (2020). Blockchain and Fog Based Architecture for Internet of Everything in Smart Cities. *Future Internet, 12*(4), 1–12. doi:10.3390/fi12040061

Suhail, S., Hussain, R., Jurdak, R., Oracevic, A., Salah, K., Matulevičius, R., & Hong, C. S. (2021). *Blockchain-based Digital Twins: Research Trends, Issues, and Future Challenges* (arXiv:2103.11585). arXiv. https://doi.org//arXiv.2103.11585 doi:10.48550

Swan, M. (2015). *Blockchain: Blueprint for a New Economy*. O'Reilly Media, Inc.

Tanwar, S., Bhatia, Q., Patel, P., Kumari, A., Singh, P. K., & Hong, W.-C. (2020). Machine Learning Adoption in Blockchain-Based Smart Applications: The Challenges, and a Way Forward. *IEEE Access : Practical Innovations, Open Solutions, 8*, 474–488. doi:10.1109/ACCESS.2019.2961372

Team DataFlair. (2018, June 1). *Advantages and Disadvantages Of Blockchain Technology*. DataFlair. https://data-flair.training/blogs/advantages-and-disadvantages-of-blockchain/

Team Etoro. (2022, March 14). *Advantages and Disadvantages of a Blockchain*. EToroX. https://etorox. com/blockchain-academy/advantages-and-disadvantages-of-a-blockchain/

Wegrzyn, K., & Wang, E. (2021, August 19). *Types of Blockchain: Public, Private, or Something in Between*. Foley & Lardner LLP. https://www.foley.com/en/insights/publications/2021/08/types-of-blockchain-public-private-between

Yang, R., Yu, F. R., Si, P., Yang, Z., & Zhang, Y. (2019). Integrated Blockchain and Edge Computing Systems: A Survey, Some Research Issues and Challenges. *IEEE Communications Surveys and Tutorials, 21*(2), 1508–1532. doi:10.1109/COMST.2019.2894727

Yli-Huumo, J., Ko, D., Choi, S., Park, S., & Smolander, K. (2016). Where Is Current Research on Blockchain Technology?—A Systematic Review. *PLoS One, 11*(10), e0163477. doi:10.1371/journal. pone.0163477 PMID:27695049

Zhao, W., Jiang, C., Gao, H., Yang, S., & Luo, X. (2021). Blockchain-Enabled Cyber–Physical Systems: A Review. *IEEE Internet of Things Journal, 8*(6), 4023–4034. doi:10.1109/JIOT.2020.3014864

Zheng, X., Zhu, Y., & Si, X. (2019). A Survey on Challenges and Progresses in Blockchain Technologies: A Performance and Security Perspective. *Applied Sciences (Basel, Switzerland), 9*(22), 4731. doi:10.3390/app9224731

Chapter 5
Mind of a Portfolio Investor:
Which Strategies Should I Use as a Basis for My Investment Decisions

Chabi Gupta

https://orcid.org/0000-0002-1927-4349

School of Commerce, Finance and Accountancy, Christ University, India

ABSTRACT

It is smart for investors to plan for a drop that may be accompanied by a recession in the late stages of a bull market. The authors examine a variety of passive and active strategies, as well as their success in different crises. However, while choosing the best of strategies in the worst of circumstances, investors must be cautious in defining 'best.' It's critical to comprehend not only the long-term performance but also the whole cost of putting various preventive measures in place. The authors analyse popular strategies like technical analysis, fundamental analysis, relying on financial news, seeking professional advice, tips from trade experts, and self-intuition while making portfolios. Our findings indicate that every investment is unique. Some defensive methods will be more effective than others in each case. As a result, diversification across several viable strategies may be the wisest course of action.

INTRODUCTION AND LITERATURE REVIEW

In this research study we analyse popular strategies that can be employed by portfolio investors like technical analysis, fundamental analysis, relying on financial news, seeking professional advice, tips from trade experts and self-intuition while making portfolio investment decisions.

1. Long-term market fluctuations can be predicted using fundamental analysis. The use of stock valuation techniques is deemed fit for investors looking to engage in long-term investments as it plays a vital role in determining the fair price at which stocks should be bought or sold. In addition, such analysis enables portfolio managers to identify and capitalize on investment opportunities that have significant potential for growth over extended periods of time. The application of these methods

DOI: 10.4018/978-1-6684-7684-0.ch005

demands an understanding of key factors influencing market trends, allowing astute investors to make informed decisions regarding their holdings while mitigating risk exposure. By adopting this approach, traders can gain an edge in navigating volatile markets and ultimately maximize returns on their invested capital through careful planning and execution strategies based upon robust research insights into various industries' fundamentals.

Investors resort to conducting in-depth fundamental research to carefully evaluate the intrinsic value of a particular stock. This is done with the aim of assessing whether it's trading at its true worth, which may be vastly different from what it appears on paper. The existing market price cannot solely determine the underlying value of a stock, as there could potentially exist undervalued stocks that are being overlooked by investors and vice versa for overvalued ones. Fundamental analysis serves as an investment strategy frequently utilized by renowned gurus like Warren Buffett and Peter Lynch to identify promising stocks poised for growth while minimizing risk exposure. It involves thoroughly analyzing key financial metrics such as revenue figures, earnings reports, cash flow statements among others before making informed decisions about purchasing shares in specific companies that have demonstrated strong potential returns. It aids the investor in better portfolio investment decision making. It looks at the fair value of a stock. Investors are also able to evaluate the company's health and effectiveness of any firm by looking at critical indicators and macroeconomic variables, making predictions about future fluctuations in price, and deciding if a stock is fair or overpriced. It is a tool for evaluating a company's strengths and ability to outperform its competitors.

A thorough comprehension of a company's business model and management techniques is integral to informed decision-making when it comes to investment selection. To gain this understanding, fundamental stock analysis serves as an important tool in the investor's arsenal. By digging deeper into a company's financial statements and market trends, investors can ascertain not only its current performance but also potential future growth prospects that will ultimately affect their returns on investments. Therefore, having a comprehensive knowledge about these key aspects provides better insights into the workings of any organization which helps investors make sound judgments with confidence.

Through their research, (Asquith and Meulbroek 1996) indicate that short sellers as a group are successful in identifying assets that underperform the market through fundamental analysis. Several researchers illustrate that fundamental-to-market-value ratios are a strategic approach of forecasting future stock returns. Accounting data-based estimates of "intrinsic" values are as compared to market prices which can be visible through these ratios. According to (Lakonishok et al 1994), "naive" investors are overly enthusiastic about the returns of investing in under-priced stocks. The method may include computing simple financial ratios (Fama and French 1995, Lakonishok et al. 1994), or slightly more complex techniques of valuation (Ohlson 1995), as well as everything between (Frankel and Lee 1998, Dechow et al. 1999). According to the research presented by Piotroski (2000), it is possible to differentiate profitable businesses from ineffective ones by determining the core value of an organisation as well as any systemic defects in the expectations of the market. Using the information obtained from the analysis of financial statements, he formulates an investment plan for businesses with a high BM or value. Recent research looked at the effectiveness of a fundamental analysis method that is based on financial statements for screening companies in Vietnam (Ho T et al 2022).

Figure 1. Fundamental analysis strategy for a portfolio investor
(Author's diagram)

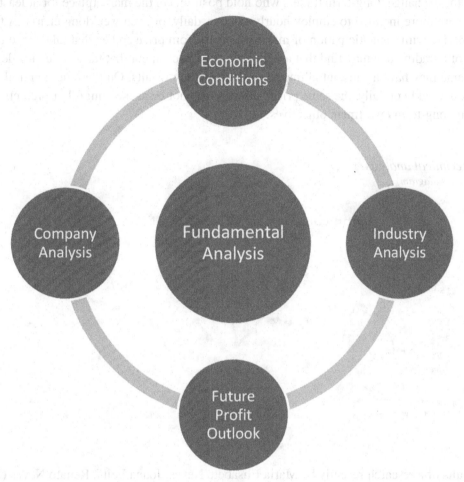

2. Charts are used in the investing approach known as technical analysis, which analyses price trends and patterns to assess assets and identify potential trading opportunities. According to the opinions of technical analysts, an asset's historical trading activity and price spikes might be helpful indicators of the asset's potential future price fluctuations. The viability of technical analysis is predicated on the assumption that the cumulative activities of all market makers, including both buying and selling, accurately depict all pertinent information about an income stream to come to a final price. Technical analysts are of the opinion that the price behaviour of the markets either at the present time or in the past is the most dependable signal of future price fluctuations.

More than only technical investors use the technical analysis techniques. After deciding whether or not to purchase into a sector based on basic valuation models, many fundamental speculators turn to technical analysis to find the optimal, low risk buy entry price levels. Once they have made their decision, they may then implement their strategy. The technique with which an individual trader approaches portfolio investments on a personal level often influences the period in which he or she analyses the possible scenarios to purchase and sell. Intraday traders prefer to assess price changes using charts with short timeframes, such as 5-10-15-minute charts, since they reach a position within a trading day. When examining the exchange, long-term traders who hold positions in the marketplace for at least one night or for more are more inclined to employ hourly, 5-hour, daily, or even weeklong charts. A trader who invests intra-day with the anticipation of making a profit from price spikes that take place throughout the course of a trading day may find that a very little price movement that takes place inside a 15-minute time frame may have a substantial impact on their trading results. On the other hand, if we design a chart that is weekly or daily, the same price variance may not be as meaningful or predictive in terms of achieving long-term investment objectives.

Figure 2. Technical analysis .
(Source: Author's diagram)

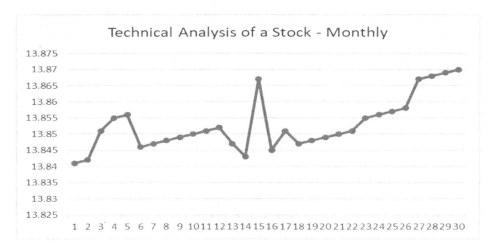

The results of a research recently by Maria Elisabete Neves, Joana Leite, Renato Neves (2022) recommend that an investor should have a technical analysis-based strategy in place when the market is bearish or ambiguous, and he should utilise than one indicator to get significant information from the market. Baumeister, C., & Kilian, L. (2016) in their research advocated the technical analysis in terms of forty long years of fluctuations in oil price and the reason it may still surprise us. Serkan Unal (2022) discovered that deductive approach and trading are quite prominent among those who have a bachelor's degree or higher. This is even though the effectiveness of technical analysis and the level of success achieved in high-frequency trading are both contingent on the ability of the investor to interpret data. They are financially illiterate, defy logic and unreasonable expectations of high returns within a short timeframe. The study by Vijaya Kittu Manda (2022) finds that the technical analysis through various stock training programs have given substantial edge to trading and investing activities and are worth spending time and money.

3. Relying on financial news is another strategy for keeping in close touch with the financial happenings around an investor who's looking to post profits in the long run and selecting the optimum strategy. Financial news plays a critical role in shaping the investment decisions of portfolio investors. By providing insights into market trends and the performance of various financial stocks, it

offers invaluable guidance that helps investors navigate through complex financial markets with confidence and precision. Moreover, financial news empowers investors to make informed choices by presenting them with detailed information on factors affecting stock prices such as economic indicators, corporate earnings reports, industry developments and regulatory changes. Ultimately, keeping abreast of current events in finance is essential for anyone looking to build a successful portfolio that maximizes returns while minimizing risks.

Financial news can be obtained from a variety of sources. Investors' financial decisions can however be largely influenced by fake or ineffective news. They may take the news at its value and invest their money accordingly. This can result in significant losses and make a significant dent in the investor's earnings in the long term. Financial news can be compared to a crying baby: it's all over the place. First, as prices increase and fall, there is a lot of noise and disturbance. The obvious explanations are considered next, followed by the less obvious ones. The portfolio investors are perplexed after that, so they conjecture and hypothesise. The action usually comes first, followed by the actual story – if it comes at all. The question of whether political or economic media is the primary driver of price movements in financial markets has been the theme of an appropriate measure of investigation, both empirical and theoretical (Smales et al 2014, Broadstock & Zhang et al 2019, Shi and Ho et al 2020). A news monitor database has already been utilised by (Smales 2014) and (Shi and Ho 2020) in their research to study the relationship between insider information perception and implied stock volatility. Financial markets are influenced to a big extent by the dissemination of financial information. (Da et al 2011, Pollock, Rindova 2003, Tetlock et al 2007). The equities market's responses might be irregular or volatile depending on variables such as financial announcements, advancements in the stock market, business pronouncements, or strategist projections. These factors all have a role in shaping the expectations and views of investors (Tetlock, 2014). Several studies, on the other hand, (Lev 1989, Liu & Thomas 2000, Lehavy & Sloan 2008) have solely investigated the recognition of a firm by portfolio investors and the effect that recognition has on the volatility of stock market values, which results in a turbulent stock market.

4.   Seeking professional advice is also a good strategy with the growing number of advisors in the market ready to share their expertise in investing in stock markets. Professional financial advisors can assist the portfolio investors in creating a financial plan for their individual financial objectives and provide in depth analysis and guidance on how to attain them. Before advising any investment in stocks they will consider relevant demographics and risk profile of a portfolio investor. They can assist in preparing for subsequent inflation and protecting the initial capital invested and interests.

Portfolio investors often make the erroneous assumption that professional guidance is unnecessary when it comes to managing their stock funds. However, this mistaken belief frequently leads them astray and jeopardizes their financial wellbeing. The truth of the matter is that whether an investor decides to enlist the aid of a seasoned financial planner depends on multiple factors, including but not limited to his or her level of knowledge about investments, intricacies in personal finances, and suitability for handling such matters with precision and composure. By delving into these considerations with greater depth before making investment decisions, portfolio investors can avoid costly mistakes down the road. Financial goals such as purchasing a home, going on an exotic vacation, funding a child's further education, or saving for retirement all require adequate direction and financial planning. An advisor can assist in the protection of a portfolio from significant losses by investing in variable return investments.

Especially in a volatile market seeking professional advice is a good strategy for portfolio investors to profit in the long run and build their wealth (Katherine H. M. Hunt 2022).

Portfolio investors are often plagued by behavioral biases that can have a detrimental impact on their financial decisions. These biases, stemming from emotional and psychological factors such as overconfidence, loss aversion, and herding behavior, can cloud an investor's judgment and lead to poor investment choices. However, advisors with specialized knowledge of these tendencies can offer invaluable support in identifying and mitigating these biases through tailored strategies aimed at maximizing portfolio returns while minimizing risk. By doing so, investors stand to benefit greatly from the guidance of professionals who possess a deep understanding of both market trends and human psychology – ultimately resulting in greater long-term success for all parties involved. The recent research by Yuan-LinHsu (2022) analyses how behavioural bias influences professional financial advice seeking using data from an online survey of experienced individual investors. Those who receive financial guidance from a professional advisor are around four times better off financially than those who do not bother at all. (Dhama, Jon 2022). Sommer, Matthew, Lim, HanNa, MacDonald, Maurice. (2022) concluded through their research that working with a financial advisor can help generate long term profits. Many portfolio investors maintain strong, productive, and high-quality working relationships with their financial advisors seeking their professional advice from time to time and gaining on their experience in investing in stock markets for a considerable number of years. (Katherine H. M. Hunt 2022)

5. Tips from trade experts is also an effective strategy for portfolio investors to choose especially when they lack the time to do sufficient research on the stocks themselves or lack basic financial literacy. To be successful in trading, trade experts conduct thorough and regular day to day or even intraday research and market analysis. Master traders develop their expertise to completely analyse all significant information relevant to the stocks for which they offer advice and, more critically, to accurately evaluate the effect that such information is anticipated to have on a given sector. The trade experts are players in the game of stock markets and adapt their market analysis to forever volatile market conditions. Their needs to be sufficient trust in the mind of a portfolio investor to blindly follow and act on the tips from trade experts.

Master trade experts build tactics and trading approaches over time that they utilise repeatedly and build their own toolkit of approaches, manoeuvres, strategies, and trading tactics throughout time. More recent studies like (Han, Yang, 2013, Stein 2008, Andrei Cujean, 2015) have focused on the spread of information directly to investors by trade experts. These models predict that the spread of information through WhatsApp or Messenger apps as trade expert tips is critical for a wide range of financial outcomes, including trading profit heterogeneity, market efficiency, momentum investing, and cognitive bias. (Hvide and Östberg, 2015). Top officials help spread the word about certain business news that influence the price of a stock (Kenneth R. Ahern 2017). Ozsoylev, Walden, Yavuz & Bildak 2014 in their research highlight the new portfolio investors and their competence levels that are not sufficient to make portfolio investment decisions. For such new investors tips from trade experts can help them to invest sometimes for short term profits. Thomas Schuster (2003) however concluded through his research that there existed no evidence that expert stock recommendations have a long-term probability of outperforming the market and generating wealth. In fact, the research suggests the exact opposite: that portfolio investors who follow such advise would end up losing money in the long run eroding their wealth.

6. Self-Intuition is another strategy for portfolio investors who are mature and competent enough to act on their instincts by themselves with experience of investing in stock markets. Portfolio investors can choose to go with the unassailable powers of the humans over the machine, courtesy intuition, creativity, curiosity, and of course, intellect. Skilled investors are able to make quick, definitive conclusions by relying on their self-intuition. Going with the "gut" instinct can be really accurate at times. However, there are situations when self-intuition is completely inaccurate and nothing more than wishful thinking.

Trading in the zone is a highly coveted state of mind that veteran investors strive to achieve. It represents an advanced level of investment mastery where one's self-intuition becomes the guiding force, enabling them to swiftly recognize and seize lucrative market opportunities with confidence and poise. In essence, trading in the zone involves tapping into one's innate abilities as an investor, allowing them to act decisively amidst uncertainty and capitalize on rare chances for significant profit gains. This requires a deep understanding of market dynamics coupled with mental agility, discipline, and emotional intelligence - all crucial elements that contribute towards achieving success within this elusive realm of investing expertise. However, to build these skills investors need time, experience, and practise else it may lead to a loss of wealth. (Kudryavtsev A et al 2012) in their research highlight the presence of behavioural biases for investors who rely on self-intuition to invest in stocks. (Kudryavtsev A et al 2013) also correlated self-intuition with behavioural biases and irrational decision making especially for long term investment. (B M Barber & T Odean 2008) find that for more experienced investors, the coefficients of correlation between the behavioural biases are higher in value, implying that these groups of investors simplify decision-making techniques through self-intuition.

Research Methodology

The sample comprises of 450 portfolio management investors actively trading in the equity stock market. Here we have taken the Indian stock market into consideration. The necessary data was collected using the convenience sampling method. All of the respondents have been using equity market investment strategies in the Indian stock market and have a equity trading or investing experience varying from 2 to 17 years. Most of the respondents (60.9 percent) had 2 to 7 years of stock market experience.

The portfolios are created by ranking the strategies based on their performance over last year, which is normalized by the past 12-month volatility. All of the portfolios' performance data are based on monthly averaging. Several panels further present the findings of regression analyses based on the returns from various tactics using (Fama and French 1992) plus (Carhart's 1997) investing momentum factor. In Panel C, the data findings from regressing the returns from these six strategies against a series of generalized risk indicators are provided. The t-statistics of Newey & West (1997) are provided in square brackets. The F-statistic is used to examine the significance jointly of the independent regression factors in Prob F.

The Table 8 presents the mean returns which are unconditional in nature and "Average", generated by the six different investment strategies being researched. Combining trend following and investing momentum can be done in two ways. One strategy is that of Faber (2010), who employs a wide equity market index's trend following signal to determine if it would be beneficial to buy or sell securities that are part of a surging portfolio. The outcome of this volatility momentum is either a cent percent investment in riskier assets or a 0% investment in riskier assets. Individual trend following is an approach used by Gwilym et al (2010) in which the rule is applied to each individual strategy separately. The attribute data which was used was all standardised. This approach balances the numerical instances, lowering the probability of computational inaccuracies. Alpha = Rp – Rf – β * (Rm – Rf) where we take the values of the average capital appreciation displayed by the portfolio in last 1 year. This will help calculate the performance of each stock in the market with respect to a risk-free return considering the investor chooses to base his decision making on these six strategies. A positive alpha value indicates a strategy that has outperformed in terms of profits generated, conversely a negative alpha indicates a strategy that has underperformed.

Table 1. Comparison of outcomes from the six chosen methodologies

Panel A: Benchmark Returns	Fundamental Analysis	Technical Analysis	Financial News	Professional Advice	Tips from trade experts	Self-Intuition
Annualized Return (in %)	6.10	5.58	5.12	6.14	7.04	6.19
Annualized Volatility (in %)	15.62	23.54	3.07	14.98	17.88	16.88
Sharpe Ratio	0.20	0.10	0.66	0.19	0.21	0.19
Maximum Return (Monthly in %)	11.42	17.14	3.45	12.00	20.70	13.10
Minimum Return (Monthly in %)	-18.73	-28.91	-1.99	-21.38	-26.85	-21.38
Maximum Drawdown (in %)	53.65	61.44	4.69	54.26	67.20	54.45
Skewness	-0.72	-0.71	-0.01	-0.62	-0.97	-0.76

Table 2. Comparison of outcomes from the six methodologies

Panel B: Equal Weight Model	Fundamental Analysis	Technical Analysis	Financial News	Professional Advice	Tips from trade experts	Self-Intuition
Annualized Return (in %)	6.71	8.35	9.11	9.16	8.73	8.51
Annualized Volatility (in %)	12.65	6.92	7.01	7.03	6.93	7.08
Sharpe Ratio	0.28	0.76	0.86	0.86	0.81	0.88
Maximum Return (Monthly in %)	10.21	7.61	6.75	6.75	6.22	6.55
Minimum Return (Monthly in %)	-18.99	-6.55	-6.55	-6.55	-6.55	-6.95
Maximum Drawdown (in %)	46.60	10.27	6.86	7.41	9.85	7.86
Skewness	-1.07	-0.05	-0.14	-0.23	-0.44	-0.14

Table 3. Statistics for risk-shared responsibility

Panel C: Risk-Shared Data	Risk-Shared Responsibility	Risk Parity Trend Following
Annualized Return (in %)	6.79	7.82
Annualized Volatility (in %)	6.34	5.17
Sharpe Ratio	0.55	1.08
Maximum Return (Monthly in %)	3.89	4.80
Minimum Return (Monthly in %)	-7.50	-4.92
Maximum Drawdown (in %)	20.46	4.92
Skewness	-1.91	-1.60

Table 4. The annualised profit trend metrics (adjusted for 6,8,10,12 months)

Panel D: Profit Trend Data	No TF	6	8	10	12
Annualized Return (in %)	8.81	10.65	10.58	10.36	10.10
Annualized Volatility (in %)	14.20	8.71	7.65	7.47	7.45
Sharpe Ratio	0.43	0.78	0.97	0.99	0.97
Maximum Return (Monthly in %)	12.05	10.16	8.29	7.49	7.42
Minimum Return (Monthly in %)	-22.95	-5.57	-5.30	-5.82	-6.50
Maximum Drawdown (in %)	46.44	7.89	7.73	8.19	8.88
Skewness	-1.06	0.48	0.43	0.07	0.04

Observations and Analysis

With the addition of a volatility adjusted momentum and investing momentum, we find that risk-adjusted performance improves significantly for all six different strategies. In all cases, returns are higher, and volatility is lower, albeit only slightly in the case of tips from trade experts' strategy. There is little difference in performance between risk parity and equal weighted trend following outcomes highlighting that it does not matter much whichever strategy is chosen in this case. Because of the outstanding risk-adjusted returns of stocks, these findings imply the probability that risk parity has been extremely incremental, which in contrast to trend-following approaches, account for a significant component of these portfolios; and has very little to do with the strategy chosen for portfolio investment. We also observe much higher Sharpe ratios with the volatility momentum and investing momentum and much lower experienced drawdowns highlighting the value of experience in investing as one of the major factors to choose a particular strategy. In the last table we observe the average values for each strategy comparable to one another and it might be because the strategy did not matter overall. The values of alpha are little on the higher side for fundamental and technical analysis suggesting that these strategies could be more profitable than the others.

Table 5. Six-strategies risk - likelihood and correlation

Panel E: Risk Parity and Trend Following	Fundamental Analysis	Technical Analysis	Financial News	Professional Advice	Tips from trade experts	Self-Intuition
Annualized Return (in %)	11.88	12.43	8.43	8.22	11.02	8.27
Annualized Volatility (in %)	9.84	12.18	9.66	8.02	8.65	8.90
Sharpe Ratio	0.89	0.73	0.46	0.66	0.90	5.64
Maximum Return (Monthly in %)	9.43	11.45	9.10	10.72	10.53	9.72
Minimum Return (Monthly in %)	-9.81	-9.43	-8.25	-8.10	-7.87	-7.10
Maximum Drawdown (in %)	10.80	24.43	19.54	14.99	8.45	9.99

Table 6. Using the six most successful strategies for investing in trend

Panel F: Investing in Trend	Fundamental Analysis	Technical Analysis	Financial News	Professional Advice	Tips from trade experts	Self-Intuition
Annualized Return (in %)	9.88	8.80	7.76	12.38	11.15	10.89
Annualized Volatility (in %)	18.00	24.64	10.14	16.11	17.34	13.71
Sharpe Ratio	0.39	0.37	0.85	0.48	0.71	0.57
Maximum Return (Monthly in %)	12.66	19.67	10.91	15.37	16.21	11.00
Minimum Return (Monthly in %)	-21.52	-30.05	-8.49	-21.32	-24.18	-20.53
Maximum Drawdown (in %)	56.02	59.80	20.99	50.45	56.01	43.83
Skewness	-0.76	-0.73	0.25	-0.72	-0.58	-1.03

Table 7. Momentum reweighted for volatility based on six model strategies

Panel F: Volatility Adjusted Momentum	Fundamental Analysis	Technical Analysis	Financial News	Professional Advice	Tips from trade experts	Self-Intuition
Annualized Return (in %)	9.46	11.00	8.02	12.82	09.44	10.07
Annualized Volatility (in %)	18.84	25.60	10.25	17.48	17.25	14.96
Sharpe Ratio	0.35	0.32	0.48	0.64	0.33	0.67
Maximum Return (Monthly in %)	15.02	20.01	10.91	15.37	16.21	11.37
Minimum Return (Monthly in %)	-26.03	-31.58	-8.49	-21.04	-24.91	-22.03
Maximum Drawdown (in %)	62.48	62.42	30.77	58.64	65.97	35.22
Skewness	-0.97	-0.35	0.95	-0.41	-0.59	-1.81

Table 8. Alpha values are estimated for six trading techniques

	Average	Alpha	Fundamental Analysis	Technical Analysis	Financial News	Professional Advice	Tips from trade experts	Self-Intuition	Prob (F)
Benchmark Returns	2.23 [0.861]	0.467 [0.211]	0.657 [0.24]	0.0935 [0.41]	0.163 [0.119]	-0.0242 [-0.32]	0.0369 [-0.02]	-0.326 [0.11]	0
Equal Weight Model	4.32 [2.61]	3.56 [2.32]	3.332 [10.7]	4.51 [1.79]	4.404 [3.43]	4.112 [0.92]	5.902 [9.34]	5.50 [0.45]	0
Risk Parity	0.892 [1.12]	0.668 [0.22]	0.286 [0.43]	0.0547 [-3.32]	0.0955 [0.31]	0.0758 [0.04]	0.0193 [0.01]	-1.36 [-0.11]	0
Profit Trend	5.53 [5.51]	4.41 [5.18]	5.11 [7.07]	4.321 [1.61]	5.211 [2.00]	4.309 [3.71]	4.112 [3.85]	3.23 [2.17]	0
Risk Parity and Trend Following	1.283 [5.50]	0.785 [3.31]	0.679 [2.10]	0.0387 [1.10]	0.0375 [2.23]	0.2596 [1.12]	0.0478 [0.34]	-2.37 [0.31]	0
Investing Momentum	5.45 [4.06]	5.34 [3.35]	3.31 [11.4]	2.39 [0.57]	5.43 [0.62]	8.32 [5.32]	3.44 [4.55]	4.53 [1.09]	0
Volatility Adjusted Momentum	5.51 [2.10]	5.16 [1.19]	6.78 [0.03]	0.56 [1.14]	0.99 [-0.03]	2.21 [5.13]	2.24 [5.51]	3.32 [5.16]	0

CONCLUSION

The most common strategies that are most common to assess the viability of long-term stock market investments are these six that have been considered in this research. Long-term investors seek assets that will allow them to maximize their earnings over a longer period. Here we have not considered any other investment objectives except profits due to which results may vary over time. Here we have also considered annual profits, but many financial trade professionals recommend waiting 5-10 years or longer to amass significant wealth. Long-term investors can select any of these six useful stock-picking strategies for making lucrative investing selections by knowing the pros and cons for each. Portfolio investors who seek to maximize their long-term investment returns often employ a comprehensive analysis strategy, combining fundamental, technical, and quantitative methodologies. While some may prefer a single approach for simplicity's sake, the benefits of utilizing multiple strategies cannot be ignored. This multi-faceted approach allows investors to gain greater depth and breadth in assessing potential investments through an examination of both qualitative factors (such as management quality) and quantitative metrics (such as financial ratios), while also considering market trends and indicators. By embracing this holistic perspective towards investment evaluation, portfolio investors can increase their chances of making informed decisions that align with their overall objectives. When it comes to making investment decisions, there are several factors that one must consider. For individuals who have limited knowledge of financial matters, lack confidence or experience in trading stocks, seeking advice from trade experts could be an excellent choice. This is especially true for those interested in intraday trading where every second counts and the slightest market movement can affect the outcome. However, for portfolio investors who have a more long-term strategy and prefer to take control of their own investments, relying on self-intuition after conducting comprehensive research can prove fruitful. It's important for these investors to analyze market trends thoroughly while keeping their goals and risk tolerance in mind before finally deciding which stock(s) they wish to invest in. In conclusion, regardless of whether one is a novice or seasoned investor with varying degrees of financial literacy and expertise; investing wisely requires careful consideration based on their individual circumstances as well as due diligence when analyzing potential opportunities.

REFERENCES

Aghion, P., & Stein, J. C. (2008). Growth versus margins: Destabilizing consequences of giving the stock market what it wants. *The Journal of Finance, 63*(3), 1025–1058. doi:10.1111/j.1540-6261.2008.01351.x

Ahern, K. R. (2017). Information networks: Evidence from illegal insider trading tips. *Journal of Financial Economics, 125*(1), 26–47. doi:10.1016/j.jfineco.2017.03.009

Alsakka, R., & ap Gwilym, O. (2012). Foreign exchange market reactions to sovereign credit news. *Journal of International Money and Finance, 31*(4), 845–864. doi:10.1016/j.jimonfin.2012.01.007

Alti, A., & Tetlock, P. C. (2014). Biased beliefs, asset prices, and investment: A structural approach. *The Journal of Finance, 69*(1), 325–361. doi:10.1111/jofi.12089

Andrei, D., & Cujean, J. (2017). Information percolation, momentum and reversal. *Journal of Financial Economics, 123*(3), 617–645. doi:10.1016/j.jfineco.2016.05.012

Barber, B. M., & Odean, T. (2008). All that glitters: The effect of attention and news on the buying behavior of individual and institutional investors. *Review of Financial Studies, 21*(2), 785–818. doi:10.1093/rfs/hhm079

Baumeister, C., & Kilian, L. (2016). Forty years of oil price fluctuations: Why the price of oil may still surprise us. *The Journal of Economic Perspectives, 30*(1), 139–160. doi:10.1257/jep.30.1.139

Broadstock, D. C., & Zhang, D. (2019). Social-media and intraday stock returns: The pricing power of sentiment. *Finance Research Letters, 30*, 116–123. doi:10.1016/j.frl.2019.03.030

Carhart, M. M. (1997). On persistence in mutual fund performance. *The Journal of Finance, 52*(1), 57–82. doi:10.1111/j.1540-6261.1997.tb03808.x

Da, Z., Engelberg, J., & Gao, P. (2011). In search of attention. *The Journal of Finance*, 66(5), 1461–1499. doi:10.1111/j.1540-6261.2011.01679.x

Dechow, P., Hutton, A. P., Meulbroek, L. K., & Sloan, R. G. (1999). Short interests, fundamental analysis, and stock returns. *Fundamental Analysis, and Stock Returns (May 1999)*.

Dechow, P. M., Hutton, A. P., Meulbroek, L., & Sloan, R. G. (2001). Short-sellers, fundamental analysis, and stock returns. *Journal of Financial Economics*, 61(1), 77–106. doi:10.1016/S0304-405X(01)00056-3

Dechow, P. M., Hutton, A. P., & Sloan, R. G. (1999). An empirical assessment of the residual income valuation model. *Journal of Accounting and Economics*, 26(1-3), 1–34. doi:10.1016/S0165-4101(98)00049-4

Dhama, J. (2022). *The future of financial advice*.

Faber, N., Jorna, R., & Van Engelen, J. O. (2010). The sustainability of "sustainability"—A study into the conceptual foundations of the notion of "sustainability". In Tools, techniques and approaches for sustainability: Collected writings in environmental assessment policy and management (pp. 337-369). IEEE.

Fama, E. F., & French, K. R. (1992). The cross-section of expected stock returns. *The Journal of Finance, 47*(2), 427-465.

Fama, E. F., & French, K. R. (1995). Size and book-to-market factors in earnings and returns. *The Journal of Finance*, 50(1), 131–155. doi:10.1111/j.1540-6261.1995.tb05169.x

Feltham, G. A., & Ohlson, J. A. (1995). Valuation and clean surplus accounting for operating and financial activities. *Contemporary Accounting Research*, 11(2), 689–731. doi:10.1111/j.1911-3846.1995.tb00462.x

Frankel, R., & Lee, C. M. (1998). Accounting valuation, market expectation, and cross-sectional stock returns. *Journal of Accounting and Economics*, 25(3), 283–319. doi:10.1016/S0165-4101(98)00026-3

Ho, T., Nguyen, Y. T., Tran, H. T. M., & Vo, D. T. (2022). Fundamental analysis and the use of financial statement information to separate winners and losers in frontier markets: evidence from Vietnam. *International Journal of Emerging Markets*.

Hon-Snir, S., Kudryavtsev, A., & Cohen, G. (2012). Stock market investors: Who is more rational, and who relies on intuition. *International Journal of Economics and Finance*, 4(5), 56–72. doi:10.5539/ijef.v4n5p56

Hunt, K. H., Brimble, M., & Freudenberg, B. (2022). A Move in the Right Direction: Client Relationships in Financial Advice. *The Journal of Wealth Management*, 25(1), 50–81. doi:10.3905/jwm.2022.1.167

Hvide, H. K., & Östberg, P. (2015). Social interaction at work. *Journal of Financial Economics*, 117(3), 628–652. doi:10.1016/j.jfineco.2015.06.004

Kudryavtsev, A., Cohen, G., & Hon-Snir, S. (2013). 'Rational 'or' Intuitive': Are behavioral biases correlated across stock market investors? *Contemporary economics, 7*(2), 31-53.

Lakonishok, J., Shleifer, A., & Vishny, R. W. (1994). Contrarian investment, extrapolation, and risk. *The Journal of Finance*, 49(5), 1541–1578. doi:10.1111/j.1540-6261.1994.tb04772.x

Lehavy, R., & Sloan, R. G. (2008). Investor recognition and stock returns. *Review of Accounting Studies*, *13*(2), 327–361. doi:10.100711142-007-9063-y

Lev, B. (1989). On the usefulness of earnings and earnings research: Lessons and directions from two decades of empirical research. *Journal of Accounting Research*, *27*, 153–192. doi:10.2307/2491070

Liu, J., & Thomas, J. (2000). Stock returns and accounting earnings. *Journal of Accounting Research*, *38*(1), 71–101. doi:10.2307/2672923

Manda, V. K. (2022). Are Stock Market Training Programs worth it? *Indonesian Journal of Contemporary Education*, *4*(1), 8–18. doi:10.33122/ijoce.v4i1.20

Micucci, C. (2022). *L'educazione Finanziaria E L'evoluzione Del Social Trading: l'indagine per capire la relazione esistente*.

Neves, M. E., Leite, J., & Neves, R. (2022). Does Technical Analysis Win?: Evidence From the Period Between Donald Trump's Campaign and the First Date for Brexit. In Handbook of Research on New Challenges and Global Outlooks in Financial Risk Management (pp. 354-383). IGI Global.

Ohlson, J. A. (1995). Earnings, book values, and dividends in equity valuation. *Contemporary Accounting Research*, *11*(2), 661–687. doi:10.1111/j.1911-3846.1995.tb00461.x

Piotroski, J. D. (2000). Value investing: The use of historical financial statement information to separate winners from losers. *Journal of Accounting Research*, *38*, 1–41. doi:10.2307/2672906

Pollock, T. G., & Rindova, V. P. (2003). Media legitimation effects in the market for initial public offerings. *Academy of Management Journal*, *46*(5), 631–642. doi:10.2307/30040654

Schuster, T. (2003). Fifty-fifty. Stock recommendations and stock prices. Effects and benefits of investment advice in the business media.

Serkan, U. N. A. L. Is Popularity of Technical Analysis a Product of Low Financial Literacy and Overconfidence Among Stock Market Investors?. *Eskişehir Osmangazi Üniversitesi İktisadi ve İdari Bilimler Dergisi*, *17*(1), 146-169.

Smales, L. A. (2014). News sentiment in the gold futures market. *Journal of Banking & Finance*, *49*, 275–286. doi:10.1016/j.jbankfin.2014.09.006

Sommer, M., Lim, H., & MacDonald, M. (2022). Financial advisor use, life events, and the relationship with beneficial intentions. *Financial Services Review*, *30*(1), 69–88.

Tetlock, P. C. (2007). Giving content to investor sentiment: The role of media in the stock market. *The Journal of Finance*, *62*(3), 1139–1168. doi:10.1111/j.1540-6261.2007.01232.x

West, K. D. (1997). Another heteroskedasticity-and autocorrelation-consistent covariance matrix estimator. *Journal of Econometrics*, *76*(1-2), 171–191. doi:10.1016/0304-4076(95)01788-7

Wu, X., Ma, C., & Han, Y. (2020). Forecasting Stock Market Volatility: An Asymmetric Conditional Autoregressive Range Mixed Data Sampling (ACARR-MIDAS) Model. *The Journal of Risk, 23*(6).

Yang, Z., Ho, K. C., Shen, X., & Shi, L. (2020). Disclosure Quality Rankings and Stock Misvaluation–Evidence from Chinese Stock Market. *Emerging Markets Finance & Trade, 56*(14), 3468–3489. doi:10.1080/1540496X.2019.1700499

Chapter 6
Modelling of Engineering Systems With Small Data:
A Comparative Study

Morteza Mohammadzaheri
ⓘ https://orcid.org/0000-0002-8187-6375
Birmingham City University, UK

Mojtaba Ghodsi
University of Portsmouth, UK

Hamidreza Ziaiefar
University of South-Eastern Norway, Norway

Issam Bahadur
Sultan Qaboos University, Oman

Musaab Zarog
Sultan Qaboos University, Oman

Mohammadreza Emadi
ⓘ https://orcid.org/0000-0002-1127-1311
Sultan Qaboos University, Oman

Payam Soltani
Birmingham City University, UK

Amirhosein Amouzadeh
ⓘ https://orcid.org/0000-0002-1535-8684
Sultan Qaboos University, Oman

ABSTRACT

This chapter equitably compares five different artificial intelligence (AI) models and a linear model to tackle two real-world engineering data-driven modelling problems with small number of experimental data samples, one with sparse and one with dense data. The models of both cases are shown to be highly nonlinear. In the case with available dense data, multi-layer perceptron (MLP) evidently outperforms other AI models and challenges the claims in the literature about superiority of fully connected cascade (FCC). However, the results of the problem with sparse data shows superiority of FCC, closely followed by MLP and neuro-fuzzy network.

DOI: 10.4018/978-1-6684-7684-0.ch006

INTRODUCTION

Nowadays, engineering world witnesses two partly conflicting realities:

1. Model-based design/optimisation/control are on rise (Madni & Sievers, 2018; Pal et al., 2022), and analytical and numerical models of many engineering systems cannot serve their purpose satisfactorily, e.g. as detailed in (Li et al., 2022; Mohammadzaheri et al., 2012a; Mohammadzaheri et al., 2020; Rahbar et al., 2022). This leads to an ascending demand for data-driven models, developed with experimental data.
2. Experiments take time and cost. Hence, experimental data sets often consist of limited number of samples, or they are small.

That is, engineers are more likely to deal with small data rather than big data (Mohammadzaheri et al., 2018a). Thus, developing accurate models out of small data is a crucial task for engineers (Chang et al., 2015; Zhang et al., 2022). There are a lot of piecemeal research in the literature reporting development of data-driven models for engineering systems with small data, e.g. (Kokol et al., 2022; Liu et al., 2023; Taajobian et al., 2018). However, no comparative research was found on modelling of engineering systems with small data, though a few were found in other areas (Collins et al., 2017; Steyerberg et al., 2000), as the value of models developed with small data is not limited to engineering (Goel et al., 2023; Kitchin & Lauriault, 2015).

AI provides powerful tools to model intricate engineering systems with their input-output data (Castro, 2018; Garg et al., 2015; Li et al., 2022). The research question is which AI method suits best to data-driven modelling of engineering systems, when only a small set of data is available. The answer to this question, which necessitates an unprecedented even-handedly comparison of the AI techniques for data-driven modelling of engineering system with small data, is the main contribution of this chapter. In order to answer the aforementioned research question, several AI-based data-driven models were developed with small data to solve two real-world engineering problems: (i) head estimation of an electrical submersible pump (ESP) lifting two-phase petroleum fluids, detailed in (Mohammadzaheri & Ghodsi, 2018) and (ii) selection of the sensing resistor in a charge estimator of a piezoelectric actuator, detailed in (Mohammadzaheri et al., 2019). Neuro-fuzzy and FCC networks, MLPs, and exact and efficient Radial Basis Function Network (RBFN) models as well as linear models have been developed to tackle problems (i) and (ii).

PROBLEM STATEMENT

This section briefly explains dual engineering problems, mentioned in the introduction, which were solved in this research using AI data-driven modelling techniques. The AI techniques will be compared based on their performance in solving these problems:

Head Estimation of Two-Phase Petroleum Fluids Lifted by ESPs

A variety of empirical models are used to estimate head of two-phase petroleum fluids, H_m, lifted by ESPs. Most of them have three inputs. One input is either intake pressure, p_{in}, or density and the other two are among oil flow rate, gas flow rate, mixed fluid flow rate, q_m, or gas void ratio, α (volumetric ratio of gas to mixed fluid) (Mohammadzaheri & Ghodsi, 2018). Temperature has been overlooked in this data-driven modelling problem so far (Mohammadzaheri & Ghodsi, 2018). Pump rotational speed definitely affect the head; however, its role is considered through the affinity law, and the empirical models are usually developed for a single rotational speed (Mohammadzaheri et al., 2016). Inspired by prevalent empirical models, following general model was employed in this work:

$$H_m = f_{ESP}(\alpha, p_{in}, q_m).$$
(1)

In this research, the two-phase fluid is a mixture of carbon dioxide and diesel fuel pumped by eight stages of an I-42B radial ESP, as detailed in (Lea & Bearden, 1982; Mohammadzaheri et al., 2015). In total, the results of 109 experiments are available. 74, 17 and 18 data samples were used as modelling, validation and test data sets to identify/approximate and cross-validate f_{ESP}. The exact use of these triple data sets will be detailed in Modelling section. Input space of these data, depicted in Fig.1, is fairly sparse. For instance, few data samples are available from operating areas with high pressure and low flow rate and in operating areas with high gas void ratio. The units of p_{in} and q_m in this research are ksi and gpm (gallons per minute), and α is unit-less.

Figure 1. Distribution of modelling, validation and test data to approximate/identify and cross-validate fESP, only input

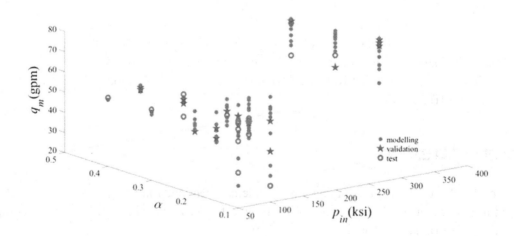

Selection of Sensing Resistor in a Charge Estimator of a Piezoelectric Actuator

Figure 2 depicts a resistor-based, or digital (Bazghaleh et al., 2013; Mohammadzaheri et al., 2022), charge estimator of a piezoelectric actuator. The excitation voltage, V_e, is applied on the actuator, leading to a voltage across the sensing resistor, V_S. Since the current passing analogue to digital convertor, A/D, is negligible, the current passing the actuator almost equals the current passing the resistor $= V_S / R_S$. Charge of the actuator is integral of its current. High pass filter removes drift phenomenon as detailed in (Bazghaleh et al., 2018).

Figure 2. A schematic of a resistor-based charge estimator for a piezoelectric actuator

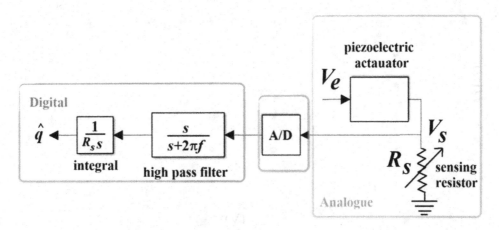

According to (Mohammadzaheri, Ziaiefar, & Ghodsi, 2022) as a selection criterion, an apt R_S should lead to a V_S just within the smallest range of A/D input voltage. For instance, if A/D has input voltage ranges of [-1 1] V, [-5 5] V and [-10 10] V, R_S should be selected so that V_S takes the widest possible span within the range of [-1 1] V. However, experiments have shown that a fixed sensing resistor cannot meet the aforesaid criterion for all operating conditions (Mohammadzaheri et al., 2019). In other words, the apt sensing resistor should be selected based on operating conditions e.g. waveform, amplitude and frequency of excitation voltage (V_e in Fig.2). It has been also shown that analytical models are inaccurate in finding such an apt R_S (Mohammadzaheri et al., 2019). Thus, the remaining alternative is to develop data-driven models to estimate apt R_S based on operating conditions. In this research, it is assumed that V_e is a sinusoidal function of time, with the range of v (in V) and the frequency of f (in Hz). Hence, v and f are the only operating conditions. That is, (2) is the data-driven model to estimate apt R_S:

$$R_S = f_{\text{PIEZO}} (v,f). \tag{2}$$

The data of 42 experimental tests on a 5×5×36 mm³ piezoelectric stack actuator are available to approximate and cross-validate f_{PIEZO}. v has the values of 5,7.5,10,12.5,15 and 17.5 V, and the frequencies (f) are 20,30,40,50,60,70 and 80 Hz. In each experiment, with a pair of v and f, R_S was tuned so that eventually met the aforementioned selection criterion. Ideally, such an R_S is the output of (2). The input-output data of 30, 6 and 6 randomly selected experiments were used as modelling, validation and test data sets, respectively. Fig. 3 shows that the available data of the second case study are quite dense. Having dense data does not contradict with small size of the data. In data-driven modelling, the inputs of a dense data set are distributed in the input space rather uniformly (Foster et al., 2021). A data set is small, if its size (number of samples) is small compared to the number of parameters of an appropriate model for such a problem.

Figure 3. Distribution of modelling, validation and test data to approximate/identify and cross-validate f_{PIEZO}, only input space

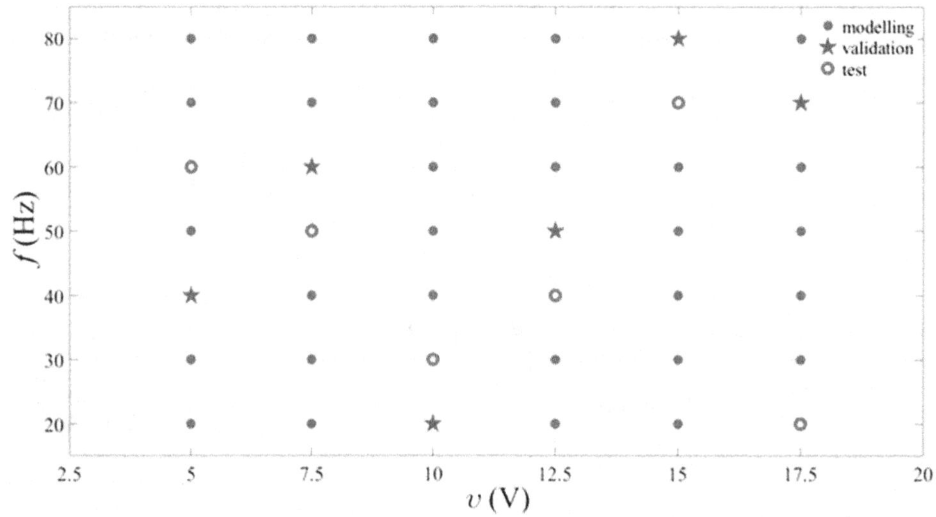

MODELLING

Development of a reliable data-driven model may include four tasks:

1- Mathematical Structure Definition
2- Parameter Identification
3- Overfitting Avoidance
4- Cross Validation

Up to three separate data sets, modelling, validation and test data, were used to perform the listed tasks for each problem defined in Problem Statement section. Generally speaking, the purpose of these quadruple steps is to minimise *error*, 'the discrepancy between the real output, from an experiment, and the estimated output by the model'. If the error is calculated using modelling, validation or test data, it is called modelling, validation or test error, respectively.

Equation 3 mathematically defines the error in this research (Mohammadzaheri et al., 2020):

$$E = \frac{\sum_{i=1}^{n_d} \left(\hat{y}_i - y_i\right)^2}{n_d}. \tag{3}$$

where y is an output, n_d is the number of samples in the data set used to calculate the error and ^ refers to estimated values. Aforementioned quadruple tasks performed in data-driven modelling are briefly introduced in the following:

Mathematical Structure Definition: In some models, the mathematical structure is not certain from the beginning. For instance, in a neuro-fuzzy network (or in short, fuzzy model), the number of rules can be defined using the modelling data through subtractive clustering (Alibak et al., 2022), or in exact RBFNs, the size of the model depends on the modelling data (Mohammadzaheri et al., 2020).

Parameter Identification: Parameters of a data-driven model, with a known mathematical structure, are identified using the modelling data. Methods of parameter identification, generally, minimise the modelling error and have two categories: single-step and iterative methods. Some models, e.g. linear and RBFN models, use single-step identification methods such as non-recursive least square of error (LSE) (Mohammadzaheri et al., 2009; Saini et al., 2022). In iterative methods, e.g. the ones based on error propagation (Haykin, 1999), the parameters are tuned step by step to minimise the modelling error (also known as the training error, as detailed in Appendix A of (Mohammadzaheri et al., 2020)).

Overfitting Avoidance: Overfitting refers to excessive focus on decrease of the modelling error, which diminishes the generality of data-driven models (Cawley & Talbot, 2010; Mohammadzaheri et al., 2007). In iterative parameter identification, e.g. for MLPs, FCCs and neuro-fuzzy networks, at each iteration, the error is both calculated for the modelling and the validation data sets; while, the latter is not used for parameter identification. A discrepancy in trend of these dual errors (normally, increase of the validation error and ongoing decrease of the modelling error) is considered as a sign of overfitting and triggers to stop parameter identification (Mohammadzaheri et al., 2020). In models with single-step parameter identifications, e.g. RBFNs, some specific parameters are identified with the validation data rather than with the modelling data to avoid overfitting (Mohammadzaheri et al., 2018a).

Cross Validation: Any data-driven model should fulfil the requirements of cross validation. In this paper, one round cross-validation or hold-out was employed, which requires that the estimation error of the model calculated with the test data (neither used in parameter identification nor in overfitting avoidance) is acceptable (Lendasse et al., 2003). In short, the test error should be reasonably low to cross validate a model. It should be noted that the validation data were not used to perform cross validation.

Six types of data-driven models were developed in this research to tackle problems detailed in Problem Statement section. In following subsections, a brief explanation of each model is presented with a focus on four aforementioned tasks for data driven modelling and correct use of the modelling and the validation data. All the developed models have a single output of y and n inputs of u_i, $i=1,...,n$.

Linear Models

In these models, the output is a linear combination of inputs

$$y = \sum_{j=1}^{n} \mathbf{A}_i u_i + \mathbf{A}_{i+1}. \tag{4}$$

Nothing needs to be done to define the mathematical structure of this model (i.e. task 1 in the list of quadruple tasks at the beginning of Modelling section), as the mathematical structure is evident. Model parameters (elements of **A**) were identified with single-step method of LSE (Mohammadzaheri et al., 2009). Overfitting was disregarded in development of (4) (i.e. task 3 was not performed); thus, both the modelling and the validation data were used for modelling.

Multi-Layer Perceptrons (MLPs)

The employed MLPs have one hidden layer with m neurons and activation function of ϕ.

$$y = \sum_{j=1}^{m} \mathbf{B}_j \phi \left(\sum_{i=1}^{n} \mathbf{C}_{ij} u_i + \mathbf{D}_i \right) + \mathbf{D}_{i+1}, \tag{5}$$

where

$$\phi(x) = \frac{2}{1+\exp(-2x)} - 1. \tag{6}$$

MLPs, presented by (5) and (6), are universal approximators. That is, the model has a proven capability to model any system when sufficient data are available (Chen & Chen, 1995; Mohammadzaheri et al., 2012) .

In this research, $m=2n+1$, (7), based on recommendation of (Haykin, 1999). Considering (7), the mathematical structure would be known. Nguyen-Widrow algorithm was used to suggest initial values for parameters (Nguyen & Widrow, 1990). Then, error back propagation with Levenberg-Marquardt algorithm (Mohammadzaheri & Chen, 2010) was utilised to minimise the modelling error iteratively and to identify MLP parameters. At each iteration, the validation error was calculated. Parameter identification stopped as the trend of the modelling and the validation errors became discrepant, i.e. overfitting happened. Even with use of parameter initialisation algorithms, some initial values of parameters may push the utilised parameter identification method to be trapped in local minima of the modelling error, leading to low accuracy of the model (Mohammadzaheri et al., 2021). Consequently, parameter identification was repeated with different initial parameters. The model with the lowest validation error was chosen in the end.

Fully Connected Cascade (FCC) Networks

The employed FCC networks are very similar to the MLPs, with extra parameters (**E** elements) which connect the inputs directly to the output.

$$y = \sum_{j=1}^{n} \bar{\mathbf{B}}_j \phi \left(\sum_{i=1}^{m} \bar{\mathbf{C}}_{ij} u_i + \bar{\mathbf{D}}_i \right) + \sum_{i=1}^{n} \bullet_i u_i + \bar{\mathbf{D}}_{i+1}. \tag{8}$$

FCC networks have shown their merit in solving some non-engineering benchmarks (Hunter et al., 2012). The number of hidden layer neurons, m, was considered same as the one of MLPs, as the same recommendation of (7) is valid for FCC networks (Hunter et al., 2012). Parameter identification, over-fitting avoidance and evasion from local minima of the modelling error in FCC networks are similar to the ones of MLPs.

Neurofuzzy Networks

Linear Sugeno-type fuzzy models were used in this research which are convertible to neuro-fuzzy networks (Ahmadpour et al., 2009). Such fuzzy models have k rules, each with n membership functions (one per input). For j^{th} rule and i^{th} input, the Gaussian membership function of (9) was employed to produce a membership grade, μ_{ij}, based on the input, u_i (Mehrabi et al., 2017):

$$\mu_{ij} = \exp\left(-\frac{(u_i - \mathbf{F}_{ij})^2}{2\mathbf{G}_{ij}^2}\right). \tag{9}$$

The product of membership grades of a rule was considered as the weight of the rule, a real number between zero and one. The output of the whole model is the weighted sum of rule outputs (Mehrabi et al., 2017):

$$y = \frac{\sum_{j=1}^{k}\left(\overbrace{\left(\sum_{i=1}^{n}\mathbf{H}_{ij}u_i + \mathbf{I}_j\right)}^{j^{th}\ rule\ output}\prod_{i=1}^{n}\mu_{ij}\right)}{\underbrace{\sum_{j=1}^{k}\prod_{i=1}^{n}\mu_{ij}}_{i^{th}\ rule\ weight}}. \tag{10}$$

Neuro-fuzzy models, presented by (9) and (10), are universal approximators (Ying, 1998). The mathematical structure of the fuzzy model, e.g. the number of rules (k), was defined through subtractive clustering with use of the modelling data, the utilised subtractive clustering algorithm is similar to the one detailed subsection 2-3 of (Mohammadzaheri et al., 2012b).

Parameters were identified using an iterative method. At each iteration, gradient descent error back propagation algorithm was used to adjust elements of $\mathbf{F}$ and $\mathbf{G}$, and LSE was used to adjust elements of $\mathbf{H}$ and $\mathbf{I}$ (Jang et al., 2006; Mohammadzaheri et al., 2018). The validation error, calculated at every iteration, was used to stop parameter identification procedure and to avoid overfitting, in the same way as used for MLPs.

Radial Basis Function Networks

RBFNs, which are universal approximators too (Park & Sandberg, 1993), are presented as a combination of (11) and (12). They receive an array of inputs rather than inputs of a single data sample; a data sample has n inputs. An RBFN can estimate the output of maximum w data samples, where w is the number of data samples used to develop the model. If the input of fewer number of data samples, i.e. z, are fed into the model, first z columns of $\mathbf{O}$ and $\mathbf{L}$ are used.

$$\ddot{\mathbf{Y}}_{ik} = \exp\left(-\left(S\underbrace{\sum_{j=1}^{n}\left(\mathbf{J}_{ij}-\mathbf{U}_{jk}\right)^2}_{\substack{\text{distance between input} \\ \text{and weight arrays}}}\right)^2\right). \tag{11}$$

$$\widehat{\mathbf{Y}}_{1\times w} = \mathbf{K}_{1\times w}\times\mathbf{O}_{w\times w}+\mathbf{L}_{1\times w}. \tag{12}$$

(12) indicates that greater elements of $\mathbf{O}$ are more influential on the network's output. In addition, (11) shows that (i) the range of $\mathbf{O}$ elements is [0 1] and (ii) if the ith row of $\mathbf{J}$ is identical to the kth column of $\mathbf{U}$, then $\mathbf{O}_{ik}$ will be maximum, 1.

In RBFN modelling, arrays of $\mathbf{J}_{w\times n}$, $\mathbf{K}$ and $\mathbf{L}$ and the scalar of S namely 'spread' should be identified. At model development stage, where modelling data were used, (13) was used instead of (12). ^ is unnecessary in (13), since no estimation happens during model development:

$$\mathbf{Y}_{1\times w} = \begin{bmatrix}\mathbf{K} & \mathbf{L}\end{bmatrix}_{1\times 2w}\begin{bmatrix}\mathbf{O} \\ \mathbf{I}\end{bmatrix}_{2w\times w}. \tag{13}$$

In exact RBFNs, $\mathbf{J}=\mathbf{U_M}^T$ (14), where $\mathbf{U_M}^T$ is the transpose of an array of all inputs of the modelling data. Hence, w equals the number of modelling data samples, and the mathematical structure is identified. For instance, for the second problem of Problem Statement section, $\mathbf{U_M}^T$ has the size of 2×30. Considering (11) and (14), $\mathbf{O}$ elements on the output, calculated with the modelling data, will be 1. Here is a pseudo-algorithm of exact RBFN modelling (to find $\mathbf{J}$, $\mathbf{K}$, $\mathbf{L}$ and S using the input and output arrays of the modelling data, $\mathbf{U_M}$ and $\mathbf{Y_M}$)

1. Set $\mathbf{J}=\mathbf{U_M}^T$
2. Set $\mathbf{O}_{w\times w}=\text{ones}(w\times w)$
3. Form and solve (13) with $\mathbf{Y_M}$ and $\mathbf{O}$ from step 2 to find $\mathbf{K}_{1\times w}$.
4. Find S, with trial and error, so as to minimise the validation error of the developed RBFN (anti-overfitting step)

An alternative to exact RBFN modelling is efficient RBFN modelling, which may produce RBFNs with fewer parameters. In this research, despite exact RBFNs, that employ the transpose of inputs array of the modelling data as $\mathbf{J}$, in efficient RBFN modelling, some columns of $\mathbf{U_M}$ were selected and transposed to form $\mathbf{J}$ (Mohammadzaheri et al., 2018b). Hence, the number of $\mathbf{J}$ rows, w, is smaller or equal to the number of the columns of $\mathbf{U_M}$, named w_{max} in this paper.

Prior to select $\mathbf{U_M}$ columns to be used as $\mathbf{J}$ rows, S, and a target error, E_t should be defined. For each set of S and E_t, every single column of $\mathbf{U_M}$ was transposed and tried as a single-row $\mathbf{J}$. Then, the corresponding RBFN was created using $\mathbf{K}$ and $\mathbf{L}$ calculated with (13). The column of $\mathbf{U_M}$ leading to the smallest modelling error was selected, transposed and used as the first row of $\mathbf{J}$. Afterwards, the remaining columns of $\mathbf{U}$ were examined to find the one in which addition of its transpose to $\mathbf{J}$ led to the largest drop in the modelling error. Transposed of such a column was added to $\mathbf{J}$. This continued till the modelling error reached E_t. Thus, the mathematical structure of efficient RBFNs is defined with use of the modelling data. In this research, the entire process of finding $\mathbf{J}$ was repeated for different pairs of S and E_t, and the validation error was calculated for each pair.

Here is a pseudo-algorithm of efficient RBFN modelling:

1. $\mathbf{J}$=null, $\mathbf{U}_{rem}$= $\mathbf{U}_M$, $\mathbf{U}_{opt}$=null, E=VEX=1000 (a large number), $^T\mathbf{J}$=null (temporary weight matrix)
2. Choose a large S and a target modelling error, E_t
3. Set w=1
4. Set k=1
5. Add transpose of kth column of $\mathbf{U}_{rem}$ to $\mathbf{J}$ to form $^T\mathbf{J}$
6. Set $\mathbf{O}_{w \times w}$=ones($w \times w$)
7. Solve (13) to find $\mathbf{K}$ and $\mathbf{L}$ ($\mathbf{Y}_M$ and $\mathbf{O}$ are available from the modelling data and step 6)
8. Find the modelling error, ME. The model (11 and 12) needs to be rum more than once as $w < w_{max}$.
9. If $ME < E$, then E=ME and $\mathbf{U}_{opt}$=$\mathbf{U}_k$
10. k=k+1
11. If $k \leq (w_{max} - w + 1)$ then go to 5
12. Remove $\mathbf{U}_{opt}$ from $\mathbf{U}_{rem}$ and add it to $\mathbf{J}$
13. w=w+1
14. if $E > E_t$ then go to 4
15. Find the validation error, VE
16. If $VE < VEX$ then VEX=VE
17. If VEX is unacceptable go to 2

Choice of S and E_t was performed using full space search with zooming (use of smaller step-size) at low error areas.

Line 4 of exact RBFN modelling pseudo-codes and lines 14-17 of efficient RBFN modelling pseudo-codes use the validation data to tackle overfitting. Use of the modelling data at these lines would diminished the generality of the model, and use of the test data would violate the conditions of cross validation.

Section Summary

Table 1 summarises the tasks performed in development of each model and the data used for each task. MD and VD refer to the modelling and the validation data, respectively. Two last columns refer to avoidance of overfitting through different strategies: (1) stopping parameter identification in the case of discrepancy in trend of modelling and validation errors, used for MLP, FCC and neuro-fuzzy networks, and (2) identifying some parameters with the validation data to improve generality of the models, or dual identification, used for RBFNs.

Table 1. Development stages for different models and their associated data

Model	Structure Definition	Parameter Identification	Over-fitting Avoidance-Stop Process	Over-fitting Avoidance- Dual Identification
Linear		MD+VD		
MLP		MD	VD	
FCC		MD	VD	
Fuzzy	MD	MD	VD	
RBFN	MD	MD		VD

RESULTS AND ANALYSIS

The models, reported in the previous section, were developed to approximate f_{ESP} and f_{PIEZO} introduced in Problem Statement section. For (neuro-) fuzzy modelling, subtractive clustering was performed with the influence range of 0.5 and squash factor of 1.25 for both problems. Also, accept ratios of 0.1 and 0.5 and reject ratios of 0.05 and 0.15 were used for subtractive clustering for the purpose of f_{ESP} and f_{PIEZO} approximation, respectively. The aforementioned factors have been explained in (Mohammadzaheri et al., 2012b). Exact RBFNs were developed with the spreads (S) of 76 and 41 for the first and the second problem, respectively. Efficient RBFNs were developed with S and E_t of 58 and 30 for the first problem (to approximate f_{ESP}) and 83.5 and 1.2 for the second problem. The results showed that targeting a too small modelling error (e.g. 0) increases the validation error or rises the chance of overfitting.

Tables 2 and 3 present different statistics for the developed models, all calculated with the test data, for the purpose of comparison of different techniques. MAE and MSE stand for mean of absolute error and mean of squared error. The range of output for the problems associated with Tables 2 and 3 are [28,72] ft and [17.5,225] Ω, respectively. The results evidently show that both systems are highly nonlinear, as linear models practically fail to approximate both f_{ESP} and f_{PIEZO}.

Table 2. Different statistics of estimation error for different models to approximate f_{ESP}

	MLP	FCC	Fuzzy	RBFN Efficient	RBFN Exact	Linear
MAE	2.692	2.342	2.824	8.006	8.611	174.50
Error Bias	1.975	1.360	0.967	0.929	0.473	174.50
Error Variance	14.124	8.732	16.832	96.49	240.44	8484.3
MSE	18.025	10.582	17.767	97.35	240.66	38934
Number of Parameters	36	39	80	26	371	4

Table 3. Different statistics of estimation error for different models to approximate f_{PIEZO}

	MLP	FCC	Fuzzy	RBFN Efficient	RBFN Exact	Linear
MAE	0.623	1.386	2.652	1.537	2.000	54.916
Error Bias	0.127	1.265	0.370	1.070	-1.081	44.177
Error Variance	0.555	2.020	11.44	1.792	11.146	2682.8
MSE	0.571	3.620	11.58	2.937	12.315	4634.4
Number of Parameters	21	23	56	37	121	3

For the first case study (approximation of f_{ESP}, presented in Table 2), with fairly sparse data, FCC outperforms other models, with a sizably lower estimation error variance. This result is in agreement with the conclusions of (Hunter et al., 2012). The performance of MLP and Fuzzy models are fairly close to the FCC. MAE, a sensible criterion of accuracy, of the MLP is only around 15% larger than the one of FCC. Fuzzy and RBFN models which convert the parameter identification problem to a linear algebra problem, partly or in full, show small estimation biases of lower than 1 ft, almost 5 to 11 inches smaller than the bias of FCC head estimation.

MLP, however, shows evident superiority for the second case study (approximation of f_{PIEZO}, presented in Table 3) with dense data. MLP has the smallest estimation bias, estimation variance and number of parameters compared to all other nonlinear models. Alternatively, due to high density of the data, one can guess interpolation techniques may estimate the sensing resistance accurately in this case study. However, a similar research has shown that RBFN models outperform cubic interpolation and averaging methods (Mohammadzaheri et al., 2020). As a result, superiority of MLP can be also extended to these interpolation techniques.

In summary, for development of models to approximate nonlinear systems/functions with small data and for engineering purposes, three following recommendations can be drawn from the results of this research:

1. FCC is recommended to be employed in the case of sparsity of data; although, MLP and fuzzy models are also worth to be tried.
2. MLP is suggested to be employed with dense data.
3. RBFN models are not recommended, due to relatively high number of parameters and low accuracy. RBFNs were not the best models for any type of estimation purposes; the reason may be their inherited weakness against overfitting.

CONCLUSION

This chapter investigated the capability of a variety of common artificial intelligence techniques in data-driven modelling of engineering systems in the case of access to small data (small number of data samples). Five different AI models were even-handedly assessed in data-driven modelling of two case studies with sparse and dense data. Both systems were shown to be highly nonlinear.

For modelling with sparse data, FCC outperformed other techniques, closely followed by MLP and fuzzy models. This outcome is consistent with the literature claiming that FCCs are at an advantage over other AI modelling tools. However, for the problem with dense data, MLP showed an obvious superiority. RBFN models could not excel in any of the investigated data-driven modelling problems; therefore, they are recommended to be disregarded in data-driven modelling of engineering systems with small data. As a suggestion for future research, the presented comparison can be repeated for any other data-driven modelling technique not covered in this chapter or the techniques that will be developed in the future.

DISCLOSURE OF POTENTIAL CONFLICT OF INTEREST

The authors have no conflicts of interest, associated with this paper, to declare.

REFERENCES

Ahmadpour, M., Yue, W. L., & Mohammadzaheri, M. (2009). *Neuro-fuzzy Modelling of Workers Trip Production*. 32nd Australasian Transport Research Forum, Auckland, New Zealand.

Alibak, A. H., Alizadeh, S. M., Davodi Monjezi, S., Alizadeh, A., Alobaid, F., & Aghel, B. (2022). Developing a Hybrid Neuro-Fuzzy Method to Predict Carbon Dioxide ($CO2$) Permeability in Mixed Matrix Membranes Containing SAPO-34 Zeolite. *Membranes*, *12*(11), 1147. doi:10.3390/membranes12111147 PMID:36422139

Bazghaleh, M., Grainger, S., & Mohammadzaheri, M. (2018). A review of charge methods for driving piezoelectric actuators. *Journal of Intelligent Material Systems and Structures*, *29*(10), 2096–2104. doi:10.1177/1045389X17733330

Bazghaleh, M., Grainger, S., Mohammadzaheri, M., Cazzolato, B., & Lu, T. (2013). A digital charge amplifier for hysteresis elimination in piezoelectric actuators. *Smart Materials and Structures*, *22*(7), 075016. doi:10.1088/0964-1726/22/7/075016

Castro, R. (2018). Data-driven PV modules modelling: Comparison between equivalent electric circuit and artificial intelligence based models. *Sustainable Energy Technologies and Assessments*, *30*, 230–238. doi:10.1016/j.seta.2018.10.011

Cawley, G. C., & Talbot, N. L. (2010). On over-fitting in model selection and subsequent selection bias in performance evaluation. *Journal of Machine Learning Research*, *11*(Jul), 2079–2107.

Chang, C.-J., Li, D.-C., Huang, Y.-H., & Chen, C.-C. (2015). A novel gray forecasting model based on the box plot for small manufacturing data sets. *Applied Mathematics and Computation*, *265*, 400–408. doi:10.1016/j.amc.2015.05.006

Chen, T. P., & Chen, H. (1995). Approximation capability to functions of several variables, nonlinear functionals, and operators by radial basis function neural networks. *IEEE Transactions on Neural Networks*, *6*(4), 904-910. <Go to ISI>://A1995RF58200008

Collins, J., Brown, J., Schammel, C., Hutson, K., Jeffery, W., & Edenfield, M. (2017). Meaningful Analysis of Small Data Sets: A Clinician's Guide. *Clinical and Translational Research*, 2(1), 16–19.

Foster, D., Gagne, D. J., & Whitt, D. B. (2021). Probabilistic Machine Learning Estimation of Ocean Mixed Layer Depth From Dense Satellite and Sparse In Situ Observations. *Journal of Advances in Modeling Earth Systems*, 13(12), e2021MS002474.

Garg, A., Vijayaraghavan, V., Wong, C., Tai, K., Sumithra, K., Mahapatra, S., Singru, P. M., & Yao, L. (2015). Application of artificial intelligence technique for modelling elastic properties of 2D nanoscale material. *Molecular Simulation*, 41(14), 1143–1152. doi:10.1080/08927022.2014.951351

Goel, M., Sharma, A., Chilwal, A. S., Kumari, S., Kumar, A., & Bagler, G. (2023). Machine learning models to predict sweetness of molecules. *Computers in Biology and Medicine*, 152, 106441. doi:10.1016/j. compbiomed.2022.106441 PMID:36543004

Haykin, S. (1999). *Neural Networks A Comprehensive Introduction*. Prentice Hall.

Hunter, D., Yu, H., Pukish, M. S. III, Kolbusz, J., & Wilamowski, B. M. (2012). Selection of proper neural network sizes and architectures—A comparative study. *IEEE Transactions on Industrial Informatics*, 8(2), 228–240. doi:10.1109/TII.2012.2187914

Jang, J. R., Sun, C., & Mizutani, E. (2006). *Neuro-Fuzzy and Soft Computing*. Prentice-Hall of India.

Kitchin, R., & Lauriault, T. P. (2015). Small data in the era of big data. *GeoJournal*, 80(4), 463–475. doi:10.100710708-014-9601-7

Kokol, P., Kokol, M., & Zagoranski, S. (2022). Machine learning on small size samples: A synthetic knowledge synthesis. *Science Progress*, 105(1), 00368504211029777. doi:10.1177/00368504211029777 PMID:35220816

Lea, J. F., & Bearden, J. (1982). Effect of gaseous fluids on submersible pump performance. *Journal of Petroleum Technology*, 34(12), 922–930. doi:10.2118/9218-PA

Lendasse, A., Wertz, V., & Verleysen, M. (2003). Model selection with cross-validations and bootstraps—application to time series prediction with RBFN models. *Artificial Neural Networks and Neural Information Processing—ICANN/ICONIP 2003*, 174-174.

Li, W., Demir, I., Cao, D., Jöst, D., Ringbeck, F., Junker, M., & Sauer, D. U. (2022). Data-driven systematic parameter identification of an electrochemical model for lithium-ion batteries with artificial intelligence. *Energy Storage Materials*, 44, 557–570. doi:10.1016/j.ensm.2021.10.023

Li, X., Jia, R., Zhang, R., Yang, S., Chen, G., & Safety, S. (2022). A KPCA-BRANN based data-driven approach to model corrosion degradation of subsea oil pipelines. *Reliability Engineering & System Safety*, 219, 108231. doi:10.1016/j.ress.2021.108231

Liu, X., Yan, Z., Wu, J., Huang, J., Zheng, Y., Sullivan, N. P., & Pan, Z. J. J. o. E. C. (2023). *Prediction of impedance responses of protonic ceramic cells using artificial neural network tuned with the distribution of relaxation times*.

Madni, A. M., & Sievers, M. (2018). Model-based systems engineering: motivation, current status, and needed advances. In *Disciplinary Convergence in Systems Engineering Research* (pp. 311–325). Springer. doi:10.1007/978-3-319-62217-0_22

Mehrabi, D., Mohammadzaheri, M., Firoozfar, A., & Emadi, M. (2017). A fuzzy virtual temperature sensor for an irradiative enclosure. *Journal of Mechanical Science and Technology*, *31*(10), 4989–4994. doi:10.100712206-017-0947-x

Mohammadzaheri, M., Akbarifar, A., Ghodsi, M., Bahadur, I., AlJahwari, F., & Al-Amri, B. (2020). Health Monitoring of Welded Pipelines with Mechanical Waves and Fuzzy Inference Systems. International Gas Union Research Conference,

Mohammadzaheri, M., Amouzadeh, A., Doustmohammadi, M., Emadi, M., Nasiri, N., Jamshidi, E., & Soltani, P. (2021). Fault diagnosis of an automobile cylinder block with neural process of modal information. *International Journal of Mechanical and Mechatronics Engineering*, *21*(2), 1–8.

Mohammadzaheri, M., & Chen, L. (2010). Intelligent predictive control of a model helicopter's yaw angle. *Asian Journal of Control*, *12*(6), 667–679. doi:10.1002/asjc.243

Mohammadzaheri, M., Chen, L., Ghaffari, A., & Willison, J. (2009). A combination of linear and nonlinear activation functions in neural networks for modeling a de-superheater. *Simulation Modelling Practice and Theory*, *17*(2), 398–407. doi:10.1016/j.simpat.2008.09.015

Mohammadzaheri, M., Chen, L., & Grainger, S. (2012). A critical review of the most popular types of neuro control. *Asian Journal of Control*, *16*(1), 1–11. doi:10.1002/asjc.449

Mohammadzaheri, M., Emadi, M., Ghodsi, M., Bahadur, I. M., Zarog, M., & Saleem, A. (2020). Development of a Charge Estimator for Piezoelectric Actuators: A Radial Basis Function Approach. [IJAIML]. *International Journal of Artificial Intelligence and Machine Learning*, *10*(1), 31–44. doi:10.4018/IJAIML.2020010103

Mohammadzaheri, M., Emadi, M., Ghodsi, M., Jamshidi, E., Bahadur, I., Saleem, A., & Zarog, M. (2019). A variable-resistance digital charge estimator for piezoelectric actuators: An alternative to maximise accuracy and curb voltage drop. *Journal of Intelligent Material Systems and Structures*, *30*(11), 1699–1705. doi:10.1177/1045389X19844011

Mohammadzaheri, M., & Ghodsi, M. (2018). A Critical Review on Empirical Head-Predicting Models of Two-phase Petroleum Fluids in Electrical Submersible Pumps. *Petroleum & Petrochemical Engineering Journal*, *2*(4), 1–4.

Mohammadzaheri, M., Ghodsi, M., & AlQallaf, A. (2018a). Estimate of the head of the head produced by electrical submeersible pumps on gaseous petroleum fluids, a radial basis function network approach. *International Journal of Artificial Intelligence & Applications*, *9*(1), 53–62. doi:10.5121/ijaia.2018.9104

Mohammadzaheri, M., Ghodsi, M., & AlQallaf, A. (2018b). Estimate of the head produced by electrical submersible pumps on gaseous petroleum fluids, a raidal basis function netrwork approach. *International Journal of Artificial Intelligence & Applications*, *9*(1), 53–62. doi:10.5121/ijaia.2018.9104

Mohammadzaheri, M., Grainger, S., & Bazghaleh, M. (2012a). A comparative study on the use of black box modelling for piezoelectric actuators. *International Journal of Advanced Manufacturing Technology*, *63*(9-12), 1247–1255. doi:10.100700170-012-3987-5

Mohammadzaheri, M., Grainger, S., & Bazghaleh, M. (2012b). Fuzzy modeling of a piezoelectric actuator. *International Journal of Precision Engineering and Manufacturing*, *13*(5), 663–670. doi:10.100712541-012-0086-3

Mohammadzaheri, M., Mirsepahi, A., Asef-afshar, O., & Koohi, H. (2007). Neuro-fuzzy modeling of superheating system of a steam power plant. *Applied Mathematical Sciences*, *1*, 2091–2099.

Mohammadzaheri, M., Tafreshi, R., Khan, Z., Franchek, M., & Grigoriadis, K. (2015). *Modelling of Petroleum Multiphase Fluids in ESPs, an Intelliegnt Approach Offshore Mediternean Conference*, Ravenna, Italy.

Mohammadzaheri, M., Tafreshi, R., Khan, Z., Franchek, M., & Grigoriadis, K. (2016). An intelligent approach to optimize multiphase subsea oil fields lifted by electrical submersible pumps. *Journal of Computational Science*, *15*, 50–59. doi:10.1016/j.jocs.2015.10.009

Mohammadzaheri, M., Tafreshi, R., Khan, Z., Ghodsi, M., Franchek, M., & Grigoriadis, K. (2020). Modelling of petroleum multiphase flow in electrical submersible pumps with shallow artificial neural networks. *Ships and Offshore Structures*, *15*(2), 174–183. doi:10.1080/17445302.2019.1605959

Mohammadzaheri, M., Ziaiefar, H., & Ghodsi, M. (2022). Digital Charge Estimation for Piezoelectric Actuators: An Artificial Intelligence Approach. In Handbook of Research on New Investigations in Artificial Life, AI, and Machine Learning (pp. 117-140). IGI Global.

Mohammadzaheri, M., Ziaiefar, H., Ghodsi, M., Bahadur, I., Zarog, M., Saleem, A., & Emadi, M. (2019). Adaptive Charge Estimation of Piezoelectric Actuators, a Radial Basis Function Approach. *20th International Conference on Research and Education in Mechatronics Wels*, Austria. 10.1109/REM.2019.8744122

Mohammadzaheri, M., Ziaiefar, H., Ghodsi, M., Emadi, M., Zarog, M., Soltani, P., & Bahadur, I. (2022). Adaptive Charge Estimation of Piezoelectric Actuators with a Variable Sensing Resistor, an Artificial Intelligence Approach. *Engineering Letters*, *30*(1), 193–200.

Nguyen, D., & Widrow, B. (1990). *Improving the learning speed of 2-layer neural networks by choosing initial values of the adaptive weights International Joint Conference on Neural Networks*, San Diego, USA.

Pal, A., Zhu, L., Wang, Y., & Zhu, G. (2022). (in press). Data-driven model-based calibration for optimizing electrically boosted diesel engine performance. *International Journal of Engine Research*, 14680874221090307.

Park, J., & Sandberg, I. W. (1993). Approximation and radial-basis-function networks. *Neural Computation*, *5*(2), 305–316. doi:10.1162/neco.1993.5.2.305 PMID:31167308

Rahbar, A., Mirarabi, A., Nakhaei, M., Talkhabi, M., & Jamali, M. (2022). A comparative analysis of data-driven models (SVR, ANFIS, and ANNs) for daily karst spring discharge prediction. *Water Resources Management*, *36*(2), 589–609. doi:10.100711269-021-03041-9

Saini, S., Orlando, M. F., & Pathak, P. M. (2022). Intelligent Control of Master-Slave based Robotic Surgical System. *Journal of Intelligent & Robotic Systems*, *105*(4), 1–20. doi:10.100710846-022-01684-3

Steyerberg, E. W., Eijkemans, M. J., Harrell, F. E. Jr, & Habbema, J. D. F. (2000). Prognostic modelling with logistic regression analysis: A comparison of selection and estimation methods in small data sets. *Statistics in Medicine*, *19*(8), 1059–1079. doi:10.1002/(SICI)1097-0258(20000430)19:8<1059::AID-SIM412>3.0.CO;2-0 PMID:10790680

Taajobian, M., Mohammadzaheri, M., Doustmohammadi, M., Amouzadeh, A., & Emadi, M. (2018). Fault diagnosis of an automobile cylinder head using low frequency vibrational data. *Journal of Mechanical Science and Technology*, *32*(7), 3037–3045. doi:10.100712206-018-0606-x

Ying, H. (1998). *General Takagi-Sugeno fuzzy systems are universal approximators*. ISI.

Zhang, T., Chen, J., Li, F., Zhang, K., Lv, H., He, S., & Xu, E. (2022). Intelligent fault diagnosis of machines with small & imbalanced data: A state-of-the-art review and possible extensions. *ISA Transactions*, *119*, 152–171. doi:10.1016/j.isatra.2021.02.042 PMID:33736889

Chapter 7

The Theory and Applications of the Software–Based PSK Method for Solving Intuitionistic Fuzzy Solid Transportation Problems

P. Senthil Kumar

iD https://orcid.org/0000-0003-4317-1021

Mohan Babu University, India

ABSTRACT

It proposes the PSK (P. Senthil Kumar) method for solving intuitionistic fuzzy solid transportation problems (IFSTPs). In our daily life, uncertainty comes in many ways, e.g., the transportation cost (TC) is not a fixed one, it varies from time to time due to market conditions (i.e., the price of diesel is depending on the cost of crude oil), mode of the transportation, etc. So, to deal with the TP having uncertainty and hesitation in TC, in this chapter, the author divided IFSTP into 4 categories and solved type II- IFSTP by using TIFNs. The model of type II- IFSTP and its relevant CSTP both are presented. The PSK method is presented clearly with the proof of some theorems and corollary. To illustrate the PSK method with proposed models, the numerical experiment and its related graphs are presented. Real-life problems are identified and solved by the PSK method with MATLAB and LINGO software. Analysis, discussion, merits, and demerits of the PSK method are all presented. A valid conclusion and recommendations are given. Finally, some of the future research areas are also suggested.

INTRODUCTION

The linear programming problem (LPP), widely used in the areas of transportation, energy industry, agriculture, manufacturing, engineering, and so forth, In that, the transportation problem (TP) is the most important and special case of LPP. It is used in a variety of fields. Some of them are listed below.

DOI: 10.4018/978-1-6684-7684-0.ch007

1. Aggregate planning
2. Personal management
3. Economics
4. Communication network
5. Inventory control
6. Employment scheduling
7. Business, etc.

Linear programming (LP) is also called linear optimization. It is a technique for the optimization of a linear objective function, subject to linear equality (=) and linear inequality (i.e., less than (<), greater than (>), less than or equal to (≤) and greater than or equal to (≥)) constraints. Generally, LP is a special case of mathematical programming. It is also known as mathematical optimization. As we know, the TP is one of the optimization problems. Its objective is to determine the optimum schedule subject to the given set of constraints. It deals with transportation of homogeneous commodities from several number of sources to different number of destinations. In that, the constraints are all should be linear type. Similarly, the objective function is also linear. These two are the major assumptions of TP. The allocations should be satisfies the supply points constraints and demand points constraints as well as non-negative restrictions. By this way we need to optimize the objective function. The term 'optimization' can be defined as either 'maximization' or 'minimization'. If the cost/time involving the objective function then our aim is to minimize the cost/time. Such a problem is called minimization problem. Similarly, if the profit/production involving the objective function then our aim is to maximize the profit/production. Such kind of problem is called a maximization problem. Cost minimization TP and profit maximization TP both are the examples of minimization and maximization problems. Shipping the raw material from several sources to different destinations is unavoidable one. Therefore, the study of TP is also unavoidable one.

In traditional TP, there are three parameters, which are:

1. Supply/availability (the amounts available at the supply points are known as supply).
2. Demand/requirement (the amounts required at the demand points are known as demand).
3. Cost (the unit costs, i.e., the cost of transporting one unit from a particular supply point to a particular demand point).

BACKGROUND

Historical background of TP, STP, fuzzy set, FSTP, IFS and IFSTP are given in this section.

Historical Background of TP and STP

In 1941, Hitchcock introduced the TP. Further, Dantzig (1963) solved the TP by using Simplex method. Swarup et al. (1997) have solved the TP with the name of 'tracts in operations research' under the assumptions that all the parameters are crisp numbers. Xie et al. (2017) discussed TP with varying demands and supplies in crisp environment. Similarly, Quddoos (2018) introduced a mathematical model for reliable transportation problem with crisp parameters. Furthermore, some of the recent literature related to this topic is specified within these brackets (Lee, 2021; Xie & Li, 2021; Bhadane et al., 2021; Hussain et al.,

2021; Das, 2021; Stoilova & Stoilov, 2021; Kacher & Singh, 2021; Xie et al., 2022; Muralidaran & Venkateswarlu, 2022; Ali-Hussein & Shiker, 2022; Ding & Xie, 2023; Lubis, 2023; Singh & Singh, 2023).

The generalization of TP is called STP. The major difference between TP and STP is conveyance, i.e., in TP, we consider supply and demand whereas in STP we consider conveyance also. The profit/cost in STP differs from transport to transport, i.e., different types of transport have different transportation costs. For example, if we consider three types of transportation such as truck, flight and ship then the cost of these three are not same. So, the transportation cost varies from different transport to transport. We are not consider this kind of assumption (or restriction) in TP. Because of addition of this constraint in TP, the study of STP was focused by several researchers. The literature related to this topic is specified within these brackets (Shell, 1955; Haley, 1962; Appa, 1973; Basu, Pal, & Kundu, 1994; Li, Ida, Gen, & Kobuchi, 1997a). To find out the optimal solution of STP by using the algorithms specified in the bracketed references, we need $m+n+l-2$ non-negative values, which is known as a basic feasible solution.

Historical Background of Fuzzy Set and FSTP

The extension of STP is called FSTP. The difference between STP and FSTP are very small. i.e., in STP, we are using crisp parameters but in FSTP we are using fuzzy parameters instead of crisp parameters. Anyhow, the objective of both the problems are either maximize the profit or minimize the cost. The parameters of STP are all not known clearly in day-to-day life due to some unavoidable circumstance. Hence, finding the solution of STP with uncertain parameters is great attention in various researchers. Zadeh (1965) introduced the fuzzy set theory to solve STP with uncertain parameters. The related literature on this topic is given within this bracket (Gen, Ida, Li, & Kubota, 1995; Li, Ida, & Gen, 1997b; Jimenez & Verdegay, 1998, 1999; Liu, 2006; Ojha, Das, Mondal, & Maiti, 2009; Kumar & Yadav, 2012; Ojha, Mondal, & Maiti, 2014; Khalaf et al., 2021; Zhu et al., 2021; Acar et al., 2021; Sangeetha et al., 2021; Nagar et al., 2021; Kumaran, 2021; Devnath et al., 2021; Das, 2022).

The basic TP was introduced by Hitchcock (1941), it is also called crisp transportation problem (CTP). The parameters of CTP are all not certain due to many factors, which are all uncertain. So, the study of TP with uncertain parameters is important role in current thinking. Some selected and related references in this topic are given this brackets (Kumar, 2010; Mohideen & Kumar, 2010a, b; He, Li, Huang, & Lei, 2014; Singh, Thakur, & Kumar, 2016; Joshi & Chauhan, 2016; Kumar, 2016a, b, 2017). Santhoshkumar and Rabinson (2018) presented a new proposed method to solve fully fuzzy transportation problem using least allocation method. Purushothkumar et al. (2018) developed fuzzy zero suffix algorithm to solve fully fuzzy transportation problems. Kaur et al. (2020) gave fuzzy transportation and transshipment problems. Mhaske and Bondar (2020) solved FTP by using different FNs with Lagrange's polynomial to approximate fuzzy cost for nonagon and hendecagon. From the literature survey discussed in this paragraph, we can understand that good amount of researchers have solved TP with uncertain parameters.

Historical Background of IFS and IFSTP

The extension of the FSTP is called IFSTP. FSTP means fuzzy solid transportation problem. In IFSTP, the parameters are considered to be intuitionistic fuzzy numbers (IFNs) whereas in FTP, the parameters are considered to be fuzzy numbers (FNs). If the STP has the parameters in uncertainty and hesitation then it is called IFSTP. Atanassov (1983) introduced the IFS theory to solve STP with uncertain and hesitation parameters. Many researchers have solved optimization problems by using uncertain and hesitation parameters, some of them are mentioned within the following brackets (e.g. He et al., 2014; Kumar, 2019a, b, 2020b; Chhibber, et al., 2021; Traneva & Tranev, 2021; Das et al., 2021).

The concepts of IFTP and IFLPP present a great interest for professors, research scholars, practitioners, etc. As a result, these issues have been well discussed in the extant literature. Some of the important literature on the subject are given within the following bracket (Hussain & Kumar, 2012a,b,c, 2013; Kumar & Hussain, 2014a, 2015, 2016a; Jana, 2016; Aggarwal & Gupta, 2016, 2017; Malhotra & Bharati, 2016; Bharati & Malhotra, 2017; Kour, Mukherjee, & Basu, 2017; Das, Bera, & Maiti, 2017; Kumar, 2015; Gupta & Anupum, 2017; and Kumar, 2018a,b,c,d,e). Mishra and Kumar (2020) presented JMD method for transforming an unbalanced fully intuitionistic fuzzy transportation problem (UBFIFTP) into a balanced fully intuitionistic fuzzy transportation problem (BFIFTP). Kaur et al. (2020) developed new methods for solving fully fuzzy solid transportation problems with LR fuzzy parameters. Recently, Rani (2022) studied multi-objective multi-item 4-dimensional green TP in an interval-valued intuitionistic fuzzy environment. From the literature review, we see that the solution procedure for solving IFTP has been given by several authors but we need its extension, i.e., the solution procedure for solving IFSTP. Due to this, this book chapter discusses the steps for solving IFSTP in the name of the PSK method.

LITERATURE REVIEW

Allocation problems involve the distribution of available resources among competing alternatives in order to maximize total return or minimize total costs. The TP and AP are all called the allocation problems. These are all most important problems in management science. Allocation problem is also called optimization problem. Because, in an optimization problem, our objective is to minimize/maximize the objective function subject to given constraints and non-negative restrictions. That is, in this issue, our aim is to find out the optimal value and optimum solution subject to the given set of conditions (or constraints). Similarly, the objective of the allocation problem is to assign the available resources in an economic way. That is, in this issue, we need to find out the allocation of resources which optimizes (either maximize the profit/minimize the cost) our objective function subject to the given set of conditions. Clearly, the objective of TP and AP are all same. Due to this, allocation problem sometimes is also called an optimization problem.

In short, both the TP and AP can be defined as follows.

TP-the problem that related to assignment of available sources to the limited destinations is called TP. AP-the problem that related to assignment of jobs to machines on a one-to-one basis is called AP.

The AP is basically the combinatorial optimization problem. It is a special case of TP. We know that, every AP and TP can be written as LPP. So, AP refers to another special class of LPP. The major difference between AP and TP is to considered the sources are assignees (or agents) and the destinations are tasks. Further, in TP, the quantity of every supply of source and the quantity of every demand of destinations are all taken as exactly 1. That is, the objective of this problem is to find out the allocation of sources to destination which minimizes total cost/maximizes the total profit subject to the allocation of sources on 1-to-1 basis. In IFTP, if we consider the above assumption then we can write every IFTP into IFAP. Similarly, we can write every IFSTP into IFSAP. In the literature, some of the research papers are available for solving IFAP and IFSTP (Kumar & Hussain, 2014b,c,d, 2016b,c; Kumar, 2020a, b, c, d, 2021).

In 1965, Zadeh introduced the degree of membership (or truth (T)) and he defined the fuzzy set. In 1983, Atanassov introduced the degree of non-membership (or falsehood (F)) and he defined the IFS. In 1995, Smarandache introduced the degree of indeterminacy (or neutrality (I)) and he defined the neutrosophic set on 3 components. Neutrosophic set is a generalization of classical, fuzzy, and IFS. Smarandache (1998) published his first article in the name of Neutrosophy/Neutrosophic probability, set, and logic with 3 components, it is known as neutrosophic sets (NSs).

In short, Truth, Indeterminacy, Falsehood can be written as T, I, F, where T, I, F $\subset$ [0, 1]. Particularly, T, I, F may be intervals, hesitant sets, or single-values. So, neutrosophic set deals with (T, I, F). In 1995, NSs proposed by Smarandache which is a generalization of fuzzy sets and IFS, is a powerful tool to deal with incomplete, indeterminate and inconsistent information which exist in the real world. So, intuitionistic fuzzy optimization and neutrosophic optimization both are the trendy areas in applied mathematics. There are several methods that have been proposed in the literature for solving optimization problems with IFSs and neutrosophic sets, from which the following are highlighted:

- Neutrosophic number linear programming method (Ye, 2017).
- Optimisation by dual simplex approach in neutrosophic environment (Mahapatra & Bera, 2019).
- A neutrosophic solid transportation model with insufficient supply (Paul, Sarma, & Bera, 2019).
- A solution for the neutrosophic linear programming problem with a new ranking function (Darehmiraki, 2020).
- Neutrosophic linear programming problem and its application to real life (Bera & Mahapatra, 2020).
- Transportation problem in neutrosophic environment (Pratihar, Kumar, Dey & Broumi, 2020).
- Linear programming method (Kumar, 2018b).
- Integer programming approach (Kumar, 2019a).
- Software-based approach (Kumar, 2021, 2023a).
- Theoretical solution method (Kumar, 2020a).
- PSK method (Kumar, 2022, 2023b).

In this book chapter, PSK method for solving the IFTP is modified to solve the IFSTP of type-2. In addition, the optimum (maximum/minimum) objective value of the IFSTP is obtained in terms of TIFN. The optimum solution of IFSTP is obtained in terms of crisp number or IFN or mixture of all. Since the solution of IFSTP is depending on its category. The well defined TIFN ranking procedure was proposed by Varghese and Kuriakose, is used to change the IFSTP into a crisp one so that the traditional method can be applied to solve the STP. The proposed method is concentrate more on occupied cells but it is concentrate less on unoccupied cells. The occupied cells of crisp solid transportation problem (CSTP) that we obtained are all identical for the occupied cells of IFSTP. Yet, the value of occupied cells of IFSTP is differ from the value of occupied cells of CSTP, which are all depending on the maximum possible value of the supply, demand and conveyance capacities of the relevant problem. It is the key for developing the PSK method. From the discussed ideas in this paragraph, the solution approach is differs from STP to IFSTP in allocation step only. Hence, the PSK method for IFTP can be modified to solve the IFSTP. This modified method is called PSK method in IFSTP. In this book chapter, the author has proved many theorems, specially, the statement 'any solution obtained by the PSK method to an IFSTP with equality constraints is an optimal' has been proved by the author.

Finding the solution of STP by using TIFN is new in intuitionistic fuzzy operations research. The computationally simple and efficient method is presented in this chapter. A significant number of numerical illustrations have been given to show the efficiency of the presented method. The numerical illustrations, software solutions and graphs are given to illustrate the proposed model. The solution of the proposed method can be checked not only a basic linear program solver but also the modern linear program solver. To solve the IFSTP, its equivalent CSTP is formulated and both are solved either by the proposed method or by software mentioned. Real life issues are discussed and which are solved by both the proposed method and software approaches. To prove the strength of this book chapter, the real-life examples are presented. It increases both the quality and quantity of this book chapter. Many of the results and discussions are all given. In this chapter, due to solving the real life issues, there is no doubt; it is very useful to the practitioners, variety of research scholars, PhD students, professors and public. Therefore, it will take more attention to attract the various kinds of researchers in upcoming years. Those who are using the proposed method in this chapter will get the following benefits.

1.   They need not to find out the basic feasible solution.
2.   They need not to check the optimality condition to get the optimal solution at the time of calculation.
3.   They need not to use the intuitionistic fuzzy modified distribution method.
4.   They will achieve the optimal solution with less number of steps. Since this is a single stage method.

In section 4, some key definitions related to IFS, IFN, TIFN and arithmetic operations on TIFN are presented. In section 5, formulae for centroid/ranking of TIFN with some useful definitions are given. Proposed mathematical models and some important definitions are all presented in section 6. Section 7 presents PSK method clearly with the proof of some theorems and corollary. To illustrate the proposed models, the numerical experiments and its related graphs are provided by section 8. In section 9, a conclusion is presented with some perspectives for the new method. Finally, in section 10, the future research areas are suggested.

PRELIMINARIES

This section presents some key terms with definitions which is relevant to the basic ideas of the proposed chapter.

Intuitionistic Fuzzy Set

Let X be a universe of discourse/finite universal set. An IFS A ($A \subset X$) is an object having the form $A = \{x, \mu_A(x), \vartheta_A(x) | x \in X\}$. Let $\mu_A(x) = (\mu_A)_x : X \to [0,1]$ and $\vartheta_A(x) = (\vartheta_A)_x : X \to [0,1]$ denote the degree of membership and degree of non – membership of the element x and are defined for every element $x \in X$ to the set A (which is a subset of X), $0 \le (\mu_A)_x + (\vartheta_A)_x \le 1$.

Moreover, we can write $\pi_A(x) = (\pi_A)_x = 1 - ((\mu_A)_x + (\vartheta_A)_x)$. It is called the IFS index or hesitation margin of x in A.

$(\pi_A)x$ is the degree of indeterminacy of $x \in X$ to the IFS A and $(\pi_A)x \in [0,1]$ i.e., $(\pi_A)=(\pi_A)x$: $X \rightarrow [0,1]$ and $0 \le (\pi_A)x \le 1$ for every $x \in X$.

$(\pi_A)x$ expresses the lack of knowledge of whether x belongs to IFS A or not.

For example, let A be an IFS with $(\mu_A)x=0.4$ and

$$\left(\vartheta_A \right)_x = 0.5 \Rightarrow (\pi_A)_x = 1 - \left(0.4 + 0.5 \right) = 0.1.$$

It can be interpreted as "the degree that the object x belongs to IFS A is 0.4, the degree that the object x does not belongs to IFS A is 0.5 and the degree of hesitancy is 0.1".

Intuitionistic Fuzzy Number

An intuitionistic fuzzy subset $A = \{x, \mu_A\left(x\right), \vartheta_A\left(x\right) \mid x \in X\}$ of the real line R is said to be an IFN if the following holds:

1. $\exists m \in R$, $\mu_A(m) = 1$ and $\vartheta_A(m) = 0$, (m denotes the mean value of A).
2. $\mu_A(x)$ is a continuous mapping from R to the closed interval [0,1], $\forall x \in R$ (i.e., $\mu_A(x)$: $R \rightarrow [0,1]$, $\forall x \in R$), the relation $0 \le \mu_A + \vartheta_A \le 1$ holds.

Then, $\mu_A(x)$ and $\vartheta_A(x)$ of A is of the following form:

$$\mu_A\left(x\right) = \begin{cases} f_1\left(x\right), & x \in \left[m-\alpha, m\right] \\ h_1\left(x\right), & x \in \left[m, m+\beta\right] \\ 0, & -\infty < x \le m-\alpha \\ 0, & m+\beta \le x < \infty \\ 1, & x = m \end{cases}$$

Where

$f_1(x)$- strictly increasing function in $[m-\alpha, m]$.
$h_1(x)$- strictly decreasing function in $[m, n+\beta]$.

$$\vartheta_A\left(x\right) = \begin{cases} f_2\left(x\right), & x \in \left[m-\alpha', m\right]; \ 0 \le f_1\left(x\right) + f_2\left(x\right) \le 1 \\ h_2\left(x\right), & x \in \left[m, m+\beta'\right]; \ 0 \le h_1\left(x\right) + h_2\left(x\right) \le 1 \\ 1, & -\infty < x \le m-\alpha' \\ 1, & m+\beta' \le x < \infty \\ 0, & x = m \end{cases}$$

Where

m - mean value of A.

α - left spread of $\mu_A(x)$.

β - right spread of $\mu_A(x)$.

α' - left spread of $\vartheta_A(x)$.

β' - right spread of $\vartheta_A(x)$.

Symbolically, the IFN $\tilde{A}^I$ is represented as $A_{\text{IFN}} = (m; \alpha, \beta; \alpha', \beta')$.

Triangular Intuitionistic Fuzzy Number

A TIFN $\tilde{A}^I$ is an IFS in R with the following membership function ($\mu_A(x)$) and non-membership function ($\vartheta_A(x)$):

$$\mu_A(x) = \begin{cases} \dfrac{x - a_1}{a_2 - a_1}, & a_1 \leq x \leq a_2 \\[2mm] \dfrac{a_3 - x}{a_3 - a_2}, & a_2 \leq x \leq a_3 \\[2mm] 0, & x < a_1 \\ 0, & x > a_3 \\ 1, & x = a_2 \end{cases}$$

$$\vartheta_A(x) = \begin{cases} \dfrac{a_2 - x}{a_2 - a_1'}, & a_1' \leq x \leq a_2 \\[2mm] \dfrac{x - a_2}{a_3' - a_2}, & a_2 \leq x \leq a_3' \\[2mm] 1, & x < a_1' \\ 1, & x > a_3' \\ 0, & x = a_2 \end{cases}$$

where $a_1' \leq a_1 \leq a_2 \leq a_3 \leq a_3'$ and $\vartheta_A(x), \mu_A(x) \leq 0.5$ for $\vartheta_A(x) = \mu_A(x)$, $\forall x \in R$. This TIFN is denoted by $\tilde{A}^I = \left(a_1, a_2, a_3; a_1', a_2, a_3'\right)$.

Arithmetic Operations on TIFN

Several researchers (Mahapatra & Roy, 2009, 2013; Kumar & Hussain, 2016a; Al-Qudaimi et al., 2021) have proposed some arithmetic operations on TIFN.

Let $\tilde{A}^I = \left(a_1, a_2, a_3; a_1^{'}, a_2^{'}, a_3^{'}\right)$ and $\tilde{B}^I = \left(b_1, b_2, b_3; b_1^{'}, b_2^{'}, b_3^{'}\right)$ be any two different TIFNs then the arithmetic operations as follows:

1. $\tilde{A}^I \oplus \tilde{B}^I = \left(a_1 + b_1, a_2 + b_2, a_3 + b_3; a_1^{'} + b_1^{'}, a_2 + b_2, a_3^{'} + b_3^{'}\right)$

2. $\tilde{A}^I \ominus \tilde{B}^I = \left(a_1 - b_3, a_2 - b_2, a_3 - b_1; a_1^{'} - b_3^{'}, a_2 - b_2, a_3^{'} - b_1^{'}\right)$

3. $\tilde{A}^I \otimes \tilde{B}^I = \left(a_1\Re\left(\tilde{B}^I\right), a_2\Re\left(\tilde{B}^I\right), a_3\Re\left(\tilde{B}^I\right); a_1^{'}\Re\left(\tilde{B}^I\right), a_2\Re\left(\tilde{B}^I\right), a_3^{'}\Re\left(\tilde{B}^I\right)\right)$

    if $\Re\left(\tilde{A}^I\right), \Re\left(\tilde{B}^I\right) \geq 0$

4. $\rho\tilde{A}^I = \left(\rho a_1, \rho a_2, \rho a_3; \rho a_1^{'}, \rho a_2, \rho a_3^{'}\right)$, for $\rho \geq 0$

    $\rho\tilde{A}^I = \left(\rho a_3, \rho a_2, \rho a_1; \rho a_3^{'}, \rho a_2, \rho a_1^{'}\right)$, for $\rho < 0$

FORMULA FOR CENTROID/RANKING OF TIFN WITH SOME USEFUL DEFINITIONS

Finding the ranking of IFNs plays a vital role in intuitionistic fuzzy operations research problems. The definition of IFN was proposed by Burillo et al. (1994). After to development of the concept of IFN, the study of its properties was focused by several authors. Some of the most recent literature related to this topic is given within this bracket (Burillo, Bustince, & Mohedano, 1994; Grzegorzewski, 2003; Mitchell, 2004; Ban, 2008; Nayagam, Lakshmana, Venkateshwari, & Sivaraman, 2008; Li, Nan, & Zhang, 2010; Das & Guha, 2013; Kumar & Kaur, 2013; Wei & Tang, 2013; Peng & Chen, 2013; Qiang et al., 2020; Amutha & Uthra, 2021; Fahrudin & Nuraini, 2021). The most effective ranking formula consisting of both the membership and non-membership values were proposed by Varghese and Kuriakose (2012).

Definition Let $\tilde{A}^I = \left(a_1, a_2, a_3; a_1^{'}, a_2, a_3^{'}\right)$ and $\tilde{B}^I = \left(b_1, b_2, b_3; b_1^{'}, b_2, b_3^{'}\right)$ be two TIFNs. Then the set of TIFNs is defined as follows:

1. $\left(\tilde{A}^I\right)$ greater than $\left(\tilde{B}^I\right)$ if and only if $\tilde{A}^I \succ \tilde{B}^I$

2. $\left(\tilde{A}^I\right)$ less than $\left(\tilde{B}^I\right)$ if and only if $\tilde{A}^I \prec \tilde{B}^I$

3. $\left(\tilde{A}^I\right)$ equals $\left(\tilde{B}^I\right)$ if and only if $\tilde{A}^I \approx \tilde{B}^I$

where:

$$\left(\tilde{A}^{'}\right) = \frac{1}{3}\left[\frac{\left(a_3^{'} - a_1^{'}\right)\left(a_2 - 2a_3^{'} - 2a_1^{'}\right) + \left(a_3 - a_1\right)\left(a_1 + a_2 + a_3\right) + 3\left(a_3^{'2} - a_1^{'2}\right)}{a_3^{'} - a_1^{'} + a_3 - a_1}\right]$$

$$\left(\tilde{B}^I\right) = \frac{1}{3}\left[\frac{\left(b_3' - b_1'\right)\left(b_2 - 2b_3' - 2b_1'\right) + \left(b_3 - b_1\right)\left(b_1 + b_2 + b_3\right) + 3\left(b_3'^2 - b_1'^2\right)}{b_3' - b_1' + b_3 - b_1}\right]$$

Whenever the above formula doesn't provide finite value then we can make use of the following formulae.

1. The score function for the membership function $\mu_A(x)$ is denoted by $S(\mu_A(x))$ and is defined by
    $$S\left(\mu_A\left(x\right)\right) = \frac{a_1 + 2a_2 + a_3}{4}.$$

2. The score function for the non-membership function $\vartheta_A(x)$ is denoted by $S(\vartheta_A(x))$ and is defined by
    $$S\left(\vartheta_A\left(x\right)\right) = \frac{a_1' + 2a_2 + a_3'}{4}.$$

3. The accuracy function of $\tilde{A}^I$ is denoted by $f\left(\tilde{A}^I\right)$ and is defined by

$$f\left(\tilde{A}^I\right) = \frac{S\left(\mu_A\left(x\right)\right) + S\left(\vartheta_A\left(x\right)\right)}{2} = \frac{\left(a_1 + 2a_2 + a_3\right) + \left(a_1' + 2a_2 + a_3'\right)}{8}$$

From the accuracy function, we have

1. $f\left(\tilde{A}^I\right)$ greater than $f\left(\tilde{B}^I\right)$ if and only if $\tilde{A}^I \succ \tilde{B}^I$

2. $f\left(\tilde{A}^I\right)$ less than $f\left(\tilde{B}^I\right)$ if and only if $\tilde{A}^I \prec \tilde{B}^I$

3. $f\left(\tilde{A}^I\right)$ equals $f\left(\tilde{B}^I\right)$ if and only if $\tilde{A}^I \approx \tilde{B}^I$

Definition The ordering principle (i.e., $\succeq$ and $\preceq$) between any two TIFNs $\tilde{A}^I$ and $\tilde{B}^I$ are defined as follows:

1. $\tilde{A}^I \succeq \tilde{B}^I \Leftrightarrow \tilde{A}^I \succ \tilde{B}^I$ or $\tilde{A}^I \approx \tilde{B}^I$

2. $\tilde{A}^I \preceq \tilde{B}^I \Leftrightarrow \tilde{A}^I \prec \tilde{B}^I$ or $\tilde{A}^I \approx \tilde{B}^I$

Definition Let $\{\tilde{A}_i^I, \ i=1,2,\ldots,n\}$ be a set of TIFNs. If $\Re\left(\tilde{A}_k^I\right) \leq \Re\left(\tilde{A}_i^I\right)$ $\forall i$, then the TIFN $\tilde{A}_k^I$ is the minimum of $\{\tilde{A}_i^I, \ i=1,2,\ldots,n\}$. For opposite, if $\Re\left(\tilde{A}_t^I\right) \geq \Re\left(\tilde{A}_i^I\right)$ $\forall i$, then the TIFN $\tilde{A}_t^I$ is the maximum of $\{\tilde{A}_i^I, \ i=1,2,\ldots,n\}$.

MATHEMATICAL MODEL WITH SOME IMPORTANT DEFINITIONS

First of all, this section classifies the different types of IFSTP and defines the technical terms which are used in this chapter. Next, it presents mathematical model of FIFSTP and its relevant CSTP with the tabular representation of both of them, it followed by type II- IFSTP and its relevant CSTP are defined and are presented in the end of this section.

1. If at least one of the parameters in STP is an IFN then the problem is called IFSTP. Otherwise, it is called a non-IFSTP. Moreover, IFSTP can be divided into 4 categories, which are:
   i.   Type I- IFSTP.
   ii. Type II- IFSTP.
   iii. MIFSTP/Type III- IFSTP.
   iv. FIFSTP/Type IV- IFSTP.
2. If the parameters are all IFN except cost in IFSTP then the problem is called Type I- IFSTP.
3. If the cost only is IFN and the remaining are all crisp numbers in IFSTP then the problem is called Type II- IFSTP.
4. If the STP has a mixture of crisp, fuzzy and intuitionistic fuzzy parameters then the problem is called MIFSTP/Type III- IFSTP.
5. If the parameters in IFSTP are all IFNs, especially if they are all the same type of IFNs, then the problem is called FIFSTP/Type IV- IFSTP.
6. If supply, demand and conveyance capacity are all equal in IFSTP then the problem is called BIFSTP. Mathematically, this statement can be written for $m \times n \times l$ IFSTP as follows.

$$\tilde{a}_1^I + \tilde{a}_2^I + \ldots + \tilde{a}_m^I = \tilde{b}_1^I + \tilde{b}_2^I + \ldots + \tilde{b}_n^I = \tilde{e}_1^I + \tilde{e}_2^I + \ldots + \tilde{e}_l^I$$

7. If supply, demand and conveyance capacity are all not equal in IFSTP then the problem is called UBIFSTP. Symbolically, the unbalanced condition for $m \times n \times l$ IFSTP can be written as follows.

$$\tilde{a}_1^I + \tilde{a}_2^I + \ldots + \tilde{a}_m^I \neq \tilde{b}_1^I + \tilde{b}_2^I + \ldots + \tilde{b}_n^I \neq \tilde{e}_1^I + \tilde{e}_2^I + \ldots + \tilde{e}_l^I$$

8. Any solution $\{\tilde{y}_{ijk}^I > \tilde{0}^I$, $i=1,2,\ldots,m$; $j=1,2,\ldots,n$ and $k=1,2,\ldots,l\}$ to the IFSTP is said to be intuitionistic fuzzy feasible solution (IFFS) if it satisfies supply, demand and capacity constraints.
9. Intuitionistic fuzzy basic feasible solution (IFBFS) is basically a feasible solution in $m \times n \times l$ IFSTP and it has at most $(m+n+l-2)$ non-negative allocations.
10. The solution of $m \times n \times l$ IFSTP is said to be degenerate if it has less than that of $(m+n+l-2)$ non-negative allocations in its IFBFS.
11. The IFBFS of an $m \times n \times l$ IFSTP is said to be non-degenerate if it contains exactly $(m+n+l-2)$ non-negative allocations/occupied cells.
12. If any IFBFS of an IFSTP is maximizes or minimizes the total objective value of the same IFSTP then it is called an optimal solution.

The Model for FIFSTP

Consider the $m \times n \times l$ STP where m-number of origins, n- number of destinations and l- number of conveyances. In this STP, we assume the following:

1. $\tilde{c}_{ijk}^{I} = \left(c_{ijk}^{1}, c_{ijk}^{2}, c_{ijk}^{3}; c_{ijk}^{1'}, c_{ijk}^{2}, c_{ijk}^{3'} \right)$ - the unit cost (in IFN) of transporting one unit of the commodity from i^{th} origin to j^{th} destination by means of kth conveyance.

2. $\tilde{a}_{i}^{I} = \left(a_{i}^{1}, a_{i}^{2}, a_{i}^{3}; a_{i}^{1'}, a_{i}^{2}, a_{i}^{3'} \right)$ - the amount of commodity (in IFN) available at origin i.

3. $\tilde{b}_{j}^{I} = \left(b_{j}^{1}, b_{j}^{2}, b_{j}^{3}; b_{j}^{1'}, b_{j}^{2}, b_{j}^{3'} \right)$ - the amount of commodity (in IFN) needed at destination j.

4. $\tilde{e}_{k}^{I} = \left(e_{k}^{1}, e_{k}^{2}, e_{k}^{3}; e_{k}^{1'}, e_{k}^{2}, e_{k}^{3'} \right)$ - the amount of commodity (in IFN) transported by k^{th} conveyance.

5. $\tilde{y}_{ijk}^{I} = \left(y_{ijk}^{1}, y_{ijk}^{2}, y_{ijk}^{3}; y_{ijk}^{1'}, y_{ijk}^{2}, y_{ijk}^{3'} \right)$ - the number of units of commodity (in IFN) transported from i^{th} origin to j^{th} destination by means of kth conveyance.

Our aim is to minimize the total intuitionistic fuzzy transportation cost (TIFTC) satisfying the above limits (i.e., $\tilde{a}_{i}^{I}, \tilde{b}_{j}^{I}$ and $\tilde{e}_{k}^{I}$).

The mathematical model of FIFSTP can be defined as follows.

(IFSTP) Min $\tilde{Z}^{I} = \sum_{i=1}^{m} \sum_{j=1}^{n} \sum_{k=1}^{l} \left(\tilde{c}_{ijk}^{I} \right) \otimes \left(\tilde{y}_{ijk}^{I} \right)$ (Say problem R)

$$s.t. \begin{cases} \sum_{j=1}^{n} \sum_{k=1}^{l} \left(y_{ijk}^{1}, y_{ijk}^{2}, y_{ijk}^{3}; y_{ijk}^{1'}, y_{ijk}^{2}, y_{ijk}^{3'} \right) \approx \left(a_{i}^{1}, a_{i}^{2}, a_{i}^{3}; a_{i}^{1'}, a_{i}^{2}, a_{i}^{3'} \right), \quad i = 1, 2, \ldots, m & (1) \\ \sum_{i=1}^{m} \sum_{k=1}^{l} \left(y_{ijk}^{1}, y_{ijk}^{2}, y_{ijk}^{3}; y_{ijk}^{1'}, y_{ijk}^{2}, y_{ijk}^{3'} \right) \approx \left(b_{j}^{1}, b_{j}^{2}, b_{j}^{3}; b_{j}^{1'}, b_{j}^{2}, b_{j}^{3'} \right), \quad j = 1, 2, \ldots, n & (2) \\ \sum_{i=1}^{m} \sum_{j=1}^{n} \left(y_{ijk}^{1}, y_{ijk}^{2}, y_{ijk}^{3}; y_{ijk}^{1'}, y_{ijk}^{2}, y_{ijk}^{3'} \right) \approx \left(e_{k}^{1}, e_{k}^{2}, e_{k}^{3}; e_{k}^{1'}, e_{k}^{2}, e_{k}^{3'} \right), \quad k = 1, 2, \ldots, l & (3) \\ \left(y_{ijk}^{1}, y_{ijk}^{2}, y_{ijk}^{3}; y_{ijk}^{1'}, y_{ijk}^{2}, y_{ijk}^{3'} \right) \succeq \tilde{0}^{I}, \quad i = 1, 2, \ldots, m; j = 1, 2, \ldots, n \text{ and } k = 1, 2, \ldots, l & (4) \end{cases}$$

Note: m - number of supply points; n - number of demand points and l - number of conveyances.

If $\tilde{a}_{i}^{I}$ or $\tilde{b}_{j}^{I}$ or $\tilde{c}_{ijk}^{I}$ or $\tilde{e}_{k}^{I}$ is/are all in IFN(s) then the minimum total cost becomes an IFN. Generally, it can be noted as $\tilde{Z}^{I}$. Further,

$$\tilde{Z}^{I} = \sum_{i=1}^{m} \sum_{j=1}^{n} \sum_{k=1}^{l} \tilde{c}_{ijk}^{I} \otimes \tilde{y}_{ijk}^{I}.$$

It can't be minimized directly. Since both the decision variables and its coefficients are in IFNs in the objective function. So, for solving the problem we convert $\tilde{a}_{i}^{I}, \tilde{b}_{j}^{I}, \tilde{c}_{ijk}^{I}$ and $\tilde{e}_{k}^{I}$ into a_{i}, b_{j}, c_{ijk} and e_{k} (i.e., crisp numbers) by using the ranking method (Varghese and Kuriakose).

The Relevant Crisp Model for FIFSTP (i.e., CSTP)

Consider the $m \times n \times l$ STP where m-number of origins, n- number of destinations and l- number of conveyances. In this STP, we assume the following:

1. c_{ijk}- the unit cost (in crisp number) of transporting one unit of the commodity from i^{th} origin to j^{th} destination by means of kth conveyance.
2. a_i- the amount of commodity (in crisp number) available at origin i.
3. b_j- the amount of commodity (in crisp number) needed at destination j.
4. e_k- the amount of commodity (in crisp number) transported by k^{th} conveyance.
5. y_{ijk}- the number of units of commodity (in crisp number) transported from i^{th} origin to j^{th} destination by means of kth conveyance.

Our objective is to minimize the total transportation cost (TTC) satisfying the above limits (i.e., a_i, b_j and e_k).

The equivalent crisp model of FIFSTP can be defined as follows.

$$(P^*) \text{ Min } \Re(\tilde{Z}^{I*}) = \sum_{i=1}^{m} \sum_{j=1}^{n} \sum_{k=1}^{l} \Re\left(\tilde{c}_{ijk}^{I}\right) \otimes \left(\tilde{y}_{ijk}^{I}\right)$$

$$s.t. \begin{cases} \sum_{j=1}^{n} \sum_{k=1}^{l} \Re\left(\tilde{y}_{ijk}^{I}\right) \approx \Re\left(\tilde{a}_i^{I}\right), \quad i = 1, 2, \ldots, m & (5) \\ \sum_{i=1}^{m} \sum_{k=1}^{l} \Re\left(\tilde{y}_{ijk}^{I}\right) \approx \Re\left(\tilde{b}_j^{I}\right), \quad j = 1, 2, \ldots, n & (6) \\ \sum_{i=1}^{m} \sum_{j=1}^{n} \Re\left(\tilde{y}_{ijk}^{I}\right) \approx \Re\left(\tilde{e}_k^{I}\right), \quad k = 1, 2, \ldots, l & (7) \\ \Re\left(\tilde{y}_{ijk}^{I}\right) \succeq \Re\left(\tilde{0}^{I}\right), \quad i = 1, 2, \ldots, m; \, j = 1, 2, \ldots, n \text{ and } k = 1, 2, \ldots, l & (8) \end{cases}$$

$\because \Re\left(\tilde{e}_k^{I}\right), \Re\left(\tilde{a}_i^{I}\right), \Re\left(\tilde{b}_j^{I}\right)$ and $\Re\left(\tilde{c}_{ijk}^{I}\right)$ all are crisp values, this problem 'P*' is obviously the CSTP of the form R/P## which can be solved by anyone/all of the following traditional methods, namely:

*   Modified Distribution Method
    or/and
*   Min Zero- Min Cost method

Once the optimum solution y^* of Model 'P*' is found, the optimum intuitionistic fuzzy objective value $\tilde{Z}^{I*}$ of the original problem can be calculated as:

$$\tilde{Z}^{I*} = \sum_{i=1}^{m} \sum_{j=1}^{n} \sum_{k=1}^{l} \left(\tilde{c}_{ijk}^{I}\right) \otimes \left(\tilde{y}_{ijk}^{I*}\right)$$

Where:

$$\tilde{c}_{ijk}^{I} = \left(c_{ijk}^{1}, c_{ijk}^{2}, c_{ijk}^{3}; c_{ijk}^{1'}, c_{ijk}^{2}, c_{ijk}^{3'} \right); \; \tilde{y}_{ijk}^{I} = \left(y_{ijk}^{1}, y_{ijk}^{2}, y_{ijk}^{3}; y_{ijk}^{1'}, y_{ijk}^{2}, y_{ijk}^{3'} \right).$$

If the number of sources (m), the number of destinations (n), and the number of conveyances (l) are all equal to 3 (i.e., $m=n=l=3$), then the above FIFSTP and its relevant CSTP may both be written in tabular form, which is as follows (See Table 1 and Table 2):

Table 1. Tabular representation of 3×3×3 FIFSTP

										Capacity $\tilde{e}_k^I$
Conveyances $\rightarrow$ $\downarrow$	E1			E1			E1			$\tilde{e}_1^I$
		E2			E2			E2		$\tilde{e}_2^I$
			E3			E3			E3	$\tilde{e}_3^I$
Destinations $\rightarrow$ **Origins** $\downarrow$	D1			D2			D3			Supply $\tilde{a}_i^I$
O1	$\tilde{c}_{111}^I$	$\tilde{c}_{112}^I$	$\tilde{c}_{113}^I$	$\tilde{c}_{121}^I$	$\tilde{c}_{122}^I$	$\tilde{c}_{123}^I$	$\tilde{c}_{131}^I$	$\tilde{c}_{132}^I$	$\tilde{c}_{133}^I$	$\tilde{a}_1^I$
O2	$\tilde{c}_{211}^I$	$\tilde{c}_{212}^I$	$\tilde{c}_{213}^I$	$\tilde{c}_{221}^I$	$\tilde{c}_{222}^I$	$\tilde{c}_{223}^I$	$\tilde{c}_{231}^I$	$\tilde{c}_{232}^I$	$\tilde{c}_{233}^I$	$\tilde{a}_2^I$
O3	$\tilde{c}_{311}^I$	$\tilde{c}_{312}^I$	$\tilde{c}_{313}^I$	$\tilde{c}_{321}^I$	$\tilde{c}_{322}^I$	$\tilde{c}_{323}^I$	$\tilde{c}_{331}^I$	$\tilde{c}_{332}^I$	$\tilde{c}_{333}^I$	$\tilde{a}_3^I$
Demand $\tilde{b}_j^I$	$\tilde{b}_1^I$			$\tilde{b}_2^I$			$\tilde{b}_3^I$			

The Models for Type II- IFSTP and its Relevant CSTP

The model of type II- IFSTP can be defined precisely as follows.

Model P# or type II- IFSTP:

$$\text{Min } \tilde{Z}^I = \sum_{i=1}^{m} \sum_{j=1}^{n} \sum_{k=1}^{l} \tilde{c}_{ijk}^I \otimes y_{ijk} \tag{9}$$

$$s.t. \begin{cases} \sum_{j=1}^{n} \sum_{k=1}^{l} y_{ijk} = a_i, \quad i=1,2,\ldots,m & (10) \\[2mm] \sum_{i=1}^{m} \sum_{k=1}^{l} y_{ijk} = b_j, \quad j=1,2,\ldots,n & (11) \\[2mm] \sum_{i=1}^{m} \sum_{j=1}^{n} y_{ijk} = e_k, \quad k=1,2,\ldots,l & (12) \\[2mm] y_{ijk} \geq 0, \quad i=1,2,\ldots,m; j=1,2,\ldots,n \text{ and } k=1,2,\ldots,l & (13) \end{cases}$$

where m - the number of supply points (i.e., $O_1, O_2, \ldots, O_m$); n - the number of demand points (i.e., $D_1, D_2, \ldots, D_n$); l - the number of conveyances (i.e., $E_1, E_2, \ldots, E_l$)

The crisp STP which is relevant and equivalent to type II- IFSTP is given in model P^{###} Model P^{###}:

$$\text{Min } Z = \sum_{i=1}^{m} \sum_{j=1}^{n} \sum_{k=1}^{l} \Re\left(\tilde{c}_{ijk}^{I}\right) \otimes y_{ijk} \approx \sum_{i=1}^{m} \sum_{j=1}^{n} \sum_{k=1}^{l} c_{ijk} \otimes y_{ijk} \tag{14}$$

s.t. eqns. (10) - (13)

Table 2. Tabular representation of crisp 3×3×3 STP

										Capacity
	E1			E1			E1			$\Re\left(\tilde{e}_1^{I}\right)$
		E2			E2			E2		$\Re\left(\tilde{e}_2^{I}\right)$
			E3			E3			E3	$\Re\left(\tilde{e}_3^{I}\right)$
	D1			D2			D3			Supply
O1	$\Re(\tilde{c}_{111}^{I})$	$\Re\left(\tilde{c}_{112}^{I}\right)$	$\Re\left(\tilde{c}_{113}^{I}\right)$	$\Re\left(\tilde{c}_{121}^{I}\right)$	$\Re\left(\tilde{c}_{122}^{I}\right)$	$\Re\left(\tilde{c}_{123}^{I}\right)$	$\Re\left(\tilde{c}_{131}^{I}\right)$	$\Re\left(\tilde{c}_{132}^{I}\right)$	$\Re\left(\tilde{c}_{133}^{I}\right)$	$\Re\left(\tilde{a}_1^{I}\right)$
O2	$\Re\left(\tilde{c}_{211}^{I}\right)$	$\Re\left(\tilde{c}_{212}^{I}\right)$	$\Re\left(\tilde{c}_{213}^{I}\right)$	$\Re\left(\tilde{c}_{221}^{I}\right)$	$\Re\left(\tilde{c}_{222}^{I}\right)$	$\Re\left(\tilde{c}_{223}^{I}\right)$	$\Re\left(\tilde{c}_{231}^{I}\right)$	$\Re\left(\tilde{c}_{232}^{I}\right)$	$\Re\left(\tilde{c}_{233}^{I}\right)$	$\Re\left(\tilde{a}_2^{I}\right)$
O3	$\Re\left(\tilde{c}_{311}^{I}\right)$	$\Re\left(\tilde{c}_{312}^{I}\right)$	$\Re\left(\tilde{c}_{313}^{I}\right)$	$\Re\left(\tilde{c}_{321}^{I}\right)$	$\Re\left(\tilde{c}_{322}^{I}\right)$	$\Re\left(\tilde{c}_{323}^{I}\right)$	$\Re\left(\tilde{c}_{331}^{I}\right)$	$\Re\left(\tilde{c}_{332}^{I}\right)$	$\Re\left(\tilde{c}_{333}^{I}\right)$	$\Re\left(\tilde{a}_3^{I}\right)$
Demand	$\Re\left(\tilde{b}_1^{I}\right)$			$\Re\left(\tilde{b}_2^{I}\right)$			$\Re\left(\tilde{b}_3^{I}\right)$			

PSK METHOD

This section presents PSK method clearly with the proof of some theorems and corollary.

Step 0. First of all, form the IFSTP for the given data. The problem may be type I/type II/type III/type IV- IFSTP which is depending on the data.

Step 1. Check the condition for balanced IFSTP. i.e., to check

$$\tilde{a}_1^I + \tilde{a}_2^I + \ldots + \tilde{a}_m^I = \tilde{b}_1^I + \tilde{b}_2^I + \ldots + \tilde{b}_n^I = \tilde{e}_1^I + \tilde{e}_2^I + \ldots + \tilde{e}_l^I.$$

In case, if it is $m \times n \times l$ type IV- IFSTP and this condition (balanced) is not satisfied then change it, i.e., change it to a balanced one. Then, go to step 2.

Step 2. After successfully applying step 1 of the proposed method, now, transform the Type IV- IFSTP into its equivalent crisp STP by using ranking method. Then, go to step 3.

Step 3. If the crisp STP that we obtained from step 2 of the proposed method is in integer (the value/ amount of the parameters) then kept as it is. Otherwise, rewrite their decimal values into its nearest integer value and then make a new STP. Now, go to step 4.

Step 4. Solve the new STP that we obtained from step 3 of the proposed method with the help of theoretical methods (e.g. Min Zero-Min Cost method and MODI)/software package (e.g. MATLAB, LINGO, etc.). This process will give the optimum objective value and optimum allocation for the new crisp STP. This optimum allotted cell(s) in new crisp solid transportation table are referred as occupied cells. The remaining cells are known as unoccupied cells (i.e., the complement of occupied cells are called unoccupied cells). The occupied cells of new crisp STP are exactly $(m+n+l-2)$ and all have zero cost. FIFSTP have $(m+n+l-2)$ number of occupied cells with the same position of new crisp STP, but the costs of occupied cells of FIFSTP are all intuitionistic fuzzy zeros. So, both the STP and IFSTP have equal number of occupied cells with the same position. Now, we should build a new fully intuitionistic fuzzy solid transportation table (FIFSTT) where the occupied cells costs are intuitionistic fuzzy zeros and the remaining cells costs are its original cost. Now, subtract the minimum cost $(\tilde{u}_i^I, i=1,2,\ldots,m)$ of each origin/source from all the elements of that origin/source. Next, subtract the minimum cost $(\tilde{v}_j^I, i=1,2,\ldots,n)$ of each destination from all the elements of that destination. Finally, subtract the minimum cost $(\tilde{w}_k^I, i=1,2,\ldots,l)$ of each conveyance from all the elements of that conveyance. Now, the resulting table will have atleast one intuitionistic fuzzy zero in each origin, destination and conveyance. This table is known as allotment table.

Step 5. In an allotment table, if an origin/a destination/a conveyance has exactly one occupied cell, that is, if it has exactly one intuitionistic fuzzy zero then allot the maximum possible value (maximum possible value= Min {supply, demand & conveyance}) to that cell and subtract the same value to itself and its relevant supply & demand/ demand & conveyance/ conveyance & supply. If not, if the origins/destinations/conveyances are all have more than one occupied cells then select a cell in the α- origin, β- destination and γ- conveyance of the transportation table whose cost is maximum (ties may occur, i.e., if the maximum cost is more than one then to break the tie, we can select arbitrarily any one of them) and examine which one of the cells having minimum original cost (ties may occur, i.e., if the minimum original cost is more than one then to break the tie, we can select arbitrarily any one of them) among all the occupied cells of its related origin, destination and conveyance then to allot the maximum possible value in that cell. In this way, allot the maximum possible value to the selected origin, destination and conveyance entirely. If the entire origin, destination and conveyance of the occupied cells have fully allotted then select a next maximum cost of the transportation table and examine which one of the cells have minimum original cost among all the occupied cells in that origin, destination and conveyance then to allot the maximum possible value to that cell. Continue the same process until all intuitionistic fuzzy supply points are fully used, all intuitionistic fuzzy demand points are fully received and all conveyance capacities are fully used. This allotment yields the fully intuitionistic fuzzy solution (FIFS) to the given FIFSTP.

Figure 1. Steps for the PSK method

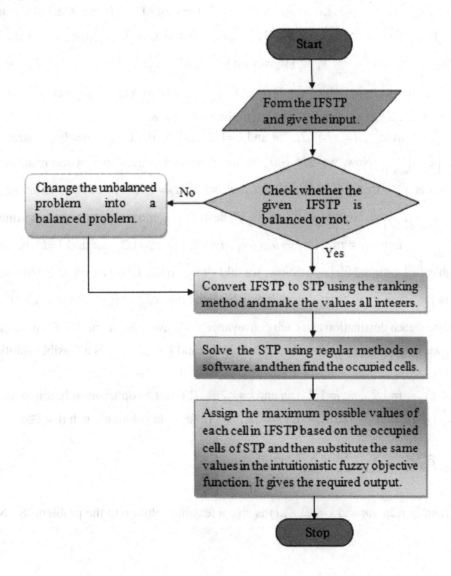

The following diagram presents the steps for the PSK method (see Figure 1).

Next, we are going to prove some theorems and corollary.

Theorem If $\{\tilde{y}_{ijk}^{I^O}$, $i=1,2,\ldots,m$; $j=1,2,\ldots,n$ and $k=1,2,\ldots,l\}$ is an optimum solution to the problem 'S'

(Problem S) Min $\sum_{i=1}^{m}\sum_{j=1}^{n}\sum_{k=1}^{l}\left(\tilde{c}_{ijk}^{I}\ominus\tilde{u}_{i}^{I}\ominus\tilde{v}_{j}^{I}\ominus\tilde{w}_{k}^{I}\right)\tilde{y}_{ijk}^{I}$

s.t. eqns. (1) - (4) &

$\left(\tilde{c}_{ijk}^{I}\ominus\tilde{u}_{i}^{I}\ominus\tilde{v}_{j}^{I}\ominus\tilde{w}_{k}^{I}\right)\succeq 0,\ \ \forall i,j$ and k (15)

where $\tilde{u}_{i}^{I}$ ($\tilde{u}_{i}^{I}=\min\{\tilde{c}_{ijk}^{I}$, $i=i$; $j=1,2,\ldots,n$ and $k=1,2,\ldots,l\}$ the cost of newly constructed transportation table $\left[\tilde{c}_{ijk}^{I}\right]_{m\times n\times l}$), $\tilde{v}_{j}^{I}$ ($\tilde{v}_{j}^{I}=\min\{\tilde{c}_{ijk}^{I}\ominus\tilde{u}_{i}^{I}$, $i=1,2,\ldots,m$; $j=j$; and $k=1,2,\ldots,l\}$ the cost of the resulting transportation table $\left[\tilde{c}_{ijk}^{I}\ominus\tilde{u}_{i}^{I}\right]_{m\times n\times l}$), $\tilde{w}_{k}^{I}$ ($\tilde{w}_{k}^{I}=\min\{\tilde{c}_{ijk}^{I}\ominus\tilde{u}_{i}^{I}\ominus\tilde{v}_{j}^{I}$, $i=1,2,\ldots,m$; $j=1,2,\ldots,n$ and $k=k\}$ the cost of resulting transportation table $\left[\tilde{c}_{ijk}^{I}\ominus\tilde{u}_{i}^{I}\ominus\tilde{v}_{j}^{I}\right]_{m\times n\times l}$), are any real values, then $\{\tilde{y}_{ijk}^{I^O}$, $i=1,2,\ldots,m$; $j=1,2,\ldots,n$ and $k=1,2,\ldots,l\}$ is an optimal solution to the problem 'R'.

Proof: Let $\tilde{u}_{i}^{I}=\min\{\tilde{c}_{ijk}^{I}$, $i=i$; $j=1,2,\ldots,n$ and $k=1,2,\ldots,l\}$ be the cost of newly constructed transportation table $\left[\tilde{c}_{ijk}^{I}\right]_{m\times n\times l}$. Now, we add $\ominus\tilde{u}_{i}^{I}$ to the ith source entries so that the resulting table is $\left[\tilde{c}_{ijk}^{I}\ominus\tilde{u}_{i}^{I}\right]_{m\times n\times l}$. Let $\tilde{v}_{j}^{I}=\min\{\tilde{c}_{ijk}^{I}\ominus\tilde{u}_{i}^{I}$, $i=1,2,\ldots,m$; $j=j$; and $k=1,2,\ldots,l\}$ be the cost of the resulting table $\left[\tilde{c}_{ijk}^{I}\ominus\tilde{u}_{i}^{I}\right]_{m\times n\times l}$. Now, we add $\ominus\tilde{v}_{j}^{I}$ to the jth destination entries so that the resulting table is $\left[\tilde{c}_{ijk}^{I}\ominus\tilde{u}_{i}^{I}\ominus\tilde{v}_{j}^{I}\right]_{m\times n\times l}$. Let $\tilde{w}_{k}^{I}=\min\{\tilde{c}_{ijk}^{I}\ominus\tilde{u}_{i}^{I}\ominus\tilde{v}_{j}^{I}$, $i=1,2,\ldots,m$; $j=1,2,\ldots,n$ and $k=k\}$ be the cost of the resulting table $\left[\tilde{c}_{ijk}^{I}\ominus\tilde{u}_{i}^{I}\ominus\tilde{v}_{j}^{I}\right]_{m\times n\times l}$. Now, we add $\ominus\tilde{w}_{k}^{I}$ to the kth conveyance entries so that the resulting table is $\left[\tilde{c}_{ijk}^{I}\ominus\tilde{u}_{i}^{I}\ominus\tilde{v}_{j}^{I}\ominus\tilde{w}_{k}^{I}\right]_{m\times n\times l}$. It may be noted that $(\tilde{c}_{ijk}^{I}\ominus\tilde{u}_{i}^{I}\ominus\tilde{v}_{j}^{I}\ominus\tilde{w}_{k}^{I})\succeq\tilde{0}^{I}$, $\forall i,j$ and k. Also, each source, each destination and each conveyance will have at least one $\tilde{0}^{I}$. From the statement of the theorem, we know that, $\{\tilde{y}_{ijk}^{I^O}$, $i=1,2,\ldots,m$; $j=1,2,\ldots,n$ and $k=1,2,\ldots,l\}$ is a feasible solution to the problem 'R'.

Suppose that $\{\tilde{y}_{ijk}^{I^O}$, $i=1,2,\ldots,m$; $j=1,2,\ldots,n$ and $k=1,2,\ldots,l\}$ is not an optimum solution to the problem 'R'. Then, $\exists\{x_{ijk}^{I}$, $i=1,2,\ldots,m$; $j=1,2,\ldots,n$ and $k=1,2,\ldots,l\}$ (a feasible solution) such that $(\ni)$

$\sum_{i=1}^{m}\sum_{j=1}^{n}\sum_{k=1}^{l}\tilde{c}_{ijk}^{I}x_{ijk}^{I}<\sum_{i=1}^{m}\sum_{j=1}^{n}\sum_{k=1}^{l}\tilde{c}_{ijk}^{I}\tilde{y}_{ijk}^{I^O}$.

$\Rightarrow\{x_{ijk}^{I}$, $i=1,2,\ldots,m$; $j=1,2,\ldots,n$ and $k=1,2,\ldots,l\}$ is also a feasible solution to the problem 'S'. Now,

$$\sum_{i=1}^{m}\sum_{j=1}^{n}\sum_{k=1}^{l}\left(\tilde{c}_{ijk}^{I}\ominus\tilde{u}_{i}^{I}\ominus\tilde{v}_{j}^{I}\ominus\tilde{w}_{k}^{I}\right)x_{ijk}^{I}\approx\sum_{i=1}^{m}\sum_{j=1}^{n}\sum_{k=1}^{l}\tilde{c}_{ijk}^{I}$$

$$\otimes x_{ijk}^{I}\ominus\sum_{i=1}^{m}\sum_{j=1}^{n}\sum_{k=1}^{l}\tilde{u}_{i}^{I}\otimes x_{ijk}^{I}\ominus\sum_{i=1}^{m}\sum_{j=1}^{n}\sum_{k=1}^{l}\tilde{v}_{j}^{I}\otimes x_{ijk}^{I}$$

$$\ominus\sum_{i=1}^{m}\sum_{j=1}^{n}\sum_{k=1}^{l}\tilde{w}_{k}^{I}\otimes x_{ijk}^{I}<\sum_{i=1}^{m}\sum_{j=1}^{n}\sum_{k=1}^{l}\tilde{c}_{ijk}^{I}\otimes\tilde{y}_{ijk}^{I^{O}}$$

$$\ominus\sum_{i=1}^{m}\sum_{j=1}^{n}\sum_{k=1}^{l}\tilde{u}_{i}^{I}\otimes\tilde{a}_{i}^{I}\ominus\sum_{i=1}^{m}\sum_{j=1}^{n}\sum_{k=1}^{l}\tilde{v}_{j}^{I}\otimes\tilde{b}_{j}^{I}\ominus\sum_{i=1}^{m}\sum_{j=1}^{n}\sum_{k=1}^{l}\tilde{w}_{k}^{I}\otimes\tilde{e}_{k}^{I}$$

(from (1) to (3)).

$$\approx\sum_{i=1}^{m}\sum_{j=1}^{n}\sum_{k=1}^{l}\left(\tilde{c}_{ijk}^{I}\ominus\tilde{u}_{i}^{I}\ominus\tilde{v}_{j}^{I}\ominus\tilde{w}_{k}^{I}\right)\tilde{y}_{ijk}^{I^{O}}$$

(from (1) to (3)).

$$\Rightarrow\sum_{i=1}^{m}\sum_{j=1}^{n}\sum_{k=1}^{l}\left(\tilde{c}_{ijk}^{I}\ominus\tilde{u}_{i}^{I}\ominus\tilde{v}_{j}^{I}\ominus\tilde{w}_{k}^{I}\right)x_{ijk}^{I}\approx\sum_{i=1}^{m}\sum_{j=1}^{n}\sum_{k=1}^{l}\left(\tilde{c}_{ijk}^{I}\ominus\tilde{u}_{i}^{I}\ominus\tilde{v}_{j}^{I}\ominus\tilde{w}_{k}^{I}\right)\tilde{y}_{ijk}^{I^{O}}$$

$\Rightarrow\Leftarrow\{\tilde{y}_{ijk}^{I^{O}}$, $i=1,2,..,m$; $j=1,2,\ldots,n$ and $k=1,2,\ldots,l\}$ is an optimal solution of the problem 'S'.

$\therefore$ we can easily conclude that any optimal solution $\{\tilde{y}_{ijk}^{I^{O}}$, $i=1,2,..,m$; $j=1,2,\ldots,n$ and $k=1,2,\ldots,l\}$ to the problem 'S' is also an intuitionistic fuzzy optimal solution (IFOS) to the problem 'R'. Hence the theorem.

Corollary

If $\{\tilde{y}_{ijk}^{o^{I}}$, $i=1,2,..,m$; $j=1,2,\ldots,n$ and $k=1,2,\ldots,l\}$ is a feasible solution to the problem 'R' and $\left(\tilde{c}_{ijk}^{I}\ominus\tilde{u}_{i}^{I}\ominus\tilde{v}_{j}^{I}\ominus\tilde{w}_{k}^{I}\right)\succeq\tilde{0}^{I}$, $\forall$ i,j and k where $\tilde{u}_{i}^{I},\tilde{v}_{j}^{I}$, and $\tilde{w}_{k}^{I}$ are some real TIFNs,

$$\ni Min\sum_{i=1}^{m}\sum_{j=1}^{n}\sum_{k=1}^{l}\left(\tilde{c}_{ijk}^{I}\ominus\tilde{u}_{i}^{I}\ominus\tilde{v}_{j}^{I}\ominus\tilde{w}_{k}^{I}\right)\tilde{y}_{ijk}^{I}$$

s.t. eqns. (1) - (4) are satisfied, is $\tilde{0}^{I}$, then $\{\tilde{y}_{ijk}^{o^{I}}$, $i=1,2,..,m$; $j=1,2,\ldots,n$ and $k=1,2,\ldots,l\}$ is an IFOS to the problem 'R'.

Proof From the above Theorem, the result follows.

Hence the theorem.

Theorem A solution obtained by the PSK method for a FIFSTP with equality constraints 'R' is a fully IFOS for the FIFSTP 'R'.

Proof Now we are going to describe the PSK method in detail.

As we said in step 0, first, we should construct the FIFSTT $\left[\tilde{c}_{ijk}^{I}\right]_{m\times n\times l}$ for the given data. Next, check the condition for balanced IFSTP. If this condition is not satisfied then change it, i.e., as we said in step 1, if the problem is not balanced then change it balanced. Afterwards, as we suggested in step 2, we should transform the FIFSTP into its equivalent crisp STP by using the ranking method (Varghese and Kuriakose).

Now, if the crisp STP that we obtained from step 2 of the PSK method is in integer (the value/amount of the parameters) then kept as it is. Otherwise, rewrite their decimal values into its nearest integer value (for example, the transportation of half part of fully filled gas cylinder is not a meaningful in real life. So, we should avoid the decimal values) and then make a new STP. So, as we mentioned in step 3 of the PSK method, we should change the value/amount of the parameters which are in decimal into integer. The STP obtained from this way is known as new crisp STP.

Now, solve the new STP that we obtained from step-3 of the PSK method with the help of theoretical methods (e.g. Min Zero-Min Cost method and MODI)/software package (e.g. MATLAB, LINGO, etc.). This process will give the optimum objective value and optimum allocation for the new crisp STP. This optimum allotted cell(s) in new crisp solid transportation table are referred as occupied cells. The remaining cells are known as unoccupied cells (i.e., the complement of occupied cells are called unoccupied cells). The occupied cells of new crisp STP are exactly $(m+n+l-2)$ and all have zero cost. FIFSTP have $(m+n+l-2)$ number of occupied cells with the same position of new crisp STP, but the costs of occupied cells of FIFSTP are all $\tilde{0}^I$'s. So, both the STP and IFSTP have equal number of occupied cells with the same position. Now, we should build a new fully intuitionistic fuzzy solid transportation table (FIFSTT) where the occupied cells costs are $\tilde{0}^I$'s and the remaining cells costs are its original cost. Now, add the maximum cost, i.e., to add max $\{\ominus \tilde{u}_i^I,\ i=1,2,\ldots,m\}$ of each origin/source to all the elements of that origin/source. Next, add the maximum cost, i.e., to add max $\{\ominus \tilde{v}_j^I,\ j=1,2,\ldots,n\}$ of each destination to all the elements of that destination. Finally, add the maximum cost, i.e., to add max $\{\ominus \tilde{w}_k^I,\ k=1,2,\ldots,l\}$ of each conveyance to all the elements of that conveyance. Now, the resulting table will have atleast one $\tilde{0}^I$ in each origin, destination and conveyance. This table is known as allotment table.

As we said in final step of the PSK method, in allotment table, if an origin/a destination/a conveyance has exactly one occupied cell, i.e., if it has exactly one $\tilde{0}^I$ then allot the maximum possible value (maximum possible value= Min {supply, demand & conveyance}) to that cell and subtract the same value to itself and its relevant supply & demand/ demand & conveyance/ conveyance & supply. If not, if the origins/destinations/conveyances are all have more than one occupied cells then select a cell in the α- origin, β- destination and γ- conveyance of the transportation table whose cost is maximum (ties may occur, i.e., if the maximum cost is more than one then to break the tie, we can select arbitrarily any one of them) and examine which one of the cells having minimum original cost (ties may occur, i.e., if the minimum original cost is more than one then to break the tie, we can select arbitrarily any one of them) among all the occupied cells of its related origin, destination and conveyance then to allot the maximum possible value in that cell. In this way, allot the maximum possible value to the selected origin, destination and conveyance entirely. If the entire origin, destination and conveyance of the occupied cells have fully allotted then select a next maximum cost of the transportation table and examine which one of the cells have minimum original cost among all the occupied cells in that origin, destination and conveyance then to allot the maximum possible value to that cell. Continue the same process until all intuitionistic fuzzy supply points are fully used, all intuitionistic fuzzy demand points are fully received and all intuitionistic fuzzy conveyance capacities are fully used. This allotment will give the FIFS to the given FIFSTP.

Because, this process will satisfies all the rim conditions. Consequently, it will satisfies the balanced condition for FIFSTP, i.e., it will satisfies

$$\tilde{a}_1^I + \tilde{a}_2^I + \ldots + \tilde{a}_m^I = \tilde{b}_1^I + \tilde{b}_2^I + \ldots + \tilde{b}_n^I = \tilde{e}_1^I + \tilde{e}_2^I + \ldots + \tilde{e}_l^I .$$

But, this is a necessary and sufficient condition for the FIFSTP.

Thus, we get a solution $\{\tilde{y}_{ijk}^I,, i=1,2,\ldots,m; j=1,2,\ldots,n$ and $k=1,2,\ldots,l\}$ for the FIFSTP whose cost matrix is $\left[\tilde{c}_{ijk}^I \ominus \tilde{u}_i^I \ominus \tilde{v}_j^I \ominus \tilde{w}_k^I \right]_{m \times n \times l}$ such that $(\ni)$ $\tilde{y}_{ijk}^I \approx \tilde{0}^I$ for

$$(\tilde{c}_{ijk}^I \ominus \tilde{u}_i^I \ominus \tilde{v}_j^I \ominus \tilde{w}_k^I) \succeq \tilde{0}^I$$

and $\tilde{y}_{ijk}^I \succ \tilde{0}^I$ for

$$(\tilde{c}_{ijk}^I \ominus \tilde{u}_i^I \ominus \tilde{v}_j^I \ominus \tilde{w}_k^I) \approx \tilde{0}^I .$$

$\therefore$ the min $\sum_{i=1}^m \sum_{j=1}^n \sum_{k=1}^l \left(\tilde{c}_{ijk}^I \ominus \tilde{u}_i^I \ominus \tilde{v}_j^I \ominus \tilde{w}_k^I \right) \tilde{y}_{ijk}^I$ s.t. eqns. (1) - (4) are satisfied, is $\tilde{0}^I$. Thus, by the Corollary, the solution $\{\tilde{y}_{ijk}^I, i=1,2,\ldots,m; j=1,2,\ldots,n$ and $k=1,2,\ldots,l\}$ is obtained by the PSK method for a FIFSTP with equality constraints is a fully IFOS for the FIFSTP. Hence the theorem.

Theorem If some/all of the costs (rupees in IFNs) in the type II- IFSTP are replaced by equivalent costs (rupees in IFNs), for example, their ranking values, the new type II- IFSTP has the same set of feasible and optimal solutions.

Proof: First of all, we know that, from the definition of type II- IFSTP, the type II-IFSTP is a STP but its cost is in the form of IFN; in particular the type II- IFSTP has crisp supply, crisp demand and crisp conveyance capacity. In every IFSTP the value of the decision parameters depends on its constraints and non-negative restriction; it is not an exemption for type II- IFSTP. So, the decision parameters of type II- IFSTP always depend on its constraints and non-negative restriction. At the same time, the right-hand side values of constraints are all crisp numbers in type II- IFSTP. Hence, now we conclude that the value of the decision variables in type II- IFSTP is always crisp number. This implies that the feasible and optimal solution of type II- IFSTP is always crisp numbers. In any IFSTP, the feasible and optimal solution is always unchanged iff the relevant parameter is unchanged. So, in type II- IFSTP, the feasible and optimal solution is always unchanged. In addition to that our assumption is to replace the existing cost with equivalent cost to the new type II- IFSTP. So, the parameters are all unchanged in a new type II- IFSTP and only the existing costs are replaced by its equivalent costs. Hence, the value/amount of the parameters are all unchanged in a new type II- IFSTP. Thus, any solution of type II- IFSTP is same as the solution of the new type II- IFSTP. Hence the theorem.

ILLUSTRATIVE EXAMPLES

The proposed model and technique both are illustrated by providing numerical examples in Section 8. Results from proposed method with software approaches are compared and presented in table. The graphical representation of the objective value is given and discussed.

Example: 1 Real-life type II- IFSTP

A company has 3 factories- O_1, O_2, and O_3 that manufacture the same kind of umbrellas in 3 different locations. The company manager/accountant would like to transport umbrellas from 3 different factories (O_1, O_2, and O_3) to 3 different retail stores- D_1, D_2 and D_3. All the factories are connected to all the retail stores by the 3 different mediums called land, water and space and umbrellas are transported by means of cars, boats and helicopters. The supply (a_i, $i=1,2,...m$) of sources, demand (b_j, $j=1,2,...,n$) of destinations and capacity (e_k, $k=1,2,..,l$) of 3 different modes of transport of umbrella are known exactly. But the transportation cost is not known exactly due to variations in rates of gas/petrol, poor road condition/traffic jam, and weather in hilly areas respectively. The transportation cost for an umbrella from factories- O_1, O_2, and O_3 to retail stores- D_1, D_2 and D_3 are given in Table 3 from the past experience.

Table 3. The tabular form of real-life type II- IFSTP that relevant to example-1

										Capacity e_k
	E1			E1			E1			e_1
		E2			E2			E2		e_2
			E3			E3			E3	e_3
Retail Stores → **Factories ↓**	D1			D2			D3			Supply a_i
O1	$\tilde{c}_{111}^I$	$\tilde{c}_{112}^I$	$\tilde{c}_{113}^I$	$\tilde{c}_{121}^I$	$\tilde{c}_{122}^I$	$\tilde{c}_{123}^I$	$\tilde{c}_{131}^I$	$\tilde{c}_{132}^I$	$\tilde{c}_{133}^I$	a_1
O2	$\tilde{c}_{211}^I$	$\tilde{c}_{212}^I$	$\tilde{c}_{213}^I$	$\tilde{c}_{221}^I$	$\tilde{c}_{222}^I$	$\tilde{c}_{223}^I$	$\tilde{c}_{231}^I$	$\tilde{c}_{232}^I$	$\tilde{c}_{233}^I$	a_2
O3	$\tilde{c}_{311}^I$	$\tilde{c}_{312}^I$	$\tilde{c}_{313}^I$	$\tilde{c}_{321}^I$	$\tilde{c}_{322}^I$	$\tilde{c}_{323}^I$	$\tilde{c}_{331}^I$	$\tilde{c}_{332}^I$	$\tilde{c}_{333}^I$	a_3
Demand b_j	b_1			b_2			b_3			

Where

$$(\tilde{c}_{111}^I, \tilde{c}_{112}^I, \tilde{c}_{113}^I, \tilde{c}_{211}^I, \tilde{c}_{212}^I, \tilde{c}_{213}^I, \tilde{c}_{311}^I, \tilde{c}_{312}^I, \tilde{c}_{313}^I, \tilde{c}_{121}^I, \tilde{c}_{122}^I, \tilde{c}_{123}^I, \tilde{c}_{221}^I,$$
$$\tilde{c}_{222}^I, \tilde{c}_{223}^I, \tilde{c}_{321}^I, \tilde{c}_{322}^I, \tilde{c}_{323}^I, \tilde{c}_{131}^I, \tilde{c}_{132}^I, \tilde{c}_{133}^I, \tilde{c}_{231}^I, \tilde{c}_{232}^I, \tilde{c}_{233}^I, \tilde{c}_{331}^I, \tilde{c}_{332}^I, \tilde{c}_{333}^I)$$

=((3,4,5; 2,4,6), (5,8,10; 1,8,11), (7,8,9; 6,8,10), (3,4,5; 2,4,6), (1,2,3; 0,2,4), (2,6,10; 1,6,11), (4,8,12; 3,8,13), (0.5,1,1.5; 0,1,2), (1,3,5; 0,3,6), (1,3,5; 0,3,6), (3,8,16; 0,8,19), (5,8,10; 1,8,11), (0.5,1,1.5; 0,1,2), (1,3,5;0,3,6), (4,8,12; 3,8,13), (3,4,5;2,4,6), (5,8,10;1,8,11), (1,3,5;0,3,6), (4,6,8; 3,6,9), (5,8,10; 1,8,11), (1,2,3; 0,2,4), (7,8,9; 6,8,10), (3,4,5; 2,4,6), (2,5,8; 1,5,9), (2,5,8; 1,5,9), (4,6,8; 3,6,9), (3,4,5; 2,4,6)).

Supply: $(a_1, a_2, a_3) = (11, 13, 10)$
Demand: $(b_1, b_2, b_3) = (7, 15, 12)$
Conveyance: $(e_1, e_2, e_3) = (11, 14, 9)$

In this issue, the objective of the manager/accountant is to find the optimal allocation (i.e., optimal transportation schedule) which minimizes TIFTC.

Solution: The ranking values of all TIFNs in Table 3 are given below.

$$\Re\left(\tilde{c}_{111}^{I}\right), \Re\left(\tilde{c}_{112}^{I}\right), \Re\left(\tilde{c}_{113}^{I}\right), \Re\left(\tilde{c}_{211}^{I}\right), \Re\left(\tilde{c}_{212}^{I}\right), \Re\left(\tilde{c}_{213}^{I}\right), \Re\left(\tilde{c}_{311}^{I}\right), \Re\left(\tilde{c}_{312}^{I}\right), \Re\left(\tilde{c}_{313}^{I}\right),$$

$$\Re\left(\tilde{c}_{121}^{I}\right), \Re\left(\tilde{c}_{122}^{I}\right), \Re\left(\tilde{c}_{123}^{I}\right), \Re\left(\tilde{c}_{221}^{I}\right), \Re\left(\tilde{c}_{222}^{I}\right), \Re\left(\tilde{c}_{223}^{I}\right), \Re\left(\tilde{c}_{321}^{I}\right), \Re\left(\tilde{c}_{322}^{I}\right), \Re\left(\tilde{c}_{323}^{I}\right),$$

$$\Re\left(\tilde{c}_{131}^{I}\right), \Re\left(\tilde{c}_{132}^{I}\right), \Re\left(\tilde{c}_{133}^{I}\right), \Re\left(\tilde{c}_{231}^{I}\right), \Re\left(\tilde{c}_{232}^{I}\right), \Re\left(\tilde{c}_{233}^{I}\right), \Re\left(\tilde{c}_{331}^{I}\right), \Re\left(\tilde{c}_{332}^{I}\right), \Re\left(\tilde{c}_{333}^{I}\right)$$

=(4, 7, 8, 4, 2, 6, 8, 1, 3, 3, 9, 7, 1, 3, 8, 4, 7, 3, 6, 7, 2, 8, 4, 5, 5, 6, 4).

From step 1 of the proposed method, we get the following.

$$a_1 + a_2 + a_3 = \sum_{i=1}^{3} a_i = 11 + 13 + 10 = 34 \quad \text{(total origin supply)}$$

$$b_1 + b_2 + b_3 = \sum_{j=1}^{3} b_j = 7 + 15 + 12 = 34 \quad \text{(total factory demand)}$$

$$e_1 + e_2 + e_3 = \sum_{k=1}^{3} e_k = 11 + 14 + 9 = 34 \quad \text{(total conveyance capacity)}$$

$\Rightarrow$ total origin supply= total factory demand= total conveyance capacity
$\therefore$ the given problem is a balanced.

Now, with the help of the steps 2 and 3 of the proposed method, in conformation to Model (P##), the given IFSTP should be transformed into its equivalent CSTP using the ranking procedure of Varghese and Kuriakose. The equivalent and relevant CSTP to example-1 is presented by Table 4.

After applying 4th step of the proposed method, now, the optimal allotment of the CSTP relevant to example-1 is obtained and it is shown by Table 5.

Table 4. Crisp form of real-life type II- IFSTP that relevant to example-1

									Capacity e_k
Conveyances → ↓	E1			E1			E1			11
		E2			E2			E2		14
			E3			E3			E3	9
Retail Stores → **Factories ↓**	D1			D2			D3			Supply a_i
O1	4	7	8	3	9	7	6	7	2	11
O2	4	2	6	1	3	8	8	4	5	13
O3	8	1	3	4	7	3	5	6	4	10
Demand b_j	7			15			12			

Table 5. The optimum table of real-life type II- IFSTP that relevant to example-1

									Capacity e_k
Conveyances → ↓	E1			E1			E1			11
		E2			E2			E2		14
			E3			E3			E3	9
Retail Stores → **Factories ↓**	D1			D2			D3			Supply a_i
O1	4	7	8	3(2)	9	7	6	7	2(9)	11
O2	4	2(0)	6	1(9)	3(4)	8	8	4	5	13
O3	8	1(7)	3	4	7	3	5	6(3)	4	10
Demand b_j	7			15			12			

The minimum objective value of CSTP that relevant to type II- IFSTP is denoted by Min Z or Z_{min} and is:

$$Z_{min}= (2)\times(0)+(1)\times(7)+(3)\times(2)+(1)\times(9)+(3)\times(4)+(6)\times(3)+(2)\times(9) =70 \qquad (16)$$

The optimal solution of the given example 1 has been obtained directly by using step 5 of the proposed method, which is as follows.

$(y_{212}, y_{121}, y_{133}, y_{221}, y_{22}, y_{312}, y_{332})=(0, 2, 9, 9, 4, 7, 3)$

The minimum objective value of IFSTP is denoted by Min $\tilde{Z}^I$ or $\tilde{Z}^I_{min}$ and is:

$\tilde{Z}^I_{min} = (1, 2, 3; 0, 2, 4) \times (0) + (0.5, 1, 1.5; 0, 1, 2) \times (7) + (1, 3, 5; 0, 3, 6) \times (2) + (0.5, 1, 1.5; 0, 1, 2) \times (9) + (1, 3, 5; 0, 3, 6) \times (4) + (1, 2, 3; 0, 2, 4) \times (9) + (4, 6, 8; 3, 6, 9) \times (3)$

$\tilde{Z}^I_{min} = (0, 0, 0; 0, 0, 0) + (3.5, 7, 10.5; 0, 7, 14) + (2, 6, 10; 0, 6, 12) + (4.5, 9, 13.5; 0, 9, 18) + (4, 12, 20; 0, 12, 24) + (9, 18, 27; 0, 18, 36) + (12, 18, 24; 9, 18, 27)$

Min $\tilde{Z}^I = \tilde{Z}^I_{min} = (35, 70, 105; 9, 70, 131)$

$$\Re\left(\tilde{Z}^I\right) = \Re\,(35, 70, 105; 9, 70, 131) = 70 \tag{17}$$

The mathematical model of Table 4 is as follows.

Min $Z = 4y_{111} + 4y_{211} + 8y_{311} + 3y_{121} + 1y_{221} + 4y_{321} + 6y_{131} + 8y_{231} + 5y_{331} + 7y_{112} + 2y_{212} + 1y_{312} + 9y_{122} + 3y_{222} + 7y_{322} + 7y_{132} + 4y_{232} + 6y_{332} + 8y_{113} + 6y_{213} + 3y_{313} + 7y_{213} + 8y_{223} + 3y_{323} + 2y_{133} + 5y_{233} + 4y_{333}$

s.t:

Constraint on factory 1: $y_{111} + y_{112} + y_{113} + y_{121} + y_{122} + y_{123} + y_{131} + y_{132} + y_{133} = 1$
Constraint on store 1: $y_{111} + y_{112} + y_{113} + y_{211} + y_{212} + y_{213} + y_{311} + y_{312} + y_{313} = 7$
Constraint on conveyance 1: $y_{111} + y_{121} + y_{131} + y_{211} + y_{221} + y_{231} + y_{311} + y_{321} + y_{331} = 11$
Constraint on factory 2: $y_{211} + y_{212} + y_{2123} + y_{221} + y_{222} + y_{223} + y_{231} + y_{232} + y_{233} = 13$
Constraint on store 2: $y_{121} + y_{122} + y_{123} + y_{221} + y_{222} + y_{223} + y_{321} + y_{322} + y_{323} = 15$
Constraint on conveyance 2: $y_{112} + y_{122} + y_{132} + y_{212} + y_{222} + y_{232} + y_{312} + y_{322} + y_{332} = 14$
Constraint on factory 3: $y_{311} + y_{312} + y_{313} + y_{321} + y_{322} + y_{323} + y_{331} + y_{332} + y_{333} = 10$
Constraint on store 3: $y_{131} + y_{132} + y_{133} + y_{231} + y_{232} + y_{233} + y_{331} + y_{332} + y_{333} = 12$
Constraint on conveyance 3: $y_{113} + y_{123} + y_{133} + y_{213} + y_{223} + y_{233} + y_{313} + y_{323} + y_{333} = 9$

Non-negative restriction:

$y_{ijk} \geq 0$, for $i = 1,2,3$; $j = 1,2,3$ and $k = 1,2,3$.

The above model's Matlab code and its output both are as follows.

```
>> clear all;
>> f=[4 4 8 3 1 4 6 8 5 7 2 1 9 3 7 7 4 6 8 6 3 7 8 3 2 5 4];
>> A=[];
>> b=[];
>> Aeq= [1 0 0 1 0 0 1 0 0 1 0 0 1 0 0 1 0 0 1 0 0 1 0 0 1 0 0; 1 1 1 0 0 0
0 0 1 1 1 0 0 0 0 0 1 1 1 0 0 0 0 0 0; 1 1 1 1 1 1 1 1 1 0 0 0 0 0 0 0 0 0
0 0 0 0 0 0 0; 0 1 0 0 1 0 0 1 0 0 1 0 0 1 0 0 1 0 0 1 0 0 1 0 0 1 0; 0 0 0
1 1 1 0 0 0 0 0 1 1 1 0 0 0 0 0 1 1 1 0 0 0; 0 0 0 0 0 0 0 1 1 1 1 1 1
1 1 1 0 0 0 0 0 0 0 0; 0 0 1 0 0 1 0 0 1 0 0 1 0 0 1 0 0 1 0 0 1 0 0 1 0 0
```

```
1; 0 0 0 0 0 0 1 1 1 0 0 0 0 0 0 1 1 1 0 0 0 0 0 0 1 1 1; 0 0 0 0 0 0 0 0 0 0
0 0 0 0 0 0 0 0 1 1 1 1 1 1 1 1 1];
>> beq= [11 7 11 13 15 14 10 12 9];
>> lb=[0 0 0 0 0 0 0 0 0 0 0 0 0 0 0 0 0 0 0 0 0 0 0 0 0 0 0];
>> ub=[];
>> [y,f]= linprog(f,A,b,Aeq,beq,lb,ub);
Optimization terminated.
>> disp(y);
    0.0000
    0.0000
    0.0000
    2.0000
    9.0000
    0.0000
    0.0000
    0.0000
    0.0000
    0.0000
    0.0000
    7.0000
    0.0000
    4.0000
    0.0000
    0.0000
    0.0000
    3.0000
    0.0000
    0.0000
    0.0000
    0.0000
    0.0000
    0.0000
    9.0000
    0.0000
    0.0000

>> disp(f);

   70.0000
```

Where:

```
clear all-clear the command window (or delete the variables created in Work-
space).
```

f-the coefficient of the objective function.
A- the left hand-side (LHS) coefficient of the < or = constraints.
b- the right-hand side (RHS) value of the < or = constraints.
Aeq- the LHS coefficient of the equality constraints.
beq- the RHS value of the equality constraints.
lb- the lower bounds of the variables.
ub- the upper bounds of the variables.
y- the variables.
linprog- the Matlab function. It can be used to solve the LPP.
disp(y)-displays the value of variable y without printing the variable name.

We notice that the solution obtained by the Matlab is same as the solution obtained by the PSK method.

Example: 2 Consider the given type II- IFSTP in Table 6.

Table 6. The tabular form of real-life type II- IFSTP that relevant to example-2

Conveyances → ↓	E1			E1			E1			Capacity e_k
		E2			E2			E2		e_1
			E3			E3			E3	e_2
										e_3
Retail Stores → Factories ↓	D1			D2			D3			Supply a_i
O1	$\tilde{c}^I_{111}$	$\tilde{c}^I_{112}$	$\tilde{c}^I_{113}$	$\tilde{c}^I_{121}$	$\tilde{c}^I_{122}$	$\tilde{c}^I_{123}$	$\tilde{c}^I_{131}$	$\tilde{c}^I_{132}$	$\tilde{c}^I_{133}$	a_1
O2	$\tilde{c}^I_{211}$	$\tilde{c}^I_{212}$	$\tilde{c}^I_{213}$	$\tilde{c}^I_{221}$	$\tilde{c}^I_{222}$	$\tilde{c}^I_{223}$	$\tilde{c}^I_{231}$	$\tilde{c}^I_{232}$	$\tilde{c}^I_{233}$	a_2
O3	$\tilde{c}^I_{311}$	$\tilde{c}^I_{312}$	$\tilde{c}^I_{313}$	$\tilde{c}^I_{321}$	$\tilde{c}^I_{322}$	$\tilde{c}^I_{323}$	$\tilde{c}^I_{331}$	$\tilde{c}^I_{332}$	$\tilde{c}^I_{333}$	a_3
Demand b_j	b_1			b_2			b_3			

Where

$$(\tilde{c}^I_{111}, \tilde{c}^I_{112}, \tilde{c}^I_{113}, \tilde{c}^I_{211}, \tilde{c}^I_{212}, \tilde{c}^I_{213}, \tilde{c}^I_{311}, \tilde{c}^I_{312}, \tilde{c}^I_{313}, \tilde{c}^I_{121}, \tilde{c}^I_{122}, \tilde{c}^I_{123}, \tilde{c}^I_{221},$$
$$\tilde{c}^I_{222}, \tilde{c}^I_{223}, \tilde{c}^I_{321}, \tilde{c}^I_{322}, \tilde{c}^I_{323}, \tilde{c}^I_{131}, \tilde{c}^I_{132}, \tilde{c}^I_{133}, \tilde{c}^I_{231}, \tilde{c}^I_{232}, \tilde{c}^I_{233}, \tilde{c}^I_{331}, \tilde{c}^I_{332}, \tilde{c}^I_{333})$$

=((3,4,5; 2,4,6), (4,6,8; 3,6,9), (2,5,8; 1,5,9), (2,5,8; 1,5,9), (3,4,5; 2,4,6), (7,8,9; 6,8,10), (1,2,3; 0,2,4), (5,8,10; 1,8,11), (4,6,8; 3,6,9), (4,8,12; 3,8,13), (0.5,1,1.5; 0,1,2), (1,3,5; 0,3,6), (3,4,5; 2,4,6), (1,2,3; 0,2,4), (2,6,10; 1,6,11), (7,8,9; 6,8,10), (5,8,10; 1,8,11), (3,4,5; 2,4,6), (3,4,5; 2,4,6), (5,8,10; 1,8,11), (1,3,5; 0,3,6), (0.5,1,1.5; 0,1,2), (1,3,5; 0,3,6), (4,8,12; 3,8,13), (1,3,5; 0,3,6), (3,8,16; 0,8,19), (5,8,10; 1,8,11)).

Supply: $(a_1, a_2, a_3) = (10, 13, 11)$
Demand: $(b_1, b_2, b_3) = (12, 7, 15)$
Conveyance: $(e_1, e_2, e_3) = (11, 14, 9)$

In this issue, the objective of the manager is to find the optimum transportation schedule which minimizes TIFTC.

Solution: The ranking values of all TIFNs in Table 6 are given below.

$$(\Re(\tilde{c}_{111}^I), \Re(\tilde{c}_{112}^I), \Re(\tilde{c}_{113}^I), \Re(\tilde{c}_{211}^I), \Re(\tilde{c}_{212}^I), \Re(\tilde{c}_{213}^I), \Re(\tilde{c}_{311}^I), \Re(\tilde{c}_{312}^I), \Re(\tilde{c}_{313}^I),$$
$$\Re(\tilde{c}_{121}^I), \Re(\tilde{c}_{122}^I), \Re(\tilde{c}_{123}^I), \Re(\tilde{c}_{221}^I), \Re(\tilde{c}_{222}^I), \Re(\tilde{c}_{223}^I), \Re(\tilde{c}_{321}^I), \Re(\tilde{c}_{322}^I), \Re(\tilde{c}_{323}^I),$$
$$\Re(\tilde{c}_{131}^I), \Re(\tilde{c}_{132}^I), \Re(\tilde{c}_{133}^I), \Re(\tilde{c}_{231}^I), \Re(\tilde{c}_{232}^I), \Re(\tilde{c}_{233}^I), \Re(\tilde{c}_{331}^I), \Re(\tilde{c}_{332}^I), \Re(\tilde{c}_{333}^I))$$

$$= (4, 6, 5, 5, 4, 8, 2, 7, 6, 8, 1, 3, 4, 2, 6, 8, 7, 4, 4, 7, 3, 1, 3, 8, 3, 9, 7).$$

From step 1 of the proposed method, we get the following.

$$a_1 + a_2 + a_3 = \sum_{i=1}^{3} a_i = 10 + 13 + 11 = 34 \quad \text{(total origin supply)}$$

$$b_1 + b_2 + b_3 = \sum_{j=1}^{3} b_j = 12 + 7 + 15 = 34 \quad \text{(total factory demand)}$$

$$e_1 + e_2 + e_3 = \sum_{k=1}^{3} e_k = 11 + 14 + 9 = 34 \quad \text{(total conveyance capacity)}$$

$\Rightarrow$ total origin supply= total factory demand= total conveyance capacity

$\therefore$ the given problem is a balanced.

Now, with the help of the steps 2 and 3 of the proposed method, in conformation to Model (P##), the given IFSTP should be transformed into its equivalent CSTP using the ranking procedure of Varghese and Kuriakose. The equivalent and relevant CSTP to example-2 is presented by Table 7.

After applying 4th step of the proposed method, now, the optimal allotment of the CSTP which corresponds to example-2 is obtained and it is shown by Table 8.

The minimum objective value of CSTP is denoted by Z_{min} and is:

$$Z_{min} = (2) \times (11) + (4) \times (1) + (1) \times (1) + (2) \times (6) + (1) \times (0) + (3) \times (6) + (3) \times (9) = 84 \tag{18}$$

The optimal solution of the given example 2 has been obtained directly by using step 5 of the proposed method, which is as follows.

$$(y_{212}, y_{311}, y_{122}, y_{22}, y_{133}, y_{231}, y_{232}) = (1, 11, 1, 6, 9, 0, 6)$$

Table 7. Crisp form of real-life type II- IFSTP that relevant to example-2

	E1	E2	E3	E1	E2	E3	E1	E2	E3	Capacity e_k
Conveyances → ↓	E1			E1			E1			11
		E2			E2			E2		14
			E3			E3			E3	9
Retail Stores → **Factories** ↓	D1			D2			D3			Supply a_i
O1	4	6	5	8	1	3	4	7	3	10
O2	5	4	8	4	2	6	1	3	8	13
O3	2	7	6	8	7	4	3	9	7	11
Demand b_j	12			7			15			

Table 8. The optimum table of real-life type II- IFSTP that relevant to example-2

	E1	E2	E3	E1	E2	E3	E1	E2	E3	Capacity e_k
Conveyances → ↓	E1			E1			E1			11
		E2			E2			E2		14
			E3			E3			E3	9
Retail Stores → **Factories** ↓	D1			D2			D3			Supply a_i
O1	4	6	5	8	1(1)	3	4	7	3(9)	10
O2	5	4(1)	8	4	2(6)	6	1(0)	3(6)	8	13
O3	2(11)	7	6	8	7	4	3	9	7	11
Demand b_j	12			7			15			

The minimum objective value of IFSTP is denoted by $\tilde{Z}^I_{min}$ or Min $\tilde{Z}^I$ and is:

$\tilde{Z}^I_{min}$ =(3, 4, 5; 2, 4, 6)×(1)+(1, 2, 3; 0, 2, 4)×(11)+(0.5, 1, 1.5; 0, 1, 2) ×(1)+(1, 2, 3; 0, 2, 4)×(6)+(1, 3, 5; 0, 3, 6)×(9)+(0.5, 1, 1.5; 0, 1, 2) ×(0)+(1, 3, 5; 0, 3, 6)×(6)

$\tilde{Z}^I_{min}$ =(3, 4, 5; 2, 4, 6)+(11, 22, 33; 0, 22, 44)+(0.5, 1, 1.5; 0, 1, 2)+(6, 12, 18; 0, 12, 24)+(9, 27, 45; 0, 27, 54)+(0, 0, 0; 0, 0, 0)+(6, 18, 30; 0, 18, 36)

$\tilde{Z}^I_{min}$ =Min $\tilde{Z}^I$ = (35.5, 84, 132.5; 2, 84, 166)

$Z_{min}= \Re\left(\tilde{Z}^I\right)= \Re(35.5, 84, 132.5; 2, 84, 166)= 84$ (19)

Lingo code of Table 7 is as follows.

```
!Objective function;
Min=4*y111+5*y211+2*y311+8*y121+4*y221+8*y321+4*y131+ 1*y231+3*y331+6*y112+4*y
212+7*y312+1*y122+2*y222+7*y322+ 7*y132+3*y232+9*y332+5*y113+8*y213+6*y313+3*y
123+6*y223+ 4*y323+3*y133+8*y233+7*y333;
!s.t:;
!Constraint on factory 1;
y111+y112+y113+y121+y122+y123+y131+y132+y133=10;
!Constraint on store 1;
y111+y112+y113+y211+y212+y213+y311+y312+y313=12;
!Constraint on conveyance 1;
y111+y121+y131+y211+y221+y231+y311+y321+y331=11;
!Constraint on factory 2;
y211+y212+y213+y221+y222+y223+y231+y232+y233=13;
!Constraint on store 2;
y121+y122+y123+y221+y222+y223+y321+y322+y323=7;
!Constraint on conveyance 2;
y112+y122+y132+y212+y222+y232+y312+y322+y332=14;
!Constraint on factory 3;
y311+y312+y313+y321+y322+y323+y331+y332+y333=11;
!Constraint on store 3;
y131+y132+y133+y231+y232+y233+y331+y332+y333=15;
!Constraint on conveyance 3;
y113+y123+y133+y213+y223+y233+y313+y323+y333=9;
!Non-negative constraints;
y111>=0;
y211>=0;
y311>=0;
y121>=0;
y221>=0;
y321>=0;
y131>=0;
y231>=0;
y331>=0;
y112>=0;
y212>=0;
y312>=0;
y122>=0;
y222>=0;
y322>=0;
```

```
y132>=0;
y232>=0;
y332>=0;
y113>=0;
y213>=0;
y313>=0;
y123>=0;
y223>=0;
y323>=0;
y133>=0;
y233>=0;
y333>=0;
```

The optimal objective value and optimal solution of Table 7 are as follows.

```
Global optimal solution found.
Objective value:                          84.00000
Infeasibilities:                          0.000000
Total solver iterations:                         7
Elapsed runtime seconds:                      0.30
Model Class:                                    LP
Total variables:                27
Nonlinear variables:             0
Integer variables:               0
Total constraints:              37
Nonlinear constraints:           0
Total non-zeros:               135
Nonlinear non-zeros:             0
Variable          Value        Reduced Cost
   Y111        0.000000         3.000000
   Y211        0.000000         3.000000
   Y311        11.00000         0.000000
   Y121        0.000000         9.000000
   Y221        0.000000         4.000000
   Y321        0.000000         8.000000
   Y131        0.000000         4.000000
   Y231        0.000000         0.000000
   Y331        0.000000         2.000000
   Y112        0.000000         3.000000
   Y212        1.000000         0.000000
   Y312        0.000000         3.000000
```

Y122	1.000000	0.000000
Y222	6.000000	0.000000
Y322	0.000000	5.000000
Y132	0.000000	5.000000
Y232	6.000000	0.000000
Y332	0.000000	6.000000
Y113	0.000000	1.000000
Y213	0.000000	3.000000
Y313	0.000000	1.000000
Y123	0.000000	1.000000
Y223	0.000000	3.000000
Y323	0.000000	1.000000
Y133	9.000000	0.000000
Y233	0.000000	4.000000
Y333	0.000000	3.000000

Row	Slack or Surplus	Dual Price
1	84.00000	-1.000000
2	0.000000	0.000000
3	0.000000	-2.000000
4	0.000000	1.000000
5	0.000000	-1.000000
6	0.000000	0.000000
7	0.000000	-1.000000
8	0.000000	-1.000000
9	0.000000	-1.000000
10	0.000000	-2.000000
11	0.000000	0.000000
12	0.000000	0.000000
13	11.00000	0.000000
14	0.000000	0.000000
15	0.000000	0.000000
16	0.000000	0.000000
17	0.000000	0.000000
18	0.000000	0.000000
19	0.000000	0.000000
20	0.000000	0.000000
21	1.000000	0.000000
22	0.000000	0.000000
23	1.000000	0.000000
24	6.000000	0.000000
25	0.000000	0.000000

26	0.000000	0.000000
27	6.000000	0.000000
28	0.000000	0.000000
29	0.000000	0.000000
30	0.000000	0.000000
31	0.000000	0.000000
32	0.000000	0.000000
33	0.000000	0.000000
34	0.000000	0.000000
35	9.000000	0.000000
36	0.000000	0.000000
37	0.000000	0.000000

Lingo solver status of example-2 is given in Figure 2.

Figure 2. Lingo solver status of given type II- IFSTP in example-2

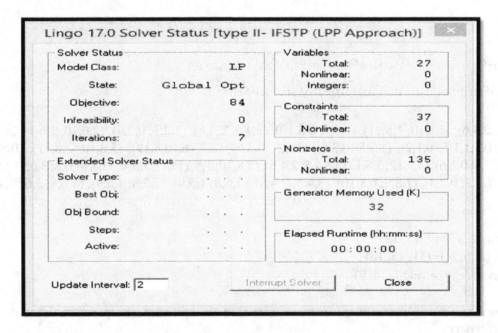

The optimal solution of example-2 obtained by the PSK method is equal to the optimal solution of example-2 obtained by the LINGO software.

Example: 3 Consider the given type II- IFSTP in Table 9.

Table 9. The tabular form of real-life type II- IFSTP that relevant to example-3

Conveyances → ↓	E1			E1			E1			Capacity e_k
		E2			E2			E2		e_1
			E3			E3			E3	e_2
										e_3
Retail Stores → Factories ↓	D1			D2			D3			Supply a_i
O1	$\tilde{c}^I_{111}$	$\tilde{c}^I_{112}$	$\tilde{c}^I_{113}$	$\tilde{c}^I_{121}$	$\tilde{c}^I_{122}$	$\tilde{c}^I_{123}$	$\tilde{c}^I_{131}$	$\tilde{c}^I_{132}$	$\tilde{c}^I_{133}$	a_1
O2	$\tilde{c}^I_{211}$	$\tilde{c}^I_{212}$	$\tilde{c}^I_{213}$	$\tilde{c}^I_{221}$	$\tilde{c}^I_{222}$	$\tilde{c}^I_{223}$	$\tilde{c}^I_{231}$	$\tilde{c}^I_{232}$	$\tilde{c}^I_{233}$	a_2
O3	$\tilde{c}^I_{311}$	$\tilde{c}^I_{312}$	$\tilde{c}^I_{313}$	$\tilde{c}^I_{321}$	$\tilde{c}^I_{322}$	$\tilde{c}^I_{323}$	$\tilde{c}^I_{331}$	$\tilde{c}^I_{332}$	$\tilde{c}^I_{333}$	a_3
Demand b_j	b_1			b_2			b_3			

where

$$(\tilde{c}^I_{111},\tilde{c}^I_{112},\tilde{c}^I_{113},\tilde{c}^I_{121},\tilde{c}^I_{122},\tilde{c}^I_{123},\tilde{c}^I_{131},\tilde{c}^I_{132},\tilde{c}^I_{133},\tilde{c}^I_{211},\tilde{c}^I_{212}\tilde{c}^I_{213},\tilde{c}^I_{221},$$

$$\tilde{c}^I_{222},\tilde{c}^I_{223},\tilde{c}^I_{231},\tilde{c}^I_{232},\tilde{c}^I_{233},\tilde{c}^I_{311},\tilde{c}^I_{312},\tilde{c}^I_{313},\tilde{c}^I_{321},\tilde{c}^I_{322},\tilde{c}^I_{323},\tilde{c}^I_{331},\tilde{c}^I_{332},\tilde{c}^I_{333})$$

=((3,4,5; 2,4,6), (5,8,10; 1,8,11), (7,8,9; 6,8,10), (3,4,5; 2,4,6), (1,2,3; 0,2,4), (2,6,10; 1,6,11), (4,8,12; 3,8,13), (0.5,1,1.5; 0,1,2), (1,3,5; 0,3,6), (1,3,5; 0,3,6), (3,8,16; 0,8,19), (5,8,10; 1,8,11), (0.5,1,1.5; 0,1,2), (1,3,5; 0,3,6), (4,8,12; 3,8,13), (3,4,5; 2,4,6), (5,8,10; 1,8,11), (1,3,5; 0,3,6), (4,6,8; 3,6,9), (5,8,10; 1,8,11), (1,2,3; 0,2,4), (7,8,9; 6,8,10), (3,4,5; 2,4,6), (2,5,8; 1,5,9), (2,5,8; 1,5,9), (4,6,8; 3,6,9), (3,4,5; 2,4,6)).

Supply: $(a_1,a_2,a_3)=(7, 15, 12)$
Demand: $(b_1,b_2,b_3)=(11, 13, 10)$
Conveyance: $(e_1,e_2,e_3)=(11, 14, 9)$

In this issue, the objective of the manager is to find the optimum transportation schedule which minimizes TIFTC.

Solution: The ranking values of all TIFNs in Table 9 are given below.

$$\Re(\tilde{c}^I_{111}),\Re(\tilde{c}^I_{112}),\Re(\tilde{c}^I_{113}),\Re(\tilde{c}^I_{121}),\Re(\tilde{c}^I_{122}),\Re(\tilde{c}^I_{123}),\Re(\tilde{c}^I_{131}),\Re(\tilde{c}^I_{132}),\Re(\tilde{c}^I_{133}),$$

$$\Re(\tilde{c}^I_{211}),\Re(\tilde{c}^I_{212}),\Re(\tilde{c}^I_{213}),\Re(\tilde{c}^I_{221}),\Re(\tilde{c}^I_{222}),\Re(\tilde{c}^I_{223}),\Re(\tilde{c}^I_{231}),\Re(\tilde{c}^I_{232}),\Re(\tilde{c}^I_{233}),$$

$$\Re(\tilde{c}^I_{311}),\Re(\tilde{c}^I_{312}),\Re(\tilde{c}^I_{313}),\Re(\tilde{c}^I_{321}),\Re(\tilde{c}^I_{322}),\Re(\tilde{c}^I_{323}),\Re(\tilde{c}^I_{331}),\Re(\tilde{c}^I_{332}),\Re(\tilde{c}^I_{333})$$

=(4, 7, 8, 4, 2, 6, 8, 1, 3, 3, 9, 7, 1, 3, 8, 4, 7, 3, 6, 7, 2, 8, 4, 5, 5, 6, 4).

From step 1 of the proposed method, we get the following.

$$a_1 + a_2 + a_3 = \sum_{i=1}^{3} a_i = 7 + 15 + 12 = 34 \quad \text{(total origin supply)}$$

$$b_1 + b_2 + b_3 = \sum_{j=1}^{3} b_j = 11 + 13 + 10 = 34 \quad \text{(total factory demand)}$$

$$e_1 + e_2 + e_3 = \sum_{k=1}^{3} e_k = 11 + 14 + 9 = 34 \quad \text{(total conveyance capacity)}$$

$\Rightarrow$ total origin supply= total factory demand= total conveyance capacity

$\therefore$ the given problem is a balanced.

Now, with the help of the steps 2 and 3 of the proposed method, in conformation to Model (P##), the given IFSTP should be transformed into its equivalent CSTP using the ranking procedure of Varghese and Kuriakose. The relevant and equivalent CSTP to example-3 is presented by Table 10.

Table 10. Crisp form of real-life type II- IFSTP that relevant to example-3

Conveyances → ↓										Capacity e_k
	E1			E1			E1			11
		E2			E2			E2		14
			E3			E3			E3	9
Retail Stores → Factories ↓	D1			D2			D3			Supply a_i
O1	4	7	8	4	2	6	8	1	3	7
O2	3	9	7	1	3	8	4	7	3	15
O3	6	7	2	8	4	5	5	6	4	12
Demand b_j	11			13			10			

After applying 4th step of the proposed method, now, the optimal allotment of the CSTP which relevant to example-3 is obtained and it is shown by Table 11.

'Z_{min}' denotes the minimum objective value of CSTP that relevant to type II- IFSTP and is:

$$Z_{min} = (3) \times (2) + (2) \times (9) + (2) \times (0) + (1) \times (9) + (3) \times (4) + (1) \times (7) + (6) \times (3) = 70 \tag{20}$$

Table 11. The optimum table of real-life type II- IFSTP that relevant to example-3

										Capacity e_k
Conveyances → ↓	E1			E1			E1			11
		E2			E2			E2		14
			E3			E3			E3	9
Retail Stores → **Factories ↓**	D1			D2			D3			Supply a_i
O1	4	7	8	4	2(0)	6	8	1(7)	3	7
O2	3(2)	9	7	1(9)	3(4)	8	4	7	3	15
O3	6	7	2(9)	8	4	5	5	6(3)	4	12
Demand b_j	11			13			10			

The optimal solution of the given example 3 has been obtained directly by using step 5 of the proposed method, which is as follows.

$(y_{211}, y_{313}, y_{122}, y_{221}, y_{222}, y_{132}, y_{332}) = (2, 9, 0, 9, 4, 7, 3)$

$\tilde{Z}^I_{min}$ or Min $\tilde{Z}^I$ denotes the minimum objective value of IFSTP and is:

$\tilde{Z}^I_{min} = (1, 3, 5; 0, 3, 6) \times (2) + (1, 2, 3; 0, 2, 4) \times (9) + (1, 2, 3; 0, 2, 4) \times (0) + (0.5, 1, 1.5; 0, 1, 2) \times (9) + (1, 3, 5; 0, 3, 6) \times (4) + (0.5, 1, 1.5; 0, 1, 2) \times (7) + (4, 6, 8; 3, 6, 9) \times (3)$

$\tilde{Z}^I_{min} = (2, 6, 10; 0, 6, 12) + (9, 18, 27; 0, 18, 36) + (0, 0, 0; 0, 0, 0) + (4.5, 9, 13.5; 0, 9, 18) + (4, 12, 20; 0, 12, 24) + (3.5, 7, 10.5; 0, 7, 14) + (12, 18, 24; 9, 18, 27)$

$\tilde{Z}^I_{min} = $ Min $\tilde{Z}^I = (35, 70, 105; 9, 70, 131)$

$\Re(\tilde{Z}^I) = Z_{min} = \Re(35, 70, 105; 9, 70, 131) = 70$ (21)

The optimal solution of example-3 obtained by the PSK method is equal to the optimal solution of the same example obtained by the LINGO and Matlab software.

RESULTS AND DISCUSSION

The comparative analysis between the PSK method and other existing methodologies, for example, Intuitionistic Fuzzy Linear Programming Method (IFLPM) and Intuitionistic Fuzzy Min-Zero Min-Cost Method (IFMZMCM) is given in Table 12 and 13. The comparison between the theoretical approaches and software approaches with proposed problems are given in Table 12. The optimum solution and objective value of the proposed type II- IFSTPs are compared with the PSK method and other already existing methodologies and are given in Table 13.

Type II- IFSTC refers to 'type II- intuitionistic fuzzy solid transportation cost'.

Table 12. Comparative analysis

Ranking method →	Varghese and Kuriakose (2012)					
	Direct solution method			Software approach		
Problem Number ↓	Linear Programming Method	Integer Programming Method	Min-Zero Min-Cost Method	TORA	MATLAB	LINGO
1	$(y_{212}, y_{121}, y_{133}, y_{221}, y_{222}, y_{312}, y_{332}; Z_{min})=(0, 2, 9, 9, 4, 7, 3; 70)$	$(y_{212}, y_{121}, y_{133}, y_{221}, y_{222}, y_{312}, y_{332}; Z_{min})=(0, 2, 9, 9, 4, 7, 3; 70)$	$(y_{212}, y_{121}, y_{133}, y_{221}, y_{222}, y_{312}, y_{332}; Z_{min})=(0, 2, 9, 9, 4, 7, 3; 70)$	$(y_{212}, y_{121}, y_{133}, y_{221}, y_{222}, y_{312}, y_{332}; Z_{min})=(0, 2, 9, 9, 4, 7, 3; 70)$	$(y_{212}, y_{121}, y_{133}, y_{221}, y_{222}, y_{312}, y_{332}; Z_{min})=(0, 2, 9, 9, 4, 7, 3; 70)$	$(y_{212}, y_{121}, y_{133}, y_{221}, y_{222}, y_{312}, y_{332}; Z_{min})=(0, 2, 9, 9, 4, 7, 3; 70)$
2	$(y_{212}, y_{311}, y_{122}, y_{222}, y_{133}, y_{231}, y_{232}; Z_{min})=(1, 11, 1, 6, 9, 0, 6; 84)$	$(y_{212}, y_{311}, y_{122}, y_{222}, y_{133}, y_{231}, y_{232}; Z_{min})=(1, 11, 1, 6, 9, 0, 6; 84)$	$(y_{212}, y_{311}, y_{122}, y_{222}, y_{133}, y_{231}, y_{232}; Z_{min})=(1, 11, 1, 6, 9, 0, 6; 84)$	$(y_{212}, y_{311}, y_{122}, y_{222}, y_{133}, y_{231}, y_{232}; Z_{min})=(1, 11, 1, 6, 9, 0, 6; 84)$	$(y_{212}, y_{311}, y_{122}, y_{222}, y_{133}, y_{231}, y_{232}; Z_{min})=(1, 11, 1, 6, 9, 0, 6; 84)$	$(y_{212}, y_{311}, y_{122}, y_{222}, y_{133}, y_{231}, y_{232}; Z_{min})=(1, 11, 1, 6, 9, 0, 6; 84)$
3	$(y_{211}, y_{313}, y_{122}, y_{221}, y_{222}, y_{132}, y_{332}; Z_{min})=(2, 9, 0, 9, 4, 7, 3; 70)$	$(y_{211}, y_{313}, y_{122}, y_{221}, y_{222}, y_{132}, y_{332}; Z_{min})=(2, 9, 0, 9, 4, 7, 3; 70)$	$(y_{211}, y_{313}, y_{122}, y_{221}, y_{222}, y_{132}, y_{332}; Z_{min})=(2, 9, 0, 9, 4, 7, 3; 70)$	$(y_{211}, y_{313}, y_{122}, y_{221}, y_{222}, y_{132}, y_{332}; Z_{min})=(2, 9, 0, 9, 4, 7, 3; 70)$	$(y_{211}, y_{313}, y_{122}, y_{221}, y_{222}, y_{132}, y_{332}; Z_{min})=(2, 9, 0, 9, 4, 7, 3; 70)$	$(y_{211}, y_{313}, y_{122}, y_{221}, y_{222}, y_{132}, y_{332}; Z_{min})=(2, 9, 0, 9, 4, 7, 3; 70)$

Table 13. Comparative analysis

Ranking method →	Varghese and Kuriakose (2012)		
Problem Number ↓	IFMZMCM	IFLPM	PSK Method
1	$(y_{212}, y_{121}, y_{133}, y_{221}, y_{222}, y_{312}, y_{332}; \tilde{Z}^I_{min}, Z_{min})=(0, 2, 9, 9, 4, 7, 3; (35, 70, 105; 9, 70, 131), 70)$	$(y_{212}, y_{121}, y_{133}, y_{221}, y_{222}, y_{312}, y_{332}; \tilde{Z}^I_{min}, Z_{min})=(0, 2, 9, 9, 4, 7, 3; (35, 70, 105; 9, 70, 131), 70)$	$(y_{212}, y_{121}, y_{133}, y_{221}, y_{222}, y_{312}, y_{332}; \tilde{Z}^I_{min}, Z_{min})=(0, 2, 9, 9, 4, 7, 3; (35, 70, 105; 9, 70, 131), 70)$
2	$(y_{212}, y_{311}, y_{122}, y_{222}, y_{133}, y_{231}, y_{232}; \tilde{Z}^I_{min}, Z_{min})=(1, 11, 1, 6, 9, 0, 6; (35.5, 84, 132.5; 2, 84, 166), 84)$	$(y_{212}, y_{311}, y_{122}, y_{222}, y_{133}, y_{231}, y_{232}; \tilde{Z}^I_{min}, Z_{min})=(1, 11, 1, 6, 9, 0, 6; (35.5, 84, 132.5; 2, 84, 166), 84)$	$(y_{212}, y_{311}, y_{122}, y_{222}, y_{133}, y_{231}, y_{232}; \tilde{Z}^I_{min}, Z_{min})=(1, 11, 1, 6, 9, 0, 6; (35.5, 84, 132.5; 2, 84, 166), 84)$
3	$(y_{211}, y_{313}, y_{122}, y_{221}, y_{222}, y_{132}, y_{332}; \tilde{Z}^I_{min}, Z_{min})=(2, 9, 0, 9, 4, 7, 3; (35, 70, 105; 9, 70, 131), 70)$	$(y_{211}, y_{313}, y_{122}, y_{221}, y_{222}, y_{132}, y_{332}; \tilde{Z}^I_{min}, Z_{min})=(2, 9, 0, 9, 4, 7, 3; (35, 70, 105; 9, 70, 131), 70)$	$(y_{211}, y_{313}, y_{122}, y_{221}, y_{222}, y_{132}, y_{332}; \tilde{Z}^I_{min}, Z_{min})=(2, 9, 0, 9, 4, 7, 3; (35, 70, 105; 9, 70, 131), 70)$

Figure 3. Graphical representation of type II- IFSTC in terms of TIFN

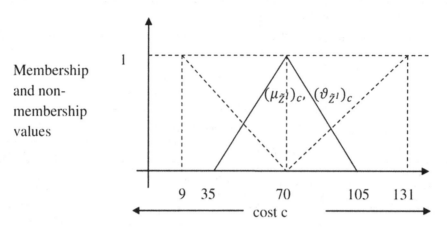

The minimum TIFTC of problem 1 is:

$$\text{Min } \tilde{Z}^I = (35, 70, 105; 9, 70, 131) \tag{17}$$

The equation (17) shows the results of problem 1 and 3, which are shown by a graph (Refer to Figure 3) and are explained as follows.

- The degree of acceptance of the transportation cost for the DM increases ($\uparrow$) if the cost $\uparrow$ from Rs.9 → Rs.35 (i.e., Rs.9 to Rs.35); while it decreases ($\downarrow$) if the cost $\uparrow$ from Rs.35 → Rs.70.
- Beyond (35, 105), the level of acceptance/the level of satisfaction for the DM is 0.
- The DM is totally satisfied/the transportation cost is totally acceptable if the transportation cost is Rs.70.
- The degree of non-acceptance of the transportation cost for the DM $\downarrow$ if the cost $\uparrow$ from Rs.9 → Rs.70 while it $\uparrow$ if the cost $\uparrow$ from Rs.70 → Rs.131.
- Beyond (9, 131), the cost is totally un-acceptable.

Let $\left(\vartheta_{\tilde{Z}^I}\right)_c$ and $\left(\mu_{\tilde{Z}^I}\right)_c$ be two functions which are denote the non-membership (non-acceptance) and membership (acceptance/level of satisfaction) of the transportation cost c, respectively. Then, the DM will get the following results.

- The degree of acceptance of the transportation cost c is $100\left(\mu_{\tilde{Z}^I}\right)_c$ % for the DM.
- The degree of non-acceptance of the transportation cost c is $100\left(\vartheta_{\tilde{Z}^I}\right)_c$ % for the DM.
- The degree of hesitation for the acceptance of the transportation cost c is $100\left(\pi_{\tilde{Z}^I}\right)_c$ % where $\left(\pi_{\tilde{Z}^I}\right)_c = \left(1 - \left(\mu_{\tilde{Z}^I}\right)_c - \left(\vartheta_{\tilde{Z}^I}\right)_c\right)$ is represents the hesitation margin/hesitation index.

Values of $\left(\vartheta_{\tilde{z}^I}\right)_c$ and $\left(\mu_{\tilde{z}^I}\right)_c$ at different values of c can be determined using the following equations.

$$\left(\vartheta_{\tilde{z}^I}\right)_c = \begin{cases} \dfrac{70.00-c}{61.00}, & 9.00 \le c \le 70.00 \\[2mm] \dfrac{c-70.00}{61.00}, & 70.00 \le c \le 131.00 \\[2mm] 1.00, & c < 9.00 \\[1mm] 1.00, & c > 131.00 \\[1mm] 0.00, & c = 70.00 \end{cases}$$

$$\left(\mu_{\tilde{z}^I}\right)_c = \begin{cases} \dfrac{c-35.00}{35.00}, & 35.00 \le c \le 70.00 \\[2mm] \dfrac{105.00-c}{35.00}, & 70.00 \le c \le 105.00 \\[2mm] 0.00, & c < 35.00 \\[1mm] 0.00, & c > 105.00 \\[1mm] 1.00, & c = 70.00 \end{cases}$$

Reviewer's General Comment on this Book Chapter: The chapter discusses the PSK method - a method for solving IFSTPs. The problem definitions of PSK is clear.

To strengthen this book chapter, some examples of the application of the PSK method in some domains are also included in the experiments and discussions.

Merits of the PSK Method

1. PSK method is logically designed. It is a theoretical method. So, this method will not work a trial and error basis.
2. If the problem has more than one optimal solution then it is known as multiple optimal solutions. The multiple optimal solutions are also known as alternative optimal solution. If the problem has an alternative optimal solution then the PSK method will give an alternative optimal solution also. But, finding alternative optimal solutions to the problem by using the existing methods are not possible.
3. It has very less computational steps.
4. It is a direct method. It doesn't depend on intuitionistic fuzzy technique. Purely, it is based on ranking technique.
5. It is easily understandable.
6. This method is always reliable. Since it is a theoretical method.
7. There is no need of any new algorithm when we use this method.
8. This is an efficient method.

9.   In this method, the optimal solution is not depending on initial basic feasible solution. But, it is depending on the optimal solution of the crisp STP equivalent to IFSTP.

10. It is very useful to solve variety of allocation problems.

11. Data mining is described as the process of extracting (or mining) useful data from a larger set of raw data. It is used in many organizations or industries to solve business problems. Similarly, the PSK method solves real-world problems (especially in industry, telecommunications, and coal transportation) from the available data.

12. IFSAP(s) is one of the special cases of IFSTP(s). So, the proposed PSK method is useful for re-source allocation problems, timetabling problems in the classroom, etc.

Demerits of the PSK Method

1.   The proposed method is based on changing TIFNs to real values. If we change TIFNs to real values then we will lose some helpful information.

2.   Without software knowledge we couldn't use PSK method.

3.   The accuracy of the results always depends on the accuracy of the data collection. That is, if the data is incorrect, the results will be incorrect. It is true for all data mining, industry, telecommunications, and coal transportation-related problems.

The author believes that the chapter clearly illustrates the issues, problems, and trend related to the proposed book. The author believes that it represents current thinking on the solid transportation problem. The chapter provides quite a detailed account of the problem, and using three examples, it takes the reader through various algorithms, which is useful and instructive. The author's fully satisfied with the balance of the chapter. Because, it clearly demonstrates how the field has developed and it demonstrates the application of some very recent work in the field. The author believes that there is an over-emphasis in this chapter. The author believes that the references are sufficient, appropriate, and current.

CONCLUSION

In this chapter, the author proposed an intuitionistic fuzzy decision making method for solving type II-IFSTPs. To illustrate the procedure of the proposed method a case study was given by the author. The type II- IFSTPs are solved by the proposed method which differ from the already existing methodologies, namely:

- intuitionistic fuzzy modified distribution method
- IFMZMCM
- IFLPM, etc.

The major advantage of this method is that the obtained solution is always optimal. Theorems have been proved by the author to substantiate that all the solutions obtained by PSK method are optimum or efficient. To apply this method, there is no need of basic feasible solution, i.e., there is no necessity to have $(m+n+l-2)$ number of non-negative allotted entries. Also, there is no need to test the optimality condition. This method is applicable for type I, type II, type III and type IV- IFSTPs.

The PSK method can help the decision-makers in the logistics related issues of real-life problems by aiding them in the decision-making process and providing an optimal solution in an easy and effective manner. So, it can be served as an important tool for a decision-maker when she/he handles various types of logistic problems having different types of parameters.

FUTURE WORK

Interested researchers can use the PSK method with TrIFNs to solve type II- IFSTP/their own work. Neutrosophic set theory is one of the trendy areas in uncertain theory. Those who are willing to solve type II- IFSTP with neutrosophic set theory, can apply the PSK method. Python is a programming language which is used to solve many real-life problems, especially, optimization problems. Nowadays, Python is an essential tool for solving real-life problems. So, solving type II- IFSTP with neutrosophic set and Python programming is an another direction of future research. In further studies of the researchers/ authors, they can use the different types of IFNs or neutrosophic numbers to solve all the four types of IFSTP with PSK method. Increasing the number of sources, number of destinations and number of conveyances in the proposed model may lead to interesting results. For future research suggestions, the proposed approach based on considering the IFSTP of type II under uncertain environment could be implemented on other IFOPs such as IFSAPs, MIFSAPs and other IFSTPs. Another future research suggestion is providing other solution methods like simple heuristic algorithms/computer programming codes to efficiently solve more realistic, large-scale instances of this type II- IFSTP.

ACKNOWLEDGMENT

The author would like to thank his teachers because he couldn't have come to this position without them. The author would also like to thank his family for their motivation and kind support.

REFERENCES

Acar, E., Bayrak, G., Jung, Y., Lee, I., Ramu, P., & Ravichandran, S. S. (2021). Modeling, analysis, and optimization under uncertainties: A review. *Structural and Multidisciplinary Optimization*, *64*(5), 1–37. doi:10.100700158-021-03026-7

Aggarwal, S., & Gupta, C. (2016). Solving intuitionistic fuzzy solid transportation problem via new ranking method based on signed distance. *International Journal of Uncertainty, Fuzziness and Knowledge-based Systems*, *24*(04), 483–501. doi:10.1142/S0218488516500240

Aggarwal, S., & Gupta, C. (2017). Sensitivity analysis of intuitionistic fuzzy solid transportation problem. *International Journal of Fuzzy Systems*, *19*(6), 1904–1915. doi:10.100740815-016-0292-8

Al-Qudaimi, A., Kaur, K., & Bhat, S. (2021). Triangular fuzzy numbers multiplication: QKB method. *Fuzzy Optimization and Modeling Journal*, *3*(2), 34–40.

Ali-Hussein, Y., & Shiker, M. A. (2022). Using the largest difference method to find the initial basic feasible solution to the transportation problem. *Journal of Interdisciplinary Mathematics*, *25*(8), 2511–2517. doi:10.1080/09720502.2022.2040852

Amutha, B., & Uthra, G. (2021). Defuzzification of symmetric octagonal intuitionistic fuzzy number. *Advances and Applications in Mathematical Sciences*, *20*(9), 1719–1728.

Appa, G. (1973). The transportation problem and its variants. *Operational Research Quarterly (1970-1977)*, *24*(1), 79-99. doi:10.2307/3008037

Atanassov, K. T. (1983). Intuitionistic Fuzzy Sets, VII ITKR Session, Sofia, 20-23 June 1983 (Deposed in Centr. Sci.-Techn. Library of the Bulg. Acad. of Sci., 1697/84) (in Bulg.). Reprinted: *Int J Bioautomation*, 2016, *20*(S1), S1-S6.

Ban, A. (2008). Trapezoidal approximations of intuitionistic fuzzy numbers expressed by value, ambiguity, width and weighted expected value. *Notes on Intuitionistic Fuzzy Sets*, *14*(1), 38–47.

Basu, M., Pal, B. B., & Kundu, A. (1994). An algorithm for finding the optimum solution of solid fixed-charge transportation problem. *Optimization*, *31*(3), 283–291. doi:10.1080/02331939408844023

Bera, T., & Mahapatra, N. K. (2020). *Neutrosophic linear programming problem and its application to real life*. Afrika Matematika. doi:10.100713370-019-00754-4

Bhadane, A. P., Manjarekar, S. D., & Dighavkar, C. G. (2021). APBs method for the IBFS of a transportation problem and comparison with North West Corner Method. *GANITA*, *71*(1), 109–114.

Bharati, S. K., & Malhotra, R. (2017). Two stage intuitionistic fuzzy time minimizing transportation problem based on generalized Zadeh's extension principle. *International Journal of System Assurance Engineering and Management*, *8*(S2), 1442–1449. doi:10.100713198-017-0613-9

Burillo, P., Bustince, H., & Mohedano, V. (1994, September). *Some definitions of intuitionistic fuzzy number. First properties*. In *1st Workshop on Fuzzy Based Expert Systems* (pp. 53-55). Bulgaria: Sofia.

Chhibber, D., Srivastava, P. K., & Bisht, D. C. (2021). From fuzzy transportation problem to non-linear intuitionistic fuzzy multi-objective transportation problem: A literature review. *International Journal of Modelling and Simulation*, 1-16. doi:10.1080/02286203.2021.1983075

Dantzig, G. B. (1963). *Linear Programming and Extensions*. Princeton Univ. Press. doi:10.1515/9781400884179

Darehmiraki, M. (2020). A solution for the neutrosophic linear programming problem with a new ranking function. *Optimization Theory Based on Neutrosophic and Plithogenic Sets*, 235–259. doi:10.1016/b978-0-12-819670-0.00011-1

Das, A. (2022). A Comprehensive Study on Neutrosophic Fuzzy Solid Transportation Model and Its Solution Technique. In *Real Life Applications of Multiple Criteria Decision Making Techniques in Fuzzy Domain* (pp. 521–531). Springer Nature Singapore. doi:10.1007/978-981-19-4929-6_24

Das, A., Bera, U. K., & Maiti, M. (2017). Defuzzification and application of trapezoidal type-2 fuzzy variables to green solid transportation problem. *Soft Computing*, 22(7), 2275–2297. doi:10.100700500-017-2491-0

Das, K. N., Das, R., & Acharjya, D. P. (2021). Least-looping stepping-stone-based ASM approach for transportation and triangular intuitionistic fuzzy transportation problems. *Complex & Intelligent Systems*, 7(6), 1–10. doi:10.100740747-021-00472-0

Das, S., & Guha, D. (2013). Ranking of intuitionistic fuzzy number by centroid point. *Journal of Industrial and Intelligent Information*, 1(2), 107–110. doi:10.12720/jiii.1.2.107-110

Das, S. K. (2021). An approach to optimize the cost of transportation problem based on triangular fuzzy programming problem. *Complex & Intelligent Systems*, 1–13. doi:10.100740747-021-00535-2

Devnath, S., Giri, P. K., & Maiti, M. (2021). Fully fuzzy multi-item two-stage fixed charge four-dimensional transportation problems with flexible constraints. *Granular Computing*, 1-19.

Ding, H., & Xie, F. (2023). A solution technique for capacitated two-level hierarchical time minimization transportation problem. *Computers &amp. Operations Research*, 151, 106125. doi:10.1016/j.cor.2022.106125

Fahrudin, M., & Nuraini, A. (2021). Performance evaluation of new ranking function methods with current ranking functions using VAM and MM-VAM. *Proceedings of the 1st International Conference on Mathematics and Mathematics Education (ICMMED 2020)*, (pp. 418-424). IEEE. 10.2991/assehr.k.210508.098

Gen, M., Ida, K., Li, Y., & Kubota, E. (1995). Solving bicriteria solid transportation problem with fuzzy numbers by a genetic algorithm. *Computers & Industrial Engineering*, 29(1), 537–541. doi:10.1016/0360-8352(95)00130-S

Grzegorzewski, P. (2003). Distance and orderings in a family of intuitionistic fuzzy numbers. In EUS-FLAT Conf., Zittau, Germany.

Gupta, G., & Anupum, K. (2017). An efficient method for solving intuitionistic fuzzy transportation problem of type-2. *International Journal of Applied and Computational Mathematics*, 3(4), 3795–3804. doi:10.100740819-017-0326-4

Haley, K. B. (1962). New methods in mathematical programming-The solid transportation problem. *Operations Research*, 10(4), 448–463. doi:10.1287/opre.10.4.448

He, D., Li, R., Huang, Q., & Lei, P. (2014). Transportation optimization with fuzzy trapezoidal numbers based on possibility theory. *PLoS One*, 9(8), e105142. doi:10.1371/journal.pone.0105142 PMID:25137239

Hitchcock, F. L. (1941). The distribution of a product from several sources to numerous localities. *Journal of Mathematics and Physics*, 20(2), 224–230. doi:10.1002apm1941201224

Hussain, R. J., & Kumar, P. S. (2012a). The transportation problem in an intuitionistic fuzzy environment. *International Journal of Mathematics Research*, 4(4), 411–420.

Hussain, R. J., & Kumar, P. S. (2012b). Algorithmic approach for solving intuitionistic fuzzy transportation problem. *Applied Mathematical Sciences*, *6*(80), 3981–3989.

Hussain, R. J., & Kumar, P. S. (2012c). The transportation problem with the aid of triangular intuitionistic fuzzy numbers. In *International Conference on MMASC Conf.* (pp. 819-825). Coimbatore Institute of Technology, Coimbatore.

Hussain, R. J., & Kumar, P. S. (2013). An optimal more-for-less solution of mixed constraints intuitionistic fuzzy transportation problems. *International Journal of Contemporary Mathematical Sciences*, *8*(12), 565–576. doi:10.12988/ijcms.2013.13056

Hussain, M. R., Qahmash, A., Alelyani, S., & Alsaqer, M. S. (2021). Optimal solution of transportation problem with effective approach mount order method: An Operational Research Tool. *Intelligent Computing*, 1151–1168. doi:10.1007/978-3-030-80126-7_81

Jana, D. K. (2016). Novel arithmetic operations on type-2 intuitionistic fuzzy and its applications to transportation problem. *Pacific Science Review A. Natural Science and Engineering*, *18*(3), 178–189.

Jimenez, F., & Verdegay, J. L. (1998). Uncertain solid transportation problems. *Fuzzy Sets and Systems*, *100*(1-3), 45–57. doi:10.1016/S0165-0114(97)00164-4

Jimenez, F., & Verdegay, J. L. (1999). Solving fuzzy solid transportation problems by an evolutionary algorithm based parametric approach. *European Journal of Operational Research*, *117*(3), 485–510. doi:10.1016/S0377-2217(98)00083-6

Joshi, N., & Chauhan, S. S. (2016). A new approach for obtaining optimal solution of unbalanced fuzzy transportation problem. *International Journal of Computers and Technology*, *15*(6), 6824–6832. doi:10.24297/ijct.v15i6.3977

Kacher, Y., & Singh, P. (2021). A comprehensive literature review on transportation problems. *International Journal of Applied and Computational Mathematics*, *7*(5), 1–49. doi:10.100740819-021-01134-y

Kaur, A., Kacprzyk, J., & Kumar, A. (2020a). *Fuzzy transportation and transshipment problems*. Studies in Fuzziness and Soft Computing., doi:10.1007/978-3-030-26676-9

Kaur, A., Kacprzyk, J., & Kumar, A. (2020b). New methods for solving fully fuzzy solid transportation problems with LR fuzzy parameters. In *Fuzzy Transportation and Transshipment Problems* (pp. 145–184). Springer., doi:10.1007/978-3-030-26676-9_7

Khalaf, W. S., Khalaf, B. A., & Abid, N. O. (2021). A plan for transportation and distribution the products based on multi-objective travelling salesman problem in fuzzy environmental. [PEN]. *Periodicals of Engineering and Natural Sciences*, *9*(4), 5–22. doi:10.21533/pen.v9i4.2253

Kour, D., Mukherjee, S., & Basu, K. (2017). Solving intuitionistic fuzzy transportation problem using linear programming. *International Journal of System Assurance Engineering and Management*, *8*(S2), 1090–1101. doi:10.100713198-017-0575-y

Kumar, P. S. (2010). *A comparative study on transportation problem in fuzzy environment* [M.Phil thesis, Jamal Mohamed College].

Kumar, P. S. (2015). *Algorithmic approach for solving allocation problems under intuitionistic fuzzy environment* [PhD thesis, Jamal Mohamed College, affiliated to the Bharathidasan University]. http://hdl.handle.net/10603/209151

Kumar, P. S. (2016a). PSK method for solving type-1 and type-3 fuzzy transportation problems. [IJFSA]. *International Journal of Fuzzy System Applications, 5*(4), 121–146. doi:10.4018/IJFSA.2016100106

Kumar, P. S. (2016b). A simple method for solving type-2 and type-4 fuzzy transportation problems. [IJFIS]. *The International Journal of Fuzzy Logic and Intelligent Systems, 16*(4), 225–237. doi:10.5391/IJFIS.2016.16.4.225

Kumar, P. S. (2017). PSK method for solving type-1 and type-3 fuzzy transportation problems. *Fuzzy Systems*, 367–392. doi:10.4018/978-1-5225-1908-9.ch017

Kumar, P. S. (2018a). A note on 'a new approach for solving intuitionistic fuzzy transportation problem of type-2'. [IJLSM]. *International Journal of Logistics Systems and Management, 29*(1), 102–129. doi:10.1504/IJLSM.2018.088586

Kumar, P. S. (2018b). Linear programming approach for solving balanced and unbalanced intuitionistic fuzzy transportation problems. [IJORIS]. *International Journal of Operations Research and Information Systems, 9*(2), 73–100. doi:10.4018/IJORIS.2018040104

Kumar, P. S. (2018c). A simple and efficient algorithm for solving type-1 intuitionistic fuzzy solid transportation problems. [IJORIS]. *International Journal of Operations Research and Information Systems, 9*(3), 90–122. doi:10.4018/IJORIS.2018070105

Kumar, P. S. (2018d). PSK method for solving intuitionistic fuzzy solid transportation problems. [IJFSA]. *International Journal of Fuzzy System Applications, 7*(4), 62–99. doi:10.4018/IJFSA.2018100104

Kumar, P. S. (2018e). Search for an optimal solution to vague traffic problems using the PSK method. In Handbook of Research on Investigations in Artificial Life Research and Development (pp. 219-257). IGI Global. doi:10.4018/978-1-5225-5396-0.ch011

Kumar, P. S. (2019a). Intuitionistic fuzzy solid assignment problems: A software-based approach. [IJSA]. *International Journal of System Assurance Engineering and Management, 10*(4), 661–675. doi:10.100713198-019-00794-w

Kumar, P. S. (2019b). PSK method for solving mixed and type-4 intuitionistic fuzzy solid transportation problems. [IJORIS]. *International Journal of Operations Research and Information Systems, 10*(2), 20–53. doi:10.4018/IJORIS.2019040102

Kumar, P. S. (2020a). Intuitionistic fuzzy zero point method for solving type-2 intuitionistic fuzzy transportation problem. [IJOR]. *International Journal of Operational Research, 37*(3), 418–451. doi:10.1504/IJOR.2020.105446

Kumar, P. S. (2020b). Algorithms for solving the optimization problems using fuzzy and intuitionistic fuzzy set. [IJSA]. *International Journal of System Assurance Engineering and Management, 11*(1), 189–222. doi:10.100713198-019-00941-3

Kumar, P. S. (2020c). Developing a new approach to solve solid assignment problems under intuitionistic fuzzy environment. [IJFSA]. *International Journal of Fuzzy System Applications*, *9*(1), 1–34. doi:10.4018/IJFSA.2020010101

Kumar, P. S. (2020d). The PSK method for solving fully intuitionistic fuzzy assignment problems with some software tools. In Theoretical and Applied Mathematics in International Business (pp. 149-202). IGI Global. doi:10.4018/978-1-5225-8458-2.ch009

Kumar, P. S. (2021). Finding the solution of balanced and unbalanced intuitionistic fuzzy transportation problems by using different methods with some software packages. In Handbook of Research on Applied AI for International Business and Marketing Applications (pp. 278-320). IGI Global. doi:10.4018/978-1-7998-5077-9.ch015

Kumar, P. S. (2022). Computationally simple and efficient method for solving real-life mixed intuitionistic fuzzy 3D assignment problems. [IJSSCI]. *International Journal of Software Science and Computational Intelligence*, *14*(1), 1–42. doi:10.4018/IJSSCI.309425

Kumar, P. S. (2023a). Algorithms and software packages for solving transportation problems with intuitionistic fuzzy numbers. In *Operational Research for Renewable Energy and Sustainable Environments*. IGI Global.

Kumar, P. S. (2023b). The PSK method: A new and efficient approach to solving fuzzy transportation problems. In J. Boukachour & A. Benaini (Eds.), *Transport and Logistics Planning and Optimization* (pp. 149–197). IGI Global. doi:10.4018/978-1-6684-8474-6.ch007

Kumaran, N. (2021). Minimize the transportation cost on fuzzy environment. *Annals of the Romanian Society for Cell Biology*, 15349–15352. https://www.annalsofrscb.ro/index.php/journal/article/view/5150

Kumar, P. S., & Hussain, R. J. (2014a). A systematic approach for solving mixed intuitionistic fuzzy transportation problems. *International Journal of Pure and Applied Mathematics*, *92*(2), 181–190. doi:10.12732/ijpam.v92i2.4

Kumar, P. S., & Hussain, R. J. (2014b, July). A method for finding an optimal solution of an assignment problem under mixed intuitionistic fuzzy environment. In *ICMS Conf.* (pp. 417-421). Elsevier.

Kumar, P. S., & Hussain, R. J. (2014c). New algorithm for solving mixed intuitionistic fuzzy assignment problem. *Elixir Appl. Math.*, *73*, 25971-25977. https://www.elixirpublishers.com/articles/1406724004_73%20(2014)%2025971-25977.pdf

Kumar, P. S., & Hussain, R. J. (2014d). A method for solving balanced intuitionistic fuzzy assignment problem. *International Journal of Engineering Research and Applications*, *4*(3), 897–903.

Kumar, P. S., & Hussain, R. J. (2015). A method for solving unbalanced intuitionistic fuzzy transportation problems. *Notes on Intuitionistic Fuzzy Sets*, *21*(3), 54–65.

Kumar, P. S., & Hussain, R. J. (2016a). Computationally simple approach for solving fully intuitionistic fuzzy real life transportation problems. [IJSA]. *International Journal of System Assurance Engineering and Management*, *7*(S1), 90–101. doi:10.100713198-014-0334-2

Kumar, P. S., & Hussain, R. J. (2016b). A simple method for solving fully intuitionistic fuzzy real life assignment problem. [IJORIS]. *International Journal of Operations Research and Information Systems, 7*(2), 39–61. doi:10.4018/IJORIS.2016040103

Kumar, P. S., & Hussain, R. J. (2016c). An algorithm for solving unbalanced intuitionistic fuzzy assignment problem using triangular intuitionistic fuzzy number. *The Journal of Fuzzy Mathematics, 24*(2), 289–302.

Kumar, A., & Kaur, M. (2013). A ranking approach for intuitionistic fuzzy numbers and its application. *Journal of Applied Research and Technology, 11*(3), 381–396. doi:10.1016/S1665-6423(13)71548-7

Kumar, A., & Yadav, S. P. (2012). A survey of multi-index transportation problems and its variants with crisp and fuzzy parameters. *Proceedings of the International Conference on Soft Computing for Problem Solving* (SocProS 2011) December 20-22, 2011, 919–932. 10.1007/978-81-322-0487-9_86

Lee, S. U. (2021). Aggregate planning using least cost first assignment algorithm of transportation problem. *The Journal of the Institute of Internet. Broadcasting and Communication, 21*(5), 181–188.

Li, Y., Ida, K., Gen, M., & Kobuchi, R. (1997a). Neural network approach for multicriteria solid transportation problem. *Computers & Industrial Engineering, 33*(3-4), 465–468. doi:10.1016/S0360-8352(97)00169-1

Li, Y., Ida, K., & Gen, M. (1997b). Improved genetic algorithm for solving multiobjective solid transportation problem with fuzzy numbers. *Journal of Japan Society for Fuzzy Theory and Systems, 9*(2), 239–250. doi:10.3156/jfuzzy.9.2_239

Li, D. F., Nan, J. X., & Zhang, M. J. (2010). A ranking method of triangular intuitionistic fuzzy numbers and application to decision making. *International Journal of Computational Intelligence Systems, 3*(5), 522–530.

Liu, S. T. (2006). Fuzzy total transportation cost measures for fuzzy solid transportation problem. *Applied Mathematics and Computation, 174*(2), 927–941. doi:10.1016/j.amc.2005.05.018

Lubis, L. A. (2023). Comparison of completion of VAM, TCOM-SUM transportation problems with stepping stone to determine optimal solutions. In Journal of Physics: Conference Series, 2421. IOP Publishing. doi:10.1088/1742-6596/2421/1/012005

Mahapatra, G. S., & Roy, T. K. (2009). Reliability evaluation using triangular intuitionistic fuzzy numbers, arithmetic operations. *International Scholarly and Scientific Research & Innovation, 3*(2), 422–429.

Mahapatra, G. S., & Roy, T. K. (2013). Intuitionistic fuzzy number and its arithmetic operation with application on system failure. *Journal of Uncertain Systems, 7*(2), 92–107.

Mahapatra, N. K., & Bera, T. (2019). Optimisation by dual simplex approach in neutrosophic environment. *International Journal of Fuzzy Computation and Modelling, 2*(4), 334. doi:10.1504/IJFCM.2019.100347

Malhotra, R., & Bharati, S. K. (2016). Intuitionistic fuzzy two stage multiobjective transportation problems. *Advances in Theoretical and Applied Mathematics, 11*(3), 305–316.

Mhaske, A. S., & Bondar, K. L. (2020). Fuzzy transportation problem by using triangular, pentagonal and heptagonal fuzzy numbers with Lagrange's polynomial to approximate fuzzy cost for nonagon and hendecagon. [IJFSA]. *International Journal of Fuzzy System Applications*, 9(1), 112–129. doi:10.4018/IJFSA.2020010105

Mishra, A., & Kumar, A. (2020). JMD method for transforming an unbalanced fully intuitionistic fuzzy transportation problem into a balanced fully intuitionistic fuzzy transportation problem. *Soft Computing*, 24(20), 15639–15654. doi:10.100700500-020-04889-6

Mitchell, H. B. (2004). Ranking intuitionistic fuzzy numbers. *International Journal of Uncertainty, Fuzziness and Knowledge-based Systems*, 12(3), 377–386. doi:10.1142/S0218488504002886

Mohideen, S. I., & Kumar, P. S. (2010a). A comparative study on transportation problem in fuzzy environment. *International Journal of Mathematics Research*, 2(1), 151–158.

Mohideen, S. I., & Kumar, P. S. (2010b). A comparative study on transportation problem in fuzzy environment. In *International Conference on Emerging Trends in Mathematics and Computer Applications (ICETMCA2010)*, MEPCO Schlenk Engineering College.

Muralidaran, C., & Venkateswarlu, B. (2022). Efficient solutions of time versus cost transportation problems. *International Journal of Logistics Systems and Management*, 43(3), 336–353. doi:10.1504/IJLSM.2022.127081

Nagar, P., Srivastava, P. K., & Srivastava, A. (2021). A new dynamic score function approach to optimize a special class of Pythagorean fuzzy transportation problem. *International Journal of System Assurance Engineering and Management*, 1-10. doi:10.1007/s13198-021-01339-w

Nayagam, G., Lakshmana, V., Venkateshwari, G., & Sivaraman, G. (2008, June). Ranking of intuitionistic fuzzy numbers. In *Proceedings of the IEEE International Conference on Fuzzy Systems FUZZ-IEEE '08* (pp. 1971-1974). IEEE. doi:10.1109/fuzzy.2008.4630639

Ojha, A., Das, B., Mondal, S., & Maiti, M. (2009). An entropy based solid transportation problem for general fuzzy costs and time with fuzzy equality. *Mathematical and Computer Modelling*, 50(1-2), 166–178. doi:10.1016/j.mcm.2009.04.010

Ojha, A., Mondal, S. K., & Maiti, M. (2014). A solid transportation problem with partial nonlinear transportation cost. *Journal of Applied and Computational Mathematics*, 3(150), 1–6.

Paul, N., Sarma, D., & Bera, U. K. (2019). A neutrosophic solid transportation model with insufficient supply. 2019 *IEEE Region 10 Symposium* (TENSYMP). IEEE. doi:10.1109/tensymp46218.2019.8971130

Peng, Z., & Chen, Q. (2013). A new method for ranking canonical intuitionistic fuzzy numbers. In *Proceedings of the International Conference on Information Engineering and Applications (IEA) 2012* (pp. 609-616). Springer, London. 10.1007/978-1-4471-4856-2_73

Pratihar, J., Kumar, R., Dey, A., & Broumi, S. (2020). Transportation problem in neutrosophic environment. *Neutrosophic Graph Theory and Algorithms*, 180–212. doi:10.4018/978-1-7998-1313-2.ch007

Purushothkumar, M. K., Ananthanarayanan, M., & Dhanasekar, S. (2018). Fuzzy zero suffix Algorithm to solve Fully Fuzzy Transportation Problems. *International Journal of Pure and Applied Mathematics*, *119*(9), 79–88.

Qiang, Z., JunHua, H., An, L., GuoMing, C., & QiMin, Y. (2020, August). New ranking methods of intuitionistic fuzzy numbers and Pythagorean fuzzy numbers. In *2020 Chinese Control And Decision Conference (CCDC)* (pp. 4661-4666). IEEE. 10.1109/CCDC49329.2020.9164633

Quddoos, A. (2018). A reliable transportation problem. *Transportation Management*, *1*(2), 1–6. doi:10.24294/tm.v1i2.570

Rani, D. (2022). Multi-objective multi-item four dimensional green transportation problem in interval-valued intuitionistic fuzzy environment. *International Journal of System Assurance Engineering and Management*, 1-18. doi:10.1007/s13198-022-01794-z

Sangeetha, V., Thirisangu, K., & Elumalai, P. (2021). Dual simplex method based solution for a fuzzy transportation problem. *Journal of Physics: Conference Series*, *1947*(1), 012017. doi:10.1088/1742-6596/1947/1/012017

Santhoshkumar, D., & Rabinson, G. C. (2018). A new proposed method to solve fully fuzzy transportation problem using least allocation method. *International Journal of Pure and Applied Mathematics*, *119*(15), 159–166.

Shell, E. (1955). Distribution of a product by several properties, directorate of management analysis. In *Proceedings of the second symposium in linear programming* (Vol. 2, pp. 615-642). IEEE.

Singh, B., & Singh, A. (2023). Hybrid particle swarm optimization for pure integer linear solid transportation problem. *Mathematics and Computers in Simulation*, *207*, 243–266. doi:10.1016/j.matcom.2022.12.019

Singh, J. P., Thakur, N. I., & Kumar, S. (2016). A new approach to solve fully fuzzy transportation problem. *Arya Bhatta Journal of Mathematics and Informatics*, *8*(2), 261–266.

Stoilova, K., & Stoilov, T. (2021). Solving transportation and travelling salesman problems in excel environment. *Advanced Aspects of Engineering Research*, *15*, 48–62. doi:10.9734/bpi/aaer/v15/9759D

Swarup, K., Gupta, P. K., & Mohan, M. (1997). Tracts in operations research. *Sultan Chand & Sons, New Delhi*, *8*, 659–692.

Traneva, V., & Tranev, S. (2021). Two-stage intuitionistic fuzzy transportation problem through the prism of index matrices. *Preprints of Position and Communication Papers of the Federated Conference on Computer Science and Information Systems* (pp. 89–96). FedCSIS. 10.15439/2021F76

Varghese, A., & Kuriakose, S. (2012). Centroid of an intuitionistic fuzzy number. *Notes on Intuitionistic Fuzzy Sets*, *18*(1), 19–24.

Wei, C., & Tang, X. (2013). A new method for ranking intuitionistic fuzzy numbers. In G. Yang (Ed.), *Multidisciplinary Studies in Knowledge and Systems Science* (pp. 45–51). IGI Global. doi:10.4018/978-1-4666-3998-0.ch004

Xie, F., Butt, M. M., Li, Z., & Zhu, L. (2017). An upper bound on the minimal total cost of the transportation problem with varying demands and supplies. *Omega, 68*, 105–118. doi:10.1016/j.omega.2016.06.007

Xie, F., & Li, Z. (2021). An iterative solution technique for capacitated two-stage time minimization transportation problem. *4OR*, 1-48.

Xie, Y., Luo, Y., & Huo, X. (2022). Solving a special type of optimal transport problem by a modified Hungarian algorithm. arXiv preprint arXiv:2210.16645. https://doi.org//arXiv.2210.16645 doi:10.48550

Ye, J. (2017). Neutrosophic number linear programming method and its application under neutrosophic number environments. *Soft Computing, 22*(14), 4639–4646. doi:10.100700500-017-2646-z

Zadeh, L. A. (1965). Fuzzy sets. *Information and Control, 8*(3), 338–353. doi:10.1016/S0019-9958(65)90241-X

Zhu, K., Ji, K., & Shen, J. (2021). A fixed charge transportation problem with damageable items under uncertain environment. *Physica A, 581*, 126234. doi:10.1016/j.physa.2021.126234

Chapter 8
Metrics for Project Management Methodologies Elicitation

Patricia R. Cristaldo
GIBD, Argentina

Daniela Lopez De Luise
iD https://orcid.org/0000-0003-3130-873X
CI2S Labs, Argentina

Lucas La Pietra
GIBD, Argentina

ABSTRACT

This chapter presents an overview of the project management field, and a set of metrics useful to evaluate the goodness of different project management methodologies considering specific features of the enterprise, project, and goals. It is a multidisciplinary problem that covers the technical analysis of main methodologies, requirements, and management perspectives. It aims to translate semantical and subjective appreciations into a combination of well-determined equations giving an approximation through automatic processing, and a systematic appreciation. The confidence levels are introduced in the indicators associated with the metrics. The entire approach considers information taken from documents and tacit biases made explicit through a questionary specifically defined. As will be shown below, one of the benefits of using these metrics is the possibility of assessing the strong association between project success and documents' scope quality. Also, a number of parameters are relevant to select a management methodology and to improve risk determination.

INTRODUCTION

From the fusion of Science and Management emerges software project management (PM) approaches. It covers management strategies, determination of scope, management of stakeholders, risks, planning and control of activities, requirements and establishment of business objectives. PM is related to Informa-

DOI: 10.4018/978-1-6684-7684-0.ch008

tion Technology (IT), and it mostly tries to avoid significant loss due to failures (Chaos Report, 2020). It is motivated by the fact that just 31% of the projects run in the planned conditions and requirements (Hoch & Dulebohn, 2013; Andrias, Matook & Vidgen, 2018), and the critical cause is considered to be the stakeholders' attitudes and how the risk is handled by the leaders (Berssaneti & Carvalho, 2015; Adywiratama et al., 2022). But there are several experts that it considers it is not possible to know in advance the success degree, since the evaluation is based on subjective evaluations of the involved people (Ramos & Mota, 2014; Montequin et al., 2016).

The process of PM for IT processes is complex because people and technology have multiple and diverse links with its environment. According to Lehtinen the complexity derives in dysfunctional communication (Lehtinen et al., 2014) and deviations in the project activity. The solution could be to evaluate carefully the technical team and its habits in the workspace prior to start the job. Many authors found that it also helps the application of good work practices (Fareed, Su, & Awan, 2021; Adywiratama et. al., 2022; Westenberger, Schuler, & Schlegel, 2022)

Among the best known PM in the market are PMBOK (PMI, 2017), PRINCE2 (Prince, 2009; Böhm, 2009), APM (Highsmith, 2010) ISO 21500 (ISO, 2012), SCRUM (Sutherland, 2014; Van Solingen & Van Lanen, 2014), KANBAN (Lei et al., 2015), and CRISP-DM (Shearer, 2000; Shafique & Qaiser, 2014). The main goal in all cases is the proper evolution of the tasks in order to fall within the predetermined resources and timeline.

This article introduces several metrics and indicators, many of them previously published. They are presented here as a tool-set to systematically evaluate requirements that allow determining critical aspects of the various components of PM methodologies. Typically, the most important part of project information is expressed textually in seminal documents during the management of the project. The collection of variables and their considerations, presented in the course of this research, establishes a framework for comparative analysis, where metrics allow a quantitative cross-evaluation of different methodologies. Then it is possible to get a suitability scoring for every methodology under consideration at every project stage. The metrics defined here are based on requirement documentation expressed in natural language by the personnel involved in the leading process. There are also indicators complementing the set, to decide on the adoption of one or another project management methodology.

This article presents and analyzes the state of the art in the field of generating evaluation metrics for PM methodologies. It also presents the set of metrics and indicators mentioned previously, for guiding in project management elicitation stage. Note that some metrics are compatible with the ones in the classical bibliography of this subject. But others are innovative, designed using subtler concerns gathered from traditional expert's criteria. The following shows the state of the art in metrics and evaluation of management control methodologies (section II), presentation metrics/indicator formulated for managing the scope of a project (section III), approach and case studies (sections IV and V respectively), and conclusions (section VI).

LITERATURE REVIEW

The reasons for success or failure in IT-related projects is a well-studied topic. From the literature between 1981 and 1987 (DeLone & McLean, 1992), six interdependent dimensions of Information Systems (IS) success were identified: system quality, information quality, usage, user satisfaction, individual impact, and organizational impact. The list has been modified, to cover recent studies that introduce the possible determinants that may affect the established dimensions (Iriarte & Bayona, 2020). On the other hand, the failure in IS projects has been also studied from the discrepancy between the real and expected requirements. After analyzing successes in IS, the community began to investigate the dimensions and determinants of failures in IS (Hou, 2020). This constitute a seminal part of the present study and frame much of the current derivations and proposals. The features considered for defining the set of metrics are based in the findings of many authors (Ramos & Mota, 2014; Iriarte & Bayona, 2020; Dwi Adywiratama et al., 2020; Adywiratama et al., 2022; Westenberger, Schuler, & Schlegel, 2022) (see Figure 1).

Figure 1. Features taken from bibliography

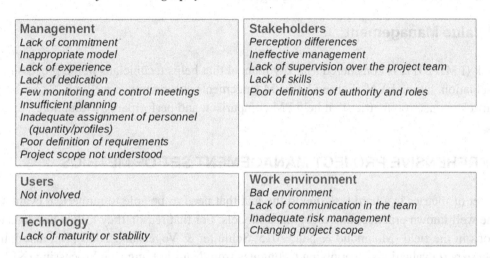

A special remark is important for systems with Artificial Intelligence (AI) (Thomas & Uminsky, 2022) in order to keep under control the risks that might emerge due to the high level of complexity in this type of software. Less dramatic is the case of open innovation projects, but also deserve attention (Shaikh & Randhawa, 2022).

For risk management GOCAME (Goal-Oriented Context-Aware Measurement and Evaluation) (Papa, 2014) is a dominant approach, and work with GQM (Becker, 2014), and C-INCAMI (Contextual-Information Need, Concept Model, Attribute, Metric and Indicator) (Rivera, 2018).

There are metrics related to specific topics like:

Risk

Meaning and scoring in PM contexts (Johansen & Rausand, 2014; Gopal & Amirthavalli, 2019), some of them use Machine Learning (ML) (Oliveira et al., 2019; Zagane, Abdi, & Alenezi, 2020; Li et al., 2022).

Measurement of developers' work as support for project management (Silva Ferreira et al, 2019).

Agile metrics to monitor and control the best practices of the ISO/IEC/IEEE 12207 and ISO/IEC standards. IEC TR 29110-5-1-2 (Mas, Mesquida, & Pacheco, 2020).

There are more metrics for controlling very specific topics

(Vanhoucke, 2011; Harclerode et.al, 2016; Wood, 2017; Meding, Staron, & Söder, 2021).

Source Code

Other metrics evaluate the readability of source code (Siddiqui & Ahmad, 2019) and to estimate defects in the source code

(He et.al, 2015; Al Mamun, Berger, & Hanson, 2019; Kapur & Sodhi, 2020).

Production Stages

There are even metrics related to the different production stages: product, process, test, maintenance and customer satisfaction, using machine learning algorithms (Siri, 2019).

Earned Value Management

The Pmbok (PMI, 2017) is considered as a key manual that helps technicians in the process of performance evaluation, taking EVM (Earned Value Management) as a reference method.

This article focuses on metrics that help PM comparison and performance evaluation.

A COMPREHENSIVE PROJECT MANAGEMENT SET OF METRICS

A proper set of metrics is a hard task due to the fact that need to be able to numerical evaluation following the well-known practices and recognized models. For that reason they follow previous relevant publications in the field (Mahmoud & Niu, 2015; Schlutter & Vogelsang, 2020), but also introduces some other expert evaluations by applying techniques from Natural Language Processing (NLP) (Guo, Cheng, & Cleland-Huang, 2017; Cristaldo et.al., 2021; Cristaldo et.al., 2021; Cristaldo et.al., 2022; Cristaldo et.al., 2022; Cristaldo, López De Luise, & La Pietra, 2022; Melluso, Grangel-González, & Fantoni, 2022; Qiu et.al., 2022). Figure 2 shows a global diagram of the process in order to evaluate methodologies' goodness at a specific project in a determined enterprise.

Figure 2. Main approach

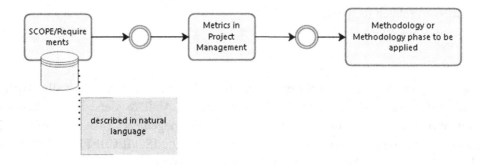

The workflow shows the main steps: the first for covering the early collection of core information that technically supports the project (Chaos Report, 2020). The second phase extracts and organizes all the information in the Business Scope Statement document. As a last step consists in the application of the set of metrics to the document.

The entire set of metrics is in Table 1. The rest of this section describes every entry.

Table 1. Summary of metrics (cont.)

ID	Metric	Formula
1	GCN	relPalCla*relParr
2	GCA	=pond(RQN)*$\log_2$(pond(RQN))+pond(RQI)*$\log_2$(pond(RQI))+pond(RQS)*$\log_2$(pond(RQS))+ pond(RQP)*$\log_2$(pond(RQP))+pond(RQC)*$\log_2$(pond(RQC))

3	RQN	$=\sum(r)/\sum$ (RQN, RQI, RQS, RQP, RQC)
		    r=count (Z>=0)
		    RQN $\mathcal{E}$ [0..1]

4	RQI	$=\sum(r)/\sum$ (RQN, RQI, RQS, RQP, RQC)
		    r= count (Z>=0)
		    RQN $\mathcal{E}$ [0..1]

5	RQS	$=\sum(r)/\sum$ (RQN, RQI, RQS, RQP, RQC)
		    r=count (Z>=0)
		    RQN ϵ [0..1]

6	RQP	$=\sum(r)/\sum$ (RQN, RQI, RQS, RQP, RQC)
		    r= count (Z>=0)
		    RQN ϵ [0..1]

7	RQC	$= \sum(r)/\sum$ (RQN, RQI, RQS, RQP, RQC)
		    r= count (Z>=0)
		    RQN ϵ [0..1]

8	CVR	= p(nec).nec+p(conc).conc + p(comp).comp + p(cons).cons + p(amb).amb+p(verif).verif
9	GradConc	= (num. nouns) + (num. verbs) / num. Words in project scope statement
10	GradCompl	= (num. Functional requirements) + (num.Non-functional requirements)/RQN
11	GradCons	= (num. Contradictions in requirement PT) + (num. Restrictions requirements) num. leaf nodes in requirement PT sub-tree.
12	GradAmb	= (num. Nodes Descriptive adjectives) + num. nodes
13	GradVerif	= $\sum$(pv) (node)/ num. nodes
14	GrTraz	= $\sum$(attribute: ID + sentence + owner + origin + priority + status)/6
15	GrComptAct	$\sum_{i=1}^{n} \dfrac{D_i + R_i + GEDAc_i + ARAct_i + C_i + GERAc_i}{8}$
16	$GEDAc_i$	$\dfrac{\sum_{j=1}^{m} G_j + H_j + RRA_j + NHS_j + FEO_j + NRI_j}{11}$ $NHS_j = NHTEA_j + NHTER_j + NHTDC_j + NHTCC_j$

continues on following page

Table 1. Contiued

ID	Metric	Formula
17	FECost$_i$	$$\frac{\sum_{j=1}^{m}G_j+\text{H}_j+\text{EvalAltCost}_j+\text{COstOpor}_j+\text{FO}_j+\text{NRI}_j}{11}$$ $\text{NHS}_j=\text{NHTEC}_j+\text{NHTPP}_j+\text{NHTCC}_j$
18	GERAc$_i$	$$\frac{\sum_{j=1}^{m}G_j+\text{H}_j+\text{Rec}_j+\text{RecGestion}_j+\text{RecLeg}_j}{9}$$ $\text{Rec}_j=\text{RecCog}_j+\text{RecComp}_j+\text{RecInfra}_j$
19	*GPCal*	$=\sum ((GMx+RetCG) + (MedLeccAp+DesPlan))$
20	*GGEPr*	$=\sum ((GMx+RetCG) + MedLeccAp+DesPlan) + Cant\_MecDesHab + Cant\_Capac + Cant\_Prem\_Rec+ Cant\_Support\_Gcia + Cant\_Resol\_Confl + Cant\_Flows\_Com + Cant\_Changes\_Aprob /10$
21	GGInt	$=\sum$ (# reg_int+ interest + influence + #expectations satisfied+ power + clasif_int + cant_HT_Identif_Int + cant_HT_Rel_Int + cant_HT_Ctrl_Int + MedLeccAp)
22	GGR$_i$	$=\sum$ (Cant_Ri_Identif + RiXEtap + (MedLeccAp+DesPlan) + Plan_Rta_Ri + cant_HT_Identif_Ri + cant_HT_Cualit_Ri + cant_HT_Ctrl_Ri + cant_HT_Cuanti_Ri + cant_HT_Plan_Rta_Ri)

Degree of Business Compressibility (GCN)

It defines the comprehensibility of the text expressed as Business Statement, typically with mission, vision, and scope. It is based in the values of:

$$relPalCla = prom\left(\frac{p}{parr}\right) \tag{1}$$

$$relParr = mPF * fPF \tag{2}$$

$$pkeywords|\,nouns{<}10\% \lor 5{-}10\;wordslessused\,| \tag{3}$$

parr paragraphs (Counted paragraphs of Business Statement)

Degree of Scope Completeness (GCA)

It evaluates whether the text covers main elements bescribing the proposal. When one of the element is not present its value is set to zero.

- Business Requirements (RQN): see ID 3 in the Table
- Stakeholders' Requirements (RQI): based on the needs of people participating, typically past of the projects requirements.
- Requirements for Solutions (RQS): features intended for the product or service.
- Project Requirements (RQP): number of activities/ processes that must be provided.

- Quality Requirements (RQC): conditions/criteria to accomplish

Requirement Validation Criteria (CVR)

CVR stands for "required validation criteria" in Spanish, **C**riterios de **V**alidación de **R**equerimientos. It is a numerical evaluation of several characteristics of the Parse Tree representing the document. Its variables are:

$$\{p(nec)=1 \ (if \ business \ risk=high), \quad 0.5 \ (if \ business \ risk\text{-}neutral), \quad 0.1 \ (if \ business \ risk=low) \tag{4}$$

$$p\left(conc\right)\frac{xx}{childnodes} \tag{5}$$

$$p\left(comp\right)=\frac{outofsubtree}{\left(descendants + \left|nodesoutofthesubtree\right|\right)} \tag{6}$$

- p(cons)= # consistencies/# requirements
- p(amb)=1
- $p(verif)=xx/\#nodes_{until \ level \ n}$
- xx=#deployable requirements=#leaf nodes in the sub-tree

Concise Degree (GradConc)

GradConc stands for Concise Degree in Spanish, **G**raduación de **C**onciso. Represents the efficiency of reduction in the linguistic expression. It is based on the noun counts combined with the same rate for verbs.

Completeness Degree (GradCompl)

GradCompl stands for Completeness degree om Spanish, **G**raduación de **C**ompleto. Represents how meaningful is the text and how well covers the relevant topics.

Consistency Degree (GradCons)

GradCons stands for Consistency (in Spanish **Grad**uación de **Cons**istente, GradCons). Counts contradictions in requirements.

Ambiguity Degree (GradAmb)

GradAmb stands for Ambiguity Degree (in Spanish **Grad**uación de **Amb**igüedad, GradAmb). If evaluates the fuzziness of semantics.

Verification Possibility (GradVerif)

GradVerif stands for its name in Spanish: **Grad**uación de **Ver**ificable (GradVerif). Determines if the requirement statement if suiTable for inspections, analysis, demonstrations and/or tests. Work with:

$$pv\left(node\right) = \begin{vmatrix} 1 : if & \exists a\ finite\ process \\ 1 : if & \exists tests\ for\ his\ requirement \\ else & 0 \end{vmatrix} \tag{7}$$

Traceability Degree of the Requirement (GrTraz)

GrTraz expresses the degree of requirement's traceability (in Spanish **Gr**ado de **Traz**abilidad del Requerimiento, GrTraz). The metric has the following variables:

- ID= {1 if there is a unique ID, else 0}
- sentence= {1 if it can be extracted from scope statement, else 0}
- priority = {1 if its priority is explicit in the requirement list, else 0}
- status= {1 if its status is explicit according status-list, else 0}
- owner = {1 if it is explicit who determined the status, else 0}
- origin= {1 if it is explicit in the statement, else 0}

The next section is a study case using these metrics in real world.

GrComplAct (Degree of Completeness of an Activity)

GrComplAct (in Spanish *Grado de Completitud de una Actividad*), evaluates the completeness of tasks in the plan. When its value is high, the model has better quality. The variables are:

$$D_i = \begin{cases} 1 : type\left(a_i\right) \in LTA \\ 0 : Type\left(a_i\right) \notin LTA \end{cases} \tag{8}$$

LTA= {technical, training, management, functional, non-functional}

$$ARAct_i = \begin{cases} 1 : role\left(a_i\right) \in LDR \\ 0 : role\left(a_i\right) \notin LDR \end{cases} \tag{9}$$

LDR = {project-manager, functional-analyst, leader, foreman, business-analyst, financial-manager, programmer, analyst, non-functional-analyst, tester}

$$R_i = \begin{cases} 1 : resource\left(a_i\right) \in LDI \\ 0 : resource\left(a_i\right) \notin LDI \end{cases} \tag{10}$$

LTI = {materials, machinery, natural, financial}

$$C_i = \begin{cases} 1 \Leftrightarrow \exists c \, / \, c = criteria\left(a_i\right) \wedge c \in T_{acc} \\ else 0 \end{cases} \tag{11}$$

The model hase *n* activities with a set of 8 features a_i to be evaluated. **LTA** is a list of available types of activities defined by the organization. When a_i is in LTA, it is valued to 1 since it is a good sign that the activity was predicted and planned.

ARAct_i uses ***role(x)*** to evaluate if the role assigned to personnel and related to activity a_i is good an gets a 1 as scoring, otherwise it is 0.

R_i represents the predicted resources related to a_i. Note that only types of resources are relevant and enumerated in **LDI**. .

C_i are acceptance criteria in order to consider if a_i can be considered as completed. If this is the case ***criteria(x)*** is 1, which indicates a healthy management. There is a Test of acceptance document to guide this evaluation (T).

GEDAC (Degree of Estimation Activities Duration)

GEDAc (in Spanish **G**rado de **E**stimación de la **D**uración de las **Ac**tividades) assess whether an activity duration was well estimated and accomplished. If this is true, the scoring is 1, indicating a good management. Here the variables are:

$G_j = GMx_j + RetCG_j$, is the granularity or detail level defined with

$$GMx_j = \{10: ManHourDefined \quad 5: MonthHourDefined \quad 1: subprojectDuration\} \tag{12}$$

$$\mathrm{Re}\,tCG_j = \begin{cases} 10 : initialization & 9 : analysis \\ 7 : design & 5 : coding\left(hybrids\right) \\ 3 : beta\left(agile\right) & 1 : alpha\left(\mathrm{P}\,rototyping\right) \end{cases} \tag{13}$$

$H_j = MedLeccAp_j + DesPlan_j$, evaluates the seniority of the project's team

$$MedLeccAp_j = \{0: no \quad 5: optional \quad 10: mandatory\} \tag{14}$$

$$DesPlan_j = \begin{cases} 0 : no & 1 :> 90\% \\ 5 : \% & 6 : \% \\ 9 : \% & 10 : \% \end{cases} \tag{15}$$

$RRA_j = \{1: \text{identified} \quad 0: \text{not identified}\}$ (16)

In this context activity a_i has m tasks. Note that G_j and H_j are also part of *GECost* and *GERAc*. It can also work by itsef as a metric.

GMx is the maximum granularity for the duration specification. The version here is not normalized (to show that even the case of a strong bias it keeps working as a measure of the duration quality). For normalizing the equation is:

$GMx_i = \{1: \text{ManHourDefined} \quad 0.5: \text{MonthHourDefined} \quad 0.1: \text{subprojectDuration}\}$ (17)

RetCG defines a scoring for any delay, with granularity *GMx*. It is close related to the current PM model. In order to make it standardized the stages declared are: initiation, analysis, design, coding, beta, alpha. The version used here is not normalized but eventually it can be used the following version:

$$\mathrm{Re}\,tCG_i = \begin{cases} 1: initiation \quad 0.9: analysis \\ 0.7: design \quad 0.5: coding\,(hybrids) \\ 0.3: beta\,(agile) \quad 0.1: alpha\,(prototyping) \end{cases}$$ (18)

MedLeccAp refer to learned lessons from past projects, its normalized version is:

$MedLeccAp_j = \{0: no \quad 0.5: optional \quad 1: mandatory\}$ (19)

DesPlan is the deviation between plan and real facts. When the project is still running, the deviation is evaluated considering the current status. The normalization is:

$$DesPlan_j = \begin{cases} 0: no\,0.1 > 90\%\,0.5: [70-90)\%\,0.6: [30-70)\%\,0.7: \\ [20-30)\%\,0.9: [10-20)\%\,1: [0-10)\% \end{cases}$$ (20)

RRA defines if there are enough foundations in requirements to determine resources. For each requirement the variables are:

- *NHTEA_j*: number of tools used to perform the activity duration prediction.
- *NHTER_j*: as *NHTEA* for the estimation for resources.
- *NHTDC_j*: similar to *NHTEA* for chronogram developing.
- *NHTCC_j*: similar to *NHTEA* for track and control of the chronogram.
- *FEO_j*: evaluates external influences. It is 1 when there are extra-organizational facts influencing the project, otherwise it is 0.
- *NRI_j*: number of risks identified. An improved version takes NRI_j^{-1}.

GECost (Degree of Cost Estimation)

Evaluates the detail/precision of costs estimation (GECost, stands for its initials in Spanish **G**rado de Estimación de **Cost**os, degree of cost estimation). The variables are:

$G_j = GMx_j + RetCG_j$, is the granularity or detail level

$H_j = MedLeccAp_j + DesPlan_j$, is seniority of the project's team

$$EvalAltCost_j = \{1: \textit{identified} \quad 0: \textit{not identified}\} \tag{21}$$

$$CostOpor_j = \{1: \textit{identified} \quad 0: \textit{not identified}\} \tag{22}$$

EvalAltCost refers to the alternative approaches chosen for costing. If there are more than one proposals for making the estimation the value is 1, otherwise it is 0.

CostOpor (opportunity cost, in Spanish *Costo de Oportunidad*) is the scoring for potential benefits from any source. It is 1 if there is a source. Other variables are:

- *NHTEC* (*Cantidad de Herramientas y Técnicas para la Estimación de Costos*): number of technical methodologies applied during the costing. Its value accumulates 1 for each of the following: Expert judgment, analog estimation, parametric estimation, bottom-up estimation, three-value estimation, reserve analysis, quality cost, and estimating software.

- *NHTPP*: number of tools and techniques used for the budget (*Cantidad de Herramientas y Técnicas para la Preparación del Presupuesto*). Adds 1 for each of the following: Sum of costs, reserve analysis, expert judgment, and historical data.

- *NHTCC*: number of tools and techniques used for expenses control (Cantidad de **H**erramientas y **T**écnicas para el **C**ontrol de los **C**ostos). Considers 1 for each of the following: Earned Value Management, Projections, Performance Review, Variance Analysis, Reserve Analysis, and Project Management Software.

- *FO_j*: organizational influences. It is 1 if there are organizational facts influencing the project.

GERAc (Degree of Estimation of Resources for Activities)

The quality of the estimation performed for every resource required for task *j* pertaining to activity a_i (in Spanish *Grado de Estimación de los Recursos para las Actividades*, *GERAc*) has the following variables:

$G_j = GMx_j + RetCG_j$, is the granularity

$H_j = MedLeccAp_j + DesPlan_j$, is the seniority of project's team.

$$RecCog_j = \{1: \textit{identified} \quad 0: \textit{not identified}\} \tag{23}$$

$$RecComp_j = \{1: \textit{identified} \quad 0: \textit{not identified}\} \tag{24}$$

$$RecInfra_j = \{1: \textit{identified} \quad 0: \textit{not identified}\} \tag{25}$$

$$RecGestion_j = \{1: \textit{identified} \quad 0: \textit{not identified}\} \tag{26}$$

$RecLeg_j = \{1:\ identified \quad 0:\ not\ identified\}$ (27)

Other variables are: **RecCog** (availability of cognitive resources for the estimation performed), **RecComp** (availability of computational resources), **RecInfra** (existence of infrastructure resources), **RecGestion** (if there are management resources for this task estimation), and **RecLeg** (whether there are resources for evaluation about lawfulness of the task).

GPCal (Degree of Quality Planning)

Evaluates the quality planning, according to business requirements, stakeholder requirements, solution requirements, project requirements and quality requirements. If one of these elements is not present, its value is 0. The variables are:

- Gmx (maximum granularity) = {HH=10, MH=5, SubProy=1}
- RetCG (delay in granular calculation) = {survey=10, analysis=9, design=7, coding(hybrid)=5, beta=3(agile), alpha(prototyping)=1}
- MedLeccAp (measures lessons learned) = {no=0, optional=5, mandatory=10}
- DesPlan (measures the deviation between what was executed and what was planned) = {no=0, >90%=1, [70-90) %=5, [30-70) %=6, [20-30) %=7, [10-20) %=9, [0-10) %=10}

GGEPr (Degree of Project Team Management)

It evaluates the management of the project team implies the evaluation of the performance of the people, the resolution of problems, the administration of changes, among others. The variables are:

- Gmx (maximum granularity) = HH=10, MH=5, SubProy=1}
- RetCG (delay in granular calculation) = {survey=10, analysis=9, design=7, coding(hybrid)=5, beta=3(agile), alpha(prototyping)=1}
- MedLeccAp (measures lessons learned) = {no=0, optional=5, mandatory=10}
- DesPlan (measures the deviation between what was executed and what was planned) = {no=0, >90%=1, [70-90) %=5, [30-70) %=6, [20-30) %=7, [10-20) %=9, [0-10) %=10}
- Cant_MecDesHab (Number of mechanisms for skills development) = {1: identified; 0: not identified}
- Cant_Capac (Number of trainings) = {1: identified; 0: not identified}
- Cant_Prem_Rec (Number of awards and recognitions) = {1: identifies; 0: not identified}
- Cant_Support_Gcia (Number of genency supports) = {1: is identified; 0: not identified}
- Cant_Resol_Confl (Amount of conflict resolution) = {1: is identified; 0: not identified}
- Cant_Flows_Com (Number of communication flows) = {1: is identified; 0: not identified}
- Cant_Changes_Aprob (Number of approved changes) = $\sum$ (changes requested, changes rejected).

GGInt (Degree of Stakeholder Management)

Calculated if along with the business requirements are the relevant requirements of the stakeholders in the project. If any of these metric elements cannot be evaluated, it is evaluated to zero. The variables are:

- #reg_int = {1: is identified in list_ident_int; 0: not identified in list_ident_int}
- list_ident_int = {name, position, role, contact}
- interest = {low=1, medium=5, high=10}
- influence = {low=1, medium=5, high=10}
- # expectations satisfied = {1: identified; 0: not identified}
- power = {low=1, medium=5, high=10}
- clasif_int = {1: is identified in list_ident_int; 0: not identified en list_ident_int}
- list_clasif_int = {internal, external, positive influence, negative influence, neutral influence}
- cant_HT_Identif_Int (Number of Tools and Techniques to identify stakeholders) = $\sum$ (expert judgment, stakeholder analysis, meetings)
- cant_HT_Rel_Int (Number of Tools and Techniques to manage the relationship with stakeholders) = $\sum$ (expert judgment, meetings, analysis techniques)
- cant_HT_Ctrl_Int (Number of Tools and Techniques to control the relationship with stakeholders) = $\sum$ (software, expert judgment, meetings)
- MedLeccAp(measures lessons learned) = {no=0, optional=5, mandatory=10}

Degree of Risk Management

This metrics involves the identification, qualitative analysis, quantitative analysis, response planning, and risk control. The variables are:

- Cant_Ri_Identif (Number of identified risks) = {1: is identified in list_Ri_identif; 0: not identified in list_Ri_identif}
- list_Ri_identif = {identifier, description, owner, identification date, prob_occurrence, impact, severity, plan_rta_ri}
- prob_ occurrence = {low=1, medium=5, high=10}
- impact = {low=1, medium=5, high=10}
- severity = {low=1, medium=5, high=10}
- Plan_Rta_Ri (Risk response plan) = {1: identified; 0: not identified}
- RiXEtap (risks by stages) = {start=10, planning=9, execution and control=7, closing=5}
- MedLeccAp (measures lessons learned) = {no=0, optional=5, mandatory=10}
- DesPlan (measures the deviation between what was executed and what was planned) = {no=0, >90%=1, [70-90) %=5, [30-70) %=6, [20-30) %=7, [10-20) %=9, [0-10) %=10}
- cant_HT_Identif_Ri (Number of Tools and Techniques to identify risks) = $\sum$ (document review, data collection techniques, checklist analysis, assumption analysis, diagramming techniques, SWOT analysis, expert judgment, meetings)
- cant_HT_Cualit_Ri (Quantity of Tools and Techniques to analyze risks qualitatively) = $\sum$ (assessment of probability and impact of risks, matrix of probability of impact, evaluation of the quality of risk data, categorization of risks, evaluation of the urgency of risks, expert judgment, meetings)
- cant_HT_Ctrl_Ri (Number of Tools and Techniques to control risks) = $\sum$ (risk reassessment, risk audits, variance and trend analysis, technical performance measurement, reserve analysis, meetings).

- cant_HT_Cuanti_Ri (Quantity of Tools and Techniques to analyze risks qualitatively) = $\sum$ (data collection and data representation, quantitative analysis, modelling techniques, expert judgment, meetings)
- cant_HT_Plan_Rta_Ri (Number of Tools and Techniques to plan responses to risks) = $\sum$ (strategies for negative risks or threats, strategies for positive risks or opportunities, contingency strategies, expert judgment, meetings)

PROTOTYPE FOR APPLICATION OF METRICS

This section introduces a measurement framework that allows, through the metrics detailed above, to evaluate the methodologies, obtaining a metric result that expresses the degree of applicability, effectiveness and efficiency in different contexts. The Python code is:

```
import pandas as pd
import numpy as np
df=pd.read_csv('Encuestas2.csv')
#New metrics
parametrosDFMetricas=['username','GPCal','GGEPr','GGInt','GradAdecHerramGesInt
','GradGesRies','GGDoc']
parametrosGPCal=['GMx','RetCG','MedLeccAp','DesPlan']
parametrosGGEPr=['DesarrolloHab','Capacitaciones','PremiosyRecon','SoportesGer
encias',
                'ResolConflictos','FlujosComunicacionales']
parametrosGGInt=['interesados','interes','influencia','expectativasSatisfchas'
,'poder']
parametrosGradAdecHerramGesInt=[]
parametrosGradGesRies=['probabilidadDeOcurrencia','riesgosIdentificados']
parametrosGGDoc=['documentos','localizacionDocumento','MedLeccAp','consultas']
parametrosMetricasHastaAhora=['username',
        'lecciones aprendidas',
        'herramientas y tecnicas para el aseguramiento de la calidad',
        'herramientas y tecnicas para el control de la calidad',
        'herramientas y tecnicas para planificar el equipo del proyecto',
        'herramientas y tecnicas para desarrollar el equipo del proyecto',
        'herramientas y tecnicas para identificar los interesados',
        'herramientas y tecnicas para identificar los riesgos',
        'herramientas y tecnicas para identificar cualitativamente los riesgos',
        'herramientas y tecnicas para identificar cuantitativamente los ries-
gos',
        'herramientas y tecnicas para planificar las respuestas a los riesgos',
        'requisitos de negocio',
        'requisitos funcionales',
        'requisitos no funcionales',
```

```
            'requisitos de interesados',
            'requisitos de proyectos',
            'requisitos de calidad',
            'grado completitud de alcance']
#Metrics calculations
#users
listUser= list(df.iloc[:,1])
#Learned lections
dictMedLeccAp={'Sí.':1,'Sí':1, 'No':0}
dictMedLeccAp2={6:10,0:0, 1:5,2:5,3:5,4:5,5:5}
dfMedLeccAp = df.filter(regex='Register Learned lections').
replace(dictMedLeccAp)
listMedLeccAp=list(dfMedLeccAp.sum(axis = 1, skipna = True).
replace(dictMedLeccAp2))
def count_tools(value,separator):
    if value!=value:
        return 0
    else:
        if value=="None of the previous.":
            return 0
        else:
            listvalue=value.split(separator)
            return len(listvalue)
#Requirement calculations requerimientos
#Business Requirement
dfReqNeg = list(df.iloc[:,20].apply(lambda x: count_tools(x,';')))
#Functional requirements
dfReqFun = list(df.iloc[:,22].apply(lambda x: count_tools(x,';')))
#Non functional requirements/sotution reqq.(RQS)
dfReqNoFun = list(df.iloc[:,24].apply(lambda x: count_tools(x,';')))
#Individuals requirements (RQI)
dfReqInt = list(df.iloc[:,26].apply(lambda x: count_tools(x,';')))
#Project requirements (RQP)
dfReqProy = list(df.iloc[:,28].apply(lambda x: count_tools(x,';')))
#Quality requirements (RQC)
dfReqCal = list(df.iloc[:,30].apply(lambda x: count_tools(x,';')))
#Completeness of activity evaluation
dfGradoCompAlc= []
for i in range(len(dfReqNeg)):
    res=dfReqNeg[i]*np.log2(dfReqNeg[i])+dfReqInt[i]*np.log2(dfReqInt[i])+ \
        dfReqNoFun[i]*np.log2(dfReqNoFun[i])+dfReqProy[i]*np.
log2(dfReqProy[i])+ \
            dfReqCal[i]*np.log2(dfReqCal[i])
    dfGradoCompAlc.append(res)
```

```
#tools/techniques for QA
dfAsegCal = list(df.iloc[:,67].apply(lambda x: count_tools(x,',')))
#toole/techniques for quality control
dfContCal = list(df.iloc[:,64].apply(lambda x: count_tools(x,';')))
#Tools/approaches to plan the project HHRR
dfPlanEq = list(df.iloc[:,68].apply(lambda x: count_tools(x,';')))
#Tools/Approaches to developr HHRR
dfDesEq = list(df.iloc[:,70].apply(lambda x: count_tools(x,';')))
#Tools/techniques to identify interested persons
dfInteres = list(df.iloc[:,74].apply(lambda x: count_tools(x,';')))
#Tools/techniques to identify risks
dfRiesgos = list(df.iloc[:,78].apply(lambda x: count_tools(x,';')))
#Tools/techniques to identify risks by quality
dfRiesgosCual = list(df.iloc[:,80].apply(lambda x: count_tools(x,';')))
#tools/techniques for qualitative risk identification
dfRiesgosCuan =list(df.iloc[:,82].apply(lambda x: count_tools(x,';')))
#tools/techniques to plan risk answers
dfRespRiesgos = list(df.iloc[:,84].apply(lambda x: count_tools(x,';')))
#generation of df
dfMetricas = pd.DataFrame(list(zip(listUser, listMedLeccAp, dfAsegCal, dfCont-
Cal,       dfPlanEq,dfDesEq,dfInteres,dfRiesgos,
dfRiesgosCual,dfRiesgosCuan,dfRespRiesgos,
dfReqNeg,dfReqFun,dfReqNoFun,dfReqInt,dfReqProy,
dfReqCal,dfGradoCompAlc)),
columns = parametrosMetricasHastaAhora)
dfMetricas.to_excel("metricas.xlsx")
```

APPLICATION OF METRICS

This section presents the application of the set of metrics to a small sample of enterprises. Figure 3 shows the volunteers' profile, while Figure 4 describes the main business of companies where they belong.

There is one dataset with the scope of the product and the project as perceived by the PM of the enterprise, and other with the same information derived from other sources.

Demographic Evaluation

Most of the enterprises belong to private sector (80%), with almost half (40%) with medium size and 30% big enterprises. Most of the volunteers are PM (65%). From the total of the cases only 20% have knowledge of methodologies and good practices. Only 60% participated in the project / product formal definition.

Figure 3. Volunteer profiles

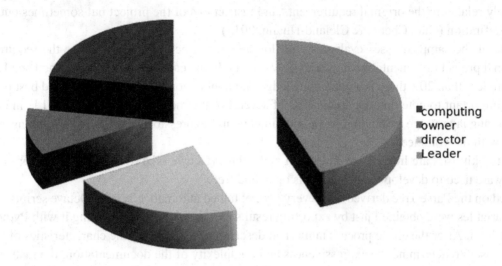

Figure 4. Company size

Metric Approaches

This section explains the effects of the working approach based on the prototype shown in section IV, which implements metrics described in the previous section. The first evidence is the complexity of the process involved in obtaining and correct evaluation of the information. There are many of the metrics introduced here that usually fall out of a numeric evaluation and are typically considered as a recommendation or subjective global appreciation (Guo, Cheng, & Cleland-Huang, 2017; Cristaldo et al., 2021; Cristaldo et al., 2021; Cristaldo et al., 2022; Cristaldo et al., 2022; Cristaldo, López De Luise, & La Pietra, 2022; Melluso, Grangel-González, & Fantoni, 2022; Qiu et al., 2022).

Table 2 is the summary of the scores obtained with the metrics implemented in the prototype. The are deeply related to the original requirements and restrictions of the project but sometimes out of the project definition (Guo, Cheng, & Cleland-Huang, 2017).

Some of the sampled cases evaluates with low scoring (Enc4 and Enc5), since the requirements and formal project documentation have very low quality. In the cases of high scores (Enc8 and Enc10), which are less than 20% there is a good knowledge and application of methodologies and best practice.

It is important to note that the application of several of the metrics requires some NLP, in order to perform language usage evaluation in the documents and expressions written in the polling used to interact with the volunteers.

The toolkit used are libraries from Python and octave (Octave NLTK(c) library). In every case all the software used to develop the prototype is open and free.

Based on the Parse Tree derived with every text, obtained automatically with Octave scripts, a number of variables were obtained just by exporting results to a log and post-processing it with Python in a batch fashion. After the entire process numerical descriptions expressing the characteristics of the PT, could be used to determine the expressiveness and complexity of the documentation, the maturity and quality of the approach involved and the applicability of one or more software management model. Table 3 shows the results of applying GGInt, from the Parse Tree, note that null values are presented for ID4 and ID5, coinciding with those expressed in Table 4.

Table 2. Preliminary results of application of metrics

	GCN	GCA	RQN	RQI	RQS	RQP	RQC	GGInt	GGRi	GPCal	GGEPr
ID1	0.3	0.01	0.3	0.2	0.25	0.05	0.05	3.69	5.41	0.33	2.31
ID2	0.6	0.02	0.13	0.13	0.38	0.38	0.0	1.98	4.33	0.03	1.73
ID3	0.25	0.11	0.1	0.1	0.0	0.28	0.0	3.01	5.12	0.01	2.12
ID4	0.33	0.26	0.03	0.03	0.35	0.64	0.02	0.03	4.03	1.03	3.93
ID5	0.15	0.01	0.15	0.0	0.0	0.01	0.58	0.05	4.99	1.05	1.99
ID6	0.35	0.22	0.31	0.32	0.11	0.08	0.12	3.31	5.32	0.31	2.32
ID7	0.63	0.22	0.25	0.29	0.12	0.24	0.17	3.97	6.12	1.07	4.12
ID8	0.61	0.21	0.68	0.67	0.70	0.16	0.15	3.18	4.27	1.18	3.17
ID9	0.68	0.32	0.51	0.33	0.41	0.62	0.72	3.92	6.33	2.02	5.31
ID10	0.74	0.31	0.41	0.55	0.52	0.41	0.75	5.29	6.59	2.82	6.52

Note that measures of many kinds are obtained systematically and automatically from data collection of information mainly expressed as texts. In this context subjective evaluations are reduced to a small bias and even used as part of the quality evaluation, not as a building block of the scoring but to differentiate cases with formal and informal procedures. Informed leaders usually match his responses to project formal documents.

There is a step with NLP accomplished with the Octave NLTK library (c). This allows obtaining numerical evaluations on the expressiveness and complexity of the descriptive language of the documents, and indirectly of the information contained.

Table 3 shows the behavior of the keyword frequencies corresponding to all the concatenated responses to determine the scope. This indicates that the companies in the sample do not consider in the description of the scope the planning of various aspects that are necessary at the beginning of their projects.

Table 3. Keyword frequencies

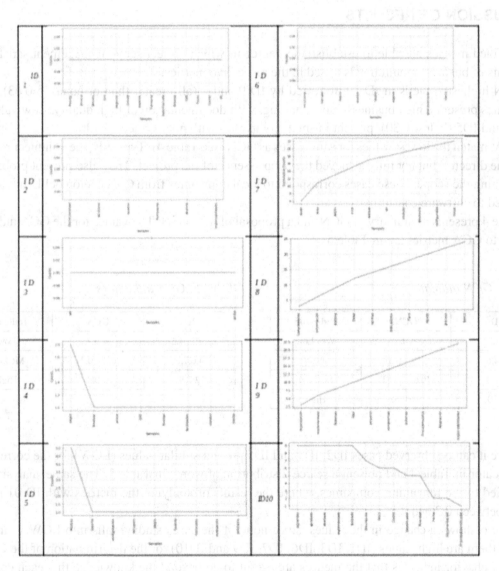

In the GCA metric, in turn, the partial values of its components RQN, RQI, RQS, RQP and RQC are discriminated. Table 4 shows the behavior of the distribution of the words in each ID. The L represent a linear behavior, where all the words have the same frequency (value 1). The entries with the value NO, correspond to the cases in which the respondent does not answer the question. The rest of the cells present words (one or more), which exceed the average value of the rest and are therefore considered of special value for the analysis.

Note that out of 50 entries, 42% have linear entries and 10% do not respond. In total they add up to 52%.

DISCUSSION OF RESULTS

The defined metrics are able to establish the degree to which project scope management satisfies the equations of business requirements raised in the respective metrics.

GCN highest value is in ID 10, followed by ID 9 and 7 (all greater than or equal to 0.63). These companies present a high business understanding, with documentation of high quality. Low values are in ID3 and ID5 (below 0.30), present in small companies with poor project results.

GCA, match the lowest values for same cases as GCN (see Table 4). Typically, the volunteer responding is the director, but not fully achieved the deep essence of the project. They also present problems in determining the scope. These cases correspond to local companies from Concepción del Uruguay, both dedicated to software consulting.

Table 4 presents a summary of GCN and a proposal of indicators. The values for the GCA indicators applied to GCA metrics are in Table 5.

Table 4. GCN indicators

ID	GCN	Indicator
3,5	< 0.3	Very Low
1,4,6	[0.3 – 0.5]	Low
2,7,8	[0.6 – 0.68]	Medium
9,10	> =0.68	High

Table 5. GCA indicators

ID	GCA	Indicator
1,2,3,4,5	< 0.2	Low
4,6,7,8	[0.2 – 0.3]	Medium
2,7,8	> 0.3	High

There it can be observed cases ID2, ID4 and ID5 present similar values (LOW) for the corresponding indicator in Table 4 and present a scarce distribution of words in Table 3. The same analysis could be applied to the remaining companies, where the results of applying the metrics with ID 01 present values between 0.3 and 0.5.

Table 6 shows a change in the values, since none of the cases studied falls into LOW values, but most of them are high values (ID1, ID3, ID6, ID7, ID9 and ID10) for the determination of the GGR_i,

This behavior indicates that the metrics are useful to go beyond the knowledge that each company about the project management. In some cases, companies with clear knowledge in project management or not, clearly define their activities according to the requirements using specific words, typically aligned to the areas of knowledge.

Table 6. GGInt indicators

ID	GGInt	Indicator
2,4,5	< 0.3	Low
1,3,6,7,8,9	[0.3 – 0.5]	Medium
10	> 0.5	High

Table 8. GPCal indicators

ID	GPCal	Indicator
1,2,3	< 0.3	Low
4,5,6,7,8,9,10	[0.3 – 0.5]	Medium
......	> 0.5	High

Table 7. GGRi indicators

ID	GGRi	Indicator
......	< 0.3	Low
2,4,5,8	[0.3 – 0.5]	Medium
1,3,6,7,9,10	> 0.5	High

Table 9. GGEPr indicators

ID	GGEPr	Indicator
1,2,5,6,7,8	< 0.3	Low
3,4,9	[0.3 – 0.5]	Medium
10	> 0.5	High

The highest GGInt occurs in ID 10, followed by ID 9, Table 1. The explanation is that these companies have a high understanding of the business and particularly that related to the management of stakeholders. They are well documented. The results match with previous results for metrics for Requirements Validation (CVR) and Requirements Traceability Degree (GrTraz), Business Comprehensibility (GCN) and Scope Completeness Degree (GCA) (Cristaldo et.al., 2021; Cristaldo et.al., 2021; Cristaldo et.al., 2022; Cristaldo et.al., 2022).

In the same way, it can be seen that in the cases of ID2, ID4 and ID5 present LOW indicator in Table 4, scarce distribution of words in Table 2. The same analysis could be applied to the rest of the cases.

The equation with ID.02 gives the results shown in Table 5. It presents a change in the values, since none of the cases studied falls into low values, and most of them have high values (ID1, ID3, ID6, ID7, ID9, and ID10) for metric GGRi.

The highest GPCal is for case ID 10, followed by case ID 9 (see Table 4). This is because these companies present high understanding of the business and particularly those linked to quality. Their documentation is well formalized, but each one has a different size. These results coincide with the results of the previously applied metrics for Requirements Validation (CVR) and Requirements Traceability Degree (GrTraz), Business Comprehensibility (GCN) and Scope Completeness Degree (GCA) (Cristaldo et.al., 2021).

With similar analysis, cases ID1, ID2, ID3, and ID6 match in values LOW for the indicator (Table 4) and present a scarce distribution of words in Table 2. Something similar is observed in the remaining companies, where the results of applying the equation ID.02 have scores between 0.3 and 0.5. Something interested is that case ID10 continues at high values, while ID3, ID4 and ID9 fall to intermediate values of GGEPr.

CONCLUSION

This article presents the problem of determining the state of PM conditions in order to evaluate the adequacy of different models to specific real cases. It also introduces a set of metrics, which also seek to fully state the scope of a project and, based on it, evaluate the appropriate methodology to manage the project. The set of metrics presented allows the application of associated indicators for an objective evaluation of project management methodologies

The use of metrics allows quality aspects to be made explicit in descriptions of the activities that make up the scope and of requirements at different levels of specificity, which are compatible with simple and traditional linguistic analyses.

While some of the failure factors in IS projects are difficult to anticipate and manage, the relevance of other typical factors for a particular organization can be easily clarified in advance. Likewise, it can be considered a contribution to the reduction of the factors that contribute to project failures, investigated in section II, allowing the project manager to choose an appropriate project management methodology. Managers are recommended to have a clear vision involving aspects related to the stakeholders, since as we have seen, in reference to the risks there is more awareness of them, from the formulation of the project scope.

Not only expand the sample of the presented use-case to generalize the findings and transfer them to other contexts but generate a friendly tool for potential users of this type of metrics as well in the future.

Furthermore, it must be related the metrics for the identification of implicit knowledge, found in texts that describe the scope of the project, applying text mining techniques, related to the process of discovering and extracting relevant and non-trivial knowledge from unstructured texts. Nevertheless, complexity of natural language makes it difficult to extract information from texts. Consequently, building general-purpose representations of meaning from text is still depending on restrictions.

Scope definition of a project must be improved using gamification techniques, not only to stimulate the definition of the same by the project managers but also to achieve greater commitment from the interested parties during the obtaining of the requirements.

REFERENCES

Adywiratama, A., Ko, C., Raharjo, T., & Wahbi, A. (2022). Critical success factors for ICT project: A case study in project colocation government data center. *Procedia Computer Science*, *197*, 385–392. doi:10.1016/j.procs.2021.12.154

Al Mamun M., Berger C., Hanson J. (2019). *Effects of measurements on correlations of software code metrics*. Springer. https://doi.org/. doi:10.1007/s10664-019-09714-9

Andrias, M., Matook, S., & Vidgen, R. (2018). Towards a typology of agile ISD leadership. *Twenty-Sixth European Conference on Information Systems (ECIS2018)*, Portsmouth, UK. 10.1177/096032717100300106

Becker, P. (2014). Visión de proceso para estrategias integradas de medición y evaluación de la calidad. [Tesis Doctoral, Facultad de Informática, Universidad Nacional de La Plata].

Berssaneti, F., & Carvalho, M. (2015). Identification of variables that impact project success in Brazilian companies. *International Journal of Project Management*, *33*(3), 638–649. doi:10.1016/j.ijproman.2014.07.002

Böhm, A. (2009). *Application of PRINCE2 and the Impact on Project Management.*

Cristaldo, P., López De Luise, D., & La Pietra, L. (2022). *Influencia de la Visión Organizacional en los riesgos de la Gestión de Proyectos. 10mo Congreso Nacional de Ingeniería Informática/Sistemas de Información (CoNaIISI).* Concepción del Uruguay. doi:10.33414/ajea.1146.2022

Cristaldo P., López De Luise D., La Pietra L., De Battista A. (2021). Metrics for validation and traceability of Project Management Requirements. *Global Research and Development Journal for Engineering (GRDJE).*

Cristaldo, P., López De Luise, D., La Pietra, L., & De Battista, A. (2022). Medición para la evaluación transversal de metodologías de gestión de proyectos. *WICC 2022; XXIV Workshop de Investigadores en Ciencias de la Computación.* Springer.

Cristaldo, P., López De Luise, D., La Pietra, L., De Battista, A., & Hemanth, J. (2021). Metrics for the Systematic Evaluation of Project Management Methodologies. [IJSSMET]. *International Journal of Service Science, Management, Engineering, and Technology.*

Cristaldo, P., López De Luise, D., La Pietra, L., Retamar, S., & De Battista, A. (2022). *Métricas para Metodologías de Gestión de Proyectos: planificación de la calidad y equipo de gestión. IEEE BIENNIAL CONGRESS OF ARGENTINA.* ARGENCON.

Davis, K. (2014). *Different stakeholder groups and their perceptions of project success.* Science Direct.

Deiva Ganesh, P. (2022). Kalpana. Future of artificial intelligence and its influence on supply chain risk management –. *Systematic Reviews.* doi:10.1016/j.cie.2022.108206

DeLone, W., & McLean, E. (1992). Information Systems Success: The Quest for the Dependent Variable. *Information Systems Research*, *3*(1), 60–95. doi:10.1287/isre.3.1.60

Dwi Adywiratama A., Ko C., Raharjo T., Wahbi A., (2020). *Critical success factors for ICT project: A case study in project colocation government data center.* Science Direct. doi:10.1016/j.procs.2021.12.154

Fareed M., Su Q., Awan A (2021). *The effect of emotional intelligence, intellectual intelligence and transformational leadership on project success; an empirical study of public projects of Pakistan.* Science Direct. . doi:10.1016/j.plas.2021.100036

Gopal M., Amirthavalli M., (2019). *Applying Machine Learning Techniques to Predict the Maintainability of Open Source Software.* Science Direct. . doi:10.35940/ijeat.E1045.0785S319

Guo, J., Cheng, J., & Cleland-Huang, J. (2017). Semantically Enhanced Software Traceability Using Deep Learning Techniques. *International Conference on Software Engineering (ICSE).* IEEE. https://doi.org/10.1109/ICSE.2017.9

Harclerode M., Macbeth T., Miller M., Gurr C., Myers T., (2016). *Early decision framework for integrating sustainable risk management for complex remediation sites: Drivers, barriers, and performance metrics*. Science Direct. . doi:10.1016/j.jenvman.2016.07.087

He, P., Li, B., Liu, X., Chen, J., & Ma, Y. (2015). Y. Ma. An empirical study on software defect prediction with a simplified metric set. *Information and Software Technology, 59*, 170–190. doi:10.1016/j.infsof.2014.11.006

Highsmith, J. (2010). *Agile project management: creating innovative products* (2nd ed.). Addison-Wesley.

Hoch, J. E., & Dulebohn, J. H. (2013). Shared leadership in enterprise resource planning and human resource management system implementation. *Human Resource Management Review, 23*(1), 114–125. doi:10.1016/j.hrmr.2012.06.007

Hou F. (2020). *Analyzing the Performance of the Unmanned Bank to Explore the Failure Reasons for AI Projects*. AIAM2020.

Illahi, H. Liu, Q. Umer, N. (2021). *Machine learning based success prediction for crowdsourcing software projects*. Science Direct. . doi:10.1016/j.jss.2021.110965

Iriarte C., Bayona S. (2020). IT projects success factors: a literature review. *International Journal of Information Systems and Project Management,* pp. 49–78.

ISO. (2012). *ISO 21500:2012 Guidance on Project Management*. ISO.

Johansen I., Rausand M., (2014). *Foundations and choice of risk metrics*. Science Direct. . doi:10.1016/j.ssci.2013.09.011

Kapur R., Sodhi B., (2020). *A Defect Estimator for Source Code: Linking Defect Reports with Programming Constructs Usage Metrics*. ACM. . doi:10.1145/3384517

Lehtinen, T., Mäntylä, M., Vanhanen, J., Itkonen, J., & Lassenius, C. (2014). Perceived causes of software project failures – An analysis of their relationships. *Information and Software Technology, 56*(6), 623–643. doi:10.1016/j.infsof.2014.01.015

Lei, H., Ganjeizadeh, F., Jayachandran, P., & Ozcan, P. (2015). A statisc al analysis of the effects of Scrum and Kanban on software development projects. *Robotics and Computer-integrated Manufacturing*. doi:10.1016/j.rcim.2015.12.001

Li X., Moreschini S., Zhang Z., Taibi D. (2022). *Exploring factors and metrics to select open source software components for integration: An empirical study*. Science Direct. . doi:10.1016/j.jss.2022.111255

Mahmoud A., Niu N., (2015). *On the role of semantics in automated requirements tracing*. Springer. . doi:10.1007/s00766-013-0199-y

Mas A., Mesquida A., Pacheco, M., (2020). Supporting the deployment of ISO-based project management processes with agile metrics. Springer. . doi:10.1016/j.csi.2019.103405

Meding W., Staron M., Söder O.. MeTeaM—A method for characterizing mature software metrics teams. , 2021. doi:10.1016/j.jss.2021.111006

Melluso N., Grangel-González I., Fantoni G. (2022). *Enhancing Industry 4.0 standads interoperability via knowledge graphs with natural language processing*. IEEE. . doi:10.1016/j.compind.2022.103676

Montequin, S., Fernandez, C., Fernandez, O., & Balsera, J. (2016). *Analysis of the Success Factors and Failure Causes in Projects: Comparison of the Spanish Information y Communication Technology (ICT)*. Sector. Journal Information Technology Project Management. doi:10.4018/978-1-5225-0196-1.ch068

Oliveira B., Da C.; Martins S., Magalhães F., Góes L., (2019). Difference based metrics for deep reinforcement learning algorithms. IEEE. . doi:10.1109/ACCESS.2019.2945879

Papa, M. (2014). *Aseguramiento de la Calidad de un Recurso Organizacional: Evaluando y Mejorando una Estrategia Integrada de Medición y Evaluación*. [Tesis Doctoral, Facultad de Informática, Universidad Nacional de La Plata].

PRINCE2. (2009). *An introduction to PRINCE2: managing and directing successful projects. Office of Government Commerce*. Stationery Office.

Project Management Institute. (2017). A Guide to the Project Management Body of Knowledge. 6 Ed. *ISBN, 10*, 9781628251845.

Qiu, S., Liu, Q., Zhou, S., & Huang, W. (2022). Adversarial attack and defense technologies in natural language processing. *Neurocomputing, 492*, 278–307. doi:10.1016/j.neucom.2022.04.020

Ramos, P., & Mota, C. (2014). Perceptions of success and failure factors in information technology projects: A study from Brazilian companies. *Procedia: Social and Behavioral Sciences, 119*, 349–357. doi:10.1016/j.sbspro.2014.03.040

Rivera, M. (2018). *Enfoque Integrado de Medición, Evaluación y Mejora de Calidad con soporte a Metas de Negocio y de Necesidad de Información: Aplicación de Estrategias a partir de Patrones de Estrategia*. [Tesis Doctoral. Facultad de Informática, Universidad Nacional de La Plata].

Schlutter A., Vogelsang A., (2020). *Knowledge Extraction from Natural Language Requirements into a Semantic Relation Graph*. ACM. . doi:10.1145/3387940.3392162

Schwalbe, K. (2015). *Information Technology Project Management.*

Shafique, U., & Qaiser, H. (2014). A Comparative Study of Process Models Data Mining (KDD, CRISP-DM and SEMMA). *International Journal of Innovation and Scientific Research*, 217–222.

Shaikh, I. & Randhawa, K. (2022). Managing the risks and motivations of technology managers in open innovation: Bringing stakeholder-centric corporate governance into focus. *Journal of Technological Innovation*. . doi:10.1016/j.technovation.2021.102437

Shearer, C. (2000). The CRISP-DM model: The new blueprint for data mining. *Journal of Data Warehousing*, (4), 13–22.

Siddiqui T., Ahmad A., (2019). Mining software repositories for software metrics (MSR-SM): conceptual framework. *IJITEE*. . doi:10.35940/ijitee.J1051.0881019

Silva Ferreira M., Almeida Martins L., Júnior P., Costa H., (2019). Measuring developer work to support the software project manager: an exploratory study. https://doi.org/. doi:10.1145/3364641.3364651

Siri, D. (2019). *Machine learning algorithm application in software quality improvement using metrics.* ACM. . doi:10.35940/ijeat.F1359.0986S319

Sutherland, J. (2014). *Scrum: The art of doing twice the work in half the time.* Crown Business.

The CHAOS Report. (2020). The Standish Group. https://secure.standishgroup.com/reports/flyers/CM2020- TOC.pdf

Thomas R., Uminsky D. (2022). Reliance on metrics is a fundamental challenge for AI. *Patterns.* . doi:10.1016/j.patter.2022.100476

Van Solingen, R., & Van Lanen, R. (2014). *Scrum voor Managers.* Academic Service. EAN.

Vanhoucke, M. (2011). On the dynamic use of project performance and schedule risk information during project tracking. *Omega, 39*(4), 416–426. doi:10.1016/j.omega.2010.09.006

Varela, L., & Domingues, L. (2022). Domingues. Risks of Data Science Projects – A Delphi Study. *Procedia Computer Science, 196,* 982–989. doi:10.1016/j.procs.2021.12.100

Wanderley, M., Menezes, J. Jr, Gusmão, C., & Lima, C. F. (2015). Proposal of risk management metrics for multiple project software development. *Procedia Computer Science, 64,* 1001–1009. doi:10.1016/j.procs.2015.08.619

Werneck Barbosa, M., Martinez Carrasco, S., & Rodriguez, P. (2022). The effect of enterprise risk management competencies on students´ perceptions of their work readiness. *International Journal of Management Education.* . 2022. doi:10.1016/j.ijme.2022.100638

Westenberger, J., Schuler, K., & Schlegel, D. (2022). Failure of AI projects: Understanding the critical factors. *Procedia Computer Science, 196,* 69–76. doi:10.1016/j.procs.2021.11.074

Wood, D. (2017). High-level integrated deterministic, stochastic and fuzzy cost-duration analysis aids project planning and monitoring, focusing on uncertainties and earned value metrics. *Journal of Natural Gas Science and Engineering, 37,* 303–326. doi:10.1016/j.jngse.2016.11.045

Zagane M., Abdi M., Alenezi M., (2020). *Deep Learning for Software Vulnerabilities Detection Using Code Metrics.* IEEE. . doi:10.1109/ACCESS.2020.2988557

Chapter 9
An Overview of Security Issues in Cognitive Radio Ad Hoc Networks

Noman Islam
Karachi Institute of Economics and Technology, Karachi, Pakistan

Muhammad Furqan Zia
ⓘ https://orcid.org/0000-0003-2769-6610
Koc University, Istanbul, Turkey

Darakhshan Syed
Bahria University, Pakistan

ABSTRACT

Cognitive radio ad hoc network (CRAHN) is an emerging discipline of network computing. It combines the advantages of cognitive radio networks and mobile ad hoc networks. This chapter starts with an overview of various research issues of CRAHN along with representative solutions for these research issues. Among the various research issues presented, security is discussed in detail due to its prime importance. A review of existing literature reveals that not much work on security has been reported for cognitive radio networks. Specifically, an overview of security issues in CRAHN, presented in this article, is a novel work of this kind. A major part of this article highlights the importance of security in CRAHN and presents an overview of major security issues and the solutions proposed to address these issues in CRAHN.

1. INTRODUCTION

A cognitive radio (CR) is a communication device that can adjust its operating properties based on its environment. It proactively observes the unlicensed communication channels in surroundings that are not in use. It then tunes itself on these free channels, and then utilizes them for communication (Yu

DOI: 10.4018/978-1-6684-7684-0.ch009

et al., 2020). This process, called dynamic channel selection, solves the spectrum scarcity issue of the wireless network. However, due to high variation in the availability of channels and various quality of service (QoS) requirements in the available spectrum, CR networks face several unique challenges. For instance, dynamic spectrum access (DSA) is required to optimize spectrum usage to solve the spectrum insufficiency issue. In DSA, there is an unlicensed device known as the secondary user (SU) or cognitive radio user. This SU leaves the band when a licensed device known as the primary user (PU) is detected.

To enable DSA, two main aspects of CR need to be considered. These are cognitive capability and re-configurability (Zhou et al., 2018). Cognitive capability enables spectrum awareness by sensing the statistics from its radio environment. Using the cognitive capability, the secondary users of the cognitive network becomes ascertain about the status of various channels and can optimally decide the spectrum to use along with its operating parameters. Re-configurability denotes the ability of a node to adjust its transmission parameters. Re-configurability of a CR demands it to be programmed dynamically for enabling transmission and reception of signals on various operating parameters and make it capable of working on multiple access technologies.

More complex strategies such as autonomous learning and action decisions are required to acquire the cognitive capability, which the system cannot learn by noticing the power of specific spectrums (Peng et al. 2020). In autonomous learning, each node autonomously learns based on its experiences and feedback obtained from the environment. Action decision techniques enable a user to achieve spatiotemporal variations in radio environment. Also, this capability provides interference avoidance between users.

Another primary concern in CR networks is to share spectrum sharing without causing interception to other nodes. The unused spectrum is represented by spectrum hole or white spaces. If the license user wants to further utilize its spectrum, the CR user has to move on to some other spectrum hole. Alternatively, if a user still wishes to continue in the same spectrum without letting the nodes to intercept, it must change the power level of transmission or modulation technique. In order to adapt the dynamic spectrum environment, the cognitive radio ad-hoc networks necessitate spectrum-aware operations, which form a cognitive cycle (Onem et al., 2013). The basic steps of the cognitive cycle consist of four spectrum management functions: spectrum sensing, spectrum decision, spectrum sharing, and spectrum mobility.

We can classify CR networks into two types based on architecture: infrastructure-based cognitive radio and cognitive radio ad-hoc networks (CRAHN). The infrastructure-based cognitive radio networks are controlled from a central location. For example, in cellular networks, the core network component is called the base station, whereas, in wireless local area networks (WLAN), it is known as an access point. On the other hand, the cognitive radio ad hoc network (CRAHN) has no infrastructure and is formed among a set of communication entities equipped with cognitive radios.

This paper discusses the security issues in CRAHN. The novelty of the paper lies in discussing not only the technical issues in CRAHN, but also social and policy issues. The next section presents an overview of security challenges pertaining to CRAHN. Then, security challenges are presented. Discussion on CRAHN security issues is presented. Finally, social and policy making issues are discussed.

2. AN OVERVIEW OF COGNITIVE RADIO AD HOC NETWORK (CRAHN)

A cognitive radio ad hoc network (CRAHN) works on infrastructure less architecture due to its ad hoc properties, has no backbone and a user can communicate only via ad hoc connection. CRAHN has the following key distinguishing properties making it unique from the simple CR networks (Mansoor et al., 2014):

§   **Infrastructure-less network:** CRAHN is formed among mobile nodes that don't have any prior infrastructure. There does not exist any centralized or dedicated entity that can perform dedicated networking tasks such as addressing, routing, spectrum management.

§   **Multi-hop architecture:** CRAHN network comprises mobile nodes that are dependent on each other to perform various network management tasks. This includes routing, security management, addressing, spectrum sensing, spectrum sharing, spectrum decision and spectrum mobility. All of these tasks are performed in distributed fashion in the multi-hopped architecture of CRAHN on both licensed and unlicensed spectrum bands.

§   **Decentralized operation:** In CRAHN, we don't have a central entity. It demands each user to have CR abilities which can lead to distributed operation by determining actions based on observation.

§   **Dynamic Network Topology:** As the nodes are mobile, the network topology varies very quickly. The links among the nodes are very shaky because of the spatiotemporal variations of spectrum availability.

Table 1. Difference between cognitive radio network and CRAHN

Property	CR Network	Ad hoc network	CRAHN
Infrastructure	Ö	×	×
Dynamism	×	Ö	Ö
Muti-hoppe architecture	×	Ö	Ö
Autonomy	×	Ö	Ö
Shaky Links	Ö	Ö	Ö
Centralized operation	Ö	×	×
Cooperation	×	Ö	Ö
Cognitive capability	Ö	×	×

Table 1 highlights the key difference between cognitive radio networks, mobile ad hoc network and CRAHN. Because of the unique properties, CRAHN suffers from various research issues. For instance, spectrum management has to be performed in cooperative fashion. There are challenges related to sensing accuracy, multipath effects, power conservation etc. The various layers such as MAC, routing layers and transport layers of CRAHN needs to be coupled with spectrum management as the protocol needs to consider the spectrum availability to make decisions. The spectrum sensing can be performed locally or in cooperative manner (Attar et al., 2012). A good overview of research issues of CRAHN has been provided in (Islam et al., 2014). The paragraphs below highlight some of these research issues.

2.1 Spectrum Sensing

The use of spectrum sensing to determine the presence of a principal user is an essential topic in CRAHN. The broadcasts of other CR users and PUs can be detected because each secondary user perceives the spectrum separately and asynchronously. It is important to note that for optimal spectrum sensing, CRAHNs must consider several other parameters as well. Figure 1 shows the overall picture.

Figure 1. The process of spectrum sharing

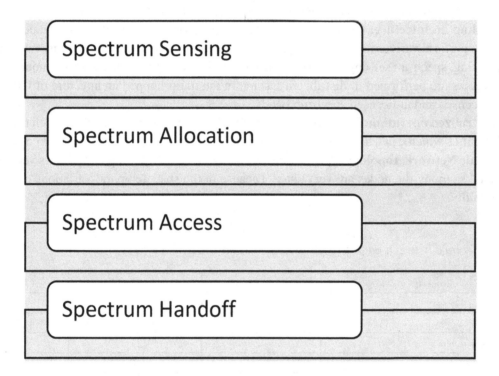

There are several methods for spectrum sensing. One of the most widely used methods is energy detection. But energy detection method also has some limitations due to which it can only detect the occurrence of a transmission, not its transmission type. This can lead to false alarms and decreased spectrum access opportunities. In this type of spectrum sensing, an important issue is to reduce the false alarm rate. However, not much work has been reported in this area (Pandya et al., 2015). As CRAHN comprises distributed and autonomous mobile nodes, spectrum sensing can be performed cooperatively. The cooperative sensing works by a set of nodes operating in collaboration to make decision regarding spectrum access. This technique makes it possible to improve the detection accuracy but with increased traffic due to the congested channel and re-transmission of the packet. Furthermore, depending on the location, each cooperative user may have varied sensing accuracies.

The majority of current spectrum sensing research is based on PU activity modeling. Nevertheless, this model is unable to capture all unique properties of the conventional primary networks. This erroneous primary network model has a negative impact on spectrum sensing; resulting in either reduced spectrum access opportunities or increased interference to primary networks. In practice, several of the empirical models on PU activities are computationally infeasible. As a result, more practical PU activity models must be developed, taking into account the unique features of access technologies and different kinds of traffic (Pandya et al., 2015).

2.1.1. Essential Functions for Spectrum Sensing

Before proceeding further, the article discusses the essential functions required by the cognitive radio ad hoc network for spectrum sensing.

2.1.1.1 Detection of PU

It is the potential to spot PU emissions using a CR individual's position assessments, and it uses that data to figure out the present spectrum availability. The most popular PU identification techniques in CRAHNs are energy and features detection approaches (Cabric et al., 2004). Depending on the energy of the signals detected, energy detector CR consumers determine if PUs are there or not. The energy detector is simple to use but is unable to distinguish between various signal kinds. As a consequence, false detection caused by unwanted signals in CRAHNs frequently occurs while using the energy detector. Additionally, it is subject to noise power unpredictability in terms of performance.

2.1.1.2. Recognition of Feature(s)

It detects the existence of PU signals by isolating their distinctive traits from its local observations, such as pilot signals, cyclic prefixes, or modulating types. The key benefit of feature recognition is that it is resistant to fluctuations in noise power. It can also discriminate between signals from multiple networks. As a result, this technique enables the CR consumer to conduct autonomous sensing processes on those of its neighbors without synchronization. The most successful method for CRAHNs is feature identification, although it is technologically challenging and necessitates a lengthy sensing period.

Additionally, in Cognitive radio-AHNs spectrum sensing demands for an effective coordination strategy to reduce the impacts of multipath-fading channels and shadowed, eliminate interference with PUs beyond of each CR participant's reach of observation, and eliminate interference with PUs.

2.1.1.3. Controller for Sensing

It oversees and coordinates the PU detecting functionality by taking into account two key factors:

- The speed with which a CR user may identify the appropriate spectrum band across a broad range of frequency for their broadcasts.
- How regularly and for how far a Cognitive radio consumer should experience the spectrum in order to obtain enough sensing precision during transmission and identify when transmission is occurring in primary channels in order to prevent disruption.

The out of band sense strategy should have a coordination system to optimize its searching sequence and choose the stopping rule for out-of-band sensing in order to perform quick and effective spectrum discovery in Cognitive radio-AHNs(Kim & Shin, 2008). Prolonged sensing times also increase accuracy in sensing, which reduces interfering.

2.1.2. Issues/ research challenges in Spectrum Sensing

Following are some of the issues with spectrum sensing.

2.1.2.1. Assistance With Asynchronous Sensing

Although each consumer in a CRAHN has a unique schedule for sensing and transmission, it is able to pick up transmissions from both CR and PU consumers during its sensing time. Nevertheless, a CR consumer can determine the existence of a transmission but cannot detect the sorts of identified transmissions when using energy detection, which is typically frequently employed for spectrum sensing. As a consequence, the transmission of CR consumers discovered through sensing procedures results in false alerts, decreasing the likelihood of gaining access to the spectrum. Therefore, a key aspect of assessing the effectiveness of CRAHNs is how to decrease these anomalies, but this topic has not yet been investigated.

2.1.2.2. Optimizing Collaborative Sensing

While increasing detection precision, collaborative sensing also generates more network traffic, which causes channel congestion and packets re-transmissions, which raise the latency of data collection. Additionally, the sensing accuracy of each cooperating user may vary depending on its location. Cognitive radio-AHNs must therefore take these things into account to pick the most appropriate operational point.

2.2 Spectrum Decision

After spectrum sensing, the transmission channel needs to be selected. This can be done by analyzing QoS criteria such as sustained rate, latency, jitters, average session time, tolerable loss rate, and spectrum parameters. These spectrum features vary significantly, due to which CR users may sometimes preserve the quality of the current session by simply re-configuring their settings. Instead of adjusting spectrum and route, adaptive modulation can be used to maintain bit rate and bit error rate (BER) when the signal-to-noise ratio (SNR) is modified.

2.2.1. Essential Functions for Spectrum Decision

The essential functions required by the Cognitive radio-AHN for spectrum decision are discussed briefly below.

2.2.1.1. Characterization of Spectrum

Using RF observations, Cognitive Radio customers describe the characteristics of the regions of spectrum that are now available by taking into account the acquired signal intensity, interruption, and the number of consumers that are actually using the spectrum. Despite of traditional ad-hoc networks, each CR individual experiencing diverse spectrum availability that changes over a period of time as a result of PU actions. This should therefore be taken into account in this regard.

2.2.1.2. Allocation of Spectrum

CR consumers choose the optimum available spectrum to meet quality of service needs based on the reported availability of spectrum. Allocating the spectrum and other routing techniques work together to choose the optimized path and spectrum. Due to the conversation session typically involves numerous hops with varying levels of spectrum availability. Therefore, it is impractical to take into account every potential link when making a spectrum option because there are so many different routes and spectrum combinations between the source and destination. Thus, route selection is carried out independently of spectrum allocation in latest literature (Wang & Zheng, 2006). Despite being very straightforward, this method is unable to offer an ideal route since it does not take into account the spectrum availability at each hop when establishing the route. As a result, CRAHNs require a hybrid spectrum and routing determination mechanism.

2.2.1.3. Protocol for Routing

Although they can be employed in a multichannel CR context, the existing on-demand routing protocols-which use the shortest route metrics and a common control channel for setup—need to be modified. Firstly, it is necessary to develop new measurements and optimized methods that encompass the total spectrum possibilities for each potential forwarding point i.e. a node. The key choice made during route configuration is whether to enable the route to pass through the area of PU activity that is impacted or to shift the spectrum while continuing to proceed in the desired direction. Additionally, routing decisions may be greatly influenced by the kind of channel allocation technology and core physical layer capacity.

2.2.1.4. Reconfigure the Communication System

The algorithms for the various network stack stages must adjust to the operational frequency's channels characteristics. Whenever the spectrum has been chosen, CR consumers must choose the appropriate communication package, such as modulation methods, error(s) control strategies, and higher layer protocols, and modify their communication system in accordance with the software needs and spectrum specifications. The potential of a given link may significantly rise or decrease when the spectrum on that connection is altered. Both of these circumstances have an impact on the end-to-end latency, which in turn affects the source's transfer rate as set by Transport Control Protocol. As a result, the congestion window must instantly represent requirements of the spectrum bandwidth on the specific link.

2.2.2. Issues in Spectrum Decision

Following are some of the issues introduced in spectrum decision.

2.2.2.1. Formation of a Shared Spectrum and Routing

It is a fairly significant challenge at the network layer even though it is crucial to concurrently determine the pathways and the availability of spectrum. Furthermore, new approaches are required to combine these potentially discontinuous routes in order to make the most efficient use of the spectrum. The route requests may travel independent routes to the target on each channel. The route requests' arrival time during the route configuration stage cannot be regarded as the performance ultimate barometer. The projected path latency requires to be further balanced with the potential for PU interference on the connections that make up the route, and new path quality metrics using knowledge of statistics of the PU knowledge require to be developed.

2.2.2.2. Spectrum Dependence on Transmission

Some frequency bands allow electromagnetic signals to propagate farther; as a result, it is crucial to evaluate the available spectrum reserves in terms of connection. When estimating the number of nodes in the route, it is important to keep in mind that the per-hop advancement towards the destination is not constant throughout all available spectrums.

2.3 Spectrum Sharing

A high number of users share the same spectrum. As a result, there is a requirement for spectrum access and cooperation. The request to send (RTS) and clear to send (CTS) techniques have been used in conventional ad hoc networks for channel management and to minimize simultaneous transmissions. The available spectrum in CR networks, on the other hand, is flexible, and users can switch channels after a corresponding pair of nodes has interchanged the channel access signal. As a result, a new series of RTS-CTS interactions may be required on the new channel to impose a silent zone among the new spectrum's nearby CR users. Furthermore, CR users tracking the earlier channel are unaware of the link's spectrum shift (Al Mojamed, et al., 2020). They keep their clocks running and wait for the entire data transfer to complete before starting their transmission. As a result, spectrum usage is inefficient. When the spectrum access circumstances change, new coordinating methods are required.

Evolution and learning are the essences of the MAC protocol. The information about the usage history of spectrum bands varies depending on the time of day and location. The MAC protocol should learn about PU activity and correspondingly adjust its spectrum selection and data transmission method. The POMDP MAC protocol has been proposed in this regard by (Zheng et al., 2020). More sophisticated and intricate learning models, are required. For example, the length of learning time and its impact on network operation should be investigated. The subject of generating detailed channel occupancy requires more investigation, so that the mobile CR user's movements at different times of the day and in different areas can be taken into account (Akyildiz et al., 2009). The long-term efficiency bounds may be guaranteed by the probabilistic spectrum selection process that employs this information.

Due to the complications in structure learning, spectrum sharing becomes complicated. Through the use of non-uniform channels, structure development is a complex operation. Without the help of the central body, the CR user selects transmission power in a distributed manner. Even if it does not detect any transmission inside its observation range, it may create interference due to the limitation of the sensing area. As a result, spectrum sharing demands complex power control algorithms to adjust time-varying radio settings so that capacity may be maximized while PU broadcasts are protected.

2.3.1. Essential Functions for Spectrum Sharing

The essential functions required by the Cognitive radio-Ad hoc Network for spectrum sharing decision are briefly discussed below.

2.3.1.1. Allocation of Resources

CR consumers must execute selecting the channel and allocating the power based on local observations, while selecting the best channel while being bound by interfering to other CRs and PUs. Cooperation among neighbors improves spectrum sharing efficiency, particularly in energy distribution, which must be mindful of PU operations in the available spectrum. The objective of all CR users is to make the most of the spectrum resource(s). The contending objectives of CR consumers, therefore, are to maximize their own part of allocation of the available spectrum. A CR consumer must also make reasonable decisions while predicting the reactions of its competitors. By defining the competition and collaboration among CR consumers and enabling each CR consumer to logically choose its optimal course of action, game theory offers an effective decentralized spectrum sharing mechanism. Despite being able to reach the Nash equilibrium, game theory methodologies cannot ensure the Pareto optimal, which results in a reduction in network capability.

2.3.1.2. Accessibility of the Spectrum

As sensing controls influences the effectiveness of spectrum access by determining the sensing and the transmitting intervals. The MAC technologies' essential functionality is represented by this (Cormio & Chowdhury, 2009). The detecting schedules of CRAHNs, nonetheless, perform independently of one another because there is a lack of user synchronization. Ad hoc CR consumers can also use periodic or on-demand sensing that is only activated by spectrum sharing procedures. The design strategies for MAC protocols in CRAHNs can be divided into three categories based on the various spectrum access methods: randomized access, fix time-scheduled and amalgamative approach. Any CR consumer may selectively acquire the network in random allocation techniques for both data and control transfer. Time-scheduled methods limit concurrent transmission by numerous CR consumers by assigning the control and data predetermined times. Furthermore, in the hybrid approach, control packets may have a defined time limit, and then they randomly access the channel before data transmission.

2.3.2. Issues in Spectrum Sensing

Following are some of the issues in spectrum sensing.

2.3.2.1. Discovering the Topology

Discovering the topology is challenging due to the use of non-uniform links by various CR consumers. If two CR users encounter distinct PU activity in their particular coverage regions, they might only be permitted to transmit on channels that are mutually exclusive. It is challenging to send out periodic beacons telling the nodes within transmission range of their own Identifier and other geographical coordinates necessary for networking because the permissible routes for the first user differs from those utilized by another.

2.3.2.2. Allocating Decentralized Power

Although if the CR ad hoc user does not identify any transmission inside its observation range, it nevertheless allocates transmission power in a distributed way without the assistance of the centralized authority, which may results in interference owing to the sensing area's limitations. Therefore, spectrum sharing requires for advanced power control techniques for adjusting to time-varying radio settings in order to optimize capacity while safeguarding PU broadcasts.

2.4 Spectrum Mobility

The mobility of nodes is a crucial problem that emerges in CRAHN. Switching the channel is essential for CR users. The use of different delay control approaches is thus required. The spectrum switching latency is determined by the algorithm used for spectrum sensing, spectrum decision, link layer, routing, and the hardware utilized, such as an RF front-end. When a CR user changes their frequency, the network protocols may necessitate adjustments to the operating settings, resulting in protocol reconfiguration delays. Moreover, CR users must also do out-of-band sensing and neighbor discovery to find the new spectrum and route while decreasing search delay through search sequence optimization. Spectrum mobility should be viewed as a multi-layer problem to lower operational overhead across all functions and achieve shorter switching times (Thakur et al., 2021). Furthermore, an accurate latency estimate in spectrum handoff is required for reliable connection management.

Because of the mobility, there is also the issue of flexible spectrum handoff. This can be done in two ways: reactively or proactively, with each having a different impact on communication performance and spectrum switching time. For example, because a PU activity region is typically more extensive than the transmission range of CR users, spectrum mobility events may affect multiple hops simultaneously, lengthening the recovery time. Spectrum handoff should also be done, depending on the type of application and network conditions. For example, instead of reactive switching, CR users can use proactive switching in the case of a delay-sensitive application (Thakur et al., 2021). The PU activities are predicted in this switching, and the CR consumers switch the spectrum before the PUs appear. As a result, the time it takes to switch between spectrums is significantly reduced.

Reactive spectrum switching is also required by energy-constrained devices such as sensors. A more effective strategy is to use flexible spectrum handoff architecture to take advantage of various switching mechanisms. Spectrum sensing, decision, sharing, and mobility are all CR functionalities that must be implemented within a wireless device's protocol stack.

2.4.1. Essential Functions for Spectrum Mobility

The necessary functions required by the cognitive radio ad hoc network for spectrum sharing mobility are briefly discussed below.

2.4.1.1. Spectrum Handover

To enable smooth communications, spectrum mobility offers rise to a new sort of handover, the so-called frequency handoff, in which users move their connections to an unoccupied spectrum band. Spectrum mobility occurrences, which are produced by both user mobility and PU activity, can be identified in CRAHNs as connection failures. Additionally, spectrum mobility is also started by the existing transmission's quality deterioration. While node mobility-related route disruptions are frequent in traditional ad hoc networks, there is a special problem with CR networks. Here, the route may still be functional, but the mobility of CR consumers may force the original path, which was originally selected to avoid PU transmissions, to go across areas that are covered by PU.

At some point, the connection will fail, at which point the spectrum handover stage will activate. Recovering the Link layer is unsuccessful in the event of a spectrum related connection failure brought on by the introduction of PUs since a significant number of channels are impacted and no mutually satisfactory route is present on the link. Local recovering is most appropriate in these circumstances, when consumers may transmit a new RREQ over the CCC in an effort to reconnect the two detached route segments on either side of the troubled PU region. Finding a new CR consumer at the initial position of the nodes that took part in channel establishment is the effective implementation strategy in failures linked to mobility. This happens because the route configuration made certain that the journey passed through areas that were largely undisturbed by the PU operations. Given the potential for recurrent spectrum and mobility related interruptions in a CRAHN, the networks' layer architecture must actively pursue local recovery solutions to lower the recovery cost.

2.4.1.2. Handling the Connection

A connection supervisory mechanism interacts with each stacking protocol in order to maintain the QoS of the current transfer of data or reduce the premature failure throughout spectrum trying to switch. The connection handling can forecast the effects of the brief disconnection on each protocol layer as soon as the new switching delay data is available, and can then sequentially rebuild the configuration each one in accordance with its predictions. The mechanisms used by the various network stack tiers should be transparent to the handover of the spectrum and the resulting latency. To prevent services from experiencing significant efficiency deterioration, novel layered mobility control mechanisms are needed. The mobility handling should be supported by these protocols and flexible to diverse application kinds.

The Multi-radio communications in which each transmitter and receiver adjusts to a separate non spectrum frequency and transmits data concurrently, are a technique that Cognitive radio consumers can utilize to prevent momentary disconnections. The other links' transmissions are undisturbed regardless of whether a PU suddenly arises in one of the existing available spectrum.

2.4.2. Issues in Spectrum Mobility

Following are some of the associated with spectrum mobility.

2.4.2.1. Minimizing the Switching Time

The improvement of algorithms for spectrum sensing, decision; link layer, and routing layer decisions, as well as hardware factors like RF front-end re-configuration times, all have a significant impact on the spectrum changeover latency. Whenever a CR client switches its frequency, the network protocols might need to make adjustments to the operating variables. This could affect the reconfiguring the protocols. Additionally, out-of-band sensing, neighbour finding, and search sequences optimization are required by CR users in order to locate the new spectrum and channel path. It is therefore preferable to create a cross-layer spectrum mobility method to save operational overhead and accomplish quicker switching durations. For dependable link management, effective latency estimations during spectrum handovers are crucial.

2.4.2.2.Dynamic Infrastructure for Spectrum Handover

The requirement to alter the routing patterns occurs in a flexible CR network where PUs may use the channels for brief periods of time. When this occurs, spectrum handover has the following decisions to make:

- Modify the terrain across which the current journey travels.
- Alter the available spectrum that is presently in use. The QoS of the current transmission is affected differently by each technique. Additionally, because PU activity regions are often bigger than CR users' transmission ranges, when a PU is detected, numerous hops may be affected simultaneously, lengthening recovery time beyond that of network connectivity. As a result, the choice of switching strategic approach must be decided to make while taking into account the different kinds of applications and mobility occurrences. It also needs to be strongly related to the assistance provided by the link layer in terms of transmission modifications, spectrum sensing data, and its own assessment of the PU activity with regard to the recent location and time, a topic that has not yet been fully researched in CRAHNs.

Summary of the advanced spectrum management techniques are presented in table 2 on the basis of essential functions and the associated challenges.

Table 2. Summary of the advanced spectrum management techniques

Sr. No.	Spectrum management technique	Essential function(s)	Introduced Issue(s)
1	Spectrum Sensing	• Detection of PU • Recognition of Feature(s) • Controller for sensing	• Assistance with Asynchronous Sensing • Optimizing Collaborative Sensing
2	Spectrum Decision	• Characterization of Spectrum • Allocation of Spectrum • Protocol for routing • Reconfigure the Communication System	• Formation of a shared spectrum and routing • Spectrum Dependence on Transmission
3	Spectrum Sharing	• Allocation Of resources • Accessibility of the Spectrum	• Discovering the topology • Allocating Decentralized Power
4	Spectrum Mobility	• Spectrum Handover • Handling the connection	• Minimizing the switching time • Dynamic Infrastructure for Spectrum Handover

2.5 Common Control Channel

Although knowing about the network environment helps CRAHNs function better, the control channel overhead must also be considered. The CCC channel must be carefully selected to ensure that it is not interrupted for long periods. While this makes CCC operation much more accessible, the key challenge is finding a generally acceptable channel throughout a substantial percentage of the network (Akyildiz et al., 2009). Furthermore, because spectrum for control messages is uniquely reserved, effort should be taken to ensure that the CCC does not reduce spectrum usage efficiency in low-traffic conditions.

The majority of existing CR MAC techniques use an out-of-band CCC, which increases spectrum utilization. Learning-based strategies must be designed to establish the optimal spectrum that ensures ongoing use even in the presence of PU activity. Furthermore, for single-transceiver systems, frequent switching of the radio transceiver from the CCC to the operational channel may be required, resulting in a finite cost in the form of switching time (Akyildiz et al., 2009). This time must be factored into the CCC plan. An 'always on' CCC might likewise be realized using novel approaches such as ultra-wideband.

2.6 Routing

Routing is also a critical issue in CRAHN. The main challenge of routing in the CRAHN environment is keeping the routing graph on each cognitive node to a bare minimum while considering additional metrics for handling interference and other requirements. The more requirements for a network are studied, the more metrics are generated to address them. As a result, each node has multiple paths available (Singh et al., 2020). Each node's routing table will face overhead path selection and routing decisions due to the massive number of routes produced. In order to decrease the end-to-end delay, long paths are used. This is done to avoid interference between them. As a result, the overall throughput of the network is increased.

2.7 Transport Protocol

Current studies in wireless ad-hoc network transport protocols have mainly addressed end-to-end packet delivery over unpredictable channel conditions, route failures owing to node mobility, and link congestion. Apart from the aforementioned concerns, numerous significant challenges must be addressed in the cognitive radio (CR) environment (Attar et al., 2012). The transport protocol must take into account the CR users' irregular spectrum sensing, the activity of the users of the spectrum, large-scale bandwidth variation based on spectrum availability, and the channel switching process.

2.8 Security

An important issue that arises in CRAHN is security problem because of the unique environment these networks operate. A CRAHN suffers from various security issues such as signal jamming, impersonation of primary user, data integrity and security of node itself. These issues arise due to various reasons such as:

a) **Heterogeneous nature of wireless network:** The data in wireless communication networks can be intercepted or manipulated without warning, and the channel could be jammed or misused by opponents. Because of its heterogeneous nature, CR technology gives eavesdroppers extra opportunities (Zhang et al., 2009).

b) **Hostile environment:** As CRAHN operates in hostile environment; they are prone to various types of physical and logical threats.

c) **Absence of infrastructure:** As CRAHN doesn't have prior infrastructure, it becomes very difficult to maintain security due to the absence of dedicated entities for authentication, authorization and key management etc.

d) **High PU Sensitivity:** Cognitive radio users should specify the primary transmission to avoid interference with licensed users. One of the demanding requirements of the CR network is to estimate temperature interference on nearby primary receivers and keep it below a criterion. As a result, sensitivity to the primary user signal is typically set to a high standard. This high sensitivity promotes false alerts in energy-based detection (Besher et al., 2019).

e) **Unknown Location Of Primary Receiver:** To minimize interference to the primary user, the cognitive radio user must know the exact location of the primary receiver. An unknown primary receiver position can generate a hidden node. The location of the primary receiver can be determined by utilizing receiver power leakage (Shams et al., 2019).

f) **Cooperative spectrum management**: As the CRAHN has no prior infrastructure-less nature, the spectrum management operations has to be performed in cooperative manner. This makes such network vulnerable to various security attacks (Yan et al.). The situation gets worst with multiple colluding attackers.

g) **Vertical spectrum access:** Unlike the conventional wireless network which is based on horizontal spectrum access, the communication in CRAHN is based on vertical right access paradigm i.e. secondary users have low priority to access the spectrum only in the absence of PU or with limited interference.

Figure 2. The factors effecting security of CRAHN

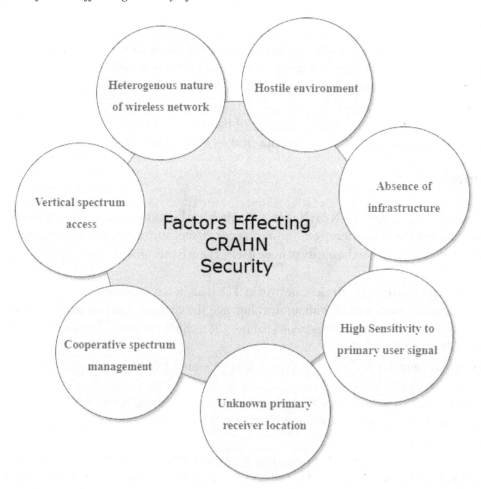

These unique challenges make security in CRAHN a very difficult job. The next section ponders upon various security issues of CRAHN.

3. SECURITY ISSUES IN CRAHN

CRAHN suffers from various types of security issues ranging across the full protocol stack. This section will review the security issues of CRAHN at each layer. Wired network is much secured as compared to wireless which is open in nature. CRAHN is very similar to wireless network and anyone can interrupt the signals more easily. CR utilizes unused spectrum of primary users for usage by secondary users. Table 3 highlights the security attacks on CRAHN.

Table 3. Security attacks on CRAHN (Dansana and Behera 2021)

Layer	Attacks	Defense mechanism
MAC	Collision Exhaustion	Error-correction code Rate Limitation
NETWORK	Selective forwarding Sinkhole Sybil Wormhole Hello Flood	Authentication monitoring Redundancy checking Authentication monitoring Authentication Packet leashes by using geographic and temporal information
TRANSPORT	SYN flooding De-synchronization	Client puzzle
APPLICATION	Logical error buffer overflow	Trusted computing
PHYSICAL	Jamming	Spread spectrum priority message
PRIVACY	Traffic analysis, attack on data privacy and location privacy	Homomorphic encryptions

3.1 Physical Layer Issues

The physical layer's goal in CRAHN is to send data in signals to the next hop. As a result, a plethora of security concerns may emerge. Planned blockage, for instance, is one of the physical layer threats. In addition, secondary users broadcast harmful signals into the principal user's spectrum, depriving the primary and secondary users of essential resources, which is a huge threat (Dung et al., 2019). If this threat goes undetected and spreads across a large geographical region, it can harm the whole communication network. The conventional method for dealing with jamming is to employ frequency hopping spread spectrum (FHSS), in which communication nodes shift frequencies based on a pseudo-random sequence (Nasser et al., 2021).

Two jamming techniques mitigate the jamming in CRAHN. The nodes can function together in cooperation or independently (Lee et al., 2021). First, in cooperative network jamming, a group of nodes operates together to resist network jamming (Wu et al., 2021). Second, in the case of uncooperative network jamming, nodes use their local statistics to reduce the jamming impact. Primary receiver jamming is yet another type of eavesdropping attack. In this threat, the eavesdropper approaches the primary receiver and begins receiving the data through secondary user transmissions, disrupting the primary receiver. A common control channel is necessary for coordination in CRAHN. A rogue node can potentially block the common control channel, causing the network to stop working. The most common attack on CRAHN is eavesdropping of information as the wireless networks have a broadcast nature (Zia et al., 2020). Several techniques are developed to overcome eavesdropping, such as a device used to collect packets and statistically analyze them to distinguish between intended information and noise. Spatial treatment, i.e. altering the position of the victim node, can be performed at the network layer to deal with jamming attacks (Felice et al., 2019). Machine learning and game theory have also been presented in some of the techniques to deal with eavesdropping and jamming attacks (Arjoune et al., 2020; Bensalem et al., 2018; Erpek et al., 2018).

In primary user emulation, the attacker uses a malicious node to impersonate the primary user (PU), misleading the secondary user to assume that the PU has reappeared. As a result, the secondary user releases its spectrum and avoids utilizing it, leading to the denial of service attack. The frequency band used by primary and secondary users must be selectable by CR. Few techniques used to fight this problem are filter detection (Salahdine et al., 2015), energy detection (Sarala et al., 2020), cyclo stationary detection (El-Hajj et al. 2011). An advanced type of primary user emulation attack can be done when a malicious user transmits during a silent period. During spectrum sensing, a silent phase is when all secondary users (SU) refrain from transmitting. By starting transmission at that moment, a malevolent SU can trick other nodes into protecting the information.

Another form of attack, known as an overlapping secondary user attack, occurs when CR utilizes several SU networks on the same spectrum simultaneously. As a result, rogue nodes in one network's signal might interfere with the PU and SU of other zones' networks. Unfortunately, this kind of attacks is challenging to detect (Rehman et al., 2017). The spectrum sensing mechanism is the cause of the security problems mentioned above. At this layer, attackers can be identified based on transmitter placement and received signal strength. Localization algorithms can be used to determine the location of CR users in the network. The following techniques mentioned below are the localization approaches used in the literature.

§ **Range based localization:** It calculated the position using the signal's travel time from the sender to the receiver.
§ **Range free Localization:** The total number of nodes in the network are determined and converted to physical distance. Received signal strength (RSS) can also pinpoint the transmitter. The attacker is detected using both location data and the received signal strength. Two RSS-based techniques are used to detect the attacker, called the distance ratio test (DRT) and the distance difference test (DDT). Details are shown in (Zhang et al., 2009).

The security concerns described above are primarily related to the spectrum sensing technique. As a result, some key elements like the transmitter's position and the strength of the received signal are used to detect attackers and provide secure communication in CRAHN (Nasser et al., 2021).

3.2 Link Layer Security Issues

Link layer which is also known as MAC layer is next to physical layer. Its main task is transfer of data from one hop to another in the network. Link layer breaks the data into chunks of frames and transmits it to next hop. In cognitive radio, this layer is responsible for addressing issues related to packet loss and delays. CRAHN suffers from various types of security attack at link layer. The following paragraphs discuss some of these attacks.

In *Byzantine attack*, a malicious user injects fake data into spectrum decision stream that is a valuable member of network. This attack has two goals (Vernekar 2012):

Increase false alarm: Malicious user generates fake alarms about the presence of primary user and nullifies the presence of real SU. Due to this reason, real SU sometimes becomes unable to get the frequency band.

Decrease detection probability: It decreases the detection probability of PU and distracts the normal operations of PU.

To counter this attack, decision fusion technique can be used (Castanedo et al., 2013). This techniquecollects all spectrum statistics and matches with a predefined threshold to identify an attack. The drawback of this technique is that threshold is fixed; uncertainty in threshold makes it inefficient.

In the bias utility attack, an illegitimate secondary node alters the utility function's values to improve its bandwidth. As a result, the genuine secondary user loses access to bandwidth.

DoS attack is also possible at link layer. In this attack, a malicious user gives an impact to other users that spectrum is full and no capacity is available to serve secondary user. It actually stops secondary users to get access to spectrum. Attacker can achieve its goal by using any of the attacks on physical layers and jamming the transmission or blocking the service. It varies with respect to system and user. To avoid this attack, we need to create trusted arch. In this technique, every neighbor evaluates suspicious activities of its neighbor and then neighbor runs sequential probability ratio test and get the results that give hint about whether a node is malicious or node (Li et. al., 2015). This counter measure enhances the performance.

A smaller back off window attack is another form of attack. The MAC layer of cognitive radio networks is the target of this assault. To access the channel, a node backs off for a considerable amount of time within a maximum duration window during medium access. So it can alleviate channel congestion in the neighborhood and provide fair chances for every node to access the channel. The back off time should generally increase with each failure to acquire access to the channel. On the other hand, a malicious node may not extend its bakeoff timeframe and instead use a lower back off window for subsequent re-transmission attempts. This is called a denial of service attack on the MAC layer. To detect and isolate nodes executing SBW attacks, a cumulative distribution function (CDF)-based method is deployed. The aim is for a node to monitor its neighbor's transmission attempts and compare the observed CDF of the backoff time window to a theoretical, hypothetical CDF predicted of a non-malicious node in the same area. The neighbor node is tagged malicious if there are a series of inconsistencies between the observed CDF and the expected hypothetical CDF within a given period. An alarm can be triggered to alert the network's intrusion detection system (IDS). There's a fair possibility that the above approach will work and result in fewer false negatives as long as the IDS node isn't compromised.

Another type of attack on link layer is called false feedback attack (Feng et al., 2018). This attack usually occurs if cognitive radio network is distributed across different nodes and regions. In decentralized or in distributed network, feedback of every node is very important for overall performance. Some malicious node in such network forces secondary node to provide wrong feedback. It impacts on the transmission of the primary user. For instance, if primary user reappears after some time and malicious node hides its reappearance, it will have a lot of impact on network.

In the literature, one of the significant threats to the development of CRAHN is the spectrum sensing data falsification (SSDF) attack, also known as the Byzantine attack. The SSDF attack in CRAHN has recently gained much attention because it hinders successful data transmission across CRAHN (Magdalene et al., 2017). In this security threat, a fraudulent secondary user sends fake local spectrum sensing information to the controllers, causing the controller to make the incorrect spectrum sensing choice (Biswas et al., 2020).

There are different kinds of security attacks that can occur via SSDF in CRAHN. Some of them are discussed in this section.

- **Selfish SSDF attack:**

In a *selfish SSDF* attack, a malicious secondary user (SU) broadcasts relatively high primary user (PU) energy to indicate the presence of a false PU. It occurs such that no PU is present or has a very low energy level. As a result, other SUs make the false assumption that PUs are accessible in the network and do not choose the spectrum to utilize. The malevolent SU will have full access to the affected spectrum (Tephillah et al., 2020).

Several works have been done to combat selfish SSDF attacks in CRAHN, but none of them promises the security of CRAHN. (Chen et al., 2009) developed a CSS model based on credibility in which the fusion center (FC) assigns credibility value to each SU depending on sensing data. The SU is then weighted based on its credibility value. The reputation level, on the other hand, cannot be changed. (Kar et al., 2017) presented multifactor trust management, in which malicious users are determined based on past actions, rewards, and reliability trust evaluations. There is no exploiting mechanism used, and it is not possible to find the selfish nodes. (Bannaeur et al., 2016) proposed a trust-based non-cooperative game in which the loss associated with defective SUs is mitigated by removing the malicious user from participating in the sensing process for a set amount of time.

It is to be noted that penalizing the genuine SUs who report erroneously due to channel circumstances would incur significant consequences. For the behavior of SUs in a distributed way, (Wang et al., 2014) recommended certificate-based trust worth respect. They also developed a strategy for combating selfish SSDF attacks by computing the potentially malicious level and reliability sense of trust for all the SUs involved in the sensing.

- **Interference SSDF attack:**

The *Interference SSDF attack* is just opposite of the *selfish SSDF* attack. In this attack, the fraudulent SU sends out false and relatively low PU energy to indicate the unavailability of PU. This casts a shadow on the availability of the PU; when the PU is present in the network and has high energy signals. As a result, SUs make the erroneous assumption that PUs do not exist (Yadav, K., et.al., 2020).

In CRAHN, there have been many efforts done in the literature to provide security against interference SSDF attacks (Wan et al., 2019). In (Zhang et al., 2014), authors developed a closed-form equation for global sensing performance at the fusion center (FC) using an enhanced probabilistic soft SSDF attacking model. To isolate rogue nodes from the selection process, (Feng et al., 2018) presented a distance-based outlier identification technique. In (Fard et al., 2017), the authors designed a flexible structure to deal with attackers' ambiguous attacking parameter settings. They proposed a soft-decision-based defense strategy employed by FC to identify attackers. Based on statistical aspects of sensing information, (Ahmed et al., 2014) introduced a Bayesian nonparametric clustering method to determine the PU's channel behavior and discover MUs' collaborative spectrum sensing. In (Althunibat et al., 2014), the authors proposed a unique resilient method to mitigate the impacts of the SSDF attack on CSS. In addition, the proposed technique may convert attackers to honest nodes, improving network energy efficiency and accuracy rate. Additionally, cryptography-based approaches are successfully used for primary and secondary user authentication, ensuring CRAHN secrecy (Soto et al., 2015).

- **Confused SSDF attack:**

In cooperative spectrum sensing, cognitive radio users either convey their sensing data to the central entity or share sensing data for cooperative decisions. During cooperative spectrum sensing, a malevolent SU sends random energy of the PU. As a result, the malevolent SU will succeed in perplexing other SUs into making spectrum decisions. There will be no consensus among SUs, making spectrum management extremely difficult (Khan et al., 2019).

Numerous methods have been presented in the literature to secure CRAHN from confused SSDF attacks. In (Du et al., 2015), the authors developed a technique to prevent SSDF attacks in CSS by computing and revising the credit value of the SUs; malevolent users are excluded to avoid SSDF attacks. In (Rauniyar et al., 2015), the authors proposed a cooperative approach based on an adaptive criterion. In this idea, an efficient energy detector is used as a first phase detector in a transparent region between signal and noise. A matched filter detector is used in the perplexing area between signal and noise as a second phase detector. The fundamental flaw of conventional detectors is their inability to detect low signal-to-noise ratios (SNR). To tackle the problem, a novel technique has been presented, in (Mamatha et. al., 2015) proposes a bilevel threshold holding technique for energy detection. A new soft fusion-based method was proposed in (Peng et al., 2016). The authors improved the standard soft fusion method by developing a reputation system based on the SU's prior service characteristics. The reputation degrees of the different SUs are used to assign weights to the SUs in the fusion, and this strategy may help reduce the impact of malicious users.

It is clear from the above discussion on different types of security attacks that an intruding node or a selfish node can carry out the SSDF attack. A two-tiered defense system can be employed to counter an SSDF attack. At the first level, during the phase of network creation, an authentication mechanism is employed. This authentication is carried out based on the findings of spectrum sensing to the data controller. This technique protects against replay attacks and false data insertion launched by any hostile cognitive user outside the network (Pratibha et. al., 2021).

The second level involves the employment of the data fusion method for network protection. Data fusion is quite effective against SSDF attacks. The data fusion approach integrates data from numerous sensors and related information from connected databases to obtain higher accuracy and more specific predictions than a single sensor alone could. These techniques can be improved by using a sequential probability ratio test (SPRT), one of the data fusion strategies that support various local spectrum sensing findings. By collecting numerous local spectrum sensing findings, SPRT ensures a bounded false alarm and bounded miss detection (Collotta et. al., 2017).

In a nutshell, the SSDF attack in the cooperative sensing spectrum (CSS) poses a significant threat to CRAHN's success. More efforts are required to address the unresolved research problems on this topic.

3.3 Network Layer Issues

A network layer ensures packet delivery from one node of a network to another node of different network. It also maintains quality of service. However, a malicious node can come in middle of transmission and redirects data to other destination drastically. Several types of attacks are possible.

In a *hole attack*, the attacker establishes a honey pot, and all other nodes believe this is the optimal path. Thus when they send packets to the worm-hole node, they are all dropped. Hole attack has following types (Babu et al., 2015):

- **Black-hole attack:** In this type of attack, the malicious node draws or requests packets from all other nodes to send them forward through this node rather than sending them to the target, and the packets are dropped.
- **Gray-hole attack:** It is a type of attack where the malicious node selectively releases the packets.
- **Worm-hole attack:** The most deadly of all the attacks is the worm-hole attack. It can hinder route finding when the source and destination are more than two hops away. A malevolent attacker uses two pairs of nodes and develops a private connection among them.

A ripple effect badly attacks the traffic. It causes such situation that no node is sure about their path because it creates a wrong path and transfers it across the network. Entire network doesn't know where to move. A *Sybil attack* changes the identity of packets dynamically and sends packets with different characteristics. It disturbs the trust schema of a network. Due to this attack, some good nodes get an impact of malicious and bad node. It impacts very badly on future routing decisions. In *Hello flood attack*, malicious node broadcasts 'Hello' message on spectrum in a manner that every other host thinks that this 'Hello' message is transmitted by neighbors. But it is actually far away from the neighbor node. This causes the packet loss and slows down the transmission due to packet losses.

In Sinkhole attack, a malicious node falsely publicizes itself as the best route towards the destination. Then, selective forwarding can be performed to drop packet of a victim node. An approach to counter such attack is geographic routing in which routing is performed based on the location of destination nodes.

In order to provide security against black hole attacks, ad hoc on-demand distance vector routing (AODV) is employed (Abbas et al., 2020). However, routing data can be encrypted using cryptographic protocols to authenticate the routing table's integrity and the nodes' identities. The watch dog system can be used to keep track of data packets as they go through the network (Dung et al., 2019). In the case of regular functioning the packets are sent between the nodes. Nevertheless, when an intermediate node behaves abnormally, it will either modify the contents of packets or drop them after receiving them from the first node. As a result, the destination node will receive the modified packet or never receive it. The watch dog idea is used to buffer packets at the sending node. After receiving the packet, the destination node compares it to the buffered one.

3.4 Transport Layer Issues

The goal of transport layer is to ensure end-to-end transmission of data. Several types of attacks are possible at transport layer. The major attacks are lion attack and key repetition attack.

An attack on transport layer is lion attack that is launched using primary user emulation. A secondary user while detecting primary user, switches its channel. As the TCP layer is not aware of the handoff occurring at lower layer, this will result in timeouts and ultimately degraded performance. To extend it further, if the malicious user is able to get hold of communication, it can claim the frequency band and hijacks the session resulting in starvation. The lion attack can be encountered by using cross-layer transport protocols. To avoid session hijacking, group key management can be employed.

As retransmissions are common in cognitive networks, single sessions only last for a limited time period, resulting in the launch of multiple sessions. At the start of each session, security protocols such as SSL and TLS create cryptographic keys in the transport layer. Because cognitive networks have a significant number of sessions, many keys are created, increasing the chance of utilizing the same key twice. The underlying cipher scheme can be broken via key repetitions. Commonly, the round trip time and the percentage of fast retransmissions are analyzed to detect the attacker. If retransmissions are too fast or the round trip time exceeds the time value, we can conclude that there is some suspicious activity in the network. Therefore an intrusion detection scheme based on RSS and RTT detection proposed in the literature can detect attacks on this layer. RSS and RTT detection can be used to detect attacks at this layer (Singh et al., 2017).

3.5 Application Layer Issues

The application layer is the final or uppermost layer of OSI protocol stack. It offers the end users with better representation when it comes to services. All other layers support the application layer. The following are the main application layer attacks:

- **Policy Attacks:** In this attack, the effect of change is not successfully passed to all nodes and that's why change is not allowed. Due to this, we can't limit the malicious use of spectrum and it keeps effecting the spectrum resources.
- **Cognitive Virus:** Radio network is vulnerable to virus. If it gets affected with some virus, it starts affecting the whole network by updating its neighbor states. The time virus takes to affect the network is directly proportional to the size of network. It uses AI virus that dynamically changes itself.

After all, the activities of other protocol layers may impact one another. Multiple protocol layers can be examined, or information can be analyzed at this layer. For instance, such anomalous behavior can be easily identified at the application layer in cases where an application creates multiple connections without doing any significant processes (Lee et al., 2021). Table 4 shows the summary of security attacks in CRAHN and the counter solutions

Table 4. Security issues in CRAHN and the countermeasures

Layer	Security issues	Countermeasures

Physical layer	Attacks that include global jamming, prime receiver's jamming, sensitivity amplification, overlapping subsidiary operator and shared operational data	• Intrusion detection system.
		• Receiving feedback from the cognitive radio devices.
		• Utilizing the networks' redundancy.
		   (Leon et al., 2009)
		   (Zhang & Lee, 2000)
		   (Leon et al., 2011)
		   (Filho et al., 2012)

Link layer	Artificially generated feedback, asynchronous detecting, and skewed utility attacks	
Network layer	Channel ecto parasite, Network endo Parasite, and Low-Loop Effect Attacks	• The adoption of an authenticating procedure between prime and secondary participants or the incorporation of a signature into an authoritative signal.
Transport layer	Lion attack, Attacks on Key Decline and Jelly-fish Denial of Service attack	• To cope with Secondary user emulation attack defenses in Cognitive radio networks, signals energy level monitoring in line with transmitter position is used.

Application layer	Since the application layer is the top tier of the transmission routing protocol, any security issue on the other layers will have an adverse effect on it.	• Using Radio frequency fingerprinting
		   (Chen et al., 2008)
		• Cross-layer approaches for improved TCP efficiency. (Hanbali et al., 2005)
		• To offer group privacy, CRNs work together to identify spectrum availability for communications.
		• To assure group privacy, a key, also described as a shared secret key is established.
		   (William & Dongwan, 2011)
		   (Marques et al., 2009)

3.6 Cross Layer Issues

Several types of cross layer attacks are possible. In these types of attacks, an attacker targets multiple layers and disturbs the cycle. The impact of attack on one layer leads the impact to the other layer and affects the whole spectrum. For instance, in *routing information jamming*, an attacker takes benefit of deferment during spectrum transfer and it causes the jamming among network nodes and slows down the routing information. This would results in indelicate routing.

A jamming attack squeezes the communication among radios of CRAHN. It is one of the major causes of denial of service (DoS) attack, compromising the availability of network. Jamming attack can be classified in four major categories (Pirayesh et al., 2021):

§ **Constant jammer:** In this jamming attack, an attacker sends data packets repeatedly without interacting with other users on the same channel.

§ **Deceptive jammer**: Here, when a genuine user perceives a steady stream of receiving data packets, an attacker tricks it into changing its status to "receive".

§ **Random jammer:** While transmitting blocking signals, an attacker takes intermittent breaks in random jamming. In this type of jamming, the attacker might act as a regular or unpredictable blocker during the phase of jamming.

§ **Reactive jammer:** In a reactive jamming scenario, the attacker constantly senses the channel and only transmits the jamming signals when it detects a transmission in the channel.

3.6.1 Jamming Attack on Other Layers

On several layers of the protocol stack, jamming attempts are possible. For example, at the physical layer, an attacker may deploy a device capable of producing signals at the same frequency as the target devices, causing communication disruption. After transmitting jamming packets, one or more cognitive radios keep switching back and forth across specific channels (Osanaiye et al., 2018). An attacker can also compromise the medium access mechanism at the link layer by sending a packet to a channel and engaging the communication channel. Due to this, all devices in the range are forced to presume that the medium is busy. As a result, all users will delay transmission (Arjoune et al., 2020).

In the literature, several strategies for detecting jamming threats have been presented. One approach at the physical layer is to use a device that gathers data packets and builds a predictive algorithm on top of it to distinguish between normal and abnormal amounts of noise on the channel (Osanaiye et al., 2018). Analyzing the relation between signal strength (SS) and packet delivery ratio (PDR) is one of the proposed jamming detection approaches (Xu et al., 2005). If the SS is high and the PDR is low, and none of its neighbors have a high SS and PDR, a node can be assumed to be a jamming attack victim. The location stability checks are another option. When the PDR values of all adjacent surrounding nodes are low, it is known that the node has either been jammed or has poor signal connections with its neighbors (Meghanathan et al., 2013).

Figure 3. The major security attacks in open systems interconnection (OSI)

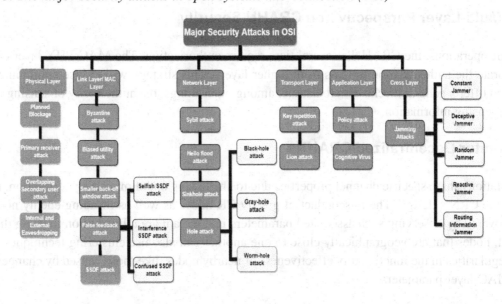

Suppose a device cannot finish the carrier-sensing phase of the link layer's carrier sensing multiple access (CSMA) medium access control protocol. In that case, it is assumed that it has already been jammed. In such a scenario, frequency hopping to a new channel is used to secure it from jamming. A network layer security mechanism known as a spatial retreat can also be used to cater this issue (Meghanathan et al., 2013). This strategy involves appropriate users changing their position to get out of an attacker's interference zone. The decision algorithm is utilized to generate the SUs' channel hopping sequence, ensuring that they are not vulnerable to physical layer jamming attacks. Each SU has simultaneous access to numerous channels through various radios in multi-channel CRNs. The defense technique is to change the transmission power of the SU on particular channels at random. Switching between control and data channels, access patterns, and detecting jamming attempts begun from several sources concurrently will improve spectrum throughput and efficiency. Collaborative jamming (one attacker per channel) is still conceivable, even though it is difficult for an attacker to determine the frequency channels that would be used between a transmitter and receiver set.

4. DISCUSSION ON SOLUTIONS PROPOSED

The scholars in this field needs to perform a more complete investigation of the security implications in a CRAHN context as they are still in their early stages. A variety of challenges are specific to cognitive transmissions, most significantly the need to protect the spectrum sensing system from outside and internal compromised nodes. While some approaches, primarily based on collaborating nodes' trust rankings, have been established to counter assaults that falsify spectrum sensing information, it is also critical to look more thoroughly at other cyber attacks, such as incumbent emulation and sensors jamming. A further important matter that needs to be addressed more thoroughly is the far-reaching impact of isolated assaults against CRAHNs because of the learning-based interaction CR nodes has with their RF environments. The following discussion introduces many prospective research directions.

4.1 A Multi-Layer Perspective on CRAHN Security

For their operations, the CRAHN's several tiers require authorization. The MAC-PHY layer can then incorporate the authentication process from higher layers. This strategy will reduce communication's costs and offer a general mechanism to handle, among other things, the authenticity of sensing devices and the sensing information.

4.2 Monitor Decentralized CRAHNs

Local stations share specific channel properties due to shadowing and diminishing correlation, regardless of the CRN's design. The misconduct of greedy CR nodes as well as invading enemy nodes can be discovered by observing such associated parameters in a certain area. In addition to using the radio channel, nodes that are geographically close to one another can also use clustering techniques to spot any irregularities in the functionality effectiveness of nearby nodes, like those caused by changes to the PHY-MAC-layer parameters.

4.3 Practicing at the Hardware Level and Collaborative Connections

Addressing the long-term effects of such breaches owing to the RF environment monitoring of CR nodes is a crucial component of defense against intrusions on CRNs. Every node will engage with and absorb knowledge from its immediate environment. The entire CRN will also gain knowledge and work to improve its performance when confronted with of node cooperation or competitiveness as well as the impact of hostile nodes. Consequently, it is crucial to create adaptable plans based on CRN learning capabilities in order to align the connection and system level objectives and enhance effectiveness of the network as a whole.

4.4 Security Measures With Incentives

In a CRN, the investigators that pose security risks were divided into three groups: external adversaries, trespassing malevolent nodes, and opportunistic CRs. Each faction will have a distinctive attack plan. In order to implement incentive-minimization strategies, it is essential to consider the motivations for bad conduct and assaults against a CRN. For instance, a greedy CR wants to improve its effectiveness even more at the expense of other nodes in the network. So long as no single node can maintain superior performance in the network, balanced resource allocation algorithms will guarantee that no one may engage in misbehavior based on false claims.

4.5 Efficient Strategies for Spectrum Sensing

Probably more importantly than any other CR security threat, countermeasures to assaults against DSS systems have been researched. However, a detailed evaluation and comparison of existing approaches, such as trust-weight fusion against consensus-based methods, can offer more understanding into the benefits and drawbacks of each plan and may inspire future investigators to create more reliable DSS alternatives.

4.6 Strategies for Preventing Jamming in CR

As mentioned in the study (Attar et al., 2012), an external attacker can interfere with CRN service by sending signals that are jammed to sensors, manage channels, or receivers. More interference-resistant communications systems are required in all of these attacks, for example, to decode the received signals in very low SNR environments or to find the primary signal hidden in the jammer's signal. To target specific solutions for different jamming threats within a CRN frame - work, more research is required.

4.6 Reliable Cognitive Connections

The methods that control how CRNs behave typically fall into two groups: those that observe or acquire the radio environment i.e. spectrum sensing and those that change it i.e. interference management via broadcast power control. Investigations that investigate at the resilience of the aforementioned processes are few and far between. It is important to conduct thorough research on robust spectrum sensing, efficient learning techniques, and reliable communication schemes, particularly when assuming incoming data error, inaccuracies, or tampering.

5. EXAMPLES AND CASE STUDIES

This section highlights some of the case studies for cognitive radio networks. Tashman and Hamouda (2020) have discussed a case study of using frequency hopping spread spectrum for physical layer requirements of cognitive radios. Chen et al. (2019) have suggested the use of artificial intelligence for managing the issues of CRAHN. They highlighted some case studies for CRAHN for different types of environments such as:

§ **Decision making:** This involves decision making across different aspects of CRAHN such as for spectrum sharing. An example of intelligent spectrum sharing has been provided in (Islam et al., 2018). The authors have proposed a deep learning based solution for spectrum sharing and decision making. By using an ad hoc network equipped with sensor, disaster management along with spectrum sharing for CRAHN have been discussed.

§ **Network management:** Network management may require use of artificial intelligence that can help in optimized solution for network management. A novel solution in this direction for data management has been proposed in (Islam et al., 2021)

§ **Resource optimization:** A deep learning based solution for resource optimization has been proposed in (Lee et al., 2021).

§ **Knowledge discovery:** Knowledge discovery can be performed in both proactive and reactive manner. Some hybrid solutions have also been proposed such as (Islam et al., 2013).

The authors in (Dai et al., 2019) have proposed an intelligent network that can combines edge computing and caching to facilitate cross-layer offloading and cooperative multi-point caching. A case study on soft data fusion schemes for SSDF attack in CRAHN has been proposed in (Bouzegag et al., 2022). Another interesting case study is cognitive IoT where the internet of things (IoT) and cognitive radio networks are combined. In this direction, physical layer security issues for CRAHN have been discussed in (Kurt & Cepheli, 2020). Monisha and Rajendran (2022) have employed CRAHN for smart grid communication.

6. SOCIAL AND POLICY IMPLICATIONS

Finally, this section discusses the social and policy implications for CRAHN. After an extensive review of literature, it has been found that CRAHN implementation requires convergence of technologies such as artificial intelligence, blockchain, internet of things and 5G networks. A number of interesting applications will emerge such as vehicular networking, machine to machine communications, military applications and smart grids. Each of these applications requires customization of spectrum sensing scheme specific to the application and their real-time needs (Gupt & Kumar, 2019). A multi-layered solution for future cognitive radio networks based on IoT has been proposed in (Molokomme et al., 2020). The role of fog computing can't be denied as it can help in mitigating latency, security and data congestion issues. Amongst the practical requirements for CRAHN include high sampling rate, high-resolution ADC and high-speed signal processors (Gupta & Kumar, 2019). The security and privacy issues must be a concern for primary user. The sharing of spectrum may also be a threat for secondary user. Conventional solutions such as intrusion detection system, cryptography and firewalls may not be enough for CRAHN. Existing literature assumes that cognitive users are honest. But, this requirement is not necessarily met. Finally, we must give a pointer (Gupta & Kumar, 2019) to hardware limitations of CRAHN.

7. CONCLUSION

In this paper, an overview of various research issues of CRAHN has been presented. The security issue of CRAHN is then discussed in detail. The security threats at different layers of cognitive radio ad hoc network have been presented. It has been found that security in CRAHN is a multilayer problem. The best approach to counter security issue is to present a cross-layer solution that is aware of events at each layer of protocol stack and can employ counter-strategies to deal with the situation.

We must highlight what a cross-layer design must entail. A cross-layer solution enables information sharing across the different layers of protocol stack. These layers include application, transport, network and physical layers. The objective is to optimize the various operations of the network. A cross layer solution must be flexible, modular, optimized, scalable, adaptable and provides support for interoperability. For instance in a cross-layer solution, physical layer can pass the information about battery status, channel characteristics to application layer to devise an SDN based solution for security management, spectrum sharing. The physical and link layer can pass the information to the transport layer to avoid trying congestion control as the spectrum is being switched off. A cross-layer design employing these strategies have been presented in (Cammarano et al.

REFERENCES

Abbas, F. & Qamar, M. (2020). Performance Analysis of Ad Hoc on-Demand Distance Vector Routing Protocol for MANET. *2020 IEEE Student Conference on Research and Development (SCOReD)*. IEEE. 10.1109/SCOReD50371.2020.9250989

Afhamisisi, K., Shahhoseini, H. S., & Meamari, E. (2019). Defense against Lion Attack in Cognitive Radio Systems using the Markov Decision Process Approach. *Frequenz (Bern)*, *68*, 191–201.

Ahmadfard, A., Jamshidi, A., & Keshavarz-Haddad, A. (2017). Probabilistic spectrum sensing data falsification attack in cognitive radio networks. *Signal Processing*, *137*, 1–9. doi:10.1016/j.sigpro.2017.01.033

Ahmed, M. E., Song, J. B., & Han, Z. (2014). Mitigating malicious attacks using Bayesian nonparametric clustering in collaborative cognitive radio networks. In: *Proceedings of the IEEE Globecom*. IEEE. https://ieeexplore.ieee.org/document/7036939

Akyildiz, I. F., Lee, W.-Y., Vuran, M. C., & Mohanty, S. (2006, September). NeXt generation/dynamic spectrum access/cognitive radio wireless networks [Elsevier North-Holland, Inc.New York, NY, USA.]. *Computer Networks*, *50*(13, 15), 2127–2159. doi:10.1016/j.comnet.2006.05.001

Althunibat, S., Di Renzo, M., & Granelli, F. (2014). Robust algorithm against spectrum sensing data falsification attack in cognitive radio networks. In: *Proceedings of VTC spring*, (pp. 1–5). IEEE. https://ieeexplore.ieee.org/document/7023078

Arjoune, Y., Salahdine, F., Islam, M., Ghribi, E., & Kaabouch, N. (2020). A Novel Jamming Attacks Detection Approach Based on Machine Learning for Wireless Communication. *International Conference on Information Networking (ICOIN)*, Barcelona, Spain. 10.1109/ICOIN48656.2020.9016462

Attar, A., Tang, H., Vasilakos, A. V., Yu, F. R., & Leung, V. C. M. (2012). A Survey of Security Challenges in Cognitive Radio Networks: Solutions and Future Research Directions. *Proceedings of the IEEE, 100*(12), 3172–3186. doi:10.1109/JPROC.2012.2208211

Attar, A., Tang, H., Vasilakos, A. V., Yu, F. R., & Leung, V. C. M. (2012). F. Richard Yu, and Victor CM Leung. "A survey of security challenges in cognitive radio networks: Solutions and future research directions.". *Proceedings of the IEEE, 100*(12), 3172–3186. doi:10.1109/JPROC.2012.2208211

Babu, B. R., Tripathi, M., Gaur, M. S., Gopalani, D., & Singh Jat, D. (2015). Cognitive radio ad-hoc networks: Attacks and its impact. *2015 International Conference on Emerging Trends in Networks and Computer Communications (ETNCC)*, (pp. 125-130). IEEE. 10.1109/ETNCC.2015.7184821

Bennaceur, J., Idoudi, H., & Saidane, L. A. (2016). *A trust game model for the cognitive radio networks.* 2016 International Conference on Performance Evaluation and Modeling in Wired and Wireless Networks (PEMWN), Paris, France. 10.1109/PEMWN.2016.7842903

Bian, K., & Park, J. M. (2006). MAC-layer Misbehaviors in Multi-hop Cognitive Radio Networks. *Proceedings of the 2006 US-Korea Conference on Science, Technology and Entrepreneurship.* IEEE.

Bouzegag, Y., Djamal, T., & Abdelmadjid, M. (2022). Comprehensive Performance Analysis of Soft Data Fusion Schemes under SSDF Attacks in Cognitive Radio Networks. *International Journal of Sensors, Wireless Communications and Control, 12*(4), 312–318. doi:10.2174/2210327912666220325155048

Cabric, D., Mishra, S. M., & Brodersen, R. W. (2004). Implementation Issues in Spectrum Sensing for Cognitive Radios. *Proc. IEEE Asilomar Conf. Signals, Sys., and Comp.*, (pp. 772–76). IEEE. 10.1109/ACSSC.2004.1399240

Cammarano, A., Presti, F. L., Maselli, G., Pescosolido, L., & Petrioli, C. (2014). Throughput-optimal cross-layer design for cognitive radio ad hoc networks. *IEEE Transactions on Parallel and Distributed Systems, 26*(9), 2599–2609. doi:10.1109/TPDS.2014.2350495

Castanedo, F. (2013). A Review of Data Fusion Techniques. The Scientific World Journal. doi:10.1155/2013/704504

Chen, H., Jin, X., & Xie, L. (2009). Reputation-based collaborative spectrum sensing algorithm in Cognitive Radio networks. In 2009 *IEEE 20th International Symposium on Personal, Indoor and Mobile Radio Communications*, (pp. 582–587). IEEE. 10.1109/PIMRC.2009.5450251

Chen, R. (2008, April). Toward Secure Distributed Spectrum Sensing in Cognitive Radio Networks. *IEEE Communications Magazine*.

Chen, R., Park, J.-M., & Reed, J. H. (2008). Defense against primary user emulation attacks in cognitive radio networks. *IEEE Journal on Selected Areas in Communications, 26*(1), 25–37. doi:10.1109/JSAC.2008.080104

Cheng, Y. & Zhou, J. (2014). S-CRAHN: A Secure Cognitive-Radio Ad-Hoc Network. *HCTL Open Science and Technology Letters (HCTL Open STL)*.

Chetan N. & Mathur, K.P. (2007). *Security issues in cognitive radio networks.* Cognitive network: Towards Self-Aware Networks.

Clancy, T. C., & Goergen, N. Security in Cognitive Radio Networks: Threats and Mitigation. *Proceedings of the International Conference on Cognitive Radio Oriented Wireless Networks and Communications*, (pp. 1-8). IEEE. 10.1109/CROWNCOM.2008.4562534

Collotta, M. (2017). A Fuzzy Data Fusion Solution to Enhance the QoS and the Energy Consumption in Wireless Sensor Networks. Wireless Communications and Mobile Computing. doi:10.1155/2017/3418284

Cormio, C., & Chowdhury, K. R. (2009). *A Survey on MAC Protocols for Cognitive Radio Networks.* Ad Hoc Net. J. doi:10.1016/j.adhoc.2009.01.002

Dai, Y., Xu, D., Maharjan, S., Qiao, G., & Zhang, Y. (2019). Artificial intelligence empowered edge computing and caching for internet of vehicles. *IEEE Wireless Communications*, 26(3), 12–18. doi:10.1109/MWC.2019.1800411

Dansana, D., & Behera, P. K. (2021). A Study of Recent Security Attacks on Cognitive Radio Ad Hoc Networks (CRAHNs). In *Soft Computing Techniques and Applications: Proceeding of the International Conference on Computing and Communication (IC3 2020)* (pp. 351-359). Springer Singapore.

Deepraj, S. (2012). *Investigation of Security Challenges in Cognitive Radio Networks.*

Di Felice, M. (2010). *Learning-Based Spectrum Selection in Cognitive Radio Ad Hoc Networks Marco Di Felice*. Springer-Verlag Berlin Heidelberg.

Du, H., Fu, S., & Chu, H. (2015). A credibility-based defense ssdf attacks scheme for the expulsion of malicious users in cognitive radio. *International Journal of Hybrid Information Technology*, 8(9), 9. doi:10.14257/ijhit.2015.8.9.25

Dung, L. T., & Choi, S. G. (2019). Connectivity Analysis of Cognitive Radio Ad-Hoc Networks with Multi-Pair Primary Networks. *Sensors (Basel)*, 19(3), 565. doi:10.339019030565 PMID:30700043

Feng, J., Li, S., Lv, S., Wang, H., & Fu, A. (2018, September). Securing Cooperative Spectrum Sensing Against Collusive False Feedback Attack in Cognitive Radio Networks. *IEEE Transactions on Vehicular Technology*, 67(9), 8276–8287. doi:10.1109/TVT.2018.2841362

Feng, J., Zhang, M., Xiao, Y., & Yue, H. (2018). Securing cooperative spectrum sensing against collusive SSDF attack using XOR distance analysis in cognitive radio networks. *Sensors (Basel)*, 18(2), 1–14. doi:10.339018020370 PMID:29382061

Gupta, M. S., & Kumar, K. (2019). Progression on spectrum sensing for cognitive radio networks: A survey, classification, challenges and future research issues. *Journal of Network and Computer Applications*, 143, 47–76. doi:10.1016/j.jnca.2019.06.005

Hanbali, A. A., Altman, E., Nain, P., & France, I. S. A. (2005). A survey of tcp over ad hoc networks. Communications Surveys and Tutorials. *IEEE Communications Surveys and Tutorials*, 7(3), 22–36. doi:10.1109/COMST.2005.1610548

Hwang, K., Chen, M., Gharavi, H., & Leung, V. C. (2019). Artificial intelligence for cognitive wireless communications. *IEEE Wireless Communications*, 26(3), 10–11. doi:10.1109/MWC.2019.8752476 PMID:31579263

Ian, F. (2009). *Akyildiz et al., "Cognitive radio ad hoc networks, Ad Hoc Networks"*. Elsevier North-Holland, Inc., doi:10.1016/j.adhoc.2009.01.001

Ian, F. (2009). *Akyildiz, "Spectrum Management in Cognitive Radio Ad Hoc Networks", Georgia Institute of Technology*. IEEE Network.

Islam, N., Shaikh, Z. A., Rehman, A. U., & Siddiqui, M. S. (2013). HANDY: A hybrid association rules mining approach for network layer discovery of services for mobile ad hoc network. *Wireless Networks, 19*(8), 1961–1977. doi:10.100711276-013-0571-3

Islam, N., Sheikh, G. S., & Islam, Z. 2018. A cognitive radio ad hoc networks based disaster management scheme with efficient spectrum management, collaboration and interoperability. arXiv preprint arXiv:1810.05090.

Islam, N., Sheikh, G. S., & Shaikh, Z. A. (2021). Using association rules mining, multi-level data representation and cross-layer operations for data management in mobile ad hoc network. *International Journal of Intelligent Engineering Informatics, 9*(3), 229–259. doi:10.1504/IJIEI.2021.118268

Islam, N., Zubair A. (2014). A study of research trends and issues in wireless ad hoc networks. IGI Global.

Kar, S., Sethi, S., & Sahoo, R. K. (2017). A Multi-factor Trust Management Scheme for Secure Spectrum Sensing in Cognitive Radio Networks. *Wireless Personal Communications, 97*(2), 2523–2540. doi:10.100711277-017-4621-5

Khan, M. S., Jibran, M., Koo, I., Kim, S. M., & Kim, J. (2019). A Double Adaptive Approach to Tackle Malicious Users in Cognitive Radio Networks. Wireless Communications and Mobile Computing. Hindawi. doi:10.1155/2019/2350694

Kim, H., & Shin, K. G. (2008, May). Efficient Discovery of Spectrum Opportunities with MAC-Layer Sensing in Cognitive Radio Networks. *IEEE Transactions on Mobile Computing, 7*(5), 533–545. doi:10.1109/TMC.2007.70751

Kurt, G. K., & Cepheli, Ö. (2020). *Physical layer security of cognitive IoT networks*. Towards Cognitive IoT Networks. doi:10.1007/978-3-030-42573-9_8

Lee, K.-E., Park, J. G., & Yoo, S.-J. (2021). Intelligent Cognitive Radio Ad-Hoc Network: Planning, Learning and Dynamic Configuration. *Electronics (Basel), 10*(3), 254. doi:10.3390/electronics10030254

Lee, K. E., Park, J. G., & Yoo, S. J. (2021). Intelligent cognitive radio ad-hoc network: Planning, learning and dynamic configuration. *Electronics (Basel), 10*(3), 254. doi:10.3390/electronics10030254

Leo'n, O., Roma'n, R., & Herna'ndez-Serrano, J. (2011). *Towards a cooperativeintrusiondetectionsystemforcognitive radio networks. In Proceedings of the IFIP TC 6th internationalconferenceonNetworking (NETWORKING'11)*. Valencia, Spain.

Leon, O., Hernandez-Serrano, J., & Soriano, M. (2010). Securing Cognitive Radio Networks. *International Journal of Communication Systems, 23*(5), 633–652.

Leon, O., Serrano, J. H., & Soriano, M. (2009). *A new cross-layer attack to TCP in cognitive radio networks.* Second international workshop on cross layer design, IWCLD '09, Mallorca, Spain. 10.1109/IWCLD.2009.5156526

Li, J., Feng, Z., Feng, Z., & Zhang, P. (2015, March). A survey of security issues in Cognitive Radio Networks. *China Communications, 12*(3), 132–150. doi:10.1109/CC.2015.7084371

Magdalene, H.S., &Thulasimani, D.L. (2017). *Analysis of Spectrum Sensing Data Falsification (SSDF) Attack in Cognitive Radio Networks: A Survey.* Semantic Scholar.

Mamatha, S., & Aparna, K. (2015). Design of an Adaptive Energy Detector based on Bi-Level Tresh holding in Cognitive Radio. *International Journal of Scientifc Engineering and Technology Research, 4*(2), 346–349.

Mansoor, N., Muzahidul Islam, A., Zareei, M., Baharun, S., Wakabayashi, T., & Komaki, S. (2014). Cognitive radio Ad-Hoc network architectures: A survey. *Wireless Personal Communications, 81*(3), 1117–1142. doi:10.100711277-014-2175-3

Marques, H., Ribeiro, J., Marques, P., Zuquete, A., & Rodriguez, J. (2009). A security framework for cognitive radio IP based cooperative protocols. In: *IEEE 20th international symposium on personal, indoor and mobile radio communications.* IEEE. 10.1109/PIMRC.2009.5449952

Minho, J. (2013). *Selfish Attacks and Detection in Cognitive Radio Ad-Hoc Networks.* IEEE Network.

Al Mojamed, M. (2020). Integrating Mobile Ad Hoc Networks withthe Internet Basedon OLSR. *Wireless Communications and Mobile Computing.* doi:10.1155/2020/8810761

Molokomme, D. N., Chabalala, C. S., & Bokoro, P. N. (2020). A review of cognitive radio smart grid communication infrastructure systems. *Energies, 13*(12), 3245. doi:10.3390/en13123245

Monisha, M., & Rajendran, V. (2022). SCAN-CogRSG: Secure channel allocation by dynamic cluster switching for cognitive radio enabled smart grid communications. *Journal of the Institution of Electronics and Telecommunication Engineers, 68*(4), 2826–2847. doi:10.1080/03772063.2020.1729259

Natarajan, M. (2013). *A Survey on the Communication Protocols and Security in Cognitive Radio Networks.* Jackson State University.

E. Onem, S. Eryigit, T. Tugcu and A. Akurgal, "QoS-Enabled Spectrum-Aware Routing for Disaster Relief and Tactical Operations over Cognitive Radio Ad Hoc Networks," *MILCOM 2013 - 2013 IEEE Military Communications Conference,* 2013, pp. 1109-1115, . doi:10.1109/MILCOM.2013.191

Osanaiye, O., Alfa, A. S., & Hancke, G. P. (2018). A Statistical Approach to Detect Jamming Attacks in Wireless Sensor Networks. *Sensors (Basel), 18*(6), 1691. doi:10.339018061691 PMID:29794994

Pandya, P., Durvesh, A., & Parekh, N. (2015). Energy Detection Based Spectrum Sensing for Cognitive Radio Network. *2015 Fifth International Conference on Communication Systems and Network Technologies.* IEEE. 10.1109/CSNT.2015.264

Peng, P., & Kievit, R. A. (2020). The development of academic achievement and cognitive abilities: A bidirectional perspective. *Child Development Perspectives*, *14*(1), 15–20. doi:10.1111/cdep.12352 PMID:35909387

Peng, T., Chen, Y., Xiao, J., Zheng, Y., & Yang, J. (2016). Improved sof fusion-based cooperative spectrum sensing defense against SSDF attacks. *Proceedings of the 2016 International Conference on Computer, Information and Telecommunication Systems, CITS*. IEEE.

Pirayesh, H., & Zeng, H. (2021). Jamming Attacks and Anti-Jamming Strategies in Wireless Networks: A Comprehensive Survey. *ArXiv, abs/2101.00292*.

Pratibha, T. S., Kumar, N., & Kumar, S. (2021). A Survey on Prevention of the Falsification Attacks on Cognitive Radio Networks. *IOP Conference Series: Materials Science and Engineering*. IOP. . doi:10.1088/1757-899X/1033/1/012021

Rauniyar, A., & Shin, S. Y. (2015). Cooperative adaptive threshold based energy and matched flter detector in cognitive radio networks. *Journal of Communication and Computer*, *12*, 13–19.

Sampath, H., Dai, H., Zheng, & Zhao, Y. (2011). *Multi-channel Jamming Attacks using Cognitive Radios*. Proceedings of the 16th International Conference on Computer Communications and Networks (ICCCN*)*, Honolulu, HI, USA

Shamir. (1984). Identity-based cryptosystems and signature schemes, Advances in Cryptology. Crypto 84, (pp. 47–53). Springer-Verlag.

Shams, S., Santhoshkumar, M., Muttath, D. J., & Premkumar, K. (2019). *Distributed Detection in Cognitive Radio Networks with Unknown Primary User's Traffic. TENCON 2019 - 2019 IEEE Region 10 Conference*. IEEE. doi:10.1109/TENCON.2019.8929431

Singh, L., & Dutta, N. (2020). Routing Protocols for CRAHN: A Comparative Evaluation. In H. Sarma, B. Bhuyan, S. Borah, & N. Dutta (Eds.), *Trends in Communication, Cloud, and Big Data. Lecture Notes in Networks and Systems* (Vol. 99). Springer. doi:10.1007/978-981-15-1624-5_1

Singh, R., Singh, J., & Singh, R. (2017). Fuzzy Based Advanced Hybrid Intrusion Detection System to Detect Malicious Nodes in Wireless Sensor Networks. Wireless Communications and Mobile Computing. doi:10.1155/2017/3548607

Soto, J., & Nogueira, M. (2015). A framework for resilient and secure spectrum sensing on cognitive radio networks. *Computer Networks*, *79*, 313–322. doi:10.1016/j.comnet.2015.01.011

Tashman, D. H., & Hamouda, W. (2020). An overview and future directions on physical-layer security for cognitive radio networks. *IEEE Network*, *35*(3), 205–211. doi:10.1109/MNET.011.2000507

Tephillah, S., & Manickam, J. M. L. (2020). An SETM Algorithm for Combating SSDF Attack in Cognitive Radio Networks. [NA.]. *Wireless Communications and Mobile Computing*, *2020*, 2020. doi:10.1155/2020/9047809

Thakur, P. (2021). Spectrum Mobility in Cognitive Radio Networks Using Spectrum Prediction and Monitoring Techniques. In *Spectrum Sharing in Cognitive Radio Networks: Towards Highly Connected Environments* (pp. 147–166). Wiley. doi:10.1002/9781119665458.ch7

Varsha, P. & Rakesh, V. (2012). Black Hole Attack and its Counter Measures in AODV Routing Protocol. *International Journal of Computational Engineering Research (ijceronline.com), 2*(5).

Wan, R., Ding, L., Xiong, N., & Zhou, X. (2019). Mitigation strategy against spectrum-sensing data falsification attack in cognitive radio sensor networks. *International Journal of Distributed Sensor Networks, 15*(9), 155014771987064. doi:10.1177/1550147719870645

Wang, B., Wu, Y., Liu, K. J. R., & Clancy, T. C. (2011, April). An Anti-Jamming Stochastic Game for Cognitive Radio Networks. *IEEE Journal on Selected Areas in Communications, 29*(4), 877–889. doi:10.1109/JSAC.2011.110418

Wang, J., & Chen, I. (2014). Trust-based data fusion mechanism design in cognitive radio networks. 2014 IEEE Conference on Communications and Network Security, (pp. 53–59). IEEE. 10.1109/CNS.2014.6997465

Wang, Q., & Zheng, H. (2006). Route and Spectrum Selection in Dynamic Spectrum Networks. *Proc. IEEE CCNC*. IEEE.

Wang, W., Chatterjee, M., & Kwiat, K. (2011). Collaborative Jamming and Collaborative Defense in Cognitive Radio Networks. *Proceedings of the IEEE International Symposium on a World of Wireless, Mobile and Multimedia Networks (WoWMoM)*. IEEE. 10.1109/WoWMoM.2011.5986172

Wang, W., Li, H., Sun, L., & Han, Z. (2009). Securing Collaborative Spectrum Sensing against Untrustworthy Secondary Users in Cognitive Radio Networks. *EURASIP Journal on Advances in Signal Processing, 2010*(1), 695750. doi:10.1155/2010/695750

Wassim, E. H. (2011). Survey of Security Issues in Cognitive Radio Networks. *Journal of Internet Technology, 12*(2).

William, R. C., & Dongwan, S. (2011). A novel node level security policy framework for wireless sensor networks. *Journal of Network and Computer Applications, 34*(1), 418–428. doi:10.1016/j.jnca.2010.03.004

Wu, Y., Wang, B., & Liu, K. J. R. (2012). Optimal Defense against Jamming Attacks in Cognitive Radio Networks using the Markov Decision Process Approach. *Proceedings of the IEEE Global Telecommunications Conference*. IEEE.

Xu, W., Trappe, W., Zhang, Y., & Wood, T. (2005). The Feasibility of Launching and Detecting Jamming Attacks in Wireless Networks. Proceedings of the ACM International Symposium on Mobile Ad hoc Networking and Computing, (pp. 46-57). ACM. 10.1145/1062689.1062697

Xu, W., Wood, T., Trappe, W., & Zhang, Y. (2004). Channel Surfing and Spatial Retreats: Defenses against Wireless Denial of Service. Proceedings of the 3rd ACM Workshop on Wireless Security, (pp. 80-89). ACM. 10.1145/1023646.1023661

Yadav, K., Roy, S. D., & Kundu, S. (2020). Defense Against Spectrum Sensing Data Falsification Attacker in Cognitive Radio Networks. *Wireless Personal Communications, 112*(2), 849–862. doi:10.100711277-020-07077-9

Yan, Q., Li, M., Jiang, T., Lou, W., & Thomas Hou, Y. (2007). Vulnerability and Protection for Distributed Consensus-based Spectrum Sensing in Cognitive Radio Networks Qing Zhao, Lang Tong, Ananthram Swami, Yunxia Chen, "Decentralized cognitive MAC for opportunistic spectrum access in ad hoc networks: A POMDP framework". *IEEE Journal on Selected Areas in Communications*, *25*(3).

Yu, H., & Zikria, Y. B. (2020). Cognitive Radio Networks for Internet of Things and Wireless Sensor Networks. *Sensors (Basel)*, *20*(18), 5288. doi:10.339020185288 PMID:32947832

Zhang, H., Liu, Z., & Hui, Q. (2012). Optimal Defense Synthesis for Jamming Attacks in Cognitive Radio Networks via Swarm Optimization. *Proceedings of the IEEE Symposium on Computational Intelligence for Security and Defense Applications*. IEEE. 10.1109/CISDA.2012.6291525

Zhang, L., Wu, Q., Ding, G., Feng, S., & Wang, J. (2014). Performance analysis of probabilistic soft SSDF attack in cooperative spectrum sensing. *EURASIP Journal on Advances in Signal Processing*, *2014*(1), 81. doi:10.1186/1687-6180-2014-81

Zhang, X., & Li, C. (2009). Constructing secure cognitive wireless networks experiences and challenges. *Wireless Communications and Mobile Computing*, *10*, 55–69.

Zhang, Y., & Lee, W. (2000). Intrusion detection in wireless ad-hoc networks. In: *Proceedings of the sixth ACM annual international conference on mobile computing and networking*. ACM.. 10.1145/345910.345958

Zheng, B., Li, Y., Cheng, W. (2020). A multi-channel load awareness-based MAC protocol for flying ad hoc networks. *J Wireless Com Network*, *181*. doi:10.1186/s13638-020-01797-z

Zhou, X., Sun, M., Li, G. Y., & Juang, B. F. (2018). Intelligent wireless communications enabled by cognitive radio and machine learning. *China Communications*, *15*, 16–48.

Chapter 10
Energy Harvesting Systems:
A Detailed Comparison of Existing Models

Afnan Khaled Elhamshari
The American University in Cairo, Egypt

Maki Habib
ⓘ https://orcid.org/0000-0001-8088-8043
The American University in Cairo, Egypt

ABSTRACT

For the past few decades, the scientific community has been paying attention to energy harvesters to reduce the use of batteries as the main power source for IoT devices and MEMS. Energy harvesters allow for the use of ambient energy, mostly a by-product of an application, to generate electricity while relying on batteries as a backup option to store the excess energy. This chapter includes a review of each energy harvester type, subtype, configuration, usage, and power output to understand the different kinds of energy harvesters and motivate a discussion between their advantages and limitations. The chapter also discusses the advantages and the limitations of current storage options for energy harvesting and how applications can benefit from future research in this area. The chapter concludes with a discussion of the challenges and future opportunities still open in the field of energy harvesters to obtain more reliable, cleaner, and cheaper energy sources.

INTRODUCTION TO ENERGY HARVESTING SYSTEMS

For the past few decades, the scientific community has been paying attention to energy harvesters to reduce the use of batteries as the main power source for IoT devices and MEMS. Energy harvesters use ambient energy, mostly a by-product of an application, to generate electricity while relying on batteries as a backup option to store the excess energy.

Low-power electronics in medical equipment, transportation, consumer devices, military, diagnostic systems, and industrial controls are the most suitable targets for energy harvesters. The goal is to reach self-sufficient, self-powered systems that rely on their surrounds as their source of energy (Ahmed,

DOI: 10.4018/978-1-6684-7684-0.ch010

2021; Foong et al., 2021; Nayak et al., 2021). The currently used harvesters reduce a device's battery dependence as the main power supply by using the kinetic energy of movement, thermal energy given by the gears' motion within a device, or other types of ambient energy. However, these devices still rely on a system battery as their main source of energy (Chetto & Queudet, 2016; Kim et al., 2009).

The most common source of ambient energy used in harvesters is vibration energy, as it is intrinsic to all materials as part of the natural vibration of atoms. Other types of harvesters include thermal, wind, radio frequency, solar, pyroelectric, geothermal, and a combination of all or some of these previously mentioned types (Safaei et al., 2019). Figure 1 shows the general classification of energy harvesters depending on the energy source.

This chapter provides an encompassing review of many energy harvester types, subtypes, configurations, usage, and power output to understand the different energy harvesters and motivate a discussion between their advantages and limitations. The chapter also discusses the advantages and the limitations of current storage options for energy harvesting and how applications can benefit from future research in this area. The chapter concludes with a discussion of the challenges and future opportunities still open in the field of energy harvesters to obtain more reliable, cleaner, and cheaper energy sources.

Figure 1. Classification of energy harvesters in relation to the energy source

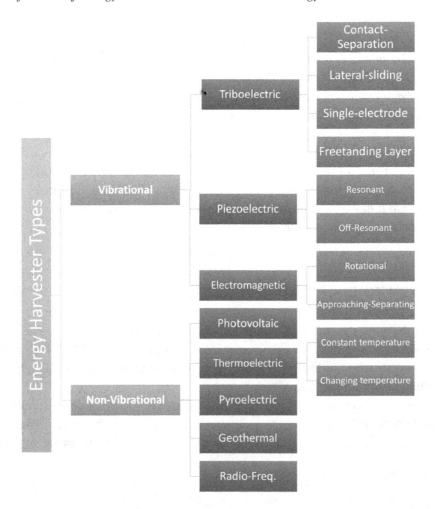

VIBRATIONAL HARVESTERS

Vibrational harvesters rely on the ambient movements of devices and components to produce electricity. It is one of the most researched types of harvesters due to the abundance and variety of natural vibrational resources in the world. These vibrations can be harvested and used in biomedical nanogenerators that rely on human movement as their power source, such as self-powered biosensors, pacemakers, implants, and degradable electronics (P. Li et al., 2019). The general model for vibration-based harvesters relies on a simple spring-damper-mass model that can be described generally using a second-order differential equation where m is the load mass, c is the damping coefficient, k is the spring constant, and U is the output voltage of the harvester. In this model, y represents the motion of the whole device, while x represents the harvester mass's relative displacement (vibration). $m\ddot{y}(t)$ represents the applied force to the dynamic structure (Kiran et al., 2020; Na et al., 2021).

$$m\ddot{x}(t) + c\dot{x}(t) + kx(t) - U = m\ddot{y}(t) \tag{1}$$

Figure 2 shows a schematic diagram of a typical vibrational harvester model using the Mass-Spring-Damper (MSD) as analogous to the kinetic energy harvester systems commonly used in harvesting energy from waves' vertical motion. The behavior of the piezoelectric energy harvesting (PEH) unit shown on the left is modeled via the spring and the damper on the right. The movement of the waves along the y-axis would cause the movement of the mass (piezoelectric disk) along the x-axis. The iterative motion causes the polarization of the piezoelectric disk, which causes the alternating current (Kiran et al., 2020). The details of how PEH works are going to be explained in 3.2.

Figure 2. Left, illustration of the use of wave movement to harvest energy. Right, mass-spring-damper system represents the operational schematics of the PEH unit.
(Kiran et al., 2020)

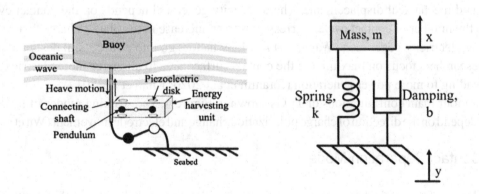

Triboelectric Nanogenerators (TENGs)

Triboelectrification is the process by which two originally uncharged bodies (with different materials) become charged when brought into contact and then separated (Mort, 2003). The electron cloud interaction theory (Figure 3) proposes a mechanism for how triboelectrification can generate electricity on the atomic level. At the beginning (figure 3a), two materials, A and B, with E_A and E_B as the occupied energy levels of electrons, respectively, are neutral and at a distance d. Before the contact, electrons could not hop from one material to the other due to the local trapping of the energy wells. As the two bodies touch (figure 3b), the electron clouds of the bodies' surfaces overlap (overlapping of the electron wells), allowing for an electron hop from material A (with escape energy E_1) to material B (with escape energy E_2). After the separation (figure 3c), the surface of material A now carries a positive charge, and surface B is now negatively charged. With no outer interference or changes in the material's surroundings, both surfaces will remain charged. With the increase in the surrounding temperature (figure 3d), the electrons can now hop the energy well due to higher energy fluctuations, returning the system to its neutral state (C. Xu et al., 2018).

The idea of triboelectrification has been recently researched as a novel method for energy harvesting based on random excitations to create Triboelectric Nanogenerators (TENGs). TENGs are characterized by their lightweight, low cost, variability of manufacturing materials, high electric output, and high conversion efficiency, especially in the low-frequency regions (W. Liu et al., 2019; H. Zhang et al., 2019).

The mechanism of how TEGs produce electricity is still under research; however, the working principle of TEGs relies on Maxwell's time-varying displacement current (J_D), defined as the following:

$$J_D = \frac{\partial D}{\partial t} = \varepsilon_0 \frac{\partial E}{\partial t} + \frac{\partial P_S}{\partial t} \tag{2}$$

Where D is the displacement field, ε_0 is the permittivity in vacuum, E is the electric field, and P_s is the polarization contributed by the presence of surface polarization charges from the triboelectric effect (Wang et al., 2017). The electrostatic charges are built-up externally by triboelectrification through vibrations and mechanical displacements. The electricity generated depends on the contact cycle; the increase in the number of contact cycles corresponds to an increase in the plate's charge density, resulting in higher electricity generation (Wang, 2017). Many factors go into a successful design of TENGs; however, researchers focus on maximizing the contact surface area to allow for more electric charge to build up, leading to more power generation (Ibrahim et al., 2020; Khan et al., 2017).

There are four main configurations of TEGs shown in Figure 4. The working modes of triboelectric generators depend on the direction of charge polarization change and electrode movement (Wu et al., 2019).

Vertical Contact Separation Mode

The basic design of the vertical contact-separation mode relies on two dielectrics with permittivity of ε1 and ε2 and thickness d1 and d2, respectively, placed between two metal electrodes. The two dielectrics must be made from different materials to create an electron affinity (that allows for the electron hop) when the two surfaces come in contact (Xu et al., 2018). These dielectrics are originally neutral after a short contact and sitting at a certain vertical separation (Figure (5a)). Due to the difference in the electron affinity between the plates, a potential drop is created within the two sides of each dielectric forming static charges on the plates (Figure (5b)). Charges then start to flow through the external load to balance the electrostatic field created by the plates until the potential drop created disappears (Figure (5c)) with charge density ($\sigma_I(z,t)$). With the external vibrations/mechanical movement, the system goes through neutrality-creating a protentional-saturation periodically (repeated vertical contact-separation cycles). This is the basis of creating alternating current (AC) flowing through the external load (Wang, 2017; Wu et al., 2019).

Figure 3. The electron cloud interaction theory of triboelectrification
(C. Xu et al., 2018)

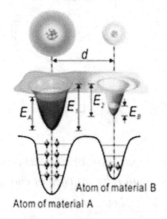

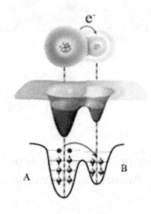

(a) Two neutral materials with their occupied energy levels at distance d

(b) Electron transfer from A to B due to the two materials touching

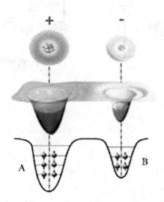

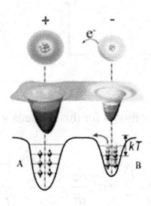

(c) Material surfaces are now charged after separation

(d) System returning to neutral states after electrons hop back from B to A

Figure 4. Working modes of triboelectric generator. X represents the vibrational motion and its direction.

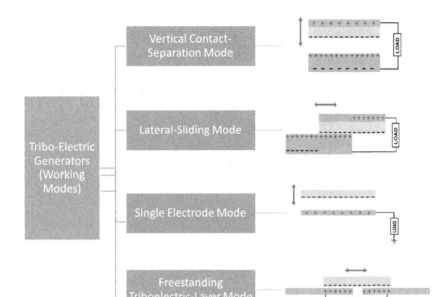

Figure 5. The working principle for the vertical contact separation TENGs. a) Neutral plates, separation after contact, b) Potential drop creation, and c) Saturation by transfer of charges through load R. (Wang, 2017)

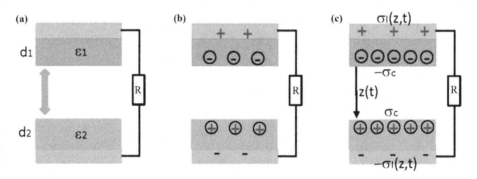

The mathematical model for this mode is given by

$$J_D = \frac{\partial D_z}{\partial t} = \frac{\partial \sigma_I(z,t)}{\partial t} = \sigma_c \frac{dz}{dt} \frac{\dfrac{d_1 \varepsilon_0}{\varepsilon_1} + \dfrac{d_2 \varepsilon_0}{\varepsilon_2}}{\left[\dfrac{d_1 \varepsilon_0}{\varepsilon_1} + \dfrac{d_2 \varepsilon_0}{\varepsilon_2} + z \right]^2} \tag{3}$$

Where $\varepsilon_{0,1,2}$ are the permittivity of space, and the dielectric plates, respectively, $d_{1,2}$ is the dielectric thickness, σ_c is the charge density accumulated between the plates, and z is the distance separating the plates (Niu et al., 2014; Wang, 2017). Based on the previous equations, figure (6) shows a more detailed diagram of the electric field distribution in a contact-separation triboelectric plate (50 mm x50 mm). This system resulted in an average power density of 0.064 µW/m² and an open-circuit voltage of 120 V.

Figure 6. a) Contact-Separation mode, b) Electric field distribution of the triboelectric plates

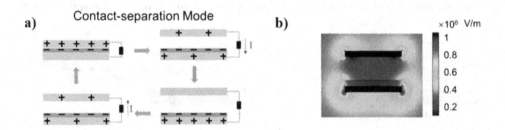

From equation 3, it is shown that the electricity generation depends on the static charge density accumulated between the plates and the rate at which the separation distance between both plates changes. It is also shown that the output current is dependent on the rate of change for the separation distance, $\frac{dz}{dt}$, as well as the separation distance itself. The separation distance between the plates ranges between 0 (when the plates are fully in contact) to $10d_0$, where d_0 is the summation of all the dielectric thicknesses between the metal electrodes. The current properties also depend on the properties of the capacitive load (specifically, resistance and area) that connects both plates (Niu & Wang, 2015; Wang, 2017).

This concept has been used to generate electricity from the sustained motion of ocean waves. The harvester is built inside a sphere with two sets of triboelectric plates with a plate size (120x100x1mm) on either side of the sphere. The device resulted in an average power density of 1.5 mW/m² and the ability to charge a 300 volts battery in 40 minutes (Wang et al., 2020).

Lateral-Sliding Mode

This mode is used for applications with horizontal or rotational mechanical vibrations and movements. The concept is very similar to that of the vertical contact separation model of having two dielectric plates; however, this mode depends on the in-plane charge separation and generating the charges based on the force of frictions between the plates with no air gaps or vertical distance between the plates (Zhang et al., 2019).

For the horizontal sliding, the initial position of the lateral-sliding mode shows complete contact between the dielectric plates (figure 7a). In this state, the system is at equilibrium with static charges forming on the inside of the plates due to the difference in the electron affinity between them. With the lateral movement of one plate (or both), the system's equilibrium is disturbed, and a potential is formed between the plates. This movement leads to alternating current (AC) generated in the external resistive load (figure 7b) when the plates are sliding further apart. The sliding distance between the plate varies depending on the application; here, the plates slide till they are completely apart and then start reversing the current direction on the way back to the original position (figure 7b,c) (Wang et al., 2016b). The sliding ratio (η) is defined as the ratio between the sliding time to the total process time (figure 7b-d), and it depends on the mechanical movement as well as the frequency of the application (Zhang et al., 2019).

Figure 7. The working principle for the lateral sliding TENGs. a) Plates at equilibrium, no sliding, b, c) Potential drop and current creation in resistive load through sliding, and d) Current reversal (Wang et al., 2016b)

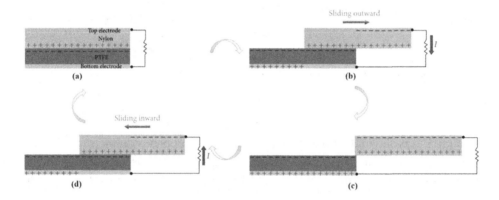

Depending on the vibration source, the sliding mode can be implemented using horizontal plates or rotational disks seen in figure 8. The geometrical design is the main difference between both implementations, as both rotational and horizontal designs follow the same physical phenomenon and contact separation cycles (Lin et al., 2013).

Figure 8. Rotational design of lateral sliding TENGs (Lin et al., 2013)

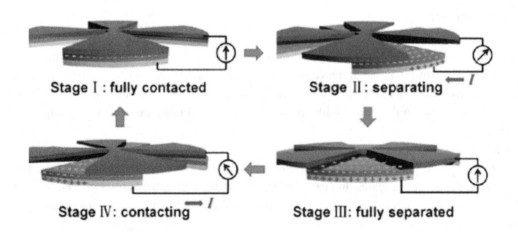

Other than the choice of material for the TENGs, many other factors affect the electric output of the lateral-sliding mode, such as the amount of mechanical loading on the plates, the friction coefficient, and the sliding ratio of the system. Theoretically, higher acceleration for the forward sliding distance can enhance the output voltage. Also, the sliding ratio plays an important role in the amount of accumulated charge and the maximum voltage generated by TENGs (Zhang et al., 2019). Modern lateral-sliding TENGs can provide high voltage approaching 3.3V with a capacitive load of 4.7 μF capacitor and a maximum power of 0.257 μW using a 7.8 MΩ resistor and 4.7 μF capacitive load (Khushboo & Azad, 2019).

Single Electrode Mode

In the single electrode mode, the TENG consists of a single electrode (a single layer or multi-layer) for freely moving objects. There are two types of the single electrode mode: Moving/vibrating TENG or Stationary TENG attached to a stationary surface. Figure 9 shows the mechanism of a stationary single-electrode TENG. In this application, TENG is made of indium tin oxide (ITO), a highly positive triboelectric material, that is paired with the less positive triboelectric such as polydimethylsiloxane (PDMS) that is used in touch pad technologies. The touch pad is coated with triboelectric layers that allow for electricity generation when touched by the human skin or any triboelectric charge-inducing material (Meng et al., 2013).

Figure 9. Mechanism of stationary single electrode TENG used to produce electricity in a touch pad application
(File, n.d.)

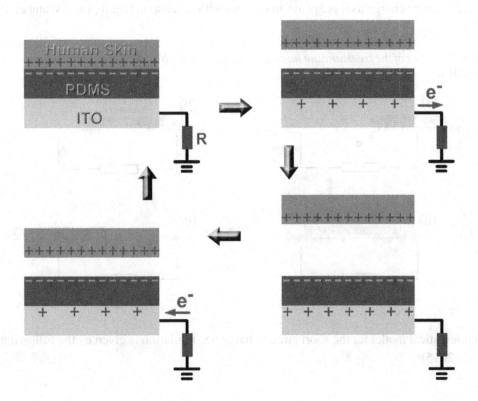

The moving single-electrode TENGs can be used in transportation applications by attaching the harvester to a rotating wheel that can generate electricity as the wheel comes into contact with a neutral road. This type of application can produce a power output of 1.79 mW and a peak current of 1.5 μA at a 10 MΩ resistive load (Mao et al., 2015). The stationary single-electrode TENG can also be used to harvest the kinetic energy from waves. For this application, the TENG is attached to a stationary wall that becomes triboelectric when a water wave impacts to generate alternating current. For this application, the power density generated was 0.344 mW/cm² using low-frequency wave impact (0.7 – 3 Hz) (Jurado et al., 2020).

Freestanding Triboelectric-Layer Mode

Freestanding triboelectric layer mode was developed to overcome the limitations of the lateral sliding, contact-separation, and single electrode modes. Typically, the single electrode TENGs are limited by a maximum charge transfer of 50% (Niu et al., 2015); however, the freestanding mode provides higher energy conversion efficiency and robustness. Freestanding mode allows for harvesting energy from arbitrary movement without needing an attached electrode, making it easier for wearable human applications (Lin & Yang, 2016). The general mechanism depends on the relative movement of the triboelectric material (or metal) across two metal electrodes (or triboelectric materials) to generate an alternating current. The idea is to increase the charge density by introducing a new surface that generates double the charges on both sides (Niu et al., 2015).

Figure 10 shows an application of freestanding, contact-sliding, dielectric-based TENG. In this application, the dielectric material Fluorinated ethylene propylene (FEP) is mounted on two conductor plates separated by distance d. In contrast with the lateral- sliding mode, the dielectric plate in the freestanding mode generates more charge as it is always in contact with at least on metal plate (Wang et al., 2016a).

Figure 10. Schematics of the freestanding lateral-sliding mode with no attached electrodes to the dielectric (Wang et al., 2016a)

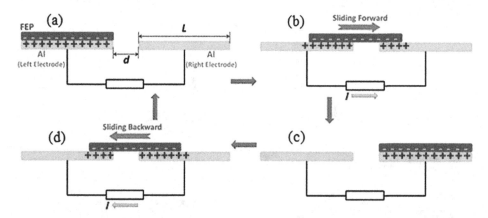

The mathematical model for the short circuit charge accumulation is given by the following equation 3 (Niu et al., 2015):

$$Q_{SC,final} = \int_0^L \frac{\sigma w}{1 + \frac{C_2(k)}{C_1(k)}_{x=d+L}} dk - \int_0^L \frac{\sigma w}{1 + \frac{C_2(k)}{C_1(k)}_{x=0}} dk \qquad (4)$$

Where x is the distance moved by the dielectric measured from the left, σ is the tribo-charge surface density, w is the width of the structure, d is the gap distance between electrodes, L is the length of the dielectric, and C_1 and C_2 are the capacitance of the two metal plates. The first integral term accounts for the charge accumulation when the triboelectric plate is closer to the right plate and the second term accounts for the left plate. This model suggests that the charge transfer efficiency can reach 100% since either plate is always going to be providing some contribution to the total charge (Niu et al., 2015).

Piezoelectric Harvesters (PEHs)

The piezoelectric effect is the accumulation of electric charges due to the mechanical stress applied to a solid crystal (Holler et al., 2007). In a non-compressed piezoelectric (PZT) crystal, the net charge is zero due to the neutrality of the crystal (figure 11a). However, when pressure is applied to the crystal, the center of the positive is moved upward, and the center of the negative charges moves downward, creating a dipole (figure 11b). This pressure causes the crystal to be slightly positive at the top surface and slightly negative at the bottom. The number of charges accumulated at the surfaces depends on the crystal material, the amount of pressure applied, and the type and frequency of vibration in the application (Sezer & Koç, 2021).

Figure 11. a) Left, neutral piezoelectric material with no pressure applied. b) Right, pressure is applied vertically to the crystal, causing a shift in the charges center.

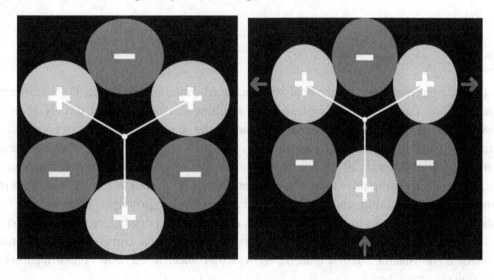

Figure 12. Classification of piezoelectric harvesters

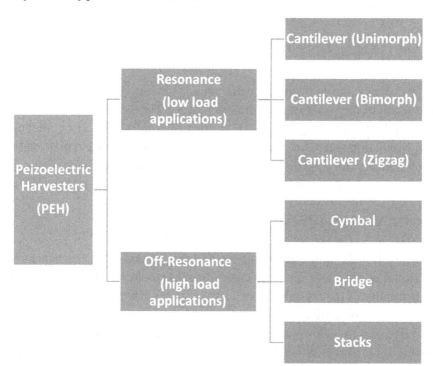

To achieve specific characteristics of the piezoelectric harvesters, the systems are fabricated using ceramics that can be characterized in multiple ways depending on the desired frequency and vibration amplitude. In theory, the piezoelectric stress-electrical displacement model constitutive equations are

$$S = E(s - de) \tag{5}$$

$$D = dS + \varepsilon e \tag{6}$$

where S (N/cm^2) represents the mechanical stress induced in the piezoelectric, E (N/cm^2) represents the elastic modulus of piezoelectric, s represents the resulting mechanical strain, d (C/N) represents the piezoelectric constant that depends on the material used in the application, D(C/m^2) represents electrical displacement, ε (C^2/N.m^2) represents the permittivity constant, and e (N/C) represents the electric field strength in the material (Na et al., 2021). This model is the basis of piezoelectric harvesters used nowadays.

Scientists have been using this concept to generate electricity from the mechanical strain resulting from ambient vibrations in different applications. The piezoelectric principle is widely used in energy harvesters by applying stresses to a cantilever beam, a diaphragm, a cymbal, or a combination of these models. The type of stress can be due to flection, torsion, compression, expansion, or any combination of these (Asthana & Khanna, 2020). Figure 12 shows a piezoelectric harvesters classification based on the application resonance type.

Resonant Harvesters

Cantilever beams are the most used design architectures in resonance piezoelectric harvesters due to their ability to provide maximum deformation compared to other beams. Since the electrical displacement of a piezoelectric material is directly correlated to the strain (higher deflections), cantilever beams are an optimum fit for most applications (Erturk & Inman, 2008). Also, the resonance frequency of the fundamental flexural modes of cantilever beams is much lower than the other vibrational modes of the piezoelectric element (H. Li et al., 2014). Cantilever harvesters have different designs and configurations based on the harvesting application and size constraints.

Most resonance piezoelectric harvesters use low-frequency applications, making it challenging to match the beam's resonance frequency to the application's frequency. To allow for lower resonance frequencies, a tip mass is added to the free end of the cantilever resulting in a resonance frequency f_r:

$$f_r = \frac{\sqrt{0.07867 v_n^2}}{2\pi L^2} \sqrt{\frac{K}{0.236 mwL + \Delta m}} \tag{7}$$

Where v_n is the eigenvalue for the fundamental vibrational mode, L (mm) is the length of the cantilever, w (mm) is the width of the cantilever, and m (g/mm^2) is the mass per unit length of the cantilever, Δm (g) is the proof mass, and K (N/mm) is the effective spring constant of the cantilever (Yi et al., 2002). This equation shows that the proof mass lowers the beam's resonance frequency, allowing for wider application of the piezoelectric harvesters.

The maximum power output from cantilever-based PEH based on the resonant is described as

$$\frac{P_{max}}{\left(B_f A\right)^2} \propto \frac{f_r}{E \zeta_m} \tag{8}$$

Where P_{max} (μW) is the maximum power output, B_f is the forcing function, A (mm/s^2) is the base acceleration, f_r (s^{-1}) is the resonant frequency, E (GPa) is the elastic modulus, and ζ_m is the mechanical dampening ratio of the system (Peddigari et al., 2018). This equation shows the best applications for piezoelectric harvesting are those with high resonant frequency and low dampening ratio.

Unimorph Cantilever

A unimorph cantilever structure has two components: an inactive substrate and an active piezoelectric layer. The inactive layer is made of metal that acts as a conductor for the generated charges. These cantilever modes operate at "31-mode," where "3" is the direction of the piezoelectric polarization and "1" is the direction of the stress in the beam (the planar direction of the beam) (Li et al., 2014). In the MEMS industry, the unimorph cantilever beams are more commonly used due to their smaller sizes and ease of manufacturing and customization (Priya et al., 2019). Typically, the sizes of the PEH layers are measured in mm^3 (less than 400 mm^3 for the piezoelectric layers and less than 500 mm^3 for the non-piezoelectric layer). Xu et al. (2022) showed that there is a need to optimize the height, width, and thickness of each layer based on the application frequency and the required output. In their application, piezoelectric layers with a thickness of 0.2 mm produced the highest voltage output (35V) at a low frequency (25 Hz) (Xu et al., 2022).

Figure 13 shows a typical structure of a unimorph cantilever beam (adapted from Li et al., 2014). The pressure from the vibration is applied to the proof mass, which results in planar strains/stresses in the piezoelectric crystals. These stresses cause the polarization of the piezoelectric surfaces generating Alternating Current (AC) between the beam surfaces.

Figure 13. Unimorph cantilever beam with applied pressure to the proof mass

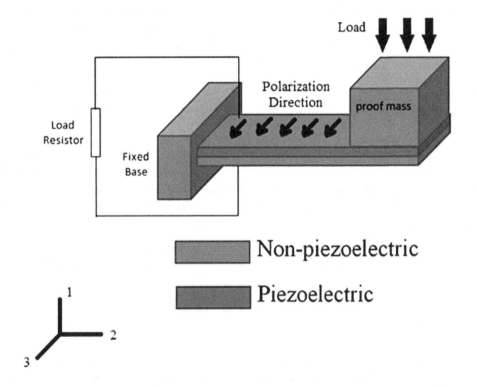

The materials used and the vibration frequency determine the unimorph cantilever beam's electrical characteristics. The common piezoelectric materials used are Lead-Zirconate Titanate (PZT), Lithium Tantalate (LiTaO$_3$), Polyvinylidene Fluoride (PVDF), Barium Titanate (BTO), and Lead Magnesium Niobate (PMN). In a (PMN-PZT) hard type single crystal piezoelectric layer with Titanium alloy plates as passive layer application, normalized volumetric power density was found as 43.4 mW/cm^3 Hz g^2 at resonant frequency if 27.4 Hz (Peddigari et al., 2018). This output is considered high-power at a low frequency.

Bimorph Cantilever

A bimorph cantilever structure consists of two active piezoelectric layers with a non-piezoelectric layer in between. Bimorph cantilevers are more commonly studied due to their higher power output (almost double) without a significant increase in size when compared to unimorph cantilevers (Li et al., 2014). Figure 14 shows a basic structure of a unimorph cantilever beam (adapted from (Li et al., 2014) and (Kuang & Zhu, 2017)).

Figure 14. Left: Bimorph cantilever structure, Right: explanation of the polarization and electricity generation process in bimorph cantilever beams
(Kuang & Zhu, 2017)

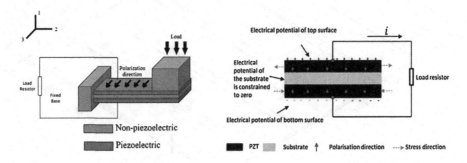

Zigzag Cantilever

Zigzag cantilevers allow for more resonance modes from bending and torsion rather than just the first mode, as in the unimorph and the simple bimorph cantilevers. It is shown that two-dimensional (zigzag) cantilever beams allow for higher power density, further reducing the PEH's size (Abdelmoula et al., 2017). Hence, zigzag cantilevers are more commonly used in MEMS applications. A typical zigzag beam consists of n members, where each member is a simple unimorph cantilever connected. Figure 15 shows a schematic of a zigzag cantilever with five members and a single PZT active layer near the harvester's clamped area (Lee et al., 2018).

In (Lee et al., 2018), study showed that torsion modes can produce more energy in the case of 2-dimensional cantilevers. Unlike the 1-D unimorph and bimorph cantilevers, the tip mass does not automatically produce higher energy output, especially in torsion modes. The power output of the zigzag model is related to the deflection in the cantilever expressed as

$$P = \frac{1}{2} \frac{\vartheta_p^2}{C_p} \omega \left(\frac{\partial v}{\partial x}\bigg|_{x=L_p+L_1} - \frac{\partial v}{\partial x}\bigg|_{x=L_1} \right)^2 \tag{9}$$

where ν is the deflection of the structure, L_p is the length of the piezoelectric layer, L_1 is the distance between the clamped side and the piezoelectric layer, ϑ_p is the piezoelectric constant, C_p is the capacitance of the piezoelectric, and ω is the resonant frequency.

Figure 15. schematic of a zigzag cantilever with five members
(Lee et al., 2018)

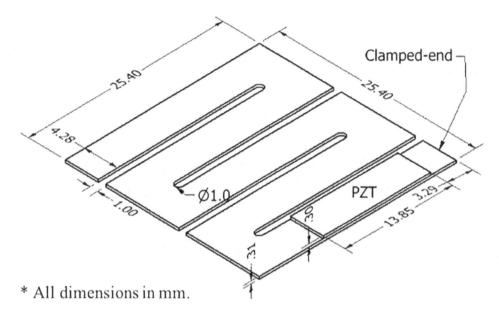

* All dimensions in mm.

In a comparative study between a zigzag 2-D cantilever and a bimorph 1-D cantilever (Sharpes et al., 2014), it was shown that the zigzag cantilevers could provide higher power density at a lower frequency when using zigzag cantilevers (65.08 µW/cm³ at 32.34 Hz) compared to bimorph cantilever (10.60 µW/cm³ at 48.75 Hz) under the same conditions.

Off-Resonant Harvesters

Despite the high-power density output provided by cantilever PEHs, designing for low resonance frequencies is challenging. Off-resonance harvesters provide a new opportunity to harvest energy from the mechanical vibrations resulting from dynamic loading, especially in the transportation field.

Cymbal Harvester

Cymbal harvesters are PEH harvesters that can work in resonance and off-resonance modes. The cymbal harvester comprises a piezoelectric disc sandwiched between two-metal cymbal-shaped endcaps. The metal caps are used to strengthen the endurance of the piezoelectric material under high-impact forces (Li et al., 2018). The cymbal architecture depends on the flattening of the metal endcaps when a high load is applied to the surface, which causes the generation of charges in the piezoelectric material in between. This effect makes cymbals the most effective candidate for road pumps, where the car's movement produces enough stress to generate electricity. The diameter sizes of the cymbal PEH range between (29-25) mm depending on the maximum loading force and application. The piezoelectric material is typically between 1-2 mm in thickness (Li et al., 2018). Figure 16 shows the schematic of a cymbal harvester (Wang et al., 2018a).

Figure 16. Cymbal Harvester with steel end caps. The loading on the top of the harvester allows for the crumpling of the plate, reducing the space between the endcap and the PZT material.
(Wang et al., 2018a)

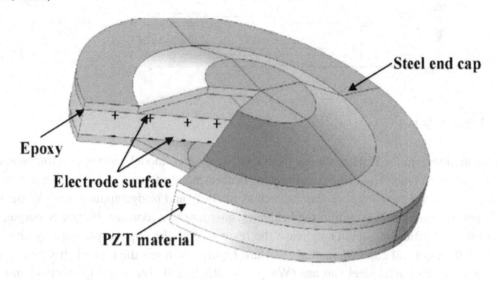

Cymbal harvesters are used commercially to produce conductive asphalt that can produce electricity from passing cars. In practice, a single cymbal can generate up to 16 µW for each pass of one heavy vehicle wheel. This application can allow for 65MW/h per year using 30,000 cymbals (Moure et al., 2016). The downfall of cymbal harvesters is that they have high overhead costs in manufacturing; however, due to their high durability, they can be cost-effective for the power generated.

The direction in research now is to combine different setups of PEH to maximize the power output and avoid the disadvantages of these models. Ren et al. combined the cantilever design with the cymbal design to reduce the system's resonance frequency, allowing for higher output (Xu et al., 2012). This CANDLE (CANtilever Driving Low-frequency Energy-harvester) system resulted in a power density of 29.6 mW/cm^3 and a peak voltage of 38 V at 102 Hz. Figure 17 shows a combined cantilever and cymbal design structure to maximize output (adopted from (Xu et al., 2012)). The piezoelectric PMNT crystal has the dimensions of 25 mm (length) x 5 mm (width) x 1 mm (thickness). The weight of the proof mass must be optimized based on the application, as it is not a direct relationship between the mass and the resultant output power. There are four contact points between the copper cantilever and the cymbal; if the bending displacement is upward, the cantilever contacts the upper cymbal at points A and B if the bending displacement is high enough. The other two contact points are A' and B' in the case of downward bending displacement (Xu et al., 2012).

Figure 17. Schematic diagram of a combined cymbal and cantilever PEH. lc = 25 mm, lt = 2.5 mm, and lb = 11 mm
(Xu et al., 2012)

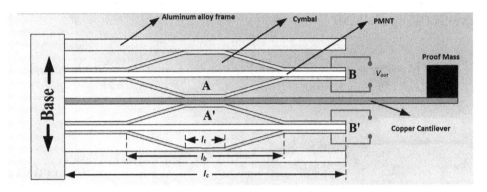

Bridge Harvester

The bridge architecture for PEH is similar to that of the cymbal model, except that the geometry is a square instead of a circle. The bridge architecture is used mainly to distribute the stress over a larger area in low-vibration frequency applications such as roadway and bridge applications (Wang & Jasim, 2020). There are many models within the bridge architecture to maximize the power output, achieve higher conversion efficiency, and/or increase the resistance of the applied pressure by changing the geometry of the steel end cap (Wang et al., 2018a). Figure 18 shows the typical structure of a bridge harvester with a trapezoidal steel end cap (Wang & Jasim, 2020). The working mechanism is similar to the cymbal architecture, where the applied pressure on the steel cap causes stress in the PZT layer resulting in an electrical field.

Figure 18. The basic geometry of a trapezoidal bridge PEH
(Wang et al., 2018a; Yao et al., 2012)

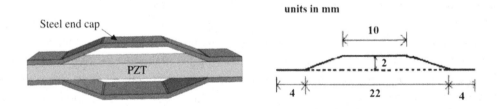

Other research has been conducted to compare the performance of the trapezoidal steel cap to other geometries. Yao et al. (2012) conducted laboratory experiments to compare the arc bridge to the trapezoidal bridge. It was found that the arc bridge produces more output voltage of 232V under 0.4 MPa and 5 Hz load compared to 106V from the trapezoidal geometry under the same conditions. However, the arc transducer could not withstand loads higher than 0.4 MPa, whereas the trapezoidal transducers could go to higher load pressures (0.7 MPa) (Yao et al., 2012).

Stacked Harvester

The stacked architecture was introduced to increase the performance of different PEH harvesters. The general idea is to arrange many thin piezoelectric layers along the direction of the electric field to allow for higher loads. There are two modes of operations in stack PEH: series and parallel. The series mode arranges the layers so that the induced stress is unidirectional, with one of the stacks surfaces producing a positive charge and the other producing a negative charge. In the parallel mode, the stress direction reverses, with each layer producing positive and negative charge accumulations at every stack layer. Figure 19 shows the general schematics of PEH stacks in both series and parallel (Sun et al., 2013).

Figure 19. a) Series and b) Parallel configurations of the stack PEH, each disk represents a PZT layer. The external force is applied vertically to the stack in each case.
(Sun et al., 2013)

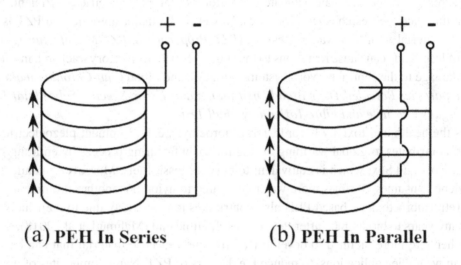

(a) PEH In Series   (b) PEH In Parallel

Using two PZT layers with a 6 MΩ load resistor, Sun et al. (Sun et al., 2013) showed that serial stacks produce higher voltage output (4.5V compared to 2.3V); however, parallel stacks produce higher power. The study also showed that the power output scales with the number of piezoelectric layers in the stack, making stacks a good design for power output maximization in applications that do not require size restrictions (Sun et al., 2013).

It can be theoretically shown that the power output of the parallel stack PEH is higher than the power output of the series stack PEH. According to (Li et al., 2018), the maximum power output of the parallel stack ($P_{max,p}$) and the series stack ($P_{max,s}$) are

$$P_{MAX,p} = \frac{n^2 d_{33}^2 F^2 \omega t_p}{4\sqrt{2} A \varepsilon_{33}} \tag{10}$$

$$P_{MAX,s} = \frac{nd_{33}^{2}F^{2}\omega t_{p}}{4\sqrt{2}A\varepsilon_{33}}$$

(11)

where ω is the frequency, t_p and A are the thickness and the area of the piezoelectric element, n is the number of piezoelectric layers, F is the applied load, d is the piezoelectric constant, and ε is the dielectric constant. As seen in equations 10 and 11, the maximum power in parallel mode scales with the square of the number of layers compared to linearly scaling with the number of layers in the series mode (Li et al., 2018).

Environmental Impact of Piezoelectric Materials

Piezoelectric Harvesters are one of the most used harvesters and sensors in many fields: wearable electronics, powering roadside assistance devices, flexible electronics, and many others. Most of these applications rely on Lead Zirconate Titanate (PZT) for its high piezoelectric coefficient, high operating temperature, and well-established properties. However, the major ingredient in PZT is lead oxide, a hazardous material with high vapor pressure (*PZT Properties & PZT Manufacturing*, n.d.). Large quantities of lead oxide can cause irritations to the skin, eyes, and respiratory tract and, in extreme cases, can cause damage to the central nervous systems, kidneys, and blood (*Sub-Chronic Inhalation of Lead Oxide Nanoparticles Revealed Their Broad Distribution and Tissue-Specific Subcellular Localization in Target Organs | Particle and Fibre Toxicology | Full Text*, n.d.).

Besides the health and toxicity hazards, tetrafluoroethylene, a prominent piezoelectric material in the market, contributes to global warming during the manufacturing process by emitting green-house gases, CO_2, Nox, and Sox, which is equivalent to burning fossil fuels. Moreover, manufacturing tetrafluoroethylene consumes 20 times more water compared to nylon 66, another prominent piezoelectric material. Tetrafluoroethylene-based PEH also contributes to ecotoxicity due to their inorganic nature, needing many years to biodegrade after the devices' lifetime end (Mahmud et al., 2018).

Researchers are more inclined to develop lead-free piezoelectric material that can be safer to use, especially in wearable applications, to reduce the dangers of PZT. Nano-composites of polyvinylidene fluoride (PVDF) have shown great promise as a non-reactive thermoplastic polymer with a high piezoelectric coefficient and flexibility (Wu et al., 2021). Other researchers turned their attention to biodegradable green polymers such as poly(L-lactic acid) (PLLA) that have high piezoelectric properties, high biocompatibility, and flexibility (Zhu et al., 2017).

Electromagnetic Harvesters (EH)

The fundamental idea behind electromagnetic harvesters is Faraday's law of electromagnetic induction, describing the electromotive force generated due to a moving magnetic field. A small vibration in the 100-200 Hz range on bridges and mechanical structures can be used to induce a current in a magnetic field. The amount of generated electricity can be quantified using the following equations where EMF is the electromotive force produced (Voltage), φ_B is the magnetic flux produced by the magnetic material, B is the magnetic field, and A is the cross-sectional area of the coil passing through the magnetic field with every vibration (*The Feynman Lectures on Physics Vol. II Ch. 1: Electromagnetism*, n.d.).

$$EMF = -\frac{d\varphi_B}{dt} \tag{12}$$

$$\varphi_B = \iint\limits_{\Sigma(t)} B(t).dA \tag{13}$$

Electromagnetic harvesters have two main models: rotational and approach-separation harvesters. Based on Faraday's law, both types rely on the interaction between coils and magnets to generate electricity.

Rotational Harvesters

Rotational magnetic harvesters concerned with ultra-low frequencies are more suitable for wearable applications (< 5Hz). Rotational harvesters rely on converting the linear motion into high-speed rotation with an inertial system by means of a twist-driving structure and a ratchet-clutch structure. Such a system can result in a peak power of 0.33 mW/cm³, enough to power 70 LEDs at a frequency as low as 1 Hz. Figure 20 shows how the harvester can convert the linear motion into a rotational motion via the ratchet-clutch system. When vertical pressure is applied to the top plate, it causes a twist in the rod which in turn causes a motion inside the system of magnets. According to Faraday's law, this motion disturbs the magnetic field, which induces a current that can be harvested (Y. (张玉龙) Zhang et al., 2020). The process of converting the linear motion into rotational motion shown in figure 20(d) can be quantified according to the following equation

$$F + mg - kx - 2f_r\sin\theta - 2f_N\cos\theta = ma \tag{14}$$

Where a and m are the acceleration and mass of the rod, θ is the threading angle of the twisting rod, x is the driven displacement, k is the spring stiffness, F is the driven force from the external vibration, fN and fr are the normal and sliding frictions on the threads.

Many designs of rotational electromagnetic harvesters are used to power human wearable devices that can harvest energy from linear reciprocating motion, rotary motion, swinging motion, and random running or walking on a treadmill. A human-wearable application of electromagnetic harvesters can generate an output of 0.69V at a frequency of 1.5 Hz. Because of their small sizes, which can be as small as 65 mm in coil diameter and 18 mm in height, electromagnetic harvesters are a good candidate for energy production in MEMS and human wearable devices (Liu et al., 2018).

Approach-Separation Harvesters

Another mode of electromagnetic harvester depends on the idea of a small silicon cantilever beam with a conduction coil at the tip mass (approach-separation paradigm to allow for freer movement of the electrons). The vibration will cause the conducting coil (e.g., Aluminum) to interact with a magnetic field generated by a magnetic material (neodymium magnet "NdFeB") placed at 100 μm away from the tip mass of the beam. Electricity is produced as the change of the magnetic flux caused by the vibrational motion of the coil through the magnetic field. Due to the small distances between the coil and the magnetic core, this system is suitable for MEMS designs to power small sensors on chips. When applied in a non-resonant low-vibration environment (10 Hz, 4 mm peak-to-peak), the simple cantilever of a total volume of 120 mm3 resul'ed in 1.44 mV RMS voltage and 24 nW RMS power (Zorlu & Kulah, 2012). Figure 21 shows a basic design of the cantilever-based electromagnetic energy harvester discussed above (Kumar et al., 2016).

Figure 20. An illustration of the rotational electromagnetic vibrational harvester that converts vertical vibrational pressure into rotational motion inside a system of magnets, inducing a current in the system (Y. (张玉龙) Zhang et al., 2020)

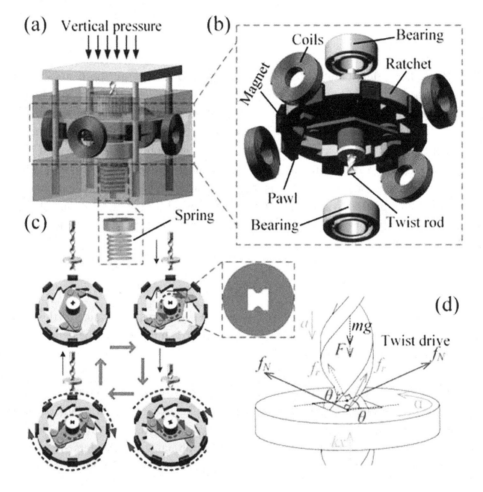

Comparison Between Vibrational Harvesters

Vibrational harvesters are highly effective at generating electricity from ambient resources by either tailoring to a resonance frequency or performing at a range of low frequencies. The vibration mode determines the amount of power generated, the harvester's efficiency, the harvester's reliability, and the harvester's design. Linear harvesters tuned to specific frequencies, such as cantilever harvesters, are easier to model and work with; however, they can be too simplistic and unreliable in outdoor applications. Bistable configurations (using low-frequency vibrations along with two stable frequencies) or nonlinear configurations (using a duffing-type frequency response) can be more reliable with their voltage output (H. Liu et al., 2021). The correct choice for a vibrational harvester depends on the intended application in size, the frequency range of vibration, and deployment location. Tables 1 and 2 list some of the general characterizations of the different types of vibrational harvesters and the limitations and advantages of each type.

Figure 21. A simple schematic of a cantilever-based electromagnetic harvester where the conduction coil made of aluminum and the magnetic core is made of neodymium magnet (Kumar et al., 2016)

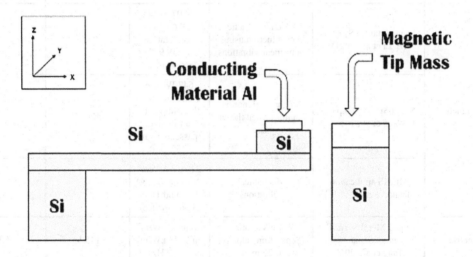

Table 1. Limitations and advantages of vibrational energy harvesters

Resource	Limitations	Advantages
Piezoelectric	- Loss of ability to generate power above the curie temperature (N. Chen, n.d.) - Cost scales with energy output demands (H. Wang et al., 2018b) - Toxicity of lead in PZT and other lead-based piezoelectric materials (Shibata et al., 2018) - High bandwidth of operation (not suited for low frequency applications) (Izadgoshasb et al., 2018) - Traditional inorganic piezoelectric material offers low durability (Siddiqui et al., 2016),(Ye et al., 2019)	- High output energy density (Sezer & Koç, 2021) - Flexibility, stretchability, and durability of design using nanofibers, composites, and organic materials (piezoelectric polymers, PVDF, PLLA) (Jin et al., 2018; J. Zhu et al., 2017) - Does not require any external electrical stimulant
Electromagnetic	- Need to operate at resonant frequency for maximum power generation (requires up-scaling of the frequency to reach resonance) (Salauddin & Park, 2017) - Miniaturization problems (power generated depends on the size of the harvester) (Struwig et al., 2018)	- High power, high voltage output in large scale applications (L. Wang et al., 2016)
Triboelectric	- Low robustness due to abrasions and heat generation (in contacting modes) (W. Xu et al., 2019) - Low reliability (performance greatly affected by dust particles and moisture) (Y. Lee et al., 2018) - High impedance (Z. L. Wang et al., 2017) - Low charge density (W. Liu et al., 2019)	- High power density - High conversion efficiency especially in the low frequency range (< 5Hz) (Invernizzi et al., 2016) - Simple fabrication process and low cost (W. Xu et al., 2017) - Happens naturally, does not require electrical signal stimulation

Table 2. Characterization of different types of vibrational energy harvesters

Resource	Case/Application	Energy Source	Electricity Characterization		
			Power Density	Open Circuit Voltage	Short Circuit Current
Piezoelectric	Wearable Technology (Smart Shoes) (Siddiqui et al., 2016)	Loading resulting from human motion (stepping, walking, running)	2.28 µW/cm^2 (under a pressure of 20 N)	3.4 V	0.67 µA/cm^2
	Space Wearable with radiation protection (Ye et al., 2019)	Applied Mechanical Stress	11.3 µW/cm^2 (under max stress 0.4 MPa)	22 V	640 nA
Electromagnetic	Transportation Systems (Z. Li et al., 2021)	Electromagnetic Transduction using non-linear vibrations	6.07 mW/cm^3 (at 1.0 g acceleration and 19.9 Hz resonance)	26 V	---
	Smart Speed Pump (L. Wang et al., 2016)	Mechanical motion of pump when the car passes	647 W/axle (When loading the pump with a full-size passenger car (1527 kg)	120 V	---
	MEMS application (Iannacci et al., 2016)	Mechanical Vibrations	240 µW/g^2/cm^3 (Normalized, @ 1.3g and 1588 Hz resonance)	---	---
Triboelectric	Liquid-Metal Vertical-Contact Separation (Tang et al., 2015)	Wave Vibration (Separation velocity: 0.25 m/s)	up to 6.7 W/m^2 and 133 kW/m^3 (@10 Hz)	145 V	5.8 µA

Case Study: Wind Harvesters

Wind is one of the sustainable resources of energy that can be harvested on a large or a small scale. Wind turbine designs are one of the energy resources that rely on different vibrational harvesters to generate electricity. Large-scale wind electricity harvesting is the most common type; however, a lot of research has been dedicated to small-scale wind harvesting in the past ten years (Yang et al., 2013).

Large Scale Wind Harvesters

Traditionally, the rotational-based electromagnetic generator is the main choice for a large-scale wind turbine. These turbines are mainly used in on-shore and off-shore sites to generate electricity based on the high-gradient wind; however, it is expensive to implement and maintain in addition to low efficiency at low wind speeds. Large-scale wind turbines account for 16% of the electricity generated by renewable resources from on-shore and off-shore turbines world-wide. According to the International Renewable Energy Agency (IRENA), Egypt is increasingly relying on onshore wind for the past ten years as its main secondary source of renewable energy, with a production of 4,245 GWh in 2020, as seen in figure 22 (IRENA, n.d.).

Figure 22. Egypt's electricity generation from off-shore wind farms in the past ten years
(IRENA, n.d.)

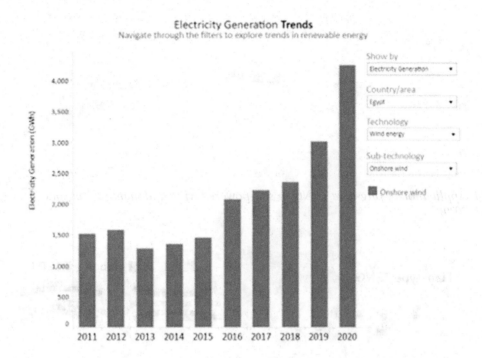

Small Scale Wind Harvesters

A new approach for more accessible large-scale wind turbines depends on the fabrication and usage of TENGs. The new designs aim to provide more wind energy access using a low gradient of wind rather than the traditional large-blade wind harvesters (Ren et al., 2022).

One of the modern designs is developed based on a vertical contact-separation TENG device for wind harvesting using a flutter-driven box. This design uses the resonance vibration from a small wind gradient to electrically charge a fluorinated ethylene–propylene (FEP) film between two aluminum foils as small as 2.5 cm x 2.5 cm x 22 cm. This system can provide an output voltage of 100 V and a power density of 1.16µW/cm³, which is enough output to self-power an array of sensors using ambient wind differences. Figure 23 shows the schematics of the TENG used in this model; the small changes in the wind gradient cause the movement of the FEP layer with the copper wire between the aluminum layers (Yang et al., 2013).

Another design uses a free-standing contact mode TENG structure that resembles a flag on a pole that flutters with low wind gradients. This design relays on two small TENGs flags, with a 35 mm gap in between, which flutter and contact each other under low wind speeds (under 7 m/s). The two TENG 150 mm x 75 mm flags generated 20.8 V and a power density of 40.8 µW/cm³. This flag-type application can be used in self-powered wind and humidity sensors, allowing for a more energy-efficient IoT system. Figure 24 shows the schematics of the wind flag design (Wang et al., 2020).

Figure 23. Schematics of the win-powered TENG
(Yang et al., 2013)

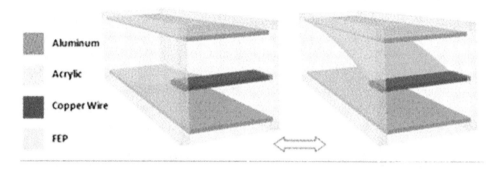

Figure 24. Application of flag-type TENG in self-powered wind and humidity sensors
(Wang et al., 2020)

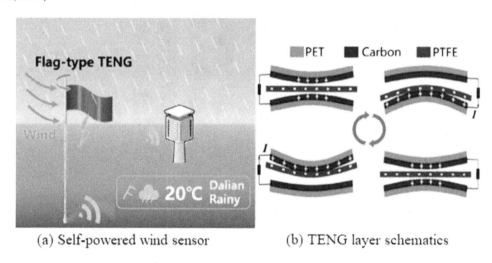

(a) Self-powered wind sensor   (b) TENG layer schematics

NON-VIBRATIONAL HARVESTERS

Another classification of harvesters is non-vibrational harvesters that use non-kinetic or non-vibrational sources of ambient energy as an energy source. Non-vibrational harvesters have been used in different applications ranging from MEMS and small IoT devices to large-scale harvesters for entire power buildings. The requirements for each type of vibrational harvester differ depending on the energy source and the application scale, offering a great range of options for reliable energy harvesting.

Photovoltaic Harvesters (PVH)

Solar energy is one of the most abundant energy resources in the world that can be harvested using a photovoltaic (PV) cell. The general idea of a PV cell relies on the freeing of electrons from metals when the sun rays excite a metal. This effect, known as the photovoltaic effect, is achieved by freeing electrons from p-n junctions when they get energized enough by a sun ray. This movement of the electrons results in an electric current that depends on the light intensity (*Photovoltaic Effect - Energy Education*, n.d.).

Solar energy harvesting is considered more efficient than other types of energy harvesting techniques for two main reasons: PV cells provide higher power output than other ambient energy harvesters due to the abundance of the source, the sun, and PV cells are comparatively cheaper to manufacture and maintain. However, one of the biggest drawbacks of solar harvesters is the intermittency of the available power, lack of solar energy prediction, and poor solar panel efficiency. Despite that, solar energy harvesters are used in Wireless Sensor Networks (WSNs) to power and store energy for the nodes and allow for real-time communication without relying solely on a conventional battery system. In most solar energy harvesters, the solar panels are connected to DC-DC converters that then connect to a rechargeable battery that can be used to power the WSNs when the PV cells are not generating electricity (Sharma et al., 2019). To overcome some of the other issues, solar harvesters are modeled with Maximum Power Point Tracking (MPPT) in mind, where the panels can track the movement of the energy source to maximize the number of rays received by the harvester (Dondi et al., 2008). Figure 25 shows a typical block diagram of solar harvesters in a WSN application.

Figure 25. Solar harvesters pipeline in a wireless sensor network
(Dondi et al., 2008)

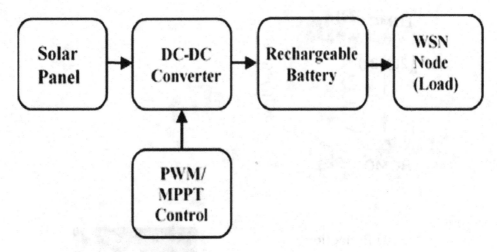

Thermoelectric Harvesters

There are two main types of thermoelectric harvesters: constant temperature and changing temperature. Unlike solar harvesters that rely on UV to generate electricity, constant thermoelectric harvesters aim to harvest the solar IR spectrum, including the Near IR (NIR) and the mid-infrared (MIR) regions, as a more stable energy source. However, most thermal generators have low efficiency that does not exceed 7.4% (J. P. Jurado et al., 2019). A constant temperature generator has three main components: a solar absorber, a thermoelectric generator, and a heat management device. The solar absorber accumulates heat by concentrating sun rays through optical means. The thermoelectric generator converts the heat into voltage difference, and the heat management system removes the excess heat from the thermoelectric generator (Kraemer et al., 2011).

A novel method of creating a solar-based thermal harvester uses organic material to create the generators. This way, the generator can act as both the solar absorber and as a means of converting heat into voltage. The process of generating electricity form the system relies mainly on the excitation of electrons to jump the LUMO-HOMO (Lowest Unoccupied Molecular Orbital-Highest Occupied Molecular Orbital) band gap creating a voltage difference. A proposed model is shown in Figure 26, showing the behavior of a solar organic thermoelectric generator that can generate electricity at 4.5 nW at 150µV. The low electricity characterization can be explained by the losses and dissipation of energies through material reflection, conduction, convection, radiation, traps, and joule heating (resistive heating) (Jurado et al., 2019).

Figure 26. The electricity generation from solar energy using the organic thermoelectric generator while showing the different means of heat loss in the system through optical, absorption, and heat loss mechanisms
(Jurado et al., 2019)

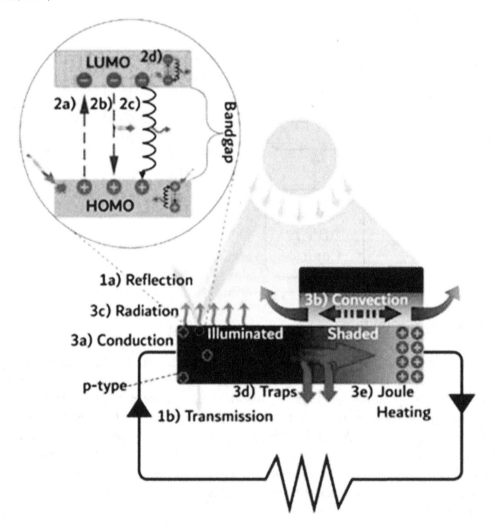

For thermoelectric generators that depend on changing temperatures, the main key in thermal harvesters is using/creating a thermal gradient resulting from the heat difference between a heat source and a cold sink. Thermoelectric generators are solid-state devices that use the spatial temperature difference to generate electrical energy based on the Seebeck thermoelectric effect. The Seebeck effect describes the creation of a hot thermoelectric junction that results in a voltage development between two dissimilar electrical semiconductors: n-type (electron saturated) and p-type (hole saturated) (Percy et al., 2014; Zabek & Morini, 2019). The Seebeck effect dictates that the voltage generated from the heat difference is given by

$$V = \int_{T_{cold}}^{T_{Hot}} S_1\left(T_{Hot}\right) - S_2\left(T_{cold}\right) dT \tag{15}$$

where S_1 and S_2 are the Seebeck coefficients at the heat sources, defined based on the material (a material property) (Percy et al., 2014).

These harvesters have many applications in MEMS technologies where the thermal energy by-product produced in the processors can be converted into electrical energy. Thermal harvesters can also be used in wearable sensor nodes in multiple locations on the human skin, relying on the natural thermal gradient between the human body heat and the ambient temperature. At an ambient temperature of 22 °C, it was shown that a thermal generator made of Bismuth Telluride (Bi_2Te_3) semiconductors could produce around 350 µW. This power can typically fuel a low-power ZigBee or a Bluetooth module to communicate data between the biosensor and the monitoring devices. Figure 27 shows a typical thermoelectric schematic of a thermoelectric generator where the semiconductors form a junction between the hot side and the cold side, driving the DC energy through the cold side (*Flexible Thermoelectric Materials and Device Optimization for Wearable Energy Harvesting - Journal of Materials Chemistry C (RSC Publishing)*, n.d.).

Pyroelectric Harvesters (PyEH)

Pyroelectric harvesting is a non-vibrational harvesting resource that depends on low-grade thermal energies at low temperatures. The main difference between pyroelectric harvesting and thermoelectric harvesting is that pyroelectric harvesters depend on the change of temperature over time, while thermoelectric harvesters depend on a huge temperature change with respect to space (Sebald et al., 2009; Thakre et al., 2019). All the materials used in pyroelectric harvesters are polar, resulting in surface charge (spontaneous polarization) that is proportional to the temperature change rate over time. This polarization results in a temporary voltage in opposition to the permanent voltage generation by thermoelectric generators (N. Han & Ho, 2014).

The general structure of a pyroelectric harvester depends on the pyroelectric crystal that generates a current expressed by

$$i = \frac{\partial P}{\partial T} A \frac{dT}{dt}$$

where P is the electric polarization, T is the temperature, and A is the area of the pyroelectric layer. Due to this fact, a lot of research has been conducted on the fabrication of thin-film-based pyroelectric devices that are used in WSNs and IoT devices by acting as a thermodynamic heat engine. Figure 28 shows the Olsen cycle used in pyroelectric power generation by employing two isothermal and two isoelectric processes at low operating frequencies. At the beginning of the cycle, the depolarized crystal goes under isothermal polarization (charging), followed by isoelectric heating and isothermal depolarization of the material (discharging), followed by isoelectric cooling at the end of the cycle (Pandya et al., 2019).

Other thermodynamic cycles, such as the Brayton cycle, are used in pyroelectric generation at high cycle frequencies. Brayton cycle depends on two adiabatic and two isoelectric processes to generate electricity, and it was shown to provide more efficient output at high cycle frequencies (50 Hz). The power density output of a thin-film pyroelectric is around 8mW/cm^3, measured at 60 °C (Hanrahan et al., 2017).

Figure 27. A general schematic of the thermoelectric generator using a junction created between one p-type and one n-type semiconductor substrate

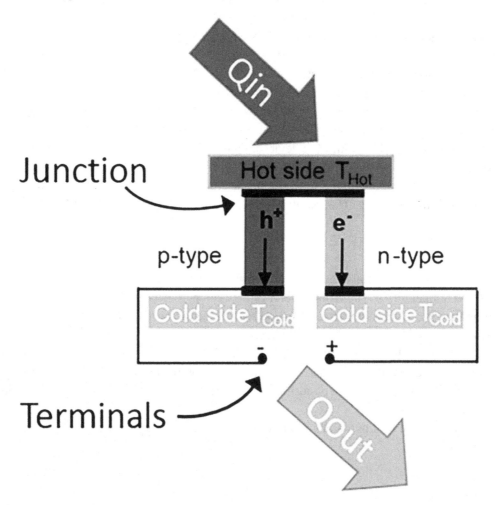

Figure 28. Olsen pyroelectric crystal polarization-heating cycle
(Pandya et al., 2019)

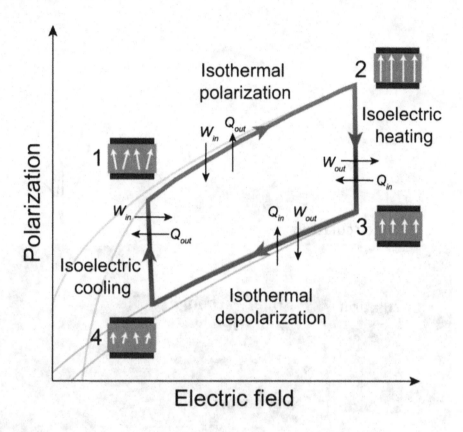

Geothermal Harvesters

Geothermal harvesting is one of the renewable energy-harvesting techniques that are aimed at reducing greenhouse emissions. The main applications of geothermal harvesters are in transportation and pavement heating. The concept depends on geothermal heat pumps (GHP) and underground energy storage systems that can be used as a more environmentally aware solution to heat pavements, providing a more sustainable way of de-icing roads. Road-deicing via geothermal harvesters is generally cheaper to maintain and operate compared to the chemical alternative (Ceylan et al., n.d.).

There are three types of GHP: groundwater heat pump systems, ground-coupled heat pump systems, and surface-water heat pump systems. The differences between these types rely mainly on the difference between the sink sources. The ground-coupled system is the most commonly used as it is spatially conscious, has smaller pipe installations, and has high heat pumping energy as a result of being directly in contact with the little heat variations in the soil (Han et al., 2018).

The main idea of ground-coupled GHP is to use the ground as a heat sink rather than the air, achieving a better heat exchange system (Ahmad et al., 2019). These systems can be used to heat and cool buildings using a heat pump and the ground. Figure 29 shows a typical heating mode by circulating water via the above ground heat pump that absorbs heat from the warmer soil and then exchanges that heat around the building, starting another circulation (US EPA, 2014).

Figure 29. Heating mode of a GHP
(US EPA, 2014)

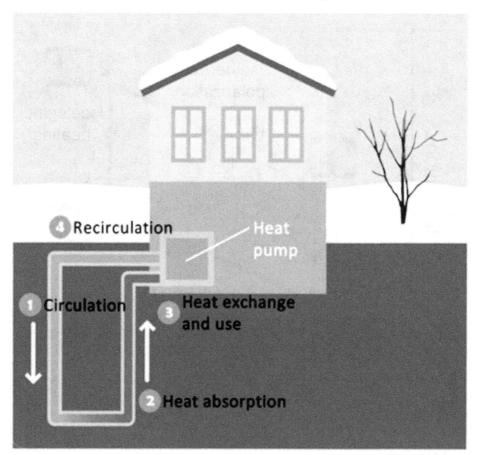

Radio-Frequency (RF) Harvesters

In IoT devices, most of the communication is sent by RF signals that are always exchanged between nodes in a network. Some of these signals are ambient and do not contain valuable system information. One of the approaches used to cultivate this ambient energy uses the RF signal during the IoT sensor's sleep cycle to charge the sensor battery to be used during the wake-up cycle. This method modifies the signal sent from the sources to account for a wake-up/sleep signal to tell the sensors if the RF signal should be used to charge the battery or interpret the signal. This scheduling system works great for ultra-low-power usage sensors and IoT. However, it is unsuitable for IoT systems with higher energy use or sensors with a longer wake cycle than sleep cycles (Rostami et al., 2018, 2020).

The main block in the RF harvesters is the RF-DC convertor which consists of rectifiers that convert the electromagnetic signal into a DC signal that can be stored in the IoT battery during the sleep cycle. The efficiency (η) of an RF-DC convertor can be calculated as $\eta = \dfrac{P_{out}}{P_{in}}$, with some designs reaching a

35% power efficiency with around 3.5 Volts at 1GHz and -12 dBm signal input (D. Khan et al., 2020). Figure 30 shows a wireless node that uses a wireless-powered wake-up receiver (WPWRx) that switches between sleep-wake schedules based on the RF signal (Rostami et al., 2018).

Figure 30. Block diagram of a wireless node that uses a wireless-powered wake-up receiver (WPWRx) (Rostami et al., 2018)

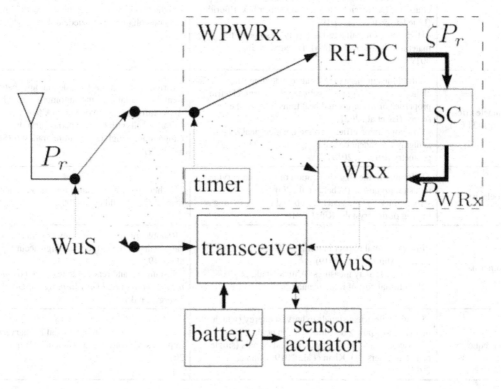

Comparison Between on Non-Vibrational Harvesters

Non-vibrational harvesters are more versatile than vibrational harvesters due to the wide variations of resources and the scale of the harvesters. These harvesters can be used on a miniature scale (MEMS and IoT applications) and larger scale applications (buildings, roads, and pavements). Energy harvesters generally help limit greenhouse emissions and aim to improve the quality of energy produced by reducing the total dependence on traditional methods of energy production that are harmful to the environment. Despite these efforts, non-vibrational harvesters still have limitations in terms of cost of implementation, environmental impacts, and amount of electricity generated, amongst others. Table 3 provides the advantages and limitations of each energy harvester discussed in this chapter. Table 4 provides the electricity characterization of these non-vibrational harvesters to serve as a way of comparing the efficiency of each harvester type.

Table 3. Limitations and advantages of non-vibrational energy harvesters

Resource	Limitations	Advantages
Photovoltaic	- Interrupted power generation and power storage when the panels are not harvesting (Farrokhi Derakhshandeh et al., 2021) - Requires regular maintenance and cleaning for optimum behavior (Farrokhi Derakhshandeh et al., 2021) - Production of solar panels can produce greenhouse gas emissions (Nitrogen trifluoride and sulfur hexafluoride) (Dziedzic & Jurczyk, 2019) - High cost of manufacturing (rarity of some of the materials used in fabrication) (Dziedzic & Jurczyk, 2019)	- High durability and long-time spans (providing regular maintenance) - Sustainable, renewable source - Reduction of CO_2 levels in cities with high volume of photovoltaic cells (Dziedzic & Jurczyk, 2019)
Thermoelectric Generators (TEGs)	- Difficulties in thermal resistance matching (the choice of the p-n couples) between the thermoelectric properties of materials and heat transfer from the heat source (Lv et al., 2021) - Low conversion efficiency and the electrical output is highly dependent on the design and the TEG leg geometry (Enescu, 2019)	- Various applications (Residential applications, wearables, solar systems, automotive, naval and spacecraft applications)(Enescu, 2019) - Works well with highly spatial varying temperatures (high temperature gradient) (Sebald et al., 2009)
Pyroelectric	- Difficulty in the characterization of the time varying temperature profile (Sebald et al., 2009) - Temporary voltage generation based on the cooling or heating of the crystals (Kittel, 2016)	- Higher power output and conversion efficiency than TEGs (Sebald et al., 2009)
Geothermal	- Environmental impact in terms of disposals and air quality (Ahmad et al., 2019) - Geological safety measures (Ahmad et al., 2019) - High Initial cost of implementation	- Reliable, high efficiency, low- operating cost, and easy to detect the output with high accuracy (Cui et al., 2019) - Sustainable and renewable resource (*What Are the Advantages and Disadvantages of Geothermal Energy?*, n.d.)
Radio Frequency	- Requires electrical signals to harvest energy (which often has low power densities) (Kuhn et al., 2015) - Low conversion efficiency using real signals (single band harvesters) (D. Khan et al., 2019; Kuhn et al., 2015)	- Stacked designs of multi-modal RF harvesters improves the conversion efficiency (Kuhn et al., 2015)

Table 4. Characterization of different types of non-vibrational energy harvesters

Resource	Case/Application	Electricity Characterization	
		Power Density	Open Circuit Voltage
Photovoltaic	Cardiac Self-powered Implantable Medical Device (Haeberlin et al., 2014)	4.94 mW/cm²	5.67 V
	Air Quality Monitoring Sensor (Yue et al., 2017)	28 mW/cm³	3.6-4.2 V
Thermoelectric Generators (TEGs)	Wearable Devices (Lv et al., 2021)	0.42 mW/cm² (temperature gradient of 30 K)	-
	Commercial wrist watches (Ando Junior et al., 2018; Fairbanks, n.d.)	13.8 µW/K	640 mV/K
Pyroelectric	Temperature Monitor (Zhao et al., 2017)	36 nW/cm²	9.1 V
	Low range thermal application (Hanrahan et al., 2017)	8mW/cm³ (@ 60 °C)	-

ENERGY STORAGE OPTIONS

Energy storage for energy harvesting devices is still one of the on-going research questions in the field. This section delivers the different energy storing options with a focus on the advantages and disadvantages.

The energy storage option depends on the type of electrical current produced by the harvester. In the case of photovoltaic cells and thermoelectric generators, the current is produced as a direct current (DC), which means that the harvester can be connected directly to the storage device without any extra circuits. In the case of piezoelectric, triboelectric, and electromagnetic, the current produced is alternative current (AC), meaning that a rectifier circuit is needed to convert the AC to DC before connecting to a storage device. The power module circuit shown in figure 31 also shows the use of a transformer to regulate the amount of charging current and voltage to a constant value (Lee et al., 2016).

Figure 31. Schematics of power module circuit used to interface between energy harvester and storage batteries
(Lee et al., 2016)

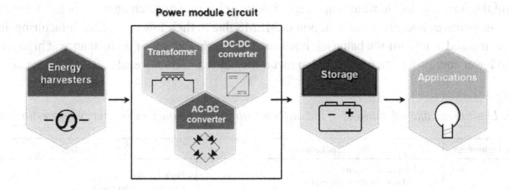

Lithium-Ion Batteries (LIBs)

Lithium-ion batteries are the most commonly used batteries to store energy generated by harvesters due to their impressive performance and efficient energy storage. LIBs rely on converting electrical energy into electrochemical energy using different variations of cathode/anode/electrolyte combinations.

LIBs have been extensively studied and optimized, leading to the current batteries used to store excess energy from harvesters. These batteries are characterized by high specific capacity and voltage, no memory, excellent cycling performance, and wide operational temperature range (Chen et al., 2021).

Despite their impressive performance, LIBs have many safety issues related to over-heating and explosions that are caused by undesirable chemical reactions, mechanical abuse (there is a high chance of this occurring in mobile systems that rely on energy harvesters), or electrical abuse caused by repeated over charge/discharge of the battery (Chen et al., 2021). Another issue with LIBs is the high production cost combined with resource scarcity, which leads to higher processing times and difficulty in large-scale distribution (Yun et al., 2019).

Zinc-Ion Batteries (ZIBs)

An electrochemical alternative to LIBs is Zinc-ion batteries which are characterized by lower levels of toxicity, more flexibility in high-impact applications, lower safety risks, and more natural abundance, which means lower costs of production and distribution (Hu et al., 2018; Wang et al., 2018). Compared to LIBs, ZIBs have lower efficiencies, shorter life cycles, and insufficient discharge capacities. This inefficiency results in a higher cost due to the frequent need to change the batteries in a given system (Wang et al., 2016).

Supercapacitors (SC)

Supercapacitors have attracted more attention in energy storage due to their long-life cycles and high power densities (Wang et al., 2019). They store energy in WSNs and photovoltaic cells; however, the technology is mainly used as a complementary storage system to already existing energy storage batteries. The supercapacitors usually exist in arrays that allow for different charging priorities, meaning they can act as back-up to other resources or even one another. Power switches usually control these arrays to control the flow and decide which supercapacitors are charging or discharging (Chen & Chou, 2010).

Micro-supercapacitors are more common in MEMS due to their low cost of manufacturing and low toxicity compared to lithium-ion batteries; however, they suffer from poor performance at high temperatures and lower energy densities compared to metal-ion batteries (Huang et al., 2019; Wang et al., 2019).

Table 5. Limitations and advantages of the different storage technologies in energy harvesting systems

Storage Technology	Limitations	Advantages
Lithium-ion Batteries	- High levels of toxicity - Risk of over-heating and explosions - Scarcity of resources leads to higher costs of production and handling	- High specific capacity - Excellent cycling performance - No memory requirements
Zinc (and other metal) -ion Batteries	- Lower efficiency compared to LIBs - Short life cycles - Insufficient discharge capacity	- Low levels of toxicity - Natural abundance (lower costs of production)
Supercapacitors	- Usually used as a complementary to a metal-ion battery - Poor performance at high temperatures - Low energy density compared to LIBs	- Long life cycles - High power densities - Easier to configure the charging and discharging cycles

ENERGY MANAGEMENT IN ENERGY HARVESTERS

With the rise of self-sufficient nodes used in IoT and WSNs, thanks to energy harvesting, more research is now dedicated to storing the harvested energy efficiently and optimizing the utilization of this energy by using different combinations of software, algorithms, and communication protocols. Some energy management systems used in state-of-the-art self-sufficient energy harvester systems are discussed below.

Task Scheduling

Task Scheduling is one of the methods used to optimize the performance of an energy-harvester-based sensor in IoT and WSNs. This method is composed of different algorithms that aim at reducing the amount of energy used in the system by managing the execution of tasks based on many factors, such as communication distance, signal sampling, data storage, and data processing (Sandhu et al., 2021).

The main idea behind task scheduling is to let the node/system decide what is the best course of action to deal with the data in a way that optimizes energy usage. That can mean the data can be sent right-away after collecting or letting the node hold-on the data until enough energy is available in the system (Sandhu et al., 2021). Task scheduling also includes wake-up/sleep schedules determined by the node that allows for the best power conservation of the system (Rostami et al., 2018).

Transmission Power Control

Transmission power control allows the system to conserve and use power more efficiently by allowing each node to change its power consumption dynamically. Systems implementing transmission power control allow more traffic on high-powered nodes and less on low-powered ones. This way, the system achieves optimized power consumption without hugely impacting performance. This algorithm leads to the re-routing of the data depending on the node energy availability, which means that the transmission time across the system network is also dynamic (Zareei et al., 2019).

Data-Driven Energy Management

Using prior data collected within a system or across systems is a new scope with great promise in energy management. This method incorporates a learning aspect by studying the patterns of energy harvesting and discharging, allowing the system to learn from its past. The system then can decide what to do based on available resources and the system history itself.

One of these new learning algorithms is PreAct which plans the future of energy utilization with the added feedback control to accommodate for unexpected or accounted-for conditions. PreAct uses real-world data collected via multiple energy harvesting systems, leading to a 28% improvement in the overall harvester IoT compared to traditional energy management systems (Geissdoerfer et al., 2019).

CHALLENGES AND FUTURE OPPORTUNITIES

Despite the impressive improvements achieved in the energy harvesting fields, whether vibrational or non-vibrational, there are still open areas for research and improvement. The main areas of open research are discussed in this section.

Stability and Amount of Energy Production

A big drawback of using energy harvesters is the minuscule amount of current that is generated by the devices, which renders most energy harvesters only suitable for small-scale and ultra-low power consumption applications. Most vibrational energy harvesters are configured to work with specific range and fail to generate adequate amounts of energy when the ambient frequency is too low (Khalid et al., 2019). Creating multi-modal energy harvesters that can use multiple operating frequencies or even different energy sources can overcome the issue of energy production stability. These multi-modal harvesters can alternate electricity generation modes from the different available sources to maximize the power generated. Depending on the system status, they can also alternate between storing and using energy. Multi-module energy harvesters are another promising solution to ensuring stable electricity output where different harvesters are integrated with a single system which allows harvesting from multiple resources depending on the availability of ambient energy (Dong & Wang, 2021; Ramírez et al., 2018; Zhu et al., 2022).

Cost of Manufacturing and Installing

Due to the small amounts of energy generated by a single harvester, more than one harvester is needed in most applications to achieve the system power requirements, meaning more harvesters must be manufactured, installed, and maintained. This process can be costly, especially in cases where the harvesters are used in remote or mobile IoT nodes.

Improving Energy Storage Options

Not all the energy generated by the harvesters is immediately used nor needed by the devices generating them, which imposes the need for reliable, low-cost, and efficient storage systems. The most promising initiatives in energy storage are the hybrid combination of supercapacitors and lithium-ion batteries, which have been proven efficient for low-voltage applications; however, it is still relying in part on toxic lithium-ion batteries. Also, although supercapacitors can store more energy than regular capacitors, supercapacitors are limited to low voltages (2.5-2.7V), which can be a challenge for higher voltage applications (Vukajlović et al., 2020).

Reducing Environmental and Health Impacts

The environmental and health impacts of energy harvesters vary depending on the material used in the harvester and the type of application, amongst others. Most currently used materials in PEH, PVHs, TENGs, and TEGs are non-biodegradable materials that use a lot of water and energy to manufacture while taking a long time to degrade after the lifetime of the device end. Specific examples of environmental issues include the use of cadmium and arsenic in the production of PV cells which are toxic chemicals, the unregulated use of geothermal energy, which can result in catastrophic impacts if safety procedures are not followed, and the generally short-life span of harvesters making the process environmentally taxing. Research aims at improving the environmental impacts by improving the lifetime of harvesting devices, improving the efficiency of biodegradable materials as a substitute to the traditionally used toxic materials, and providing better practices in the production of harvesters overall (Mahmud et al., 2018; *PZT Properties & PZT Manufacturing*, n.d.; Wang et al., 2018b).

REFERENCES

Abdelmoula, H., Sharpes, N., Abdelkefi, A., Lee, H., & Priya, S. (2017). Low-frequency Zigzag energy harvesters operating in torsion-dominant mode. *Applied Energy*, *204*, 413–419. doi:10.1016/j.apenergy.2017.07.044

Ahmad, S., Abdul Mujeebu, M., & Farooqi, M. A. (2019). Energy harvesting from pavements and roadways: A comprehensive review of technologies, materials, and challenges. *International Journal of Energy Research*, *43*(6), 1974–2015. doi:10.1002/er.4350

Ahmed, S. (2021). Realizing the Benefits of Energy Harvesting for IoT. In *Role of IoT in Green Energy Systems* (pp. 144–155). IGI Global. doi:10.4018/978-1-7998-6709-8.ch006

Ando, O. H. Junior, Maran, A. L. O., & Henao, N. C. (2018). A review of the development and applications of thermoelectric microgenerators for energy harvesting. *Renewable & Sustainable Energy Reviews*, *91*, 376–393. doi:10.1016/j.rser.2018.03.052

Asthana, P., & Khanna, G. (2020). Development of Vibration Piezoelectric Harvesters by the Optimum Design of Cantilever Structures. In *Nanogenerators*. IntechOpen. doi:10.5772/intechopen.90556

Ceylan, H., Gopalakrishnan, K., Kim, S., & Cord, W. (n.d.). *Heated transportation infrastructure systems: Existing and emerging technologies*.

Chen, C.-Y., & Chou, P. H. (2010). DuraCap: A supercapacitor-based, power-bootstrapping, maximum power point tracking energy-harvesting system. *2010 ACM/IEEE International Symposium on Low-Power Electronics and Design (ISLPED)*, (pp. 313–318). ACM/IEEE. 10.1145/1840845.1840910

Chen, N. (n.d.). *Design, Modeling, and Simulation of Piezoelectric and Magnetoelectric Devices for Multimodal Energy Harvesting Applications*. MTSU.

Chen, Y., Kang, Y., Zhao, Y., Wang, L., Liu, J., Li, Y., Liang, Z., He, X., Li, X., Tavajohi, N., & Li, B. (2021). A review of lithium-ion battery safety concerns: The issues, strategies, and testing standards. *Journal of Energy Chemistry*, *59*, 83–99. doi:10.1016/j.jechem.2020.10.017

Chetto, M., & Queudet, A. (2016). 3—Harnessing Ambient Energy for Embedded Systems. In M. Chetto & A. Queudet (Eds.), *Energy Autonomy of Real-Time Systems* (pp. 57–83). Elsevier. doi:10.1016/B978-1-78548-125-3.50003-8

Cui, Y., Zhu, J., Twaha, S., Chu, J., Bai, H., Huang, K., Chen, X., Zoras, S., & Soleimani, Z. (2019). Techno-economic assessment of the horizontal geothermal heat pump systems: A comprehensive review. *Energy Conversion and Management*, *191*, 208–236. doi:10.1016/j.enconman.2019.04.018

Dondi, D., Bertacchini, A., Brunelli, D., Larcher, L., & Benini, L. (2008). Modeling and Optimization of a Solar Energy Harvester System for Self-Powered Wireless Sensor Networks. *IEEE Transactions on Industrial Electronics*, *55*(7), 2759–2766. doi:10.1109/TIE.2008.924449

Dong, K., & Wang, Z. L. (2021). Self-charging power textiles integrating energy harvesting triboelectric nanogenerators with energy storage batteries/supercapacitors. *Journal of Semiconductors*, *42*(10), 101601. doi:10.1088/1674-4926/42/10/101601

Dziedzic, B., & Jurczyk, M. (2019). *The Pros And Cons Of Solar Energy In Poland*. Sunpower.

Enescu, D. (2019). *Green Energy Advances*. BoD – Books on Demand. doi:10.5772/intechopen.77501

Erturk, A., & Inman, D. J. (2008). A Distributed Parameter Electromechanical Model for Cantilevered Piezoelectric Energy Harvesters. *Journal of Vibration and Acoustics*, *130*(4), 041002. Advance online publication. doi:10.1115/1.2890402

Fairbanks, J. (n.d.). *DOE's Launch of High-Efficiency Thermoelectrics Projects*. 26.

Farrokhi Derakhshandeh, J., AlLuqman, R., Mohammad, S., AlHussain, H., AlHendi, G., AlEid, D., & Ahmad, Z. (2021). A comprehensive review of automatic cleaning systems of solar panels. *Sustainable Energy Technologies and Assessments*, *47*, 101518. doi:10.1016/j.seta.2021.101518

Single-electrode mode triboelectric nanogenerator.png. (n.d.). Wikipedia. https://commons.wikimedia.org/wiki/File:Single-electrode_mode_triboelectric_nanogenerator.png

Bahk, J., Fang, H., Yazawa, K., & Shakouri, A. (2015). *Flexible thermoelectric materials and device optimization for wearable energy harvesting—Journal of Materials Chemistry C*. RSC Publishing. https://pubs.rsc.org/en/content/articlelanding/2015/TC/C5TC01644D

Foong, M. F., Thein, C. K., & Ooi, B. L. (2021). Applications of Vibration-Based Energy Harvesting (VEH) Devices. In Role of IoT in Green Energy Systems (pp. 81–116). IGI Global. doi:10.4018/978-1-7998-6709-8.ch004

Geissdoerfer, K., Jurdak, R., Kusy, B., & Zimmerling, M. (2019). Getting more out of energy-harvesting systems: Energy management under time-varying utility with PreAct. *Proceedings of the 18th International Conference on Information Processing in Sensor Networks*, (pp. 109–120). ACM. 10.1145/3302506.3310393

Haeberlin, A., Zurbuchen, A., Schaerer, J., Wagner, J., Walpen, S., Huber, C., Haeberlin, H., Fuhrer, J., & Vogel, R. (2014). Successful pacing using a batteryless sunlight-powered pacemaker. *Europace*, *16*(10), 1534–1539. doi:10.1093/europace/euu127 PMID:24916431

Han, C., Wu, G., & Yu, X. (2018). Performance Analyses of Geothermal and Geothermoelectric Pavement Snow Melting System. *Journal of Energy Engineering*, *144*(6), 04018067. doi:10.1061/(ASCE)EY.1943-7897.0000585

Han, N., & Ho, J. C. (2014). 3—One-Dimensional Nanomaterials for Energy Applications. In S.-C. Tjong (Ed.), *Nanocrystalline Materials* (2nd ed., pp. 75–120). Elsevier. doi:10.1016/B978-0-12-407796-6.00003-8

Hanrahan, B. M., Sze, F., Smith, A. N., & Jankowski, N. R. (2017). Thermodynamic cycle optimization for pyroelectric energy conversion in the thin film regime: Thermodynamic cycles for pyroelectric thin films. *International Journal of Energy Research*, *41*(13), 1880–1890. doi:10.1002/er.3749

Holler, F. J., Skoog, D., Douglas, A., & Crouch, S. R. (2007). *Principles of Instrumental Analysis* (6th ed.). Cengage Learning.

Hu, P., Zhu, T., Wang, X., Wei, X., Yan, M., Li, J., Luo, W., Yang, W., Zhang, W., Zhou, L., Zhou, Z., & Mai, L. (2018). Highly Durable Na2V6O16·1.63H2O Nanowire Cathode for Aqueous Zinc-Ion Battery. *Nano Letters*, *18*(3), 1758–1763. doi:10.1021/acs.nanolett.7b04889 PMID:29397745

Huang, S., Zhu, X., Sarkar, S., & Zhao, Y. (2019). Challenges and opportunities for supercapacitors. *APL Materials*, *7*(10), 100901. doi:10.1063/1.5116146

Iannacci, J., Sordo, G., Schneider, M., Schmid, U., Camarda, A., & Romani, A. (2016). A novel toggle-type MEMS vibration energy harvester for Internet of Things applications. *2016 IEEE SENSORS*, 1–3. doi:10.1109/ICSENS.2016.7808553

Ibrahim, A., Ramini, A., & Towfighian, S. (2020). Triboelectric energy harvester with large bandwidth under harmonic and random excitations. *Energy Reports*, *6*, 2490–2502. doi:10.1016/j.egyr.2020.09.007

Invernizzi, F., Dulio, S., Patrini, M., Guizzetti, G., & Mustarelli, P. (2016). Energy harvesting from human motion: Materials and techniques. *Chemical Society Reviews*, *45*(20), 5455–5473. doi:10.1039/C5CS00812C PMID:27398416

IRENA. (n.d.). *Wind energy*. Wind. https://www.irena.org/wind

Izadgoshasb, I., Lim, Y. Y., Lake, N., Tang, L., Padilla, R. V., & Kashiwao, T. (2018). Optimizing orientation of piezoelectric cantilever beam for harvesting energy from human walking. *Energy Conversion and Management*, *161*, 66–73. doi:10.1016/j.enconman.2018.01.076

Jin, L., Ma, S., Deng, W., Yan, C., Yang, T., Chu, X., Tian, G., Xiong, D., Lu, J., & Yang, W. (2018). Polarization-free high-crystallization β-PVDF piezoelectric nanogenerator toward self-powered 3D acceleration sensor. *Nano Energy*, *50*, 632–638. doi:10.1016/j.nanoen.2018.05.068

Jurado, J. P., Dörling, B., Zapata-Arteaga, O., Roig, A., Mihi, A., & Campoy-Quiles, M. (2019). Solar Harvesting: A Unique Opportunity for Organic Thermoelectrics? *Advanced Energy Materials*, *9*(45), 1902385. doi:10.1002/aenm.201902385

Jurado, U. T., Pu, S. H., & White, N. M. (2020). Wave impact energy harvesting through water-dielectric triboelectrification with single-electrode triboelectric nanogenerators for battery-less systems. *Nano Energy*, *78*, 105204. doi:10.1016/j.nanoen.2020.105204

Khalid, S., Raouf, I., Khan, A., Kim, N., & Kim, H. S. (2019). A Review of Human-Powered Energy Harvesting for Smart Electronics: Recent Progress and Challenges. *International Journal of Precision Engineering and Manufacturing-Green Technology*, *6*(4), 821–851. doi:10.100740684-019-00144-y

Khan, D., Oh, S. J., Shehzad, K., Basim, M., Verma, D., Pu, Y. G., Lee, M., Hwang, K. C., Yang, Y., & Lee, K.-Y. (2020). An Efficient Reconfigurable RF-DC Converter With Wide Input Power Range for RF Energy Harvesting. *IEEE Access : Practical Innovations, Open Solutions*, *8*, 79310–79318. doi:10.1109/ACCESS.2020.2990662

Khan, D., Oh, S. J., Shehzad, K., Verma, D., Khan, Z. H. N., Pu, Y. G., Lee, M., Hwang, K. C., Yang, Y., & Lee, K.-Y. (2019). A CMOS RF Energy Harvester With 47% Peak Efficiency Using Internal Threshold Voltage Compensation. *IEEE Microwave and Wireless Components Letters*, *29*(6), 415–417. doi:10.1109/LMWC.2019.2909403

Khan, U., Kim, T.-H., Ryu, H., Seung, W., & Kim, S.-W. (2017). Graphene Tribotronics for Electronic Skin and Touch Screen Applications. *Advanced Materials, 29*(1), 1603544. doi:10.1002/adma.201603544 PMID:27786382

Khushboo, & Azad, P. (2019). Design and Implementation of Conductor-to-Dielectric Lateral Sliding TENG Mode for Low Power Electronics. In H. Malik, S. Srivastava, Y. R. Sood, & A. Ahmad (Eds.), *Applications of Artificial Intelligence Techniques in Engineering* (pp. 167–174). Springer. doi:10.1007/978-981-13-1819-1_17

Kim, H., Tadesse, Y., & Priya, S. (2009). Piezoelectric Energy Harvesting. In S. Priya & D. J. Inman (Eds.), *Energy Harvesting Technologies* (pp. 3–39). Springer US. doi:10.1007/978-0-387-76464-1_1

Kiran, M., Farrok, O., Mamun, M., Islam, M. R., & Xu, W. (2020). Progress in Piezoelectric Material Based Oceanic Wave Energy Conversion Technology. *IEEE Access : Practical Innovations, Open Solutions, 8*, 146428–146449. doi:10.1109/ACCESS.2020.3015821

Kittel, C. (2016). *Introduction to Solid State Physics* (8th ed.). Maruzen.

Kraemer, D., Poudel, B., Feng, H.-P., Caylor, J. C., Yu, B., Yan, X., Ma, Y., Wang, X., Wang, D., Muto, A., McEnaney, K., Chiesa, M., Ren, Z., & Chen, G. (2011). High-performance flat-panel solar thermo-electric generators with high thermal concentration. *Nature Materials, 10*(7), 532–538. doi:10.1038/nmat3013 PMID:21532584

Kuang, Y., & Zhu, M. (2017). Design study of a mechanically plucked piezoelectric energy harvester using validated finite element modelling. *Sensors and Actuators. A, Physical, 263*, 510–520. doi:10.1016/j.sna.2017.07.009

Kuhn, V., Lahuec, C., Seguin, F., & Person, C. (2015). A Multi-Band Stacked RF Energy Harvester With RF-to-DC Efficiency Up to 84%. *IEEE Transactions on Microwave Theory and Techniques, 63*(5), 1768–1778. doi:10.1109/TMTT.2015.2416233

Kumar, A., Balpande, S. S., & Anjankar, S. C. (2016). Electromagnetic Energy Harvester for Low Frequency Vibrations Using MEMS. *Procedia Computer Science, 79*, 785–792. doi:10.1016/j.procs.2016.03.104

Lee, H., Sharpes, N., Abdelmoula, H., Abdelkefi, A., & Priya, S. (2018). Higher power generation from torsion-dominant mode in a zigzag shaped two-dimensional energy harvester. *Applied Energy, 216*, 494–503. doi:10.1016/j.apenergy.2018.02.083

Lee, J.-H., Kim, J., Yun Kim, T., Hossain, M. S. A., Kim, S.-W., & Ho Kim, J. (2016). All-in-one energy harvesting and storage devices. *Journal of Materials Chemistry. A, Materials for Energy and Sustainability, 4*(21), 7983–7999. doi:10.1039/C6TA01229A

Lee, Y., Cha, S. H., Kim, Y.-W., Choi, D., & Sun, J.-Y. (2018). Transparent and attachable ionic communicators based on self-cleanable triboelectric nanogenerators. *Nature Communications, 9*(1). *Scopus, 9*(1), 1804. Advance online publication. doi:10.103841467-018-03954-x PMID:29728600

Li, H., Tian, C., & Deng, Z. (2014). Energy harvesting from low frequency applications using piezoelectric materials. *Applied Physics Reviews, 1*(4), 041301. doi:10.1063/1.4900845

Li, L., Xu, J., Liu, J., & Gao, F. (2018). Recent progress on piezoelectric energy harvesting: Structures and materials. *Advanced Composites and Hybrid Materials*, *1*(3), 478–505. doi:10.100742114-018-0046-1

Li, P., Ryu, J., & Hong, S. (2019). Piezoelectric/Triboelectric Nanogenerators for Biomedical Applications. In *Nanogenerators*. IntechOpen. doi:10.5772/intechopen.90265

Li, Z., Liu, Y., Yin, P., Peng, Y., Luo, J., Xie, S., & Pu, H. (2021). Constituting abrupt magnetic flux density change for power density improvement in electromagnetic energy harvesting. *International Journal of Mechanical Sciences*, *198*, 106363. doi:10.1016/j.ijmecsci.2021.106363

Lin, L., Wang, S., Xie, Y., Jing, Q., Niu, S., Hu, Y., & Wang, Z. L. (2013). Segmentally Structured Disk Triboelectric Nanogenerator for Harvesting Rotational Mechanical Energy. *Nano Letters*, *13*(6), 2916–2923. doi:10.1021/nl4013002 PMID:23656350

Lin, Z., & Yang, J. (2016). Recent Progress in Triboelectric Nanogenerators as a Renewable and Sustainable Power Source. *Journal of Nanomaterials*, *2016*, 1–24. doi:10.1155/2016/5651613

Liu, H., Fu, H., Sun, L., Lee, C., & Yeatman, E. M. (2021). Hybrid energy harvesting technology: From materials, structural design, system integration to applications. *Renewable & Sustainable Energy Reviews*, *137*, 110473. doi:10.1016/j.rser.2020.110473

Liu, H., Hou, C., Lin, J., Li, Y., Shi, Q., Chen, T., Sun, L., & Lee, C. (2018). A non-resonant rotational electromagnetic energy harvester for low-frequency and irregular human motion. *Applied Physics Letters*, *113*(20), 203901. doi:10.1063/1.5053945

Liu, W., Wang, Z., Wang, G., Liu, G., Chen, J., Pu, X., Xi, Y., Wang, X., Guo, H., Hu, C., & Wang, Z. L. (2019). Integrated charge excitation triboelectric nanogenerator. *Nature Communications*, *10*(1), 1. doi:10.103841467-019-09464-8 PMID:30926813

Lv, H., Liang, L., Zhang, Y., Deng, L., Chen, Z., Liu, Z., Wang, H., & Chen, G. (2021). A flexible spring-shaped architecture with optimized thermal design for wearable thermoelectric energy harvesting. *Nano Energy*, *88*, 106260. doi:10.1016/j.nanoen.2021.106260

Mahmud, M. A. P., Huda, N., Farjana, S. H., & Lang, C. (2018). Environmental profile evaluations of piezoelectric polymers using life cycle assessment. *IOP Conference Series. Earth and Environmental Science*, *154*(1), 012017. doi:10.1088/1755-1315/154/1/012017

Mao, Y., Geng, D., Liang, E., & Wang, X. (2015). Single-electrode triboelectric nanogenerator for scavenging friction energy from rolling tires. *Nano Energy*, *15*, 227–234. doi:10.1016/j.nanoen.2015.04.026

Meng, B., Tang, W., Too, Z., Zhang, X., Han, M., Liu, W., & Zhang, H. (2013). A transparent single-friction-surface triboelectric generator and self-powered touch sensor. *Energy & Environmental Science*, *6*(11), 3235–3240. doi:10.1039/c3ee42311e

Mort, J. (2003). Polymers, Electronic Properties. In R. A. Meyers (Ed.), *Encyclopedia of Physical Science and Technology* (3rd ed., pp. 645–657). Academic Press. doi:10.1016/B0-12-227410-5/00597-4

Moure, A., Izquierdo Rodríguez, M. A., Rueda, S. H., Gonzalo, A., Rubio-Marcos, F., Cuadros, D. U., Pérez-Lepe, A., & Fernández, J. F. (2016). Feasible integration in asphalt of piezoelectric cymbals for vibration energy harvesting. *Energy Conversion and Management*, *112*, 246–253. doi:10.1016/j.enconman.2016.01.030

Na, L., Yuhao, W., Huanqing, H., & Tongshuo, L. (2021). A review on vibration energy harvesting. *E3S Web of Conferences*, *245*, 01041. doi:10.1051/e3sconf/202124501041

Nayak, A., Saini, V. K., & Bhushan, B. (2021). Nanomaterials for Energy Harvesting and Storage: An Overview. In Applications of Nanomaterials in Agriculture, Food Science, and Medicine (pp. 188–203). IGI Global. doi:10.4018/978-1-7998-5563-7.ch011

Niu, S., Liu, Y., Chen, X., Wang, S., Zhou, Y. S., Lin, L., Xie, Y., & Wang, Z. L. (2015). Theory of freestanding triboelectric-layer-based nanogenerators. *Nano Energy*, *12*, 760–774. doi:10.1016/j.nanoen.2015.01.013

Niu, S., Wang, S., Liu, Y., Zhou, Y. S., Lin, L., Hu, Y., Pradel, K. C., & Wang, Z. L. (2014). A theoretical study of grating structured triboelectric nanogenerators. *Energy and Environmental Science*, *7*(7), 2339–2349. *Scopus*. Advance online publication. doi:10.1039/C4EE00498A

Niu, S., & Wang, Z. L. (2015). Theoretical systems of triboelectric nanogenerators. *Nano Energy*, *14*, 161–192. doi:10.1016/j.nanoen.2014.11.034

Pandya, S., Velarde, G., Zhang, L., Wilbur, J. D., Smith, A., Hanrahan, B., Dames, C., & Martin, L. W. (2019). New approach to waste-heat energy harvesting: Pyroelectric energy conversion. *NPG Asia Materials*, *11*(1), 1. doi:10.103841427-019-0125-y

Peddigari, M., Lim, K.-W., Kim, M., Park, C. H., Yoon, W.-H., Hwang, G.-T., & Ryu, J. (2018). Effect of elastic modulus of cantilever beam on the performance of unimorph type piezoelectric energy harvester. *APL Materials*, *6*(12), 121107. doi:10.1063/1.5070087

Percy, S., Knight, C., McGarry, S., Post, A., Moore, T., & Cavanagh, K. (2014). Thermal to Electrical Energy Converters. In S. Percy, C. Knight, S. McGarry, A. Post, T. Moore, & K. Cavanagh (Eds.), *Thermal Energy Harvesting for Application at MEMS Scale* (pp. 51–67). Springer. doi:10.1007/978-1-4614-9215-3_5

Photovoltaic effect. (n.d.). Energy Education. https://energyeducation.ca/encyclopedia/Photovoltaic_effect

Priya, S., Song, H.-C., Zhou, Y., Varghese, R., Chopra, A., Kim, S.-G., Kanno, I., Wu, L., Ha, D. S., Ryu, J., & Polcawich, R. G. (2019). A Review on Piezoelectric Energy Harvesting: Materials, Methods, and Circuits. *Energy Harvesting and Systems*, *4*(1), 3–39. doi:10.1515/ehs-2016-0028

PZT Properties & PZT Manufacturing. (n.d.). APC. https://www.americanpiezo.com/piezo-theory/pzt.html

Ramírez, J. M., Gatti, C. D., Machado, S. P., & Febbo, M. (2018). A multi-modal energy harvesting device for low-frequency vibrations. *Extreme Mechanics Letters*, *22*, 1–7. doi:10.1016/j.eml.2018.04.003

Ren, Z., Wu, L., Pang, Y., Zhang, W., & Yang, R. (2022). Strategies for effectively harvesting wind energy based on triboelectric nanogenerators. *Nano Energy*, *100*, 107522. doi:10.1016/j.nanoen.2022.107522

Rostami, S., Heiska, K., Puchko, O., Leppanen, K., & Valkama, M. (2018). Wireless powered wake-up receiver for ultra-low-power devices. *2018 IEEE Wireless Communications and Networking Conference (WCNC)*, (pp. 1–5). IEEE. 10.1109/WCNC.2018.8377436

Rostami, S., Trinh, H. D., Lagen, S., Costa, M., Valkama, M., & Dini, P. (2020). Wake-Up Scheduling for Energy-Efficient Mobile Devices. *IEEE Transactions on Wireless Communications*, *19*(9), 6020–6036. doi:10.1109/TWC.2020.2999339

Safaei, M., Sodano, H. A., & Anton, S. R. (2019). A review of energy harvesting using piezoelectric materials: State-of-the-art a decade later (2008–2018). *Smart Materials and Structures*, *28*(11), 113001. doi:10.1088/1361-665X/ab36e4

Salauddin, M., & Park, J. Y. (2017). Design and experiment of human hand motion driven electromagnetic energy harvester using dual Halbach magnet array. *Smart Materials and Structures*, *26*(3), 035011. doi:10.1088/1361-665X/aa573f

Sandhu, M. M., Khalifa, S., Jurdak, R., & Portmann, M. (2021). Task Scheduling for Energy-Harvesting-Based IoT: A Survey and Critical Analysis. *IEEE Internet of Things Journal*, *8*(18), 13825–13848. doi:10.1109/JIOT.2021.3086186

Sebald, G., Guyomar, D., & Agbossou, A. (2009). On thermoelectric and pyroelectric energy harvesting. *Smart Materials and Structures*, *18*(12), 125006. doi:10.1088/0964-1726/18/12/125006

Sezer, N., & Koç, M. (2021). A comprehensive review on the state-of-the-art of piezoelectric energy harvesting. *Nano Energy*, *80*, 105567. doi:10.1016/j.nanoen.2020.105567

Sharma, H., Haque, A., & Jaffery, Z. A. (2019). Maximization of wireless sensor network lifetime using solar energy harvesting for smart agriculture monitoring. *Ad Hoc Networks*, *94*, 101966. doi:10.1016/j.adhoc.2019.101966

Sharpes, N., Abdelkefi, A., & Priya, S. (2014). Comparative Analysis of One-Dimensional and Two-Dimensional Cantilever Piezoelectric Energy Harvesters. *Energy Harvesting and Systems*, *1*(3–4), 209–216. doi:10.1515/ehs-2014-0007

Shibata, K., Wang, R., Tou, T., & Koruza, J. (2018). Applications of lead-free piezoelectric materials. *MRS Bulletin*, *43*(8), 612–616. doi:10.1557/mrs.2018.180

Siddiqui, S., Kim, D.-I., Roh, E., Duy, L. T., Trung, T. Q., Nguyen, M. T., & Lee, N.-E. (2016). A durable and stable piezoelectric nanogenerator with nanocomposite nanofibers embedded in an elastomer under high loading for a self-powered sensor system. *Nano Energy*, *30*, 434–442. doi:10.1016/j.nanoen.2016.10.034

Struwig, M. N., Wolhuter, R., & Niesler, T. (2018). Nonlinear model and optimization method for a single-axis linear-motion energy harvester for footstep excitation. *Smart Materials and Structures, 27*(12). *Smart Materials and Structures*, *27*(12), 125007. Advance online publication. doi:10.1088/1361-665X/aae6e7

lDumkova, J., Smutna, T., Vrlikova, L., Coustumer, P., Vevera, Z., Docekal, B., Mikuska, P., Capka, L., Fictum, P., Hampl, A., & Buchtoava, M. (n.d.). *Sub-chronic inhalation of lead oxide nanoparticles revealed their broad distribution and tissue-specific subcellular localization in target organs: Particle and Fibre Toxicology.* BMC. https://particleandfibretoxicology.biomedcentral.com/articles/10.1186/s12989-017-0236-y

Sun, C., Shang, G., Zhu, X., Tao, Y., & Li, Z. (2013). Modeling for Piezoelectric Stacks in Series and Parallel. *2013 Third International Conference on Intelligent System Design and Engineering Applications*, (pp. 954–957). IEEE. 10.1109/ISDEA.2012.228

Tang, W., Jiang, T., Fan, F. R., Yu, A. F., Zhang, C., Cao, X., & Wang, Z. L. (2015). Liquid-metal electrode for high-performance triboelectric nanogenerator at an instantaneous energy conversion efficiency of 70.6%. *Advanced Functional Materials, 25*(24), 3718–3725. doi:10.1002/adfm.201501331

Thakre, A., Kumar, A., Song, H.-C., Jeong, D.-Y., & Ryu, J. (2019). Pyroelectric Energy Conversion and Its Applications—Flexible Energy Harvesters and Sensors. *Sensors (Basel), 19*(9), 2170. doi:10.339019092170 PMID:31083331

The Feynman Lectures. (n.d.). *Physics Vol. II Ch. 1: Electromagnetism.* Feynman Lectures. https://www.feynmanlectures.caltech.edu/II_01.html#Ch1-S4

US EPA. O. (2014, October 28). *Geothermal Heating and Cooling Technologies* [Overviews and Factsheets]. EPA. https://www.epa.gov/rhc/geothermal-heating-and-cooling-technologies

Vukajlović, N., Milićević, D., Dumnić, B., & Popadić, B. (2020). Comparative analysis of the supercapacitor influence on lithium battery cycle life in electric vehicle energy storage. *Journal of Energy Storage, 31*, 101603. doi:10.1016/j.est.2020.101603

Wang, H., & Jasim, A. (2020). Piezoelectric energy harvesting from pavement. In *Eco-Efficient Pavement Construction Materials* (pp. 367–382). Elsevier. doi:10.1016/B978-0-12-818981-8.00014-X

Wang, H., Jasim, A., & Chen, X. (2018a). Energy harvesting technologies in roadway and bridge for different applications – A comprehensive review. *Applied Energy, 212*, 1083–1094. doi:10.1016/j.apenergy.2017.12.125

Wang, H., Jasim, A., & Chen, X. (2018b). Energy harvesting technologies in roadway and bridge for different applications – A comprehensive review. *Applied Energy, 212*, 1083–1094. doi:10.1016/j.apenergy.2017.12.125

Wang, H., Xu, L., Bai, Y., & Wang, Z. L. (2020). Pumping up the charge density of a triboelectric nanogenerator by charge-shuttling. *Nature Communications, 11*(1), 1. doi:10.103841467-020-17891-1 PMID:32826902

Wang, J., Li, F., Zhu, F., & Schmidt, O. G. (2019). Recent Progress in Micro-Supercapacitor Design, Integration, and Functionalization. *Small Methods, 3*(8), 1800367. doi:10.1002mtd.201800367

Wang, L., Todaria, P., Pandey, A., O'Connor, J., Chernow, B., & Zuo, L. (2016). An Electromagnetic Speed Bump Energy Harvester and Its Interactions With Vehicles. *IEEE/ASME Transactions on Mechatronics, 21*(4), 1985–1994. doi:10.1109/TMECH.2016.2546179

Wang, Y., Chen, R., Chen, T., Lv, H., Zhu, G., Ma, L., Wang, C., Jin, Z., & Liu, J. (2016). Emerging non-lithium ion batteries. *Energy Storage Materials*, *4*, 103–129. doi:10.1016/j.ensm.2016.04.001

Wang, Y., Yang, E., Chen, T., Wang, J., Hu, Z., Mi, J., Pan, X., & Xu, M. (2020). A novel humidity resisting and wind direction adapting flag-type triboelectric nanogenerator for wind energy harvesting and speed sensing. *Nano Energy*, *78*, 105279. doi:10.1016/j.nanoen.2020.105279

Wang, Z., Ruan, Z., Ng, W. S., Li, H., Tang, Z., Liu, Z., Wang, Y., Hu, H., & Zhi, C. (2018). Integrating a Triboelectric Nanogenerator and a Zinc-Ion Battery on a Designed Flexible 3D Spacer Fabric. *Small Methods*, *2*(10), 1800150. doi:10.1002mtd.201800150

Wang, Z. L. (2017). On Maxwell's displacement current for energy and sensors: The origin of nanogenerators. *Materials Today*, *20*(2), 74–82. doi:10.1016/j.mattod.2016.12.001

Wang, Z. L., Jiang, T., & Xu, L. (2017). Toward the blue energy dream by triboelectric nanogenerator networks. *Nano Energy*, *39*, 9–23. doi:10.1016/j.nanoen.2017.06.035

Wang, Z. L., Lin, L., Chen, J., Niu, S., & Zi, Y. (2016a). Triboelectric Nanogenerator: Freestanding Triboelectric-Layer Mode. In Z. L. Wang, L. Lin, J. Chen, S. Niu, & Y. Zi (Eds.), *Triboelectric Nanogenerators* (pp. 109–153). Springer International Publishing. doi:10.1007/978-3-319-40039-6_5

Wang, Z. L., Lin, L., Chen, J., Niu, S., & Zi, Y. (2016b). Triboelectric Nanogenerator: Lateral Sliding Mode. In Z. L. Wang, L. Lin, J. Chen, S. Niu, & Y. Zi (Eds.), *Triboelectric Nanogenerators* (pp. 49–90). Springer International Publishing. doi:10.1007/978-3-319-40039-6_3

What are the Advantages and Disadvantages of Geothermal Energy? (n.d.). TWI Global. https://www.twi-global.com/technical-knowledge/faqs/geothermal-energy/pros-and-cons.aspx

What is Piezoelectricity? (n.d.). *OnScale*. http://https%253A%252F%252Fonscale.com%252Fpiezoelectricity%252Fwhat-is-piezoelectricity%252F

Wu, C., Wang, A. C., Ding, W., Guo, H., & Wang, Z. L. (2019). Triboelectric Nanogenerator: A Foundation of the Energy for the New Era. *Advanced Energy Materials*, *9*(1), 1802906. doi:10.1002/aenm.201802906

Wu, Y., Ma, Y., Zheng, H., & Ramakrishna, S. (2021). Piezoelectric materials for flexible and wearable electronics: A review. *Materials & Design*, *211*, 110164. doi:10.1016/j.matdes.2021.110164

Xu, C., Ren, B., Di, W., Liang, Z., Jiao, J., Li, L., Li, L., Zhao, X., Luo, H., & Wang, D. (2012). Cantilever driving low frequency piezoelectric energy harvester using single crystal material 0.71Pb(Mg1/3Nb2/3)O3-0.29PbTiO3. *Applied Physics Letters*, *101*(3), 033502. doi:10.1063/1.4737170

Xu, C., Ren, B., Liang, Z., Chen, J., Zhang, H., Yue, Q., Xu, Q., Zhao, X., & Luo, H. (2012). Nonlinear output properties of cantilever driving low frequency piezoelectric energy harvester. *Applied Physics Letters*, *101*(22), 223503. doi:10.1063/1.4768219 PMID:23284178

Xu, C., Zi, Y., Wang, A. C., Zou, H., Dai, Y., He, X., Wang, P., Wang, Y.-C., Feng, P., Li, D., & Wang, Z. L. (2018). On the Electron-Transfer Mechanism in the Contact-Electrification Effect. *Advanced Materials*, *30*(15), 1706790. doi:10.1002/adma.201706790 PMID:29508454

Xu, Q., Gao, A., Li, Y., & Jin, Y. (2022). Design and Optimization of Piezoelectric Cantilever Beam Vibration Energy Harvester. *Micromachines*, *13*(5), 5. doi:10.3390/mi13050675 PMID:35630142

Xu, W., Huang, L.-B., Wong, M.-C., Chen, L., Bai, G., & Hao, J. (2017). Environmentally Friendly Hydrogel-Based Triboelectric Nanogenerators for Versatile Energy Harvesting and Self-Powered Sensors. *Advanced Energy Materials, 7*(1). *Advanced Energy Materials*, *7*(1), 1601529. doi:10.1002/aenm.201601529

Xu, W., Wong, M.-C., & Hao, J. (2019). Strategies and progress on improving robustness and reliability of triboelectric nanogenerators. *Nano Energy*, *55*, 203–215. doi:10.1016/j.nanoen.2018.10.073

Yang, Y., Zhu, G., Zhang, H., Chen, J., Zhong, X., Lin, Z.-H., Su, Y., Bai, P., Wen, X., & Wang, Z. L. (2013). Triboelectric Nanogenerator for Harvesting Wind Energy and as Self-Powered Wind Vector Sensor System. *ACS Nano*, *7*(10), 9461–9468. doi:10.1021/nn4043157 PMID:24044652

Yao, L., Zhao, H. D., Dong, Z. Y., Sun, Y. F., & Gao, Y. F. (2012). Laboratory Testing of Piezoelectric Bridge Transducers for Asphalt Pavement Energy Harvesting. *Key Engineering Materials*, *492*, 172–175. . doi:10.4028/www.scientific.net/KEM.492.172

Ye, S., Cheng, C., Chen, X., Chen, X., Shao, J., Zhang, J., Hu, H., Tian, H., Li, X., Ma, L., & Jia, W. (2019). High-performance piezoelectric nanogenerator based on microstructured P(VDF-TrFE)/BNNTs composite for energy harvesting and radiation protection in space. *Nano Energy*, *60*, 701–714. doi:10.1016/j.nanoen.2019.03.096

Yi, J. W., Shih, W. Y., & Shih, W.-H. (2002). Effect of length, width, and mode on the mass detection sensitivity of piezoelectric unimorph cantilevers. *Journal of Applied Physics*, *91*(3), 1680–1686. doi:10.1063/1.1427403

Yue, X., Kauer, M., Bellanger, M., Beard, O., Brownlow, M., Gibson, D., Clark, C., MacGregor, C., & Song, S. (2017). Development of an Indoor Photovoltaic Energy Harvesting Module for Autonomous Sensors in Building Air Quality Applications. *IEEE Internet of Things Journal*, *4*(6), 2092–2103. doi:10.1109/JIOT.2017.2754981

Yun, S., Zhang, Y., Xu, Q., Liu, J., & Qin, Y. (2019). Recent advance in new-generation integrated devices for energy harvesting and storage. *Nano Energy*, *60*, 600–619. doi:10.1016/j.nanoen.2019.03.074

Zabek, D., & Morini, F. (2019). Solid state generators and energy harvesters for waste heat recovery and thermal energy harvesting. *Thermal Science and Engineering Progress*, *9*, 235–247. doi:10.1016/j.tsep.2018.11.011

Zareei, M., Vargas-Rosales, C., Hernndez, R. V., & Azpilicueta, El. (2019). Efficient Transmission Power Control for Energy-harvesting Cognitive Radio Sensor Network. *2019 IEEE 30th International Symposium on Personal, Indoor and Mobile Radio Communications (PIMRC Workshops)*, (pp. 1–5). IEEE. 10.1109/PIMRCW.2019.8880825

Zhang, H., Zhang, C., Zhang, J., Quan, L., Huang, H., Jiang, J., Dong, S., & Luo, J. (2019). A theoretical approach for optimizing sliding-mode triboelectric nanogenerator based on multi-parameter analysis. *Nano Energy*, *61*, 442–453. doi:10.1016/j.nanoen.2019.04.057

Zhang, Y., Luo, A., Wang, Y., Dai, X., Lu, Y., & Wang, F. (2020). Rotational electromagnetic energy harvester for human motion application at low frequency. *Applied Physics Letters*, *116*(5), 053902. doi:10.1063/1.5142575

Zhao, T., Jiang, W., Niu, D., Liu, H., Chen, B., Shi, Y., Yin, L., & Lu, B. (2017). Flexible pyroelectric device for scavenging thermal energy from chemical process and as self-powered temperature monitor. *Applied Energy*, *195*, 754–760. doi:10.1016/j.apenergy.2017.03.097

Zhu, J., Jia, L., & Huang, R. (2017). Electrospinning poly(l-lactic acid) piezoelectric ordered porous nanofibers for strain sensing and energy harvesting. *Journal of Materials Science Materials in Electronics*, *28*(16), 12080–12085. doi:10.100710854-017-7020-5

Zhu, Y., Yang, Z., Jiao, C., Ma, M., & Zhong, X. (2022). A Multi-Modal Energy Harvesting Device for Multi-Directional and Low-Frequency Wave Energy. *Frontiers in Materials*, *9*, 898921. https://www.frontiersin.org/articles/10.3389/fmats.2022.898921. doi:10.3389/fmats.2022.898921

Zorlu, Ö., & Kulah, H. (2012). A Miniature and Non-Resonant Vibration-based Energy Harvester Structure. *Procedia Engineering*, *47*, 664–667. doi:10.1016/j.proeng.2012.09.234

Chapter 11
Detecting Phishing URLs With Word Embedding and Deep Learning

Ali Selamat

(iD) https://orcid.org/0000-0001-9746-8459

Universiti Teknologi Malaysia, Malaysia & Hradec Kralove University, Czech Republic

Nguyet Quang Do

Universiti Teknologi Malaysia, Malaysia

Ondrej Krejcar

(iD) https://orcid.org/0000-0002-5992-2574

Hradec Kralove University, Czech Republic

ABSTRACT

The past decade has witnessed the rapid development of natural language processing and machine learning in the phishing detection domain. However, there needs to be more research on word embedding and deep learning for malicious URL classification. Inspired to solve this problem, this chapter aims to examine the application of word embedding and deep learning in extracting features from website URLs. To achieve this, several word embedding techniques, such as Keras, Word2Vec, GloVe, and FastText, were used to learn feature representations of webpage URLs. The obtained feature vectors were fed into a deep-learning model based on CNN-BiGRU for extraction and classification. Two different datasets were used to conduct numerous experiments, while various metrics were utilized to evaluate the phishing detection model's performance. The obtained findings indicated that when combined with deep learning, Keras outperformed other text embedding methods and achieved the best results across all evaluation metrics on both datasets.

DOI: 10.4018/978-1-6684-7684-0.ch011

INTRODUCTION

Phishing is currently a major area of interest within the field of cyber security. In recent years, there have been numerous efforts to mitigate phishing attacks and protect end users from losing their private and sensitive information to cybercriminals. Especially, the past decade has witnessed the rapid development of natural language processing (NLP) and machine learning (ML) in many phishing detection-related tasks (Bharadwaj et al., 2022; Tajaddodianfar et al., 2020; Vinayakumar et al., 2018; Yuan et al., 2018). Phishing detection is usually divided into three categories: malicious URL classification, phishing website detection, and phishing email detection. Malicious URL classification comprises related studies solely focusing on the detection of phishing attacks using URL-based features (T. Feng & Yue, 2020; Huang et al., 2019). Meanwhile, phishing website detection makes use of various features extracted from web pages to classify malicious and benign websites (J. Feng et al., 2020; Le-Nguyen et al., 2021). Phishing email detection regards emails as the medium to conduct phishing activities and extracts features from the email's header and body for classification (Hasan et al., 2021). Even though these three approaches use different types of features, these attributes can be extracted manually or automatically using numerous feature representation techniques and various learning algorithms.

NLP and ML have been widely used in phishing website and email detection to represent and extract features from the content of web pages and emails. However, the extraction of content-based features is time-consuming and computationally expensive (Ya et al., 2019). As a result, researchers and security experts have shifted their attention to phishing detection based on only URL features. Yet, much of the research on phishing URL detection up to now has focused more on word embedding and traditional ML (Bharadwaj et al., 2022; Yuan et al., 2018). On the one hand, conventional ML techniques require manual feature engineering. On the other hand, they cannot handle a substantial amount of data, resulting in a deficiency in detection accuracy (Bello et al., 2021). In addition, URL structure is different compared to website and email text. URL sometimes contains meaningless words and more information can be found at the character level. Nevertheless, the existing character embedding method disregards the relationships between characters and fails to capture meaningful information in long sequences. Whereas, the word-level embedding techniques can discover the semantic and syntactic similarities among words (Le et al., 2018). Still, there has been little research on word embedding with deep learning to identify malicious URLs.

Motivated to solve these problems, this chapter aims to investigate the application of word embedding and deep learning (DL) in extracting features from website URLs. First, word-level embedding can discover the semantic meaning and syntactic structure within URL sequences. Second, DL can prevent hand-crafted feature engineering and third-party dependency. Third, the extraction of URL-based features can reduce computational complexity. To achieve this, website URLs are used as inputs and pre-processed using several word embedding techniques (Keras, Word2Vec, GloVe, and FastText). Next, the obtained feature representations are fed into DL layers consisting of CNN and BiGRU for feature extraction and classification. Finally, website URLs are identified as malicious or benign based on the probability calculated by the Sigmoid function in the output layer. The main objectives of this chapter are as follows:

- To conduct a comparative analysis using various word embedding techniques to obtain feature representations from website URLs.
- To propose a DL-based phishing detection model using CNN-BiGRU to combine their complementary effects and improve the overall performance accuracy.

- To evaluate the performance of the proposed model using two datasets of different sizes and distributions to reflect real-world scenarios.

RELATED WORK

Human vocabulary is normally presented in the form of text that machines are unable to understand. To make traditional ML or DL models comprehend and process human natural language, linguistic data needs to be transformed into numeric values. These numerical representations should be able to capture the statistical inferences as well as the contextual and semantic meaning of the input data (Hasan et al., 2021). NLP is a method used to discover rich information in the text from syntactic and semantic perspectives. The syntactic and semantic patterns of words from the text corpus are represented by the embedded vectors via the NLP model (Zhang et al., 2021). NLP is mainly classified into two groups: non-sequential and sequential (Vinayakumar et al., 2018). Non-sequential disregards the order of information and is unable to capture the spatial relationships between characters or words. In addition, they also require hand-crafted feature engineering (Le et al., 2018), fail to detect unknown features (Rao et al., 2019), and cause a sparsity issue (Sahoo et al., 2017). Techniques that belong to this category include Term Frequency-Inverse Document Frequency (TF-IDF), Bag-of-Word (BoW), n-gram, etc. Whereas, sequential approaches are modern text representation techniques that can overcome the limitations of conventional (non-sequential) methods. Sequential representation can capture the correlations between words, preserve the word order (Vinayakumar et al., 2019), and is the main focus of this chapter. Examples of sequential methods are Keras embedding, Word2Vec, GloVe, and FastText, which will be described in the following subsections.

Keras Embedding

Keras framework offers a built-in embedding layer that can be used for neural networks to represent textual data. This embedding layer is often defined as the first layer in a neural network structure (Hiransha et al. 2018). It is a flexible layer that can be used as part of a DL model. Thereby, the embedding for all the words in the training datasets is learned simultaneously with the model itself. In Keras embedding, the input sequence is first tokenized by words and each word is then encoded by a unique integer. Each encoded sequence is normalized to the same length so that it can be processed by DL algorithms.

Keras embedding was used by Hiransha et al. (2018) to build a model based on DL for phishing email detection. Particularly, Keras was implemented as the first hidden layer in the proposed architecture, followed by the convolutional layer of the CNN algorithm. The obtained results showed that Keras embedding combined with CNN provided a dense vector representation for words. This architecture was used to classify phishing and legitimate emails with relatively high detection accuracies (94.2% with email header and 96.8% without header).

Similarly, Vinayakumar et al. (2018) proposed a model, called DeepEmailNet (DEN), for spam email detection. The proposed model used Keras embedding to convert email features into numerical vectors and utilized DL techniques to distinguish between legitimate and spam emails. The experimental results indicated that the proposed architecture outperformed the conventional ML technique (Support Vector Machine) and classical text representation (TF-IDF). This is primarily because Keras embedding can capture the semantic and contextual information in the input data, which traditional text representation methods fail to do.

Due to the benefits that Keras embedding offers, most DL models use this approach for text representation to preserve the sequence information in the input data (Vinayakumar et al., 2018). For instance, Wei et al. (2019) presented a lightweight DL architecture to detect malicious URLs in real time. In this study, word embedding was used as the first layer in the deep neural network structure. The authors claimed that word embedding is better in comparison to one-hot encoding. This is because word embedding considers the relationship among characters and enhances the performance of NLP-related problems.

Ya et al. (2019) proposed an approach called NeuralAS to detect spoofed URLs using word embedding and the DL algorithm. Word-level embedding was used to segment the URLs into sequences to learn feature representations of phishing websites effectively. At the same time, Bidirectional Long Short-Term Memory (BiLSTM) was employed as a learning algorithm to extract URL-based features efficiently. Results obtained from various experiments showed that the proposed solution provided higher accuracies than other baseline models using character-level embedding or traditional ML (Random Forest and Decision Tree).

Word2Vec

Word2Vec was first developed by Mikolov et al. (2013) at Google and since then has become one of the most well-known pre-trained word embedding techniques in the NLP domain. Word2Vec is a dense, low-dimension vector representation of words that has rich semantic and contextual information (Zheng et al. 2018). In the Word2Vec embedding method, a large textual corpus is normally used as the input to create an n-dimensional vector space (Yuan et al., 2018). The position of each word in the vector space is denoted by a vector. Similar words are assigned similar positions in space, and the similarity between words can be described by the spatial distance (Vinayakumar et al., 2018).

Yuan et al. (2018) introduced a novel framework that utilized Word2Vec to learn URL embeddings for phishing detection. According to the authors, Word2Vec is an effective text representation technique that has several advantages over traditional language modeling methods. Word2Vec does not require prior knowledge, manual information, and network load. It can be applied seamlessly with the existing classification models for fast and accurate detection of phishing websites. When compared with other embedding strategies such as Continuous Bag-of-Words (CBOW), GloVe, and Doc2Vec, it is observed that there was a slight difference in the performance accuracy. However, Word2Vec performed the best in the given dataset with an accuracy of 99.69%. Also in this study, conventional ML approaches were used as classifiers. All classification models demonstrated comparative performance, with XGBoost achieving the highest detection accuracy of 99.79%.

Afzal et al. (2021) developed an LSTM-based model, named URLdeepDetect, to identify malicious URLs. The proposed approach consisted of two different techniques, including DL and classical ML for phishing detection. The former implemented Word2Vec and LSTM, while the latter employed URL encryption and k-means clustering. In the Word2Vec-LSTM approach, word embedding generated by a vector space model was used to discover the semantics of URLs. Their embeddings were utilized as inputs to the LSTM model to encapsulate the sequential information of the entire URLs. Skip-gram was selected to train the Word2Vec model, and the resulting word vectors were given into the LSTM layer. The authors in this study believed that LSTM was the best model for classification tasks that involve the learning of word embedding.

Wang et al. (2019) suggested a phishing detection model, named PDRCNN, based on word embedding and DL to classify malicious and benign URLs. Word embedding was a part of data pre-processing where URL strings were transformed into feature vectors. These vector representations were then passed to the DL model based on the CNN-BiLSTM algorithm for feature extraction and classification. The authors also used the Bigram embedding method as a baseline model for comparison to evaluate the proposed PDRCNN's ability to detect phishing web pages. The obtained findings indicated that Bigram combined with traditional ML techniques (Naïve Bayes, Logistic Regression, and Gradient Boosting Decision Tree) produced significantly lower performance accuracies than the proposed PDRCNN model. These results demonstrated that the combination of Word2Vec and DL algorithms can outperform conventional text representation and ML methods.

Besides LSTM, GRU is another variant of the RNN classifier. Wu et al (2022) proposed a method based on Bidirectional GRU and an attention-based mechanism for malicious URL detection. In the data pre-processing phase, Word2Vec was used to obtain the word vectors of the input URLs and to facilitate subsequent feature extraction. A dropout mechanism was implemented after the embedding layer to avoid overfitting, while an attention mechanism was applied after the BiGRU layers to strengthen the importance of the key information. Thus, the dropout-attention BiGRU (DA-BiGRU) model was formed. Finally, a comparative analysis was conducted by comparing the DA-BiGRU model with other DL algorithms, such as MLP and BiLSTM. The obtained results showed that the proposed method performed better than other baseline architectures, achieving the highest accuracy of 97.92%.

All four RNN-based models, including LSTM, GRU, BiLSTM, and BiGRU, were implemented by Feng and Yue (2020) for the classification of phishing URLs. Word2Vec embedding scheme was used to encode the URL into a 16-dimension vector, and the encoded URL was fed into the input layer of each deep neural network. In this study, four RNN models achieved equivalent phishing detection accuracies (more than 99%) and were able to capture relevant features, such as protocol, IP address, special character, and different paths in URLs.

GloVe (Global Vector for Word Representation)

Like Word2Vec, GloVe is a pre-trained model for word embedding commonly used in the field of NLP. GloVe was trained on a dataset containing one billion tokens with a vocabulary of 400 thousand words and various embedding sizes, such as 50, 100, 200, and 300 dimensions. While Word2Vec is provided by Google, GloVe is a pre-trained model from Stanford with word embedding trained on Wikipedia data (*GloVe: Global Vectors for Word Representation*, n.d.).

Bharadwaj et al. (2022) constructed a malicious URL detector using NLP to obtain word vector representations from URL features. Two different types of features were used in this study, including statistical features and GloVe embedded features. The lexical features extracted from URL and word embeddings obtained from the GloVe model were fed into SVM and ANN classifiers to classify malicious and benign URLs. GloVe was used in the phishing URL detector instead of Word2Vec to extract vector representation of words. This is due to the fact that GloVe can perform better than Word2Vec in many NLP-based tasks. Results obtained from the experiments revealed that classification models using GloVe-embedded features performed better than those using only statistical features. In addition, among two malicious URL detection models using GloVe, the one with the ANN classifier produced a higher accuracy. The authors believed that the use of GloVe-based features helped enhance the accuracy of ML classifiers and improve the overall performance of the malicious URL detector.

Le-Nguyen et al. (2023) designed a system to search, extract, and analyze suspicious websites. The system determines whether these web pages are legitimate or phishing based on three different types of features: URL, graphical interfaces, and HTML content. GloVe was used for semantic comparison between two HTML documents to get the vector representation of HTML contents. Then, Cosine distance was employed to measure the resemblances between two vectors. Combined with URL and visual similarities, these values were fed into a decision model using ML classifiers (Support Vector Machine, Decision Tree, and Random Forest). Since an imbalanced dataset was used to train the phishing detection model, Recall was selected as an evaluation metric to assess the performance of the proposed solution. The experimental results showed that the Support Vector Machine achieved the highest Recall of 96%, while the other two classifiers produced a significantly lower measure of 90.19%.

Mustafa Hilal et al. (2023) developed a model based on Artificial Fish Swarm Algorithm (AFSA) and DL to distinguish between malicious and genuine URLs. The proposed model applied GloVe as a text embedding technique and GRU integrated with AFSA as a classifier. Compared with the baseline algorithms, the proposed model obtained the best performance accuracy of 99.60%.

Benavides-Astudillo et al. (2023) proposed a model for phishing detection using NLP and DL. The proposed model used two text embedding methods to extract features from the website content and utilized four DL algorithms to classify web pages as legitimate or phishing. Specifically, Keras embedding was combined with GloVe to obtain the semantic and syntactic features of the website's HTML code. LSTM, GRU, and their bidirectional versions (BiLSTM, BiGRU) were employed to determine which algorithm produced the best performance. After conducting various experiments, the authors concluded that BiGRU yielded the highest detection rate of 97.39% when integrating Keras with GloVe for text representation.

FastText

Similar to Word2Vec and GloVe, FastText is another word embedding method in the pre-trained category. FastText is an open-source library developed by Facebook AI Research (*FastText*, n.d.). It was designed to achieve scalable solutions for efficient text classification and learning word vector representations. FastText solves the problem of time complexities on very large and imbalanced datasets. FastText integrates some of the most popular techniques in the field of NLP and ML, such as Bag-of-Words, Bags of n-grams, and the Huffman algorithm.

A DL architecture, called Texception, was proposed by Tajaddodianfar et al. (2020) that leveraged both character-level and word-level embeddings for phishing URL detection. FastText was implemented for word-level embedding in constructing the Texception model. Similar to Word2Vec, FastText has two variants: CBOW and Skip-gram. Skip-gram was used in this study where the generated word embeddings served as inputs to the CNN layer. Results obtained from the study showed that FastText outperformed classical word embedding approaches (e.g., BOW). Plus, the use of word embeddings to improve classification tasks has been proven in the phishing detection domain.

Ravi et al. (2018) introduced a model to distinguish between phishing and legitimate emails using distributed representation. In the proposed model, FastText was utilized to obtain feature vectors from email text, while Softmax was used to make the final classification. Based on the observation from various experiments, the proposed solution attained a high F1-Score (99%) on both the training and testing corpus. With this result, the authors believed that FastText alone could provide reliable performance in detecting phishing emails even without any ML classifier. In addition, this distributed representation technique could also reduce computational constraints and was suitable for real-world applications.

Likewise, Tahsin et al. (2020) suggested an approach to classify emails into multiple categories (including spam) without any ML classifier. In this study, the authors used FastText for text embedding and as a linear classifier. In addition to FastText, Softmax was used for classification by calculating the probability distribution of different classes. The metrics involved in the performance evaluation of the proposed approach were precision, recall, and F1-score. Results derived from the experiments demonstrated that FastText performed well even on small datasets. Moreover, by treating the email classification task as a text classification problem, FastText provided satisfactory results as a classifier and even produced better performance than CNN during the k-fold validation phase.

Somesha and Pais (2022) also proposed a framework for phishing email classification using six word embedding techniques and five ML classifiers. The word embedding methods included TF-IDF, Count Vectorization (CV), Word2Vec (Skip-gram, CBOW), and FastText (Skip-gram, CBOW). The traditional ML learners consisted of Random Forest (RF), Support Vector Machine (SVM), Logistic Regression (LR), Decision Tree (DT), and XGBoost. Results from various experiments showed that FastText (CBOW) embedding technique and RF classifier formed the best combination with the highest detection accuracy of 99.50%. Besides accuracy, Matthews's Correlation Coefficient (MCC) was also used as an evaluation metric for an imbalanced dataset. The highest MCC value of 98.88% was achieved when FastText (skip-gram) was combined with RF classifier.

A three-step framework was introduced by Chen & Omote (2022) for malicious URL detection. The proposed framework comprised three steps: segmentation, embedding, and machine learning. The first step contained two methods: segmentation by alphabet (splitting the URL by characters) and segmentation by token (splitting the URL by separators). The second step consisted of four different embedding techniques: TF-IDF, Word2Vec, GloVe, and FastText. The final step involved five ML classifiers: RF, Light Gradient Boosting Machine (GBM), LR, DT, and CNN. The experimental results revealed that Word2Vec, GloVe, and FastText obtained higher F1 score than TF-IDF. With these findings, the authors believed that context-considering embedding methods (Word2Vec, GloVe, and FastText) played a more important role than the context-agnostic embedding technique (TF-IDF) in malicious URL classification.

Research Novelty

In short, the above studies can be viewed from three perspectives: phishing detection, feature representation, and learning algorithm. Phishing detection is categorized into three different groups, including malicious URL classification, phishing website detection, and phishing email detection. Although these three approaches use different types of features, these attributes can be extracted manually or automatically using numerous feature representation techniques and various learning algorithms. Feature representations using word embedding techniques are grouped into four categories, such as Keras embedding, Word2Vec, GloVe, and FastText as described in the previous section. Learning algorithms for feature extraction and classification are divided into two classes: traditional ML and DL.

This chapter focuses on phishing URL detection using word embedding and DL. First, malicious URL classification is one of the most common phishing detection approaches. This is because the majority of phishing activities are performed through the spreading of malicious URLs (Sahoo et al., 2017). URL features are considered lightweight and hence, can be extracted rapidly. In addition, this approach does not require the URL to be launched, or the need to visit the website content (Al-Ahmadi & Alharbi, 2020). Therefore, relying on URL-based features is sufficient as they can offer a fair trade-off between performance and detection accuracy (Pooja & Sridhar, 2020).

Second, modern word embedding techniques (sequential) solve the problems of the classical methods (non-sequential). BoW, an example of a non-sequential approach, is frequently used for feature extraction with conventional ML classifiers. This approach fails to discover the word order in the URL sequence, requires hand-crafted feature engineering to select relevant features, is unable to recognize unseen words, and needs a large vocabulary for model training (Rao et al., 2019). Meanwhile, sequential techniques take into consideration the order of input information, preserving the relationships between words, and maintaining their semantic and syntactic similarities.

Third, DL offers several advantages over traditional ML. For example, conventional ML approaches depend heavily on manually engineered features. Meanwhile, DL techniques can automatically extract unprocessed data and learn the relationships among features generated from the input information, even with unstructured data (Iqbal et al., 2021; Lee et al., 2021). Moreover, DL is able to handle a large amount of information and demonstrates strong learning capability when training on massive datasets (Ozcan et al., 2021). Furthermore, DL can detect zero-day attacks more efficiently as it is more flexible in adapting to more complicated behaviors in phishing patterns (Yang et al., 2019).

Consequently, this chapter examines modern word embedding techniques and uses DL to detect malicious URLs. Tables 1 and 2 summarize the related works on word embedding and ML for phishing detection and highlight the novelty of this research. It is observed that some of the previous studies focused on email classification (Hasan et al., 2021; Hiransha & Unnithan, n.d.; Ravi et al., n.d.; Somesha & Pais, 2022; Tahsin et al., 2020; Vinayakumar et al., 2018), while others emphasized phishing website detection (Le-Nguyen et al., 2023; Rao et al., 2022). On the one hand, email text is different from URL string. An email usually consists of numerous sentences. Each sentence is constructed by various words and each word is separated by a space. Whereas, a URL string is a sequence of characters. URL sometimes contains words without any specific meaning, where each word is separated by a special character or symbol. On the other hand, phishing website detection involves the extraction of multiple features from webpage content. Acquiring a large number of features and performing feature selection requires a substantial amount of time, effort, and cost. Due to these reasons, this chapter pays more attention to URL-based features in order to reduce computational complexities and achieve fast and accurate detection of phishing attacks.

Besides, most of the related work used only a single type of word embedding technique. For instance, Hiransha & Unnithan (2018), Wei et al. (2019), and Ya et al. (2019) only used Keras embedding in their studies. Afzal et al. (2021), Feng & Yue (2020), Wang et al. (2019), and Wu et al. (2022) only applied Word2Vec for text representation. Bharadwaj et al. (2022), Mustafa Hilal et al. (2023) and Le-Nguyen et al. (2023) employed GloVe as their word embedding technique, while Ravi et al. (2018), Tahsin et al. (2020), and Tajaddodianfar et al. (2020) implemented FastText to obtain feature vector representations. Although several text embedding methods were used by Hasan et al. (2021), Somesha & Pais (2022), Rao et al. (2022), Chen & Omote (2022), Vinayakumar et al. (2018), and Yuan et al. (2018), their major limitations were the use of conventional ML classifiers or single DL algorithms. Besides, multiple features were utilized for extraction, while inappropriate metrics were applied for evaluation in imbalanced datasets.

Plus, even when DL was implemented in previous studies, none of them combined CNN with Bi-GRU for classification. CNN is a well-known algorithm that can learn spatial representation and extract features from raw input data. BiGRU can learn the temporal representation of URL features and regard both directions of information in the URL sequence. However, their combination has not been fully explored for malicious URL classification. Overall, there is a lack of a comparative study that provides a comprehensive comparison among all four modern text embedding methods using DL technologies. To the best of the authors' knowledge, this chapter is the first study that provides a comparative analysis of different word embedding techniques with DL algorithms.

Table 1. Comparison between the related work and this study

Reference	Feature	Word embedding				DL algorithm
	URL	Keras	Word2Vec	GloVe	FastText	CNN-BiGRU
(Hiransha & Unnithan, 2018)		✓				
(Wei et al., 2019)	✓	✓				
(Ya et al., 2019)	✓	✓				
(Yuan et al., 2018)	✓		✓	✓		
(W. Wang et al., 2019)	✓		✓			
(T. Feng & Yue, 2020)	✓		✓			
(Afzal et al., 2021)	✓		✓			
(Wu et al., 2022)	✓		✓			
(Bharadwaj et al., 2022)	✓			✓		
(Le-Nguyen et al., 2023)				✓		
(Mustafa Hilal et al., 2023)	✓			✓		
(Tajaddodianfar et al., 2020)	✓				✓	
(Ravi et al., 2018)					✓	
(Tahsin et al., 2020)					✓	
(Hasan et al., 2021)		✓		✓		
(Somesha & Pais, 2022)			✓		✓	
(Rao et al., 2022)			✓	✓	✓	
(Chen & Omote, 2022)			✓	✓	✓	
(Vinayakumar et al., 2018)		✓	✓		✓	
This study	✓	✓	✓	✓	✓	✓

MATERIALS AND METHODS

The Proposed Model

Figure 1 illustrates the general architecture of the proposed phishing detection model consisting of three phases. In Phase 1, website URLs are collected from public datasets (Ebbu2017 and 420K-PD) and pre-processed using several word embedding techniques. During this procedure, raw URLs are converted to feature vectors through tokenizing, encoding, and padding. Tokenization is the first step in the text representation process where each URL string is separated into a sequence of individual words. Each word is encoded using a unique integer, and the encoded sequence is standardized into a fixed length through padding or truncating. Except for Keras which uses a built-in layer for text embedding, other word embedding techniques (Word2Vec, GloVe, and FastText) are pre-trained models. The weights obtained from these pre-trained models can be used to replace the random weights initially assigned by the Keras embedding layer. Outputs from the embedding layers are vector representations of URL sequences and served as inputs to the subsequent DL layers.

Table 2. Strengths and limitations of previous studies

Reference	Strengths	Limitations
(Afzal et al., 2021; Bharadwaj et al., 2022; T. Feng & Yue, 2020; Mustafa Hilal et al., 2023; Tajaddodianfar et al., 2020; W. Wang et al., 2019; Wei et al., 2019; Ya et al., 2019)	• Use DL algorithms.	• Employ a single type of word embedding technique.
(Wu et al., 2022)	• Apply attention-based mechanism.	• Employ a single type of word embedding technique. • Use a single type of DL algorithm.
(Hiransha & Unnithan, 2018)	• Use DL algorithms.	• Apply to email classification.
(Ravi et al., 2018; Tahsin et al., 2020)	• Classify without learning algorithms.	• Apply to email classification.
(Le-Nguyen et al., 2023)	• Train on an imbalanced dataset.	• Extract multiple features from webpage content. • Use unsuitable metrics for an imbalanced dataset.
(Somesha & Pais, 2022)	• Train on multiple imbalanced datasets. • Use various text embedding methods. • Use a suitable metric (MCC) for imbalanced datasets.	• Apply traditional ML classifiers.
(Benavides-Astudillo et al., 2023)	• Use various text embedding methods.	• Use a single type of DL algorithm.
(Chen & Omote, 2022)	• Use various text embedding methods.	• Apply traditional ML classifiers. • Use a single type of DL algorithm.
(Yuan et al., 2018)	• Train on large and multiple datasets. • Use various text embedding methods.	• Apply traditional ML classifiers. • Use inappropriate metrics for imbalanced datasets.
(Hasan et al., 2021)	• Compare Keras embedding with GloVe.	• Use a single type of DL algorithm. • Apply to email classification.
(Rao et al., 2022)	• Use numerous text embedding methods.	• Extract content-based features. • Employ traditional ML classifiers.
(Vinayakumar et al., 2018)	• Use multiple text embedding methods.	• Apply to email classification.

Figure 1. The proposed phishing detection model

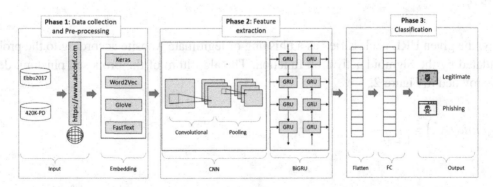

In Phase 2, URL features are extracted using DL algorithms. An ensemble DL architecture based on CNN-BiGRU was proposed to address the limitations of the individual algorithms and join their complementary effects. Specifically, CNN performs convolutional operations on the input vectors and uses a pooling layer to reduce the dimension of the feature maps created by the convolutional layer.

$$c_i = f\left(W \otimes x_{i:i+h-1} + b_i\right) \tag{1}$$

$$p_i = max(c_i) \tag{2}$$

In the above equations, c_i and p_i denote the outputs of the convolutional and max pooling layers, $f()$ is the activation function, W refers to the convolutional filer, $\otimes$, h, and b_i are the convolution operation, kernel size, and bias, respectively. Outputs from the CNN layers are fed into the GRU layers, where each GRU unit consists of an update gate and a reset gate given as follows:

$$z_t = \sigma\left(W_z x_t + R_z h_{t-1} + b_z\right) \tag{3}$$

$$r_t = \sigma\left(W_r x_t + R_r h_{t-1} + b_r\right) \tag{4}$$

where z_t and r_t refer to the update gate and reset gate, x_t is the embedding vector at time t, W and R denote the weight matrices for recurrent hidden and input layer, and σ represents an activation function. The hidden state ($\tilde{h}_t$) and output (h_t) of the GRU layer are mathematically presented by:

$$\tilde{h}_t = \tanh\left(W_h x_t + r_t R_h h_{t-1} + b_h\right) \tag{5}$$

$$h_t = z_t \tilde{h}_t + \left(1 - z_t\right) h_{t-1} \tag{6}$$

BiGRU combines the past ($\overleftarrow{h}_t$) and future ($\overrightarrow{h}_t$) information of the input data and its outputs (H_t) are flattened before passing to a fully-connected (FC) layer.

$$H_t = \overrightarrow{h}_t \oplus \overleftarrow{h}_t \tag{7}$$

Finally, the given URL is classified as a phishing or legitimate website according to the probability (y_p) calculated by the Sigmoid activation function. The algorithm of the proposed phishing detection model is provided in Figure 2.

$$y_p = Sigmoid\left(y^*\right) = \frac{1}{1 + y^*} \tag{8}$$

Figure 2. Pseudo code of the proposed phishing detection model

---

Algorithm 1: Phishing URL detection based on word embedding and DL

Input: *U*

Output: *Pr, Rc, F₁, Acc*

  1    $U_{train}, U_{val}, U_{test} \leftarrow$ train_valid_test_split (*U*);

  2   *filters* ← '!"#\$%&()*+,-./:;<=>?@[\\]^_`{|}~\t\n';

  3   *token_word ← Tokenize(U_{train}, filters);*

  4   *Index_seq ← Indexing(U_{train}, U_{val}, U_{test}, token_word);*

  5    $E_{w\_train}, E_{w\_val}, E_{w\_test} \leftarrow$ Padding(*Index _seq*);

  6   *weights ← Load(Keras, Word2Vec, GloVe, FastText)*

  7   *Input_tensor ← Input(URL_length);*

  8   *Input_layer ← Embedding(vocab_size, dimension, weights)(Input_tensor);*

  9   *Conv ← CNN(Input_layer);*

 10   *Max ← Max_Pooling_1D(Conv);*

 11   *Drop ← Drop_out(Max);*

 12   *BiG ← Bidirectional_GRU(Drop);*

 13   *Flat ← Flatten(BiG);*

 14   *FC ← Dense(Flat);*

 15   *M ← Sigmoid(FC);*

 16   $M_c \leftarrow$ Model_compile(*Adam_optimizer, Learning_rate*);

 17   **for** *i* in *Epoch* **do**

 18        $M_f \leftarrow$ Model_fit(E_{w_train}, E_{w_val}, *Batch_size*);

 19   **end for**

 20   *Pr, Rc, F₁, Acc* ← Model_evaluate(E_{w_test});

Dataset

In real-world scenarios, the number of phishing or malicious URLs is significantly lower than legitimate or benign samples. Consequently, two datasets of different distributions (balanced and imbalanced) are used to reflect real-life situations. Moreover, to emphasize the potential of DL in handling a large amount of data and to highlight the robustness of the proposed model, different data sizes are utilized to conduct numerous experiments. Ebbu2017 dataset (Sahingoz et al., 2019) consists of 73,575 samples, with 37,175 phishing URLs and 36,400 legitimate URLs. The 420K-PD dataset (Yuan et al., 2018) contains 420,464 instances, including 75,643 malicious URLs and 344,821 benign URLs as shown in Figure 3. Figure 4 demonstrates the distribution of phishing (bad) and legitimate (good) URLs in both datasets. The former (D1) is a balanced dataset with 49.5% of phishing and 50.5% of legitimate URLs. The latter (D2) is an imbalanced dataset with only 18% of malicious URLs.

Detailed statistics of D1 and D2 are provided in Tables 3 and 4. The longest and shortest URLs in D1 are phishing URLs with a length of 3992 and 9, respectively. Similarly, malicious URLs in D2 have a maximal length of 2307 and a minimal length of 1. The distributions of URL length for both classes in two datasets are displayed in Figure 5 and Figure 6. The normal ranges for phishing and legitimate URLs for D1 are 0 to 400 and 0 to 250, while those for D2 are 0 to 250 and 0 to 200. Maximal URL length is an essential value as it will later be used in the parameter setting for the phishing detection model.

Figure 3. Size of datasets D1 and D2

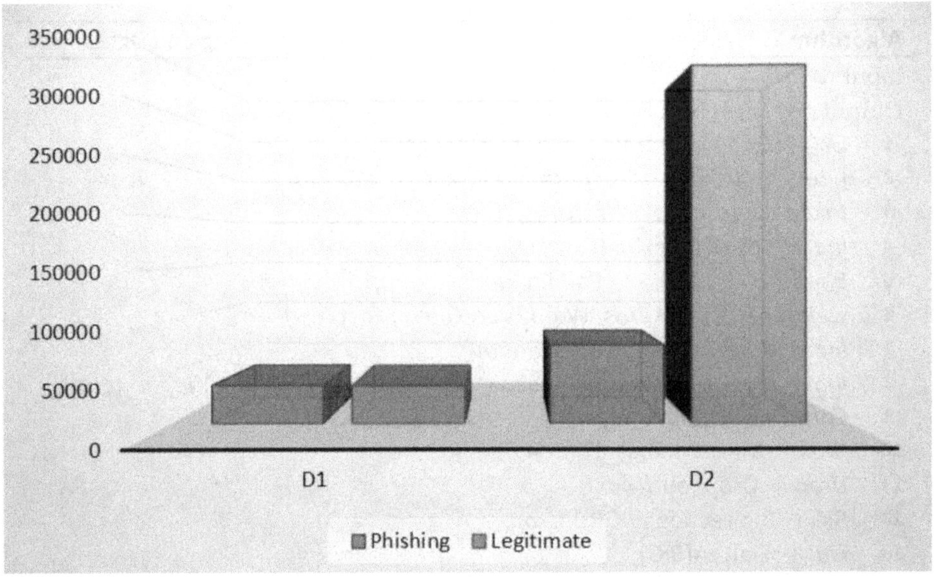

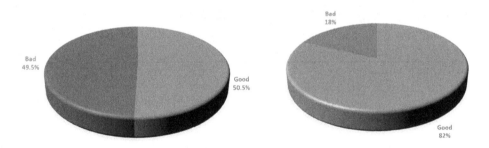

Figure 4. Distribution of phishing and legitimate URLs in a) D1 and b) D2

Table 3. Statistics of D1

D1	Min. URL length	Max. URL length	Avg. URL length	Standard deviation	Median
Phishing	9	3992	78.51	69.07	59
Legitimate	14	341	59.36	23.53	55
Total	9	3992	69.04	52.68	56

Table 4. Statistics of D2

D2	Min. URL length	Max. URL length	Avg. URL length	Standard deviation	Median
Phishing	1	2307	54.45	61.72	38
Legitimate	6	1025	47.00	25.49	42
Total	1	2307	48.34	35.02	41

Figure 5. Distribution of URL length in D1 by a) Dataset and b) Class label

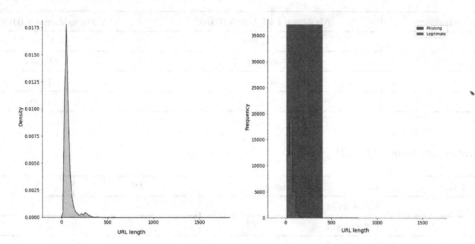

Figure 6. Distribution of URL length in D2 by a) Dataset and b) Class label

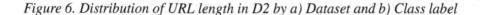

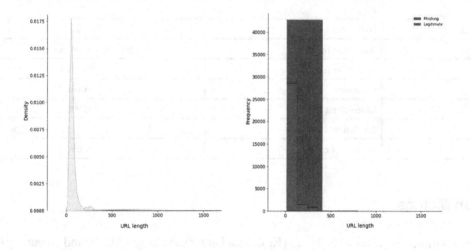

Parameter Settings

Parameter settings for several layers in the proposed phishing detection model are given in Tables 5 and 6. The maximum URL length and embedding dimension vary according to the size of the datasets and the type of embedding techniques. For the DL algorithm, convolutional layers with 32 and 16 kernels of size 3 are used for D1 and D2, followed by a max pooling layer with the same window size and stride. GRU layers with 64 units for D1 and 16 units for D2 in each direction (forward and backward) are utilized to form the BiGRU architecture. Additionally, dropout layers (dropout rate = 0.5) are implemented in between DL layers to avoid overfitting (Jabir & Falih, 2021). Finally, a fully-connected layer with 8 neurons is applied before the output layer. For model compilation, Rectified Linear Unit (ReLU) and Sigmoid are used as activation functions in the hidden and output layers. Adam is chosen as an optimizer with a learning rate of 0.005. For model training, batch size and epochs are set as specified in the table.

Table 5. Parameter settings for word embedding

Word embedding	Maximum URL length (D1/D2)	Embedding size (D1/D2)
Keras	200/100	16/16
Word2Vec	400/200	225/175
GloVe	400/100	100/100
FastText	200/300	300/300

Table 6. Parameter settings for DL

Layer	Parameter	D1	D2
CNN	Number of kernels	32	16
	Kernel size	3	
Max pooling	Window size	2	
	Stride	2	
BiGRU	Number of units	64	16
Dropout	Rate	0.5	
Fully Connected	Number of neurons	8	
Hidden	Activation function	Rectified Linear Unit (ReLU)	
Output	Activation function	Sigmoid	
Training	Optimizer	Adam	
	Learning rate	0.005	
	Batch size	1024	256
	Number of epochs	10	

Evaluation Metrics

For model evaluation, Precision (Pr), Recall (Rc), Area Under the Curve (AUC), and Accuracy (Acc) are used as performance metrics for D1. The formulas of these metrics are mathematically given as follows:

$$Pr = \frac{TP}{TP + FP} \tag{1}$$

$$Rc = \frac{TP}{TP + FN} \tag{2}$$

$$Acc = \frac{TP + TN}{TP + TN + FP + FN} \tag{3}$$

where TP, FP, TN, and FN refer to True Positive, False Positive, True Negative, and False Negative, respectively.

Since D2 is an imbalanced dataset, conventional metrics are not suitable to assess the performance of the phishing detection model. In scenarios where imbalanced class distribution is involved, F1-score (F1) and MCC (Misra & Rayz, 2022; Sahoo et al., 2017; Somesha & Pais, 2022) are more appropriate metrics than AUC or Acc. F1 and MCC can be measured using the following formulas:

$$F1 = 2.\frac{Pr.Rc}{Pr + Rc} \qquad (4)$$

$$MCC = \frac{TP.TN - FP.FN}{\sqrt{(TP + FP)(TP + FN)(TN + FP)(TN + FN)}} \qquad (5)$$

RESULTS AND DISCUSSION

Several experiments were conducted to provide a comparative analysis among different word embedding techniques. Table 7 and Table 8 summarize the results obtained when training the proposed phishing detection model on D1 and D2, respectively. Their graphical representations are illustrated in Figures 5 and 6. It can be seen that among four text embedding methods, Keras produced the best results across all performance metrics for both datasets. This can be explained by the fact that pre-trained models (Word-2Vec, GloVe, and FastText) may not be suitable for malicious URL classification since these publicly available word embeddings are trained using human-readable corpora. Whereas, URLs are different from these corpora since they sometimes contain unreadable words to human eyes (Huang et al., 2019).

Among pre-trained text embedding models, Word2Vec displays the worst performance, while FastText performed the best. A possible explanation for this is that Word2Vec only learns feature representations from the local perspective, while GloVe can extract features from the global aspect. In addition, FastText can identify rare words which is an advantage over Word2Vec and GloVe.

Table 7. Performance metrics of various word embedding techniques on D1

Word Embedding	Pr (%)	Rc (%)	AUC (%)	Acc (%)
Word2Vec	92.13	91.98	97.72	92.01
GloVe	96.73	96.35	99.47	96.48
FastText	96.68	97.72	99.63	97.15
Keras	**99.05**	**98.68**	**99.90**	**98.86**

Table 8. Performance metrics of various word embedding techniques on D2

Word Embedding	Pr (%)	Rc (%)	F1 (%)	MCC (%)
Word2Vec	90.30	72.36	80.34	77.26
GloVe	89.52	77.40	83.02	79.97
FastText	94.10	78.11	85.36	82.98
Keras	**95.66**	**95.00**	**95.33**	**94.31**

Figure 7. Performance comparison of four word embedding techniques on D1

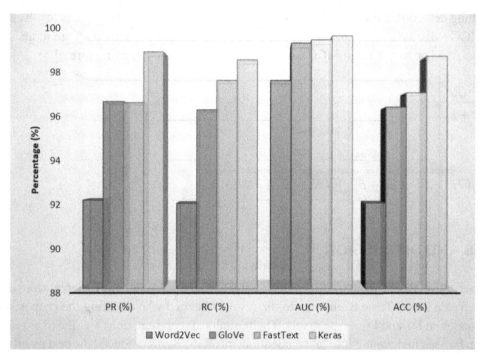

Figure 8. Performance comparison of four word embedding techniques on D2

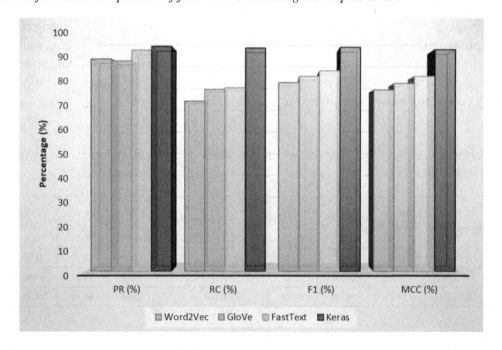

The effect of an ensemble DL architecture on phishing URL detection was examined by comparing the proposed model with individual DL classifiers (CNN and BiGRU separately). Results given in Tables 9 and 10 showed that for both D1 and D2, BiGRU outperformed CNN and the proposed model when GloVe and FastText were used. Meanwhile, ensemble DL produced better performance when Word2Vec and Keras were applied. These findings indicate that ensemble architectures do not necessarily achieve better results than single classifiers. Instead, their performance also depends on the type of text embedding technique used in the data pre-processing phase. Figure 7 displays the Receiver Operating Characteristic (ROC) curves of four word embedding techniques with different DL algorithms on D1. Since D2 is an imbalanced dataset, AUC is not used as an appropriate metric to evaluate the phishing detection model's performance. Therefore, ROC curves of four embedding methods with various DL algorithms on D2 are not shown.

Table 9. Comparison with single DL algorithms on D1

Word Embedding	DL algorithm	Pr (%)	Rc (%)	AUC (%)	Acc (%)
Word2Vec	CNN	98.78	80.09	97.98	89.34
	BiGRU	95.88	8.065	97.48	88.37
	Proposed	92.13	91.98	97.83	**92.01**
GloVe	CNN	95.19	96.35	99.27	95.75
	BiGRU	97.61	95.43	99.59	**96.55**
	Proposed	96.73	96.35	99.30	96.48
FastText	CNN	96.61	97.77	99.63	97.13
	BiGRU	97.05	97.75	99.67	**97.35**
	Proposed	96.68	97.72	99.64	97.15
Keras	CNN	98.28	99.13	99.93	98.70
	BiGRU	98.48	98.72	99.90	98.60
	Proposed	99.05	98.68	99.90	**98.86**

Table 10. Comparison with single DL algorithms on D2

Word Embedding	DL algorithm	Pr (%)	Rc (%)	F1 (%)	MCC (%)
Word2Vec	CNN	82.22	78.93	80.54	76.40
	BiGRU	80.00	81.53	80.76	76.49
	Proposed	90.30	72.36	80.34	**77.26**
GloVe	CNN	95.32	73.00	82.68	80.44
	BiGRU	95.17	76.67	84.92	**82.69**
	Proposed	89.52	77.40	83.02	79.97
FastText	CNN	95.40	76.47	84.89	82.75
	BiGRU	92.06	82.69	87.13	**84.68**
	Proposed	94.10	78.11	85.36	82.98
Keras	CNN	93.69	92.91	93.30	91.81
	BiGRU	95.66	94.67	95.16	94.09
	Proposed	95.66	95.00	95.33	**94.31**

To highlight the potential of CNN-BiGRU, the proposed phishing detection model was also compared with another ensemble DL architecture using CNN-BiLSTM. Results provided in Table 11 and Table 12 revealed that regardless of which embedding method was used, the proposed model outperformed the baseline architecture in both D1 and D2. This suggests that BiGRU can provide competitive performance to BiLSTM although the former is less popular than the latter. Figure 8 demonstrates the ROC curve comparison between the proposed model and CNN-BiLSTM using four different word embedding methods on D1. Among four word embedding techniques, the combination of GloVe and CNN-BiLSTM displayed the worst performance, while Keras produced the best outcomes.

Figure 9. ROC curves of four word embedding techniques with different DL algorithms on D1

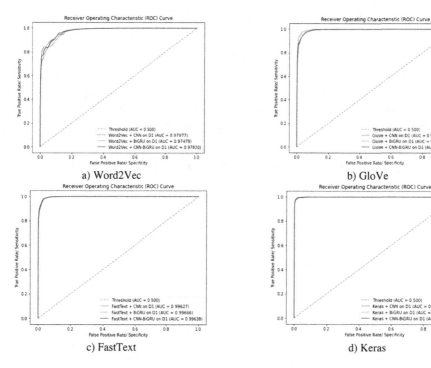

a) Word2Vec

b) GloVe

c) FastText

d) Keras

Table 11. Comparison with another DL model on D1

Word Embedding	DL model	Pr (%)	Rc (%)	AUC (%)	Acc (%)
Word2Vec	CNN-BiLSTM	91.52	84.99	96.44	88.46
	Proposed	92.13	91.98	97.42	**92.01**
GloVe	CNN-BiLSTM	87.23	65.62	82.28	77.85
	Proposed	96.73	96.35	99.47	**96.48**
FastText	CNN-BiLSTM	91.40	89.40	97.01	90.51
	Proposed	96.68	97.72	99.59	**97.15**
Keras	CNN-BiLSTM	97.68	98.55	99.85	98.08
	Proposed	99.05	98.68	99.92	**98.86**

Table 12. Comparison with another DL model on D2

Word Embedding	DL model	Pr (%)	Rc (%)	F1 (%)	MCC (%)
Word2Vec	CNN-BiLSTM	94.38	55.80	70.14	68.64
	Proposed	90.30	72.36	80.34	**77.26**
GloVe	CNN-BiLSTM	82.83	80.37	81.58	77.68
	Proposed	89.52	77.40	83.02	**79.97**
FastText	CNN-BiLSTM	97.76	59.74	74.16	73.01
	Proposed	94.10	78.11	85.36	**82.98**
Keras	CNN-BiLSTM	91.69	95.88	93.74	92.40
	Proposed	95.66	95.00	95.33	**94.31**

Figure 10. ROC curve comparison between the proposed model and CNN-BiLSTM on D1

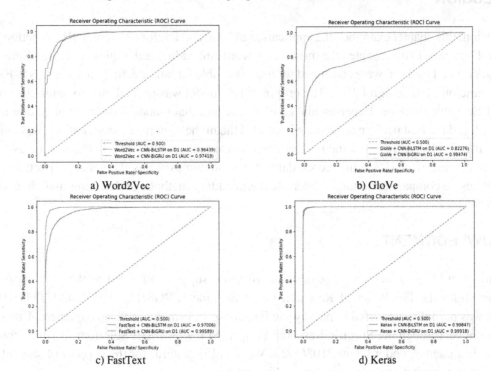

a) Word2Vec

b) GloVe

c) FastText

d) Keras

FUTURE RESEARCH DIRECTIONS

In the field of NLP, besides the aforementioned word embedding techniques, there are other methods to convert linguistic data to numerical values. One of them is a transformer-based approach that employs unsupervised learning. Bidirectional Embedding Representations from Transformers (BERT) is a type of transformer model that has gained tremendous attention among researchers in various NLP-related tasks. Unlike other unidirectional language modeling techniques, BERT considers both directions (forward and backward) of text sequence to produce bidirectional representations of words. It is more advanced than any of the word embedding techniques discussed above. As a result, one possible direction for future research is employing BERT to distinguish between legitimate and phishing URLs.

Additionally, researchers can also apply the attention-based mechanism to eliminate irrelevant features and further improve the performance accuracy of phishing detection models. The attention mechanism focuses on more important features by assigning them higher weights. It can be implemented in the data pre-processing phase after the embedding layer. Alternatively, an attention mechanism can also be deployed in the feature extraction and classification phases after the DL algorithm.

CONCLUSION

In conclusion, this chapter examined the application of NLP and DL for phishing URL detection through a comparative study. In this chapter, the most recent word embedding techniques, including Keras, Word-2Vec, GloVe, and FastText, were combined with an ensemble DL architecture based on CNN-BiGRU to classify malicious and benign URLs. The proposed DL model was trained on two datasets of different sizes and class distributions. Experimental results indicated that among four text embedding methods, Keras displayed the best performance since it yielded the highest scores across multiple evaluation metrics. Specifically, Keras achieved the highest detection accuracy of 98.86% in the first dataset and the highest MCC value of 94.31% in the second dataset. The outcomes of this chapter are expected to provide a comprehensive comparison among modern text embedding methods in detecting malicious URLs.

ACKNOWLEDGMENT

The authors would like to acknowledge that this work was supported/funded by the Ministry of Higher Education under the Fundamental Research Grant Scheme [FRGS/1/2022/ICT08/UTM/01/1]; and, this work was partially supported in part by the Faculty of Informatics and Management, University of Hradec Králové, through the Specific Research Project (SPEV), "Smart Solutions in Ubiquitous Computing Environments", under Grant 2102/2023. We are also grateful for the support of student Michal Dobrovolny in consultations regarding application aspects.

REFERENCES

Afzal, S., Asim, M., Javed, A. R., Beg, M. O., & Baker, T. (2021). URLdeepDetect: A Deep Learning Approach for Detecting Malicious URLs Using Semantic Vector Models. *Journal of Network and Systems Management*, 29(3), 1–27. doi:10.100710922-021-09587-8

Al-Ahmadi, S., & Alharbi, Y. (2020). A Deep Learning Technique For Web Phishing Detection Combined Url Features And Visual Similarity. *International Journal of Computer Networks and Communications*, 12(5), 41–54. doi:10.5121/ijcnc.2020.12503

Bello, I., Chiroma, H., Abdullahi, U. A., Gital, A. Y., Jauro, F., Khan, A., Okesola, J. O., & Abdulhamid, S. M. (2021). Detecting ransomware attacks using intelligent algorithms: Recent development and next direction from deep learning and big data perspectives. *Journal of Ambient Intelligence and Humanized Computing*, 12(9), 8699–8717. doi:10.100712652-020-02630-7

Benavides-Astudillo, E., Fuertes, W., Sanchez-Gordon, S., Nuñez-Agurto, D., & Rodríguez-Galán, G. (2023). A Phishing-Attack-Detection Model Using Natural Language Processing and Deep Learning. *Applied Sciences, 13*(9), 5275. doi:10.3390/app13095275

Bharadwaj, R., Bhatia, A., Divya Chhibbar, L., Tiwari, K., & Agrawal, A. (2022). *Is this URL Safe: Detection of Malicious URLs Using Global Vector for Word Representation*. IEEE. doi:10.1109/ICOIN53446.2022.9687204

Chen, Q., & Omote, K. (2022). *A Three-Step Framework for Detecting Malicious URLs*. doi:10.1109/ISNCC55209.2022.9851734

fastText. (n.d.). *Home*. fastText. https://fasttext.cc/

Feng, J., Zou, L., Ye, O., & Han, J. (2020). Web2Vec: Phishing Webpage Detection Method Based on Multidimensional Features Driven by Deep Learning. *IEEE Access : Practical Innovations, Open Solutions*, *8*, 221214–221224. doi:10.1109/ACCESS.2020.3043188

Feng, T., & Yue, C. (2020). Visualizing and interpreting RNN Models in URL-based phishing detection. *Proceedings of ACM Symposium on Access Control Models and Technologies, SACMAT*, (pp. 13–24). ACM. 10.1145/3381991.3395602

GloVe. (n.d.). *Global Vectors for Word Representation*. GloVe. https://nlp.stanford.edu/projects/glove/

Hasan, M. M., Zaman, S. M., Talukdar, M. A., Siddika, A., & Rabiul Alam, M. G. (2021). An Analysis of Machine Learning Algorithms and Deep Neural Networks for Email Spam Classification using Natural Language Processing. *2021 IEEE International Conference on Service Operations and Logistics, and Informatics, SOLI 2021*. IEEE. 10.1109/SOLI54607.2021.9672398

Hiransha, C.-D. M., & Unnithan, N. A. (2018). *Deep Learning Based Phishing E-mail Detection*. Cuer. http://ceur-ws.org

Huang, Y., Yang, Q., Qin, J., & Wen, W. (2019). Phishing URL detection via CNN and attention-based hierarchical RNN. *Proceedings - 2019 18th IEEE International Conference on Trust, Security and Privacy in Computing and Communications/13th IEEE International Conference on Big Data Science and Engineering, TrustCom/BigDataSE 2019*, (pp. 112–119). IEEE. 10.1109/TrustCom/BigDataSE.2019.00024

Iqbal, K., Khan, S. A., Anisa, S., Tasneem, A., & Mohammad, N. (2021). A Preliminary Study on Personalized Spam E-mail Filtering Using Bidirectional Encoder Representations from Transformers (BERT) and TensorFlow 2.0. *International Journal of Computing and Digital Systems*, *11*(1), 893–903. doi:10.12785/ijcds/110173

Jabir, B., & Falih, N. (2021). Dropout, a basic and effective regularization method for a deep learning model: A case study. *Indonesian Journal of Electrical Engineering and Computer Science*, *24*(2), 1009–1016. doi:10.11591/ijeecs.v24.i2.pp1009-1016

Le, H., Pham, Q., Sahoo, D., & Hoi, S. C. H. (2018). URLNet: Learning a URL Representation with Deep Learning for Malicious URL Detection. https://doi.org/ doi:10.48550/arxiv.1802.03162

Le-Nguyen, M.-K., Nguyen, T.-C.-H., Le, D.-T., & Chi Minh City, H. Lab Ho Chi Minh City, V., vanhoa, V., Long-Phuoc Tôn, verichainsio, & Nguyen-An, K. (2021). Hunting Phishing Websites Using a Hybrid Fuzzy-Semantic-Visual Approach; Hunting Phishing Websites Using a Hybrid Fuzzy-Semantic-Visual Approach. *2021 15th International Conference on Advanced Computing and Applications (ACOMP)*. 10.1109/ACOMP53746.2021.00012

Le-Nguyen, M.-K., Nguyen, T.-C.-H., Le, D.-T., Nguyen, V.-H., Tôn, L.-P., & Nguyen-An, K. (2023). Phishing Website Detection as a Website Comparing Problem. *SN Computer Science*, *4*(2), 122. doi:10.100742979-022-01544-9

Lee, J., Tang, F., Ye, P., Abbasi, F., Hay, P., & Divakaran, D. M. (2021). D-Fence: A flexible, efficient, and comprehensive phishing email detection system. *Proceedings - 2021 IEEE European Symposium on Security and Privacy, Euro S and P 2021*, 578–597. 10.1109/EuroSP51992.2021.00045

Mikolov, T., Chen, K., Corrado, G., & Dean, J. (n.d.). *Efficient Estimation of Word Representations in Vector Space*. Retrieved November 3, 2022, from https://ronan.collobert.com/senna/

Misra, K., & Rayz, J. T. (2022). *LMs go Phishing: Adapting Pre-trained Language Models to Detect Phishing Emails*. doi:10.1109/WI-IAT55865.2022.00028

Mustafa Hilal, A., Hassan Abdalla Hashim, A., Mohamed, H. G., Nour, M. K., Asiri, M. M., Al-Sharafi, A. M., Othman, M., Motwakel, A., & Author, C. (2023). *Malicious URL Classification Using Artificial Fish Swarm Optimization and Deep Learning*. doi:10.32604/cmc.2023.031371

Ozcan, A., Catal, C., Donmez, E., & Senturk, B. (2021). A hybrid DNN–LSTM model for detecting phishing URLs. *Neural Computing & Applications*. doi:10.100700521-021-06401-z PMID:34393380

Pooja, A. S. S. V. L., & Sridhar, M. (2020). Analysis of Phishing Website Detection Using CNN and Bidirectional LSTM. *Proceedings of the 4th International Conference on Electronics, Communication and Aerospace Technology, ICECA 2020*, (pp. 1620–1629). IEEE. 10.1109/ICECA49313.2020.9297395

Rao, R. S., Umarekar, A., Alwyn, & Pais, R. (2022). *Application of word embedding and machine learning in detecting phishing websites*. *79*, 33–45. doi:10.1007/s11235-021-00850-6

Rao, R. S., Vaishnavi, T., & Pais, A. R. (2019). PhishDump: A multi-model ensemble based technique for the detection of phishing sites in mobile devices. *Pervasive and Mobile Computing*, *60*, 101084. doi:10.1016/j.pmcj.2019.101084

Ravi, V., Anand Kumar, M., Ganesh, B. H., & Kumar, A. M. (2018). *Distributed Representation Using Target Classes: Bag of Tricks for Security and Privacy Analytics Amrita-NLP@IWSPA 2018 Distributed Representation using Target Classes: Bag of Tricks for Security and Privacy Analytics*. 21–24. Ceur. http://ceur-ws.org

Sahingoz, O. K., Buber, E., Demir, O., & Diri, B. (2019). Machine learning based phishing detection from URLs. *Expert Systems with Applications*, *117*, 345–357. doi:10.1016/j.eswa.2018.09.029

Sahoo, D., Liu, C., & Hoi, S. C. H. (2017). Malicious URL Detection using Machine Learning. *Survey (London, England)*. Advance online publication. doi:10.48550/arxiv.1701.07179

Somesha, M., & Pais, A. R. (2022). Classification of Phishing Email Using Word Embedding and Machine Learning Techniques. *Journal of Cyber Security and Mobility, 11*(3), 279–320–279–320. doi:10.13052/jcsm2245-1439.1131

Tahsin, R., Mozumder, M. H., Shahriyar, S. A., & Salim Mollah, M. A. (2020). A Novel Approach for E-mail Classification Using FastText. *2020 IEEE Region 10 Symposium, TENSYMP 2020*, 1392–1395. 10.1109/TENSYMP50017.2020.9230961

Tajaddodianfar, F., Stokes, J. W., & Gururajan, A. (2020). Texception: A Character/Word-Level Deep Learning Model for Phishing URL Detection. *ICASSP, IEEE International Conference on Acoustics, Speech and Signal Processing - Proceedings, 2020-May*, (pp. 2857–2861). IEEE. 10.1109/ICASSP40776.2020.9053670

Vinayakumar, R., Barathi Ganesh, H. B., Anand Kumar, M., Soman, K. P., & Poornachandran, P. (2018). DeepAnti-PhishNet: Applying deep neural networks for phishing email detection CEN-AISecurity@IWSPA-2018. *CEUR Workshop Proceedings, 2124*(March), 39–49.

Vinayakumar, R., Soman, K. P., Poornachandran, P., Mohan, V. S., & Kumar, A. D. (2019). ScaleNet: Scalable and Hybrid Frameworkfor Cyber Threat Situational AwarenessBased on DNS, URL,and Email Data Analysis. *Journal of Cyber Security and Mobility, 8*(2), 189–240. doi:10.13052/jcsm2245-1439.823

Wang, H., Yu, L., Tian, S., Peng, Y., & Pei, X. (2019). Bidirectional LSTM Malicious webpages detection algorithm based on convolutional neural network and independent recurrent neural network. *Applied Intelligence, 49*(8), 3016–3026. doi:10.100710489-019-01433-4

Wang, W., Zhang, F., Luo, X., & Zhang, S. (2019). PDRCNN: Precise Phishing Detection with Recurrent Convolutional Neural Networks. *Security and Communication Networks, 2019*, 1–15. doi:10.1155/2019/2595794

Wei, B., Ali Hamad, R., Yang, L., He, X., Wang, H., Gao, B., & Woo, W. L. (2019). A Deep-Learning-Driven Light-Weight Phishing Detection Sensor. *Sensors 2019, 19*(19), 4258. doi:10.3390/s19194258

Wu, T., Wang, M., Xi, Y., & Zhao, Z. (2022). Malicious URL Detection Model Based on Bidirectional Gated Recurrent Unit and Attention Mechanism. *Applied Sciences 2022, 12*(23), 12367. doi:10.3390/app122312367

Ya, J., Liu, T., Zhang, P., Shi, J., Guo, L., & Gu, Z. (2019). NeuralAS: Deep Word-Based Spoofed URLs Detection against Strong Similar Samples. *Proceedings of the International Joint Conference on Neural Networks, 2019-July*(July), (pp. 1–7). IEEE. 10.1109/IJCNN.2019.8852416

Yang, W., Zuo, W., & Cui, B. (2019). Detecting Malicious URLs via a Keyword-Based Convolutional Gated-Recurrent-Unit Neural Network. *IEEE Access : Practical Innovations, Open Solutions, 7*, 29891–29900. doi:10.1109/ACCESS.2019.2895751

Yuan, H., Yang, Z., Chen, X., Li, Y., & Liu, W. (2018). URL2Vec: URL Modeling with Character Embeddings for Fast and Accurate Phishing Website Detection. *2018 IEEE Intl Conf on Parallel & Distributed Processing with Applications, Ubiquitous Computing & Communications, Big Data & Cloud Computing, Social Computing & Networking, Sustainable Computing & Communications (ISPA/IUCC/BDCloud/SocialCom/SustainCom)*. IEEE. 10.1109/BDCloud.2018.00050

Zhang, Y., Yuan, X., & Tzeng, N. F. (2021). Platform-Oblivious Anti-Spam Gateway. *ACM International Conference Proceeding Series*, (pp. 1064–1077). ACM.. 10.1145/3485832.3488024

Zheng, H.-T., Chen, J.-Y., Yao, X., Kumar Sangaiah, A., Jiang, Y., & Zhao, C.-Z. (2018). Clickbait Convolutional. *Symmetry, 10*(5), 138. doi:10.3390ym10050138

Chapter 12
Prospects of Deep Learning and Edge Intelligence in Agriculture:
A Review

Ali Shaheen
 https://orcid.org/0000-0002-3669-8899
Dakota State University, USA

Omar El-Gayar
 https://orcid.org/0000-0001-8657-8732
Dakota State University, USA

ABSTRACT

Agriculture is one of the high labor occupations around the globe. To meet the population growth and its demand, with the increase in labor cost, there is a need to explore efficient autonomous systems which may replace the traditional methods. Computer vision, edge, and deep learning (DL) models have become a promising area of research. This new paradigm of deep edge intelligence is most appropriate for agriculture activities where real-time decision-making is very important. In this chapter, the authors conduct a systematic literature review on deep learning-aided edge intelligence (EI) applications in agriculture to gather the evidence for prospects of DL at edge in agriculture. They discuss how DL models have shown outstanding performance within limited time and computation resources, and also provide future research directions to enhance the viability and applicability of complex deep learning (DL) models deployed at edge devices in agricultural applications.

1. INTRODUCTION

Agriculture is the foundation of society and national economies, and one of the most important industries for every country. The United Nations Food and Agriculture Organization (FAO) defines food security to be existent when all people will always have economic and physical access to food that is secure, adequate, and has nutritional value for a healthy life. However, with the consistent growth in population,

DOI: 10.4018/978-1-6684-7684-0.ch012

recent studies indicate a need to increase food production by 70-90% by 2050 to cater to 9 billion people (Gulzar et al., 2020). Agriculture problems have been always one of the critical challenges for humans. Owing to a continuous decline in global cultivable land, increasing the productivity of the existing agricultural land is highly necessary (Chandra et al., 2020). Agriculture problems have been always one of the critical challenges for humans. Technology advancement has been seen in agriculture to change the conventional methods of farming through modern technologies.

Smart farming has become very popular and is important for tackling various challenges of agricultural production such as productivity, environmental impact, food security, and sustainability (Kamilaris & Prenafeta-Boldú, 2018). The rise in food demand poses several challenges to agriculture and this need has led to the scientific community focusing their efforts on developing efficient and sustainable ways to increase crop yield. Due to the disruption in the cycles of rainfall, increasing atmospheric temperatures and a rise in CO_2 emissions has brought food security to be at risk globally. This has posed severe threats to food availability, quality, quantity, and livelihoods of the stakeholders in the agricultural industry (Gulzar et al., 2020).

We have seen technology has played a vital role in agricultural advancement. Acquiring timely and reliable agriculture information such as crop growth and yields is crucial to the establishment of related policies and plans for food security, poverty reduction, and sustainable development. In recent years precision agriculture (PA) has developed rapidly, which refers to a management strategy that gathers, processes, and analyzes temporal, spatial, and individual data in agricultural production (Liu et al., 2021). The era of smart agriculture 4.0 emphasizes unmanned operations by use of the latest technology. The application of technology in agriculture aims to provide farmers with the appropriate tools to support them in their decision making and automation activities by offering products, knowledge, and services for better productivity, quality, and profit. (Friha et al., 2021).

Theories and technologies of Artificial Intelligence (AI) have made great progress when it comes to AI and computer vision (Wang et al., 2020). AI applications are based on machine learning (ML) which have long been applied in a variety of applications to discover patterns and correlations due to their capability to address linear and non-linear issues from large numbers of inputs (Liu et al., 2021). In recent years, due to the tremendous progress and popularity of image acquisition equipment, the image has become a huge amount of data and easy to obtain, which makes image analysis very challenging with traditional ML methods (Zhang et al., 2020).

Deep Learning belongs to machine learning (Zhang et al., 2020), is the most dazzling sector, and has made substantial breakthroughs in a wide spectrum of fields, ranging from computer vision, natural language processing, and big data analysis (Zhou et al., 2019), based on representation learning of data, which realizes artificial intelligence by means of artificial neural networks with many hidden layers and massive training data. Recently, DL based algorithms have achieved much higher recognition in accuracy than traditional algorithms based on shallow learning, and compared to other machine learning techniques, DL has shown powerful information extraction and processing capabilities (C.-J. Chen et al., 2021). DL methods have consistently outperformed traditional methods for object recognition and detection in the Computer Vision Competition since 2012 (Chen & Ran, 2019). In agriculture also DL has been successfully applied in applications such as weed detection, crop picking, pest control, and disease detect. The expressive power and robustness of deep learning systems can be effectively leveraged researchers to identify complex patterns from raw data and devise efficient precision agriculture methodologies (Chandra et al., 2020).

Table 1. Comparison between cloud and edge computing

	Edge Computing	Cloud Computing
Description	Computing devices are deployed at the edge of the network close to data sources. These devices are with built-in processors enabling onboard analytics or AI (e.g., UAVs and Internet of Things gateways) (Liu et al., 2021).	Cloud computing is a computing paradigm that provides end-users with infrastructure, platforms, computing resources over an Internet connection (Liu et al., 2021).
Data storage	On site (edge devices)	In the cloud
Analytics	On site (edge devices)	In the cloud
Latency	Network traffic is largely reduced since the local processing avoids much data transmission, which also reduces the cost (Wang et al., 2020)	Brings high latency and consumes much bandwidth, unable to satisfy those latency-sensitive applications, for real-time decisions (Wang et al., 2020).
Feasibility	Cost-effective, accurate, and deployable in rural area for farming (Mishra et al., 2020).	Challenging as the vast majority of farming is in rural area with limited Internet connectivity (Mishra et al., 2020).
Example	Real-time decision-making in orchards, require computer vision models to run on edge devices while performing inferences at high speed (Assunção et al., 2022).	UAVs are utilized to acquire pine trees imagery over the test sites, and then these images are transferred to the cloud to identify the infected trees (Li et al., 2021).

Edge computing has recently emerged as a complement to cloud computing for running online applications with low latency or high bandwidth needs. In the past because of computing and storage limitations the traditional method relies on cloud computing for content processing where data is streamed back to cloud servers and later the processed results are delivered to the frontend devices. This processing mode however brings high latency and consumes much bandwidth, unable to satisfy those latency-sensitive applications, for real-time decisions (Wang et al., 2020). Edge computing has many advantages over cloud computing, on one hand, data computing is put closer to the data source, which greatly facilitates the development of delay-sensitive applications. On the other hand, the network traffic is largely reduced since the local processing avoids much data transmission, which remarkably saves the cost (Wang et al., 2020). Table 1 illustrates the difference between edge and cloud computing.

The fusion between edge and AI brought in new terminology known as Edge Intelligence (EI) in the year 2018. The emergence of EI, although still in the early stages, provides a promising solution for AI applications on edge devices at the edge of the network close to data sources and has emerged as a powerful alternative to enable learning using the concepts of Edge Computing. The fundamental idea is to run AI models on intelligent edge devices. These devices have built-in processors enabling onboard analytics (e.g., UAVs, smartphones, and Internet of Things), which helps to increase productivity (Liu et al., 2021). This technology offers the ability to process certain amounts of data directly, while reducing latency, bandwidth requirement, cost, and privacy threats. Deep Learning-based EI is a rapidly evolving domain in general, especially in the agriculture sector, and is most appropriate for agriculture activities where real-time decision-making at edge is very critical (Mishra et al., 2020). A schematic illustration of EI is illustrated in Figure 1. Intelligent application tasks are done at the edge with locally generated data in a distributed manner.

There are surveys about deep learning and agriculture in various contexts but when the authors focused DL with Edge, they did not find any comprehensive review. Chandra et al., (2020) did a survey about deep learning-based plant phenotyping techniques, Kamilaris and Prenafeta-Boldú (2018) did a review of the use of convolutional neural networks (CNNs) in agriculture, Santos et al. (2019) did a survey about the deep learning techniques applied to various agricultural problems, Wang et al. (2021) in their survey compared DL with traditional machine learning for image analysis, and Zhang et al. (2020) did a review of DL in dense agricultural scenes. Overall, all studies (Chandra et al., 2020; Kamilaris & Prenafeta-Boldú, 2018; Santos et al., 2019; Wang et al., 2021; Zhang et al., 2020) suggested Deep learning as a promising technique with high performance in terms of precision and classification accuracy, outperforming existing commonly used image-processing techniques, but they were missing the aspect of fusion between DL and Edge computing.

Figure 1. Edge intelligence

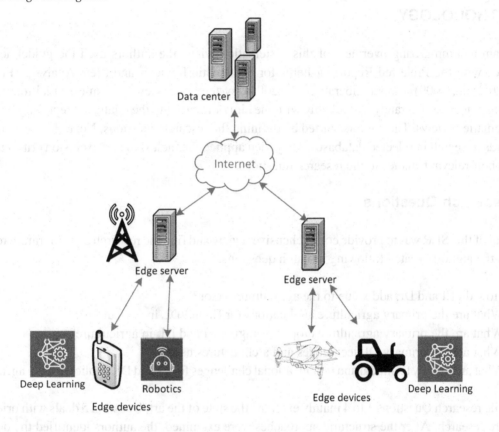

The authors only found one study about deep learning with EI; Liu et al.'s (2021) review focused only on UAV without a comprehensive review on the other edge devices like smartphone, robots, and other Internet of things (IOT). This is where the authors found this as a gap and did this study to bring a bird's eye view of the advancements in the field of deep learning and edge computing.

The research and practice of EI with DL are still in an early stage, and to the best of the authors' knowledge there is a research gap of a comprehensive review related to this paradigm. A complete survey on the current cutting-edge research is required at this time to provide a thorough review on deep learning enabled EI applications specific to agriculture and illuminate the potential future directions. In particular, the contribution of this work is as follows,

1.   A systematic literature review (SLR) is conducted to create a comprehensive presentation of existing deep learning-based applications for edge devices in the field of agriculture.
2.   Research gaps are brought to attention for future research.

This remainder of this paper is organized as follows. Section 2 explains the methodology of the conducted SLR. Section 3 presents the investigated literature and further classifies it along multiple dimensions. Section 4 discusses findings and provides impulses for further research and Section 5 concludes the paper with a summary and future work.

2. METHODOLOGY

To obtain a summarizing overview of this systematic review, the authors used the guidelines in accordance with the Preferred Reporting Items for Systematic Reviews and Meta-Analyses (PRISMA) (Liberati et al., 2009). As per Liberati et al. (2009), systematic reviews are an essential tool for summarizing evidence accurately and reliably with the aim of improving the quality of reporting by authors of systematic reviews. The authors started by defining the research questions. Next, they used different keywords to search in selected databases. They then applied the inclusion and exclusion criteria to filter out the non-relevant studies to the research questions.

2.1 Research Questions

The goal of this SLR was to provide comprehensive review and find the research gaps for future research, for this the authors created following research questions:

RQ1. How do EI and DL add value to the agriculture sector?
RQ2. What are the primary agriculture applications for EI and DL in agriculture?
RQ3. What are the primary agriculture crops leveraging EI and DL in agriculture?
RQ4. What are the primary DL techniques and architectures used?
RQ5. What are the key technical and organizational challenges for EI and DL applications in agriculture?

While research Questions 1 to 4 mainly examine the state of the art, Question 5 deals with orientation of future research. After the structural approaches were examined, the authors identified the dominant concepts. The final question aim is to focus these concepts and propose in a way which makes it easier to find starting points for future research.

2.2 Search Criteria

For existing literature, the authors systematically reviewed studies from common databases (IEEE Xplore digital library, ABI/INFORM, Web of science, and ScienceDirect). They used search query consisting of keywords/strings including Deep Learning, Edge Intelligence, Smart Framing, and AI Agriculture. The main challenge was to gather the relevant literature; authors have used DL in agriculture, but the focus of this study is DL at edge.

Due to the overlap of some databases, duplicates had to be excluded. The next section presents the inclusion and exclusion criteria that was considered in this SLR.

2.3 Inclusion and Exclusion Criteria

To filter out the relevant studies, the authors defined the following inclusion and exclusion criteria. A study had to comply with all inclusion criteria and none of the exclusion criteria to be considered in this systematic literature review.

Inclusion criteria:

1. The study is related to the deep learning in agriculture and reports evaluated approach.
2. The study application is at edge, i.e., some kind of edge device is used for inference.

Exclusion criteria:

1. The study is not published in English.
2. The study is not freely accessible through the standard university libraries.
3. The study or the presented approach is not related to the field of Agriculture.
4. The study was published prior 2018.

Figure 2 shows PRISMA flow of articles reviewed in the different phases of conducting an SLR. It maps out the number of articles identified, included, and excluded from further analysis. A total number of 46 articles were found from all searched libraries. After removing 12 duplicate articles, 34 articles remained. Subsequently, the titles and abstracts of the found articles were analyzed and at the end 26 articles were found relevant as per research questions.

To further enrich the data retrieved, only peer review publications were included in our research. The survey targeted the literature published from 2018 till this year. AI at edge is a relatively new subject area, edge artificial intelligence emerges in the Gartner Hype Cycle for the first time in August 2018 (Zhou et al., 2019), and this is the reason we just included studies from 2018 or afterwards. Furthermore, due to the language barrier, only English language publications were considered for this study.

Publications focusing other than AI in agriculture were excluded and furthermore livestock applications were excluded as well. In classification of papers, the authors refer to their research questions and applications in the field of agriculture using DL at edge.

3. RESULTS

This section summarizes the in-depth analysis of the findings from the filtered studies. The general structure provides the primary information of studies included. In Table 2 the authors have bifurcated the source of publications. In total they have included 26 studies; among those 12 articles were presented in conferences and 14 were published in journals.

Figure 2. Study selection process for systematic review

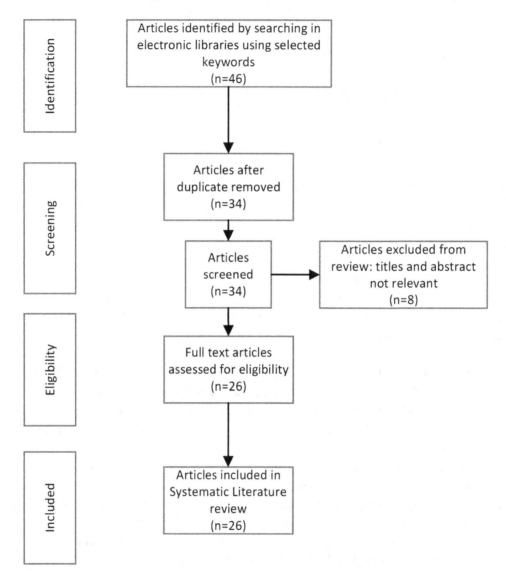

Precision Agriculture
1
Grand Total
26

Table 2. Source of publications

	Count
Conference Paper	
2018 5th International Conference on Systems and Informatics (ICSAI)	1
2019 18th IEEE International Conference On Machine Learning And Applications (ICMLA)	1
2019 IEEE International Instrumentation and Measurement Technology Conference (I2MTC)	1
2020 IEEE 17th Annual Consumer Communications & Networking Conference (CCNC)	1
2020 IEEE 3rd International Conference on Computer and Communication Engineering Technology (CCET)	1
2020 IEEE International Conference on Robotics and Automation (ICRA)	1
2021 6th International Conference for Convergence in Technology (I2CT)	1
2021 International Conference on Computer Information Science and Artificial Intelligence (CISAI)	1
2021 International Conference on Control, Automation, Power and Signal Processing (CAPS)	1
2021 XIX Workshop on Information Processing and Control (RPIC)	1
2022 IEEE International Conference on Consumer Electronics (ICCE)	1
2022 International Conference for Advancement in Technology (ICONAT)	1
Journal Article	
Artificial Intelligence in Agriculture	1
Computers and Electronics in Agriculture	1
IEEE Access	3
IEEE Geoscience and Remote Sensing Letters	1
IEEE Transactions on Computers	1
Information Processing in Agriculture	1
International Journal of Applied Earth Observation and Geoinformation	1
Procedia Computer Science	1
Smart Agricultural Technology	2
Future Internet	1

3.1 Prospects of EI and DL to the Agriculture Sector

Agriculture has conventionally been a labor-intensive occupation. To provide for the rapidly increasing population, in the face of rising labor costs, there is a need to explore autonomous alternatives in place of traditional methods. At the same time edge and AI technology have merged into a new paradigm of EI. This paradigm has become the new hotspot in research for the agriculture sector as well. DL model has shown outstanding accuracy within limited time and computation resources, compared with other machine learning methods such as Support Vector Machine, Random Forest (Liu et al., 2019). The deep learning-based models can extract the relevant features automatically and do not require manual intervention (Ismail & Malik, 2022).

With the development of unmanned aerial vehicles (UAV), research on using UAV to assist in developing precision agricultural management has become a mainstream trend. In recent years, some researchers have adopted UAV technology and DL models to predict strawberry yield, monitor and control diseases in strawberries, detect powdery mildew disease in squash, and detect citrus greening, all of which have achieved good results (Zhou et al., 2021).

The widespread distribution of smartphones among crop growers around the world offers the potential of turning the smartphone into a valuable tool for diverse communities growing food. One potential application is the development of mobile disease diagnostics through machine learning and crowdsourcing. With the help of state of art technologies like DL and cloud computing, the same can was achieved on a real-time basis with a mere click of leaf picture (S et al., 2021).

Potato, the world's most important root and tuber crop, is grown in more than 125 countries and consumed almost daily by over a billion people. Yield loss due to diseases can be serious; for example, disseminated viruses in tubers can reduce yields by 50 percent. Abnormal potato leaf detection in the mid-growth stage consists of an existing deep learning model for leaf detection and the developed explainable deep classification model to classify the detected leaves (Oishi et al., 2021).

DL can reveal the nonlinear features hidden in the data through multi-layer processing mechanism, and can obtain ''feature learning'' from a large number of training data sets; the DL based models have proven to be an effective and promising approach (C.-J. Chen et al., 2021; S. Chen et al., 2021; Li et al., 2021; Menshchikov et al., 2021; Mishra et al., 2020; Tetila et al., 2020; Xiong et al., 2020; Xu et al., 2020; Yang et al., 2020). The authors see a lot of research going and potential for future research the use of more complex DL models at edge devices with limited hardware environment which eventually will help in using smart solutions to improve production efficiency.

3.2 EI and DL Applications in Agriculture

The authors have noticed DL models have been incorporated for smart agriculture in different segments. Disease detection, crop picking, pest control, and visual classification are the main areas where DL models have been deployed for EI.

3.2.1 Disease Detection

Disease to any crop affects the demand-supply and threatens food availability. Included studies in table 3 are related to disease detection using DL and EI. Currently, infectious diseases reduce the potential yield by an average of 40% with many farmers in the developing world experiencing yield losses as high as 100% (S et al., 2021). Weeds are a big problem in agriculture because they are a major part of agricultural losses (Czymmek et al., 2019; Hafeez et al., 2021; Menshchikov et al., 2021). In fields, the prime job to fight these diseases is to continuously monitor the fields, which is laborious work. The recent adoption of smart devices is being utilized to provide automatic detection of diseases which in the end prevents severe losses. Menshchikov et al. (2021) addressed the problem of Hogweed detection, reporting on an aerial drone platform with an embedded system on board capable of real-time image processing using FCNN. Similarly, Oishi et al. (2021) developed an automated abnormal potato plant detection system that utilizes a portable video camera and DL models and detects abnormal plants or leaves considering the stage of growth. In another work, Hafeez et al. (2021) proposed a fully automatic method for weed detection by using drone and CNN. S et al., (2021) with the help of CNN architectures, proposed a system that focuses on detection and identification of the plant disease with a mere click of a leaf picture and provides solutions. Mishra et al. (2020) presented a real-time method based on deep CNN for corn leaf disease recognition. Czymmek et al. (2019) proposed a state-of-the-art DL detector to realize an efficient real-time classification of weeds on a carrot dam.

Faster R-CNN/ YOLO
Potato
Leave classification: AP 90.5%;
potato plant: AP 90%

Table 3. Previous studies on disease detection through application of deep learning and edge

Study	Specific Application	Technique/Model	Crop	
	Results		Czymmek et al. (2019)	Method detecting multiple weed species
CNN/ YOLOv3	-	Precision of 89% and recall of 86%. The average precision is 75.07%.	Hafeez et al. (2021)	Weed detection system
CNN+SVM	-	Accuracy of 96.4% in real time	Li et al. (2021)	Fast detection of pine wilt disease
CNN/ YOLOv4-tiny, YOLOv3, MobileNetv2	-	YOLOv4-tiny highest AP of 84.88%.	Menshchikov et al. (2021)	Realtime hogweed detection
CNN/ SegNet, U-Net & RefineNet	-	SegNet has the best ROC AUC 0.969	Mishra et al. (2020)	Real time corn diseases
CNN	Corn	Average accuracy of 88.66%.	Oishi et al. (2021)	Detects abnormal plants or leaves

3.2.2 Crop Picking

Picking is one of the high laborious jobs throughout the agriculture life cycle. To automate this a lot of engineering approaches have been worked on. One of the key challenges is the complex scenes with backlighting, direct sunlight, overlapping fruit and branches, blocking leaves, etc. AI has brought some very promising solutions for this, and we see more advancement in this by researchers using DL technique. Studies in table 4 are related to crop picking through DL and EI. Liu et al. (2018) distinguished not only citrus fruits but also leaves, branches, and fruits occluded by branch or leaves using YOLOv3, ResNet50, and ResNet152, which are the advanced deep CNNs. Similarly, Xu et al. (2020) proposed for the challenge of complex scenes a fast tomato detection method based on an improved YOLOv3-tiny model. Mangaonkar et al. (2022) proposed a design using DL algorithm which can identify fruits with the help of a camera module using image preprocessing supplemented with object detection. YOLO v3 model is adopted to analyze mature and unripe pitaya using AI Edge computing module; research has demonstrated that image processing based on the YOLO v3-tiny model can reach recognition accuracy up to 95% (Huang et al., 2022). A faster and more accurate vision system was developed by Xiong et al. (2021) that combined YOLOv4 and DeepSORT, two neural networks for strawberry detection, tracking and localization in real-time, which was a contunation of previous work where they used R-CNN to segment the objects in pixel level (Xiong et al., 2020). Chen et al., (2021) proposed a novel cognition framework for citrus picking robots to realize harvesting sequence planning inspired by human cognitive behaviors, using YOLOv4 model to detect the citrus fruits. He et al. (2020) proposed that transfer learning-based fruits image segmentation not only alleviates the stringent need of a large image dataset but also saves much time for training and did a comparison with three different backbone networks using Mobilenet_v2, Xception_65, and Resnet_v1_50_beta.

Table 4. Previous studies on crop picking through application of deep learning and edge

Study	Specific Application	Technique/Model	Crop	Results
Chen et al. (2021)	Framework for citrus picking robots	CNN/ YOLO V4	Citrus	Mean average precision is 97.19%
He et al. (2020)	Image Segmentation for Robots	CNN/ Xception_65, Mobilenet_v2, Resnet_v1_50_beta	Vegetables	Xception_65 mean intersection over union (MIoU) 94.9%
Huang et al. (2022)	Robotic arm for pitaya picking	CNN/ YOLO v3-tiny	Pitaya	Recognition accuracy up to 95%
Liu et al. (2018)	Citrus picking using CNN	CNN/ MaskRCNN-152	Citrus	MaskRCNN-152 highest comprehensive detection rate 86.83%
Mangaonkar et al. (2022)	Robotic arm for harvesting	CNN/ YOLOv3	Fruits	Yolo algorithm was observed to be much more accurate than others
Xiong et al. (2020)	Complex clusters of fruits to be harvested	R-CNN	fruits	Proposed method improves picking performance
Xiong et al. (2021)	Two neural networks for fruit picking	CNN/ YOLO V4 & Deep Sort	fruits	Improved picking success rate to 62.4%
Xu et al. (2020)	Tomatoes detection in complex scenes	CNN/ YOLOv3-tiny	Tomatoes	Ripe and unripe AP 91.8% and 81.5%

3.2.3 Pest Control

The pest attack on agricultural fields brings one of the most vital concerns for farmers around the world. Early and automatic identification of pest numbers and type could identify the level of damage and bring in efficient application of pesticides which reduce production cost and lower the impact on the environment, human health, and food safety. Technology has been in use to bring better and more effective solutions to these problems, using automatic and efficient image recognition methods using AI. Studies in table 5 are related to pest control through DL and EI. Suarez et al. (2021) proposed automatic pest detection and classification in the context of fruit crops based on image processing and Deep Neural Networks, employing an image collection obtained from in-field traps. Chen et al. (2021) developed a novel application for an intelligent pest recognition system to manage this pest problem, using a drone to photograph the pest with a Tiny-YOLOv3 neural network model built on an embedded system to spray pesticides only where needed. Tetila et al. (2020) observed that DenseNet-201 is the most appropriate model for the classification of soybean insect pests in their study with respect to other models.

Table 5. Previous studies on pest control through application of deep learning and edge

Study	Specific Application	Technique/Model	Crop	
	Results		Chen et al. (2021)	Real-time pest detection
CNN/ YOLO v3-tiny	longan	Mean average precision increased to 95.33% and 89.72%	Suarez et al. (2021)	Pest detection
CNN/ VGG-16	Fruits	Accuracy of 84%, with 89% and 76.7% for precision and recall respectively	Tetila et al. (2020)	Automatic diagnosis of insect pests' numbers

CNN/ DenseNet-201, Inception-Resnet-v2, ResNet-50
Soybean
DenseNet-201 achieved 94.89% accuracy

3.2.4 Visual Classification

Methods to evaluate fruits and vegetable growth are evaluated with certain objective criteria including color, texture, size, etc. These methods are time-consuming and labor-intensive with inconsistency in the inspection and classification process. In recent years edge computing and DL have shown promising results in the agriculture field. Studies in table 6 are related to crop visual classification through DL and EI. Liu et al. (2019) designed and implemented an edge computing visual system to classify vegetables and fruits. Their system has shown outstanding performance in image categorization with limited memory consumption in a short time frame. Gao et al. (2020) proposed a portable system to estimate the strawberry ripeness in real-time, which could provide support for precision strawberry harvesting infield farmers and producers. Yang et al. (2020) developed a system for real-time image segmentation and identification of agricultural crops, which can clearly identify and calculate the current agricultural production status and save the current manpower expenses by quickly scanning unmanned aerial vehicles. Zhou et al. (2021) developed an automatic strawberry maturity classification system for the rapid and accurate classification of different strawberry maturity stages with a You Only Look Once (YOLOv3).

CNN/ YOLO v3
Strawberry
0.96 AP on RF

Ismail and Malik (2022) proposed an efficient and effective machine vision system based on the state-of-the-art deep learning techniques and stacking ensemble methods to offer a non-destructive and cost-effective solution for automating the visual inspection of fruit's freshness and appearance. Manual identification of barley varieties by the naked eye is challenging and time-consuming for all stakeholders; for that Shah et al. (2022) proposed an efficient deep learning-based technique that can classify barley varieties from reg, green and blue (RGB) images.

Table 6. Previous studies on crop classification through application of deep learning and edge

Study	Specific Application	Technique/Model	Crop	
	Results		Assunção et al. (2022)	Peach maturity classification
CNN/ MobileNet	peaches	Average precision (AP) of 88.2%	Gao et al. (2020)	Strawberry ripeness with deep learning
CNN/ AlexNet	Strawberry	Prediction accuracy of 98.6%	Ismail & Malik (2022)	Real-time grading fruits
CNN/ EfficientNet, ResNet, MobileNet, Dense Net, NASNet	Fruits	Highest value of 93.8% for EfficientNetB2	Liu et al. (2019)	Vegetable and fruit image classification
CNN/ MobileNet	Vegetables & fruits	MobileNet model can achieve the state-of-art accuracy in all datasets	Osco et al. (2021)	Semantic segment citrus-trees
FCN, U-Net, SegNet, DeepLab, DDCN	citrus	DDCN achieved accuracy of 95.46%	Shah et al. (2022)	Barley classification
CNN/ VGG-16	Barley	Average accuracy of 94%	Yang et al. (2020)	Identification of agricultural crops
CNN/ SegNet, FCN-AlexNet	Rice/Corn	SegNet is relatively complete in detail processing, Rice Accuracy 96.07% & Corn 90.61%	Zhou et al. (2021)	Strawberry maturity classification

3.3 Agriculture Crops Leveraging EI and DL in Agriculture

Traditionally the field and the crops were manually handled with the help of equipment and labor. Farmers have seen substantial economic losses at times because of these traditional practices. Technology has brought a great deal in the field of agriculture, which leads to smart and digital agriculture (Zhou et al., 2021). Earlier crop disease caused great amounts of loss but now with the help of technology, if disease symptoms are identified at an early stage and remedial measures are taken then yield and quality may be preserved. In the agriculture field all kinds of crops have been leveraging the benefits of machine learning. In this study as the primary focus is towards DL at edge, the authors observed that the majority of filtered past research have focused on fruits. Figure 3 shows that focus of around 63% of studies has been towards fruits.

3.4 Existing DL Techniques and Architectures Used at Edge

Applications, such as robot vision in orchards, require computer vision models to run on edge devices while performing inferences at high speed (Assunção et al., 2022). Selection of an architecture is one of the critical decisions for EI applications, especially when models run on limited computational resources. In the authors' selected studies DL applications at edge had one technique in common, CNN-based DL architectures. CNN constitutes probably the most popular and widely used technique in agricultural research today, in problems related to image analysis (Kamilaris & Prenafeta-Boldú, 2018).

Figure 3. Type of crop

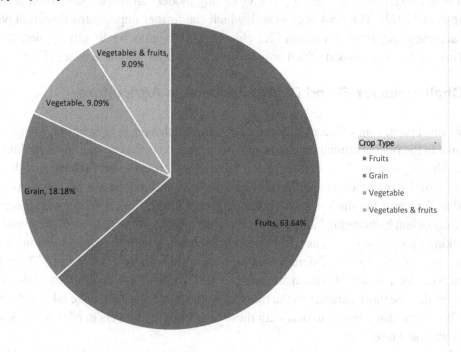

YOLO (You only look once) series is currently the most widely used technology for object detection. Table 7 highlights articles where YOLO series models were used. YOLOv3 not only has higher detection accuracy and speed compared to other architectures but also performs well in the detection of small targets (Chen et al., 2021; Czymmek et al., 2019; Mangaonkar et al., 2022; Oishi et al., 2021; Xiong et al., 2021; Zhou et al., 2021). However, this has a complex architecture, but there are Tiny-YOLO with layer optimization and parameter reduction which are more suitable for processing units with limitations. Tiny-YOLO model reduces the computational complexity and is built on embedded systems like Jetson

Table 7. Studies with YOLO applications

Reference	Architecture	Inference	Edge Device
Chen et al. (2021)	YOLO V4	CPU	Robot
Chen et al. (2021)	YOLO v3-tiny	Single board CPU	Drone
Czymmek et al. (2019)	YOLOv3	CPU	Robot
Huang et al. (2022)	YOLO v3-tiny	Single board CPU	Robot
Li et al. (2021)	YOLOv4-tiny	Single board CPU	UAV
Mangaonkar et al. (2022)	YOLOv3	Single board CPU	Robot
Oishi et al. (2021)	YOLO & Faster R-CNN	CPU	Portable camera
Xiong et al. (2021)	YOLO V4 & Deep Sort	CPU	Robot
Xu et al. (2020)	YOLOv3-tiny	CPU	Robot
Zhou et al. (2021)	YOLO v3	Embedded CPU	UAV

TX2 (Chen et al., 2021; Xu et al., 2020). YOLO v3-tiny model can reach recognition accuracy up to 95% (Huang et al., 2022). YOLOv4 is proposed, which can further improve the detection performance in terms of accuracy and speed. On Jetson TX2 chip YOLOv4 cannot be directly applied; a lightweight YOLOv4-Tiny method is proposed which only utilizes a two-layer output network (Li et al., 2021).

3.5 Key Challenges for EI and DL Applications in Agriculture

DL is one the most promising solutions addressing existing challenges in agriculture, because of its magnificent results in the field of computer vision. EI's main essence is the capability of providing inference in real-time. Although during the evolution period, technology brings some challenges with it. One main challenge is the high computation requirement for DL based solutions. One of the solutions is to go with cloud-based architecture, but this brings in the constraint of latency and real time data processing. This will not be as efficient by bringing latency in access and retrieval of the data from the cloud. Real-time decision-making applications, such as robot vision in orchards, require computer vision models to run on edge devices while performing inferences at high speed (Assunção et al., 2022). These high-speed inferences at edge are a tradeoff between accuracy, model size, and inference speed of the architecture. It demonstrates that the more parameters the model has, the more time inference takes (Menshchikov et al., 2021). One of the challenges is to deal with these high complex models in edge devices with limitation of computational resources.

Transfer learning and incremental learning for intelligent models on edge devices are helpful but can be challenging. The performance of many DL models is mainly dependent on the quantity and quality of data sets (Liu et al., 2021). Edge devices may collect data with different distributions like smooth, backlit, dark, dense, occluded, and complex scenes or even data belonging to an unknown class compared with the original training data. Accuracy of the system depends upon the quality of image data collected, image processing, feature extraction methods and real time weather condition of field (Hafeez et al., 2021).

Real-time scene-parsing through object detection running on an embedded device is very challenging due to the limited memory and computing power of embedded devices (Xu et al., 2020). Limited memory is also one of the main challenges for real-time scene parsing.

4. DISCUSSION

DL brings the ability to automatically identify patterns and detect anomalies in the large data generated from edge devices. However, this poses significant challenges in deploying and running complex model architectures on edge nodes because of their resource constraints and brings in high significance of technique selection. The current analysis shows with DL, CNN offers superior performance at edge in most of the related work, in particular to disease detection, pest control, harvesting and visual classification. Authors have included primary information of selected studies in table 8.

The performance of many DL models is mainly dependent on the quantity and quality of data sets (Liu et al., 2021). It is difficult to collect large amounts of data with labels. Because of this Transfer learning is also one of the areas which is considered very helpful for EI. With transfer learning at the time of inference this can affect the performance of the model, as train data and test data may belong to different conditions. To verify the effectiveness and performance of architectures, it is necessary to evaluate under various conditions.

Table 8. Primary Information of 26 Articles Used in This Study

Study	Task	Specific Application	Technique/ Model	Crop	Results	Dataset	Data Types	Edge Device
Chen et al. (2021)	Crop picking	Framework for citrus picking	CNN/ YOLO V4	Citrus	Mean average precision is 97.19%	Private	RGB-D	Robot
He et al. (2020)	Crop picking	Image Segmentation for robots	CNN/ Xception_65, Mobilenet_v2, Resnet_v1_50_beta	Vegetables	Xception_65 mean intersection over union (MIoU) 94.9%.	Average accuracy of 88.66%.	RGB	Robot
Huang et al. (2022).	Crop picking	Robotic arm for pitaya picking.	CNN/ YOLO v3-tiny	Pitaya	Recognition accuracy up to 95%	Private	RGB/ Video	Robot
Liu et al. (2018)	Crop picking	Citrus picking using CNN	CNN/ MaskRCNN-152	Citrus	MaskRCNN-152 highest comprehensive detection rate 86.83%	Private	RGB	Robot
Mangaonkar et al. (2022)	Crop picking	Robotic arm for harvesting	CNN/ YOLOv3	Fruits	YOLO algorithm was observed to be more accurate.	COCO	Grayscale	Robot
Xiong et al. (2020)	Crop picking	Complex clusters of fruits to be harvested.	R-CNN	Fruits	Proposed method improves picking performance	Private	RGB/ RGB-D	Robot
Xiong et al. (2021)	Crop picking	Two neural networks for fruit picking.	CNN/ YOLO V4 & Deep Sort	Fruits	Improved picking success rate to 62.4%	Private	RGB/ RGB-D	Robot
Xu et al. (2020)	Disease detection	Tomatoes detection in complex scenes	CNN/ YOLOv3-tiny	Tomatoes	Ripe and unripe AP 91.8% and 81.5%	Private	RGB/HSI	Robot
Czymmek et al. (2019)	Disease detection	Method detecting multiple weed species	CNN/ YOLOv3		Precision of 89% and recall of 86%. The average precision is 75.07%.	Private	RGB	Robot
Hafeez et al. (2021)	Disease detection	Weed detection system	CNN–SVM		Accuracy of 96.4% in real time	Private	RGB	UAV
Li et al. (2021)	Disease detection	Fast detection of pine wilt disease	CNN/ YOLOv4-tiny, YOLOv3, MobileNetv2		YOLOv4-tiny highest AP of 84.88%.	Private	RGB	UAV
Menshchikov et al. (2021)	Disease detection	Realtime hogweed detection	CNN/ SegNet, U-Net & RefineNet		SegNet has the best ROC AUC 0.969	Private	RGB	UAV
Mishra et al. (2020)	Disease detection	Real time corn diseases	CNN	Corn	Average accuracy of 88.66%.	Private/ Village Disease Classification	RGB	Smart phone

continues on following page

Table 8. Continued

Study	Task	Specific Application	Technique/ Model	Crop	Results	Dataset	Data Types	Edge Device
Oishi et al. (2021)	Disease detection	Detects abnormal plants or leaves	Faster R-CNN/ YOLO	Potato	Leaf classification: AP 90.5% potato plant: AP 90%	Private/plant /COCO/ Pascal VOC 2007	RGB/ Video	Portable CPU
S et al. (2021)	Disease detection	Real-time detection plant disease.	CNN/ MobileNetV2, ResNet50V2, InceptionResNetV2	Vegetables & fruits	ResNet50V2 with augmentation: Train Accuracy 99.10% & Test 98.65%	PlantVillage	RGB	Smart phone
Chen et al. (2021)	PEST control	Real-time pest detection	CNN/ YOLO v3-tiny	Longan	MAP increased to 95.33% and 89.72%.	Web	RGB	UAV
Suarez et al. (2021)	PEST control	Pest detection	CNN/ VGG-16	Fruits	Accuracy of 84%, with 89% and 76.7% precision and recall respectively	ImageNet	RGB/ Grayscale	UAV
Tetila et al. (2020)	PEST control	Automatic diagnosis of insect pests numbers	CNN/ DenseNet-201, Inception-Resnet-v2, ResNet-50	Soybean	DenseNet-201 achieved 94.89% accuracy	Private	RGB	UAV
Assunção et al. (2022)	Visual classification	Peach maturity classification	CNN/ MobileNe	Peach	Average precision (AP) of 88.2%	Private	RGB	Raspberry Pi
Gao et al. (2020)	Visual classification	Strawberry ripeness with DL	CNN/ AlexNet	Strawberry	Prediction accuracy of 98.6%	Private	RGB-D/ HIS	Portable CPU
Ismail & Malik (2022)	Visual classification	Real-time grading fruits	CNN/ EfficientNet, ResNet, MobileNet, Dense Net, NASNet	Fruits	Highest value of 93.8% for EfficientNetB2	IFW	RGB	Raspberry Pi
Liu et al. (2019)	Visual classification	Vegetable and fruit image classification	CNN/ MobileNet	Vegetables & fruits	MobileNet model achieve state of art accuracy in all datasets	Vegfru/ Fru92/ VegFru292	RGB	Smart phone
Shah et al. (2022)	Visual classification	Barley classification	CNN/ VGG-16	Barley	Average accuracy of 94%	Private	RGB	Smart phone
Yang et al. (2020)	Visual classification	Identification of agricultural crops	CNN/ SegNet, FCN-AlexNet	Rice/Corn	SegNet relatively complete in processing, Rice Accuracy 96.07% & Corn 90.61%	Private	RGB	UAV
Zhou et al. (2021)	Visual classification	Strawberry maturity classification	CNN/ YOLO v3	Strawberry	0.96 AP on RF	Private	RGB	UAV
Osco et al. (2021)	Visual classification	Semantic segment citrus-trees	FCN, U-Net, SegNet, DeepLab, DDCN	Citrus	DDCN achieved accuracy of 95.46%	Private	Near-infrared, red, red-edge	UAV

Moreover, the authors observed the application of deep learning models has been found more accurate in classification of crops as compared to the results previously reported while applying traditional machine learning techniques using the feature extraction methods (Ismail & Malik, 2022). The authors have also seen higher accuracy of models is a tradeoff with their complexities (Xinshao & Cheng, 2015). To overcome the complexity model compression is one approach which reduces complexity and increases the efficiency of DL architectures. To further improve performance, an ensemble strategy allows models to generalize better by using a combination of individual predictions from two or more models (Rokach, 2019). Tang et al. (2017) achieved 92.89% accuracy using k-Means feature learning combined with a CNN for soybean classification. Such approaches, despite the performance gains, also increase the complexity of the models (Xinshao & Cheng, 2015). Ofori (2021) combined ensemble learning with model compression to reduce complexity and increase the efficiency of DL in low resource conditions by using two models. The study used a dataset of plant species captured both in field and lab settings. However, as Ofori (2021) noted, the models relied on past work for various parameters, most importantly, the number of layers to freeze for each model, and further research is warranted to further optimize these models with respect to hyperparameters tuning.

5. CONCLUSION

In this chapter, the authors conducted a systematic and comprehensive literature review about DL and EI's latest development in the agriculture sector. They used SLR methodology to filter the articles and gather the evidence for their research questions. According to the findings, the articles are grouped on the basis of four application segments: crop picking, disease detection, pest control, and visual classification using different edge devices. The authors also observed DL model has shown outstanding accuracy within limited time and computation resources, compared to other machine learning methods, and YOLO series models are currently the most widely used for intelligence on edge devices. This deep-edge intelligence paradigm is still in its early stage. The authors hope this study will attract attention and inspire future research ideas on deep EI, which may include design and implementation of complex DL models with different approaches like ensemble models, compression, and hyper parameter tuning to improve the outcome.

REFERENCES

Assunção, E., Gaspar, P. D., Alibabaei, K., Simões, M. P., Proença, H., Soares, V. N. G. J., & Caldeira, J. M. L. P. (2022). Real-time image detection for edge devices: A peach fruit detection application. *Future Internet*, *14*(11), 323. doi:10.3390/fi14110323

Chandra, A. L., Desai, S. V., Guo, W., & Balasubramanian, V. N. (2020). *Computer vision with deep learning for plant phenotyping in agriculture: A survey*. Advanced Computing and Communications., doi:10.34048/ACC.2020.1.F1

Chen, C.-J., Huang, Y.-Y., Li, Y.-S., Chen, Y.-C., Chang, C.-Y., & Huang, Y.-M. (2021). Identification of fruit tree pests with deep learning on embedded drone to achieve accurate pesticide spraying. *IEEE Access : Practical Innovations, Open Solutions*, *9*, 21986–21997. doi:10.1109/ACCESS.2021.3056082

Chen, J., & Ran, X. (2019). Deep learning with edge computing: A review. *Proceedings of the IEEE*, *107*(8), 1655–1674. doi:10.1109/JPROC.2019.2921977

Chen, S., Xiong, J., He, Z., Jiao, J., Xie, Z., & Han, Y. (2021). Citrus fruits harvesting sequence planning method based on visual attention mechanism: A novel cognition framework for citrus picking robots. In *2021 International Conference on Computer Information Science and Artificial Intelligence (CISAI)* (pp. 806–809). 10.1109/CISAI54367.2021.00162

Czymmek, V., Harders, L. O., Knoll, F. J., & Hussmann, S. (2019). Vision-based deep learning approach for real-time detection of weeds in organic farming. In *2019 IEEE International Instrumentation and Measurement Technology Conference (I2MTC)* (pp. 1–5). 10.1109/I2MTC.2019.8826921

Friha, O., Ferrag, M. A., Shu, L., Maglaras, L., & Wang, X. (2021). Internet of things for the future of smart agriculture: A comprehensive survey of emerging technologies. *IEEE/CAA Journal of Automatica Sinica, 8*(4), 718–752. doi:10.1109/JAS.2021.1003925

Gao, Z., Shao, Y., Xuan, G., Wang, Y., Liu, Y., & Han, X. (2020). Real-time hyperspectral imaging for the in-field estimation of strawberry ripeness with deep learning. *Artificial Intelligence in Agriculture*, *4*, 31–38. doi:10.1016/j.aiia.2020.04.003

Gulzar, M., Abbas, G., & Waqas, M. (2020). Climate smart agriculture: A survey and taxonomy. In *2020 International Conference on Emerging Trends in Smart Technologies (ICETST)* (pp. 1–6). 10.1109/ICETST49965.2020.9080695

Hafeez, A., Tiwari, V., Verma, V. K., Ansari, A. S., Husain, M. A., Singh, S. P., & Khan, A. N. (2021). Crop monitoring and automatic weed detection using drone. In *2021 International Conference on Control, Automation, Power and Signal Processing (CAPS)* (pp. 1–4). 10.1109/CAPS52117.2021.9730682

He, Y., Pan, F., Wang, B., Teng, Z., & Wu, J. (2020). Transfer learning based fruits image segmentation for fruit-picking robots. In *2020 IEEE 3rd International Conference on Computer and Communication Engineering Technology (CCET)* (pp. 71–75). 10.1109/CCET50901.2020.9213127

Huang, X.-R., Chen, W.-H., Hu, W.-C., & Chen, L.-B. (2022). An AI edge computing-based robotic arm automated guided vehicle system for harvesting pitaya. In *2022 IEEE International Conference on Consumer Electronics (ICCE)* (pp. 1–2). 10.1109/ICCE53296.2022.9730442

Ismail, N., & Malik, O. A. (2022). Real-time visual inspection system for grading fruits using computer vision and deep learning techniques. *Information Processing in Agriculture*, *9*(1), 24–37. doi:10.1016/j.inpa.2021.01.005

Kamilaris, A., & Prenafeta-Boldú, F. X. (2018). A review of the use of convolutional neural networks in agriculture. *Journal of Agricultural Science*, *156*(3), 312–322. doi:10.1017/S0021859618000436

Li, F., Liu, Z., Shen, W., Wang, Y., Wang, Y., Ge, C., Sun, F., & Lan, P. (2021). A remote sensing and airborne edge-computing based detection system for pine wilt disease. *IEEE Access : Practical Innovations, Open Solutions*, *9*, 66346–66360. doi:10.1109/ACCESS.2021.3073929

Liberati, A., Altman, D. G., Tetzlaff, J., Mulrow, C., Gøtzsche, P. C., Ioannidis, J. P. A., Clarke, M., Devereaux, P. J., Kleijnen, J., & Moher, D. (2009). The PRISMA statement for reporting systematic reviews and meta-analyses of studies that evaluate health care interventions: Explanation and elaboration. *Annals of Internal Medicine*, 30. PMID:19622512

Liu, C., Wang, X., Ni, J., Cao, Y., & Liu, B. (2019). An edge computing visual system for vegetable categorization. In *2019 18th IEEE International Conference On Machine Learning And Applications (ICMLA)* (pp. 625–632). 10.1109/ICMLA.2019.00115

Liu, J., Xiang, J., Jin, Y., Liu, R., Yan, J., & Wang, L. (2021). Boost precision agriculture with unmanned aerial vehicle remote sensing and edge intelligence: A survey. *Remote Sensing (Basel)*, *13*(21), 4387. doi:10.3390/rs13214387

Liu, Y.-P., Yang, C.-H., Ling, H., Mabu, S., & Kuremoto, T. (2018). A visual system of citrus picking robot using convolutional neural networks. In *2018 5th International Conference on Systems and Informatics (ICSAI)* (pp. 344–349). 10.1109/ICSAI.2018.8599325

Mangaonkar, S. M., Khandelwal, R., Shaikh, S., Chandaliya, S., & Ganguli, S. (2022). Fruit harvesting robot using computer vision. In *2022 International Conference for Advancement in Technology (ICONAT)* (pp. 1–6). 10.1109/ICONAT53423.2022.9726126

Menshchikov, A., Shadrin, D., Prutyanov, V., Lopatkin, D., Sosnin, S., Tsykunov, E., Iakovlev, E., & Somov, A. (2021). Real-time detection of hogweed: UAV platform empowered by deep learning. *IEEE Transactions on Computers*, *70*(8), 1175–1188. doi:10.1109/TC.2021.3059819

Mishra, S., Sachan, R., & Rajpal, D. (2020). Deep convolutional neural network based detection system for real-time corn plant disease recognition. *Procedia Computer Science*, *167*, 2003–2010. doi:10.1016/j.procs.2020.03.236

Ofori, M. (2021). *Transfer-Learned Pruned Deep Convolutional Neural Networks for Efficient Plant Classification in Resource-Constrained Environments* [Masters Theses & Doctoral Dissertations]. https://scholar.dsu.edu/theses/371

Oishi, Y., Habaragamuwa, H., Zhang, Y., Sugiura, R., Asano, K., Akai, K., Shibata, H., & Fujimoto, T. (2021). Automated abnormal potato plant detection system using deep learning models and portable video cameras. *International Journal of Applied Earth Observation and Geoinformation*, *104*, 102509. doi:10.1016/j.jag.2021.102509

Osco, L. P., Nogueira, K., Marques Ramos, A. P., Faita Pinheiro, M. M., Furuya, D. E. G., Gonçalves, W. N., de Castro Jorge, L. A., Marcato, J. Junior, & dos Santos, J. A. (2021). Semantic segmentation of citrus-orchard using deep neural networks and multispectral UAV-based imagery. *Precision Agriculture*, *22*(4), 1171–1188. doi:10.100711119-020-09777-5

Rokach, L. (2019). *Ensemble Learning: Pattern Classification Using Ensemble Methods* (2nd ed., Vol. 85). World Scientific. doi:10.1142/11325

S, C., Ghana, S., Singh, S., & Poddar, P. (2021). Deep learning model for image-based plant diseases detection on edge devices. In *2021 6th International Conference for Convergence in Technology (I2CT)* (pp. 1–5). doi:10.1109/I2CT51068.2021.9418124

Santos, L., Santos, F., Oliveira, P. M., & Shinde, P. (2019). Deep learning applications in agriculture: A short review. In M. F. Silva, J. Luís Lima, L. P. Reis, A. Sanfeliu, & D. Tardioli (Eds.), *Robot 2019: Fourth Iberian Robotics Conference* (pp. 139–151). Springer International Publishing. 10.1007/978-3-030-35990-4_12

Shah, S. A. A., Luo, H., Pickupana, P. D., Ekeze, A., Sohel, F., Laga, H., Li, C., Paynter, B., & Wang, P. (2022). Automatic and fast classification of barley grains from images: A deep learning approach. *Smart Agricultural Technology*, 2, 100036. doi:10.1016/j.atech.2022.100036

Suarez, A., Molina, R. S., Ramponi, G., Petrino, R., Bollati, L., & Sequeiros, D. (2021). Pest detection and classification to reduce pesticide use in fruit crops based on deep neural networks and image processing. In *2021 XIX Workshop on Information Processing and Control (RPIC)* (pp. 1–6). 10.1109/RPIC53795.2021.9648485

Tang, J., Wang, D., Zhang, Z., He, L., Xin, J., & Xu, Y. (2017). Weed identification based on K-means feature learning combined with convolutional neural network. *Computers and Electronics in Agriculture*, 135, 63–70. doi:10.1016/j.compag.2017.01.001

Tetila, E. C., Brandoli Machado, B., Menezes, G. V., de Souza Belete, N. A., Astolfi, G., & Pistori, H. (2020). A deep-learning approach for automatic counting of soybean insect pests. *IEEE Geoscience and Remote Sensing Letters*, 17(10), 1837–1841. doi:10.1109/LGRS.2019.2954735

Wang, C., Liu, B., Liu, L., Zhu, Y., Hou, J., Liu, P., & Li, X. (2021). A review of deep learning used in the hyperspectral image analysis for agriculture. *Artificial Intelligence Review*, 54(7), 5205–5253. doi:10.100710462-021-10018-y

Wang, F., Zhang, M., Wang, X., Ma, X., & Liu, J. (2020). Deep learning for edge computing applications: A state-of-the-art survey. *IEEE Access : Practical Innovations, Open Solutions*, 8, 58322–58336. doi:10.1109/ACCESS.2020.2982411

Xinshao, W., & Cheng, C. (2015). Weed seeds classification based on PCANet deep learning baseline. *2015 Asia-Pacific Signal and Information Processing Association Annual Summit and Conference (APSIPA)*, 408–415. 10.1109/APSIPA.2015.7415304

Xiong, Y., Ge, Y., & From, P. J. (2020). Push and drag: An active obstacle separation method for fruit harvesting robots. In *2020 IEEE International Conference on Robotics and Automation (ICRA)* (pp. 4957–4962). 10.1109/ICRA40945.2020.9197469

Xiong, Y., Ge, Y., & From, P. J. (2021). An improved obstacle separation method using deep learning for object detection and tracking in a hybrid visual control loop for fruit picking in clusters. *Computers and Electronics in Agriculture*, 191, 106508. doi:10.1016/j.compag.2021.106508

Xu, Z.-F., Jia, R.-S., Liu, Y.-B., Zhao, C.-Y., & Sun, H.-M. (2020). Fast method of detecting tomatoes in a complex scene for picking robots. *IEEE Access : Practical Innovations, Open Solutions*, 8, 55289–55299. doi:10.1109/ACCESS.2020.2981823

Yang, M. D., Tseng, H. H., Hsu, Y. C., & Tseng, W. C. (2020). *Real-time crop classification using edge computing and deep learning. In 2020 IEEE 17th Annual Consumer Communications & Networking Conference.* CCNC. doi:10.1109/CCNC46108.2020.9045498

Zhang, Q., Liu, Y., Gong, C., Chen, Y., & Yu, H. (2020). Applications of deep learning for dense scenes analysis in agriculture: A review. *Sensors (Basel)*, *20*(5), 5. Advance online publication. doi:10.339020051520 PMID:32164200

Zhou, X., Lee, W. S., Ampatzidis, Y., Chen, Y., Peres, N., & Fraisse, C. (2021). Strawberry maturity classification from UAV and near-ground imaging using deep learning. *Smart Agricultural Technology*, *1*, 100001. doi:10.1016/j.atech.2021.100001

Zhou, Z., Chen, X., Li, E., Zeng, L., Luo, K., & Zhang, J. (2019). Edge Intelligence: Paving the Last Mile of Artificial Intelligence With Edge Computing. *Proceedings of the IEEE*, *107*(8), 1738–1762. doi:10.1109/JPROC.2019.2918951

KEY TERMS AND DEFINITIONS

AI: Artificial intelligence.
CNN: Convolutional neural networks.
DL: Deep learning.
EI: Edge intelligence.
ML: Machine learning.
RGB: Red, green, and blue.
UAV: Unmanned aerial vehicles.
YOLO: You only look once.

Chapter 13
Study on Healthcare Security System–Integrated Internet of Things (IoT)

S. A. Karthik
BMS Institute of Technology and Management, India

M. Deivakani
PSNA College of Engineering and Technology, India

R. Hemalatha
St. Joseph's College of Engineering, India

R. Vijaya Kumar Reddy
Koneru Lakshmaiah Education Foundation, India

R. Aruna
AMC Engineering College, India

Sampath Boopathi
Muthayammal Engineering College, India

ABSTRACT

The internet of things (IoT) has the potential to transform healthcare by fusing the most significant technological and scientific advances in the fields of automation, mobility, and data analytics to improve patient care. IoT links sensors, actuators, and other devices to a network in order to collect and disseminate communication messages that an organization may then evaluate. To track health parameters, the suggested paradigm focuses on sensors, communications protocols, and cloud technologies. The study looks at the crucial elements of a healthcare IoT system. For the control, security, and protection of IoT networks, data confidentiality and authentication are crucial. For the purpose of resolving security challenges, flexible infrastructure is necessary. The goal of the chapter is to discuss IoT security concerns in healthcare devices and offer recommendations for future research to enhance the use of IoT devices.

INTRODUCTION

Thanks to the abundance of IoT devices that are available in various locations and the enormous amounts of data and information they contain, Internet of Things (IoT) healthcare systems offer a solid foundation for smart sensor technology. Huge volumes of data are released by IoT-based healthcare systems, yet

DOI: 10.4018/978-1-6684-7684-0.ch013

security and privacy are crucial concerns. IoT sensors and their released data can be supported by object and cloud network topologies. The Internet of Things (IoT) is a system of linked, intelligent sensors that can perceive their surroundings and share data and processes from many areas. It is utilised in a variety of industries, including smart transportation, finance, railroads, and healthcare. Different domains are involved with smart IoT-based sensors, particularly in smart healthcare systems. The majority are offered in stores. IoT infrastructure security design is crucial for a variety of technological, scientific, and commercial reasons, including privacy and security. Security concerns are governed by IoT architectures, technologies, and design approaches. The internet of things architecture is divided into layers, and each layer makes use of a different topology and piece of hardware to maintain sensor data standardisation, privacy protection, and parameter coordination(Polu, 2019).

To track and manage the healthcare system, IoT systems need a range of data and sensors. Wireless sensors are crucial for distant security, whereas vision-based sensors improve monitoring capacity. These sensors use the concept of physical position based and are vision-based. Home-based deployment of a wireless sensor for patient eyesight that is linked to an LPWAN base station and a cloud with machine learning capabilities (Toghuj & Turab, 2022).

- Smart gadgets are those that can communicate with one another and are connected to a network or other devices. Since they only make up a minor portion of the notion, it is inaccurate to refer to them as IoT. It is preferable to refer to intelligent objects or intelligent things rather than merely devices. IoT may be used for basic calculations, communication, discovery, message reception and response (Janardhana et al., 2023; Reddy et al., 2023; Selvakumar et al., 2023). The ability to make anything intelligent is made possible by the fact that sensors are now more affordable, simple to install, and affordable than ever. They are not required for intelligent things, though.
- Bluetooth, NFC, Wi-Fi, low-power wide-area networks, and LoRa are just a few examples of the smart objects that require wireless networks to communicate with one another.
- RFID technology is a significant advancement over conventional barcodes because it makes it possible to create microchips for wireless data exchange. It has writing capabilities, requires no line-of-sight contact, and can read several tags simultaneously.
- Big data from intelligent objects, such as temperature, pressure, altitude, motion, proximity to other objects, biometrics, sound, etc., must be combined and analysed using cloud computing. One of the main problems with IoT is the integration of all this data. A platform called cloud computing enables on-demand network access to computational resources. It receives data from intelligent devices, processes and interprets it, and then presents web-based visualisations. As a result, there will be a large market with lots of potential to add value for IoT application users. These data are analysed using machine learning techniques and big data analytics. Artificial intelligence known as machine learning enables computers to become smarter by learning from the data they are fed. The quantity of data produced by IoT applications necessitates a large increase in storage space, despite the fact that big data has been a hot issue. Big businesses utilise edge computing to preprocess data before sending it to the cloud.

Confidentiality is at the nexus of privacy and security in healthcare, where both are mutually advantageous. The foundation of network security systems are security, privacy, and protection, and IOT healthcare systems offer five levels: perception layers, edge layers, transport layers, processing layers, application layers, and business layers. IoT focuses on the autonomous interaction of smart items without requiring people as an intermediary station, in contrast to present technology, which focuses on communication primarily from gadgets to the end-user. The background interactions, data collection, and sharing of the connected smart items produce information that is helpful to the end user or have an impact on their behaviour (Koutras et al., 2020).

The functions of the layers:

- Perception or edge technology layers are critical hardware components that are crucial to the healthcare industry. Examples include EDI, Smart Camera, WSTN, GSM networks, GPS, PCS, and RIFD systems. They also include smart remotes, embedded processors, intelligence terminals, and smart processors for monitoring and controlling objects. RFID is a technology that is utilised for data information and personal identification. It is a mobile, secure device that gathers data and information for processing and to assist activities related to healthcare monitoring. The wireless gadget and sensors gather sinks' data while the chip reader gathers real-time data for objects and tags for each individual (Boopathi, Siva Kumar, et al., 2023; Harikaran et al., 2023; Jeevanantham et al., 2023).
- Middleware layer (Network Layer): The network layer or transport layer together with the middleware layer is in charge of managing the hardware and software in healthcare systems. Data mining, data aggregation, semantic and syntactic analysis, data fermentation, data filtering, data control, data framing, Electronic Product Code (EPC), and Object Naming Service are all involved (ONS). Data gateway between the network layer and the transport layer is handled by the access gateway layer. It uses Ethernet, wireless technology, or any other network technology to collect data from the perception layer.
- Applications layer: Interfacing at the application layer that is answerable, machine-to-machine communication, end-user services, controlling and interacting with cloud services, and LPWAN applications.

The Internet of Things (IoT) is a system of linked smart items that may be utilised to change and enhance our way of life. It may be used to smart and private spaces, healthcare, transportation, and logistics (Babu et al., 2023; Kumara et al., 2023; Senthil et al., 2023; Vanitha et al., 2023). One significant industry that stands to gain from IoT advancements is logistics. Businesses can swiftly respond to changes in the supply chain thanks to real-time tracking using RFID (Radio Frequency Identification) and NFC (near-field communication), which helps them plan more effectively and cut back on safety supplies. This is crucial for transportation in particular (Kang et al., 2021).

Sensors may be installed in vehicles to guarantee safety, and the Internet of Things (IoT) can deliver real-time data regarding traffic congestion and the healthcare industry. To stop left-in things during surgery and tool and medicine theft, the IoT enables tracking of moving tags that may be affixed to any person or object. Real-time, global patient condition monitoring is possible with the use of implanted or outpatient sensors. The IoT can also help other sectors, such as intelligent environments. In addition to helping in the personal & social sector, the IoT may assist avoid accidents and conserve energy in homes, workplaces, and industrial facilities (Chakravarthi et al., 2022; Jeevanantham et al., 2023; Samikannu et al., 2023).

By reviewing the most recent location information and looking for keywords, RFID devices can assist us in recovering lost things. Although the Internet of Things (IoT) includes numerous innovative technologies that show promise, security issues still exist. One of the most valuable resources in any stream is information, which should be properly preserved. To secure the integrity and confidentiality of data and operational procedures, security combines technology, operations, and internal controls. By reviewing the most recent location information and looking for keywords, RFID devices can assist us in recovering lost things. Although they may be used to track theft, the Internet of Things has security issues. Any stream's most valuable asset is information, which should be safeguarded by integrating internal controls, systems, and operations to guarantee integrity and confidentiality (Boopathi, Arigela, et al., 2023; Domakonda et al., 2023; Palaniappan et al., 2023; Vennila et al., 2023). Confidentiality, integrity, availability, authorisation, and non-repudiation are the five information security objectives.

- **Confidentiality**: Confidentiality means upholding confidentiality while information is being sent.
- **Integrity:** Information storage modifications must be made by authorised parties through allowed procedures in order to maintain integrity.
- **Availability**: Data must be available in order for authorised drugs to use it.
- **Authorization:** Those with permission to use the information must have access to it.
- **Non-repudiation:** Who, when, and where must all be mentioned in change documents.

Although the Internet of Things offers numerous innovative technologies that show promise, security issues still exist. The majority of IoT architectures that have been suggested use server-side design, in which the server interacts with all of the linked parts, handles all of the administrations, and serves as a single point of contact for customers. The fundamental layer is the bottom layer and comprises a database that holds information about every device, including its characteristics, flaws, and connections. While the Application layer offers services to clients, the Component layer includes programming related to devices (Boopathi, Khare, et al., 2023; S. et al., 2022; Samikannu et al., 2023; Sampath, C., et al., 2022).

The object layer enables communication between devices and data sharing, while the social layer controls user application execution, handles requests, and communicates with the application layer on the server. Multi-sensor imaging is the process of combining relevant data from two or more sensors to produce a single image that is more informative than each of the input images alone. Thanks to RFID and sensor technologies, computers can now monitor and understand the environment without being restricted by human-entered data. In order to collect data and change the types of things that may communicate via an IP network, sensor-equipped devices connect to other items and/or systems. To wirelessly access physical items, such as temperature, humidity, fire alarms, push buttons, buzzers, rotary encoders, etc., sensors must be given distinct identities. The most used Internet protocol is IPv4, whereas IPv6 offers 128 bits of capacity for object tracking (Garg et al., 2022).

HEALTHCARE SECURITY LAYERS

Data secrecy, information acuity, and information accessibility are the three most crucial requirements, and each of the four tiers of the IoT network system must fulfil them. Data confidentiality refers to the idea that the information gathered by sensors and nodes shouldn't be shared with unauthorised parties. This may be done by the use of data encryption, and two-step verification is another way to guarantee data secrecy. Instances like server failure or power outages might potentially have an impact on the integrity of the data. At the basic level, data integrity is ensured via cyclic redundancy check (CRC).

- **Application layer:** Healthcare system monitoring and management are the responsibility of the application layer, which offers features like availability services, anti-virus services, and Spam Filtering System.
- **Processing layer:** This layer is in charge of transporting data from the Transport Layer to lower levels, storing it for analysis, and mining network data.
- **Network layer:** In order to receive and process information, the network layer links servers, equipment, and smart devices.
- **Perception layer:** Physical parameters are used by the physical layer to get information from the environment.

Benefits

- **Enhanced treatment administration:** Better administration power, system monitoring, medicine and record tracking, and medical problem solving are all made possible by IoT devices.
- **Remote Real-life monitoring**: The ideal option for healthcare systems utilising Internet of Things-based smart devices is remote monitoring.
- **Investigation**: IoT devices gather medical data for research.
- **Preclusion**: To maintain living quality, smart sensors collect and analyse everyday data.
- **Decrease healthcare costs**: IoT healthcare system can reduce medical costs.
- **Ease of use**: IoT devices collect data and send it to cloud for future use and investigation.
- **Enhanced healthcare Supervision**: Data and information are essential for IoT healthcare.

Objectives

With an emphasis on device configuration, device administration, device security, and IEEE standards, this thesis investigates IoT architecture and middleware layers with devices utilised on network security in healthcare systems. The strength of IoT-based security solutions is increased by the cooperation of middleware.

- Controlling and setting up the apparatus.
- Create secure infrastructure.
- Keeping an eye on the tools and equipment.
- Fix the security issues with IoT.
- Observing sensing equipment.
- Address the healthcare IoT challenges.
- Layers of network security should be created.
- Describe IoT topologies and layers.
- Fix the security issues with the 5G network.
- Make sure the gadgets are coordinated.

To maintain, configure, and distribute sensitive, crucial, and domain-specific issues, IoT devices require personal attention. Artificial smart sensors are more adaptable, simple, controllable, trackable, and available. The primary goal of this thesis is to develop an architecture for an Internet of Things (IoT)-based security healthcare system that assesses the privacy and safety of linked networks, boosts productivity, and addresses pressing challenges in remote locations. The traditional system uses cryptography to encode data through encryption, whereas the more recent IOT-based healthcare system makes use of a five-layer protection protocol, high level security, secure algorithm/protocol, secure system architecture, short-range communication, and RFID chip to expand medical services at remote hospitals, assign smart medical agents, and address sensitive and serious activity. This study looks at the benefits and drawbacks of IoT-based hospital security solutions. It emphasises the potency, practicality, and security of medical sensors (Boopathi et al., 2022; Chakravarthi et al., 2022; Sampath, Pandian, et al., 2022; Sampath, Yuvaraj, et al., 2022). While the sensor containing all data and information reading healthcare and leakage of such information impacts the sensitivity of the healthcare care system, the IOT security architecture is meant to promote privacy and confidentiality.

The Internet of Things (IoT) technologies are cutting-edge trends in the rapidly expanding field of technology used in healthcare to track patients, devices, and sensor-based monitoring systems. They offer practical, on-the-spot answers to heath care issues and are crucial for COVID and other unobservable disorders. Additionally, they support various healthcare applications, develop (personal information healthcare systems), and offer the commercial link between hospitals and the Internet of Things. Hospitals, the medical industry, and its applications are currently intimately linked to RFID. Many industries, including data mining, cloud computing, fog computing, artificial intelligence, context-based intelligence, etc., employ IoT-based devices. The foundation of many organisations, including hospitals, synthetic pharmaceutical labs, remote healthcare facilities, controlling biosensor medications and devices, offering intelligent therapy, and amplifying cumulative demise, is healthcare. Security and service providers are looking for a strong security and protection framework for the healthcare industry, particularly for the creation of RFID and smart medicines. Security for personal information, payment applications, remote healthcare applications, SQL database administration, relationships between businesses and hospitals, and common control gateways are all required for IOT healthcare (Bin Zikria et al., 2020; Hireche et al., 2022).

Disadvantages of Existing Healthcare Security System

- **Lack of security is only one of the numerous drawbacks of IoT-based healthcare technologies.**
- **Protection and Retreat**: Since the sensor that holds all of the data and information reading healthcare is sensitive, healthcare security and protection are crucial for monitoring and controlling IOT-based healthcare systems.
- **Hazard of failure**: Standardization, protocol, and consistency amongst manufacturers are needed for sensors and IoT devices.
- **Integration**: Standardization and protocol are needed for sensors and IoT devices, as well as consistency between manufacturers.

Performance Metrics

Both IoT and traditional network devices have distinct security settings and functionalities. Frequency hopping communication and public key encryption are challenging to use to safeguard IoT devices on sensor nodes due to their low processing capacity and storage space. Lightweight encryption technology is used to IoT computers. The purpose of this exercise is to offer a helpful handbook of readily available security risks and vulnerabilities, particularly for various IoT contexts, and to make doable recommendations for enhancing the design of IoT security. Modern device implementation dangers and vulnerabilities have been evaluated, and the IoT's structural architecture has been researched.

Based on the flaws and restrictions of current approaches, a viable solution to the security issue is put forth. The E2E stable key-managing protocol for e-health applications developed by Abdmeziem and Tandjaoui is restricted to the release of heavy cryptographic primitives and does not specify the necessary trade-off between communication overhead and the number of third parties. Flauzac proposed a new SDN-based security architecture for the IoT, however it has drawbacks, including difficulties in protecting both desirable and undesired traffic and issues with enterprise security. A method of lightweight authentication and authorisation for limited smart objects was proposed by Hernández-Ramos, however it has not yet been put into practise.

NEW IoT INTEGRATED HEALTHCARE SECURITY SYSTEM

A technique called picture mixing mixes data from many photos of an identical scene. The two kinds of image fusion methods are spatial domain and frequency domain. The problems and vulnerabilities of IoT architecture and applications are examined in this survey along with potential fixes. It assumes that building a global IoT security architecture can secure IoT applications (Boopathi, 2019, 2022a, 2022b, 2022c; Sampath & Myilsamy, 2021). The effectiveness of any of the existing defence tactics has not been established. A safe IoT architecture should be developed to handle translations, provide positional privacy, and define mobility for dormant IoT nodes. symmetric cryptography as a third-party offloading option. Convergence of the control and data planes, which enables the adoption of applications like encryption, analysis, and traffic categorization, is the only method to increase SDN efficiency. In order to establish shared keys with wireless objects with whom no prior common knowledge has been established, third parties are committed to assisting limited nodes. E2E code makes sure that nobody can obtain the shared secret. IoT integrated Health care -Architecture is illustrated in Figure 1.

Figure 1. IoT integrated healthcare: Architecture

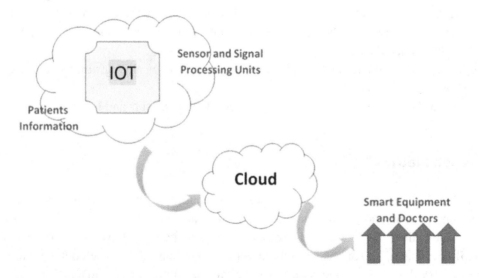

Components

- Application layer is a term used to describe the smart grid, healthcare system, transportation, and environment.
- The Perception layer includes sensor nodes, gateways, RFID, network protocols, and mobile devices.

Smart metres, smart appliances, renewable energy sources, and energy efficiency are just a few of the operational and energy efforts that make up a smart grid, which is an electrical system. With the help of a trustworthy and dispersed approach, intelligent backdrops combine the functions of many stockholders and grow in the direction of consumers. By offering an IoT device a security risk and a communication route, RFID technology is redefining the embedded common. Various functions of complex messaging of IoT devices are provided by Wi-Fi, Ultra-wideband, ZigBee, Bluetooth, LTE, LTE-A structure, citizens verification, Privacy, Eavesdropping, permission, Smart grid, Smart metres, Smart readers, Health care's system, Bluetooth and ZigBee Sensors, Smart wearable devices, authentication authorization, DoS, Intelligent transportation DSRC 5.8 GHz EFC, RSU, OBUs Jamming, Congestion, security and spectrum sharing model. There are two different kinds of RFID tags: active and passive. Although active RFID tags have limited processing power and storage, they can send signals to readers and communicate instantly. However, their lifespans are also confined. Sensor gateways use a 2.4 GHz IEEE 802.15.4 radio for communication and manage wireless networks and aggregate data from dispersed WSN nodes. Sensor nodes link to other network nodes and collect and interpret sensory input (Garg et al., 2022; Gupta et al., 2021).

- Controller manages output and data processing.
- A transceiver sends and receives radio waves.
- A memory used for computer programming is called programming memory.
- Data about the environment is collected via hardware.
- Nodes get electricity from a power source.

Smart Healthcare

Our framework's design depends on three primary entities to carry out analysis activities while protecting user privacy.

- **Community Members (CM):** Bio signal data from CMs is collected via wired and wireless sensors, and after encryption, is sent to cloud-enabled storage.
- **IoT gateway:** This intelligent IoT device gathers data from CMs and transmits it securely to the cloud for additional analysis.
- **Cloud-enabled Database (CD):** Encrypted cloud storage for CM's medical information.
- **Abnormality Detection Model (ADM):** This allows for the examination of encrypted data from several smart communities.

Cloud Architecture for Health: Security, collaboration, and collaboration are the three main features that cloud technology provide healthcare applications.

- Healthcare practitioners can use apps using Software as a Service (SaaS) to complete tasks and retrieve patient data.
- Tools for virtualization, networking, database administration, and other tasks are available through platform as a service.
- Storage, servers, and other physical infrastructure are provided through infrastructure as a service.

Big Data Management: The five Vs—volume, velocity, variety, veracity, and value—define big data. The terms "volume," "velocity," "variety," "truthfulness," and "value" all refer to different aspects of the generation of data: its quantity, speed, diversity, veracity, and uncertainty over potential future contributions.

Security and Privacy: A patient's health information must be easily available to authorised parties on the cloud. Additionally, it is crucial to maintain patient confidentiality since sharing private information can have a detrimental impact on the patient, such as making it more difficult for them to get insurance or becoming a victim of identity theft. The patient's health might suffer if an unintentional attacker makes changes to the health record.

Data Processing and Analytics: Machine learning and computational offloading are two examples of data processing that may be carried out utilising cloud technology. Machine learning uses the computing power of multiple computers to analyse disconnected mobile tools and offer incentives, whereas computational offloading uses the cloud to carry out complicated data processing that is beyond the capacity of low-resource wearable devices. In cloud-based systems, security and privacy are crucial concerns.

In a healthcare setting, it is crucial that a patient's health information is easily available to authorised individuals because it is sensitive and need to be kept private. The patient may have negative effects, such as identity theft or difficulty obtaining insurance, if hostile assaults disclosed their health information. The patient's health may suffer if the attacker changed their record, if they did so.

IoT ATTACKS

There are different type occur in current healthcare system (Garg et al., 2022; Mohd Aman et al., 2021).

- *Physical attacks*: Due to the small size and wireless connectivity of IoT devices, it is crucial to preserve the gathered perception data and provide secure storage. 23 mechanisms, including those related to people, technological ecology, development, and intelligent objectives, round up the overall structural arrangement. Recognition, faith, isolation, security, auto-immunity, consistency, and liability are all protective elements. A perimeter expertise layer can also be divided into sub-layers with distinct security requirements.
- *Incorporating RFID into IoT*: RFID technology has been employed in IoT applications for item recognition, tracking, and recovery, however it is attackable owing to resource constraints. The three mechanisms that make up IoT-supported RFID are the RFID system, the middleware system, and the Internet system. These components are protected by a number of security, including risks associated with wireless communication, eavesdropping, man-in-the-middle attacks, denial of service, spoofing, cloning, tracking, and tag misuse. To protect and regulate access to data via RFID labels, certain security measures are necessary.

- In order to prevent unauthorised RFID readers from obtaining statistics, RFID protection techniques and tactics including symmetric and asymmetric cyphers are utilised. Elliptic Curve Cryptography and the MD5 method work together to improve user verification, dependability, protection, and isolation of information conveyed from mark to reader.

- *Incorporating WSNs into IoT*: Individuals are vulnerable to assault by hostile nodes because they have insufficient computing and power resources. Critical data, including security standards, source code, and other data, can be accessed physically. WSNs must be safeguarded using encryption, MACs, and laws and regulations for protected location and accessibility since they are utilised in numerous IoT requests for healthcare. At a lower cost, signcryption can shield a channel from the CIA.

- *Denial of Service (DoS) attacks*: DDoS assaults prevent disabled users from accessing server resources or data. The majority of generic DoS attacks are explained using knowledge of RFID and WSNs, such as how crowding and machine-transmitted radio signals interfere with neighbouring RFID readers. Attackers can deactivate RFID tags, launch kill commands against WSNs, wipe off knobs, jam networks, flood them with SYN traffic, leave servers with no resources, and use fake source addresses in desynchronizing assaults.

- *Denial of sleep attack:* Access control is crucial to preventing admittance terrorization, which may result in life-threatening threats in the IoT, and unauthorised organisations from accessing system resources. To check for forbidden user interaction, efficient verification knowledge should be acquired.

Following are the security qualities of access control

- *Identification*: Various identification methods, like RFID, IPv4, IPv6, EPCglobal, Near Field Communications Forum (NFC), etc., should be used to uniquely identify IoT items. PONS is a scalable physical-object naming system that issues URL-based semantic identities and reuses existing ontologies. The main division of PONS is made up of IoT substance recording and possessions, S-URL storage partitions, individuality regulators, and programmes that describe S-URLs. IdP and SP are two sorts of entities that make up the IdM structure, which offers access and individuality management services.

- *Authentication*: To establish a communication channel and mutual confidence between objects or users, authentication entails confirming an entity's identity and data source. It is an IoT access control and authentication technique.

IoT HEALTHCARE PROTOCOL

By utilising efficient communication protocols like CoAP, effective filtering and sampling methods, combined computation and network resource optimization, and efficient filtering and sampling approaches, HTTP/2 can lower energy usage in fog situations.

Constraints: The Internet Engineering Task Force (IETF) created the limited application protocol, which is an HTTP-compatible synchronous request/response protocol. It utilises UDP and supports both multicast and unicast, lowering bandwidth needs. The CoAP is intended for devices with limited resources, like mobile phones, tablets, laptops, and low-power consumption gadgets.

Transport Protocol: The IBM-powered MQTT application layer protocol was created to adhere to the demands of low-bandwidth and battery utilisation. MQTT, which has less delays, is the protocol used by Facebook Messenger, although CoAP offers smaller package losses and more dependability.

BLE Communication Layer Protocol: Bluetooth is a constrained connectivity technology that works well for many different purposes. Bluetooth Low Energy (BLE), often known as Bluetooth 4.0, is the most recent version of the wireless technology. It boosts power use and energy level for ultra-low energy operation during low-power inactive times. However, the maximum information speed for BLE is just 100 kbps, which is slower than Bluetooth's EDR mode.

BLE protocol stack: The host and controller components of the Bluetooth protocol stack are separated. The middleware protocols RFCOMM and L2CAP make up the host stack. Data from the higher layer is converted by the controller stack into a format that the controller stack can understand. Bluetooth services in the area may be found and advertised using SDP (Service Discovery Protocol). For the purpose of running services, the intermediate HCI transport layer directly accesses Bluetooth hardware. The HTTP transaction over the Internet is the same as Transport Layer Security (TLS)/SSL.

Queuing Protocol: QP is an asynchronous 68 publish/subscribe messaging system that is utilised in the financial sector. It transmits 1 billion messages every day and has inherent dependability when running over the TCP protocol. With message delivery assurances and TLS/SSL security, it assures dependability.

Extensible Messaging and Presence Protocol: The Extensible Messaging and Presence Protocol (XMPP), which the IETF has standardised, is not suitable for M2M communications since it supports TLS/SSL and includes QoS settings. It recently regained importance as a suitable protocol for the Internet of Things.

Data Flow: CoAP is a condensed form of HTTP. It is generally made for inter-device communication between devices with limited resources. Proxy devices act as a bridge between the constrained environment and the internet environment. Data collection, data transmission, data storage, and data analysis are the four phases that make up the IoT's data flow. Token, option, or multi-options come after the final two bytes in big-endian order, with no payload coming after the options.

DQAL Protocol: The distributed collision resolution queue proposed by the DQAL protocol has two counters for each MD: RQ and pRQ. At the start of each CRI, each MD performs initialization based on broadcast information. The Allow Transmission Interval (ETI), which measures the amount of time the MD spends waiting for the start of the next CRI, represents the disciplinary law of queuing, which states that any clashing preamble must rejoin the queue. Each virtual community in the DQAL may be modelled as a queueing architecture, with a single server. The distributed crash declaration line, which consists of two offsets, is the most crucial step in the proposed DQAL operation (RQ and pRQ). Every MD establishes a number of initializations that are supported by the transmission information at the beginning of every CRI. Queuing regulation rule is the name of this kind of initialization, and demand broadcast regulation is utilised to identify the crash. The DQAL may be used to provide accurate unique access time allocation in a queuing mechanism. As the MD waits for the start of the next CRI to begin broadcasting its preamble, it uses an instance known as the Enable Transmission Interval (ETI).

LTE RACH Protocol: LTE RACH is made up by PRBs, which provide the bandwidth for six physical resource blocks, and RA slots, which are provided for access needs. In LTE, the RA process consists of four grip communications between the UE device and the eNodeB and is both reliant on and free from congestion. Random-Access Preamble broadcasting is the first kind of communication, in which workstations broadcast the preamble in the RA window whenever they have information to send. Preambles are sent via RBs on subframes and are specifically created for erratic access. In order for the UE mechanism to disseminate communication, the eNodeB broadcasts an uplink supply distribution. Access Classes are used to categorise the EAB techniques (ACs). If the system is overloaded, this method is used to prevent short priory ACs. A paging message is sent to inform the MDs when a bitmap message is modified.

The UE system can wait until the changed bitmap is received by the paging cycle after taking into account how many sub frames there are between two successive paging cycles. There are several studies outlining the period at which the EAB will be permitted and the conventional LTE access methods will be deactivated. MDs access the device through the standard LTE technique when there is little to no traffic. The overcrowding coefficient, which can be calculated from the difference between the number of crashing UE procedures and the number of booming UE operations in a fixed period, was used by Intel to create an algorithm for formative altering slot.

PROPOSED SECURITY WORKING METHODOLOGY

Use of READ and WRITE security approaches as well as the application of get/set techniques are part of the suggested methodology to enhance IoT healthcare security. Figure 2 depicts the block diagram for the IoT -integrated Security working model.

Figure 2. IoT-integrated healthcare security block diagram

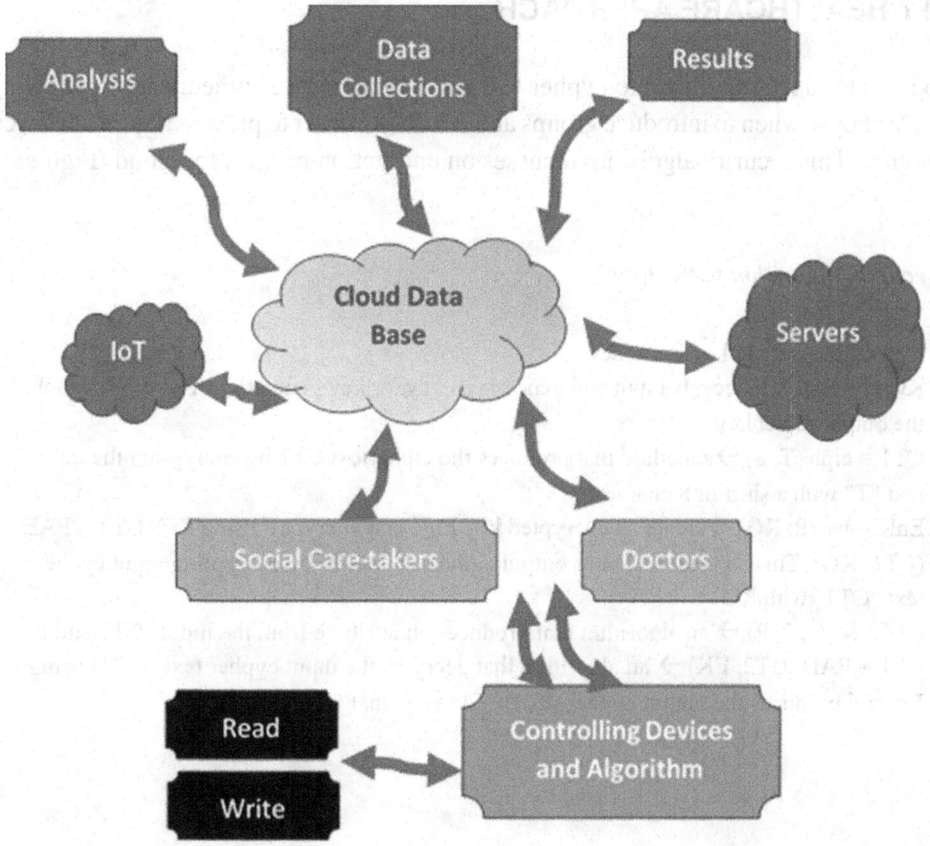

Global Security READ/WRITE Method

IoT services have distinct communication requirements than human-based communications do. Two key differences are:

IoT devices report events using small message sizes. To give a comprehensive understanding of the IoT, we concentrate on standardised cellular networks that offer large area coverage, security, permit roaming and mobility, and operate in permitted bands. Disciplines collaborate through problem-oriented cooperation or by borrowing ideas and techniques from one another to research a phenomenon. A growing number of people are using cloud storage to store their data, which is why it is growing in popularity. Users may upload, download, and share files thanks to user-centric encryption and decryption, which also makes them shareable. Data security in a cloud environment is split into two categories. The first end deals with data that is sent into the network after being collected from the user site, and the second end is concerned with data that is kept on a cloud disc. Researchers have proposed a hybrid ciphering technique to protect data files stored in cloud storage. It is hybrid in nature and offers preliminary level security and more accurate key. The second stage of projected effort is to create a new encryption algorithm based on a cryptographic encryption technique. To ensure the security of the data, it is important to verify authentication privileges of the different users accessing the cloud-disk stored data. This will increase the utilization factor of healthcare systems(Garg et al., 2022; Polu, 2019).

SECURITY HEALTHCARE APPROACH

This method creates a feature linked to cypher text and manages user authentication, allowing creative appearances to choose when to introduce groups above GRQ in order to prevent requests from conflicting with one another. This security algorithm focusses on encryption process for cloud (Figures 3 and 4).

Figure 3. Security algorithm with cloud

P $\rightarrow$ Cloud private key for nodes.

KG $\rightarrow$ Gen(s): It accepts input and generates a key, or key generator, of size "s," which is the output secret key.

CT1 = ciph (T, 8) $\rightarrow$ a method that produces the ciphertext CT1 by encrypting the input text "T" with a shift of 8 characters.

EnK = En (P, KG) $\rightarrow$ create an encrypted key EnK and encrypt P using KG. CT2 = PAE (CT1, KG): This algorithm creates output ciphertext "CT2" by encrypting input cypher text "CT1" with KG.

α= RSK (CT2, P) $\rightarrow$ an algorithm that produces an attribute from the inputs CT2 and P.

CT1 = PAD (CT2, EK) $\rightarrow$ an algorithm that decrypts the input cypher text "CT2" using EK and produces the output cypher text "CT1" such that CT1' == CT1.

Figure 4. Cloud encryption algorithm (128-bits)

Start

Add text data (D) and a 128-bit private key (P) by a cloud user.

Key (P) and user text data (D) arrive at the end of the cloud server.

At the cloud end, read the user text data and key (128 bits).

Apply the RSA to T algorithm.

Create the CT1 Initial Level Cipher text.

Assemble the encrypted key (EK)

Create KG with an algorithm.

Apply the "EnK" algorithm to produce KG.

To the next level of the algorithm, pass CT1 and KG.

Apply algorithm to create Second Level of Cipher Text CT2

Send CT2 to the "ABC to produce an attribute" method.

Stop

SECURITY ALGORITHM

In order to combine information from two input pictures, image fusion involves inversely twisting a wavelet transform array. User authentication and confidentiality are included together with the three level security concepts of robustness, low execution time, encrypted keys, and ease of understanding.

Nordic nRF52832 Chip

The Cortex-M4F processor of the nRF52832 provides DSP instructions, FPU, single cycle multiplies and accumulates, and hardware divisions for computationally intensive processes that use little power. The nRF52832 SoC is a potent device that can operate between 1.7V and 3.6V and has a full set of automated and adaptive authority administration functions. The IC functions cover a wide spectrum, including power supply switching, peripheral bus/Easy DMA memory management, and automatic shutdown of crucial peripherals.

Security Protocol

The distributed collision resolution queue, which consists of the two counters RQ and PRQ, is the most crucial operation for the proposed DQAL protocol. MDs demand the use of broadcast rules to identify collision and produce initialization that is supported by RQ value and foreword recognition category. Algorithm is used to show DQAL protocol(Figure 5).

Figure 5. Algorithm for security protocol

Algorithm

LTE dispersed queue admission process (DQAL):
For each CRI, the following actions and practises are repeated.

Initialization

The RQ rate and the foreword recognition category are sent via eNodeB.
Each MD increased the RQ by one to account for the colliding forewords.
if (RQ > 0) then
RQ rates are lowered by MDs by means of [min (RQ, *NNgg*)]
if (MD's foreword is collided) then
Determine the pRQ that the foreword order supports.

Preamble selection

if (RQ < *NNgg*) do
if (pRQ =0) then
Choose at random one of the group's preambles. GRQ+1
Else, Pick one of the foreword clusters at random. from GpRQ
Else, Await the following CRI
end if

The main goal is to be successful and let the cluster decide how the new appearance will proceed, avoiding conflicts with already-existing demands. The approach helps MDs select an efficient cluster and lessens the chance of collision, hence reducing access time and increasing access rate. AES- A symmetric-key encryption standard with a 128-bit block size and 128-bit key size is called the Advanced Encryption Standard (AES). It ensures that the hash code being used for encryption is encrypted using a very secure method.

Its algorithm is as follows:

- Key Expansion
- Initial Round
- Add Round Key
- Rounds
- Sub Bytes—Bytes are restored using a non-linear replacement technique in accordance with a lookup table.
- Shift Rows—Transposition involves moving lines to suit the circumstance.
- Mix Columns—Four bytes in each line are used for integration.
- Add Round Key—Using a key programme, round keys are created from the cypher key.
- Final Round (no Mix Columns)
- Sub Bytes
- Shift Rows

- Add Round Key
- **Encryption:** Statistics are transformed into plain text using cypher text, and the opposite is true when it is decrypted.
- **Protection Assaults:** Thanks to cloud computing frameworks, sellers may generate predictable income by renting out spaces on their physical equipment on an hourly basis.
- **Threats:** DDoS assaults are used by extortionists to disrupt services and flood nodes with messages.
- **The DDos Attack Tools Complex:** Agobot, Mstream, Trinoo
- **Straightforward:** The Denial of Service functionalities are present in XML and HTTP (H-DoS).
- **X-DoS:** Attacks using coercive parsing may result in an increase in CPU utilisation.
- **H-DoS:** The HTTP Flooder drains a victim's communications channel by using random HTTP needs.

XDoS attacks are defended against in cloud computing using Cloud Traceback. To defend Iran against H-DoS assaults, Cloud Protector is employed to train a reverse broadcast neural network. Back propagation neural network for Cloud Protector.

QUALITY EVALUATION MEASURES

Risks of Patients' Privacy Exposure

PHR is an electronic media-based confirmation tool that promotes and offers interoperability principles throughout the nation. It is subject to human supervision, mutual prohibition, and prohibition. To safeguard patient PHRs, one-to-many encryption methods like ABE and AES are utilised, along with encryption algorithms like AES and MD5. Two security areas that are based on the classification of users' data supply needs are PUDs and PSDs. PSDs are sovereign financial divisions, whereas PUDs are made up of clients who need access to support their specialised activities. Customers can obtain PHRs supported by the access credentials granted by the proprietor when connecting through a statistics proprietor. It is possible to gauge how much isolation is around and decide about whether to provide sensitive material or not.

Threats of Cyber-Attacks on Privacy

IoT operations can suffer substantial harm from cyberattacks, thus it's critical to have strong protections in place to prevent them. It's challenging to install typical security solutions on IoT devices due to their resource limitations, thus it's crucial to develop a system to detect and respond to cyberattacks. A brand-new distributed method for detecting cyberattacks was put out and is based on simulations, system characteristics, experiment variables, and simulation limits. Iterative local processing and message transmission are necessary for organisational progress.

- To guarantee uniformity and significance, experiments are carried out utilising an Intel Core i5, 240 GHz, 4GB RAM system.

- To guarantee uniformity and significance, experiments are carried out utilising an Intel Core i5, 240 GHz, 4GB RAM system.
- The suggested algorithms are compared based on how quickly they can save or retrieve data blocks from cloud storage.

The essential parameters include key analysis, Avalanche effect, execution time, encryption time, and decryption time. The identity authentication paradigm for the IoT capabilities based on access control was proposed by simulation software. All electronic devices, distributed devices, and mobile/portable devices that meet certain requirements can use the suggested working model for a public key approach. To prevent a Mit M attack, it concerns the substantiation message as well as communication equipment and boosts usage factor over time. Three steps of authentication are completed one after the other.

- An procedure called Key Generation Phase (KGP) is used to create secret keys.
- Phase of concern: The authentication mechanism used to verify identity might be either one-way or mutual.
- Phase of implementation: Reliable device communication requires access control and permission management.

Future Extension of Work

The various parameters of the system have been optimized by traditional and non-traditional multi-criteria optimization techniques (Boopathi et al., 2022; Boopathi & Sivakumar, 2013, 2016; Haribalaji et al., 2021; Sampath, C., et al., 2022; Saravanan et al., 2022; Vanitha et al., 2023; Vennila et al., 2023; Yupapin et al., 2023). The real time experiments are conducted to continue the future work.

SUMMARY

This chapter covers a variety of IoT healthcare strategies, performance indicators, and security solutions for the IoT architecture and applications' dangers and weaknesses. Additionally, it discusses wireless assaults on various pieces of equipment connected to IoT healthcare systems as well as protocols for security mechanisms for IoT healthcare. Algorithms for encryption and decryption are used in the READ and WRITE security method. User-centric encryption and decryption of data files enable for upload, download, and sharing mode. The chapter's objective is to develop a new appearance to select the foreword from the group.

ABBREVIATIONS

- ADM - Abnormality Detection Model
- AES - Advanced Encryption Standard
- CM - Community Members
- COVID - Corona Virus Disease 2019 caused by SARS
- CPU - Central Processing Unit

- DoS - Denial of Service
- DQAL - Date Structured Query Language
- HTTP - Hypertext Transfer Protocol
- IETF - Internet Engineering Task Force
- IoT - Internet-of-Things
- KGP - Key Generation Phase
- NFC - Near Field Communications Forum
- ONS - Object Naming Service
- RFID – Radio Frequency Identification
- TLS -Transport Layer Security
- XML - Extensible Mark-up Language

REFERENCES

Babu, B. S., Kamalakannan, J., Meenatchi, N., M, S. K. S., S, K., & Boopathi, S. (2023). Economic impacts and reliability evaluation of battery by adopting Electric Vehicle. *IEEE Explore*, 1–6. doi:10.1109/ICPECTS56089.2022.10046786

Bin Zikria, Y., Khalil Afzal, M., & Won Kim, S. (2020). Internet of multimedia things (Iomt): Opportunities, challenges and solutions. *Sensors (Basel)*, *20*(8), 2334. doi:10.339020082334 PMID:32325944

Boopathi, S. (2019). Experimental investigation and parameter analysis of LPG refrigeration system using Taguchi method. In SN Applied Sciences (Vol. 1, Issue 8). doi:10.100742452-019-0925-2

Boopathi, S. (2022a). Experimental investigation and multi-objective optimization of cryogenic Friction-stir-welding of AA2014 and AZ31B alloys using MOORA technique. *Materials Today. Communications*, *33*, 104937. doi:10.1016/j.mtcomm.2022.104937

Boopathi, S. (2022b). Performance Improvement of Eco-Friendly Near-Dry Wire-Cut Electrical Discharge Machining Process Using Coconut Oil-Mist Dielectric Fluid. *Journal of Advanced Manufacturing Systems*. Advance online publication. doi:10.1142/S0219686723500178

Boopathi, S. (2022c). An Extensive Review on Sustainable Developments of Dry and Near-Dry Electrical Discharge Machining Processes. *Journal of Manufacturing Science and Engineering*, *144*(5), 1–37. doi:10.1115/1.4052527

Boopathi, S., Arigela, S. H., Raman, R., Indhumathi, C., Kavitha, V., & Bhatt, B. C. (2023). Prominent Rule Control-based Internet of Things: Poultry Farm Management System. *IEEE Explore*, 1–6. doi:10.1109/ICPECTS56089.2022.10047039

Boopathi, S., Haribalaji, V., Mageswari, M., & Asif, M. M. (2022). Influences of Boron Carbide Particles on the Wear Rate and Tensile Strength of Aa2014 Surface Composite Fabricated By Friction-Stir Processing. *Materiali in Tehnologije*, *56*(3), 263–270. doi:10.17222/mit.2022.409

Boopathi, S., Khare, R., Jaya Christiyan, K. G., Muni, T. V., & Khare, S. (2023). Additive manufacturing developments in the medical engineering field. In Development, Properties, and Industrial Applications of 3D Printed Polymer Composites (pp. 86–106). IGI Global. doi:10.4018/978-1-6684-6009-2.ch006

Boopathi, S., Siva Kumar, P. K., & Meena, R. S. J., S. I., P., S. K., & Sudhakar, M. (2023). Sustainable Developments of Modern Soil-Less Agro-Cultivation Systems. In Human Agro-Energy Optimization for Business and Industry (pp. 69–87). IGI Global. doi:10.4018/978-1-6684-4118-3.ch004

Boopathi, S., & Sivakumar, K. (2013). Experimental investigation and parameter optimization of near-dry wire-cut electrical discharge machining using multi-objective evolutionary algorithm. *International Journal of Advanced Manufacturing Technology, 67*(9–12), 2639–2655. doi:10.100700170-012-4680-4

Boopathi, S., & Sivakumar, K. (2016). Optimal parameter prediction of oxygen-mist near-dry Wire-cut EDM. *International Journal of Manufacturing Technology and Management, 30*(3–4), 164–178. doi:10.1504/IJMTM.2016.077812

Chakravarthi, P. K., Yuvaraj, D., & Venkataramanan, V. (2022). IoT-based smart energy meter for smart grids. *ICDCS 2022 - 2022 6th International Conference on Devices, Circuits and Systems*, 360–363. 10.1109/ICDCS54290.2022.9780714

Domakonda, V. K., Farooq, S., Chinthamreddy, S., Puviarasi, R., Sudhakar, M., & Boopathi, S. (2023). Sustainable Developments of Hybrid Floating Solar Power Plants. In *Human Agro-Energy Optimization for Business and Industry* (pp. 148–167). IGI Global. doi:10.4018/978-1-6684-4118-3.ch008

Garg, N., Wazid, M., Singh, J., Singh, D. P., & Das, A. K. (2022). Security in IoMT -driven smart healthcare: A comprehensive review and open challenges. *Security and Privacy, 5*(5), e235. doi:10.1002py2.235

Gupta, D., Gupta, M., Bhatt, S., & Tosun, A. S. (2021). Detecting Anomalous User Behavior in Remote Patient Monitoring. *Proceedings - 2021 IEEE 22nd International Conference on Information Reuse and Integration for Data Science, IRI 2021*, 33–40. 10.1109/IRI51335.2021.00011

Haribalaji, V., Boopathi, S., & Asif, M. M. (2021). Optimization of friction stir welding process to join dissimilar AA2014 and AA7075 aluminum alloys. *Materials Today: Proceedings, 50*, 2227–2234. doi:10.1016/j.matpr.2021.09.499

Harikaran, M., Boopathi, S., Gokulakannan, S., & Poonguzhali, M. (2023). Study on the Source of E-Waste Management and Disposal Methods. In *Sustainable Approaches and Strategies for E-Waste Management and Utilization* (pp. 39–60). IGI Global. doi:10.4018/978-1-6684-7573-7.ch003

Hireche, R., Mansouri, H., & Pathan, A.-S. K. (2022). Security and Privacy Management in Internet of Medical Things (IoMT): A Synthesis. *Journal of Cybersecurity and Privacy, 2*(3), 640–661. doi:10.3390/jcp2030033

Janardhana, K., Singh, V., Singh, S. N., Babu, T. S. R., Bano, S., & Boopathi, S. (2023). Utilization Process for Electronic Waste in Eco-Friendly Concrete: Experimental Study. In Sustainable Approaches and Strategies for E-Waste Management and Utilization (pp. 204–223). IGI Global.

Jeevanantham, Y. A., A, S., V, V., J, S. I., Boopathi, S., & Kumar, D. P. (2023). Implementation of Internet-of-Things (IoT) in Soil Irrigation System. *IEEE Explore*, 1–5. doi:10.1109/ICPECTS56089.2022.10047185

Kang, J., Fan, K., Zhang, K., Cheng, X., Li, H., & Yang, Y. (2021). An ultra light weight and secure RFID batch authentication scheme for IoMT. *Computer Communications, 167*, 48–54. doi:10.1016/j.comcom.2020.12.004

Koutras, D., Stergiopoulos, G., Dasaklis, T., Kotzanikolaou, P., Glynos, D., & Douligeris, C. (2020). Security in iomt communications: A survey. *Sensors (Basel), 20*(17), 1–49. doi:10.339020174828 PMID:32859036

Kumara, V., Mohanaprakash, T. A., Fairooz, S., Jamal, K., Babu, T., & B., S. (2023). Experimental Study on a Reliable Smart Hydroponics System. In *Human Agro-Energy Optimization for Business and Industry* (pp. 27–45). IGI Global. doi:10.4018/978-1-6684-4118-3.ch002

Mohd Aman, A. H., Hassan, W. H., Sameen, S., Attarbashi, Z. S., Alizadeh, M., & Latiff, L. A. (2021). IoMT amid COVID-19 pandemic: Application, architecture, technology, and security. *Journal of Network and Computer Applications, 174*, 102886. doi:10.1016/j.jnca.2020.102886 PMID:34173428

Palaniappan, M., Tirlangi, S., Mohamed, M. J. S., Moorthy, R. M. S., Valeti, S. V., & Boopathi, S. (2023). Fused deposition modelling of polylactic acid (PLA)-based polymer composites: A case study. In Development, Properties, and Industrial Applications of 3D Printed Polymer Composites (pp. 66–85). IGI Global. doi:10.4018/978-1-6684-6009-2.ch005

Polu, S. K. (2019). IoMT Based Smart Health Care Monitoring System. *CEUR Workshop Proceedings, 2544*(11), 58–64.

Reddy, M. A., Reddy, B. M., Mukund, C. S., Venneti, K., Preethi, D. M. D., & Boopathi, S. (2023). Social Health Protection During the COVID-Pandemic Using IoT. In *The COVID-19 Pandemic and the Digitalization of Diplomacy* (pp. 204–235). IGI Global. doi:10.4018/978-1-7998-8394-4.ch009

S., P. K., Sampath, B., R., S. K., Babu, B. H., & N., A. (2022). Hydroponics, Aeroponics, and Aquaponics Technologies in Modern Agricultural Cultivation. In *IGI:Trends, Paradigms, and Advances in Mechatronics Engineering* (pp. 223–241). IGI Global. doi:10.4018/978-1-6684-5887-7.ch012

Samikannu, R., Koshariya, A. K., Poornima, E., Ramesh, S., Kumar, A., & Boopathi, S. (2023). Sustainable Development in Modern Aquaponics Cultivation Systems Using IoT Technologies. In *Human Agro-Energy Optimization for Business and Industry* (pp. 105–127). IGI Global. doi:10.4018/978-1-6684-4118-3.ch006

Sampath, B., & Myilsamy, S. (2021). Experimental investigation of a cryogenically cooled oxygen-mist near-dry wire-cut electrical discharge machining process. *Strojniski Vestnik. Jixie Gongcheng Xuebao, 67*(6), 322–330. doi:10.5545v-jme.2021.7161

Sampath, B., Pandian, M., Deepa, D., & Subbiah, R. (2022). Operating parameters prediction of liquefied petroleum gas refrigerator using simulated annealing algorithm. *AIP Conference Proceedings, 2460*(1), 070003. doi:10.1063/5.0095601

Sampath, B., Yuvaraj, D., & Velmurugan, D. (2022). Parametric analysis of mould sand properties for flange coupling casting. *AIP Conference Proceedings, 2460*(1), 070002. doi:10.1063/5.0095599

Sampath, B. C. S., & Myilsamy, S. (2022). Application of TOPSIS Optimization Technique in the Micro-Machining Process. In IGI:Trends, Paradigms, and Advances in Mechatronics Engineering (pp. 162–187). IGI Global. doi:10.4018/978-1-6684-5887-7.ch009

Saravanan, M., Vasanth, M., Boopathi, S., Sureshkumar, M., & Haribalaji, V. (2022). Optimization of Quench Polish Quench (QPQ) Coating Process Using Taguchi Method. *Key Engineering Materials*, *935*, 83–91. doi:10.4028/p-z569vy

Selvakumar, S., Adithe, S., Isaac, J. S., Pradhan, R., Venkatesh, V., & Sampath, B. (2023). A Study of the Printed Circuit Board (PCB) E-Waste Recycling Process. In Sustainable Approaches and Strategies for E-Waste Management and Utilization (pp. 159–184). IGI Global.

Senthil, T. S. R., Ohmsakthi vel, Puviyarasan, M., Babu, S. R., Surakasi, R., & Sampath, B. (2023). Industrial Robot-Integrated Fused Deposition Modelling for the 3D Printing Process. In Development, Properties, and Industrial Applications of 3D Printed Polymer Composites (pp. 188–210). IGI Global. doi:10.4018/978-1-6684-6009-2.ch011

Toghuj, W., & Turab, N. (2022). A survey on security threats in the internet of medical things (IoMT). *Journal of Theoretical and Applied Information Technology*, *100*(10), 3361–3371.

Vanitha, S. K. R., & Boopathi, S. (2023). Artificial Intelligence Techniques in Water Purification and Utilization. In *Human Agro-Energy Optimization for Business and Industry* (pp. 202–218). IGI Global., doi:10.4018/978-1-6684-4118-3.ch010

Vennila, T., Karuna, M. S., Srivastava, B. K., Venugopal, J., Surakasi, R., & B., S. (2023). New Strategies in Treatment and Enzymatic Processes. In *Human Agro-Energy Optimization for Business and Industry* (pp. 219–240). IGI Global. doi:10.4018/978-1-6684-4118-3.ch011

Yupapin, P., Trabelsi, Y., Nattappan, A., & Boopathi, S. (2023). Performance Improvement of Wire-Cut Electrical Discharge Machining Process Using Cryogenically Treated Super-Conductive State of Monel-K500 Alloy. *Iranian Journal of Science and Technology. Transaction of Mechanical Engineering*, *47*(1), 267–283. doi:10.100740997-022-00513-0

Compilation of References

IDumkova, J., Smutna, T., Vrlikova, L., Coustumer, P., Vevera, Z., Docekal, B., Mikuska, P., Capka, L., Fictum, P., Hampl, A., & Buchtoava, M. (n.d.). *Sub-chronic inhalation of lead oxide nanoparticles revealed their broad distribution and tissue-specific subcellular localization in target organs: Particle and Fibre Toxicology.* BMC. https://particleandfibretoxicology.biomedcentral.com/articles/10.1186/s12989-017-0236-y

Abbas, F. & Qamar, M. (2020). Performance Analysis of Ad Hoc on-Demand Distance Vector Routing Protocol for MANET. *2020 IEEE Student Conference on Research and Development (SCOReD).* IEEE. 10.1109/SCOReD50371.2020.9250989

Abd-Alrazaq, A., Al-Jafar, E., Alajlani, M., Toro, C., Alhuwail, D., Ahmed, A., Reagu, S. M., Al-Shorbaji, N., & Househ, M. (2022). The effectiveness of serious games for alleviating depression: Systematic review and meta-analysis. *JMIR Serious Games, 10*(1), e32331. doi:10.2196/32331 PMID:35029530

Abdelmoula, H., Sharpes, N., Abdelkefi, A., Lee, H., & Priya, S. (2017). Low-frequency Zigzag energy harvesters operating in torsion-dominant mode. *Applied Energy, 204,* 413–419. doi:10.1016/j.apenergy.2017.07.044

Acar, E., Bayrak, G., Jung, Y., Lee, I., Ramu, P., & Ravichandran, S. S. (2021). Modeling, analysis, and optimization under uncertainties: A review. *Structural and Multidisciplinary Optimization, 64*(5), 1–37. doi:10.100700158-021-03026-7

Adywiratama, A., Ko, C., Raharjo, T., & Wahbi, A. (2022). Critical success factors for ICT project: A case study in project colocation government data center. *Procedia Computer Science, 197,* 385–392. doi:10.1016/j.procs.2021.12.154

Afhamisisi, K., Shahhoseini, H. S., & Meamari, E. (2019). Defense against Lion Attack in Cognitive Radio Systems using the Markov Decision Process Approach. *Frequenz (Bern), 68,* 191–201.

Afzal, S., Asim, M., Javed, A. R., Beg, M. O., & Baker, T. (2021). URLdeepDetect: A Deep Learning Approach for Detecting Malicious URLs Using Semantic Vector Models. *Journal of Network and Systems Management, 29*(3), 1–27. doi:10.100710922-021-09587-8

Aggarwal, S., & Gupta, C. (2016). Solving intuitionistic fuzzy solid transportation problem via new ranking method based on signed distance. *International Journal of Uncertainty, Fuzziness and Knowledge-based Systems, 24*(04), 483–501. doi:10.1142/S0218488516500240

Aggarwal, S., & Gupta, C. (2017). Sensitivity analysis of intuitionistic fuzzy solid transportation problem. *International Journal of Fuzzy Systems, 19*(6), 1904–1915. doi:10.100740815-016-0292-8

Aghion, P., & Stein, J. C. (2008). Growth versus margins: Destabilizing consequences of giving the stock market what it wants. *The Journal of Finance, 63*(3), 1025–1058. doi:10.1111/j.1540-6261.2008.01351.x

Aguilar-Lazcano, C. A., & Rechy-Ramirez, E. J. (2020). Performance analysis of Leap motion controller for finger rehabilitation using serious games in two lighting environments. *Measurement, 157,* 107677. doi:10.1016/j.measurement.2020.107677

Ahern, K. R. (2017). Information networks: Evidence from illegal insider trading tips. *Journal of Financial Economics*, *125*(1), 26–47. doi:10.1016/j.jfineco.2017.03.009

Ahmadfard, A., Jamshidi, A., & Keshavarz-Haddad, A. (2017). Probabilistic spectrum sensing data falsification attack in cognitive radio networks. *Signal Processing*, *137*, 1–9. doi:10.1016/j.sigpro.2017.01.033

Ahmadpour, M., Yue, W. L., & Mohammadzaheri, M. (2009). *Neuro-fuzzy Modelling of Workers Trip Production*. 32nd Australasian Transport Research Forum, Auckland, New Zealand.

Ahmad, S., Abdul Mujeebu, M., & Farooqi, M. A. (2019). Energy harvesting from pavements and roadways: A comprehensive review of technologies, materials, and challenges. *International Journal of Energy Research*, *43*(6), 1974–2015. doi:10.1002/er.4350

Ahmed, M. E., Song, J. B., & Han, Z. (2014). Mitigating malicious attacks using Bayesian nonparametric clustering in collaborative cognitive radio networks. In: *Proceedings of the IEEE Globecom*. IEEE. https://ieeexplore.ieee.org/document/7036939

Ahmed, S. (2021). Realizing the Benefits of Energy Harvesting for IoT. In *Role of IoT in Green Energy Systems* (pp. 144–155). IGI Global. doi:10.4018/978-1-7998-6709-8.ch006

Akyildiz, I. F., Lee, W.-Y., Vuran, M. C., & Mohanty, S. (2006, September). NeXt generation/dynamic spectrum access/cognitive radio wireless networks [Elsevier North-Holland, Inc.New York, NY, USA.]. *Computer Networks*, *50*(13, 15), 2127–2159. doi:10.1016/j.comnet.2006.05.001

Al Mamun M., Berger C., Hanson J. (2019). *Effects of measurements on correlations of software code metrics*. Springer. https://doi.org/. doi:10.1007/s10664-019-09714-9

Al Mojamed, M. (2020). Integrating Mobile Ad Hoc Networks withthe Internet Basedon OLSR. *Wireless Communications and Mobile Computing*. doi:10.1155/2020/8810761

Al-Ahmadi, S., & Alharbi, Y. (2020). A Deep Learning Technique For Web Phishing Detection Combined Url Features And Visual Similarity. *International Journal of Computer Networks and Communications*, *12*(5), 41–54. doi:10.5121/ijcnc.2020.12503

Alibak, A. H., Alizadeh, S. M., Davodi Monjezi, S., Alizadeh, A., Alobaid, F., & Aghel, B. (2022). Developing a Hybrid Neuro-Fuzzy Method to Predict Carbon Dioxide (CO_2) Permeability in Mixed Matrix Membranes Containing SAPO-34 Zeolite. *Membranes*, *12*(11), 1147. doi:10.3390/membranes12111147 PMID:36422139

Ali-Hussein, Y., & Shiker, M. A. (2022). Using the largest difference method to find the initial basic feasible solution to the transportation problem. *Journal of Interdisciplinary Mathematics*, *25*(8), 2511–2517. doi:10.1080/09720502.2022.2040852

Al-Qudaimi, A., Kaur, K., & Bhat, S. (2021). Triangular fuzzy numbers multiplication: QKB method. *Fuzzy Optimization and Modeling Journal*, *3*(2), 34–40.

Alsakka, R., & ap Gwilym, O. (2012). Foreign exchange market reactions to sovereign credit news. *Journal of International Money and Finance*, *31*(4), 845–864. doi:10.1016/j.jimonfin.2012.01.007

Althunibat, S., Di Renzo, M., & Granelli, F. (2014). Robust algorithm against spectrum sensing data falsification attack in cognitive radio networks. In: *Proceedings of VTC spring*, (pp. 1–5). IEEE. https://ieeexplore.ieee.org/document/7023078

Alti, A., & Tetlock, P. C. (2014). Biased beliefs, asset prices, and investment: A structural approach. *The Journal of Finance*, *69*(1), 325–361. doi:10.1111/jofi.12089

Alvarez-Perez, M. G., Garcia-Murillo, M. A., & Cervantes-Sánchez, J. J. (2020). Robot-assisted ankle rehabilitation: A review. *Disability and Rehabilitation. Assistive Technology, 15*(4), 394–408. doi:10.1080/17483107.2019.1578424 PMID:30856032

American Physical Therapy Association. (2001). Guide to physical therapist practice. Physical therapy, 81(1), 9–746.

Amutha, B., & Uthra, G. (2021). Defuzzification of symmetric octagonal intuitionistic fuzzy number. *Advances and Applications in Mathematical Sciences, 20*(9), 1719–1728.

Ando, O. H. Junior, Maran, A. L. O., & Henao, N. C. (2018). A review of the development and applications of thermo-electric microgenerators for energy harvesting. *Renewable & Sustainable Energy Reviews, 91*, 376–393. doi:10.1016/j.rser.2018.03.052

Andrade, K. D. O., Fernandes, G., Caurin, G. A., Siqueira, A. A., Romero, R. A., & Pereira, R. D. L. (2014, October). Dynamic player modelling in serious games applied to rehabilitation robotics. *In 2014 Joint Conference on Robotics: SBR-LARS Robotics Symposium and Robocontrol* (pp. 211-216). IEEE. 10.1109/SBR.LARS.Robocontrol.2014.41

Andrade, K. O., Ito, G. G., Joaquim, R. C., Jardim, B., Siqueira, A. A., Caurin, G. A., & Becker, M. (2010, November). A robotic system for rehabilitation of distal radius fracture using games. *In 2010 Brazilian symposium on games and digital entertainment* (pp. 25-32). IEEE. 10.1109/SBGAMES.2010.26

Andrade, K. O., Joaquim, R. C., Caurin, G. A., & Crocomo, M. K. (2018). Evolutionary algorithms for a better gaming experience in rehabilitation robotics. [CIE]. *Computers in Entertainment, 16*(2), 1–15. doi:10.1145/3180657

Andrei, D., & Cujean, J. (2017). Information percolation, momentum and reversal. *Journal of Financial Economics, 123*(3), 617–645. doi:10.1016/j.jfineco.2016.05.012

Andrias, M., Matook, S., & Vidgen, R. (2018). Towards a typology of agile ISD leadership. *Twenty-Sixth European Conference on Information Systems (ECIS2018)*, Portsmouth, UK. 10.1177/096032717100300106

Andrychowicz, M., Wolski, F., Ray, A., Schneider, J., Fong, R., Welinder, P., McGrew, B., Tobin, J., Abbeel, P., Zaremba W. (2017). *Hindsight Experience Replay, Advances in Neural Information Processing Systems 30*. NeurIPS. https://arxiv.org/pdf/1707.01495.pdf

Anwar, H. (2018, August 25). Consensus Algorithms: The Root of Blockchain Technology. *101 Blockchains*. https://101blockchains.com/consensus-algorithms-blockchain/

Anwar, H. (2021, June 2). What is a Private Blockchain? Beginner's Guide. *101 Blockchains*. https://101blockchains.com/what-is-a-private-blockchain/

Appa, G. (1973). The transportation problem and its variants. *Operational Research Quarterly (1970-1977), 24*(1), 79-99. doi:10.2307/3008037

Arjoune, Y., Salahdine, F., Islam, M., Ghribi, E., & Kaabouch, N. (2020). A Novel Jamming Attacks Detection Approach Based on Machine Learning for Wireless Communication. *International Conference on Information Networking (ICOIN)*, Barcelona, Spain. 10.1109/ICOIN48656.2020.9016462

Arsenault, D. (2009). Video game genre, evolution and innovation. *Eludamos (Göttingen), 3*(2), 149–176. doi:10.7557/23.6003

Assunção, E., Gaspar, P. D., Alibabaei, K., Simões, M. P., Proença, H., Soares, V. N. G. J., & Caldeira, J. M. L. P. (2022). Real-time image detection for edge devices: A peach fruit detection application. *Future Internet, 14*(11), 323. doi:10.3390/fi14110323

Asthana, P., & Khanna, G. (2020). Development of Vibration Piezoelectric Harvesters by the Optimum Design of Cantilever Structures. In *Nanogenerators*. IntechOpen. doi:10.5772/intechopen.90556

Atanassov, K. T. (1983). Intuitionistic Fuzzy Sets, VII ITKR Session, Sofia, 20-23 June 1983 (Deposed in Centr. Sci.-Techn. Library of the Bulg. Acad. of Sci., 1697/84) (in Bulg.). Reprinted: *Int J Bioautomation*, 2016, *20*(S1), S1-S6.

Attar, A., Tang, H., Vasilakos, A. V., Yu, F. R., & Leung, V. C. M. (2012). A Survey of Security Challenges in Cognitive Radio Networks: Solutions and Future Research Directions. *Proceedings of the IEEE, 100*(12), 3172–3186. doi:10.1109/JPROC.2012.2208211

Babu, B. R., Tripathi, M., Gaur, M. S., Gopalani, D., & Singh Jat, D. (2015). Cognitive radio ad-hoc networks: Attacks and its impact. *2015 International Conference on Emerging Trends in Networks and Computer Communications (ETNCC)*, (pp. 125-130). IEEE. 10.1109/ETNCC.2015.7184821

Babu, B. S., Kamalakannan, J., Meenatchi, N., M, S. K. S., S, K., & Boopathi, S. (2023). Economic impacts and reliability evaluation of battery by adopting Electric Vehicle. *IEEE Explore*, 1–6. doi:10.1109/ICPECTS56089.2022.10046786

Bahk, J., Fang, H., Yazawa, K., & Shakouri, A. (2015). *Flexible thermoelectric materials and device optimization for wearable energy harvesting—Journal of Materials Chemistry C.* RSC Publishing. https://pubs.rsc.org/en/content/articlelanding/2015/TC/C5TC01644D

Baiod, W., Light, J., & Mahanti, A. (2021). Blockchain Technology and its Applications Across Multiple Domains: A Survey. *Journal of International Technology and Information Management, 29*(4), 78–119. doi:10.58729/1941-6679.1482

Ban, A. (2008). Trapezoidal approximations of intuitionistic fuzzy numbers expressed by value, ambiguity, width and weighted expected value. *Notes on Intuitionistic Fuzzy Sets, 14*(1), 38–47.

Barber, B. M., & Odean, T. (2008). All that glitters: The effect of attention and news on the buying behavior of individual and institutional investors. *Review of Financial Studies, 21*(2), 785–818. doi:10.1093/rfs/hhm079

Barbuzzi, D., Massaro, A., Galiano, A., Pellicani, L., Pirlo, G., & Sageese, M. (2020). Multi-Domain Intelligent System for Document Image Retrieval. *International Journal of Adaptive and Innovative Systems, 2*(4), 282–297. doi:10.1504/IJAIS.2019.108381

Barnes, S., & Prescott, J. (2018). Empirical evidence for the outcomes of therapeutic video games for adolescents with anxiety disorders: Systematic review. *JMIR Serious Games, 6*(1), e9530. doi:10.2196/games.9530 PMID:29490893

Basu, M., Pal, B. B., & Kundu, A. (1994). An algorithm for finding the optimum solution of solid fixed-charge transportation problem. *Optimization, 31*(3), 283–291. doi:10.1080/02331939408844023

Baumeister, C., & Kilian, L. (2016). Forty years of oil price fluctuations: Why the price of oil may still surprise us. *The Journal of Economic Perspectives, 30*(1), 139–160. doi:10.1257/jep.30.1.139

Bazghaleh, M., Grainger, S., & Mohammadzaheri, M. (2018). A review of charge methods for driving piezoelectric actuators. *Journal of Intelligent Material Systems and Structures, 29*(10), 2096–2104. doi:10.1177/1045389X17733330

Bazghaleh, M., Grainger, S., Mohammadzaheri, M., Cazzolato, B., & Lu, T. (2013). A digital charge amplifier for hysteresis elimination in piezoelectric actuators. *Smart Materials and Structures, 22*(7), 075016. doi:10.1088/0964-1726/22/7/075016

Becker, P. (2014). Visión de proceso para estrategias integradas de medición y evaluación de la calidad. [Tesis Doctoral, Facultad de Informática, Universidad Nacional de La Plata].

Bello, I., Chiroma, H., Abdullahi, U. A., Gital, A. Y., Jauro, F., Khan, A., Okesola, J. O., & Abdulhamid, S. M. (2021). Detecting ransomware attacks using intelligent algorithms: Recent development and next direction from deep learning and big data perspectives. *Journal of Ambient Intelligence and Humanized Computing, 12*(9), 8699–8717. doi:10.100712652-020-02630-7

Benavides-Astudillo, E., Fuertes, W., Sanchez-Gordon, S., Nuñez-Agurto, D., & Rodríguez-Galán, G. (2023). A Phishing-Attack-Detection Model Using Natural Language Processing and Deep Learning. *Applied Sciences, 13*(9), 5275. doi:10.3390/app13095275

Bennaceur, J., Idoudi, H., & Saidane, L. A. (2016). *A trust game model for the cognitive radio networks.* 2016 International Conference on Performance Evaluation and Modeling in Wired and Wireless Networks (PEMWN), Paris, France. 10.1109/PEMWN.2016.7842903

Bera, T., & Mahapatra, N. K. (2020). *Neutrosophic linear programming problem and its application to real life.* Afrika Matematika. doi:10.100713370-019-00754-4

Berssaneti, F., & Carvalho, M. (2015). Identification of variables that impact project success in Brazilian companies. *International Journal of Project Management, 33*(3), 638–649. doi:10.1016/j.ijproman.2014.07.002

Bhadane, A. P., Manjarekar, S. D., & Dighavkar, C. G. (2021). APBs method for the IBFS of a transportation problem and comparison with North West Corner Method. *GANITA, 71*(1), 109–114.

Bharadwaj, R., Bhatia, A., Divya Chhibbar, L., Tiwari, K., & Agrawal, A. (2022). *Is this URL Safe: Detection of Malicious URLs Using Global Vector for Word Representation.* IEEE. doi:10.1109/ICOIN53446.2022.9687204

Bharati, S. K., & Malhotra, R. (2017). Two stage intuitionistic fuzzy time minimizing transportation problem based on generalized Zadeh's extension principle. *International Journal of System Assurance Engineering and Management, 8*(S2), 1442–1449. doi:10.100713198-017-0613-9

Bhardwaj, C. (2019, October 21). Analysis of the Blockchain Consensus Algorithms. *Appinventiv.* https://appinventiv.com/blog/blockchain-consensus-algorithms-guide/

Bian, K., & Park, J. M. (2006). MAC-layer Misbehaviors in Multi-hop Cognitive Radio Networks. *Proceedings of the 2006 US-Korea Conference on Science, Technology and Entrepreneurship.* IEEE.

Bin Zikria, Y., Khalil Afzal, M., & Won Kim, S. (2020). Internet of multimedia things (Iomt): Opportunities, challenges and solutions. *Sensors (Basel), 20*(8), 2334. doi:10.339020082334 PMID:32325944

Bitstamp Team. (2021, August 18). *What is Block Size?* Bitstamp Blog. https://blog.bitstamp.net/post/what-is-block-size/

Böhm, A. (2009). *Application of PRINCE2 and the Impact on Project Management.*

Boopathi, S. (2019). Experimental investigation and parameter analysis of LPG refrigeration system using Taguchi method. In SN Applied Sciences (Vol. 1, Issue 8). doi:10.100742452-019-0925-2

Boopathi, S., Arigela, S. H., Raman, R., Indhumathi, C., Kavitha, V., & Bhatt, B. C. (2023). Prominent Rule Control-based Internet of Things: Poultry Farm Management System. *IEEE Explore*, 1–6. doi:10.1109/ICPECTS56089.2022.10047039

Boopathi, S., Khare, R., Jaya Christiyan, K. G., Muni, T. V., & Khare, S. (2023). Additive manufacturing developments in the medical engineering field. In Development, Properties, and Industrial Applications of 3D Printed Polymer Composites (pp. 86–106). IGI Global. doi:10.4018/978-1-6684-6009-2.ch006

Boopathi, S., Siva Kumar, P. K., & Meena, R. S. J., S. I., P., S. K., & Sudhakar, M. (2023). Sustainable Developments of Modern Soil-Less Agro-Cultivation Systems. In Human Agro-Energy Optimization for Business and Industry (pp. 69–87). IGI Global. doi:10.4018/978-1-6684-4118-3.ch004

Boopathi, S. (2022a). Experimental investigation and multi-objective optimization of cryogenic Friction-stir-welding of AA2014 and AZ31B alloys using MOORA technique. *Materials Today. Communications*, *33*, 104937. doi:10.1016/j.mtcomm.2022.104937

Boopathi, S. (2022b). Performance Improvement of Eco-Friendly Near-Dry Wire-Cut Electrical Discharge Machining Process Using Coconut Oil-Mist Dielectric Fluid. *Journal of Advanced Manufacturing Systems*. Advance online publication. doi:10.1142/S0219686723500178

Boopathi, S. (2022c). An Extensive Review on Sustainable Developments of Dry and Near-Dry Electrical Discharge Machining Processes. *Journal of Manufacturing Science and Engineering*, *144*(5), 1–37. doi:10.1115/1.4052527

Boopathi, S., Haribalaji, V., Mageswari, M., & Asif, M. M. (2022). Influences of Boron Carbide Particles on the Wear Rate and Tensile Strength of Aa2014 Surface Composite Fabricated By Friction-Stir Processing. *Materiali in Tehnologije*, *56*(3), 263–270. doi:10.17222/mit.2022.409

Boopathi, S., & Sivakumar, K. (2013). Experimental investigation and parameter optimization of near-dry wire-cut electrical discharge machining using multi-objective evolutionary algorithm. *International Journal of Advanced Manufacturing Technology*, *67*(9–12), 2639–2655. doi:10.100700170-012-4680-4

Boopathi, S., & Sivakumar, K. (2016). Optimal parameter prediction of oxygen-mist near-dry Wire-cut EDM. *International Journal of Manufacturing Technology and Management*, *30*(3–4), 164–178. doi:10.1504/IJMTM.2016.077812

Bouzegag, Y., Djamal, T., & Abdelmadjid, M. (2022). Comprehensive Performance Analysis of Soft Data Fusion Schemes under SSDF Attacks in Cognitive Radio Networks. *International Journal of Sensors, Wireless Communications and Control*, *12*(4), 312–318. doi:10.2174/2210327912666220325155048

Broadstock, D. C., & Zhang, D. (2019). Social-media and intraday stock returns: The pricing power of sentiment. *Finance Research Letters*, *30*, 116–123. doi:10.1016/j.frl.2019.03.030

Brockmyer, J. H., Fox, C. M., Curtiss, K. A., McBroom, E., Burkhart, K. M., & Pidruzny, J. N. (2009). The development of the game engagement questionnaire: A measure of engagement in video game-playing. *Journal of Experimental Social Psychology*, *45*(4), 624–634. doi:10.1016/j.jesp.2009.02.016

Burillo, P., Bustince, H., & Mohedano, V. (1994, September). *Some definitions of intuitionistic fuzzy number. First properties*. In *1st Workshop on Fuzzy Based Expert Systems* (pp. 53-55). Bulgaria: Sofia.

BYJU'S Team. (2022, November 8). *Difference between Client-Server and Peer-to-Peer Network*. BYJUS. https://byjus.com/gate/difference-between-client-server-and-peer-to-peer-network/

Cabric, D., Mishra, S. M., & Brodersen, R. W. (2004). Implementation Issues in Spectrum Sensing for Cognitive Radios. *Proc. IEEE Asilomar Conf. Signals, Sys., and Comp.*, (pp. 772–76). IEEE. 10.1109/ACSSC.2004.1399240

Cammarano, A., Presti, F. L., Maselli, G., Pescosolido, L., & Petrioli, C. (2014). Throughput-optimal cross-layer design for cognitive radio ad hoc networks. *IEEE Transactions on Parallel and Distributed Systems*, *26*(9), 2599–2609. doi:10.1109/TPDS.2014.2350495

Cardia da Cruz, L., Sierra-Franco, C. A., Silva-Calpa, G. F. M., & Barbosa Raposo, A. (2020, July). A Self-adaptive serious game for eye-hand coordination training. *In International Conference on Human-Computer Interaction* (pp. 385-397). Springer, Cham. 10.1007/978-3-030-50164-8_28

Carhart, M. M. (1997). On persistence in mutual fund performance. *The Journal of Finance, 52*(1), 57–82. doi:10.1111/j.1540-6261.1997.tb03808.x

Casino, F., Dasaklis, T. K., & Patsakis, C. (2019). A Systematic Literature Review Of Blockchain-Based Applications: Current Status, Classification And Open Issues. *Telematics and Informatics, 36*, 55–81. doi:10.1016/j.tele.2018.11.006

Castanedo, F. (2013). A Review of Data Fusion Techniques. The Scientific World Journal. doi:10.1155/2013/704504

Castro, R. (2018). Data-driven PV modules modelling: Comparison between equivalent electric circuit and artificial intelligence based models. *Sustainable Energy Technologies and Assessments, 30*, 230–238. doi:10.1016/j.seta.2018.10.011

Castro, R. Q., & Au-Yong-Oliveira, M. (2021). Blockchain and Higher Education Diplomas. *European Journal of Investigation in Health, Psychology and Education, 11*(1), 1. Advance online publication. doi:10.3390/ejihpe11010013 PMID:34542456

Cawley, G. C., & Talbot, N. L. (2010). On over-fitting in model selection and subsequent selection bias in performance evaluation. *Journal of Machine Learning Research, 11*(Jul), 2079–2107.

Ceylan, H., Gopalakrishnan, K., Kim, S., & Cord, W. (n.d.). *Heated transportation infrastructure systems: Existing and emerging technologies.*

Chakravarthi, P. K., Yuvaraj, D., & Venkataramanan, V. (2022). IoT-based smart energy meter for smart grids. *ICDCS 2022 - 2022 6th International Conference on Devices, Circuits and Systems*, 360–363. 10.1109/ICDCS54290.2022.9780714

Chandra, A. L., Desai, S. V., Guo, W., & Balasubramanian, V. N. (2020). *Computer vision with deep learning for plant phenotyping in agriculture: A survey.* Advanced Computing and Communications., doi:10.34048/ACC.2020.1.F1

Chandrayan, P. (2020, September 21). BlockChain Principle, Type & Application & Why You Should Care About It? *SysopsMicro.* https://medium.com/the-programmer/blockchain-principle-type-application-why-you-should-care-about-it-249417b516cc

Chang, C.-J., Li, D.-C., Huang, Y.-H., & Chen, C.-C. (2015). A novel gray forecasting model based on the box plot for small manufacturing data sets. *Applied Mathematics and Computation, 265*, 400–408. doi:10.1016/j.amc.2015.05.006

Chen, C.-Y., & Chou, P. H. (2010). DuraCap: A supercapacitor-based, power-bootstrapping, maximum power point tracking energy-harvesting system. *2010 ACM/IEEE International Symposium on Low-Power Electronics and Design (ISLPED)*, (pp. 313–318). ACM/IEEE. 10.1145/1840845.1840910

Chen, H., Jin, X., & Xie, L. (2009). Reputation-based collaborative spectrum sensing algorithm in Cognitive Radio networks. In 2009 *IEEE 20th International Symposium on Personal, Indoor and Mobile Radio Communications*, (pp. 582–587). IEEE. 10.1109/PIMRC.2009.5450251

Chen, L., Lu, K., Rajeswaran, A., Lee, K., Grover, A., Laskin, M., Abbeel, P., Srinivas, A. and Mordatch, I. (2021). Decision Transformer: Reinforcement Learning via Sequence Modeling. arXiv. https://arxiv.org/abs/2106.01345

Chen, N. (n.d.). *Design, Modeling, and Simulation of Piezoelectric and Magnetoelectric Devices for Multimodal Energy Harvesting Applications.* MTSU.

Chen, Q., & Omote, K. (2022). *A Three-Step Framework for Detecting Malicious URLs.* doi:10.1109/ISNCC55209.2022.9851734

Chen, T. P., & Chen, H. (1995). Approximation capability to functions of several variables, nonlinear functionals, and operators by radial basis function neural networks. *IEEE Transactions on Neural Networks, 6*(4), 904-910. <Go to ISI>://A1995RF58200008

Chen, C.-J., Huang, Y.-Y., Li, Y.-S., Chen, Y.-C., Chang, C.-Y., & Huang, Y.-M. (2021). Identification of fruit tree pests with deep learning on embedded drone to achieve accurate pesticide spraying. *IEEE Access : Practical Innovations, Open Solutions*, 9, 21986–21997. doi:10.1109/ACCESS.2021.3056082

Chen, F., Wan, H., Cai, H., & Cheng, G. (2021). Machine Learning In/For Blockchain: Future and Challenges. *The Canadian Journal of Statistics*, 49(4), 1364–1382. doi:10.1002/cjs.11623

Cheng, Y. & Zhou, J. (2014). S-CRAHN: A Secure Cognitive-Radio Ad-Hoc Network. *HCTL Open Science and Technology Letters (HCTL Open STL)*.

Chen, J., & Ran, X. (2019). Deep learning with edge computing: A review. *Proceedings of the IEEE*, 107(8), 1655–1674. doi:10.1109/JPROC.2019.2921977

Chen, R. (2008, April). Toward Secure Distributed Spectrum Sensing in Cognitive Radio Networks. *IEEE Communications Magazine*.

Chen, R., Park, J.-M., & Reed, J. H. (2008). Defense against primary user emulation attacks in cognitive radio networks. *IEEE Journal on Selected Areas in Communications*, 26(1), 25–37. doi:10.1109/JSAC.2008.080104

Chen, S., Xiong, J., He, Z., Jiao, J., Xie, Z., & Han, Y. (2021). Citrus fruits harvesting sequence planning method based on visual attention mechanism: A novel cognition framework for citrus picking robots. In *2021 International Conference on Computer Information Science and Artificial Intelligence (CISAI)* (pp. 806–809). 10.1109/CISAI54367.2021.00162

Chen, Y., Kang, Y., Zhao, Y., Wang, L., Liu, J., Li, Y., Liang, Z., He, X., Li, X., Tavajohi, N., & Li, B. (2021). A review of lithium-ion battery safety concerns: The issues, strategies, and testing standards. *Journal of Energy Chemistry*, 59, 83–99. doi:10.1016/j.jechem.2020.10.017

Chesham, A., Wyss, P., Müri, R. M., Mosimann, U. P., & Nef, T. (2017). What older people like to play: Genre preferences and acceptance of casual games. *JMIR Serious Games*, 5(2), e7025. doi:10.2196/games.7025 PMID:28420601

Chetan N. & Mathur, K.P. (2007). *Security issues in cognitive radio networks*. Cognitive network: Towards Self-Aware Networks.

Chetto, M., & Queudet, A. (2016). 3—Harnessing Ambient Energy for Embedded Systems. In M. Chetto & A. Queudet (Eds.), *Energy Autonomy of Real-Time Systems* (pp. 57–83). Elsevier. doi:10.1016/B978-1-78548-125-3.50003-8

Chhibber, D., Srivastava, P. K., & Bisht, D. C. (2021). From fuzzy transportation problem to non-linear intuitionistic fuzzy multi-objective transportation problem: A literature review. *International Journal of Modelling and Simulation*, 1-16. doi:10.1080/02286203.2021.1983075

Christidis, K., & Devetsikiotis, M. (2016). Blockchains and Smart Contracts for the Internet of Things. *IEEE Access : Practical Innovations, Open Solutions*, 4, 2292–2303. doi:10.1109/ACCESS.2016.2566339

Clancy, T. C., & Goergen, N. Security in Cognitive Radio Networks: Threats and Mitigation. *Proceedings of the International Conference on Cognitive Radio Oriented Wireless Networks and Communications*, (pp. 1-8). IEEE. 10.1109/CROWNCOM.2008.4562534

Coinbase Team. (2022, April 24). *What Is 'Proof Of Work' Or 'Proof Of Stake'?* https://www.coinbase.com/learn/crypto-basics/what-is-proof-of-work-or-proof-of-stake

Colas, C., Fournier, P., Sigaud, O., Chetouani, M., Oudeyer, P. (2019). CURIOUS: Intrinsically Motivated Modular Multi-Goal Reinforcement Learning. *Proc. of the 36th International Conference on Machine Learning, 2019*. arXiv. https://arxiv.org/pdf/1810.06284v4.pdf

Collins, J., Brown, J., Schammel, C., Hutson, K., Jeffery, W., & Edenfield, M. (2017). Meaningful Analysis of Small Data Sets: A Clinician's Guide. *Clinical and Translational Research*, 2(1), 16–19.

Collotta, M. (2017). A Fuzzy Data Fusion Solution to Enhance the QoS and the Energy Consumption in Wireless Sensor Networks. Wireless Communications and Mobile Computing. doi:10.1155/2017/3418284

Conway, L. (2022, February 18). *Proof-of-Work vs. Proof-of-Stake: Which Is Better?* Blockworks. https://blockworks. co/proof-of-work-vs-proof-of-stake-whats-the-difference/

Cormio, C., & Chowdhury, K. R. (2009). *A Survey on MAC Protocols for Cognitive Radio Networks*. Ad Hoc Net. J. doi:10.1016/j.adhoc.2009.01.002

Cristaldo P., López De Luise D., La Pietra L., De Battista A. (2021). Metrics for validation and traceability of Project Management Requirements. *Global Research and Development Journal for Engineering (GRDJE)*.

Cristaldo, P., López De Luise, D., La Pietra, L., & De Battista, A. (2022). Medición para la evaluación transversal de metodologías de gestión de proyectos. *WICC 2022; XXIV Workshop de Investigadores en Ciencias de la Computación*. Springer.

Cristaldo, P., López De Luise, D., & La Pietra, L. (2022). *Influencia de la Visión Organizacional en los riesgos de la Gestión de Proyectos. 10mo Congreso Nacional de Ingeniería Informática/Sistemas de Información (CoNaIISI)*. Concepción del Uruguay. doi:10.33414/ajea.1146.2022

Cristaldo, P., López De Luise, D., La Pietra, L., De Battista, A., & Hemanth, J. (2021). Metrics for the Systematic Evaluation of Project Management Methodologies. [IJSSMET]. *International Journal of Service Science, Management, Engineering, and Technology*.

Cristaldo, P., López De Luise, D., La Pietra, L., Retamar, S., & De Battista, A. (2022). *Métricas para Metodologías de Gestión de Proyectos: planificación de la calidad y equipo de gestión. IEEE BIENNIAL CONGRESS OF ARGENTINA*. ARGENCON.

Cui, Y., Zhu, J., Twaha, S., Chu, J., Bai, H., Huang, K., Chen, X., Zoras, S., & Soleimani, Z. (2019). Techno-economic assessment of the horizontal geothermal heat pump systems: A comprehensive review. *Energy Conversion and Management*, *191*, 208–236. doi:10.1016/j.enconman.2019.04.018

Czikszentmihalyi, M. (1990). *Flow: the psychology of optimal experience*. Harper & Row.

Czymmek, V., Harders, L. O., Knoll, F. J., & Hussmann, S. (2019). Vision-based deep learning approach for real-time detection of weeds in organic farming. In *2019 IEEE International Instrumentation and Measurement Technology Conference (I2MTC)* (pp. 1–5). 10.1109/I2MTC.2019.8826921

Dai, Y., Xu, D., Maharjan, S., Qiao, G., & Zhang, Y. (2019). Artificial intelligence empowered edge computing and caching for internet of vehicles. *IEEE Wireless Communications*, *26*(3), 12–18. doi:10.1109/MWC.2019.1800411

Dansana, D., & Behera, P. K. (2021). A Study of Recent Security Attacks on Cognitive Radio Ad Hoc Networks (CRAHNs). In *Soft Computing Techniques and Applications: Proceeding of the International Conference on Computing and Communication (IC3 2020)* (pp. 351-359). Springer Singapore.

Dantzig, G. B. (1963). *Linear Programming and Extensions*. Princeton Univ. Press. doi:10.1515/9781400884179

Darehmiraki, M. (2020). A solution for the neutrosophic linear programming problem with a new ranking function. *Optimization Theory Based on Neutrosophic and Plithogenic Sets*, 235–259. doi:10.1016/b978-0-12-819670-0.00011-1

Das, A. (2022). A Comprehensive Study on Neutrosophic Fuzzy Solid Transportation Model and Its Solution Technique. In *Real Life Applications of Multiple Criteria Decision Making Techniques in Fuzzy Domain* (pp. 521–531). Springer Nature Singapore. doi:10.1007/978-981-19-4929-6_24

Das, A., Bera, U. K., & Maiti, M. (2017). Defuzzification and application of trapezoidal type-2 fuzzy variables to green solid transportation problem. *Soft Computing*, *22*(7), 2275–2297. doi:10.100700500-017-2491-0

Das, K. N., Das, R., & Acharjya, D. P. (2021). Least-looping stepping-stone-based ASM approach for transportation and triangular intuitionistic fuzzy transportation problems. *Complex & Intelligent Systems*, *7*(6), 1–10. doi:10.100740747-021-00472-0

Das, S. K. (2021). An approach to optimize the cost of transportation problem based on triangular fuzzy programming problem. *Complex & Intelligent Systems*, 1–13. doi:10.100740747-021-00535-2

Das, S., & Guha, D. (2013). Ranking of intuitionistic fuzzy number by centroid point. *Journal of Industrial and Intelligent Information*, *1*(2), 107–110. doi:10.12720/jiii.1.2.107-110

Davis, K. (2014). *Different stakeholder groups and their perceptions of project success*. Science Direct.

Da, Z., Engelberg, J., & Gao, P. (2011). In search of attention. *The Journal of Finance*, *66*(5), 1461–1499. doi:10.1111/j.1540-6261.2011.01679.x

Dazeley, R., Vamplew, P. and Cruz, F. (2023). *Explainable reinforcement learning for broad-XAI: a conceptual framework and survey*. Neural Computing and Applications. https://link.springer.com/article/10.1007/s00521-023-08423-1

Dechow, P., Hutton, A. P., Meulbroek, L. K., & Sloan, R. G. (1999). Short interests, fundamental analysis, and stock returns. *Fundamental Analysis, and Stock Returns (May 1999)*.

Dechow, P. M., Hutton, A. P., Meulbroek, L., & Sloan, R. G. (2001). Short-sellers, fundamental analysis, and stock returns. *Journal of Financial Economics*, *61*(1), 77–106. doi:10.1016/S0304-405X(01)00056-3

Dechow, P. M., Hutton, A. P., & Sloan, R. G. (1999). An empirical assessment of the residual income valuation model. *Journal of Accounting and Economics*, *26*(1-3), 1–34. doi:10.1016/S0165-4101(98)00049-4

Deepa, N., Pham, Q.-V., Nguyen, D. C., Bhattacharya, S., Prabadevi, B., Gadekallu, T. R., Maddikunta, P. K. R., Fang, F., & Pathirana, P. N. (2021). *A Survey on Blockchain for Big Data: Approaches, Opportunities, and Future Directions* (arXiv:2009.00858). arXiv. https://doi.org//arXiv.2009.00858 doi:10.48550

Deepraj, S. (2012). *Investigation of Security Challenges in Cognitive Radio Networks*.

Deiva Ganesh, P. (2022). Kalpana. Future of artificial intelligence and its influence on supply chain risk management –. *Systematic Reviews*. doi:10.1016/j.cie.2022.108206

DeLone, W., & McLean, E. (1992). Information Systems Success: The Quest for the Dependent Variable. *Information Systems Research*, *3*(1), 60–95. doi:10.1287/isre.3.1.60

Devlin, S. M., & Kudenko, D. (2012). Dynamic Potential-Based Reward Shaping. *Proceedings of the 11th International Conference on Autonomous Agents and Multiagent Systems (AAMAS 2012)*, 433-440. https://eprints.whiterose.ac.uk/75121/1/aamas2012.pdf

Devnath, S., Giri, P. K., & Maiti, M. (2021). Fully fuzzy multi-item two-stage fixed charge four-dimensional transportation problems with flexible constraints. *Granular Computing*, 1-19.

Dhama, J. (2022). *The future of financial advice*.

Di Felice, M. (2010). *Learning-Based Spectrum Selection in Cognitive Radio Ad Hoc Networks Marco Di Felice*. Springer-Verlag Berlin Heidelberg.

Dias, L. P. S., Barbosa, J. L. V., & Vianna, H. D. (2018). Gamification and serious games in depression care: A systematic mapping study. *Telematics and Informatics*, *35*(1), 213–224. doi:10.1016/j.tele.2017.11.002

Ding, H., & Xie, F. (2023). A solution technique for capacitated two-level hierarchical time minimization transportation problem. *Computers &amp. Operations Research*, *151*, 106125. doi:10.1016/j.cor.2022.106125

Domakonda, V. K., Farooq, S., Chinthamreddy, S., Puviarasi, R., Sudhakar, M., & Boopathi, S. (2023). Sustainable Developments of Hybrid Floating Solar Power Plants. In *Human Agro-Energy Optimization for Business and Industry* (pp. 148–167). IGI Global. doi:10.4018/978-1-6684-4118-3.ch008

Dondi, D., Bertacchini, A., Brunelli, D., Larcher, L., & Benini, L. (2008). Modeling and Optimization of a Solar Energy Harvester System for Self-Powered Wireless Sensor Networks. *IEEE Transactions on Industrial Electronics*, *55*(7), 2759–2766. doi:10.1109/TIE.2008.924449

Dong, K., & Wang, Z. L. (2021). Self-charging power textiles integrating energy harvesting triboelectric nanogenerators with energy storage batteries/supercapacitors. *Journal of Semiconductors*, *42*(10), 101601. doi:10.1088/1674-4926/42/10/101601

Du, H., Fu, S., & Chu, H. (2015). A credibility-based defense ssdf attacks scheme for the expulsion of malicious users in cognitive radio. *International Journal of Hybrid Information Technology*, *8*(9), 9. doi:10.14257/ijhit.2015.8.9.25

Dung, L. T., & Choi, S. G. (2019). Connectivity Analysis of Cognitive Radio Ad-Hoc Networks with Multi-Pair Primary Networks. *Sensors (Basel)*, *19*(3), 565. doi:10.339019030565 PMID:30700043

Dziedzic, B., & Jurczyk, M. (2019). *The Pros And Cons Of Solar Energy In Poland*. Sunpower.

E. Onem, S. Eryigit, T. Tugcu and A. Akurgal, "QoS-Enabled Spectrum-Aware Routing for Disaster Relief and Tactical Operations over Cognitive Radio Ad Hoc Networks," *MILCOM 2013 - 2013 IEEE Military Communications Conference*, 2013, pp. 1109-1115, . doi:10.1109/MILCOM.2013.191

Edgar, T. (2021, June 29). Advantages and Disadvantages of Blockchain. *BBVA.CH*. https://www.bbva.ch/en/news/advantages-and-disadvantages-of-blockchain/

Elnaggar, A., & Reichardt, D. (2016, December). Digitizing the hand rehabilitation using serious games methodology with user-centered design approach. *In 2016 International Conference on Computational Science and Computational Intelligence (CSCI)* (pp. 13-22). IEEE. 10.1109/CSCI.2016.0011

Enescu, D. (2019). *Green Energy Advances*. BoD – Books on Demand. doi:10.5772/intechopen.77501

Entertainment Software Association. (2022). *2022 Essential Facts About the Video Game Industry. Player habits and preferences*. The ESA. https://www.theesa.com/resource/2022-essential-facts-about-the-video-game-industry/

Erturk, A., & Inman, D. J. (2008). A Distributed Parameter Electromechanical Model for Cantilevered Piezoelectric Energy Harvesters. *Journal of Vibration and Acoustics*, *130*(4), 041002. Advance online publication. doi:10.1115/1.2890402

Evans, J. (2022, April 24). *Blockchain Nodes: How They Work (All Types Explained)*. Nodes.com. https://nodes.com/

Evett, L., Burton, A., Battersby, S., Brown, D., Sherkat, N., Ford, G., & Standen, P. (2011, November). Dual camera motion capture for serious games in stroke rehabilitation. *In 2011 IEEE 1st International Conference on Serious Games and Applications for Health (SeGAH)* (pp. 1-4). IEEE. 10.1109/SeGAH.2011.6165460

Faber, N., Jorna, R., & Van Engelen, J. O. (2010). The sustainability of "sustainability"—A study into the conceptual foundations of the notion of "sustainability". In Tools, techniques and approaches for sustainability: Collected writings in environmental assessment policy and management (pp. 337-369). IEEE.

Fahrudin, M., & Nuraini, A. (2021). Performance evaluation of new ranking function methods with current ranking functions using VAM and MM-VAM. *Proceedings of the 1st International Conference on Mathematics and Mathematics Education (ICMMED 2020)*, (pp. 418-424). IEEE. 10.2991/assehr.k.210508.098

Fairbanks, J. (n.d.). *DOE's Launch of High-Efficiency Thermoelectrics Projects*. 26.

Fama, E. F., & French, K. R. (1992). The cross-section of expected stock returns. *The Journal of Finance, 47*(2), 427-465.

Fama, E. F., & French, K. R. (1995). Size and book-to-market factors in earnings and returns. *The Journal of Finance, 50*(1), 131–155. doi:10.1111/j.1540-6261.1995.tb05169.x

Fareed M., Su Q., Awan A (2021). *The effect of emotional intelligence, intellectual intelligence and transformational leadership on project success; an empirical study of public projects of Pakistan*. Science Direct. . doi:10.1016/j.plas.2021.100036

Farrokhi Derakhshandeh, J., AlLuqman, R., Mohammad, S., AlHussain, H., AlHendi, G., AlEid, D., & Ahmad, Z. (2021). A comprehensive review of automatic cleaning systems of solar panels. *Sustainable Energy Technologies and Assessments, 47*, 101518. doi:10.1016/j.seta.2021.101518

fastText. (n.d.). *Home*. fastText. https://fasttext.cc/

Feltham, G. A., & Ohlson, J. A. (1995). Valuation and clean surplus accounting for operating and financial activities. *Contemporary Accounting Research, 11*(2), 689–731. doi:10.1111/j.1911-3846.1995.tb00462.x

Feng, J., Chen, K., Zhang, C., & Li, H. (2018, December). A virtual reality-based training system for ankle rehabilitation. *In 2018 IEEE International Conference on Progress in Informatics and Computing (PIC)* (pp. 255-259). IEEE. 10.1109/PIC.2018.8706143

Feng, J., Li, S., Lv, S., Wang, H., & Fu, A. (2018, September). Securing Cooperative Spectrum Sensing Against Collusive False Feedback Attack in Cognitive Radio Networks. *IEEE Transactions on Vehicular Technology, 67*(9), 8276–8287. doi:10.1109/TVT.2018.2841362

Feng, J., Zhang, M., Xiao, Y., & Yue, H. (2018). Securing cooperative spectrum sensing against collusive SSDF attack using XOR distance analysis in cognitive radio networks. *Sensors (Basel), 18*(2), 1–14. doi:10.339018020370 PMID:29382061

Feng, J., Zou, L., Ye, O., & Han, J. (2020). Web2Vec: Phishing Webpage Detection Method Based on Multidimensional Features Driven by Deep Learning. *IEEE Access: Practical Innovations, Open Solutions, 8*, 221214–221224. doi:10.1109/ACCESS.2020.3043188

Feng, T., & Yue, C. (2020). Visualizing and interpreting RNN Models in URL-based phishing detection. *Proceedings of ACM Symposium on Access Control Models and Technologies, SACMAT*, (pp. 13–24). ACM. 10.1145/3381991.3395602

Fernández-Caramés, T. M., & Fraga-Lamas, P. (2018). A Review on the Use of Blockchain for the Internet of Things. *IEEE Access: Practical Innovations, Open Solutions, 6*, 32979–33001. doi:10.1109/ACCESS.2018.2842685

Fernández-González, P., Carratalá-Tejada, M., Monge-Pereira, E., Collado-Vázquez, S., Sánchez-Herrera Baeza, P., Cuesta-Gómez, A., Oña-Simbaña, E., Jardón-Huete, A., Molina-Rueda, F., Balaguer-Bernaldo de Quirós, C., Miangolarra-Page, J., & Cano-de la Cuerda, R. (2019). Leap motion controlled video game-based therapy for upper limb rehabilitation in patients with Parkinson's disease: A feasibility study. *Journal of Neuroengineering and Rehabilitation, 16*(1), 1–10. doi:10.118612984-019-0593-x PMID:31694653

Ferrag, M. A., Derdour, M., Mukherjee, M., Derhab, A., Maglaras, L., & Janicke, H. (2019). Blockchain Technologies for the Internet of Things: Research Issues and Challenges. *IEEE Internet of Things Journal, 6*(2), 2188–2204. doi:10.1109/JIOT.2018.2882794

Foong, M. F., Thein, C. K., & Ooi, B. L. (2021). Applications of Vibration-Based Energy Harvesting (VEH) Devices. In Role of IoT in Green Energy Systems (pp. 81–116). IGI Global. doi:10.4018/978-1-7998-6709-8.ch004

Forestier, S., Portelas, R., Mollard, Y., Oudeyer, P. (2022). Intrinsically Motivated Goal Exploration Processes with Automatic Curriculum Learning. *Journal of Machine Learning Research, 23*, 1–41. https://arxiv.org/pdf/1708.02190v3.pdf

Foster, D., Gagne, D. J., & Whitt, D. B. (2021). Probabilistic Machine Learning Estimation of Ocean Mixed Layer Depth From Dense Satellite and Sparse In Situ Observations. *Journal of Advances in Modeling Earth Systems, 13*(12), e2021MS002474.

Frankel, R., & Lee, C. M. (1998). Accounting valuation, market expectation, and cross-sectional stock returns. *Journal of Accounting and Economics, 25*(3), 283–319. doi:10.1016/S0165-4101(98)00026-3

Friha, O., Ferrag, M. A., Shu, L., Maglaras, L., & Wang, X. (2021). Internet of things for the future of smart agriculture: A comprehensive survey of emerging technologies. *IEEE/CAA Journal of Automatica Sinica, 8*(4), 718–752. doi:10.1109/JAS.2021.1003925

Gadekallu, T. R., Pham, Q.-V., Nguyen, D. C., Maddikunta, P. K. R., Deepa, N., Prabadevi, B., Pathirana, P. N., Zhao, J., & Hwang, W.-J. (2022). Blockchain for Edge of Things: Applications, Opportunities, and Challenges. *IEEE Internet of Things Journal, 9*(2), 964–988. doi:10.1109/JIOT.2021.3119639

Gao, Z., Shao, Y., Xuan, G., Wang, Y., Liu, Y., & Han, X. (2020). Real-time hyperspectral imaging for the in-field estimation of strawberry ripeness with deep learning. *Artificial Intelligence in Agriculture, 4*, 31–38. doi:10.1016/j.aiia.2020.04.003

Garg, A., Vijayaraghavan, V., Wong, C., Tai, K., Sumithra, K., Mahapatra, S., Singru, P. M., & Yao, L. (2015). Application of artificial intelligence technique for modelling elastic properties of 2D nanoscale material. *Molecular Simulation, 41*(14), 1143–1152. doi:10.1080/08927022.2014.951351

Garg, N., Wazid, M., Singh, J., Singh, D. P., & Das, A. K. (2022). Security in IoMT -driven smart healthcare: A comprehensive review and open challenges. *Security and Privacy, 5*(5), e235. doi:10.1002py2.235

Geissdoerfer, K., Jurdak, R., Kusy, B., & Zimmerling, M. (2019). Getting more out of energy-harvesting systems: Energy management under time-varying utility with PreAct. *Proceedings of the 18th International Conference on Information Processing in Sensor Networks*, (pp. 109–120). ACM. 10.1145/3302506.3310393

Gen, M., Ida, K., Li, Y., & Kubota, E. (1995). Solving bicriteria solid transportation problem with fuzzy numbers by a genetic algorithm. *Computers & Industrial Engineering, 29*(1), 537–541. doi:10.1016/0360-8352(95)00130-S

Geroni, D. (2021, April 5). Blockchain Nodes: An In-Depth Guide. *101 Blockchains*. https://101blockchains.com/blockchain-nodes/

GloVe. (n.d.). *Global Vectors for Word Representation*. GloVe. https://nlp.stanford.edu/projects/glove/

Goel, M., Sharma, A., Chilwal, A. S., Kumari, S., Kumar, A., & Bagler, G. (2023). Machine learning models to predict sweetness of molecules. *Computers in Biology and Medicine, 152*, 106441. doi:10.1016/j.compbiomed.2022.106441 PMID:36543004

Gopal M., Amirthavalli M., (2019). *Applying Machine Learning Techniques to Predict the Maintainability of Open Source Software*. Science Direct. . doi:10.35940/ijeat.E1045.0785S319

Grech, A., Sood, I., & Ariño, L. (2021). Blockchain, Self-Sovereign Identity and Digital Credentials: Promise Versus Praxis in Education. *Frontiers in Blockchain, 4*. https://www.frontiersin.org/articles/10.3389/fbloc.2021.616779

Grzegorzewski, P. (2003). Distance and orderings in a family of intuitionistic fuzzy numbers. In EUSFLAT Conf., Zittau, Germany.

Gulzar, M., Abbas, G., & Waqas, M. (2020). Climate smart agriculture: A survey and taxonomy. In *2020 International Conference on Emerging Trends in Smart Technologies (ICETST)* (pp. 1–6). 10.1109/ICETST49965.2020.9080695

Gunning, D., Vorm, E., Wang, J.Y. and Turek, M. (2021). DARPA's explainable AI (XAI) program: A retrospective. *APPLIED AI LETTERS, 2*(4). Wiley Online Library. doi:10.1002/ail2.61

Guo, J., Cheng, J., & Cleland-Huang, J. (2017). Semantically Enhanced Software Traceability Using Deep Learning Techniques. *International Conference on Software Engineering (ICSE)*. IEEE. https://doi.org/10.1109/ICSE.2017.9

Gupta, A. (2018, July 18). Introduction to Blockchain Technology. *GeeksforGeeks*. https://www.geeksforgeeks.org/blockchain-technology-introduction/

Gupta, D., Gupta, M., Bhatt, S., & Tosun, A. S. (2021). Detecting Anomalous User Behavior in Remote Patient Monitoring. *Proceedings - 2021 IEEE 22nd International Conference on Information Reuse and Integration for Data Science, IRI 2021*, 33–40. 10.1109/IRI51335.2021.00011

Gupta, G., & Anupum, K. (2017). An efficient method for solving intuitionistic fuzzy transportation problem of type-2. *International Journal of Applied and Computational Mathematics, 3*(4), 3795–3804. doi:10.100740819-017-0326-4

Gupta, M. S., & Kumar, K. (2019). Progression on spectrum sensing for cognitive radio networks: A survey, classification, challenges and future research issues. *Journal of Network and Computer Applications, 143*, 47–76. doi:10.1016/j.jnca.2019.06.005

Haber, S., & Stornetta, W. S. (1991). How to time-stamp a digital document. *Journal of Cryptology, 3*(2), 99–111. doi:10.1007/BF00196791

Haeberlin, A., Zurbuchen, A., Schaerer, J., Wagner, J., Walpen, S., Huber, C., Haeberlin, H., Fuhrer, J., & Vogel, R. (2014). Successful pacing using a batteryless sunlight-powered pacemaker. *Europace, 16*(10), 1534–1539. doi:10.1093/europace/euu127 PMID:24916431

Hafeez, A., Tiwari, V., Verma, V. K., Ansari, A. S., Husain, M. A., Singh, S. P., & Khan, A. N. (2021). Crop monitoring and automatic weed detection using drone. In *2021 International Conference on Control, Automation, Power and Signal Processing (CAPS)* (pp. 1–4). 10.1109/CAPS52117.2021.9730682

Haley, K. B. (1962). New methods in mathematical programming-The solid transportation problem. *Operations Research, 10*(4), 448–463. doi:10.1287/opre.10.4.448

Hanbali, A. A., Altman, E., Nain, P., & France, I. S. A. (2005). A survey of tcp over ad hoc networks. Communications Surveys and Tutorials. *IEEE Communications Surveys and Tutorials, 7*(3), 22–36. doi:10.1109/COMST.2005.1610548

Han, C., Wu, G., & Yu, X. (2018). Performance Analyses of Geothermal and Geothermoelectric Pavement Snow Melting System. *Journal of Energy Engineering, 144*(6), 04018067. doi:10.1061/(ASCE)EY.1943-7897.0000585

Han, N., & Ho, J. C. (2014). 3—One-Dimensional Nanomaterials for Energy Applications. In S.-C. Tjong (Ed.), *Nanocrystalline Materials* (2nd ed., pp. 75–120). Elsevier. doi:10.1016/B978-0-12-407796-6.00003-8

Hanrahan, B. M., Sze, F., Smith, A. N., & Jankowski, N. R. (2017). Thermodynamic cycle optimization for pyroelectric energy conversion in the thin film regime: Thermodynamic cycles for pyroelectric thin films. *International Journal of Energy Research*, *41*(13), 1880–1890. doi:10.1002/er.3749

Harclerode M., Macbeth T., Miller M., Gurr C., Myers T., (2016). *Early decision framework for integrating sustainable risk management for complex remediation sites: Drivers, barriers, and performance metrics*. Science Direct. . doi:10.1016/j.jenvman.2016.07.087

Haribalaji, V., Boopathi, S., & Asif, M. M. (2021). Optimization of friction stir welding process to join dissimilar AA2014 and AA7075 aluminum alloys. *Materials Today: Proceedings*, *50*, 2227–2234. doi:10.1016/j.matpr.2021.09.499

Harikaran, M., Boopathi, S., Gokulakannan, S., & Poonguzhali, M. (2023). Study on the Source of E-Waste Management and Disposal Methods. In *Sustainable Approaches and Strategies for E-Waste Management and Utilization* (pp. 39–60). IGI Global. doi:10.4018/978-1-6684-7573-7.ch003

Hasan, M. M., Zaman, S. M., Talukdar, M. A., Siddika, A., & Rabiul Alam, M. G. (2021). An Analysis of Machine Learning Algorithms and Deep Neural Networks for Email Spam Classification using Natural Language Processing. *2021 IEEE International Conference on Service Operations and Logistics, and Informatics, SOLI 2021*. IEEE. 10.1109/SOLI54607.2021.9672398

Hassan, F. ul, Ali, A., Rahouti, M., Latif, S., Kanhere, S., Singh, J., AlaAl-Fuqaha, Janjua, U., Mian, A. N., Qadir, J., & Crowcroft, J. (2020). Blockchain And The Future of the Internet: A Comprehensive Review. *ArXiv:1904.00733 [Cs]*. https://arxiv.org/abs/1904.00733

Hasselgren, A., Kralevska, K., Gligoroski, D., Pedersen, S. A., & Faxvaag, A. (2020). Blockchain In Healthcare And Health Sciences—A Scoping Review. *International Journal of Medical Informatics*, *134*, 104040. doi:10.1016/j.ijmedinf.2019.104040 PMID:31865055

Hayes, A. (2022, September 27). *Blockchain Facts: What Is It, How It Works, and How It Can Be Used*. Investopedia. https://www.investopedia.com/terms/b/blockchain.asp

Haykin, S. (1999). *Neural Networks A Comprehensive Introduction*. Prentice Hall.

He, Y., Pan, F., Wang, B., Teng, Z., & Wu, J. (2020). Transfer learning based fruits image segmentation for fruit-picking robots. In *2020 IEEE 3rd International Conference on Computer and Communication Engineering Technology (CCET)* (pp. 71–75). 10.1109/CCET50901.2020.9213127

He, D., Li, R., Huang, Q., & Lei, P. (2014). Transportation optimization with fuzzy trapezoidal numbers based on possibility theory. *PLoS One*, *9*(8), e105142. doi:10.1371/journal.pone.0105142 PMID:25137239

Hendrickx, R., van der Avoird, T., Pilot, P., Kerkhoffs, G., & Schotanus, M. (2021). Exergaming as a Functional Test Battery in Patients Who Received Arthroscopic Ankle Arthrodesis: Cross-sectional Pilot Study. *JMIR Rehabilitation and Assistive Technologies*, *8*(2), e21924. doi:10.2196/21924 PMID:33949311

He, P., Li, B., Liu, X., Chen, J., & Ma, Y. (2015). Y. Ma. An empirical study on software defect prediction with a simplified metric set. *Information and Software Technology*, *59*, 170–190. doi:10.1016/j.infsof.2014.11.006

Herrera-Luna, I. (2019. *Fusión de características geométricas y señales electromiográficas para la identificación off-line de movimientos de muñeca utilizados en rehabilitación* [Unpublished dissertation, Universidad Veracruzana, Xalapa, Veracruz, México]. https://www.uv.mx/mia/files/2021/07/tesis-IHL-1.pdf

Highsmith, J. (2010). *Agile project management: creating innovative products* (2nd ed.). Addison-Wesley.

Hiransha, C.-D. M., & Unnithan, N. A. (2018). *Deep Learning Based Phishing E-mail Detection*. Cuer. http://ceur-ws.org

Hireche, R., Mansouri, H., & Pathan, A.-S. K. (2022). Security and Privacy Management in Internet of Medical Things (IoMT): A Synthesis. *Journal of Cybersecurity and Privacy*, 2(3), 640–661. doi:10.3390/jcp2030033

Hitchcock, F. L. (1941). The distribution of a product from several sources to numerous localities. *Journal of Mathematics and Physics*, 20(2), 224–230. doi:10.1002apm1941201224

Ho, T., Nguyen, Y. T., Tran, H. T. M., & Vo, D. T. (2022). Fundamental analysis and the use of financial statement information to separate winners and losers in frontier markets: evidence from Vietnam. *International Journal of Emerging Markets*.

Hoch, J. E., & Dulebohn, J. H. (2013). Shared leadership in enterprise resource planning and human resource management system implementation. *Human Resource Management Review*, 23(1), 114–125. doi:10.1016/j.hrmr.2012.06.007

Hocine, N., Gouaich, A., & Cerri, S. A. (2014, April). Dynamic difficulty adaptation in serious games for motor rehabilitation. In *International Conference on Serious Games* (pp. 115-128). Springer, Cham. 10.1007/978-3-319-05972-3_13

Hocine, N., Gouaïch, A., Cerri, S. A., Mottet, D., Froger, J., & Laffont, I. (2015). Adaptation in serious games for upper-limb rehabilitation: An approach to improve training outcomes. *User Modeling and User-Adapted Interaction*, 25(1), 65–98. doi:10.100711257-015-9154-6

Holler, F. J., Skoog, D., Douglas, A., & Crouch, S. R. (2007). *Principles of Instrumental Analysis* (6th ed.). Cengage Learning.

Hon-Snir, S., Kudryavtsev, A., & Cohen, G. (2012). Stock market investors: Who is more rational, and who relies on intuition. *International Journal of Economics and Finance*, 4(5), 56–72. doi:10.5539/ijef.v4n5p56

Horiachko, A. (2022, June 10). *Top 9 Blockchain Technology Trends to Follow in 2022*. Softermii. https://www.softermii.com/blog/hot-trends-in-blockchain-app-development

Hou F. (2020). *Analyzing the Performance of the Unmanned Bank to Explore the Failure Reasons for AI Projects*. AIAM2020.

Huang, Y., Yang, Q., Qin, J., & Wen, W. (2019). Phishing URL detection via CNN and attention-based hierarchical RNN. *Proceedings - 2019 18th IEEE International Conference on Trust, Security and Privacy in Computing and Communications/13th IEEE International Conference on Big Data Science and Engineering, TrustCom/BigDataSE 2019*, (pp. 112–119). IEEE. 10.1109/TrustCom/BigDataSE.2019.00024

Huang, S., Zhu, X., Sarkar, S., & Zhao, Y. (2019). Challenges and opportunities for supercapacitors. *APL Materials*, 7(10), 100901. doi:10.1063/1.5116146

Huang, X.-R., Chen, W.-H., Hu, W.-C., & Chen, L.-B. (2022). An AI edge computing-based robotic arm automated guided vehicle system for harvesting pitaya. In *2022 IEEE International Conference on Consumer Electronics (ICCE)* (pp. 1–2). 10.1109/ICCE53296.2022.9730442

Hunter, D., Yu, H., Pukish, M. S. III, Kolbusz, J., & Wilamowski, B. M. (2012). Selection of proper neural network sizes and architectures—A comparative study. *IEEE Transactions on Industrial Informatics*, 8(2), 228–240. doi:10.1109/TII.2012.2187914

Hunt, K. H., Brimble, M., & Freudenberg, B. (2022). A Move in the Right Direction: Client Relationships in Financial Advice. *The Journal of Wealth Management*, 25(1), 50–81. doi:10.3905/jwm.2022.1.167

Hu, P., Zhu, T., Wang, X., Wei, X., Yan, M., Li, J., Luo, W., Yang, W., Zhang, W., Zhou, L., Zhou, Z., & Mai, L. (2018). Highly Durable Na2V6O16·1.63H2O Nanowire Cathode for Aqueous Zinc-Ion Battery. *Nano Letters*, 18(3), 1758–1763. doi:10.1021/acs.nanolett.7b04889 PMID:29397745

Hussain, M. R., Qahmash, A., Alelyani, S., & Alsaqer, M. S. (2021). Optimal solution of transportation problem with effective approach mount order method: An Operational Research Tool. *Intelligent Computing*, 1151–1168. doi:10.1007/978-3-030-80126-7_81

Hussain, R. J., & Kumar, P. S. (2012a). The transportation problem in an intuitionistic fuzzy environment. *International Journal of Mathematics Research*, 4(4), 411–420.

Hussain, R. J., & Kumar, P. S. (2012b). Algorithmic approach for solving intuitionistic fuzzy transportation problem. *Applied Mathematical Sciences*, 6(80), 3981–3989.

Hussain, R. J., & Kumar, P. S. (2012c). The transportation problem with the aid of triangular intuitionistic fuzzy numbers. In *International Conference on MMASC Conf.* (pp. 819-825). Coimbatore Institute of Technology, Coimbatore.

Hussain, R. J., & Kumar, P. S. (2013). An optimal more-for-less solution of mixed constraints intuitionistic fuzzy transportation problems. *International Journal of Contemporary Mathematical Sciences*, 8(12), 565–576. doi:10.12988/ijcms.2013.13056

Hussain, S., Jamwal, P. K., & Ghayesh, M. H. (2017). State-of-the-art robotic devices for ankle rehabilitation: Mechanism and control review. *Proceedings of the Institution of Mechanical Engineers. Part H, Journal of Engineering in Medicine*, 231(12), 1224–1234. doi:10.1177/0954411917737584 PMID:29065774

Hussain, S., Jamwal, P. K., Vliet, P. V., & Brown, N. A. (2021). Robot assisted ankle neuro-rehabilitation: State of the art and future challenges. *Expert Review of Neurotherapeutics*, 21(1), 111–121. doi:10.1080/14737175.2021.1847646 PMID:33198522

Hutsebaut-Buysse, M., Mets, K., & Steven Latré, S. (2022). Hierarchical Reinforcement Learning: A Survey and Open Research Challenges, *Machine Learning Knowledge*, 4(1), 172-221. https://www.mdpi.com/2504-4990/4/1/9

Hvide, H. K., & Östberg, P. (2015). Social interaction at work. *Journal of Financial Economics*, 117(3), 628–652. doi:10.1016/j.jfineco.2015.06.004

Hwang, K., Chen, M., Gharavi, H., & Leung, V. C. (2019). Artificial intelligence for cognitive wireless communications. *IEEE Wireless Communications*, 26(3), 10–11. doi:10.1109/MWC.2019.8752476 PMID:31579263

Hyperledger Team. (2022, May 16). About – Hyperledger Foundation. *Hyperledger Foundation*. https://www.hyperledger.org/about

Ian, F. (2009). *Akyildiz et al., "Cognitive radio ad hoc networks, Ad Hoc Networks"*. Elsevier North-Holland, Inc., doi:10.1016/j.adhoc.2009.01.001

Ian, F. (2009). *Akyildiz, "Spectrum Management in Cognitive Radio Ad Hoc Networks", Georgia Institute of Technology*. IEEE Network.

Iannacci, J., Sordo, G., Schneider, M., Schmid, U., Camarda, A., & Romani, A. (2016). A novel toggle-type MEMS vibration energy harvester for Internet of Things applications. *2016 IEEE SENSORS*, 1–3. doi:10.1109/ICSENS.2016.7808553

Ibrahim, A., Ramini, A., & Towfighian, S. (2020). Triboelectric energy harvester with large bandwidth under harmonic and random excitations. *Energy Reports*, 6, 2490–2502. doi:10.1016/j.egyr.2020.09.007

Illahi, H. Liu, Q. Umer, N. (2021). *Machine learning based success prediction for crowdsourcing software projects*. Science Direct. . doi:10.1016/j.jss.2021.110965

Invernizzi, F., Dulio, S., Patrini, M., Guizzetti, G., & Mustarelli, P. (2016). Energy harvesting from human motion: Materials and techniques. *Chemical Society Reviews*, 45(20), 5455–5473. doi:10.1039/C5CS00812C PMID:27398416

Iqbal, K., Khan, S. A., Anisa, S., Tasneem, A., & Mohammad, N. (2021). A Preliminary Study on Personalized Spam E-mail Filtering Using Bidirectional Encoder Representations from Transformers (BERT) and TensorFlow 2.0. *International Journal of Computing and Digital Systems*, *11*(1), 893–903. doi:10.12785/ijcds/110173

Iredale, G. (2021, January 6). What Are The Different Types of Blockchain Technology? *101 Blockchains*. https://101blockchains.com/types-of-blockchain/

IRENA. (n.d.). *Wind energy*. Wind. https://www.irena.org/wind

Iriarte C., Bayona S. (2020). IT projects success factors: a literature review. *International Journal of Information Systems and Project Management,* pp. 49–78.

Islam, N., Sheikh, G. S., & Islam, Z. 2018. A cognitive radio ad hoc networks based disaster management scheme with efficient spectrum management, collaboration and interoperability. arXiv preprint arXiv:1810.05090.

Islam, N., Zubair A. (2014). A study of research trends and issues in wireless ad hoc networks. IGI Global.

Islam, N., Shaikh, Z. A., Rehman, A. U., & Siddiqui, M. S. (2013). HANDY: A hybrid association rules mining approach for network layer discovery of services for mobile ad hoc network. *Wireless Networks*, *19*(8), 1961–1977. doi:10.100711276-013-0571-3

Islam, N., Sheikh, G. S., & Shaikh, Z. A. (2021). Using association rules mining, multi-level data representation and cross-layer operations for data management in mobile ad hoc network. *International Journal of Intelligent Engineering Informatics*, *9*(3), 229–259. doi:10.1504/IJIEI.2021.118268

Ismail, N., & Malik, O. A. (2022). Real-time visual inspection system for grading fruits using computer vision and deep learning techniques. *Information Processing in Agriculture*, *9*(1), 24–37. doi:10.1016/j.inpa.2021.01.005

ISO. (2012). *ISO 21500:2012 Guidance on Project Management*. ISO.

Izadgoshasb, I., Lim, Y. Y., Lake, N., Tang, L., Padilla, R. V., & Kashiwao, T. (2018). Optimizing orientation of piezoelectric cantilever beam for harvesting energy from human walking. *Energy Conversion and Management*, *161*, 66–73. doi:10.1016/j.enconman.2018.01.076

Jabbar, R., Kharbeche, M., Al-Khalifa, K., Krichen, M., & Barkaoui, K. (2020). Blockchain for the Internet of Vehicles: A Decentralized IoT Solution for Vehicles Communication Using Ethereum. *Sensors (Basel)*, *20*(14), 3928. doi:10.339020143928 PMID:32679671

Jabir, B., & Falih, N. (2021). Dropout, a basic and effective regularization method for a deep learning model: A case study. *Indonesian Journal of Electrical Engineering and Computer Science*, *24*(2), 1009–1016. doi:10.11591/ijeecs.v24.i2.pp1009-1016

Jaikaran, C. (2018). *Blockchain: Background and Policy Issues*. Congressional Research Service.

Jana, D. K. (2016). Novel arithmetic operations on type-2 intuitionistic fuzzy and its applications to transportation problem. *Pacific Science Review A: Natural Science and Engineering*, *18*(3), 178–189.

Janardhana, K., Singh, V., Singh, S. N., Babu, T. S. R., Bano, S., & Boopathi, S. (2023). Utilization Process for Electronic Waste in Eco-Friendly Concrete: Experimental Study. In Sustainable Approaches and Strategies for E-Waste Management and Utilization (pp. 204–223). IGI Global.

Jang, J. R., Sun, C., & Mizutani, E. (2006). *Neuro-Fuzzy and Soft Computing*. Prentice-Hall of India.

Jeevanantham, Y. A., A, S., V, V., J, S. I., Boopathi, S., & Kumar, D. P. (2023). Implementation of Internet-of Things (IoT) in Soil Irrigation System. *IEEE Explore*, 1–5. doi:10.1109/ICPECTS56089.2022.10047185

Jimenez, F., & Verdegay, J. L. (1998). Uncertain solid transportation problems. *Fuzzy Sets and Systems*, *100*(1-3), 45–57. doi:10.1016/S0165-0114(97)00164-4

Jimenez, F., & Verdegay, J. L. (1999). Solving fuzzy solid transportation problems by an evolutionary algorithm based parametric approach. *European Journal of Operational Research*, *117*(3), 485–510. doi:10.1016/S0377-2217(98)00083-6

Jin, L., Ma, S., Deng, W., Yan, C., Yang, T., Chu, X., Tian, G., Xiong, D., Lu, J., & Yang, W. (2018). Polarization-free high-crystallization β-PVDF piezoelectric nanogenerator toward self-powered 3D acceleration sensor. *Nano Energy*, *50*, 632–638. doi:10.1016/j.nanoen.2018.05.068

Johansen I., Rausand M., (2014). *Foundations and choice of risk metrics*. Science Direct. . doi:10.1016/j.ssci.2013.09.011

Joshi, N., & Chauhan, S. S. (2016). A new approach for obtaining optimal solution of unbalanced fuzzy transportation problem. *International Journal of Computers and Technology*, *15*(6), 6824–6832. doi:10.24297/ijct.v15i6.3977

Jurado, J. P., Dörling, B., Zapata-Arteaga, O., Roig, A., Mihi, A., & Campoy-Quiles, M. (2019). Solar Harvesting: A Unique Opportunity for Organic Thermoelectrics? *Advanced Energy Materials*, *9*(45), 1902385. doi:10.1002/aenm.201902385

Jurado, U. T., Pu, S. H., & White, N. M. (2020). Wave impact energy harvesting through water-dielectric triboelectrification with single-electrode triboelectric nanogenerators for battery-less systems. *Nano Energy*, *78*, 105204. doi:10.1016/j.nanoen.2020.105204

Kacher, Y., & Singh, P. (2021). A comprehensive literature review on transportation problems. *International Journal of Applied and Computational Mathematics*, *7*(5), 1–49. doi:10.100740819-021-01134-y

Kamilaris, A., & Prenafeta-Boldú, F. X. (2018). A review of the use of convolutional neural networks in agriculture. *Journal of Agricultural Science*, *156*(3), 312–322. doi:10.1017/S0021859618000436

Kang, J., Fan, K., Zhang, K., Cheng, X., Li, H., & Yang, Y. (2021). An ultra light weight and secure RFID batch authentication scheme for IoMT. *Computer Communications*, *167*, 48–54. doi:10.1016/j.comcom.2020.12.004

Kaplan, A., Figge, H., & Hirsch-Allen, J. (2022). The Next Evolution Of Digital Identity: Scalable, Secure, And Trusted Digital Credentials. *IBM Institute for Business Value*. https://www.ibm.com/thought-leadership/institute-business-value/en-us/report/digital-identity

Kapur R., Sodhi B., (2020). *A Defect Estimator for Source Code: Linking Defect Reports with Programming Constructs Usage Metrics*. ACM. . doi:10.1145/3384517

Kar, S., Sethi, S., & Sahoo, R. K. (2017). A Multi-factor Trust Management Scheme for Secure Spectrum Sensing in Cognitive Radio Networks. *Wireless Personal Communications*, *97*(2), 2523–2540. doi:10.100711277-017-4621-5

Karthikeyan, A., & Priyakumar, U. (2022). Artificial Intelligence: Machine Learning For Chemical Sciences. *Journal of Chemical Sciences*, *134*(1), 2. doi:10.100712039-021-01995-2 PMID:34955617

Kaur, A., Kacprzyk, J., & Kumar, A. (2020a). *Fuzzy transportation and transshipment problems*. Studies in Fuzziness and Soft Computing., doi:10.1007/978-3-030-26676-9

Kaur, A., Kacprzyk, J., & Kumar, A. (2020b). New methods for solving fully fuzzy solid transportation problems with LR fuzzy parameters. In *Fuzzy Transportation and Transshipment Problems* (pp. 145–184). Springer., doi:10.1007/978-3-030-26676-9_7

Khalaf, W. S., Khalaf, B. A., & Abid, N. O. (2021). A plan for transportation and distribution the products based on multi-objective travelling salesman problem in fuzzy environmental. [PEN]. *Periodicals of Engineering and Natural Sciences*, *9*(4), 5–22. doi:10.21533/pen.v9i4.2253

Khalid, S., Raouf, I., Khan, A., Kim, N., & Kim, H. S. (2019). A Review of Human-Powered Energy Harvesting for Smart Electronics: Recent Progress and Challenges. *International Journal of Precision Engineering and Manufacturing-Green Technology*, *6*(4), 821–851. doi:10.100740684-019-00144-y

Khan, M. S., Jibran, M., Koo, I., Kim, S. M., & Kim, J. (2019). A Double Adaptive Approach to Tackle Malicious Users in Cognitive Radio Networks. Wireless Communications and Mobile Computing. Hindawi. doi:10.1155/2019/2350694

Khan, D., Oh, S. J., Shehzad, K., Basim, M., Verma, D., Pu, Y. G., Lee, M., Hwang, K. C., Yang, Y., & Lee, K.-Y. (2020). An Efficient Reconfigurable RF-DC Converter With Wide Input Power Range for RF Energy Harvesting. *IEEE Access : Practical Innovations, Open Solutions*, *8*, 79310–79318. doi:10.1109/ACCESS.2020.2990662

Khan, D., Oh, S. J., Shehzad, K., Verma, D., Khan, Z. H. N., Pu, Y. G., Lee, M., Hwang, K. C., Yang, Y., & Lee, K.-Y. (2019). A CMOS RF Energy Harvester With 47% Peak Efficiency Using Internal Threshold Voltage Compensation. *IEEE Microwave and Wireless Components Letters*, *29*(6), 415–417. doi:10.1109/LMWC.2019.2909403

Khan, U., Kim, T.-H., Ryu, H., Seung, W., & Kim, S.-W. (2017). Graphene Tribotronics for Electronic Skin and Touch Screen Applications. *Advanced Materials*, *29*(1), 1603544. doi:10.1002/adma.201603544 PMID:27786382

Khushboo, & Azad, P. (2019). Design and Implementation of Conductor-to-Dielectric Lateral Sliding TENG Mode for Low Power Electronics. In H. Malik, S. Srivastava, Y. R. Sood, & A. Ahmad (Eds.), *Applications of Artificial Intelligence Techniques in Engineering* (pp. 167–174). Springer. doi:10.1007/978-981-13-1819-1_17

Kim, H., & Shin, K. G. (2008, May). Efficient Discovery of Spectrum Opportunities with MAC-Layer Sensing in Cognitive Radio Networks. *IEEE Transactions on Mobile Computing*, *7*(5), 533–545. doi:10.1109/TMC.2007.70751

Kim, H., Tadesse, Y., & Priya, S. (2009). Piezoelectric Energy Harvesting. In S. Priya & D. J. Inman (Eds.), *Energy Harvesting Technologies* (pp. 3–39). Springer US. doi:10.1007/978-0-387-76464-1_1

Kiran, M., Farrok, O., Mamun, M., Islam, M. R., & Xu, W. (2020). Progress in Piezoelectric Material Based Oceanic Wave Energy Conversion Technology. *IEEE Access : Practical Innovations, Open Solutions*, *8*, 146428–146449. doi:10.1109/ACCESS.2020.3015821

Kitchin, R., & Lauriault, T. P. (2015). Small data in the era of big data. *GeoJournal*, *80*(4), 463–475. doi:10.100710708-014-9601-7

Kittel, C. (2016). *Introduction to Solid State Physics* (8th ed.). Maruzen.

Kokol, P., Kokol, M., & Zagoranski, S. (2022). Machine learning on small size samples: A synthetic knowledge synthesis. *Science Progress*, *105*(1), 00368504211029777. doi:10.1177/00368504211029777 PMID:35220816

Kour, D., Mukherjee, S., & Basu, K. (2017). Solving intuitionistic fuzzy transportation problem using linear programming. *International Journal of System Assurance Engineering and Management*, *8*(S2), 1090–1101. doi:10.100713198-017-0575-y

Koutras, D., Stergiopoulos, G., Dasaklis, T., Kotzanikolaou, P., Glynos, D., & Douligeris, C. (2020). Security in iomt communications: A survey. *Sensors (Basel)*, *20*(17), 1–49. doi:10.339020174828 PMID:32859036

Kraemer, D., Poudel, B., Feng, H.-P., Caylor, J. C., Yu, B., Yan, X., Ma, Y., Wang, X., Wang, D., Muto, A., McEnaney, K., Chiesa, M., Ren, Z., & Chen, G. (2011). High-performance flat-panel solar thermoelectric generators with high thermal concentration. *Nature Materials*, *10*(7), 532–538. doi:10.1038/nmat3013 PMID:21532584

Kuang, Y., & Zhu, M. (2017). Design study of a mechanically plucked piezoelectric energy harvester using validated finite element modelling. *Sensors and Actuators. A, Physical*, *263*, 510–520. doi:10.1016/j.sna.2017.07.009

Kudryavtsev, A., Cohen, G., & Hon-Snir, S. (2013). 'Rational 'or' Intuitive': Are behavioral biases correlated across stock market investors? *Contemporary economics, 7*(2), 31-53.

Kuhn, V., Lahuec, C., Seguin, F., & Person, C. (2015). A Multi-Band Stacked RF Energy Harvester With RF-to-DC Efficiency Up to 84%. *IEEE Transactions on Microwave Theory and Techniques, 63*(5), 1768–1778. doi:10.1109/TMTT.2015.2416233

Kumar, A., & Yadav, S. P. (2012). A survey of multi-index transportation problems and its variants with crisp and fuzzy parameters. *Proceedings of the International Conference on Soft Computing for Problem Solving* (SocProS 2011) December 20-22, 2011, 919–932. 10.1007/978-81-322-0487-9_86

Kumar, A., Hong, J., Singh, A., Levine, S. (2022). When Should We Prefer Offline Reinforcement Learning Over Behavioral Cloning? The International Conference on Learning Representations (ICLR 2022). arXiv. https://arxiv.org/abs/2204.05618

Kumar, P. S. (2010). *A comparative study on transportation problem in fuzzy environment* [M.Phil thesis, Jamal Mohamed College].

Kumar, P. S. (2015). *Algorithmic approach for solving allocation problems under intuitionistic fuzzy environment* [PhD thesis, Jamal Mohamed College, affiliated to the Bharathidasan University]. http://hdl.handle.net/10603/209151

Kumar, P. S. (2017). PSK method for solving type-1 and type-3 fuzzy transportation problems. *Fuzzy Systems*, 367–392. doi:10.4018/978-1-5225-1908-9.ch017

Kumar, P. S. (2020d). The PSK method for solving fully intuitionistic fuzzy assignment problems with some software tools. In Theoretical and Applied Mathematics in International Business (pp. 149-202). IGI Global. doi:10.4018/978-1-5225-8458-2.ch009

Kumar, P. S. (2021). Finding the solution of balanced and unbalanced intuitionistic fuzzy transportation problems by using different methods with some software packages. In Handbook of Research on Applied AI for International Business and Marketing Applications (pp. 278-320). IGI Global. doi:10.4018/978-1-7998-5077-9.ch015

Kumar, P. S., & Hussain, R. J. (2014c). New algorithm for solving mixed intuitionistic fuzzy assignment problem. *Elixir Appl. Math., 73*, 25971-25977. https://www.elixirpublishers.com/articles/1406724004_73%20(2014)%2025971-25977.pdf

Kumara, V., Mohanaprakash, T. A., Fairooz, S., Jamal, K., Babu, T., & B., S. (2023). Experimental Study on a Reliable Smart Hydroponics System. In *Human Agro-Energy Optimization for Business and Industry* (pp. 27–45). IGI Global. doi:10.4018/978-1-6684-4118-3.ch002

Kumar, A., Balpande, S. S., & Anjankar, S. C. (2016). Electromagnetic Energy Harvester for Low Frequency Vibrations Using MEMS. *Procedia Computer Science, 79*, 785–792. doi:10.1016/j.procs.2016.03.104

Kumar, A., & Kaur, M. (2013). A ranking approach for intuitionistic fuzzy numbers and its application. *Journal of Applied Research and Technology, 11*(3), 381–396. doi:10.1016/S1665-6423(13)71548-7

Kumaran, N. (2021). Minimize the transportation cost on fuzzy environment. *Annals of the Romanian Society for Cell Biology*, 15349–15352. https://www.annalsofrscb.ro/index.php/journal/article/view/5150

Kumar, P. S. (2016a). PSK method for solving type-1 and type-3 fuzzy transportation problems. [IJFSA]. *International Journal of Fuzzy System Applications, 5*(4), 121–146. doi:10.4018/IJFSA.2016100106

Kumar, P. S. (2016b). A simple method for solving type-2 and type-4 fuzzy transportation problems. [IJFIS]. *The International Journal of Fuzzy Logic and Intelligent Systems, 16*(4), 225–237. doi:10.5391/IJFIS.2016.16.4.225

Kumar, P. S. (2018). Search for an Optimal Solution to Vague Traffic Problems Using the PSK Method. In *Handbook of Research on Investigations in Artificial Life Research and Development* (pp. 219–257). IGI Global. doi:10.4018/978-1-5225-5396-0.ch011

Kumar, P. S. (2018a). A note on 'a new approach for solving intuitionistic fuzzy transportation problem of type-2'. [IJLSM]. *International Journal of Logistics Systems and Management*, 29(1), 102–129. doi:10.1504/IJLSM.2018.088586

Kumar, P. S. (2018b). Linear programming approach for solving balanced and unbalanced intuitionistic fuzzy transportation problems. [IJORIS]. *International Journal of Operations Research and Information Systems*, 9(2), 73–100. doi:10.4018/IJORIS.2018040104

Kumar, P. S. (2018c). A simple and efficient algorithm for solving type-1 intuitionistic fuzzy solid transportation problems. [IJORIS]. *International Journal of Operations Research and Information Systems*, 9(3), 90–122. doi:10.4018/IJORIS.2018070105

Kumar, P. S. (2018d). PSK method for solving intuitionistic fuzzy solid transportation problems. [IJFSA]. *International Journal of Fuzzy System Applications*, 7(4), 62–99. doi:10.4018/IJFSA.2018100104

Kumar, P. S. (2019). PSK Method for Solving Mixed and Type-4 Intuitionistic Fuzzy Solid Transportation Problems. [IJORIS]. *International Journal of Operations Research and Information Systems*, 10(2), 20–53. doi:10.4018/IJORIS.2019040102

Kumar, P. S. (2019a). Intuitionistic fuzzy solid assignment problems: A software-based approach. [IJSA]. *International Journal of System Assurance Engineering and Management*, 10(4), 661–675. doi:10.100713198-019-00794-w

Kumar, P. S. (2020a). Intuitionistic fuzzy zero point method for solving type-2 intuitionistic fuzzy transportation problem. [IJOR]. *International Journal of Operational Research*, 37(3), 418–451. doi:10.1504/IJOR.2020.105446

Kumar, P. S. (2020b). Algorithms for solving the optimization problems using fuzzy and intuitionistic fuzzy set. [IJSA]. *International Journal of System Assurance Engineering and Management*, 11(1), 189–222. doi:10.100713198-019-00941-3

Kumar, P. S. (2020c). Developing a new approach to solve solid assignment problems under intuitionistic fuzzy environment. [IJFSA]. *International Journal of Fuzzy System Applications*, 9(1), 1–34. doi:10.4018/IJFSA.2020010101

Kumar, P. S. (2022). Computationally simple and efficient method for solving real-life mixed intuitionistic fuzzy 3D assignment problems. [IJSSCI]. *International Journal of Software Science and Computational Intelligence*, 14(1), 1–42. doi:10.4018/IJSSCI.309425

Kumar, P. S. (2023a). Algorithms and software packages for solving transportation problems with intuitionistic fuzzy numbers. In *Operational Research for Renewable Energy and Sustainable Environments*. IGI Global.

Kumar, P. S. (2023b). The PSK method: A new and efficient approach to solving fuzzy transportation problems. In J. Boukachour & A. Benaini (Eds.), *Transport and Logistics Planning and Optimization* (pp. 149–197). IGI Global. doi:10.4018/978-1-6684-8474-6.ch007

Kumar, P. S., & Hussain, R. J. (2014a). A systematic approach for solving mixed intuitionistic fuzzy transportation problems. *International Journal of Pure and Applied Mathematics*, 92(2), 181–190. doi:10.12732/ijpam.v92i2.4

Kumar, P. S., & Hussain, R. J. (2014b, July). A method for finding an optimal solution of an assignment problem under mixed intuitionistic fuzzy environment. In *ICMS Conf.* (pp. 417-421). Elsevier.

Kumar, P. S., & Hussain, R. J. (2014d). A method for solving balanced intuitionistic fuzzy assignment problem. *International Journal of Engineering Research and Applications*, 4(3), 897–903.

Kumar, P. S., & Hussain, R. J. (2015). A method for solving unbalanced intuitionistic fuzzy transportation problems. *Notes on Intuitionistic Fuzzy Sets*, *21*(3), 54–65.

Kumar, P. S., & Hussain, R. J. (2016a). Computationally simple approach for solving fully intuitionistic fuzzy real life transportation problems. [IJSA]. *International Journal of System Assurance Engineering and Management*, *7*(S1), 90–101. doi:10.100713198-014-0334-2

Kumar, P. S., & Hussain, R. J. (2016b). A simple method for solving fully intuitionistic fuzzy real life assignment problem. [IJORIS]. *International Journal of Operations Research and Information Systems*, *7*(2), 39–61. doi:10.4018/IJORIS.2016040103

Kumar, P. S., & Hussain, R. J. (2016c). An algorithm for solving unbalanced intuitionistic fuzzy assignment problem using triangular intuitionistic fuzzy number. *The Journal of Fuzzy Mathematics*, *24*(2), 289–302.

Kuo, T.-T., Kim, H.-E., & Ohno-Machado, L. (2017). Blockchain Distributed Ledger Technologies For Biomedical And Health Care Applications. *Journal of the American Medical Informatics Association : JAMIA*, *24*(6), 1211–1220. doi:10.1093/jamia/ocx068 PMID:29016974

Kurt, G. K., & Cepheli, Ö. (2020). *Physical layer security of cognitive IoT networks*. Towards Cognitive IoT Networks. doi:10.1007/978-3-030-42573-9_8

Lakonishok, J., Shleifer, A., & Vishny, R. W. (1994). Contrarian investment, extrapolation, and risk. *The Journal of Finance*, *49*(5), 1541–1578. doi:10.1111/j.1540-6261.1994.tb04772.x

Lastbitcoder. (2022, February 2). Advantages and Disadvantages of Blockchain. *GeeksforGeeks*. https://www.geeksforgeeks.org/advantages-and-disadvantages-of-blockchain/

Le, H., Pham, Q., Sahoo, D., & Hoi, S. C. H. (2018). URLNet: Learning a URL Representation with Deep Learning for Malicious URL Detection. https://doi.org/ doi:10.48550/arxiv.1802.03162

Lea, J. F., & Bearden, J. (1982). Effect of gaseous fluids on submersible pump performance. *Journal of Petroleum Technology*, *34*(12), 922–930. doi:10.2118/9218-PA

Leap Motion Controller. (n.d.) *Overview. Which hand tracking product is right for you? Leap Motion controller.* Ultra Leap. https://www.ultraleap.com/product/leap-motion-controller/

Lee, J., Tang, F., Ye, P., Abbasi, F., Hay, P., & Divakaran, D. M. (2021). D-Fence: A flexible, efficient, and comprehensive phishing email detection system. *Proceedings - 2021 IEEE European Symposium on Security and Privacy, Euro S and P 2021*, 578–597. 10.1109/EuroSP51992.2021.00045

Lee, H., Sharpes, N., Abdelmoula, H., Abdelkefi, A., & Priya, S. (2018). Higher power generation from torsion-dominant mode in a zigzag shaped two-dimensional energy harvester. *Applied Energy*, *216*, 494–503. doi:10.1016/j.apenergy.2018.02.083

Lee, J.-H., Kim, J., Yun Kim, T., Hossain, M. S. A., Kim, S.-W., & Ho Kim, J. (2016). All-in-one energy harvesting and storage devices. *Journal of Materials Chemistry. A, Materials for Energy and Sustainability*, *4*(21), 7983–7999. doi:10.1039/C6TA01229A

Lee, K.-E., Park, J. G., & Yoo, S.-J. (2021). Intelligent Cognitive Radio Ad-Hoc Network: Planning, Learning and Dynamic Configuration. *Electronics (Basel)*, *10*(3), 254. doi:10.3390/electronics10030254

Lee, S. U. (2021). Aggregate planning using least cost first assignment algorithm of transportation problem. *The Journal of the Institute of Internet. Broadcasting and Communication*, *21*(5), 181–188.

Lee, Y., Cha, S. H., Kim, Y.-W., Choi, D., & Sun, J.-Y. (2018). Transparent and attachable ionic communicators based on self-cleanable triboelectric nanogenerators. *Nature Communications, 9*(1). *Scopus, 9*(1), 1804. Advance online publication. doi:10.103841467-018-03954-x PMID:29728600

Lehavy, R., & Sloan, R. G. (2008). Investor recognition and stock returns. *Review of Accounting Studies, 13*(2), 327–361. doi:10.100711142-007-9063-y

Lehtinen, T., Mäntylä, M., Vanhanen, J., Itkonen, J., & Lassenius, C. (2014). Perceived causes of software project failures – An analysis of their relationships. *Information and Software Technology, 56*(6), 623–643. doi:10.1016/j.infsof.2014.01.015

Lei, H., Ganjeizadeh, F., Jayachandran, P., & Ozcan, P. (2015). A statisc al analysis of the effects of Scrum and Kanban on software development projects. *Robotics and Computer-integrated Manufacturing.* doi:10.1016/j.rcim.2015.12.001

Lendasse, A., Wertz, V., & Verleysen, M. (2003). Model selection with cross-validations and bootstraps—application to time series prediction with RBFN models. *Artificial Neural Networks and Neural Information Processing—ICANN/ICONIP 2003*, 174-174.

Le-Nguyen, M.-K., Nguyen, T.-C.-H., Le, D.-T., & Chi Minh City, H. Lab Ho Chi Minh City, V., vanhoa, V., Long-Phuoc Tôn, verichainsio, & Nguyen-An, K. (2021). Hunting Phishing Websites Using a Hybrid Fuzzy-Semantic-Visual Approach; Hunting Phishing Websites Using a Hybrid Fuzzy-Semantic-Visual Approach. *2021 15th International Conference on Advanced Computing and Applications (ACOMP)*. 10.1109/ACOMP53746.2021.00012

Le-Nguyen, M.-K., Nguyen, T.-C.-H., Le, D.-T., Nguyen, V.-H., Tôn, L.-P., & Nguyen-An, K. (2023). Phishing Website Detection as a Website Comparing Problem. *SN Computer Science, 4*(2), 122. doi:10.100742979-022-01544-9

Leo'n, O., Roma'n, R., & Herna'ndez-Serrano, J. (2011). *Towards a cooperative intrusion detection system for cognitive radio networks.* In *Proceedings of the IFIP TC 6th international conference on Networking (NETWORKING'11)*. Valencia, Spain.

Leon, O., Serrano, J. H., & Soriano, M. (2009). *A new cross-layer attack to TCP in cognitive radio networks.* Second international workshop on cross layer design, IWCLD '09, Mallorca, Spain. 10.1109/IWCLD.2009.5156526

Leon, O., Hernandez-Serrano, J., & Soriano, M. (2010). Securing Cognitive Radio Networks. *International Journal of Communication Systems, 23*(5), 633–652.

Lev, B. (1989). On the usefulness of earnings and earnings research: Lessons and directions from two decades of empirical research. *Journal of Accounting Research, 27*, 153–192. doi:10.2307/2491070

Li X., Moreschini S., Zhang Z., Taibi D. (2022). *Exploring factors and metrics to select open source software components for integration: An empirical study.* Science Direct. . doi:10.1016/j.jss.2022.111255

Liberati, A., Altman, D. G., Tetzlaff, J., Mulrow, C., Gøtzsche, P. C., Ioannidis, J. P. A., Clarke, M., Devereaux, P. J., Kleijnen, J., & Moher, D. (2009). The PRISMA statement for reporting systematic reviews and meta-analyses of studies that evaluate health care interventions: Explanation and elaboration. *Annals of Internal Medicine, 30*. PMID:19622512

Li, D. F., Nan, J. X., & Zhang, M. J. (2010). A ranking method of triangular intuitionistic fuzzy numbers and application to decision making. *International Journal of Computational Intelligence Systems, 3*(5), 522–530.

Li, F., Liu, Z., Shen, W., Wang, Y., Wang, Y., Ge, C., Sun, F., & Lan, P. (2021). A remote sensing and airborne edge-computing based detection system for pine wilt disease. *IEEE Access : Practical Innovations, Open Solutions, 9*, 66346–66360. doi:10.1109/ACCESS.2021.3073929

Li, H., Tian, C., & Deng, Z. (2014). Energy harvesting from low frequency applications using piezoelectric materials. *Applied Physics Reviews, 1*(4), 041301. doi:10.1063/1.4900845

Li, J., Feng, Z., Feng, Z., & Zhang, P. (2015, March). A survey of security issues in Cognitive Radio Networks. *China Communications*, *12*(3), 132–150. doi:10.1109/CC.2015.7084371

Li, L., Xu, J., Liu, J., & Gao, F. (2018). Recent progress on piezoelectric energy harvesting: Structures and materials. *Advanced Composites and Hybrid Materials*, *1*(3), 478–505. doi:10.100742114-018-0046-1

Lindner, P., Rozental, A., Jurell, A., Reuterskiöld, L., Andersson, G., Hamilton, W., Miloff, A., & Carlbring, P. (2020). Experiences of gamified and automated virtual reality exposure therapy for spider phobia: Qualitative study. *JMIR Serious Games*, *8*(2), e17807. doi:10.2196/17807 PMID:32347803

Lin, L., Wang, S., Xie, Y., Jing, Q., Niu, S., Hu, Y., & Wang, Z. L. (2013). Segmentally Structured Disk Triboelectric Nanogenerator for Harvesting Rotational Mechanical Energy. *Nano Letters*, *13*(6), 2916–2923. doi:10.1021/nl4013002 PMID:23656350

Lin, Z., & Yang, J. (2016). Recent Progress in Triboelectric Nanogenerators as a Renewable and Sustainable Power Source. *Journal of Nanomaterials*, *2016*, 1–24. doi:10.1155/2016/5651613

Li, P., Ryu, J., & Hong, S. (2019). Piezoelectric/Triboelectric Nanogenerators for Biomedical Applications. In *Nanogenerators*. IntechOpen. doi:10.5772/intechopen.90265

Lissounov, K. (2018, June 28). *What's The Difference Between Peer-To-Peer (P2P) Networks And Client-Server?* Resilio Blog. https://www.resilio.com/blog/whats-the-difference-between-peer-to-peer-and-client-server

Liu, C., Wang, X., Ni, J., Cao, Y., & Liu, B. (2019). An edge computing visual system for vegetable categorization. In *2019 18th IEEE International Conference On Machine Learning And Applications (ICMLA)* (pp. 625–632). 10.1109/ICMLA.2019.00115

Liu, X., Yan, Z., Wu, J., Huang, J., Zheng, Y., Sullivan, N. P., & Pan, Z. J. J. o. E. C. (2023). *Prediction of impedance responses of protonic ceramic cells using artificial neural network tuned with the distribution of relaxation times.*

Liu, Y.-P., Yang, C.-H., Ling, H., Mabu, S., & Kuremoto, T. (2018). A visual system of citrus picking robot using convolutional neural networks. In *2018 5th International Conference on Systems and Informatics (ICSAI)* (pp. 344–349). 10.1109/ICSAI.2018.8599325

Liu, H., Fu, H., Sun, L., Lee, C., & Yeatman, E. M. (2021). Hybrid energy harvesting technology: From materials, structural design, system integration to applications. *Renewable & Sustainable Energy Reviews*, *137*, 110473. doi:10.1016/j.rser.2020.110473

Liu, H., Hou, C., Lin, J., Li, Y., Shi, Q., Chen, T., Sun, L., & Lee, C. (2018). A non-resonant rotational electromagnetic energy harvester for low-frequency and irregular human motion. *Applied Physics Letters*, *113*(20), 203901. doi:10.1063/1.5053945

Liu, J., & Thomas, J. (2000). Stock returns and accounting earnings. *Journal of Accounting Research*, *38*(1), 71–101. doi:10.2307/2672923

Liu, J., Xiang, J., Jin, Y., Liu, R., Yan, J., & Wang, L. (2021). Boost precision agriculture with unmanned aerial vehicle remote sensing and edge intelligence: A survey. *Remote Sensing (Basel)*, *13*(21), 4387. doi:10.3390/rs13214387

Liu, S. T. (2006). Fuzzy total transportation cost measures for fuzzy solid transportation problem. *Applied Mathematics and Computation*, *174*(2), 927–941. doi:10.1016/j.amc.2005.05.018

Liu, W., Wang, Z., Wang, G., Liu, G., Chen, J., Pu, X., Xi, Y., Wang, X., Guo, H., Hu, C., & Wang, Z. L. (2019). Integrated charge excitation triboelectric nanogenerator. *Nature Communications*, *10*(1), 1. doi:10.103841467-019-09464-8 PMID:30926813

Liu, Y., Yu, F. R., Li, X., Ji, H., & Leung, V. C. M. (2020). Blockchain and Machine Learning for Communications and Networking Systems. *IEEE Communications Surveys and Tutorials*, *22*(2), 1392–1431. doi:10.1109/COMST.2020.2975911

Li, W., Demir, I., Cao, D., Jöst, D., Ringbeck, F., Junker, M., & Sauer, D. U. (2022). Data-driven systematic parameter identification of an electrochemical model for lithium-ion batteries with artificial intelligence. *Energy Storage Materials*, *44*, 557–570. doi:10.1016/j.ensm.2021.10.023

Li, X., Jia, R., Zhang, R., Yang, S., Chen, G., & Safety, S. (2022). A KPCA-BRANN based data-driven approach to model corrosion degradation of subsea oil pipelines. *Reliability Engineering & System Safety*, *219*, 108231. doi:10.1016/j.ress.2021.108231

Li, Y., Ida, K., & Gen, M. (1997b). Improved genetic algorithm for solving multiobjective solid transportation problem with fuzzy numbers. *Journal of Japan Society for Fuzzy Theory and Systems*, *9*(2), 239–250. doi:10.3156/jfuzzy.9.2_239

Li, Y., Ida, K., Gen, M., & Kobuchi, R. (1997a). Neural network approach for multicriteria solid transportation problem. *Computers & Industrial Engineering*, *33*(3-4), 465–468. doi:10.1016/S0360-8352(97)00169-1

Li, Z., Liu, Y., Yin, P., Peng, Y., Luo, J., Xie, S., & Pu, H. (2021). Constituting abrupt magnetic flux density change for power density improvement in electromagnetic energy harvesting. *International Journal of Mechanical Sciences*, *198*, 106363. doi:10.1016/j.ijmecsci.2021.106363

Lohse, K., Shirzad, N., Verster, A., Hodges, N., & Van der Loos, H. M. (2013). Video games and rehabilitation: Using design principles to enhance engagement in physical therapy. *Journal of Neurologic Physical Therapy; JNPT*, *37*(4), 166–175. doi:10.1097/NPT.0000000000000017 PMID:24232363

Lubis, L. A. (2023). Comparison of completion of VAM, TCOM-SUM transportation problems with stepping stone to determine optimal solutions. In Journal of Physics: Conference Series, 2421. IOP Publishing. doi:10.1088/1742-6596/2421/1/012005

Luo, C., Xu, L., Li, D., & Wu, W. (2020). Edge Computing Integrated with Blockchain Technologies. In D.-Z. Du & J. Wang (Eds.), *Complexity and Approximation: In Memory of Ker-I Ko* (pp. 268–288). Springer International Publishing., doi:10.1007/978-3-030-41672-0_17

Lv, H., Liang, L., Zhang, Y., Deng, L., Chen, Z., Liu, Z., Wang, H., & Chen, G. (2021). A flexible spring-shaped architecture with optimized thermal design for wearable thermoelectric energy harvesting. *Nano Energy*, *88*, 106260. doi:10.1016/j.nanoen.2021.106260

Machine Learning. (2022). In *Wikipedia*. https://en.wikipedia.org/w/index.php?title=Machine_learning&oldid=1125574586#Approaches

Madni, A. M., & Sievers, M. (2018). Model-based systems engineering: motivation, current status, and needed advances. In *Disciplinary Convergence in Systems Engineering Research* (pp. 311–325). Springer. doi:10.1007/978-3-319-62217-0_22

Magaletti, N., Massaro, A., Cosoli, G., & Leogrande, A. (2023). Smart District 4.0 Project: Validation of Results and Exploitation Perspectives. G. Agapito et al. (Eds.): ICWE 2022 Workshops, (pp. 149-159). IEEE.

Magdalene, H.S., &Thulasimani, D.L. (2017). *Analysis of Spectrum Sensing Data Falsification (SSDF) Attack in Cognitive Radio Networks: A Survey*. Semantic Scholar.

Mahapatra, G. S., & Roy, T. K. (2009). Reliability evaluation using triangular intuitionistic fuzzy numbers, arithmetic operations. *International Scholarly and Scientific Research & Innovation*, *3*(2), 422–429.

Mahapatra, G. S., & Roy, T. K. (2013). Intuitionistic fuzzy number and its arithmetic operation with application on system failure. *Journal of Uncertain Systems*, *7*(2), 92–107.

Mahapatra, N. K., & Bera, T. (2019). Optimisation by dual simplex approach in neutrosophic environment. *International Journal of Fuzzy Computation and Modelling*, 2(4), 334. doi:10.1504/IJFCM.2019.100347

Mahmoud A., Niu N., (2015). *On the role of semantics in automated requirements tracing.* Springer. . doi:10.1007/s00766-013-0199-y

Mahmud, M. A. P., Huda, N., Farjana, S. H., & Lang, C. (2018). Environmental profile evaluations of piezoelectric polymers using life cycle assessment. *IOP Conference Series. Earth and Environmental Science*, 154(1), 012017. doi:10.1088/1755-1315/154/1/012017

Malcom, A. (2021, October 6). Blockchain Principles: Understanding Blockchain Technology. *Businesstechweekly.com.* https://www.businesstechweekly.com/finance-and-accounting/fintech/blockchain-principles/

Malhotra, R., & Bharati, S. K. (2016). Intuitionistic fuzzy two stage multiobjective transportation problems. *Advances in Theoretical and Applied Mathematics*, 11(3), 305–316.

Mamatha, S., & Aparna, K. (2015). Design of an Adaptive Energy Detector based on Bi-Level Tresh holding in Cognitive Radio. *International Journal of Scientifc Engineering and Technology Research*, 4(2), 346–349.

Manda, V. K. (2022). Are Stock Market Training Programs worth it? *Indonesian Journal of Contemporary Education*, 4(1), 8–18. doi:10.33122/ijoce.v4i1.20

Manela, B. (2019). Bias-Reduced Hindsight Experience Replay with Virtual Goal Prioritization. *Papers With Code.* https://paperswithcode.com/paper/bias-reduced-hindsight-experience-replay-with

Mangaonkar, S. M., Khandelwal, R., Shaikh, S., Chandaliya, S., & Ganguli, S. (2022). Fruit harvesting robot using computer vision. In *2022 International Conference for Advancement in Technology (ICONAT)* (pp. 1–6). 10.1109/ICONAT53423.2022.9726126

Mansoor, N., Muzahidul Islam, A., Zareei, M., Baharun, S., Wakabayashi, T., & Komaki, S. (2014). Cognitive radio Ad-Hoc network architectures: A survey. *Wireless Personal Communications*, 81(3), 1117–1142. doi:10.100711277-014-2175-3

Mao, Y., Geng, D., Liang, E., & Wang, X. (2015). Single-electrode triboelectric nanogenerator for scavenging friction energy from rolling tires. *Nano Energy*, 15, 227–234. doi:10.1016/j.nanoen.2015.04.026

Marques, H., Ribeiro, J., Marques, P., Zuquete, A., & Rodriguez, J. (2009). A security framework for cognitive radio IP based cooperative protocols. In: *IEEE 20th international symposium on personal, indoor and mobile radio communications.* IEEE. 10.1109/PIMRC.2009.5449952

Marr, B. (2021a, July 2). Why Use Blockchain Technology? *Bernard Marr.* https://bernardmarr.com/why-use-blockchain-technology/

Marr, B. (2021b, November 19). The 5 Biggest Blockchain Trends In 2022. *Forbes.* https://www.forbes.com/sites/bernardmarr/2021/11/19/the-5-biggest-blockchain-trends-in-2022/

Mas A., Mesquida A., Pacheco, M., (2020). Supporting the deployment of ISO-based project management processes with agile metrics. Springer. . doi:10.1016/j.csi.2019.103405

Massaro, A. (2020). Image Processing and Post-Data Mining Processing for Security in Industrial Applications: Security in Industry. Handbook of Research on Intelligent Data Processing and Information Security Systems. IGI Global. doi:10.4018/978-1-7998-1290-6.ch006

Massaro, A. (2021 a). *Electronic in Advanced Research Industry: From Industry 4.0 to Industry 5.0 Advances.* Wiley. doi:10.1002/9781119716907

Massaro, A. (2021 b). *Electronic and Reverse Engineering*. Wiley. doi:10.1002/9781119716907.ch8

Massaro, A. (2021 c). *Information Technology Infrastructures Supporting Industry 5.0 Facilities*. Wiley. doi:10.1002/9781119716907.ch2

Massaro, A. (2022a). Advanced Control Systems in Industry 5.0 Enabling Process Mining. *Sensors (Basel)*, *22*(22), 1–18. doi:10.339022228677 PMID:36433272

Massaro, A. (2022c). Multi-Level Decision Support System in Production and Safety Management. *Knowledge (Beverly Hills, Calif.)*, *2*(4), 682–701.

Massaro, A. (2023). Advanced Electronic and Optoelectronic Sensors, Applications, Modelling and Industry 5.0 Perspectives. *Applied Sciences (Basel, Switzerland)*, *13*(7), 1–26. doi:10.3390/app13074582

Massaro, A., Cosoli, G., Magaletti, N., & Costantiello, A. (2022b). A Search Methodology Based on Industrial Ontology and Machine Learning to Analyze Georeferenced Italian Districts. *Knowledge (Beverly Hills, Calif.)*, *2*(2), 243–265.

Massaro, A., Gargaro, M., Dipierro, G., Galiano, A. M., & Buonopane, S. (2020). Prototype Cross Platform Oriented on Cybersecurity, Virtual Connectivity, Big Data and Artificial Intelligence Control. *IEEE Access : Practical Innovations, Open Solutions*, *8*, 197939–197954. doi:10.1109/ACCESS.2020.3034399

McGovern, A., & Barto, A. G. (2002). *Automatic Discovery of Subgoals in Reinforcement Learning using Diverse Density*. Scholar Works. https://scholarworks.umass.edu/cgi/viewcontent.cgi?article=1017&context=cs_faculty_pubs

Meding W., Staron M., Söder O.. MeTeaM—A method for characterizing mature software metrics teams. , 2021. doi:10.1016/j.jss.2021.111006

Mehrabi, D., Mohammadzaheri, M., Firoozfar, A., & Emadi, M. (2017). A fuzzy virtual temperature sensor for an irradiative enclosure. *Journal of Mechanical Science and Technology*, *31*(10), 4989–4994. doi:10.100712206-017-0947-x

Melluso N., Grangel-González I., Fantoni G. (2022). *Enhancing Industry 4.0 standads interoperability via knowledge graphs with natural language processing*. IEEE. . doi:10.1016/j.compind.2022.103676

Meng, B., Tang, W., Too, Z., Zhang, X., Han, M., Liu, W., & Zhang, H. (2013). A transparent single-friction-surface triboelectric generator and self-powered touch sensor. *Energy & Environmental Science*, *6*(11), 3235–3240. doi:10.1039/c3ee42311e

Menshchikov, A., Shadrin, D., Prutyanov, V., Lopatkin, D., Sosnin, S., Tsykunov, E., Iakovlev, E., & Somov, A. (2021). Real-time detection of hogweed: UAV platform empowered by deep learning. *IEEE Transactions on Computers*, *70*(8), 1175–1188. doi:10.1109/TC.2021.3059819

Mhaske, A. S., & Bondar, K. L. (2020). Fuzzy transportation problem by using triangular, pentagonal and heptagonal fuzzy numbers with Lagrange's polynomial to approximate fuzzy cost for nonagon and hendecagon. [IJFSA]. *International Journal of Fuzzy System Applications*, *9*(1), 112–129. doi:10.4018/IJFSA.2020010105

Micucci, C. (2022). *L'educazione Finanziaria E L'evoluzione Del Social Trading: l'indagine per capire la relazione esistente*.

Mikolov, T., Chen, K., Corrado, G., & Dean, J. (n.d.). *Efficient Estimation of Word Representations in Vector Space*. Retrieved November 3, 2022, from https://ronan.collobert.com/senna/

Minho, J. (2013). *Selfish Attacks and Detection in Cognitive Radio Ad-Hoc Networks*. IEEE Network.

Miraz, M. H. (2020). Blockchain of Things (BCoT): The Fusion of Blockchain and IoT Technologies. In S. Kim & G. C. Deka (Eds.), *Advanced Applications of Blockchain Technology* (pp. 141–159). Springer. doi:10.1007/978-981-13-8775-3_7

Mishra, A., & Kumar, A. (2020). JMD method for transforming an unbalanced fully intuitionistic fuzzy transportation problem into a balanced fully intuitionistic fuzzy transportation problem. *Soft Computing*, *24*(20), 15639–15654. doi:10.100700500-020-04889-6

Mishra, S., Sachan, R., & Rajpal, D. (2020). Deep convolutional neural network based detection system for real-time corn plant disease recognition. *Procedia Computer Science*, *167*, 2003–2010. doi:10.1016/j.procs.2020.03.236

Misra, K., & Rayz, J. T. (2022). *LMs go Phishing: Adapting Pre-trained Language Models to Detect Phishing Emails*. doi:10.1109/WI-IAT55865.2022.00028

Mitchell, H. B. (2004). Ranking intuitionistic fuzzy numbers. *International Journal of Uncertainty, Fuzziness and Knowledge-based Systems*, *12*(3), 377–386. doi:10.1142/S0218488504002886

Mnih, Kavukcuoglu, K., Silver, D., Rusu, A. A., Veness, J., Bellemare, M. G., Graves, A., Riedmiller, M., Fidjeland, A. K., Ostrovski, G., Petersen, S., Beattie, C., Sadik, A., Antonoglou, I., King, H., Kumaran, D., Wierstra, D., Legg, S., & Hassabis, D. (2015). Mnih, V., Kavukcuoglu, K., Silver, D., Rusu, A. A., Veness, J., Bellemare, M. G., & Petersen, S. (2015). Human-level control through deep reinforcement learning. *Nature*, *518*(7540), 529–533. doi:10.1038/nature14236 PMID:25719670

Mohammadzaheri, M., Akbarifar, A., Ghodsi, M., Bahadur, I., AlJahwari, F., & Al-Amri, B. (2020). Health Monitoring of Welded Pipelines with Mechanical Waves and Fuzzy Inference Systems. International Gas Union Research Conference,

Mohammadzaheri, M., Ziaiefar, H., & Ghodsi, M. (2022). Digital Charge Estimation for Piezoelectric Actuators: An Artificial Intelligence Approach. In Handbook of Research on New Investigations in Artificial Life, AI, and Machine Learning (pp. 117-140). IGI Global.

Mohammadzaheri, M., Amouzadeh, A., Doustmohammadi, M., Emadi, M., Nasiri, N., Jamshidi, E., & Soltani, P. (2021). Fault diagnosis of an automobile cylinder block with neural process of modal information. *International Journal of Mechanical and Mechatronics Engineering*, *21*(2), 1–8.

Mohammadzaheri, M., & Chen, L. (2010). Intelligent predictive control of a model helicopter's yaw angle. *Asian Journal of Control*, *12*(6), 667–679. doi:10.1002/asjc.243

Mohammadzaheri, M., Chen, L., Ghaffari, A., & Willison, J. (2009). A combination of linear and nonlinear activation functions in neural networks for modeling a de superheater. *Simulation Modelling Practice and Theory*, *17*(2), 398–407. doi:10.1016/j.simpat.2008.09.015

Mohammadzaheri, M., Chen, L., & Grainger, S. (2012). A critical review of the most popular types of neuro control. *Asian Journal of Control*, *16*(1), 1–11. doi:10.1002/asjc.449

Mohammadzaheri, M., Emadi, M., Ghodsi, M., Bahadur, I. M., Zarog, M., & Saleem, A. (2020). Development of a Charge Estimator for Piezoelectric Actuators: A Radial Basis Function Approach. [IJAIML]. *International Journal of Artificial Intelligence and Machine Learning*, *10*(1), 31–44. doi:10.4018/IJAIML.2020010103

Mohammadzaheri, M., Emadi, M., Ghodsi, M., Jamshidi, E., Bahadur, I., Saleem, A., & Zarog, M. (2019). A variable-resistance digital charge estimator for piezoelectric actuators: An alternative to maximise accuracy and curb voltage drop. *Journal of Intelligent Material Systems and Structures*, *30*(11), 1699–1705. doi:10.1177/1045389X19844011

Mohammadzaheri, M., & Ghodsi, M. (2018). A Critical Review on Empirical Head-Predicting Models of Two-phase Petroleum Fluids in Electrical Submersible Pumps. *Petroleum & Petrochemical Engineering Journal*, *2*(4), 1–4.

Mohammadzaheri, M., Ghodsi, M., & AlQallaf, A. (2018a). Estimate of the head of the head produced by electrical submeersible pumps on gaseous petroleum fluids, a radial basis function network approach. *International Journal of Artificial Intelligence & Applications, 9*(1), 53–62. doi:10.5121/ijaia.2018.9104

Mohammadzaheri, M., Grainger, S., & Bazghaleh, M. (2012a). A comparative study on the use of black box modelling for piezoelectric actuators. *International Journal of Advanced Manufacturing Technology, 63*(9-12), 1247–1255. doi:10.100700170-012-3987-5

Mohammadzaheri, M., Grainger, S., & Bazghaleh, M. (2012b). Fuzzy modeling of a piezoelectric actuator. *International Journal of Precision Engineering and Manufacturing, 13*(5), 663–670. doi:10.100712541-012-0086-3

Mohammadzaheri, M., Mirsepahi, A., Asef-afshar, O., & Koohi, H. (2007). Neuro-fuzzy modeling of superheating system of a steam power plant. *Applied Mathematical Sciences, 1*, 2091–2099.

Mohammadzaheri, M., Tafreshi, R., Khan, Z., Franchek, M., & Grigoriadis, K. (2015). *Modelling of Petroleum Multiphase Fluids in ESPs, an Intelliegnt Approach Offshore Mediternean Conference*, Ravenna, Italy.

Mohammadzaheri, M., Tafreshi, R., Khan, Z., Franchek, M., & Grigoriadis, K. (2016). An intelligent approach to optimize multiphase subsea oil fields lifted by electrical submersible pumps. *Journal of Computational Science, 15*, 50–59. doi:10.1016/j.jocs.2015.10.009

Mohammadzaheri, M., Tafreshi, R., Khan, Z., Ghodsi, M., Franchek, M., & Grigoriadis, K. (2020). Modelling of petroleum multiphase flow in electrical submersible pumps with shallow artificial neural networks. *Ships and Offshore Structures, 15*(2), 174–183. doi:10.1080/17445302.2019.1605959

Mohammadzaheri, M., Ziaiefar, H., Ghodsi, M., Bahadur, I., Zarog, M., Saleem, A., & Emadi, M. (2019). Adaptive Charge Estimation of Piezoelectric Actuators, a Radial Basis Function Approach. *20th International Conference on Research and Education in Mechatronics Wels*, Austria. 10.1109/REM.2019.8744122

Mohammadzaheri, M., Ziaiefar, H., Ghodsi, M., Emadi, M., Zarog, M., Soltani, P., & Bahadur, I. (2022). Adaptive Charge Estimation of Piezoelectric Actuators with a Variable Sensing Resistor, an Artificial Intelligence Approach. *Engineering Letters, 30*(1), 193–200.

Mohd Aman, A. H., Hassan, W. H., Sameen, S., Attarbashi, Z. S., Alizadeh, M., & Latiff, L. A. (2021). IoMT amid COVID-19 pandemic: Application, architecture, technology, and security. *Journal of Network and Computer Applications, 174*, 102886. doi:10.1016/j.jnca.2020.102886 PMID:34173428

Mohideen, S. I., & Kumar, P. S. (2010a). A comparative study on transportation problem in fuzzy environment. *International Journal of Mathematics Research, 2*(1), 151–158.

Mohideen, S. I., & Kumar, P. S. (2010b). A comparative study on transportation problem in fuzzy environment. In *International Conference on Emerging Trends in Mathematics and Computer Applications (ICETMCA2010)*, MEPCO Schlenk Engineering College.

Mollah, M. B., Zhao, J., Niyato, D., Guan, Y. L., Yuen, C., Sun, S., Lam, K.-Y., & Koh, L. H. (2021). Blockchain for the Internet of Vehicles towards Intelligent Transportation Systems: A Survey. *IEEE Internet of Things Journal, 8*(6), 4157–4185. doi:10.1109/JIOT.2020.3028368

Molokomme, D. N., Chabalala, C. S., & Bokoro, P. N. (2020). A review of cognitive radio smart grid communication infrastructure systems. *Energies, 13*(12), 3245. doi:10.3390/en13123245

Monisha, M., & Rajendran, V. (2022). SCAN-CogRSG: Secure channel allocation by dynamic cluster switching for cognitive radio enabled smart grid communications. *Journal of the Institution of Electronics and Telecommunication Engineers, 68*(4), 2826–2847. doi:10.1080/03772063.2020.1729259

Montequin, S., Fernandez, C., Fernandez, O., & Balsera, J. (2016). *Analysis of the Success Factors and Failure Causes in Projects: Comparison of the Spanish Information y Communication Technology (ICT).* Sector. Journal Information Technology Project Management. doi:10.4018/978-1-5225-0196-1.ch068

Mort, J. (2003). Polymers, Electronic Properties. In R. A. Meyers (Ed.), *Encyclopedia of Physical Science and Technology* (3rd ed., pp. 645–657). Academic Press. doi:10.1016/B0-12-227410-5/00597-4

Moure, A., Izquierdo Rodríguez, M. A., Rueda, S. H., Gonzalo, A., Rubio-Marcos, F., Cuadros, D. U., Pérez-Lepe, A., & Fernández, J. F. (2016). Feasible integration in asphalt of piezoelectric cymbals for vibration energy harvesting. *Energy Conversion and Management, 112,* 246–253. doi:10.1016/j.enconman.2016.01.030

Muralidaran, C., & Venkateswarlu, B. (2022). Efficient solutions of time versus cost transportation problems. *International Journal of Logistics Systems and Management, 43*(3), 336–353. doi:10.1504/IJLSM.2022.127081

Mustafa Hilal, A., Hassan Abdalla Hashim, A., Mohamed, H. G., Nour, M. K., Asiri, M. M., Al-Sharafi, A. M., Othman, M., Motwakel, A., & Author, C. (2023). *Malicious URL Classification Using Artificial Fish Swarm Optimization and Deep Learning.* doi:10.32604/cmc.2023.031371

Na, L., Yuhao, W., Huanqing, H., & Tongshuo, L. (2021). A review on vibration energy harvesting. *E3S Web of Conferences, 245,* 01041. doi:10.1051/e3sconf/202124501041

Nagar, P., Srivastava, P. K., & Srivastava, A. (2021). A new dynamic score function approach to optimize a special class of Pythagorean fuzzy transportation problem. *International Journal of System Assurance Engineering and Management,* 1-10. doi:10.1007/s13198-021-01339-w

Nair, S. (2020, May 30). How AI & Blockchain Can Combine To Boost The Healthcare Industry. *Blockchain for Everyone.* https://medium.com/blockchain-for-everyone/how-ai-blockchain-can-combine-to-boost-the-healthcare-industry-bcfb6aef2b96

Nakamoto, S. (2009). *Bitcoin: A Peer-to-Peer Electronic Cash System.* Bitcoin. https://bitcoin.org/bitcoin.pdf

Narayan, J., Kalita, B., & Dwivedy, S. K. (2021). Development of robot-based upper limb devices for rehabilitation purposes: A systematic review. *Augmented Human Research, 6*(1), 1–33. doi:10.100741133-020-00043-x

Narbayeva, S., Bakibayev, T., Abeshev, K., Makarova, I., Shubenkova, K., & Pashkevich, A. (2020). Blockchain Technology on the Way of Autonomous Vehicles Development. *Transportation Research Procedia, 44,* 168–175. doi:10.1016/j.trpro.2020.02.024

Nasri, N., Orts-Escolano, S., & Cazorla, M. (2020). An semg-controlled 3d game for rehabilitation therapies: Real-time time hand gesture recognition using deep learning techniques. *Sensors (Basel), 20*(22), 6451. doi:10.339020226451 PMID:33198083

Natarajan, M. (2013). *A Survey on the Communication Protocols and Security in Cognitive Radio Networks.* Jackson State University.

Nayagam, G., Lakshmana, V., Venkateshwari, G., & Sivaraman, G. (2008, June). Ranking of intuitionistic fuzzy numbers. In *Proceedings of the IEEE International Conference on Fuzzy Systems FUZZ-IEEE '08* (pp. 1971-1974). IEEE. doi:10.1109/fuzzy.2008.4630639

Nayak, A., Saini, V. K., & Bhushan, B. (2021). Nanomaterials for Energy Harvesting and Storage: An Overview. In Applications of Nanomaterials in Agriculture, Food Science, and Medicine (pp. 188–203). IGI Global. doi:10.4018/978-1-7998-5563-7.ch011

Neves, M. E., Leite, J., & Neves, R. (2022). Does Technical Analysis Win?: Evidence From the Period Between Donald Trump's Campaign and the First Date for Brexit. In Handbook of Research on New Challenges and Global Outlooks in Financial Risk Management (pp. 354-383). IGI Global.

Ng, A. Y., Harada, D., & Russell, S.J. (1999). Policy invariance under reward transformations: Theory and application to reward shaping. *Proceedings of International Conference on Machine Learning (ICML-1999)*, (pp. 278–287). EECS. https://people.eecs.berkeley.edu/~pabbeel/cs287-fa09/readings/NgHaradaRussell-shaping-ICML1999.pdf

Nguyen, D. C., Pathirana, P. N., Ding, M., & Seneviratne, A. (2020). Integration of Blockchain and Cloud of Things: Architecture, Applications and Challenges. *IEEE Communications Surveys and Tutorials*, *22*(4), 2521–2549. doi:10.1109/COMST.2020.3020092

Nguyen, D., & Widrow, B. (1990). *Improving the learning speed of 2-layer neural networks by choosing initial values of the adaptive weights International Joint Conference on Neural Networks*, San Diego, USA.

Niu, S., Liu, Y., Chen, X., Wang, S., Zhou, Y. S., Lin, L., Xie, Y., & Wang, Z. L. (2015). Theory of freestanding tribo-electric-layer-based nanogenerators. *Nano Energy*, *12*, 760–774. doi:10.1016/j.nanoen.2015.01.013

Niu, S., Wang, S., Liu, Y., Zhou, Y. S., Lin, L., Hu, Y., Pradel, K. C., & Wang, Z. L. (2014). A theoretical study of grating structured triboelectric nanogenerators. *Energy and Environmental Science, 7*(7), 2339–2349. *Scopus*. Advance online publication. doi:10.1039/C4EE00498A

Niu, S., & Wang, Z. L. (2015). Theoretical systems of triboelectric nanogenerators. *Nano Energy*, *14*, 161–192. doi:10.1016/j.nanoen.2014.11.034

Norkin, C. C. (2016). *Measurement of joint motion: a guide to goniometry*. FA Davis.

Ofori, M. (2021). *Transfer-Learned Pruned Deep Convolutional Neural Networks for Efficient Plant Classification in Resource-Constrained Environments* [Masters Theses & Doctoral Dissertations]. https://scholar.dsu.edu/theses/371

Ohlson, J. A. (1995). Earnings, book values, and dividends in equity valuation. *Contemporary Accounting Research*, *11*(2), 661–687. doi:10.1111/j.1911-3846.1995.tb00461.x

Oishi, Y., Habaragamuwa, H., Zhang, Y., Sugiura, R., Asano, K., Akai, K., Shibata, H., & Fujimoto, T. (2021). Automated abnormal potato plant detection system using deep learning models and portable video cameras. *International Journal of Applied Earth Observation and Geoinformation*, *104*, 102509. doi:10.1016/j.jag.2021.102509

Ojha, A., Das, B., Mondal, S., & Maiti, M. (2009). An entropy based solid transportation problem for general fuzzy costs and time with fuzzy equality. *Mathematical and Computer Modelling*, *50*(1-2), 166–178. doi:10.1016/j.mcm.2009.04.010

Ojha, A., Mondal, S. K., & Maiti, M. (2014). A solid transportation problem with partial nonlinear transportation cost. *Journal of Applied and Computational Mathematics*, *3*(150), 1–6.

Oliveira B., Da C.; Martins S., Magalhães F., Góes L., (2019). Difference based metrics for deep reinforcement learning algorithms. IEEE. . doi:10.1109/ACCESS.2019.2945879

Osanaiye, O., Alfa, A. S., & Hancke, G. P. (2018). A Statistical Approach to Detect Jamming Attacks in Wireless Sensor Networks. *Sensors (Basel)*, *18*(6), 1691. doi:10.339018061691 PMID:29794994

Osco, L. P., Nogueira, K., Marques Ramos, A. P., Faita Pinheiro, M. M., Furuya, D. E. G., Gonçalves, W. N., de Castro Jorge, L. A., Marcato, J. Junior, & dos Santos, J. A. (2021). Semantic segmentation of citrus-orchard using deep neural networks and multispectral UAV-based imagery. *Precision Agriculture, 22*(4), 1171–1188. doi:10.100711119-020-09777-5

Ozcan, A., Catal, C., Donmez, E., & Senturk, B. (2021). A hybrid DNN–LSTM model for detecting phishing URLs. *Neural Computing & Applications.* doi:10.100700521-021-06401-z PMID:34393380

Pal, A., Zhu, L., Wang, Y., & Zhu, G. (2022). (in press). Data-driven model-based calibration for optimizing electrically boosted diesel engine performance. *International Journal of Engine Research*, 14680874221090307.

Palaniappan, M., Tirlangi, S., Mohamed, M. J. S., Moorthy, R. M. S., Valeti, S. V., & Boopathi, S. (2023). Fused deposition modelling of polylactic acid (PLA)-based polymer composites: A case study. In Development, Properties, and Industrial Applications of 3D Printed Polymer Composites (pp. 66–85). IGI Global. doi:10.4018/978-1-6684-6009-2.ch005

Pandya, P., Durvesh, A., & Parekh, N. (2015). Energy Detection Based Spectrum Sensing for Cognitive Radio Network. *2015 Fifth International Conference on Communication Systems and Network Technologies*. IEEE. 10.1109/CSNT.2015.264

Pandya, S., Velarde, G., Zhang, L., Wilbur, J. D., Smith, A., Hanrahan, B., Dames, C., & Martin, L. W. (2019). New approach to waste-heat energy harvesting: Pyroelectric energy conversion. *NPG Asia Materials, 11*(1), 1. doi:10.103841427-019-0125-y

Papa, M. (2014). *Aseguramiento de la Calidad de un Recurso Organizacional: Evaluando y Mejorando una Estrategia Integrada de Medición y Evaluación.* [Tesis Doctoral, Facultad de Informática, Universidad Nacional de La Plata].

Parizo, C. (2021, May 28). *What Are The 4 Different Types of Blockchain Technology?* SearchCIO. https://www.techtarget.com/searchcio/feature/What-are-the-4-different-types-of-blockchain-technology

Park, J., & Sandberg, I. W. (1993). Approximation and radial-basis-function networks. *Neural Computation, 5*(2), 305–316. doi:10.1162/neco.1993.5.2.305 PMID:31167308

Pateria, Subagdja, B., Tan, A., & Quek, C. (2021). Pateria, S., Subagdja, B., Tan, A., Quek, C., Hierarchical Reinforcement Learning: A Comprehensive Survey. *ACM Computing Surveys, 54*(5), 1–35. doi:10.1145/3453160

Paul, N., Sarma, D., & Bera, U. K. (2019). A neutrosophic solid transportation model with insufficient supply. 2019 *IEEE Region 10 Symposium* (TENSYMP). IEEE. doi:10.1109/tensymp46218.2019.8971130

Peddigari, M., Lim, K.-W., Kim, M., Park, C. H., Yoon, W.-H., Hwang, G.-T., & Ryu, J. (2018). Effect of elastic modulus of cantilever beam on the performance of unimorph type piezoelectric energy harvester. *APL Materials, 6*(12), 121107. doi:10.1063/1.5070087

Peng, T., Chen, Y., Xiao, J., Zheng, Y., & Yang, J. (2016). Improved sof fusion-based cooperative spectrum sensing defense against SSDF attacks. *Proceedings of the 2016 International Conference on Computer, Information and Telecommunication Systems, CITS*. IEEE.

Peng, P., & Kievit, R. A. (2020). The development of academic achievement and cognitive abilities: A bidirectional perspective. *Child Development Perspectives, 14*(1), 15–20. doi:10.1111/cdep.12352 PMID:35909387

Peng, Z., & Chen, Q. (2013). A new method for ranking canonical intuitionistic fuzzy numbers. In *Proceedings of the International Conference on Information Engineering and Applications (IEA) 2012* (pp. 609-616). Springer, London. 10.1007/978-1-4471-4856-2_73

Percy, S., Knight, C., McGarry, S., Post, A., Moore, T., & Cavanagh, K. (2014). Thermal to Electrical Energy Converters. In S. Percy, C. Knight, S. McGarry, A. Post, T. Moore, & K. Cavanagh (Eds.), *Thermal Energy Harvesting for Application at MEMS Scale* (pp. 51–67). Springer. doi:10.1007/978-1-4614-9215-3_5

Photovoltaic effect. (n.d.). Energy Education. https://energyeducation.ca/encyclopedia/Photovoltaic_effect

Piotroski, J. D. (2000). Value investing: The use of historical financial statement information to separate winners from losers. *Journal of Accounting Research, 38,* 1–41. doi:10.2307/2672906

Pirayesh, H., & Zeng, H. (2021). Jamming Attacks and Anti-Jamming Strategies in Wireless Networks: A Comprehensive Survey. *ArXiv, abs/2101.00292.*

Plaat, A., Kosters, W., & Preuss, M. (2020). *Deep Model-Based Reinforcement Learning for High-Dimensional Problems, a Survey.* arXiv. https://arxiv.org/pdf/2008.05598.pdf

Plappert, M., Andrychowicz, M., Ray, A., McGrew, B., Baker, B., Powell, G., Schneider, J., Tobin, J., Chociej, M., Welinder, P., Kumar, V., Zaremba. W. (2018). *Multi-Goal Reinforcement Learning: Challenging Robotics Environments and Request for Research, 2018.* arXiv. https://arxiv.org/pdf/1802.09464v2.pdf

Pollock, T. G., & Rindova, V. P. (2003). Media legitimation effects in the market for initial public offerings. *Academy of Management Journal, 46*(5), 631–642. doi:10.2307/30040654

Polu, S. K. (2019). IoMT Based Smart Health Care Monitoring System. *CEUR Workshop Proceedings, 2544*(11), 58–64.

Pooja, A. S. S. V. L., & Sridhar, M. (2020). Analysis of Phishing Website Detection Using CNN and Bidirectional LSTM. *Proceedings of the 4th International Conference on Electronics, Communication and Aerospace Technology, ICECA 2020,* (pp. 1620–1629). IEEE. 10.1109/ICECA49313.2020.9297395

Poston, H. (2022, April 24). *Blockchain Tutorial: Part 2—Nodes.* Ghost Vault. https://ghostvolt.com/articles/blockchain_nodes.html

Pratibha, T. S., Kumar, N., & Kumar, S. (2021). A Survey on Prevention of the Falsification Attacks on Cognitive Radio Networks. *IOP Conference Series: Materials Science and Engineering.* IOP. . doi:10.1088/1757-899X/1033/1/012021

Pratihar, J., Kumar, R., Dey, A., & Broumi, S. (2020). Transportation problem in neutrosophic environment. *Neutrosophic Graph Theory and Algorithms,* 180–212. doi:10.4018/978-1-7998-1313-2.ch007

PRINCE2. (2009). *An introduction to PRINCE2: managing and directing successful projects. Office of Government Commerce.* Stationery Office.

Priya, S., Song, H.-C., Zhou, Y., Varghese, R., Chopra, A., Kim, S.-G., Kanno, I., Wu, L., Ha, D. S., Ryu, J., & Polcawich, R. G. (2019). A Review on Piezoelectric Energy Harvesting: Materials, Methods, and Circuits. *Energy Harvesting and Systems, 4*(1), 3–39. doi:10.1515/ehs-2016-0028

Project Management Institute. (2017). A Guide to the Project Management Body of Knowledge. 6 Ed. *ISBN, 10,* 9781628251845.

Puiutta, E. & Veith, E. (2020). MSP, Explainable Reinforcement Learning. *Survey (London, England)*https://arxiv.org/pdf/2005.06247.pdf

Purushothkumar, M. K., Ananthanarayanan, M., & Dhanasekar, S. (2018). Fuzzy zero suffix Algorithm to solve Fully Fuzzy Transportation Problems. *International Journal of Pure and Applied Mathematics, 119*(9), 79–88.

Puterman, M. L. (1994). *Markov Decision Processes: Discrete Stochastic Dynamic Programming.* John Wiley & Sons, Inc. doi:10.1002/9780470316887

PZT Properties & PZT Manufacturing. (n.d.). APC. https://www.americanpiezo.com/piezo-theory/pzt.html

Qiang, Z., JunHua, H., An, L., GuoMing, C., & QiMin, Y. (2020, August). New ranking methods of intuitionistic fuzzy numbers and Pythagorean fuzzy numbers. In *2020 Chinese Control And Decision Conference (CCDC)* (pp. 4661-4666). IEEE. 10.1109/CCDC49329.2020.9164633

Qiu, S., Liu, Q., Zhou, S., & Huang, W. (2022). Adversarial attack and defense technologies in natural language processing. *Neurocomputing*, *492*, 278–307. doi:10.1016/j.neucom.2022.04.020

Quddoos, A. (2018). A reliable transportation problem. *Transportation Management*, *1*(2), 1–6. doi:10.24294/tm.v1i2.570

Rahbar, A., Mirarabi, A., Nakhaei, M., Talkhabi, M., & Jamali, M. (2022). A comparative analysis of data-driven models (SVR, ANFIS, and ANNs) for daily karst spring discharge prediction. *Water Resources Management*, *36*(2), 589–609. doi:10.100711269-021-03041-9

Rahman, M. A. (2017). Web-based multimedia hand-therapy framework for measuring forward and inverse kinematic data. *Multimedia Tools and Applications*, *76*(6), 8227–8255. doi:10.100711042-016-3447-6

Ramírez, J. M., Gatti, C. D., Machado, S. P., & Febbo, M. (2018). A multi-modal energy harvesting device for low-frequency vibrations. *Extreme Mechanics Letters*, *22*, 1–7. doi:10.1016/j.eml.2018.04.003

Ramos, P., & Mota, C. (2014). Perceptions of success and failure factors in information technology projects: A study from Brazilian companies. *Procedia: Social and Behavioral Sciences*, *119*, 349–357. doi:10.1016/j.sbspro.2014.03.040

Rani, D. (2022). Multi-objective multi-item four dimensional green transportation problem in interval-valued intuitionistic fuzzy environment. *International Journal of System Assurance Engineering and Management*, 1-18. doi:10.1007/s13198-022-01794-z

Rao, R. S., Umarekar, A., Alwyn, & Pais, R. (2022). *Application of word embedding and machine learning in detecting phishing websites. 79*, 33–45. doi:10.1007/s11235-021-00850-6

Rao, R. S., Vaishnavi, T., & Pais, A. R. (2019). PhishDump: A multi-model ensemble based technique for the detection of phishing sites in mobile devices. *Pervasive and Mobile Computing*, *60*, 101084. doi:10.1016/j.pmcj.2019.101084

Rauniyar, A., & Shin, S. Y. (2015). Cooperative adaptive threshold based energy and matched flter detector in cognitive radio networks. *Journal of Communication and Computer*, *12*, 13–19.

Ravi, V., Anand Kumar, M., Ganesh, B. H., & Kumar, A. M. (2018). *Distributed Representation Using Target Classes: Bag of Tricks for Security and Privacy Analytics Amrita-NLP@IWSPA 2018 Distributed Representation using Target Classes: Bag of Tricks for Security and Privacy Analytics. 21–24.* Ceur. http://ceur-ws.org

Rechy-Ramirez, E. J., Marin-Hernandez, A., & Rios-Figueroa, H. V. (2019). A human–computer interface for wrist rehabilitation: A pilot study using commercial sensors to detect wrist movements. *The Visual Computer*, *35*(1), 41–55. doi:10.100700371-017-1446-x

Reddy, M. A., Reddy, B. M., Mukund, C. S., Venneti, K., Preethi, D. M. D., & Boopathi, S. (2023). Social Health Protection During the COVID-Pandemic Using IoT. In *The COVID-19 Pandemic and the Digitalization of Diplomacy* (pp. 204–235). IGI Global. doi:10.4018/978-1-7998-8394-4.ch009

Ren, Z., Wu, L., Pang, Y., Zhang, W., & Yang, R. (2022). Strategies for effectively harvesting wind energy based on triboelectric nanogenerators. *Nano Energy*, *100*, 107522. doi:10.1016/j.nanoen.2022.107522

Rivera, M. (2018). *Enfoque Integrado de Medición, Evaluación y Mejora de Calidad con soporte a Metas de Negocio y de Necesidad de Información: Aplicación de Estrategias a partir de Patrones de Estrategia.* [Tesis Doctoral. Facultad de Informática, Universidad Nacional de La Plata].

Rokach, L. (2019). *Ensemble Learning: Pattern Classification Using Ensemble Methods* (2nd ed., Vol. 85). World Scientific. doi:10.1142/11325

Rosa, A., Massaro, A., & McDermott, O. (2023). Process Mining Applied to Lean Management Model Improving Decision Making in Healthcare Organizations. In 18th International Forum on Knowledge Asset Dynamics, Matera, Italy.

Rostami, S., Heiska, K., Puchko, O., Leppanen, K., & Valkama, M. (2018). Wireless powered wake-up receiver for ultra-low-power devices. *2018 IEEE Wireless Communications and Networking Conference (WCNC)*, (pp. 1–5). IEEE. 10.1109/WCNC.2018.8377436

Rostami, S., Trinh, H. D., Lagen, S., Costa, M., Valkama, M., & Dini, P. (2020). Wake-Up Scheduling for Energy-Efficient Mobile Devices. *IEEE Transactions on Wireless Communications*, *19*(9), 6020–6036. doi:10.1109/TWC.2020.2999339

S, C., Ghana, S., Singh, S., & Poddar, P. (2021). Deep learning model for image-based plant diseases detection on edge devices. In *2021 6th International Conference for Convergence in Technology (I2CT)* (pp. 1–5). doi:10.1109/I2CT51068.2021.9418124

S., P. K., Sampath, B., R., S. K., Babu, B. H., & N., A. (2022). Hydroponics, Aeroponics, and Aquaponics Technologies in Modern Agricultural Cultivation. In *IGI:Trends, Paradigms, and Advances in Mechatronics Engineering* (pp. 223–241). IGI Global. doi:10.4018/978-1-6684-5887-7.ch012

Safaei, M., Sodano, H. A., & Anton, S. R. (2019). A review of energy harvesting using piezoelectric materials: State-of-the-art a decade later (2008–2018). *Smart Materials and Structures*, *28*(11), 113001. doi:10.1088/1361-665X/ab36e4

Sahingoz, O. K., Buber, E., Demir, O., & Diri, B. (2019). Machine learning based phishing detection from URLs. *Expert Systems with Applications*, *117*, 345–357. doi:10.1016/j.eswa.2018.09.029

Sahoo, D., Liu, C., & Hoi, S. C. H. (2017). Malicious URL Detection using Machine Learning. *Survey (London, England)*. Advance online publication. doi:10.48550/arxiv.1701.07179

Saini, S., Orlando, M. F., & Pathak, P. M. (2022). Intelligent Control of Master-Slave based Robotic Surgical System. *Journal of Intelligent & Robotic Systems*, *105*(4), 1–20. doi:10.100710846-022-01684-3

Salauddin, M., & Park, J. Y. (2017). Design and experiment of human hand motion driven electromagnetic energy harvester using dual Halbach magnet array. *Smart Materials and Structures*, *26*(3), 035011. doi:10.1088/1361-665X/aa573f

Salha, R. A., El-Hallaq, M. A., & Alastal, A. I. (2019). Blockchain in Smart Cities: Exploring Possibilities in Terms of Opportunities and Challenges. *Journal of Data Analysis and Information Processing*, *7*(3), 3. doi:10.4236/jdaip.2019.73008

Samikannu, R., Koshariya, A. K., Poornima, E., Ramesh, S., Kumar, A., & Boopathi, S. (2023). Sustainable Development in Modern Aquaponics Cultivation Systems Using IoT Technologies. In *Human Agro-Energy Optimization for Business and Industry* (pp. 105–127). IGI Global. doi:10.4018/978-1-6684-4118-3.ch006

Sampath, B. C. S., & Myilsamy, S. (2022). Application of TOPSIS Optimization Technique in the Micro-Machining Process. In IGI:Trends, Paradigms, and Advances in Mechatronics Engineering (pp. 162–187). IGI Global. doi:10.4018/978-1-6684-5887-7.ch009

Sampath, H., Dai, H., Zheng, & Zhao, Y. (2011). *Multi-channel Jamming Attacks using Cognitive Radios*. Proceedings of the 16th International Conference on Computer Communications and Networks (ICCCN), Honolulu, HI, USA

Sampath, B., & Myilsamy, S. (2021). Experimental investigation of a cryogenically cooled oxygen-mist near-dry wire-cut electrical discharge machining process. *Strojniski Vestnik. Jixie Gongcheng Xuebao*, *67*(6), 322–330. doi:10.5545v-jme.2021.7161

Sampath, B., Pandian, M., Deepa, D., & Subbiah, R. (2022). Operating parameters prediction of liquefied petroleum gas refrigerator using simulated annealing algorithm. *AIP Conference Proceedings, 2460*(1), 070003. doi:10.1063/5.0095601

Sampath, B., Yuvaraj, D., & Velmurugan, D. (2022). Parametric analysis of mould sand properties for flange coupling casting. *AIP Conference Proceedings, 2460*(1), 070002. doi:10.1063/5.0095599

Sandhu, M. M., Khalifa, S., Jurdak, R., & Portmann, M. (2021). Task Scheduling for Energy-Harvesting-Based IoT: A Survey and Critical Analysis. *IEEE Internet of Things Journal, 8*(18), 13825–13848. doi:10.1109/JIOT.2021.3086186

Sangeetha, V., Thirisangu, K., & Elumalai, P. (2021). Dual simplex method based solution for a fuzzy transportation problem. *Journal of Physics: Conference Series, 1947*(1), 012017. doi:10.1088/1742-6596/1947/1/012017

Santhoshkumar, D., & Rabinson, G. C. (2018). A new proposed method to solve fully fuzzy transportation problem using least allocation method. *International Journal of Pure and Applied Mathematics, 119*(15), 159–166.

Santos, L., Santos, F., Oliveira, P. M., & Shinde, P. (2019). Deep learning applications in agriculture: A short review. In M. F. Silva, J. Luís Lima, L. P. Reis, A. Sanfeliu, & D. Tardioli (Eds.), *Robot 2019: Fourth Iberian Robotics Conference* (pp. 139–151). Springer International Publishing. 10.1007/978-3-030-35990-4_12

Saravanan, M., Vasanth, M., Boopathi, S., Sureshkumar, M., & Haribalaji, V. (2022). Optimization of Quench Polish Quench (QPQ) Coating Process Using Taguchi Method. *Key Engineering Materials, 935*, 83–91. doi:10.4028/p-z569vy

Sarker, S., Saha, A. K., & Ferdous, M. S. (2020). *A Survey on Blockchain & Cloud Integration* (arXiv:2012.02644). arXiv. /arXiv.2012.02644 doi:10.1109/ICCIT51783.2020.9392748

Schlutter A., Vogelsang A., (2020). *Knowledge Extraction from Natural Language Requirements into a Semantic Relation Graph.* ACM. . doi:10.1145/3387940.3392162

Schuster, T. (2003). Fifty-fifty. Stock recommendations and stock prices. Effects and benefits of investment advice in the business media.

Schwalbe, K. (2015). *Information Technology Project Management.*

Sebald, G., Guyomar, D., & Agbossou, A. (2009). On thermoelectric and pyroelectric energy harvesting. *Smart Materials and Structures, 18*(12), 125006. doi:10.1088/0964-1726/18/12/125006

Selvakumar, S., Adithe, S., Isaac, J. S., Pradhan, R., Venkatesh, V., & Sampath, B. (2023). A Study of the Printed Circuit Board (PCB) E-Waste Recycling Process. In Sustainable Approaches and Strategies for E-Waste Management and Utilization (pp. 159–184). IGI Global.

Senthil, T. S. R., Ohmsakthi vel, Puviyarasan, M., Babu, S. R., Surakasi, R., & Sampath, B. (2023). Industrial Robot-Integrated Fused Deposition Modelling for the 3D Printing Process. In Development, Properties, and Industrial Applications of 3D Printed Polymer Composites (pp. 188–210). IGI Global. doi:10.4018/978-1-6684-6009-2.ch011

Serkan, U. N. A. L. Is Popularity of Technical Analysis a Product of Low Financial Literacy and Overconfidence Among Stock Market Investors?. *Eskişehir Osmangazi Üniversitesi İktisadi ve İdari Bilimler Dergisi, 17*(1), 146-169.

Sezer, N., & Koç, M. (2021). A comprehensive review on the state-of-the-art of piezoelectric energy harvesting. *Nano Energy, 80*, 105567. doi:10.1016/j.nanoen.2020.105567

Shafay, M., Ahmad, R. W., Salah, K., Yaqoob, I., Jayaraman, R., & Omar, M. (2022). Blockchain For Deep Learning: Review and Open Challenges. *Cluster Computing*. Advance online publication. doi:10.100710586-022-03582-7 PMID:35309043

Shafique, U., & Qaiser, H. (2014). A Comparative Study of Process Models Data Mining (KDD, CRISP-DM and SEMMA). *International Journal of Innovation and Scientific Research*, 217–222.

Shah, S. A. A., Luo, H., Pickupana, P. D., Ekeze, A., Sohel, F., Laga, H., Li, C., Paynter, B., & Wang, P. (2022). Automatic and fast classification of barley grains from images: A deep learning approach. *Smart Agricultural Technology*, 2, 100036. doi:10.1016/j.atech.2022.100036

Shaikh, I. & Randhawa, K. (2022). Managing the risks and motivations of technology managers in open innovation: Bringing stakeholder-centric corporate governance into focus. *Journal of Technological Innovation.* . doi:10.1016/j.technovation.2021.102437

Shamir. (1984). Identity-based cryptosystems and signature schemes, Advances in Cryptology. Crypto 84, (pp. 47–53). Springer-Verlag.

Shams, S., Santhoshkumar, M., Muttath, D. J., & Premkumar, K. (2019). *Distributed Detection in Cognitive Radio Networks with Unknown Primary User's Traffic. TENCON 2019 - 2019 IEEE Region 10 Conference*. IEEE. doi:10.1109/TENCON.2019.8929431

Sharma, T. K. (2020, January 7). 5 Biggest Blockchain Trends In 2022. *Blockchain Council*. https://www.blockchain-council.org/blockchain/5-biggest-blockchain-trends/

Sharma, H., Haque, A., & Jaffery, Z. A. (2019). Maximization of wireless sensor network lifetime using solar energy harvesting for smart agriculture monitoring. *Ad Hoc Networks*, *94*, 101966. doi:10.1016/j.adhoc.2019.101966

Sharpes, N., Abdelkefi, A., & Priya, S. (2014). Comparative Analysis of One-Dimensional and Two-Dimensional Cantilever Piezoelectric Energy Harvesters. *Energy Harvesting and Systems*, *1*(3–4), 209–216. doi:10.1515/ehs-2014-0007

Shearer, C. (2000). The CRISP-DM model: The new blueprint for data mining. *Journal of Data Warehousing*, (4), 13–22.

Shell, E. (1955). Distribution of a product by several properties, directorate of management analysis. In *Proceedings of the second symposium in linear programming* (Vol. 2, pp. 615-642). IEEE.

Shibata, K., Wang, R., Tou, T., & Koruza, J. (2018). Applications of lead-free piezoelectric materials. *MRS Bulletin*, *43*(8), 612–616. doi:10.1557/mrs.2018.180

Siddiqui T., Ahmad A., (2019). Mining software repositories for software metrics (MSR-SM): conceptual framework. *IJITEE.* . doi:10.35940/ijitee.J1051.0881019

Siddiqui, S., Kim, D.-I., Roh, E., Duy, L. T., Trung, T. Q., Nguyen, M. T., & Lee, N.-E. (2016). A durable and stable piezoelectric nanogenerator with nanocomposite nanofibers embedded in an elastomer under high loading for a self-powered sensor system. *Nano Energy*, *30*, 434–442. doi:10.1016/j.nanoen.2016.10.034

Siegel, S., & Smeddinck, J. (2012, September). Adaptive difficulty with dynamic range of motion adjustments in exergames for Parkinson's disease patients. *In International Conference on Entertainment Computing* (pp. 429-432). Springer, Berlin, Heidelberg 10.1007/978-3-642-33542-6_45

Silva Ferreira M., Almeida Martins L., Júnior P., Costa H., (2019). Measuring developer work to support the software project manager: an exploratory study. https://doi.org/. doi:10.1145/3364641.3364651

Silva, G. M., Souto, J. J. D. S., Fernandes, T. P., Bolis, I., & Santos, N. A. (2021). Interventions with serious games and entertainment games in autism spectrum disorder: A systematic review. *Developmental Neuropsychology*, *46*(7), 463–485. doi:10.1080/87565641.2021.1981905 PMID:34595981

Singh, R., Singh, J., & Singh, R. (2017). Fuzzy Based Advanced Hybrid Intrusion Detection System to Detect Malicious Nodes in Wireless Sensor Networks. Wireless Communications and Mobile Computing. doi:10.1155/2017/3548607

Singh, B., & Singh, A. (2023). Hybrid particle swarm optimization for pure integer linear solid transportation problem. *Mathematics and Computers in Simulation, 207*, 243–266. doi:10.1016/j.matcom.2022.12.019

Singh, J. P., Thakur, N. I., & Kumar, S. (2016). A new approach to solve fully fuzzy transportation problem. *Arya Bhatta Journal of Mathematics and Informatics, 8*(2), 261–266.

Singh, L., & Dutta, N. (2020). Routing Protocols for CRAHN: A Comparative Evaluation. In H. Sarma, B. Bhuyan, S. Borah, & N. Dutta (Eds.), *Trends in Communication, Cloud, and Big Data. Lecture Notes in Networks and Systems* (Vol. 99). Springer. doi:10.1007/978-981-15-1624-5_1

Singh, P., Nayyar, A., Kaur, A., & Ghosh, U. (2020). Blockchain and Fog Based Architecture for Internet of Everything in Smart Cities. *Future Internet, 12*(4), 1–12. doi:10.3390/fi12040061

Single-electrode mode triboelectric nanogenerator.png. (n.d.). Wikipedia. https://commons.wikimedia.org/wiki/File:Single-electrode_mode_triboelectric_nanogenerator.png

Siri, D. (2019). *Machine learning algorithm application in software quality improvement using metrics.* ACM. . doi:10.35940/ijeat.F1359.0986S319

Smales, L. A. (2014). News sentiment in the gold futures market. *Journal of Banking & Finance, 49*, 275–286. doi:10.1016/j.jbankfin.2014.09.006

Smeddinck, J. D., Siegel, S., & Herrlich, M. (2013, May). Adaptive difficulty in exergames for Parkinson's disease patients. In Graphics Interface (pp. 141-148).

Somesha, M., & Pais, A. R. (2022). Classification of Phishing Email Using Word Embedding and Machine Learning Techniques. *Journal of Cyber Security and Mobility, 11*(3), 279–320–279–320. doi:10.13052/jcsm2245-1439.1131

Sommer, M., Lim, H., & MacDonald, M. (2022). Financial advisor use, life events, and the relationship with beneficial intentions. *Financial Services Review, 30*(1), 69–88.

Song, X., van de Ven, S. S., Chen, S., Kang, P., Gao, Q., Jia, J., & Shull, P. B. (2022). Proposal of a wearable multimodal sensing based serious games approach for hand movement training after stroke. *Frontiers in Physiology, 13*, 811950. doi:10.3389/fphys.2022.811950 PMID:35721546

Soto, J., & Nogueira, M. (2015). A framework for resilient and secure spectrum sensing on cognitive radio networks. *Computer Networks, 79*, 313–322. doi:10.1016/j.comnet.2015.01.011

Soviany, P., Ionescu, R. T., Rota, P., Sebe, N. (2022). Curriculum Learning. *Survey (London, England)*, arXiv. https://arxiv.org/abs/2101.10382

Steiner, B., Elgert, L., Saalfeld, B., & Wolf, K. H. (2020). Gamification in rehabilitation of patients with musculoskeletal diseases of the shoulder: Scoping review. *JMIR Serious Games, 8*(3), e19914. doi:10.2196/19914 PMID:32840488

Steyerberg, E. W., Eijkemans, M. J., Harrell, F. E. Jr, & Habbema, J. D. F. (2000). Prognostic modelling with logistic regression analysis: A comparison of selection and estimation methods in small data sets. *Statistics in Medicine, 19*(8), 1059–1079. doi:10.1002/(SICI)1097-0258(20000430)19:8<1059::AID-SIM412>3.0.CO;2-0 PMID:10790680

Stoilova, K., & Stoilov, T. (2021). Solving transportation and travelling salesman problems in excel environment. *Advanced Aspects of Engineering Research, 15*, 48–62. doi:10.9734/bpi/aaer/v15/9759D

Struwig, M. N., Wolhuter, R., & Niesler, T. (2018). Nonlinear model and optimization method for a single-axis linear-motion energy harvester for footstep excitation. *Smart Materials and Structures, 27*(12). *Smart Materials and Structures, 27*(12), 125007. Advance online publication. doi:10.1088/1361-665X/aae6e7

Suarez, A., Molina, R. S., Ramponi, G., Petrino, R., Bollati, L., & Sequeiros, D. (2021). Pest detection and classification to reduce pesticide use in fruit crops based on deep neural networks and image processing. In *2021 XIX Workshop on Information Processing and Control (RPIC)* (pp. 1–6). 10.1109/RPIC53795.2021.9648485

Sun, C., Shang, G., Zhu, X., Tao, Y., & Li, Z. (2013). Modeling for Piezoelectric Stacks in Series and Parallel. *2013 Third International Conference on Intelligent System Design and Engineering Applications*, (pp. 954–957). IEEE. 10.1109/ISDEA.2012.228

Sutherland, J. (2014). *Scrum: The art of doing twice the work in half the time.* Crown Business.

Swan, M. (2015). *Blockchain: Blueprint for a New Economy.* O'Reilly Media, Inc.

Swarup, K., Gupta, P. K., & Mohan, M. (1997). Tracts in operations research. *Sultan Chand & Sons, New Delhi, 8*, 659–692.

Taajobian, M., Mohammadzaheri, M., Doustmohammadi, M., Amouzadeh, A., & Emadi, M. (2018). Fault diagnosis of an automobile cylinder head using low frequency vibrational data. *Journal of Mechanical Science and Technology, 32*(7), 3037–3045. doi:10.100712206-018-0606-x

Tahsin, R., Mozumder, M. H., Shahriyar, S. A., & Salim Mollah, M. A. (2020). A Novel Approach for E-mail Classification Using FastText. *2020 IEEE Region 10 Symposium, TENSYMP 2020*, 1392–1395. 10.1109/TENSYMP50017.2020.9230961

Tajaddodianfar, F., Stokes, J. W., & Gururajan, A. (2020). Texception: A Character/Word-Level Deep Learning Model for Phishing URL Detection. *ICASSP, IEEE International Conference on Acoustics, Speech and Signal Processing - Proceedings, 2020-May*, (pp. 2857–2861). IEEE. 10.1109/ICASSP40776.2020.9053670

Tang, J., Wang, D., Zhang, Z., He, L., Xin, J., & Xu, Y. (2017). Weed identification based on K-means feature learning combined with convolutional neural network. *Computers and Electronics in Agriculture, 135*, 63–70. doi:10.1016/j.compag.2017.01.001

Tang, W., Jiang, T., Fan, F. R., Yu, A. F., Zhang, C., Cao, X., & Wang, Z. L. (2015). Liquid-metal electrode for high-performance triboelectric nanogenerator at an instantaneous energy conversion efficiency of 70.6%. *Advanced Functional Materials, 25*(24), 3718–3725. doi:10.1002/adfm.201501331

Tanwar, S., Bhatia, Q., Patel, P., Kumari, A., Singh, P. K., & Hong, W.-C. (2020). Machine Learning Adoption in Blockchain-Based Smart Applications: The Challenges, and a Way Forward. *IEEE Access : Practical Innovations, Open Solutions, 8*, 474–488. doi:10.1109/ACCESS.2019.2961372

Tashman, D. H., & Hamouda, W. (2020). An overview and future directions on physical-layer security for cognitive radio networks. *IEEE Network, 35*(3), 205–211. doi:10.1109/MNET.011.2000507

Team DataFlair. (2018, June 1). *Advantages and Disadvantages Of Blockchain Technology.* DataFlair. https://data-flair.training/blogs/advantages-and-disadvantages-of-blockchain/

Team Etoro. (2022, March 14). *Advantages and Disadvantages of a Blockchain.* EToroX. https://etorox.com/blockchain-academy/advantages-and-disadvantages-of-a-blockchain/

Tephillah, S., & Manickam, J. M. L. (2020). An SETM Algorithm for Combating SSDF Attack in Cognitive Radio Networks. [NA.]. *Wireless Communications and Mobile Computing, 2020*, 2020. doi:10.1155/2020/9047809

Tetila, E. C., Brandoli Machado, B., Menezes, G. V., de Souza Belete, N. A., Astolfi, G., & Pistori, H. (2020). A deep-learning approach for automatic counting of soybean insect pests. *IEEE Geoscience and Remote Sensing Letters*, *17*(10), 1837–1841. doi:10.1109/LGRS.2019.2954735

Tetlock, P. C. (2007). Giving content to investor sentiment: The role of media in the stock market. *The Journal of Finance*, *62*(3), 1139–1168. doi:10.1111/j.1540-6261.2007.01232.x

Thakre, A., Kumar, A., Song, H.-C., Jeong, D.-Y., & Ryu, J. (2019). Pyroelectric Energy Conversion and Its Applications—Flexible Energy Harvesters and Sensors. *Sensors (Basel)*, *19*(9), 2170. doi:10.339019092170 PMID:31083331

Thakur, P. (2021). Spectrum Mobility in Cognitive Radio Networks Using Spectrum Prediction and Monitoring Techniques. In *Spectrum Sharing in Cognitive Radio Networks: Towards Highly Connected Environments* (pp. 147–166). Wiley. doi:10.1002/9781119665458.ch7

The CHAOS Report. (2020). The Standish Group. https://secure.standishgroup.com/reports/flyers/CM2020- TOC.pdf

The Feynman Lectures. (n.d.). *Physics Vol. II Ch. 1: Electromagnetism*. Feynman Lectures. https://www.feynmanlectures.caltech.edu/II_01.html#Ch1-S4

Thomas R., Uminsky D. (2022). Reliance on metrics is a fundamental challenge for AI. *Patterns*. . doi:10.1016/j.patter.2022.100476

Toghuj, W., & Turab, N. (2022). A survey on security threats in the internet of medical things (IoMT). *Journal of Theoretical and Applied Information Technology*, *100*(10), 3361–3371.

Traneva, V., & Tranev, S. (2021). Two-stage intuitionistic fuzzy transportation problem through the prism of index matrices. *Preprints of Position and Communication Papers of the Federated Conference on Computer Science and Information Systems* (pp. 89–96). FedCSIS. 10.15439/2021F76

Tsikinas, S., & Xinogalos, S. (2019). Studying the effects of computer serious games on people with intellectual disabilities or autism spectrum disorder: A systematic literature review. *Journal of Computer Assisted Learning*, *35*(1), 61–73. doi:10.1111/jcal.12311

US EPA. O. (2014, October 28). *Geothermal Heating and Cooling Technologies* [Overviews and Factsheets]. EPA. https://www.epa.gov/rhc/geothermal-heating-and-cooling-technologies

Van Solingen, R., & Van Lanen, R. (2014). *Scrum voor Managers*. Academic Service. EAN.

Vanhoucke, M. (2011). On the dynamic use of project performance and schedule risk information during project tracking. *Omega*, *39*(4), 416–426. doi:10.1016/j.omega.2010.09.006

Vanitha, S. K. R., & Boopathi, S. (2023). Artificial Intelligence Techniques in Water Purification and Utilization. In *Human Agro-Energy Optimization for Business and Industry* (pp. 202–218). IGI Global., doi:10.4018/978-1-6684-4118-3.ch010

Varela, L., & Domingues, L. (2022). Domingues. Risks of Data Science Projects – A Delphi Study. *Procedia Computer Science*, *196*, 982–989. doi:10.1016/j.procs.2021.12.100

Varghese, A., & Kuriakose, S. (2012). Centroid of an intuitionistic fuzzy number. *Notes on Intuitionistic Fuzzy Sets*, *18*(1), 19–24.

Varsha, P. & Rakesh, V. (2012). Black Hole Attack and its Counter Measures in AODV Routing Protocol. *International Journal of Computational Engineering Research (ijceronline.com)*, *2*(5).

Vennila, T., Karuna, M. S., Srivastava, B. K., Venugopal, J., Surakasi, R., & B., S. (2023). New Strategies in Treatment and Enzymatic Processes. In *Human Agro-Energy Optimization for Business and Industry* (pp. 219–240). IGI Global. doi:10.4018/978-1-6684-4118-3.ch011

Verhulst, A., Yamaguchi, T., & Richard, P. (2015, February). Physiological-based Dynamic difficulty adaptation in a theragame for children with cerebral palsy. *In Proceedings of the 2nd International Conference on Physiological Computing Systems (PhyCS-2015)* (pp. 164-171). Scitepress. 10.5220/0005271501640171

Viglialoro, R. M., Condino, S., Turini, G., Mamone, V., Carbone, M., Ferrari, V., Ghelarducci, G., Ferrari, M., & Gesi, M. (2020). Interactive serious game for shoulder rehabilitation based on real-time hand tracking. *Technology and Health Care*, *28*(4), 403–414. doi:10.3233/THC-192081 PMID:32444586

Vinayakumar, R., Barathi Ganesh, H. B., Anand Kumar, M., Soman, K. P., & Poornachandran, P. (2018). DeepAnti-PhishNet: Applying deep neural networks for phishing email detection CEN-AISecurity@IWSPA-2018. *CEUR Workshop Proceedings*, *2124*(March), 39–49.

Vinayakumar, R., Soman, K. P., Poornachandran, P., Mohan, V. S., & Kumar, A. D. (2019). ScaleNet: Scalable and Hybrid Frameworkfor Cyber Threat Situational AwarenessBased on DNS, URL,and Email Data Analysis. *Journal of Cyber Security and Mobility*, *8*(2), 189–240. doi:10.13052/jcsm2245-1439.823

Vukajlović, N., Milićević, D., Dumnić, B., & Popadić, B. (2020). Comparative analysis of the supercapacitor influence on lithium battery cycle life in electric vehicle energy storage. *Journal of Energy Storage*, *31*, 101603. doi:10.1016/j.est.2020.101603

Walsh, C. M., Gull, K., & Dooley, D. (2022). Motor rehabilitation as a therapeutic tool for spinal cord injury: New perspectives in immunomodulation. *Cytokine & Growth Factor Reviews*. doi:10.1016/j.cytogfr.2022.08.005 PMID:36114092

Wanderley, M., Menezes, J. Jr, Gusmão, C., & Lima, C. F. (2015). Proposal of risk management metrics for multiple project software development. *Procedia Computer Science*, *64*, 1001–1009. doi:10.1016/j.procs.2015.08.619

Wang, J., & Chen, I. (2014). Trust-based data fusion mechanism design in cognitive radio networks. 2014 IEEE Conference on Communications and Network Security, (pp. 53–59). IEEE. 10.1109/CNS.2014.6997465

Wang, Q., & Zheng, H. (2006). Route and Spectrum Selection in Dynamic Spectrum Networks. *Proc. IEEE CCNC*. IEEE.

Wang, W., Chatterjee, M., & Kwiat, K. (2011). Collaborative Jamming and Collaborative Defense in Cognitive Radio Networks. *Proceedings of the IEEE International Symposium on a World of Wireless, Mobile and Multimedia Networks (WoWMoM)*. IEEE. 10.1109/WoWMoM.2011.5986172

Wang, B., Wu, Y., Liu, K. J. R., & Clancy, T. C. (2011, April). An Anti-Jamming Stochastic Game for Cognitive Radio Networks. *IEEE Journal on Selected Areas in Communications*, *29*(4), 877–889. doi:10.1109/JSAC.2011.110418

Wang, C., Liu, B., Liu, L., Zhu, Y., Hou, J., Liu, P., & Li, X. (2021). A review of deep learning used in the hyperspectral image analysis for agriculture. *Artificial Intelligence Review*, *54*(7), 5205–5253. doi:10.100710462-021-10018-y

Wang, F., Zhang, M., Wang, X., Ma, X., & Liu, J. (2020). Deep learning for edge computing applications: A state-of-the-art survey. *IEEE Access : Practical Innovations, Open Solutions*, *8*, 58322–58336. doi:10.1109/ACCESS.2020.2982411

Wang, H., & Jasim, A. (2020). Piezoelectric energy harvesting from pavement. In *Eco-Efficient Pavement Construction Materials* (pp. 367–382). Elsevier. doi:10.1016/B978-0-12-818981-8.00014-X

Wang, H., Jasim, A., & Chen, X. (2018a). Energy harvesting technologies in roadway and bridge for different applications – A comprehensive review. *Applied Energy*, *212*, 1083–1094. doi:10.1016/j.apenergy.2017.12.125

Wang, H., Xu, L., Bai, Y., & Wang, Z. L. (2020). Pumping up the charge density of a triboelectric nanogenerator by charge-shuttling. *Nature Communications*, *11*(1), 1. doi:10.103841467-020-17891-1 PMID:32826902

Wang, H., Yu, L., Tian, S., Peng, Y., & Pei, X. (2019). Bidirectional LSTM Malicious webpages detection algorithm based on convolutional neural network and independent recurrent neural network. *Applied Intelligence*, *49*(8), 3016–3026. doi:10.100710489-019-01433-4

Wang, J., Li, F., Zhu, F., & Schmidt, O. G. (2019). Recent Progress in Micro-Supercapacitor Design, Integration, and Functionalization. *Small Methods*, *3*(8), 1800367. doi:10.1002mtd.201800367

Wang, L., Chen, J. L., Wong, A. M., Liang, K. C., & Tseng, K. C. (2022). Game-Based Virtual Reality System for Upper Limb Rehabilitation After Stroke in a Clinical Environment: Systematic Review and Meta-Analysis. *Games for Health Journal*, *11*(5), 277–297. doi:10.1089/g4h.2022.0086 PMID:36252097

Wang, L., Todaria, P., Pandey, A., O'Connor, J., Chernow, B., & Zuo, L. (2016). An Electromagnetic Speed Bump Energy Harvester and Its Interactions With Vehicles. *IEEE/ASME Transactions on Mechatronics*, *21*(4), 1985–1994. doi:10.1109/TMECH.2016.2546179

Wang, W., Li, H., Sun, L., & Han, Z. (2009). Securing Collaborative Spectrum Sensing against Untrustworthy Secondary Users in Cognitive Radio Networks. *EURASIP Journal on Advances in Signal Processing*, *2010*(1), 695750. doi:10.1155/2010/695750

Wang, W., Zhang, F., Luo, X., & Zhang, S. (2019). PDRCNN: Precise Phishing Detection with Recurrent Convolutional Neural Networks. *Security and Communication Networks*, *2019*, 1–15. doi:10.1155/2019/2595794

Wang, Y., Chen, R., Chen, T., Lv, H., Zhu, G., Ma, L., Wang, C., Jin, Z., & Liu, J. (2016). Emerging non-lithium ion batteries. *Energy Storage Materials*, *4*, 103–129. doi:10.1016/j.ensm.2016.04.001

Wang, Y., Yang, E., Chen, T., Wang, J., Hu, Z., Mi, J., Pan, X., & Xu, M. (2020). A novel humidity resisting and wind direction adapting flag-type triboelectric nanogenerator for wind energy harvesting and speed sensing. *Nano Energy*, *78*, 105279. doi:10.1016/j.nanoen.2020.105279

Wang, Z. L. (2017). On Maxwell's displacement current for energy and sensors: The origin of nanogenerators. *Materials Today*, *20*(2), 74–82. doi:10.1016/j.mattod.2016.12.001

Wang, Z. L., Jiang, T., & Xu, L. (2017). Toward the blue energy dream by triboelectric nanogenerator networks. *Nano Energy*, *39*, 9–23. doi:10.1016/j.nanoen.2017.06.035

Wang, Z. L., Lin, L., Chen, J., Niu, S., & Zi, Y. (2016a). Triboelectric Nanogenerator: Freestanding Triboelectric-Layer Mode. In Z. L. Wang, L. Lin, J. Chen, S. Niu, & Y. Zi (Eds.), *Triboelectric Nanogenerators* (pp. 109–153). Springer International Publishing. doi:10.1007/978-3-319-40039-6_5

Wang, Z. L., Lin, L., Chen, J., Niu, S., & Zi, Y. (2016b). Triboelectric Nanogenerator: Lateral Sliding Mode. In Z. L. Wang, L. Lin, J. Chen, S. Niu, & Y. Zi (Eds.), *Triboelectric Nanogenerators* (pp. 49–90). Springer International Publishing. doi:10.1007/978-3-319-40039-6_3

Wang, Z., Ruan, Z., Ng, W. S., Li, H., Tang, Z., Liu, Z., Wang, Y., Hu, H., & Zhi, C. (2018). Integrating a Triboelectric Nanogenerator and a Zinc-Ion Battery on a Designed Flexible 3D Spacer Fabric. *Small Methods*, *2*(10), 1800150. doi:10.1002mtd.201800150

Wan, R., Ding, L., Xiong, N., & Zhou, X. (2019). Mitigation strategy against spectrum-sensing data falsification attack in cognitive radio sensor networks. *International Journal of Distributed Sensor Networks*, *15*(9), 155014771987064. doi:10.1177/1550147719870645

Wassim, E. H. (2011). Survey of Security Issues in Cognitive Radio Networks. *Journal of Internet Technology, 12*(2).

Wegrzyn, K., & Wang, E. (2021, August 19). *Types of Blockchain: Public, Private, or Something in Between.* Foley & Lardner LLP. https://www.foley.com/en/insights/publications/2021/08/types-of-blockchain-public-private-between

Wei, B., Ali Hamad, R., Yang, L., He, X., Wang, H., Gao, B., & Woo, W. L. (2019). A Deep-Learning-Driven Light-Weight Phishing Detection Sensor. *Sensors 2019, 19*(19), 4258. doi:10.3390/s19194258

Wei, C., & Tang, X. (2013). A new method for ranking intuitionistic fuzzy numbers. In G. Yang (Ed.), *Multidisciplinary Studies in Knowledge and Systems Science* (pp. 45–51). IGI Global. doi:10.4018/978-1-4666-3998-0.ch004

Werneck Barbosa, M., Martinez Carrasco, S., & Rodriguez, P. (2022). The effect of enterprise risk management competencies on students´ perceptions of their work readiness. *International Journal of Management Education. . 2022.* doi:10.1016/j.ijme.2022.100638

Westenberger, J., Schuler, K., & Schlegel, D. (2022). Failure of AI projects: Understanding the critical factors. *Procedia Computer Science, 196,* 69–76. doi:10.1016/j.procs.2021.11.074

West, K. D. (1997). Another heteroskedasticity-and autocorrelation-consistent covariance matrix estimator. *Journal of Econometrics, 76*(1-2), 171–191. doi:10.1016/0304-4076(95)01788-7

What are the Advantages and Disadvantages of Geothermal Energy ? (n.d.). TWI Global. https://www.twi-global.com/technical-knowledge/faqs/geothermal-energy-pros-and-cons.aspx

What is Piezoelectricity? (n.d.). *OnScale.* http://https%253A%252F%252Fonscale.com%252Fpiezoelectricity%252Fwhat-is-piezoelectricity%252F

William, R. C., & Dongwan, S. (2011). A novel node level security policy framework for wireless sensor networks. *Journal of Network and Computer Applications, 34*(1), 418–428. doi:10.1016/j.jnca.2010.03.004

Wirth, W., Hartmann, T., Böcking, S., Vorderer, P., Klimmt, C., Schramm, H., Saari, T., Laarni, J., Ravaja, N., Gouveia, F. R., Biocca, F., Sacau, A., Jäncke, L., Baumgartner, T., & Jäncke, P. (2007). A process model of the formation of spatial presence experiences. *Media Psychology, 9*(3), 493–525. doi:10.1080/15213260701283079

Wood, D. (2017). High-level integrated deterministic, stochastic and fuzzy cost-duration analysis aids project planning and monitoring, focusing on uncertainties and earned value metrics. *Journal of Natural Gas Science and Engineering, 37,* 303–326. doi:10.1016/j.jngse.2016.11.045

Wu, T., Wang, M., Xi, Y., & Zhao, Z. (2022). Malicious URL Detection Model Based on Bidirectional Gated Recurrent Unit and Attention Mechanism. *Applied Sciences 2022, 12*(23), 12367. doi:10.3390/app122312367

Wu, Y., Wang, B., & Liu, K. J. R. (2012). Optimal Defense against Jamming Attacks in Cognitive Radio Networks using the Markov Decision Process Approach. *Proceedings of the IEEE Global Telecommunications Conference.* IEEE.

Wu, C., Wang, A. C., Ding, W., Guo, H., & Wang, Z. L. (2019). Triboelectric Nanogenerator: A Foundation of the Energy for the New Era. *Advanced Energy Materials, 9*(1), 1802906. doi:10.1002/aenm.201802906

Wu, X., Ma, C., & Han, Y. (2020). Forecasting Stock Market Volatility: An Asymmetric Conditional Autoregressive Range Mixed Data Sampling (ACARR-MIDAS) Model. *The Journal of Risk, 23*(6).

Wu, Y., Ma, Y., Zheng, H., & Ramakrishna, S. (2021). Piezoelectric materials for flexible and wearable electronics: A review. *Materials & Design, 211,* 110164. doi:10.1016/j.matdes.2021.110164

Xie, F., & Li, Z. (2021). An iterative solution technique for capacitated two-stage time minimization transportation problem. *4OR, 1-48.*

Xie, F., Butt, M. M., Li, Z., & Zhu, L. (2017). An upper bound on the minimal total cost of the transportation problem with varying demands and supplies. *Omega*, *68*, 105–118. doi:10.1016/j.omega.2016.06.007

Xinshao, W., & Cheng, C. (2015). Weed seeds classification based on PCANet deep learning baseline. *2015 Asia-Pacific Signal and Information Processing Association Annual Summit and Conference (APSIPA)*, 408–415. 10.1109/APSIPA.2015.7415304

Xiong, Y., Ge, Y., & From, P. J. (2020). Push and drag: An active obstacle separation method for fruit harvesting robots. In *2020 IEEE International Conference on Robotics and Automation (ICRA)* (pp. 4957–4962). 10.1109/ICRA40945.2020.9197469

Xiong, Y., Ge, Y., & From, P. J. (2021). An improved obstacle separation method using deep learning for object detection and tracking in a hybrid visual control loop for fruit picking in clusters. *Computers and Electronics in Agriculture*, *191*, 106508. doi:10.1016/j.compag.2021.106508

Xu, W., Trappe, W., Zhang, Y., & Wood, T. (2005). The Feasibility of Launching and Detecting Jamming Attacks in Wireless Networks. Proceedings of the ACM International Symposium on Mobile Ad hoc Networking and Computing, (pp. 46-57). ACM. 10.1145/1062689.1062697

Xu, W., Wood, T., Trappe, W., & Zhang, Y. (2004). Channel Surfing and Spatial Retreats: Defenses against Wireless Denial of Service. Proceedings of the 3rd ACM Workshop on Wireless Security, (pp. 80-89). ACM. 10.1145/1023646.1023661

Xu, C., Ren, B., Di, W., Liang, Z., Jiao, J., Li, L., Li, L., Zhao, X., Luo, H., & Wang, D. (2012). Cantilever driving low frequency piezoelectric energy harvester using single crystal material 0.71Pb(Mg1/3Nb2/3)O3-0.29PbTiO3. *Applied Physics Letters*, *101*(3), 033502. doi:10.1063/1.4737170

Xu, C., Ren, B., Liang, Z., Chen, J., Zhang, H., Yue, Q., Xu, Q., Zhao, X., & Luo, H. (2012). Nonlinear output properties of cantilever driving low frequency piezoelectric energy harvester. *Applied Physics Letters*, *101*(22), 223503. doi:10.1063/1.4768219 PMID:23284178

Xu, C., Zi, Y., Wang, A. C., Zou, H., Dai, Y., He, X., Wang, P., Wang, Y.-C., Feng, P., Li, D., & Wang, Z. L. (2018). On the Electron-Transfer Mechanism in the Contact-Electrification Effect. *Advanced Materials*, *30*(15), 1706790. doi:10.1002/adma.201706790 PMID:29508454

Xu, Q., Gao, A., Li, Y., & Jin, Y. (2022). Design and Optimization of Piezoelectric Cantilever Beam Vibration Energy Harvester. *Micromachines*, *13*(5), 5. doi:10.3390/mi13050675 PMID:35630142

Xu, W., Huang, L.-B., Wong, M.-C., Chen, L., Bai, G., & Hao, J. (2017). Environmentally Friendly Hydrogel-Based Triboelectric Nanogenerators for Versatile Energy Harvesting and Self-Powered Sensors. *Advanced Energy Materials*, *7*(1). *Advanced Energy Materials*, *7*(1), 1601529. doi:10.1002/aenm.201601529

Xu, W., Wong, M.-C., & Hao, J. (2019). Strategies and progress on improving robustness and reliability of triboelectric nanogenerators. *Nano Energy*, *55*, 203–215. doi:10.1016/j.nanoen.2018.10.073

Xu, Z.-F., Jia, R.-S., Liu, Y.-B., Zhao, C.-Y., & Sun, H.-M. (2020). Fast method of detecting tomatoes in a complex scene for picking robots. *IEEE Access : Practical Innovations, Open Solutions*, *8*, 55289–55299. doi:10.1109/ACCESS.2020.2981823

Ya, J., Liu, T., Zhang, P., Shi, J., Guo, L., & Gu, Z. (2019). NeuralAS: Deep Word-Based Spoofed URLs Detection against Strong Similar Samples. *Proceedings of the International Joint Conference on Neural Networks, 2019-July*(July), (pp. 1–7). IEEE. 10.1109/IJCNN.2019.8852416

Yadav, K., Roy, S. D., & Kundu, S. (2020). Defense Against Spectrum Sensing Data Falsification Attacker in Cognitive Radio Networks. *Wireless Personal Communications*, *112*(2), 849–862. doi:10.100711277-020-07077-9

Yang, M. D., Tseng, H. H., Hsu, Y. C., & Tseng, W. C. (2020). *Real-time crop classification using edge computing and deep learning. In 2020 IEEE 17th Annual Consumer Communications & Networking Conference.* CCNC. doi:10.1109/CCNC46108.2020.9045498

Yang, R., Yu, F. R., Si, P., Yang, Z., & Zhang, Y. (2019). Integrated Blockchain and Edge Computing Systems: A Survey, Some Research Issues and Challenges. *IEEE Communications Surveys and Tutorials*, *21*(2), 1508–1532. doi:10.1109/COMST.2019.2894727

Yang, W., Zuo, W., & Cui, B. (2019). Detecting Malicious URLs via a Keyword-Based Convolutional Gated-Recurrent-Unit Neural Network. *IEEE Access : Practical Innovations, Open Solutions*, *7*, 29891–29900. doi:10.1109/ACCESS.2019.2895751

Yang, Y., Zhu, G., Zhang, H., Chen, J., Zhong, X., Lin, Z.-H., Su, Y., Bai, P., Wen, X., & Wang, Z. L. (2013). Triboelectric Nanogenerator for Harvesting Wind Energy and as Self-Powered Wind Vector Sensor System. *ACS Nano*, *7*(10), 9461–9468. doi:10.1021/nn4043157 PMID:24044652

Yang, Z., Ho, K. C., Shen, X., & Shi, L. (2020). Disclosure Quality Rankings and Stock Misvaluation–Evidence from Chinese Stock Market. *Emerging Markets Finance & Trade*, *56*(14), 3468–3489. doi:10.1080/1540496X.2019.1700499

Yan, Q., Li, M., Jiang, T., Lou, W., & Thomas Hou, Y. (2007). Vulnerability and Protection for Distributed Consensus-based Spectrum Sensing in Cognitive Radio Networks Qing Zhao, Lang Tong, Ananthram Swami, Yunxia Chen, "Decentralized cognitive MAC for opportunistic spectrum access in ad hoc networks: A POMDP framework". *IEEE Journal on Selected Areas in Communications*, *25*(3).

Yao, L., Zhao, H. D., Dong, Z. Y., Sun, Y. F., & Gao, Y. F. (2012). Laboratory Testing of Piezoelectric Bridge Transducers for Asphalt Pavement Energy Harvesting. *Key Engineering Materials*, *492*, 172–175. . doi:10.4028/www.scientific.net/KEM.492.172

Ye, J. (2017). Neutrosophic number linear programming method and its application under neutrosophic number environments. *Soft Computing*, *22*(14), 4639–4646. doi:10.100700500-017-2646-z

Ye, S., Cheng, C., Chen, X., Chen, X., Shao, J., Zhang, J., Hu, H., Tian, H., Li, X., Ma, L., & Jia, W. (2019). High-performance piezoelectric nanogenerator based on microstructured P(VDF-TrFE)/BNNTs composite for energy harvesting and radiation protection in space. *Nano Energy*, *60*, 701–714. doi:10.1016/j.nanoen.2019.03.096

Yi, J. W., Shih, W. Y., & Shih, W.-H. (2002). Effect of length, width, and mode on the mass detection sensitivity of piezoelectric unimorph cantilevers. *Journal of Applied Physics*, *91*(3), 1680–1686. doi:10.1063/1.1427403

Ying, H. (1998). *General Takagi-Sugeno fuzzy systems are universal approximators*. ISI.

Yli-Huumo, J., Ko, D., Choi, S., Park, S., & Smolander, K. (2016). Where Is Current Research on Blockchain Technology?—A Systematic Review. *PLoS One*, *11*(10), e0163477. doi:10.1371/journal.pone.0163477 PMID:27695049

Yuan, B., Folmer, E., & Harris, F. C. Jr. (2011). Game accessibility: A survey. *Universal Access in the Information Society*, *10*(1), 81–100. doi:10.100710209-010-0189-5

Yuan, H., Yang, Z., Chen, X., Li, Y., & Liu, W. (2018). URL2Vec: URL Modeling with Character Embeddings for Fast and Accurate Phishing Website Detection. *2018 IEEE Intl Conf on Parallel & Distributed Processing with Applications, Ubiquitous Computing & Communications, Big Data & Cloud Computing, Social Computing & Networking, Sustainable Computing & Communications (ISPA/IUCC/BDCloud/SocialCom/SustainCom)*. IEEE. 10.1109/BDCloud.2018.00050

Yue, X., Kauer, M., Bellanger, M., Beard, O., Brownlow, M., Gibson, D., Clark, C., MacGregor, C., & Song, S. (2017). Development of an Indoor Photovoltaic Energy Harvesting Module for Autonomous Sensors in Building Air Quality Applications. *IEEE Internet of Things Journal*, *4*(6), 2092–2103. doi:10.1109/JIOT.2017.2754981

Yu, H., & Zikria, Y. B. (2020). Cognitive Radio Networks for Internet of Things and Wireless Sensor Networks. *Sensors (Basel)*, *20*(18), 5288. doi:10.339020185288 PMID:32947832

Yun, S., Zhang, Y., Xu, Q., Liu, J., & Qin, Y. (2019). Recent advance in new-generation integrated devices for energy harvesting and storage. *Nano Energy*, *60*, 600–619. doi:10.1016/j.nanoen.2019.03.074

Yupapin, P., Trabelsi, Y., Nattappan, A., & Boopathi, S. (2023). Performance Improvement of Wire-Cut Electrical Discharge Machining Process Using Cryogenically Treated Super-Conductive State of Monel-K500 Alloy. *Iranian Journal of Science and Technology. Transaction of Mechanical Engineering*, *47*(1), 267–283. doi:10.100740997-022-00513-0

Zabek, D., & Morini, F. (2019). Solid state generators and energy harvesters for waste heat recovery and thermal energy harvesting. *Thermal Science and Engineering Progress*, *9*, 235–247. doi:10.1016/j.tsep.2018.11.011

Zadeh, L. A. (1965). Fuzzy sets. *Information and Control*, *8*(3), 338–353. doi:10.1016/S0019-9958(65)90241-X

Zagane M., Abdi M., Alenezi M., (2020). *Deep Learning for Software Vulnerabilities Detection Using Code Metrics*. IEEE. . doi:10.1109/ACCESS.2020.2988557

Zareei, M., Vargas-Rosales, C., Hernndez, R. V., & Azpilicueta, El. (2019). Efficient Transmission Power Control for Energy-harvesting Cognitive Radio Sensor Network. *2019 IEEE 30th International Symposium on Personal, Indoor and Mobile Radio Communications (PIMRC Workshops)*, (pp. 1–5). IEEE. 10.1109/PIMRCW.2019.8880825

Zhang, H., Liu, Z., & Hui, Q. (2012). Optimal Defense Synthesis for Jamming Attacks in Cognitive Radio Networks via Swarm Optimization. *Proceedings of the IEEE Symposium on Computational Intelligence for Security and Defense Applications*. IEEE. 10.1109/CISDA.2012.6291525

Zhang, Y., & Lee, W. (2000). Intrusion detection in wireless ad-hoc networks. In: *Proceedings of the sixth ACM annual international conference on mobile computing and networking*. ACM.. 10.1145/345910.345958

Zhang, H., Zhang, C., Zhang, J., Quan, L., Huang, H., Jiang, J., Dong, S., & Luo, J. (2019). A theoretical approach for optimizing sliding-mode triboelectric nanogenerator based on multi-parameter analysis. *Nano Energy*, *61*, 442–453. doi:10.1016/j.nanoen.2019.04.057

Zhang, L., Wu, Q., Ding, G., Feng, S., & Wang, J. (2014). Performance analysis of probabilistic soft SSDF attack in cooperative spectrum sensing. *EURASIP Journal on Advances in Signal Processing*, *2014*(1), 81. doi:10.1186/1687-6180-2014-81

Zhang, Q., Liu, Y., Gong, C., Chen, Y., & Yu, H. (2020). Applications of deep learning for dense scenes analysis in agriculture: A review. *Sensors (Basel)*, *20*(5), 5. Advance online publication. doi:10.339020051520 PMID:32164200

Zhang, T., Chen, J., Li, F., Zhang, K., Lv, H., He, S., & Xu, E. (2022). Intelligent fault diagnosis of machines with small & imbalanced data: A state-of-the-art review and possible extensions. *ISA Transactions*, *119*, 152–171. doi:10.1016/j.isatra.2021.02.042 PMID:33736889

Zhang, X., & Li, C. (2009). Constructing secure cognitive wireless networks experiences and challenges. *Wireless Communications and Mobile Computing*, *10*, 55–69.

Zhang, Y., Luo, A., Wang, Y., Dai, X., Lu, Y., & Wang, F. (2020). Rotational electromagnetic energy harvester for human motion application at low frequency. *Applied Physics Letters*, *116*(5), 053902. doi:10.1063/1.5142575

Zhang, Y., Yuan, X., & Tzeng, N. F. (2021). Platform-Oblivious Anti-Spam Gateway. *ACM International Conference Proceeding Series*, (pp. 1064–1077). ACM.. 10.1145/3485832.3488024

Zhao, T., Jiang, W., Niu, D., Liu, H., Chen, B., Shi, Y., Yin, L., & Lu, B. (2017). Flexible pyroelectric device for scavenging thermal energy from chemical process and as self-powered temperature monitor. *Applied Energy*, *195*, 754–760. doi:10.1016/j.apenergy.2017.03.097

Zhao, W., Jiang, C., Gao, H., Yang, S., & Luo, X. (2021). Blockchain-Enabled Cyber–Physical Systems: A Review. *IEEE Internet of Things Journal*, *8*(6), 4023–4034. doi:10.1109/JIOT.2020.3014864

Zheng, B., Li, Y., Cheng, W. (2020). A multi-channel load awareness-based MAC protocol for flying ad hoc networks. *J Wireless Com Network*, *181*. doi:10.1186/s13638-020-01797-z

Zheng, H.-T., Chen, J.-Y., Yao, X., Kumar Sangaiah, A., Jiang, Y., & Zhao, C.-Z. (2018). Clickbait Convolutional. *Symmetry*, *10*(5), 138. doi:10.3390ym10050138

Zheng, X., Zhu, Y., & Si, X. (2019). A Survey on Challenges and Progresses in Blockchain Technologies: A Performance and Security Perspective. *Applied Sciences (Basel, Switzerland)*, *9*(22), 4731. doi:10.3390/app9224731

Zhou, X., Lee, W. S., Ampatzidis, Y., Chen, Y., Peres, N., & Fraisse, C. (2021). Strawberry maturity classification from UAV and near-ground imaging using deep learning. *Smart Agricultural Technology*, *1*, 100001. doi:10.1016/j.atech.2021.100001

Zhou, X., Sun, M., Li, G. Y., & Juang, B. F. (2018). Intelligent wireless communications enabled by cognitive radio and machine learning. *China Communications*, *15*, 16–48.

Zhou, Z., Chen, X., Li, E., Zeng, L., Luo, K., & Zhang, J. (2019). Edge Intelligence: Paving the Last Mile of Artificial Intelligence With Edge Computing. *Proceedings of the IEEE*, *107*(8), 1738–1762. doi:10.1109/JPROC.2019.2918951

Zhu, J., Jia, L., & Huang, R. (2017). Electrospinning poly(l-lactic acid) piezoelectric ordered porous nanofibers for strain sensing and energy harvesting. *Journal of Materials Science Materials in Electronics*, *28*(16), 12080–12085. doi:10.100710854-017-7020-5

Zhu, K., Ji, K., & Shen, J. (2021). A fixed charge transportation problem with damageable items under uncertain environment. *Physica A*, *581*, 126234. doi:10.1016/j.physa.2021.126234

Zhu, Y., Yang, Z., Jiao, C., Ma, M., & Zhong, X. (2022). A Multi-Modal Energy Harvesting Device for Multi-Directional and Low-Frequency Wave Energy. *Frontiers in Materials*, *9*, 898921. https://www.frontiersin.org/articles/10.3389/fmats.2022.898921. doi:10.3389/fmats.2022.898921

Zohaib, M. (2018). Dynamic difficulty adjustment (DDA) in computer games: A review. *Advances in Human-Computer Interaction*, *2018*, 1–12. doi:10.1155/2018/5681652

Zorlu, Ö., & Kulah, H. (2012). A Miniature and Non-Resonant Vibration-based Energy Harvester Structure. *Procedia Engineering*, *47*, 664–667. doi:10.1016/j.proeng.2012.09.234

Zyda, M. (2005). From visual simulation to virtual reality to games. *Computer*, *38*(9), 25–32. doi:10.1109/MC.2005.297

About the Contributors

Maki K. Habib obtained Doctor of Eng. Sciences in Intelligent and Autonomous Robotics, Univ. of Tsukuba Japan. Selected research scientist at RIKEN Japan. Senior researcher at RISO-Labs Japan. Visiting researcher at EPFL, Switzerland. Visiting expert under ADB, Associate Prof. UTM, Malaysia. Senior Manager MCRIA Malaysia. Senior research scientist with GMD-Japan. Associate Prof. with Monash Univ. leading Mechatronics program. A full Prof. Robotics and Mechatronics at Swinburne Univ. Invited Prof. KAIST South Korea, Visiting Prof. at Saga Univ. Japan. Since Sept. 2007 he is full Professor of Robotics and Mechatronics at AUC. He also served consultant and technical adviser for Toyota group, ABB, etc. He published 10 books, 24 book chapters, more than 275 papers at international journals and intern. confs. His main research focus: Human and Friendly Mechatronics, Intelligent and Autonomous Robotics/Vehicles: Control, Mapping-Localization, Navigation and Learning. Service Robots for Humanitarian Demining, Biomimetic and Biomedical Robotics, Telecooperation Distributed Teleoperation, and Collaborative Control, Intelligent and Nonlinear Control, Wireless Sensor Networks, Industry 4, Flying Robots.

* * *

Issam Bahadur obtained his M.Sc. in 2006 and his Ph.D. in 2013 in the field of Mechanical and Mechatronics Engineering from University of Toronto, Canada. He is currently an assistant professor at the Department of Mechanical and Industrial Engineering at Sultan Qaboos University, Sultanate of Oman. Dr. Bahadur is motivated in the research of Micro-Electro-Mechanical Systems (MEMS), Instrumentations, and Smart Materials applications in vibration-based energy harvesters.

Sampath Boopathi completed his undergraduate in Mechanical Engineering and postgraduate in the field of Computer-Aided Design. He completed his Ph.D. from Anna University and his field of research includes Manufacturing and optimization. He published 100 more research articles in Internationally Peer-reviewed journals, one Patent grant, and three published patents. He has 16 more years of academic and research experiences in the various Engineering Colleges in Tamilnadu, India.

Patricia Raquel Cristaldo is an Information Systems Engineer from the National Technological University. Specialist in Information Systems Engineering. Master in Information Systems Engineering. Professional experience as a Project Manager. Teacher and Researcher in the area of Information

Systems and Engineering Management. Director of the Information Systems Engineering Career at the Regional Faculty of Concepción del Uruguay, National Technological University. Professor of Higher Education in Information Systems. Undergraduate and graduate professor. Co-director in the R&D Project: Generation of a measurement framework for the transversal evaluation of project management methodologies, executed at the National Technological University.

Quang D. N. received the B.S. degree in Electrical and Electronics Engineering, and the master's degree in Electrical Engineering from Universiti Tenaga Nasional (UNITEN), Malaysia, in 2011 and 2014, respectively. She is currently pursuing the PhD degree with Malaysia-Japan International Institute of Technology (MJIIT), Universiti Teknologi Malaysia (UTM). She received a scholarship for her bachelor's degree from Electricity of Vietnam (EVN). She is also an awardee of Malaysia International Scholarship (MIS) from Ministry of Higher Education (MoHE), Malaysia for her postgraduate studies. Her research interests include wireless communication network, Smart Grid, network testing, cybersecurity, phishing detection, artificial intelligence, machine learning, and deep learning.

Omar El-Gayar, Ph.D., is a Professor of Information Systems. His research interests include: analytics, business intelligence, and decision support with applications in problem domain areas such as healthcare, environmental management, and security planning and management. His inter-disciplinary educational background and training is in information technology, computer science, economics, and operations research. Dr. El-Gayar's industry experience includes working as an analyst, modeler, and programmer. His numerous publications appear in various IT related fields. He is a member of AIS, ACM, INFORMS, and DSI.

Afnan Elhamshari received her MSc degree in Robotics, Control, and Smart Systems from the American University in Cairo. She graduated from The University of Kansas in 2020 with a BSc in Engineering Physics with a concentration in Electromechanical Control Systems and a minor in Mathematics. Her research interests are Applications of Optimization Algorithms in different fields including Cardiac Simulation and Energy Harvesting.

Mohammadreza Emadi is a Ph.D. candidate of Mechanical Engineering in the area of System Dynamics, Vibrations and Control at Shahrood University of Technology, Iran.

Mojtaba Ghodsi received his Ph.D. in Precision Engineering from the University of Tokyo in 2007. He has then served 2 years as a postdoctoral researcher and 13 years as a faculty member, including 7 years at Sultan Qaboos University, Oman. His main research interest is smart materials and structures. Dr. Mojtaba Ghodsi is currently a Senior Lecturer of Instrumentation and Measurement Systems at the School of Energy and Electronic Engineering at the University of Portsmouth, UK.

Chabi Gupta, Ph.D., is with Christ University, India. She is an alumnus of Shri Ram College of Commerce, Delhi University. She has over 21 years of rich teaching and industry experience. To her credit, there are several national and international publications and presentations in conferences. Her research areas of interest are Finance, Banking, and Analytics. Her published book on Investment Banking, based on the NYU curriculum has been ranked as second best e-book in the world to read amongst the seven best books on Mergers and Acquisitions by Booksauthority.org.

S. A. Karthik is currently working as an Assistant Professor in the Department of Information Science And Engineering, BMS Institute of Technology and Management, Bangalore. He has 10 years of teaching experience and published 2 patents and 20+ research articles in various conferences and international journals. He is an active researcher in the field of Machine learning, Deep learning, image processing.

Ondrej Krejcar received the Ph.D. degree in technical cybernetics from the VSB—Technical University of Ostrava, Ostrava, Czech Republic, in 2008.,From 2016 to 2020, he was the Vice Dean of science and research with the Faculty of Informatics and Management, University of Hradec Kralove (UHK), Hradec Kralove, Czech Republic, where he is currently a Full Professor in systems engineering and informatics with the Center for Basic and Applied Research, Faculty of Informatics and Management, UHK, and a Research Fellow with the Malaysia–Japan International Institute of Technology, University Technology Malaysia, Kuala Lumpur, Malaysia. He has been a Vice Rector for science and creative activities with UHK since 2020, where he is also the Director of the Center for Basic and Applied Research. From 2014 to 2019, he was the Deputy Chairperson of Panel 7 (processing industry, robotics, and electrical engineering) of the Epsilon Program, Technological Agency of the Czech Republic. He has also been a Management Committee Member Substitute with the COST CA16226 Project since 2017. He has been the Vice Leader and a Management Committee Member at WG4 with the COST CA17136 Project since 2018. Since 2019, he has been the Chairperson of the Program Committee of the KAPPA Program, Technological Agency of the Czech Republic. He is a Regulator of the EEA/Norwegian Financial Mechanism in the Czech Republic for 2019–2024. Since 2020, he has been Chairperson of Panel 1 (computer, physical, and chemical sciences) of the ZETA Program, Technological Agency of the Czech Republic. His research interests include technical cybernetics, ubiquitous computing, control systems, smart sensors, wireless technology, biomedicine, image segmentation and recognition, biometrics, biotelemetric system architectures, including portable device architectures and wireless biosensors, and the development of applications for mobile/remote devices with the use of remote or embedded biomedical sensors. Dr. Krejcar is currently on the Editorial Board of the Multidisciplinary Digital Publishing Institute (MDPI) Sensors Impact Factor (IF) journal (Q1/Q2 at Journal Citation Reports (JCR)) and several other Emerging Sources Citation Index (ESCI)-indexed journals. In 2018, he was the 14th Top Peer Reviewer in Multidisciplinary in the World according to Publons. He received the Top Reviewer in the Global Peer Review Award from Publons in 2019. His h-index is 27 according to the Web of Science, with more than 3300 citations received in the Web of Science, where more than 160 IF journal articles are indexed in the JCR index (h-index 30 at SCOPUS with more than 4200 citations).

P. Senthil Kumar is an Associate Professor (Mathematics) at the School of Liberal Arts & Science of Mohan Babu University, Tirupati, Andhra Pradesh, India. He received BSc, MSc, and MPhil degrees from Jamal Mohamed College (JMC), Tiruchirappalli in 2006, 2008, and 2010, respectively. Furthermore, he received a B.Ed. degree from the Jamal Mohamed College of Teacher Education in 2009. Additionally, he completed PGDCA in 2011 at Bharathidasan University and PGDAOR in 2012 at Annamalai University, Tamil Nadu, India. He completed his PhD at JMC in 2017. He has published many research papers in peer-reviewed journals. He has also presented research papers at various conferences. He has introduced the PSK (P. Senthil Kumar) method and PSK theorem for solving transportation problems (TPs) in uncertain environments. And also, he has proved the supporting theorem, which states that the solution obtained by the PSK method for solving fuzzy TPs is always an optimal solution. Its relevant articles have been published in Springer and IGI Global Journals which are indexed in Scopus and WoS. His areas of research interest include operations research and fuzzy and intuitionistic fuzzy optimization.

Lucas Ezequiel La Pietra is an Information Systems Engineer full time at ITSynch, a Software development company for the maritime industry. From June 2022 to the Present full time at Globant, working as a full stack developer for Ernst & Young. Works since 2018 as a Data Scientist in the GDBD researching group at the UTN University. Responsible of several freelance projects involving software development and data science.

Daniela Lopez De Luise graduated in System Analysis and in Public communication of Science and Technology. Eng. in Computer Science, Expert System Eng. specialization, doctor in Computer Science. Current research interests are in Natural Language Processing, Machine Learning and Intelligent reasoning, Chatter-bots, Morphosyntactic Linguistic Wavelets, Harmonics Systems and Time mining, Video-Games/Gamification for educational purposes, and Automatic Reasoning. Theories created: Morphosyntactic Linguistic Wavelets (MLW) for automatic semantic by a wavelet-wise decomposition, Harmonics Systems (HS) for a lightweight time prediction approach, Bacterial consciousness (BC), and Currently working on Caos & Language Theory (CLT), to produce and process Natural Language in Spanish Dialogs Current activity: CETI coordination at National Acedemy of Sciences in Buenos Aires (Since 2019), coordinator outreach of de Scientific Society of Argentina, Director of Specialization for Software Quality Assurance Management. Universidad Autónoma de Entre Ríos (UADER), Director of/researcher in CI2S Lab (since June 2013), Founder of the local branch and leading member of IEEE CIS Game Technical Committee (Since 2015), Director of IDTI Lab (since March 2017) at University UADER, Entre Ríos, Argentina. Undergraduate and graduate teacher of Universidad Autónoma de Entre Ríos (UADER), National Technological University (UTN), National University of Cuyo (UNCU), Open Interamerican university (UAI), and Cuenca del Plata University (UCP).Member of GIBD research center @ UTN(since 2019), Member of CAETI research center @ UAI University (since 2013) and director of several projects there. Consultant in Intelligent Systems (Computational Intelligence), soft computing (Since 1997) Member of IEEE WCI (Woman in Computational Intelligence) and leader of Argentina branch since 2015.

Alessandro Massaro (ING/INF/01, FIS/01, FIS/03) carried out scientific research at the Polytechnic University of Marche, at CNR, and at Italian Institute of Technology (IIT) as Team Leader by activating laboratories for nanocomposite sensors for industrial robotics. He is in MIUR register as scientific expert in competitive Industrial Research and social development, and he was head of the Research and Development section and scientific director of MIUR Research Institute Dyrecta Lab Srl. Member of the International Scientific Committee of Measurers IMEKO and IEEE Senior member. He received an award from the National Council of Engineers as Best Engineer of Italy 2018 (Top Young Engineer 2018). Actually he is Professor and researcher at LUM University of Casamassima (BA, Italy).

Morteza Mohammadzaheri received his PhD in Intelligent Control Systems in 2011 from the University of Adelaide, Australia. He has served 3.5 years as a postdoctoral associate and 8 years as a faculty member at different institutes. He is now a Senior Lecturer in Mechatronics at Birmingham City University, UK. Dr Mohammadzaheri has published 127 peer-reviewed book chapters and journal and conference papers mainly in the area of data-driven techniques for modelling, control, monitoring and optimisation of engineering systems.

Ericka Janet Rechy-Ramirez is a full time researcher in the Instituto de Investigaciones en Inteligencia Artificial at Universidad Veracruzana (Mexico). She holds a PhD in Computer Science from the University of Essex (United Kingdom). She received a MPhil in Computer Science from the Laboratorio Nacional de Informática Avanzada (Mexico) and BSc degree in Administrative Computer Systems from the Universidad Veracruzana (Mexico). Her research interests include human computer interaction, serious games, biosignals, sensor fusion, and assistive technology.

Ali Selamat received the B.Sc. degree (Hons.) in IT from Teesside University, U.K., in 1997, the M.Sc. degree in distributed multimedia interactive systems from Lancaster University, U.K., in 1998, and the Dr.Eng. degree from Osaka Prefecture University, Japan, in 2003. He is currently the Dean of the Malaysia–Japan International Institute of Technology (MJIIT), which is an educational institute that is established by the Ministry of Higher Education, Malaysia, to enhance Japanese oriented engineering education in Malaysia and Asia with the support from the Government of Japan through the Japanese International Cooperation Agency (JICA) and Universiti Teknologi Malaysia (UTM) together with 29 Japanese University Consortium (JUC). He is also a Visiting Professor with the University of Hradec Králové, Czech Republic, and the Kagoshima Institute of Technology, Japan. Prior to that, he was the Chief Information Officer (CIO) and the Director of Communication and Information Technology with UTM. He was previously assuming the position of the Research Dean on the knowledge economy research alliance with UTM. He was a Visiting Professor with Kuwait University and few other universities in Japan, Saudi Arabia, and Indonesia. His research interests include data analytics, digital transformations, knowledge management in higher education, key performance indicators, cloud-based software engineering, software agents, information retrievals, pattern recognition, genetic algorithms, neural networks, and soft computing. He was elected as the Chair of IEEE Computer Society, Malaysia Section, under the Institute of Electrical and Electronics Engineers (IEEE), USA. He was a Principal Consultant of big data analytics with the Ministry of Higher Education, in 2010, a member of the Malaysia Artificial Intelligence Roadmaps, from 2020 to 2021, and a keynote speaker in many international conferences.

Ali Shaheen is currently a fourth year Ph.D. student in Information Systems at the Dakota State University. His research interests are analytics and decision support systems. His educational background is in information technology and computer sciences. Ali Shaheen industry experience includes working as analyst, engineer and program manager.

Payam Soltani completed his PhD in Nonlinear Structural Dynamics in 2012. Since then, he has served in academia in Iran, Belgium and UK. He has an outstanding research record in piezoelectric-based smart structures; this includes the projects carried out at the University of Brussels and the University of Liege, Belgium. Dr Soltani is now a Senior Lecturer and the Course Lead of Mechanical Engineering at Birmingham City University, UK.

Juan Ignacio Vargas-Bustos holds a MPhil in Artificial Intelligence from Universidad Veracruzana (Mexico). He received a BSc degree in Mechatronics from Universidad Veracruzana (Mexico) His research interests include serious games, robotics and multiagent systems.

Tomohiro Yamaguchi received his M.E. degree from Osaka University, Japan, in 1987. He joined Mitsubishi Electric Corporation in 1987 and moved to Matsushita Electric Industrial in 1988. He worked at Osaka University from 1991 to 1998 as a research associate and got Doctor of Engineering Degree from Osaka University in 1996. He moved to Nara National College of Technology as associate professor in 1998 and is currently a professor from 2007. His research interests include interactive recommender system, music information retrieval, multiagent reinforcement learning, autonomous learning agent, human-agent interaction, learning support system, human learning process and mastery process. He is a member of The Japanese Society for Artificial Intelligence and The Society of Instrument and Control Engineers, Japan.

Oluwaleke Yusuf holds a Bachelor's degree in Mechanical Engineering from the University of Ibadan, Nigeria, and a Master's degree in Robotics, Control, and Smart Systems from The American University in Cairo, Egypt. He has worked in the Construction Industry as a field maintenance personnel and later as an operations management expert in the Telecommunications Industry. His research interests lie at the intersection of Machine Learning and Computer Vision, with a focus on utilizing advances in data-driven neural network architectures and algorithms to address the problem of perception in robotics and machine intelligence. He is currently pursuing his PhD at the Norwegian University of Science and Technology, Norway, where his research is centred on developing Digital Twins of urban mobility infrastructures using AI and Big Data, with the ultimate objective of achieving carbon neutrality in mobility.

Muhammad Furqan Zia received his B.E. degree in Electrical engineering from DHA Suffa University, Karachi, Pakistan, in 2017 and M.S. degree in Electrical and Computer engineering from Antalya Bilim University, Turkey in Jan. 2021. Currently, he is working as a researcher and teaching assistant in Electrical and Electronics engineering department at Koc University, Istanbul, Turkey. In the past he worked as a researcher at the Wireless Intelligent Systems laboratory in Antalya Bilim University. He is an author of multiple peer-reviewed articles and the inventor of a patent application. Furqan's primary research interests include 5G/6G wireless systems, MIMO systems, RIS, NOMA, physical layer security and deep learning for communication systems.

Hamidreza Ziaiefar is a researcher at Universitetet i Sørøst-Norge in Norway. Before joining USN, he served as a research assistant at Sultan Qaboos University in Oman from 2016 to 2020. Mr. Ziaiefar received his M.Sc. degree in Mechanical Engineering (Mechatronics) from Tarbiat Modares University (Iran) in 2013, and B.Sc. degree in Mechanical Engineering (Manufacturing) from Iran University of Science & Technology (Iran) in 2011. His main research interests include mechatronics, smart material applications and hybrid renewable energy systems.

Index

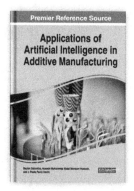
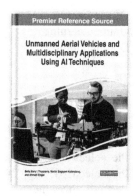

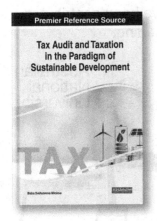

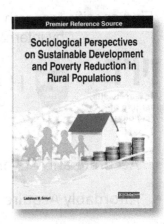

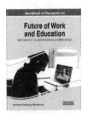

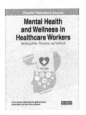

Printed in the United States
by Baker & Taylor Publisher Services